Inside Forensic Psychology

Inside Forensic Psychology

Tiffany R. Masson, PsyD, Editor

 PRAEGER™

An Imprint of ABC-CLIO, LLC
Santa Barbara, California • Denver, Colorado

Library of Congress Cataloging-in-Publication Data

Names: Masson, Tiffany R., editor.
Title: Inside forensic psychology / Tiffany R. Masson, editor.
Description: Santa Barbara, California : Praeger, [2016] | Includes
   bibliographical references and index.
Identifiers: LCCN 2015041770 | ISBN 9781440803031 (hardback) | ISBN
   9781440803048 (e-book)
Subjects: LCSH: Forensic psychology. | BISAC: PSYCHOLOGY / Forensic
   Psychology.
Classification: LCC RA1148 .I57 2016 | DDC 614/.15—dc23 LC record available at
http://lccn.loc.gov/2015041770

ISBN: 978-1-4408-0303-1
EISBN: 978-1-4408-0304-8

20 19 18 17 16   1 2 3 4 5

This book is also available on the World Wide Web as an eBook.
Visit www.abc-clio.com for details.

Praeger
An Imprint of ABC-CLIO, LLC

ABC-CLIO, LLC
130 Cremona Drive, P.O. Box 1911
Santa Barbara, California 93116-1911

This book is printed on acid-free paper ∞
Manufactured in the United States of America

Contents

Part II   Cases, Approaches, and Practices with Specialized Populations

Preface

Inside Forensic Psychology was written to provide readers with a broad and in-depth understanding of forensic psychology cases as presented by distinguished experts working throughout this multifaceted field. This book is intended as a learning tool that professors can use to encourage critical thinking and facilitate understanding in students. At present, many professors supplement their own experience by asking one another for redacted clinical cases or court reports that can bring to life the complex set of issues often found in forensic psychology cases and in conducting competent forensic evaluations. Few books are currently available that balance an understanding of the literature with relevant case law, best practices, and clinical case vignettes. By bringing together this assortment of theory, required background knowledge, and real-life experience across numerous areas of forensic psychology, we hope to help students share in the thinking and mindset of the clinician or evaluator grappling with the multidimensional aspects of a case, and to highlight best practices and case law that can be used when conducting evaluations or working with a particular population.

This book is also intended to underscore the complexity of the forensic psychology field. Many case summaries available to students err on the side of simplicity, carrying with them the danger of infusing a false sense of black and white, precise formulas and easy answers. This could not be further from reality. Every case a student or clinician will encounter is unique; while there are basic tasks to perform and information to gather that are vital to every case (e.g., knowledge of relevant case law, review of case records, relevant background information, outcomes of psychological testing/assessment), the way this information is evaluated and used can depend on a great many factors. For this reason, several chapters herein include a section on common pitfalls and considerations, including factors and possibilities we wish we had considered when starting out in this challenging but rewarding field.

I was motivated to compile this book after teaching for several years and reflecting on learning methodologies that had the greatest impact on my students. As a professor, I found myself wanting to bring to life important concepts in ways that challenged students to think critically about complex human and ethical issues that they will face every day as forensic clinicians and evaluators. *The case vignettes, which highlight varying types of forensic evaluations, were created or adapted into case summaries based on the authors' professional experience, and any likeness to an actual case is purely coincidental. The case vignettes are not meant to serve as a comprehensive forensic report. Rather, the emphasis is intended as a means of encouraging students to synthesize, evaluate, and apply information and concepts learned.*

Forensic psychology is not an exact science. This book is intended as a collection of case vignettes that provide students with multiple viewpoints into the work of a forensic evaluator and into a variety of professional approaches. As a result, the reader may or may not agree with the opinions reached or the methodologies used in the cases described. The goal is to encourage readers to think critically about the challenges posed in each specific case, articulate opposing positions, argue differing points of view, and evaluate all courses of potential action. It is through this type of thoughtful discourse that students can be expected to grow into practices and confident professionals.

Acknowledgments

The compilation of this book would not be possible without the support of family and friends, colleagues—Judy Beaupre, MS, and Alisha DeWalt, MA—and research assistant—Jenna Hedglen, MA. Moreover, it is with great appreciation that I thank the authors who wrote tirelessly and remained committed to the vision of this book.

Part I

Cases, Approaches, and Practices

Ethical Considerations in Cross-Cultural Assessment

Rebecca Weiss and Amanda Rosinski

The goal of forensic assessment is to utilize psychologically based measures to aid in legal contexts (Heilbrun, 1992). Forensic assessment represents an important juxtaposition regarding its emphasis on normative and individual factors. As the evaluations are a form of scientific evidence potentially used in a courtroom, it is important to utilize empirically supported measures that rely on normative data (i.e., comparing individual scores with a representative sample). However, this reliance is problematic, considering the increasing diversity rates in the United States, which threaten the validity of those normative data. This trend is likely to become increasingly problematic. Demographic statistics in the United States reveal a distinct increase in rates of diversity, with Hispanic and Asian populations increasing 43% from 2000 to 2010 while the non-Hispanic white population decreased over the same period (U.S. Census Bureau, 2011). While these rates do reveal a nation growing in diversity, this trend is more pronounced in forensic populations. In 2012, more than 60% of the United States prison population was classified as minority (Carson & Golinelli, 2013), an imbalance that is unlikely to change as immigration offenses are among the fastest growing segments of the federal prison system (Carson & Sabol, 2012).

Relevant Case Law

Cross-cultural forensic assessment is continually shaped by legal precedent. While there are cases addressing culture that date back to the 1970s, cultural issues are recurrent in the courtroom. In 1970, *United States ex rel. Negron v. State of New York* recognized the need for interpreters and translators in the trial process. This case held that basic and fundamental fairness of the trial process includes a non-English speaking defendant's right to a translator or interpreter at criminal trials, which will be provided at the state's expense in the case of an indigent defendant. *Iao v. Gonzalez* (2005) recognized that interpreters of intricate languages might misunderstand statements and that there is an insensitivity to the challenges associated with determining the credibility of a person from another culture. This lack of consideration was apparent in this case, in which the refusal to make eye contact was interpreted as unreliable, whereas it is a symbol of respect in Asian culture. *Diaz v. State of Delaware* (1999) held that the Administrative Office of the Courts (AOC) would regularly provide all court interpreters with a mandatory orientation to cover the training of court interpreters, the role of the interpreter in the courtroom, the ethics and structure of the court system, the social and cultural diversity issues, and other various topics. Post-*Diaz*, the Consortium for State Court Interpreter Certification also increased its standards to advance the proficiency assessment of court-appointed interpreters and to promote due process (Griffin, 2002). Higher standards were necessary to train interpreters to mirror the language and style of presentation without changing meaning or tone. If court-appointed interpreters misinterpret to the level of plain error, then defendants may be entitled to a new trial (Griffin, 2002).

Dia v. Ashcroft (2003) established that cross-cultural differences could increase the complexity of immigration hearings. However, cultural differences do not necessarily reflect variability in credibility. It was determined that immigration judges might have a cultural bias in which they rely on their own experiences to assess cross-cultural testimony. The court held that cultural biases might affect even a well-intentioned and meticulous fact finder. *Chouchkov v. Immigration and Naturalization Service* (2000) strengthened this finding by stating that an idiosyncrasy in one country might be a cultural norm in another country. *Chen v. Holder* (2009) held that an immigration judge must be thoughtful and careful before determining that a specific gesture, tone, or facial expression weakens credibility. *Zhang v. District of Columbia Department of Consumer and Regulatory Affairs* (2003) held that while cross-cultural differences might make the review of evidence more difficult, review boards must consider this information to ensure due process. Overall, an awareness for potential cross-cultural differences might help reduce biases.

Models set forth regarding cross-cultural barriers are applied to a forensic assessment setting. *Dusky v. United States* (1960) set forth the notion that every defendant has a right to a competency evaluation before proceeding to trial. The *Dusky* standard for determining competency is that the defendant is capable of working with an attorney and must have a "reasonable degree of rational and factual understanding of the proceedings against him" (*Dusky v. United States*, 1960, p. 1). The *Matter of M-A-M-* (2011) held that immigration proceedings must follow similar standards. Therefore, immigration judges must make mental competency determinations and justify their reasoning so that proceedings are fundamentally fair. *State of Washington v. Sisouvanh* (2012) reasoned that although cultural competency is important and a requirement for court-appointed mental health evaluators, there is no minimum requirement for the qualification to assess competency to stand trial. Cultural competency includes research and investigation into the defendant's background and culture, but there is no standard protocol for the minimum cultural competency requirement.

Review of the Literature

When reviewing cross-cultural differences in assessment, acculturation is a relevant but understudied factor. Acculturation is a process in which members adopt characteristics of another culture (Berry, 1980). Acculturation exists on a spectrum for both the culture of origin and the adopted culture. An assessment of acculturation is crucial as it provides a gauge for how adherent one is to his or her culture and, therefore, provides an estimate of the importance of cultural effects on measures of assessment.

Psychologists should try to use culturally specific and culturally valid measures whenever possible (Dana, 1998). This is not an easy task. The forensic population is quite diverse, and therefore, an individual being evaluated is unlikely to resemble the groups that were used to develop psychological assessment instruments. Additionally, cultural variability may increase as psychopathology increases (Fields, 2010). Even when objective measures with standardized scoring are used to aid in the assessment process, cultural variables may affect the results. Common problems identified by Okawa (2008) include a lack of orientation to time and cognitive functioning. While many Americans value the ability to complete tasks quickly, this is not the case in all cultures. Therefore, assessments that include timed tests could be problematic. Furthermore, basic cognitive processes, such as attention and memory, can vary significantly across cultures (Nisbett, Peng, Choi, & Norenzayan, 2001). Specifically, attention and memory may reflect what an individual considers to be important. Nisbett et al. (2001) found that East Asians attend more to the context of a visual object than Westerners do, who tend to separate an object from its context. Additionally, Nisbett et al. (2001) suggested that thinking patterns and abstract concepts are often affected by culture. Some researchers have theorized that at least part of the cultural differences in thought patterns may result from differences in language (e.g., Hebrew has relatively few abstract terms; Friedman & Schustack, 2010). The American Psychological Association (APA) Presidential Task Force on Immigration (2011) acknowledged many of these concerns and put forth a general call for researchers to address the gap in available literature regarding cultural-specific expressions of well-being and distress. However, until this research is conducted, evaluators need to navigate how to conduct an assessment with culturally diverse individuals.

It is important for the evaluator to be aware of these cultural influences and not misattribute differences from the norm as necessarily abnormal. However, interpreting abnormal neuropsychological results is a delicate balance. Not all deviations from the norm are culturally based, as researchers estimate that between 25% and 87% of inmates have experienced traumatic brain injury and are therefore at greater risk to display related cognitive deficits (Diamond, Harzke, Magaletta, Cummins, & Frankowski, 2007). Although the paucity of published literature limits the applicability of some forms of testing with diverse populations, there is a growing literature on the utility of neuropsychological testing in non-English speaking samples. For instance, Tuokko et al. (2009) utilized a factor-analytic technique that provided equal support for the validity of the latent variables (and therefore construct validity) in a neuropsychological battery administered in English and French. Similarly, Siedlecki and her colleagues (2010) found factor structure and loading that supported the use of a neuropsychological battery across English and Spanish-speaking groups in a community-based sample. However, numerous studies have found a disproportionate rate of false-positive classifications for neuropsychological disorders in African American and Latino samples (Rivera-Mindt, Byrd, Saez, & Manly, 2010). The limitations of neuropsychological data with diverse populations are similar to those for other types of psychological testing, including a dearth of research support, reliance on Western norms and a basis in Western culture and linguistics. Therefore, considerable clinical judgment is necessary in the choice and interpretation of the measures used.

When the construct validity of a measure is considered sound, the measure often needs to be translated into another language. Translation can be a very tedious process, as it requires more than the literal translation and is subject to several different types of biases. Construct bias is when a construct is conceptualized differently in different cultures. Method bias occurs when factors that threaten validity are present during assessment. Item bias is when items are translated with poor wording or inaccurately for a specific cultural group (Van de Vijver & Hambleton, 1996). Trait bias occurs when the assessment contains factors that invalidate scores for a particular group (Hambleton & Kanjee, 1995). Joint effects of language and culture differences are likely to produce the highest amount of bias (Candell & Hulin, 1986).

The International Test Commission (ITC) Guidelines for Translating and Adapting Tests (2010) provided a commonly adopted method for the advance translation of measures. Linguistic and cultural equivalence must be considered in each stage of the translation. After the measure has been translated, a second individual, who is unfamiliar with the original version of the measure, will then back-translate the measure. The initial and back-translated versions should be compared, and final adjustments should be made. Without these procedures, the evaluator risks jeopardizing the accuracy of the translated measure and generates assessment data of unknown reliability and validity. However, regardless of the applied method, psychologists should clearly state limitations with any translation process, as this limits test interpretations (Leong, Park, & Leach, 2013).

After the psychological assessments are completed, cultural differences must also be considered during the interpretation of results. Interpretations of assessments should consider the individual's cultural background (Leong et al., 2013). Cultural studies should examine the clinical setting and develop an understanding of the individual's cultural beliefs (Fields, 2010). Psychologists should research the cultural reliability and validity of the assessments used. If the statistics are insufficient, psychologists should consider the use of another measure (Weiss & Rosenfeld, 2012).

Cultural differences also present challenges when conducting psychological assessments. Cultural competence is not only the understanding of cultural knowledge but also the ability to implement that into practice (Fields, 2010). Cultural psychology focuses on the individual's symbolic culture. *Culture* implies shared knowledge, values, and communication. According to some researchers, these values aren't universal or cross-culturally equal (Greenfield, 1997). The cultural factors that may affect an individual's assessment include motivation, values, experiences, and degree of test anxiety (Hambleton & Bollwark, 1991). An example of cross cultural differences includes the notion of indigenous conceptions of intelligence, which requires the assessment of individual differences when measuring IQ. In addition, knowledge might not be individualized in some cultures, so cooperative construction of knowledge should be allowed (Greenfield, 1997). To reduce the effects of cultural differences, all assessment items must measure the same behaviors across populations (Hambleton & Bollwark, 1991). Also, some cultures may focus on learning instead of speaking, so questions that focus on doing rather than saying may be more beneficial (Greenfield, 1997). Finally, free-response assessments may be more beneficial than fixed-response assessments (Ibrahim & Arrendondo, 1986).

In addition to cultural differences, professionals who are conducting the psychological assessments may experience cultural biases. Psychologists should be aware of their cultural biases and not allow them to lead to unjust work (Leong et al., 2013; Weiss & Rosenfeld, 2012). To reduce these biases, cross-cultural knowledge should be a comprehensive curriculum. In assessment, psychologists should first consider the individual as a psychological entity. Assessment begins with an understanding of the individual's culture (Ibrahim & Arrendondo, 1986). Information on an individual's cultural background should be gathered prior to the assessment (Leong et al., 2013). Assessments should use multimethod approaches to measure potentials and limitations of the individual (Ibrahim & Arrendondo, 1986). Psychologists should learn culturally competent service delivery styles. Acculturation measures are suggested to help correct for cultural differences between the psychologist and the individual (Dana, 1998; Weiss & Rosenfeld, 2012). Psychologists should try to use culturally specific and culturally valid measures when possible (Dana, 1998).

Research on the impact of language and culture in forensic assessment is essential for professionals working in the field. It is essential because it provides professionals with the most current empirical support for the optimal method of cross-cultural assessment. It is also essential because, currently, there is no universally accepted standard of care in forensic mental health assessment. Instead, professional conduct is currently supported by best practice guidelines (Heilbrun, DeMatteo, Marczyk, & Goldstein, 2008).

Best Practices

The field of psychology is guided by both enforced standards and aspirational guidelines, which are distinct practices. The APA provides professionals in the field with the "Ethical Principles of Psychologists and Code of Conduct" (APA Ethics Code; American Psychological Association, 2002a), which is a set of mandatory standards. Violations of the APA Ethics Code may result in sanctions, felony convictions, expulsion from the state psychological association, and suspension or loss of licensure (APA, 2002a). The APA Ethics Code provides several instructions regarding psychological assessment. Psychological assessments must be based on scientific and professional judgments (Standard 9.01). Assessments must be purposeful, reliable, valid, and appropriate for the individual (Standard 9.02). Psychological assessments require obtaining informed consent from the individual (in forensic settings, this may not always be the case; Standard 9.03). Psychologists must interpret the individual's test results based on the individual's holistic background characteristics, including both cultural and linguistic differences (Standard 9.06; APA, 2002a).

On the other hand, APA also provides the specific field of forensic psychology with aspirational guidelines, which are the "Specialty Guidelines for Forensic Psychologists" (American Psychological Association, 2013). These are considered guidelines because they are a set of recommendations that professionals in the field strive to achieve. However, unlike the standards, guidelines do not have enforceable violations and do not supersede professional judgment. Included in these guidelines are several goals for working in cross-cultural populations. For example, forensic psychologists must recognize their own cultural bias and work to limit such bias in practice (Guideline 2.08). Psychologists must also appreciate cross-cultural differences and their potential effects on psychological services (Guideline 2.08). Appropriate training or a referral may be necessary (Guideline 2.08; American Psychological

Association, 2013). In addition, several aspirations regarding forensic assessment are noted. Cultural differences are particularly important to consider when interpreting the results of a psychological assessment, as well as the strengths and limitations of these interpretations (Guideline 10.03). Psychologists must focus on the psycholegal issue during the individual's assessment (Guideline 10.01). The forensic context of the evaluation must be considered during interpretation (Guideline 10.04). All data intended to be presented in the courtroom must be documented, and the psychologist must keep the records (Guidelines 10.07, 10.08; American Psychological Association, 2013).

When considering forensic assessment in a multicultural context, one must also consider cultural guidelines. APA has developed a set of cultural guidelines, which are known as the "Guidelines on Multicultural Education, Training, Research, Practice, and Organizational Change for Psychologists" (APA, 2002b). APA has set out six guidelines regarding multicultural issues. First, psychologists should reflect on their own cultural biases. Second, psychologists should research the significance of diverse populations. Third, psychologists who instruct others should teach about multiculturalism in a psychological context. Fourth, culture-centered psychological research should be established as essential in the field. Fifth, culturally based training skills should be implemented in psychological practice. And sixth, policy development should be updated in a cultural context by psychologists (APA, 2002b).

Case Vignette

Mr. Smith was a middle-aged man from Western Africa, referred for a psychological evaluation by his attorney. At the time of the evaluation, the client was facing numerous charges, including conspiracy, auto theft, and assault. A former associate had recently agreed to a plea deal and provided extensive evidence against other individuals, including Mr. Smith. If Mr. Smith was convicted, he would likely face deportation.

Reason for Referral

The referral question was regarding potential mitigating factors. His attorney reported that Mr. Smith suffered from a traumatic brain injury as a child, which had resulted in memory impairments. Mr. Smith's attorney asked for a general report regarding personality functioning and any neurological deficits.

In many ways, this type of referral resembles a typical neuropsychological evaluation. However, as in many forensic cases, there is a considerable motivation for external gain (reduce jail time, avoid deportation). These desires can

---

The case vignette has been redacted and all identifying information removed. It is not meant to serve as a forensic report. Any likeness to a case is purely coincidental.

motivate individuals to present themselves in a specific (inaccurate) manner so it is crucial to include measures of feigned symptoms and suspect effort. As evaluators are asked to be objective, these measures are crucial. However, even from the perspective of a defense attorney, they can be helpful in that they support the validity of a client's presentation. Additionally, it is crucial to establish the potential impact of culture and language, as this client entered the country relatively recently and as English was not his first language.

Summary of Relevant Records

In forensic evaluations, collateral information can provide key clues regarding the validity of a client's self-report. However, access to this information can be limited for individuals from other countries. This limitation was true for Mr. Smith, as he came from a country with an unstable government, which resulted in an inability to review any medical or educational records prior to the last few years. Only Mr. Smith's recent employment records were available, which supported his self-report.

Relevant Background Information

Mr. Smith grew up in Western Africa in the midst of a civil war. He had become separated from his family during his teenage years, and he believed that his parents, brothers, and sisters remained in Africa. His first language was an African dialect, and he was also fluent in English and French. He reported that he was an average student and attended school until the eighth grade. His schooling was in French and occasionally in English. When questioned further, he reported that his schooling was inconsistent since the school closed down when rebel groups came through the town, which occurred every few months. He was unused to paper-and-pencil tests, and he reported that his testing had been primarily verbal. However, he enjoyed reading, and he was capable of reading in all three languages.

He denied major health concerns as he was growing up, but he reported one incident in which rebels had caught him on his way home from school. He was a target due to his ethnicity. He was severely beaten, specifically around the head. He believed that he fell unconscious during the beating. He received stitches at a nearby hospital, but he did not report any lasting physical impairments although he felt his memory was affected by this incident. He had scars on his forehead that supported this story. He denied any legal history prior to the instant offense. He reported occasionally drinking with friends, but denied any alcohol or drug abuse. Although he acknowledged high levels of current fears and depression, he denied any history of notable psychological symptoms or treatment.

Mr. Smith reported that he had come to the United States approximately four years prior to the evaluation. A man in Mr. Smith's village had helped Mr. Smith escape his country, and Mr. Smith gained refugee status prior to entering the United States, but he was not naturalized (i.e., was not a citizen). This difference is crucial, as citizenship generally cannot be revoked, but a lawful refugee can face mandatory deportation if convicted of certain offenses, such as the ones Mr. Smith faced [Immigration and Nationality Act of 1952]. At the time of the evaluation, he lived alone and worked full time in construction. His support network consisted of the men from his country, several of whom were accused of the same crimes. He denied any lasting romantic relationships since arriving in the United States and stated that he did not have any children.

Mental Status Examination

Prior to the assessment, Mr. Smith was informed of the purpose of testing and the limits to confidentiality. Despite being verbally proficient in English, he was offered the option of an interpreter, which he refused. The evaluator described the purpose of the testing and informed Mr. Smith that some of the tests would evaluate the validity of his responses (those specific tests were not identified). Testing was conducted on two occasions with frequent breaks. He dressed appropriately and displayed good hygiene. Mr. Smith was consistently on time and engaged during testing. His thought processes were clear and logical, he was alert and oriented, and no delusions were evident. He denied a history of hallucinations, and no hallucinations were apparent during the interview. His affect was appropriate to the content of his speech. He reported distress regarding his current situation and specifically the potential for deportation but denied suicidal and homicidal ideation.

Psychological Measures

In adherence to the APA Ethical Code (APA, 2002a), and due to the potential risk regarding the effect of cultural variables on testing, the evaluator consulted with two experts in the field, both with experience regarding neurological or forensic testing with minority samples (Standard 2.01b). This consultation resulted in several decisions regarding the selection of assessments. Mr. Smith's English proficiency should be established, as this could directly pertain to testing results. Additionally, as language and culture could be confounding variables, the evaluator chose to avoid standard measures of intelligence and memory that often rely on English language, timed ability testing, and Western concepts. However, if his English abilities were appropriate, standard personality measures were recommended. Although acculturation was considered, at the time there were no validated measures of acculturation for African samples. Lastly, as there was substantial external gain in this case, it was advised that both suspect effort and psychiatric feigning be assessed.

Mr. Smith's reading level was assessed with STAR Reading (Renaissance Learning, 2009), a brief reading ability test for children and adults that can produce scores indicating grade-equivalent reading levels. His general mental ability was assessed using a nonverbal test that utilizes abstract geometric designs to assess reasoning and problem solving, the General Ability Measure for Adults (GAMA; Naglieri & Bardos, 1997). The GAMA was designed to be used for diverse cultural and educational samples, and the test is recommended in neuropsychological and forensic evaluations. His memory was assessed using the Hopkins Verbal Learning Test–Revised (HVLT-R; Brandt & Benedict, 2001), a widely used test of verbal learning and memory; the Brief Visuospatial Memory Test–Revised (BVMT-R; Benedict, 1997), a short test of visual memory; and the Stroop Color and Word Test (Stroop; Golden & Freshwater, 2002), a brief test of working memory. His level of effort in testing was assessed using two primarily nonverbal brief measures: the Test of Memory Malingering (TOMM; Tombaugh, 1996) and the Dot Counting Test (DCT; Boone, Lu, & Herzberg, 2002). Lastly, personality functioning and psychiatric feigning were assessed with the Personality Assessment Inventory, Second Edition (PAI-2; Morey, 2007).

On the STAR Reading Test, Mr. Smith obtained a score consistent with a sixth-grade reading level, which indicated that he was capable of completing the PAI-2, the test with the highest required reading level. Although language might not have interfered with the accuracy of the tests, Mr. Smith produced scores that were highly indicative of suspect effort on the tests designed to assess the validity of his responses. His scores on the TOMM and DCT were well below the standard cutoffs, as well as the cutoffs for individuals with cognitive impairment and dementia. Thus, the results of cognitive testing administered during the same evaluation are unlikely to adequately reflect his current intellectual functioning. On the GAMA, the nonverbal test of general intellectual abilities, Mr. Smith earned a score of 61, with a 95% chance that his true score falls between 57 and 74. This score is well below average and is equal to or lower than 99.5% of the population. Although Mr. Smith might have suffered from intellectual deficits, a general ability score this low is highly inconsistent with his presentation and level of achievement and unlikely to represent his genuine abilities. He scored similarly on the HVLT-R, BVMT-R, and Stroop, producing scores equivalent to bottom 1%–5% of the normative sample. These types of scores would be inconsistent with an individual capable of navigating a major city and regularly attending his appointments without assistance.

Lastly, the results of the PAI-2 were invalid. Mr. Smith was consistent in his responses, and he did not endorse infrequent symptoms. However, he scored higher than did 99% of similarly aged peers on a scale measuring negative impression management, which combines exaggerated/distorted self-impression items and bizarre or unlikely symptoms. Therefore, his responses on the clinical scales should be interpreted as the symptoms he desired to report rather than actually experienced. His responses to all clinical scales were at clinically relevant levels; his scores were more than two standard deviations above the mean for a sample of clinical patients on scales assessing somatic, depressive, manic, paranoid, psychotic, suicidal, and antisocial symptoms. As Mr. Smith indicated suicidal ideation on the PAI-2 (although he denied it during the clinical interview), the evaluator called to follow up. He denied imminent suicidal intent, and the evaluator connected Mr. Smith with outpatient services. He began attending these services within a week following the evaluation.

Clinical Summary and Opinion

Throughout an evaluation, a clinician should keep the referring attorney or agency apprised of the progress and developments. For instance, information resulting from an evaluation might suggest a change in legal strategy. Additionally, not all cases referred from attorneys will result in a written report. After the clinician verbally presented the results of the evaluation described above, the referring attorney decided that a written report would not be in the client's best interest. While it remains important for evaluators to discuss the case prior to writing a report, this act became less crucial after the 2010 amendments to Federal Rule of Civil Procedure 26(b)(4)(B) (2010), which allows for trial-preparation protection for draft reports and disclosures.

The evaluation results bring to light the potential negative repercussions of forensic testing, as well as considerations regarding appropriate testing choices. Upon providing the referral, Mr. Smith's attorney indicated that Mr. Smith appeared to be capable of reading in English, although he occasionally asked for definitions of legal terms. Language ability is often a crucial element of psychological assessment, and lack of that ability is confounding factor in the interpretation of results. However, Mr. Smith's ability to respond to the STAR Reading Test, as well as his consistency on the PAI-2 questions, make it unlikely that language was a factor in his response profile.

There is little doubt that Mr. Smith exaggerated his deficits throughout the exam. However, the potential effect of cultural variables remains. When a client does not resemble the normative population, the use of any measure must be carefully considered and the limitations of the measures must be carefully explained (APA, 2002a; Standard 9.02b). While this requirement could increase the temptation of relying on clinical interviews rather than assessments, personal interviews are just as (if not more) susceptible to cultural biases. Refusing a referral is also an option, but when a more qualified expert is hard to find, the repercussions regarding the lack of psychological evaluations for specific clients must also be considered (APA, 2002a; Principle A). There is no easy answer for this situation, as it involves conflicting duties and a substantial amount of clinical judgment.

Common Pitfalls and Considerations

When evaluators choose to move forward with clinical evaluations for minority groups, it is crucial to carefully examine the literature. At the time of Mr. Smith's evaluation, there were no published studies regarding the efficacy of measures of feigning and suspect effort with a non-Western sample. More recently, one published article questioned the efficacy of the DCT in a non-Western sample and examined a sample in which participants who were thought to be honest produced exceedingly high scores (Weiss & Rosenfeld, 2010).

Additionally, a potentially confounding variable based on culture is one of intent. The definition of malingering is the intentional creation or exaggeration of symptoms motivated by external gain (American Psychiatric Association, 2013). However, Mr. Smith's presentation was inconsistent with those of many other individuals in similar situations who were attempting to feign symptoms. When questioned about his responses after the evaluation to assess his imminent risk, he did not seem to understand the discrepancy between endorsing items referring to specific symptoms (such as hearing voices) and describing general distress. He was generally unfamiliar with psychiatric diagnoses and had a categorical view of all psychological symptoms. Despite conversations with his clinician and attorney prior to the evaluation, he felt that he could most adequately represent his current distress during testing by endorsing all symptoms. His explanations after the assessment highlight the need for an adequate informed consent prior to the evaluation. Even when a client can understand and repeat instructions and explanations in his own words, it is important to assess his personal understanding of the purposes and goals of an evaluation. While Mr. Smith's interpretations might be idiosyncratic, they do bring up the importance of research that evaluates the expression of psychiatric symptoms in a variety of cultures. At every stage of the assessment process, it is crucial to carefully consider the potential for cultural biases and miscommunication.

References

American Psychiatric Association. (2013). *Diagnostic and statistical manual of mental disorders* (5th ed.). Washington, DC: Author.

American Psychological Association. (2002a). Ethical principles of psychologists and code of conduct. *American Psychologist, 57,* 1060–1073.

American Psychological Association. (2002b). Guidelines on multicultural education, training, research, practice, and organizational change for psychologists. *American Psychologist, 58,* 377–402.

American Psychological Association. (2013). Specialty guidelines for forensic psychology. *American Psychology, 68,* 7–19.

American Psychological Association Presidential Task Force on Immigration. (2011). *Crossroads: The psychology of immigration in the new century.* Retrieved from http://www.apa.org/topics/immigration/executive-summary.pdf

Benedict, R. (1997). *Brief Visuospatial Memory Test–Revised.* Odessa, FL: Psychological Assessment Resources.

Berry, J. W. (1980). Acculturation as varieties of adaptation. In A. M. Padilla (Ed.), *Acculturation: Theory, models and some new findings* (pp. 9–25). Boulder, CO: Westview.

Boone, K. B., Lu, P., & Herzberg, D. (2002). *The Dot Counting Test manual.* Los Angeles, CA: Western Psychological Services.

Brandt, J., & Benedict, R. (2001). *Hopkins Verbal Learning Test–Revised.* Lutz, FL: Psychological Assessment Resources.

Candell, G. L., & Hulin, C. L. (1986). Cross-language and cross-cultural comparisons in scale translations independent sources of information about item nonequivalence. *Journal of Cross-Cultural Psychology, 17,* 417–440. doi:10.1177/0022002186017004003

Carson, E. A., & Golinelli, D. (2013). *Prisoners in 2012.* Washington, DC: Bureau of Justice Statistics.

Carson, E. A., & Sabol, W. J. (2012). *Prisoners in 2011.* Washington, DC: Bureau of Justice Statistics.

Chen v. Holder, 579 F.3d 73, 79 (1st Cir. 2009).

Chouchkov v. Immigration and Naturalization Service, 220 F.3d 1077 (2000).

Dana, R. H. (1998). Multicultural assessment of personality and psychopathology in the United States: Still art, not yet science, and controversial. *European Journal of Psychological Assessment, 14,* 62–70. doi:10.1027/1015-5759.14.1.62

Dia v. Ashcroft, 353 F.3d 228 (2003).

Diamond, P. M., Harzke, A. J., Magaletta, P. R., Cummins, A. G., & Frankowski, R. (2007). Screening for traumatic brain injury in an offender sample: A first look at the reliability and validity of the Traumatic Brain Injury Questionnaire. *Journal of Head Trauma Rehabilitation, 22*(6), 330–338. doi:10.1097/01.HTR.0000300228.05867.5c

Diaz v. State, 743 A.2d 1166 (Del. 1999).

Dusky v. United States, 362 U.S. 402, 80 S. Ct. 788, 4 L. Ed. 2d 824 (1960).

Fed. R. Civ. P. 26(b)(4) (2010).

Fields, A. J. (2010). Multicultural research and practice: Theoretical issues and maximizing cultural exchange. *Professional Psychology: Research and Practice, 41,* 196–201. doi:10.1037/a0017938

Friedman, H. S., & Schustack, M. W. (2010). *Personality: Classic theories and modern research* (5th ed.). Boston, MA: Pearson Higher Education.

Golden, C. J., & Freshwater, S. M. (2002). *Stroop Color and Word Test: A manual for clinical and experimental uses.* Lutz, FL: Psychological Assessment Resources.

Greenfield, P. M. (1997). You can't take it with you: Why ability assessments don't cross cultures. *American Psychologist, 52,* 1115–1124. doi:10.1037/0003-066X.52.10.1115

Griffin, P. W. (2002). Beyond State v. Diaz: How to interpret "access to justice" for non-English speaking defendants? *Delaware Law Review, 5,* 131–154.

Hambleton, R. K., & Bollwark, J. (1991). Adapting tests for use in different cultures: Technical issues and methods. *Bulletin of the International Test Commission, 18,* 3–32. doi:10.1027/1015-5759.11.3.147

Hambleton, R. K., & Kanjee, A. (1995). Increasing the validity of cross-cultural assessments: Use of improved methods for test adaptations. *European Journal of Psychological Assessment, 11,* 147–157.

Heilbrun, K. (1992). The role of psychological testing in forensic assessment. *Law and Human Behavior, 16,* 257–272. doi:10.1007/BF01044769

Heilbrun, K., DeMatteo, D., Marczyk, G., & Goldstein, A. M. (2008). Standards of practice and care in forensic mental health assessment: Legal, professional, and principles-based consideration. *Psychology, Public Policy, and Law, 14,* 1–26. doi:10.1037/1076-8971.14.1.1

Iao v. Gonzalez, 400 F.3d 530 (2005).

Ibrahim, F. A., & Arrendondo, P. M. (1986). Ethical standards for cross-cultural counseling: Counselor preparation, practice, assessment, and research. *Journal of Counseling & Development, 64,* 349–351. doi:10.1002/j.1556-6676.1986.tb01131.x

Immigration and Nationality Act of 1952, § 235(b)(2)(A).

International Test Commission (2010). International Test Commission guidelines for translating and adapting tests. Retrieved from http://www.intestcom.org

Leong, F. L., Park, Y., & Leach, M. M. (2013). Ethics in psychological testing and assessment. In K. F. Geisinger, B. A. Bracken, J. F. Carlson, J. C. Hansen, N. R. Kuncel, S. P. Reise, & M. C. Rodriguez (Eds.), *APA handbook of testing and assessment in psychology: Vol. 1. Test theory and testing and assessment in industrial and organizational psychology* (pp. 65–282). Washington, DC: American Psychological Association.

Matter of M-A-M-, 25 I&N Dec. 474 (2011).

Morey, L. C. (2007). *The Personality Assessment Inventory* (2nd ed.). Lutz, FL: Psychological Assessment Resources.

Naglieri, J. A., & Bardos, A. N. (1997). *Manual for the General Ability Measure for Adults.* Minneapolis, MN: National Computer Systems.

Nisbett, R. E., Peng, K., Choi, I., & Norenzayan, A. (2001). Culture and systems of thought: Holistic versus analytic cognition. *Psychological Review, 108,* 291–310. doi:10.1037//0033-295X.108.2.291

Okawa, J. B. (2008). Considerations for the cross-cultural evaluation of refugees and asylum seekers. In L. A. Suzuki & J. G. Ponterottto (Eds.), *Handbook of multicultural assessment: Clinical, psychological, and education application* (3rd ed., pp. 165–194). San Francisco, CA: Wiley.

Renaissance Learning. (2009). *STAR Reading: Technical manual.* Wisconsin Rapids, WI: Author.

Rivera-Mindt, M., Byrd, D., Saez, P., & Manly, J. (2010). Increasing culturally competent neuropsychological services for ethnic minority populations: A call to action. *Clinical Neuropsychology, 24,* 429–453. doi:10.1080/13854040903058960

Siedlecki, K. L., Manly, J. J., Brickman, A. D., Schupf, N., Tang, M. X., & Stern, Y. (2010). Do neuropsychological tests have the same meaning in Spanish speakers as they do in English speakers? *Neuropsychology, 24,* 402–411. doi:10.1037/a0017515

State v. Sisouvanh, 175 Wn.2d 607, 290 P.3d 942 (Wash. 2012).

Tombaugh, T. N. (1996). *TOMM: Test of Memory Malingering.* North Tonawanda, NY: Multi-Health Systems.

Tuokko, H. A., Chou, P. H. B., Bowden, S. C., Simartd, M., Ska, B., & Crossley, M. (2009). Partial measurement equivalence of French and English versions of the Canadian Study of Health and Aging neuropsychological battery. *Journal of the International Neuropsychological Society, 15,* 416–425. doi:10.1017/S1355617709090602

United States Census Bureau. (2011). *2010 Census shows America's diversity.* Retrieved from https://www.census.gov/newsroom/releases/archives/2010_census/cb11-cn125.html

United States Department of Labor, Bureau of Labor Statistics. (2013). *Household data annual averages.* Retrieved from http://www.bls.gov/cps/cpsaat11.pdf

United States ex rel. Negron v. State of New York, 434 F.2d 386 (1970).

Van de Vijver, F., & Hambleton, R. K. (1996). Translating tests: Some practical guidelines. *European Psychologist, 1,* 89–128. doi:10.1027/1016-9040.1.2.89

Weiss, R., & Rosenfeld, B. (2010). Cross-cultural validity in malingering assessment: The DCT in a rural Indian sample. *The International Journal of Forensic Mental Health, 9,* 300–307. doi:10.1080/14999013.2010.526680

Weiss, R. A., & Rosenfeld, B. (2012). Navigating cross-cultural issues in forensic assessment: Recommendations for practice. *Professional Psychology: Research and Practice, 43,* 234–240. doi:10.1037/a0025850

Zhang v. Dept. of Consumer and Regulatory AFF, 834 A.2d 97 (D.C. 2003).

2

Competency to Stand Trial

Michelle Hoy-Watkins and Megan E. Shaal

Often, individuals with serious mental illness (SMI) become involved in the criminal justice system. Since the widespread deinstitutionalization of state psychiatric institutions beginning in the 1950s, an unfortunate result in the United States has been that our jails and prisons house individuals with SMI and provide psychiatric care. According to the Department of Justice, 1.2 million inmates reported mental health problems in state, local, and federal custody: 64% in jails, 56% in state prisons, and 45% in federal prisons (U.S. Department of Justice, 2006).

For some criminal defendants, mental or cognitive deficits interfere with their ability to understand the legal system and the charges against them. Frequently, forensic mental health practitioners are asked to intervene and assess an individual's knowledge about the legal system and the individual's ability to assist in his or her defense. This occurs in evaluations for competency to stand trial (CST).

Evaluations for CST involve the assessment of an individual's mental state during a specific period in the legal process (i.e., prior to and during trial). Accordingly, this focuses on the individual's psychological functioning in the present. This is in contrast to criminal responsibility—or sanity—evaluations, which center on the individual's mental state at the time a crime was committed and therefore focuses on the individual's functioning in the past. Additionally, in some states (e.g., Illinois), CST is referred to as "fitness" to stand trial (Illinois Code of Criminal Procedure, Fitness for Trial, to Plead or to be Sentenced, 1963). In the last several years, some empirical research has referred to CST as *adjudicative competence* or *competence to proceed* (Bonnie, 1992; Poythress, Bonnie, Monahan, Otto, & Hoge, 2002). For the purposes of this chapter, these terms are used interchangeably.

The American legal system recognizes many different types of competencies for a defendant: competency to stand trial, to testify, to be executed, and to make a will. While the issues for these competencies are similar, the focus in this chapter is on CST.

Relevant Case Law and Review of Literature

The modern view of CST is that an individual has a fundamental constitutional right to a fair trial, which includes the right to participate in one's own defense (Meyer & Weaver, 2006; Slobogin, Rei, & Reisner, 2008; Zapf & Roesch, 2009). These rights are grounded in the 14th Amendment, specifically the Due Process Clause. If an individual suffers from mental illness, to what extent does he or she understand that his or her life and liberty are at stake? Is that due process? The 1899 case of *Youtsey v. United States* opines on this very issue (Zapf & Roesch, 2009). The court stated it is not due process of law.

Evaluations for CST are one of the most common assessments performed by forensic mental health practitioners. The most recent estimates are that approximately 60,000 evaluations are conducted annually (Bonnie & Grisso, 2000). Additionally, between 2% and 8% of all felony defendants are referred for competency evaluations (Bonnie, 1992; Golding, 1993; Hoge, Bonnie, Poythress, & Monahan, 1992).

The modern legal standard of CST was established by the 1960 United States Supreme Court case of *Dusky v. United States*. On August 19, 1958, Milton Dusky was charged with assisting in the rape, kidnapping, and transport of a 15-year-old female across state lines (from Kansas to Missouri). Dusky was described as "the product of a disorganized home situation" (p. 4). He was discharged from the Navy due to mental illness. He made suicidal gestures and attempts. He also engaged in heavy alcohol use. Shortly before his arrest, Dusky's psychotic symptoms apparently worsened.

At arraignment, Dusky's defense counsel raised the issue of his CST. Dusky was committed to the United States Medical Center for Federal Prisoners (USMCFP) in Springfield, Missouri, to undergo an evaluation to determine his CST. While at USMCFP, he was diagnosed with Schizophrenia. A competency hearing was held, and a psychiatrist testified that because of Dusky's severity of mental illness, he was unable to properly understand the legal proceedings or assist in his defense. However, the psychiatrist also testified that Dusky was oriented to person, place, and time, and as a result, the district court found him competent to stand trial. He was convicted and sentenced to 45 years. Dusky appealed the district court's finding of CST and his conviction; the Court of Appeals for the Eighth Circuit affirmed both issues.

The Supreme Court of the United States granted certiorari. The question for the Supreme Court was, what is the test for determining a defendant's CST? In a rare unanimous opinion, the Court reversed the lower courts' decisions to convict Dusky, and the case was remanded back to the district court to determine Dusky's present CST. If Dusky were to be found competent, then the court would determine the appropriateness of a new trial.

In its reasoning, the Supreme Court found there was not sufficient evidence that Dusky was competent to stand trial. Specifically, the court questioned the psychiatric testimony. They opined that the finding that Dusky was oriented to person/place/time (i.e., a mental status examination) was not enough to make a determination of CST. To be found competent, an individual must have (a) a sufficient present ability to consult with his attorney with a reasonable degree of rational understanding and (b) a rational and factual understanding of the proceedings against him.

Dusky was a landmark case outlining the basic standards for CST, although those standards include minor variations or modifications from state to state (e.g., some states do not incorporate the necessity of rational understanding). Unfortunately, the case defines neither the meaning of the legal language nor the specific abilities necessary for CST (Frederick, DeMier, & Smith, 2014). The challenge for practitioners is to communicate data that is relevant to CST within the purview of mental health rather than commenting on the ultimate legal question (i.e., whether the defendant is or is not competent to stand trial; Frederick, DeMier, & Smith, 2014).

Every state has adopted the *Dusky* standard verbatim or with minor revisions or expansions (Zapf & Roesch, 2009). For example, Illinois is one state that has modified its competency (i.e., fitness) standard and expanded it to include specific functional abilities. The Illinois Statute (725 ILCS 5/104-10, 1963) states:

> A defendant is unfit if, because of his mental or physical condition, he is unable to understand the nature and purpose of the proceedings against him or to assist in his defense. (n.p.)

Because states differ on this issue, this highlights the importance of practitioners consulting their state statutes for competency standards prior to conducting CST evaluations (Grisso, 2003; Zapf & Roesch, 2009).

Although the *Dusky* ruling does not clearly identify mental illness as a factor in CST decisions, most state laws require the presence of a mental illness or defect or a physical disorder (Zapf, 2002; see Zapf & Roesch, 2009) as a condition for denying a defendant's competence. Some examples of mental health symptoms that may interfere with an individual's CST include psychotic symptoms, such as disorganized thinking and behavior, hallucinations, and delusions; difficulties concentrating; rapid thoughts or speech associated with mania, or the opposite, slowed thoughts or speech associated with depression; memory problems; and intellectual and developmental deficits.

The presence of a mental illness or defect has been described as a necessary but not sufficient condition for CST. That is, possessing a mental illness does not automatically lead to a finding of incompetence. The U.S. Court of

Appeals case for the Ninth Circuit, *Higgins v. McGrath* (1951), outlined that CST is not to be equated with the presence or absence of psychosis or psychotic symptoms.

There are important behaviors and abilities one must demonstrate in order to be found competent to stand trial. Zapf and Roesch (2009) refer to these as *psycholegal abilities*. In 1961, the U.S. District Court case for the Western District of Missouri, *Wieter v. Settle*, delineated eight minimal functional abilities related to *Dusky* that must be demonstrated by a competent defendant. They included: (a) the mental capacity to appreciate his presence in relation to time, place, and things; (b) the elementary mental processes to grasp that he is in a court of law charged with a criminal offense; (c) an understanding that there is a judge on the bench; (d) an understanding that the prosecutor will try to convict him of a criminal charge; (e) an understanding that he has a lawyer who will defend him against his charge; (f) an understanding that he will be expected to tell his lawyer of the legal circumstances to the best of his mental ability, including the facts of his personal and legal circumstances; (g) an understanding that a jury will be present to review evidence; and (h) memory sufficient to relate those things to his personal circumstances (p. 320).

To be found competent to stand trial, a defendant basically must have factual knowledge of the charges and roles of the legal players, demonstrate rational knowledge and understanding, and have a reasonable ability to assist counsel.

Factual Knowledge of the Charges and Roles of the Legal Players

This refers to possessing general knowledge about the court and the roles of the key players (i.e., judge, jury, witness, defendant, defense attorney, and prosecutor). This understanding may comprise an awareness of the current charges, the components of an offense, the duties of the various courtroom personnel, and the consequences of a conviction (Zapf & Roesch, 2009). Referring back to the *Dusky* standard, this is under the prong of *factual understanding*.

Rational Knowledge and Understanding

An individual found competent to stand trial must have an appreciation for the legal case in the context of his or her knowledge of the legal system. That is, the defendant must possess an ability to recognize information about the legal system and apply it to his own case. This involves such information as the possible penalties, the various legal defenses, decision making regarding testimony, and the likelihood of being found guilty (Zapf & Roesch, 2009). In summary, this is the ability to make rational, reality-based decisions regarding one's own case. Referring back to the *Dusky* standard, this is under the prong of *rational understanding*.

An individual competent to stand trial must also be able to demonstrate reasoning and decision-making abilities. This involves the ability to discriminate relevant information. This also refers to the ability to weigh and evaluate the available legal options and their consequences (Zapf & Roesch, 2009). The importance of this factor lies in the defendant's ability to reason appropriately and not necessarily in the "rightness" or "wrongness" of the decisions he or she makes. Referring back to the *Dusky* standard, this is under the prong of *rational understanding*.

Ability to Assist Counsel

This delineates the ability to consult, relate, and plan a legal strategy with his or her attorney. A competent defendant should participate in planning his or her defense. This also involves the abilities to challenge witnesses, testify relevantly, engage in a discussion, and manage courtroom behavior properly (Zapf & Roesch, 2009). Referring back to the *Dusky* standard, this is under the prong of a *sufficient present ability to rationally consult with their attorney*.

CST Process and Procedures

In most legal jurisdictions, the defense, the prosecution, or the judge can raise the question of a defendant's CST at any stage prior to or during the trial (as outlined in *Pate v. Robinson* and *Drope v. Missouri*). Once the issue of competency is raised, a CST evaluation is conducted. The majority of states allow such evaluations to include testimony by psychologists (Farkas, DeLeon, & Newman, 1997). CST evaluations can take place in a variety of settings, including inpatient psychiatric hospitals, forensic hospitals, outpatient mental health clinics, jails, or prisons. However, many states have moved from relying on inpatient competency evaluations to conducting evaluations at the outpatient service level (e.g., at mental health clinics or private practices; Grisso, 2003; Zapf & Roesch, 2009). CST evaluations are typically due to the courts in 30 days with possible extensions of up to 60 days (Grisso, 2003).

Once the competency evaluation has been submitted to the court, there is a judicial determination of competence. The judge may schedule a hearing to adjudicate the issue; however, a hearing is not always required if all court players agree on the defendant's competence (Grisso, 2003). Often, when one expert conducts a CST evaluation, the court agrees with the expert's opinion regarding CST and recommendations approximately 90% of the time (Zapf, Hubbard, Cooper, Wheeles, & Ronan, 2004). Hearings are more frequent when two experts are asked to conduct CST evaluations (Zapf & Roesch, 2009).

When a defendant is found competent, trial proceedings resume. If a defendant is found incompetent, the court determines whether the provision of treatment is likely to render the defendant competent to stand trial (Grisso, 2003). In *Jackson v. Indiana* (1972) the U.S. Supreme Court held that incompetent defendants cannot be held for treatment longer than the nature of their disorder warranted. Thus, courts must address the likelihood that the defendant can be restored to competence. When the disorder cannot be treated, the state must either drop the charges and release the defendant or initiate commitment proceedings under the state's civil commitment criteria. Medication is the most common form of treatment for incompetent defendants (Zapf & Roesch, 2009). If they respond to the treatment, they can return to court for a rehearing on their competence. In *Riggins v. Nevada* (1992), the court held that incompetent defendants have the right to refuse involuntary medications if they can demonstrate that the side effects interfere with their abilities in court.

When a defendant is undergoing treatment, reevaluations and rehearings on his or her competence are held approximately every three to six months (Grisso, 2003).

Best Practices

When conducting a CST evaluation and incorporating best practices, information is typically collected from three sources: the clinical interview, forensic assessment instruments, and third-party/collateral sources (Zapf & Roesch, 2009).

The Clinical Interview

The clinical interview is the primary method for conducting a CST evaluation. When evaluating an individual in any context, it is best practice to conduct a thorough clinical interview; however, this is particularly important in CST evaluations due to the contextual nature of the evaluation and the strong emphasis on psycholegal abilities (Zapf & Roesch, 2009).

The clinical interview should involve relevant notification information and informed consent, which includes the nature and purpose of the evaluation, who the report is submitted to, the procedures used, the possibility of testimony by the evaluator, the limits to confidentiality, and the right of refusal and consequences of the refusal (Zapf & Roesch, 2009). Additionally, a thorough background history should be obtained, including developmental and family history, educational history, marital history, military history, occupational history, mental health history, medical history, substance abuse history, and legal history. A mental status examination should be conducted, along with questions pertaining to psychiatric diagnosis. Furthermore, the evaluator should inquire about the individual's knowledge of the charges, his or her understanding of the legal system, his or her reasoning and decision making about a variety of legal scenarios, his involvement with the attorney and legal defense, and his or her proper courtroom behavior. Finally, the individual should be evaluated within the context of his or her legal charge against him or her and the typical requirements of defendants with similar legal circumstances.

Forensic Assessment Instruments

Research has found that the reliability of competency determinations increases when utilizing competency assessment instruments (Nicholson & Kugler, 1991; Skeem, Golding, Cohn, & Berge, 1998). Grisso (2003) expanded on this, stating that utilizing forensic assessment instruments (FAI) in evaluations of CST (a) provides structure to the evaluation process, (b) improves communication to the court, and (c) provides the evaluation with empirical support by associating psychological findings with legally relevant behaviors.

One such FAI is the Evaluation of Competency to Stand Trial-Revised (ECST-R; Rogers, Tillbrook, & Sewell, 2004), which was utilized in the case vignette that appears below. The ECST-R was designed to be consistent with the prongs of the *Dusky* standard. The first 18 items are divided into four scales, each producing total scores: (a) Factual Understanding of the Courtroom Proceedings (FAC), (b) Rational Understanding of the Courtroom Proceedings (RAC), (c) Consult with Counsel (CWC), and (d) Overall Rational Ability. The last 28 items are divided into five scales producing total scores that outline a defendant's style of responding to questions: realistic, psychotic, nonpsychotic, impairment, or both psychotic and nonpsychotic. The total scores on all of the scales are compared with similar peers who also were administered the instrument. The ECST-R takes approximately 30 minutes to administer. There are no cutoffs used to determine whether a defendant is competent to stand trial. The information derived from the ECST-R should be used along with other information gathered in the course of the evaluation.

Collateral or Third-Party Sources

It is vital to gather outside information from collateral sources that include information pertaining to the defendant's charges and allegations surrounding the alleged crime, reasons for the referral, and the expectations of the defendant moving forward. Other relevant information could be prior criminal history records and interactions with the legal system and interviews with collateral sources, including mental health professionals, jail personnel, jail medical staff, and anyone with which he or she has had recent contact (Zapf & Roesch, 2009).

It is important to note that all third-party records/sources should be reviewed for accuracy and reliability (Zapf & Roesch, 2009).

Case Vignette

Reason for Referral

Albert Krupen, a 26-year-old man from Northern Europe, was referred for a court-ordered evaluation. The defendant was charged with unlawful reentry. Mr. Krupen was referred for a CST evaluation. According to the court order, dated August 12, 2013, the defendant initially entered the United States on a work visa. Upon completion of his 12-month service as an au pair, Mr. Krupen failed to reapply for entrance into the United States.

Relevant Notifications

Upon the initial interview, on September 10, 2013, Mr. Krupen was notified of the nature and purpose of the evaluation. He was also informed of the unique limits of confidentiality, given the court-ordered nature of the evaluation. Mr. Krupen was informed that the evaluation would be conducted in compliance with a court order and that the information we discussed was not confidential. Specifically, he was told that clinical interviews would be conducted, psychological testing would be administered, behavioral observations would be completed, collateral information would be collected, and findings would be summarized in a report and submitted to the court. He was also told that the court might require that the evaluator testify in court about the assessment.

There are legal, ethical, and cultural considerations with regard to the discussion and assessment of the defendant's understanding of the limits of confidentiality. These considerations are equally as important in disclosing the nature and purpose of the evaluation. With regard to legal considerations, the ruling from *Estelle v. Smith* (1981) requires forensic evaluators to inform defendants of the purpose of the evaluation and the specific limits of confidentiality relevant to the evaluation (Grisso, 2003).

In terms of ethical considerations, the APA (2002) ethical code indicates that when services are court ordered, psychologists are required to notify the defendant that the court has mandated the evaluation. The code (APA, 2002) also recommends that, prior to the onset of the evaluation, the evaluator inform the defendant of the specific services that will be provided as well as the limits of confidentiality.

With regard to cultural considerations, the evaluation must be delivered in a language that is preferred and understandable to the defendant (APA, 2002; Dana, 2000; Geisinger, 2003). Mr. Krupen was fluent in English, and he indicated that he preferred to communicate in this language throughout the evaluation.

Assessment of the defendant's understanding and appreciation of the nature and purpose of the evaluation, as well as the limits of confidentiality, are

---

The case vignette has been redacted and all identifying information removed. It is not meant to serve as a forensic report. Any likeness to a case is purely coincidental.

important aspects of the evaluation process. The defendant's ability to accurately interpret the nature, purpose, and limits of confidentiality of the evaluation may be one of the first indicators of the presence of a mental impairment as well as the ability to appreciate her or his legal situation. As the evaluator, consideration must be given to whether the defendant's mental impairment and failure to articulate an understanding of these disclosures represents impairment in one of several competency-related functional abilities. In this case, it may provide information about the defendant's ability to engage, communicate, and assist in one's defense (Zapf & Roesch, 2009).

In this case, Mr. Krupen's understanding of the charges and reason for the psychological evaluation suggested a gross misperception due to delusional ideation. He insisted that the evaluation was a mistake, that he did not need a psychological evaluation, and that he did not have a mental illness. Mr. Krupen continued to explain that the family that he worked for had him sent to the jail. Mr. Krupen verbalized erotomanic delusions about his perceived relationship with the wife of his host family. He was also read and provided a typed Statement of Understanding. The Statement of Understanding summarized the purpose of the court-ordered evaluation and the processes involved in the evaluation, and the statement clearly defined the limits of confidentiality. Mr. Krupen refused to sign the document and refused participation in the evaluation. Thus, he was informed that this evaluator would contact his attorney and would return within a couple of days. Mr. Krupen spoke to his attorney and agreed to be interviewed. However, he refused to complete any paper-and-pencil-formatted psychological tests. Prior to subsequent interviews, he was reminded of the purpose of the evaluation and limits to confidentiality. Each time, he verbalized delusional ideation about the reason for his detainment.

Evaluation Procedures

A total of four clinical interviews with Mr. Krupen were conducted that totaled 7 hours and 45 minutes. The clinical interviews were conducted on September 10, 2013, September 16, 2013, September 23, 2013, and September 29, 2013.

Summary of Relevant Records (Sources of Information)

Court order dated August 12, 2013

Jail Intake Notes dated September 5, 2013

Relevant Background Information

It is important to address the defendant's reliability as a historian. The goal is to assess whether the defendant's mental impairment impacts his ability to recall remote information and to communicate effectively. Another goal is to assess the level of effort and overall approach to the assessment process as demonstrated by defendant. In this case, Mr. Krupen's ability to provide historical information was limited given his guarded presentation and systematized delusions.

Mr. Krupen reported that he was born and raised in Northern Europe to an intact family. He reported that, although English was his second language, he spoke the language fluently. Mr. Krupen described an uneventful upbringing. He stated that he had a close and meaningful relationship with his parents and three siblings.

Regarding education, Mr. Krupen indicated that he completed elementary and high school with honors. He reportedly began an associate's degree program in elementary education in the United States. It was during this time period that he obtained his first job, which was as an au pair. He reported that his work with the family ended after two months indicating, "My girlfriend did discuss how much she loved me." Mr. Krupen reported that he began a "love life" with the mother of the host family. However, corroborative documentation indicated that he had no relationship with her other than to work for the family. He stated that he never made his feelings of love for Mrs. Host known to anyone. However, he said he left love notes regarding his feelings for her. Since the time he stopped working for the family, he had reportedly e-mailed Mrs. Host more than 100 times. However, he said that Mrs. Host never wrote back. Mr. Krupen had never been married and has no children.

Mr. Krupen denied a significant history of medical treatment. Likewise, he denied a history of mental health symptoms and treatment. In terms of legal history, Mr. Krupen reported that he had never been arrested or in trouble with the law.

Mental Status Examination

The jail intake progress note dated September 5, 2013, was reviewed to assess Mr. Krupen's mental status upon arrival to the institution. According to the note completed by Dr. Intake, Mr. Krupen presented as oriented to person, place, and time. His demeanor was described as agitated and argumentative. His hygiene and grooming were reportedly fair. The note indicated Mr. Krupen articulated paranoid ideations with regard to the purpose of his stay at the jail. The content of his thoughts reportedly focused on his release from jail and return to his former employer's home. His insight into his need for mental health treatment as well as the reason for the referral was regarded to be poor.

Mr. Krupen was interviewed five times during his competency evaluation. During each interview, his clinical presentation remained relatively unchanged. He was dressed in a jail uniform, his hygiene and grooming appeared adequate, and his attitude was pleasant toward the examiner. However, he made clear that he was not in agreement with the need for the evaluation. Mr. Krupen displayed the ability to communicate his thoughts. He was well engaged during each clinical interview.

With regard to cognition, Mr. Krupen was fully oriented to person, place, and time. However, he had an impaired understanding of his legal situation. Specifically, he communicated the belief that there was no legal basis for his detainment at the jail, and he was waiting for Mrs. Host to pick him up. His insight into his legal situation was limited. His judgment was questionable.

> Mr. Krupen's mood appeared euthymic, and his affect was congruent. He denied thoughts a suicidal or homicidal nature. He reported having a good appetite and sleep habits. He displayed adequate energy throughout the evaluation process.

At times it was very difficult to follow Mr. Krupen's flow of conversation. His speech was tangential and irrelevant at times. The content of his speech was replete with erotomanic themes and persecutory delusions as it related to the purpose of the evaluation, his misperceived relationship with Mrs. Host, and the pending charges. His responses to questions regarding the charges were clearly distorted and based on delusional ideation. Mr. Krupen stated that Mrs. Host was coming to get him and would "release" him. By the third session, when asked why he believed Mrs. Host did not come to pick him up, he said that he thought she had to work and could not be excused to come get him. He added that Mrs. Host wanted to keep him detained as long as possible to ensure that "I don't stop loving her." He consistently denied hallucinatory processes and evidenced no overt signs suggestive of responding to internal stimuli. He displayed no insight into his illness. His judgment appeared tenuous.

Psychological Measures and Results

The use of psychological tests in CST evaluations to assess for competency-related functional abilities may vary from evaluator to evaluator. However, when psychological tests are used, competency-specific forensic assessment tools may be most relevant in addressing the psycholegal questions and in adding empirical support to the evaluation (Heilbrun, 1992; Grisso, 2003; Heilbrun, Grisso, & Goldstein, 2009; Zapf & Roesch, 2009).

The ECST-R was selected for the purpose of this CST evaluation for several reasons. First, as discussed earlier in this chapter, the ECST-R was developed based on the *Dusky* standard. The scales on the ECST-R also provide information directly relevant to the psycholegal issue, competency to stand trial.

Mr. Krupen was administered the ECST-R to assess the psycholegal domains relevant to the legal standard for competency to stand trial. This test is administered in an interview format and assesses three primary areas: the defendant's ability to consult with counsel, the defendant's factual understanding of the courtroom procedures, and the defendant's rational understanding of the courtroom proceedings.

Mr. Krupen appeared to put forth sufficient effort in answering competency-related questions. The results suggested a severe impairment in Mr. Krupen's ability to consult with his legal counsel as it relates to assisting and planning a successful defense strategy. While Mr. Krupen articulated a positive view of his attorney and his attorney's ability to represent him, he expressed the belief that his attorney's services were unnecessary due the defendant's false belief that the charges against him do not exist. When asked to provide information about how he would go about settling a disagreement with his attorney, Mr. Krupen continued to verbalize delusional ideation. Specifically, he said that Mrs. Host hired his attorney. Mr. Krupen was able to articulate that if a defendant disagreed with his attorney, then he could hire a new one. With regard to his own legal situation, Mr. Krupen stated that he would not look for a new attorney because "Mrs. Host wants me to be here."

Mr. Krupen's test results suggested knowledge of specific factual information of the courtroom proceedings. His overall score in the area of factual understanding of courtroom proceedings fell within the normal range. On the other hand, he continued to express an inaccurate understanding of the criminal charges against him. When asked to discuss the criminal charges against him, he insisted that Mrs. Host was responsible for his stay in jail and that there were no charges against him. After being informed of the documented charges, he was asked about the possible penalties, such as prison time. Again, his delusional ideation limited his ability to appreciate the charges against him. Specifically, he indicated that the only outcome would be to return to live with Mrs. Host.

Legal Statute

Under U.S. Code 4241, the defendant must "be presently suffering from a mental disease or defect rendering him mentally incompetent to the extent that he is unable to understand the nature and consequences of the proceedings against him or to assist properly in his defense."

Clinical Summary and Opinion

The summary and opinion section of a CST report must convey to the court the defendant's functional abilities as it relates to the issue of competency to proceed (Grisso, 2003; Zapf & Roesch, 2000). A long-standing debate among forensic evaluators exists as to whether or not it is appropriate to address the legal issue in the report or if the ultimate legal issue is to be determined by the trier of fact. Some researchers suggest that the forensic evaluator must speak only to the defendant's functional capacities and abilities (Ogloff & Douglas, 2003; Melton, Petrila, Poythress, & Slobogin, 2008; Heilbrun, Grisso, & Goldstein, 2009; Zapf & Roesch, 2009). The authors of this chapter agree with the latter. Thus, the summary and opinion section will speak to the defendant's functional abilities.

Mr. Krupen was interviewed regarding functional abilities relevant to competency to stand trial on several occasions. His ability to provide a factual and rational account of the charges against him and the circumstances that led to his arrest were significantly impaired by his delusional thought process. Consequently, he would have difficulty providing the necessary information in order to assist in his defense. As previously mentioned, Mr. Krupen appeared to suffer from Delusional Disorder, Mixed type with erotomanic and persecutory features. His false beliefs about having a romantic relationship with Mrs. Host and persecutory themes of being conspired against by all court personnel and prison staff (including the undersigned evaluator) dominated all discussions as it related to his actual charges.

Mr. Krupen was asked questions to assess his factual knowledge of the legal proceedings against him. He consistently reported the idea that he believes the charges against him are false despite having reviewed court documents, which specify the charges and reason for the referral. He was unable to provide a factual or rational explanation of the charges against him or the events that led to his arrest. It was evident during each interview that he did not retain or believe the explanation given to him about the pending charges. Rather, he asserted that the court documents were "bogus." By the third interview, he stated that he did not believe the charges were real and that his "girlfriend" [Mrs. Host] would come to pick him up the next day. He went on to describe the delusional themes. Mr. Krupen had no appreciation as to whether or not the charges against him were a felony or misdemeanor. He simply said, "The whole thing is fake." When asked whether a felony or misdemeanor is a more serious charge, he indicated that he did not know.

Another aspect of factual understanding is having knowledge of the members or roles of courtroom personnel and participants. Overall, Mr. Krupen's awareness of the roles of courtroom participants during a trial was good. He was able to accurately define the role of the judge, defense attorney, prosecutor, witness, and defendant.

The assessment of Mr. Krupen's understanding of the possible pleas and consequences and appreciation of the potential outcomes were also key elements of factual understanding. Mr. Krupen was questioned regarding his understanding of the possible pleas. It was unclear as to his true level of knowledge regarding these terms because he never directly addressed the question. Instead, he continued to deny the validity of the charges against him. He was unable to examine the available defenses. His appreciation of the possible penalties was also impaired. Mr. Krupen was asked to articulate his understanding of what could occur if he were found guilty. He said, "These charges aren't real. There is no way I have to leave this country." Mr. Krupen denied awareness of the concept of a plea bargain. Although this concept was explained to him, he was unable to appreciate how this legal concept pertained to him because of the belief that all aspects of his case are "superficial" or have been made up.

Mr. Krupen's ability to assist in his defense was also assessed. Mr. Krupen indicated that he knew his attorney and provided his correct name. He stated that he had confidence in his attorney. Nevertheless, he also expressed the belief that Mrs. Host hired his attorney. When asked to discuss the meaning of confidentiality between him and his attorney, Mr. Krupen's response was irrelevant to the question asked. Mr. Krupen's delusional beliefs also markedly impaired his appreciation of the collaborative relationship between himself and his attorney. He stated that he must do what Mrs. Host instructs him to do, not his attorney. He also indicated that he would contact Mrs. Host to get her advice on whether he should work with his attorney. He was asked how his attorney could assist him. Mr. Krupen stated that his attorney could not help him get released. He explained that the only person that could get him out of jail was Mrs. Host. With regard to settling disagreements with his attorney, he said that he would not terminate him because Mrs. Host hired him. In terms of appropriate courtroom behavior, Mr. Krupen expressed an understanding of the potential consequences of engaging in inappropriate behavior in court.

Mr. Krupen articulated a limited appreciation for courtroom procedures. He articulated some confusion about the process of testimony. He said he thought that defendants were always required to testify in their own cases. Based on his comments, he did not appear to have an appreciation for the adversarial nature of cross-examination.

Based on the totality of the information previously outlined, Mr. Krupen was unable to provide a factual understanding of the charges against him or to assist in his defense. His ability to do so was markedly impaired by his delusional thought processes. Mr. Krupen lacked an ability to consider and integrate information based on own legal situation due to his delusional beliefs. He was unable to provide a logical, factual, or sequential account of the events that led to his arrest due to his psychosis. His explanation of his legal situation was based upon false beliefs or delusions related to his idealized romantic relationship with Mrs. Host. Thus, he lacked an appreciation of the potential consequences of his legal situation.

Mr. Krupen displayed a limited ability to reason and engage in appropriate decision making as it related to his case. He refused to sign any documents and negated the relevance of court documentation. Given Mr. Krupen's firm delusions surrounding his relationship with the victim as it relates to the alleged offense, it was likely that he would not be able to assist in planning effective legal strategies.

Mr. Krupen's reasoning abilities were also impaired due to his mental condition. Based on his most recent mental status, Mr. Krupen would not be able to consider relevant information as it relates to his case. Likewise, he was unable to consider his legal options or potential consequences due to his impaired thinking.

Mr. Krupen's ability to explain the basic roles of courtroom members was fair; however, he expressed a belief that the alleged victim hired his attorney. His ability to fully participate in the undersigned evaluation was impacted by his psychosis.

In summary, it was the evaluator's opinion that Mr. Krupen was presently suffering from a mental disease or defect that limited his ability to understand the nature and consequences of the proceedings against him or to assist properly in his defense.

Common Pitfalls and Considerations

CST evaluations are the most commonly requested evaluations performed by psychologists in criminal court (Stafford, 2003). The assessment of CST requires familiarity with relevant nomenclature and statutes. The language used to describe "competency" or "fitness" to stand trial may vary across state and federal jurisdictions. The use of the wrong terminology in an evaluation may lead to confusion about the referral question at hand. Having a rote understanding of the legal system and procedures in the United States will enable a deeper understanding of how to assess a defendant in a CST evaluation. In fact, this basic understanding of the legal system and legal principles is an ethical obligation of psychologists. Furthermore, evaluators must be knowledgeable of relevant case law and statutory criteria. Inclusion of the applicable state or federal statute in the report articulates the functional abilities that are to be assessed according to the law. Thus, it is important to have an understanding of what the jurisdiction requires of the defendant with regard to functional abilities. The type of questions in a CST evaluation may differ by jurisdiction.

This chapter offered a case vignette to illustrate the key components of a CST evaluation. This case also discussed and applied best practices regarding competency-related abilities as recommended by leaders in the field of forensic psychology (Frederick, DeMier, & Smith, 2014; Zapf & Roesch, 2009; Goldstein & Weiner, 2003; Grisso, 2003; Melton, Petrila, Poythress, &

Slobogin, 2007). A common pitfall is that some evaluators fail to use multiple sources of data and multiple methods to evaluate the defendant and to form their hypotheses and conclusions regarding competency to stand trial. When multiple sources of data (e.g., collateral contacts, records, etc.) are available, it is a best practice to obtain and integrate the information.

Additionally, evaluators must determine whether they would like to utilize a specific forensic test to assist in their determination of competence. Thus, another pitfall is the use of clinical assessment tools that are not relevant to the referral question. As stated previously, research has shown that utilizing a competency assessment instrument increases the reliability of competency determinations. However, the disadvantage of incorporating assessment instruments is that it opens up more diverse and potentially challenging lines of questioning in cross-examination if expert witness testimony takes place.

How and to what degree does the presence of mental illness affect the adjudication of incompetence? When conducting CST evaluations, it is important to know that the presence of a mental illness or related symptoms does not necessarily mean that the individual lacks the functional abilities for competency to stand trial. Conducting CST evaluations requires consideration of the defendant's relevant functional abilities. The evaluation must address the impact of the defendant's mental illness and the severity of the defendant's symptoms on competency relevant functional abilities.

Another pitfall is the lack of awareness of the constitutional rights of the defendant. Given that the CST evaluation is conducted at the pretrial stage, it is important to exclude incriminating information regarding the defendant's role in the criminal act. For example, to understand the defendant's ability to communicate his or her version of the alleged events, the evaluator may ask him or her to speak about this. Another example is to assess the defendant's ability to reason and weigh the relevance between multiple defense strategies. The defendant may discuss which strategy he or she feels would be most beneficial. Because this information may speak to the defendant's admission of guilt, the evaluator should take caution to not include the details of these inquiries in the evaluation report. Instead, the evaluator could summarize the quality of the defendant's overall psycholegal abilities in those areas. In summary, inclusion of information in the report regarding the defendant's criminal responsibility is a mistake that is often made. Such information is a post-adjudicative legal matter that does not belong in a pretrial assessment of competency to stand trial.

With regard to evaluation and conclusions, there are varying opinions about whether the evaluator must address the ultimate legal question by documenting whether or not the defendant "is competent" or "is not competent." According to the "Specialty Guidelines for Forensic Psychology" (APA, 2013), evaluators are cautioned against answering the legal question at hand; this is the job of the trier of fact (i.e., the judge). Offering such conclusions is not within the professional competence of psychologists. However, jurisdictions differ on what they require of experts in submitting reports and in expert testimony. Often evaluators may feel pressure from various members of the legal profession to offer such conclusions (Melton et al., 2007). As specified in the APA ethical code (2002) when professional and legal obligations conflict, psychologists are to make known professional obligations first and proceed accordingly. Ultimately, the CST evaluation must be driven by the psycholegal issue documented in the court order, the requirements of the law, and the functional abilities necessary to be adjudicated to competence to stand trial by the court.

References

American Psychological Association. (2002). *American Psychological Association ethical principles of psychologists and code of conduct*. Retrieved May 20, 2015, from http://www.apa.org/ethics/code2002.html

American Psychological Association. (2013). Specialty guidelines for forensic psychology. *American Psychologist, 68*(1), 7–19. doi:10.1037/a0029889

Bonnie, R. J. (1992). The competence of criminal defendants: A theoretical formulation. *Behavioral Sciences and the Law, 10*, 291–316.

Bonnie, R. J., & Grisso, T. (2000). Adjudicative competence and youthful offenders. In T. Grisso & R. Schwartz (Eds.), *Youth on trial: A developmental perspective on juvenile justice* (pp. 73–103). Chicago, IL: University of Chicago Press.

Dana, R.H. (2000). *Handbook of cross-cultural and multicultural personality assessment*. New York: Psychology Press.

Drope v. Missouri, 420 U.S. 162 (1975).

Dusky v. United States, 362 U.S. 402 (1960).

Estelle v. Smith 451 U.S. 454 (1981).

Farkas, G. M., DeLeon, P. H., & Newman, R. (1997). Sanity examiner certification: An evolving national agenda. *Professional Psychology: Research and Practice, 28*(1), 73–76.

Frederick, R. I., DeMier, R. L., & Smith, M. S. (2014). *Examinations of competency to stand trial: Foundations in mental health case law* (2nd ed.). Sarasota, FL: Professional Resource Press.

Geisinger, K. F. (2003). Testing and assessment in cross-cultural psychology. In J. R. Graham & J. A. Naglieri (Eds.), *Handbook of psychology: Assessment psychology* (pp. 95–117). New York: Wiley.

Goldstein, A. M., & Weiner, I. B. (Eds.). (2003). *Handbook of psychology: Vol. 11. Forensic psychology*. Hoboken, NJ: Wiley.

Grisso, T. (2003). *Evaluating competencies: Forensic assessments and instruments* (2nd ed.). New York, NY: Kluwer Academic/Plenum.

Heilbrun, K. (1992). The role of psychological testing in forensic assessment. *Law and Human Behavior, 16* (3), 257–272.

Heilbrun, K., Grisso, T., & Goldstein, A. (2009). *The foundations of forensic mental health assessment*. New York: Oxford University Press.

Higgins v. McGrath, 205 F.2d 650 (9th Cir. 1953).

Hoge, S. K., Bonnie, R., Poythress, N. G., & Monahan, J. (1992). Attorney-client decision-making in criminal cases: Client competence and participation as perceived by their attorneys. *Behavioral Sciences and the Law, 10*, 385–394.

Illinois Code of Criminal Procedure, Fitness for trial, to plead or to be sentenced, 725 ILCS 5/104 (1963).

Jackson v. Indiana, 406 U.S. 715 (1972).

Melton, G. B., Petrila, J., Poythress, N. G., & Slobogin, C., with Lyons, P. M., Jr., & Otto, R. K. (2007). *Psychological evaluations for the courts: A handbook for mental health professionals and lawyers* (3rd ed.). New York, NY: Guilford Press.

Meyer, R. G., & Weaver, C. M. (2006). *Law and mental health: A case-based approach.* New York, NY: Guilford Press.

Nicholson, R., & Kugler, K. (1991). Competent and incompetent criminal defendants: A quantitative review of comparative research. *Psychological Bulletin, 109*, 355–370.

Ogloff, J. R., & Douglas, K. S. (2003). Psychological assessment in forensic settings. In J. R. Graham, J. A. Naglieri, & I. B. Weiner (Eds.), *Handbook of psychology: Volume 10: Assessment psychology* (pp. 345–363). New York, NY: Wiley.

Pate v. Robinson, 383 U.S. 375 (1966).

Poythress, N. G., Bonnie, R. J., Monahan, J., Otto, R., & Hoge, S. K. (2002). *Adjudicative competence: The MacArthur studies (Perspective in Law & Psychology, Volume 15).* New York, NY: Kluwer Academic/Plenum.

Riggins v. Nevada, 504 U.S. 127 (1992).

Rogers, R., Tillbrook, C. E., & Sewell, K. W. (2004). *Evaluation of Competency to Stand Trial—Revised (ECST-R).* Odessa, FL: Psychological Assessment Resources.

Skeem, J., Golding, S., Cohn, N., & Berge, G. (1998). Logic and reliability of evaluations of competence to stand trial. *Law and Human Behavior, 22*, 519–547.

Slobogin, C., Rai, A., & Reisner, R. (2008). *American Casebook Series: Law and the mental health system: Civil and criminal aspects* (5th ed.). St. Paul, MN: West Academic.

Stafford, K. P. (2003). Assessment of competency to stand trial. In A. M. Goldstein & I. B. Weiner (Eds.), *Handbook of psychology: Vol. 11. Forensic psychology* (pp. 359–380). New York, NY: Wiley.

United States Department of Justice (2006, September). Bureau of Justice Statistics: Mental health problems of prison and jail inmates (NCJ 213600). Washington, DC: Office of Justice Programs.

Wieter v. Settle, 193 F. Supp. 318 18 U.S.C. 4241.

Zapf, P. A., & Roesch, R. (2009). *Best practices in forensic mental health assessment: Evaluation of competence to stand trial.* New York, NY: Oxford University Press.

Zapf, P. A., Hubbard, K. L., Cooper, V. G., Wheeles, M., & Ronan, K. A. (2004). Have the courts abdicated their responsibility for determination of competency to stand trial to clinicians? *Journal of Forensic Psychology Practice, 4*, 27–44.

3

Conducting Criminal Responsibility Evaluations

Allison M. Schenk, Emily D. Gottfried, and Michael J. Vitacco

Criminal responsibility evaluations are one of the most controversial and contentious areas of mental health law. On one hand, the insanity defense is vastly misunderstood by the general public due to its sensationalized portrayal in the media. On the other hand, the notion of convicting someone who was unable to form intent or understand the wrongfulness of his or her actions, due to a mental disease or defect, is considered unjust. Despite their contentiousness, criminal responsibility evaluations are arguably one of the most complex, challenging, and fascinating in the field of forensic psychology. A criminal responsibility evaluation assesses the defendant's mental state at the time of an alleged crime; the retrospective nature of the evaluation adds to its complexity. The criminal justice system requires those it prosecutes to have committed a criminal act (actus reus) and also to have had intent or knowledge the act was criminal (mens rea).

History and Relevant Case Law of Criminal Responsibility

An examination of ancient texts reveals references to criminal actions being excused for reasons of "madness," being an "idiot" or "madman," or possessing the understanding of a child (Melton, Petrila, Poythress, & Slobogin, 2007; Packer, 2009). In 1723, the concept of insanity was initially defined as follows: "a man must be totally deprived of his understanding and memory so as not to know what he is doing; no more than an infant, brute, or wild beast" (*Rex v. Arnold*, 1724). It was not until the mid-nineteenth century that the first formal test of insanity was put forth. Known as the "Wild Beast" test, this standard would set an almost unattainable bar for a defendant to meet in order to be found not responsible.

In England, Daniel M'Naghten believed he was being persecuted by England's right-wing political party and sought to kill Prime Minister Robert Peel, the person he thought was most at fault for his persecution (Meyer & Weaver, 2006). He was unsuccessful in killing the prime minister, but he did kill the prime minister's secretary. Many medical experts testified about M'Naghten's mental state at the time of the crime, which led to his acquittal. To prevent an insurgence of politically motivated acts of violence, the House of Lords defined a test for subsequent insanity defenses that stipulated a defendant had to be "laboring under such a defect of reason, from disease of the mind" that he did not know the nature or quality of his actions or that they were wrong (M'Naghten Case, 1843). A century and a half later, there is still a required link between the "disease of the mind" and the individual's inability to understand the consequences and wrongfulness of his or her actions (Rogers, 2008a).

The M'Naghten standard remains the oldest and most widely used test for legal insanity, and the standard is still employed directly or in some variation in 26 states today. It has faced some criticism as people have argued this standard is too rigid or places too much emphasis on assessing the defendant's cognitive awareness or ability to know right from wrong (e.g., cognitive prong). This standard is typically referred to as the "right versus wrong" test.

In response to criticisms of the M'Nagthen standard, many jurisdictions chose to add a volitional prong to their insanity standard. Coined the "irresistible impulse test," this component allows a defendant to be found insane if he knew what he was doing was wrong (cognitive prong) but, because of a mental disease or defect, could not keep himself from engaging in the crime (volitional prong). A major criticism of the "irresistible impulse test," which is founded on a long-standing debate, is successfully differentiating between an impulse that *was not* resisted and one that *could not* be resisted (see Packer, 2009).

The Durham Rule (*Durham v. U.S.*, 1954), or "product test," was adopted by several jurisdictions in the United States. This standard allowed the defendant to be found insane if the criminal actions were the result, or product, of a mental illness. As with M'Naghten, there must be a direct link between the mental illness and the criminal act. This standard allowed significant leeway in the expertise of mental health practitioners regarding mental illness and its influence on criminal behavior (Bartol & Bartol, 2015). Unfortunately, the courts found the testimony of experts confusing and "difficult to interpret" (Meyer & Weaver, 2006, p. 118), as well as inconsistent (Packer, 2009). Ultimately, the "product test" was overturned in favor of a more restrictive insanity defense in all jurisdictions except for one (*U.S. v. Brawner*, 1973). This standard is currently employed only by New Hampshire, and this standard remains the least restrictive insanity standard.

In 1962, the American Law Institute (ALI) wrote the Model Penal Code, which was a new formulation of the standards for the insanity defense. The goal of the ALI was to strike a balance between the broadness of the Durham Rule and the rigidity of the cognitively focused M'Naghten standard. In *U.S. v. Brawner* (1972), Judge Bazelon modified the Model Penal Code slightly and devised what is now referred to as either the ALI rule or Brawner rule. The ALI/Brawner rule incorporates both cognitive and volitional components for insanity. It states that an individual should be found not guilty by reason of insanity (NGRI) "if at the time of his unlawful conduct his mental or emotional processes or behavior controls were impaired to such an extent that he could not justly be held responsible for his act" (as cited in Melton et al., 2007, p. 207). The ALI/Brawner standard was the first to specify diagnoses related to criminal conduct (e.g., Antisocial Personality Disorder) did not constitute a mental disease or defect in the eyes of the court. The ALI/Brawner standard is still used in many states but was abandoned as the standard for insanity by the federal government in 1984, following the attempted assassination of President Reagan.

The landscape of the insanity defense changed dramatically after John Hinckley was found NGRI for his attempted assassination of the President and his shooting of two others in 1981. The Insanity Defense Reform Act (IDRA) in 1984 removed the volitional prong from the insanity defense. For a defendant to be found NGRI under the IDRA, he or she must have been "unable to appreciate the nature and quality or wrongfulness" of the act (Insanity Defense Reform Act, 1984). The IDRA also shifted the burden to the defendant to prove he or she met this standard at the time of the crime and limited the testimony that could be given by expert witnesses. Most notably, expert witnesses are not allowed to provide an ultimate opinion regarding the question of insanity when testifying (see FRE, 704[b]).

Another change in many jurisdictions was the creation of the guilty but mentally ill (GBMI) defense. This standard allows a defendant to be found guilty of the crime but also acknowledges the presence of a mental illness. A successful GBMI defense still results in a finding of guilt, and the defense may (but does not have to) reduce the seriousness of the charge or the penalty. In theory, offenders found GBMI would have some form of treatment for their mental illness incorporated into their punishment. One of the criticisms surrounding this defense is that effective treatment for these offenders is not guaranteed, and many can still face the most serious of penalties, including the death penalty (Bartol & Bartol, 2015; Roesch, Zapf, & Hart, 2010).

To date, four states have chosen to abolish the insanity defense completely: Idaho, Montana, Utah, and Kansas. Nevada also attempted to eliminate this defense, but the Nevada Supreme Court ruled that doing so violated both state and federal constitutions (*Finger v. State*, 2001). The U.S. Supreme Court has consistently declined to rule on the issue regarding the constitutionality of the insanity defense. As recently as 2012, this issue was brought to the U.S.

Supreme Court (*Delling v. Idaho*, 2012), but only three of the nine justices voted to hear the case, which was insufficient to grant certiorari (Bartol & Bartol, 2015). The U.S. Supreme Court did rule in *Clark v. Arizona* (2006) that there was no specific language or minimum standard that needed to be included in a state's statute surrounding the insanity defense.

In addition to the controversy about the various insanity standards, there has been a great deal of debate generated regarding the definition of key words or phrases in these different standards. For example, does wrongfulness refer to moral wrongfulness, legal wrongfulness, or both? Unfortunately, a complete discussion of the existing case law and debated definitions of these terms is outside the scope of this chapter. Readers are encouraged to refer to Packer (2009) or Melton et al. (2007) for a more thorough account of these terms and their debated meanings within the insanity standards.

Given the variety of standards and requirements surrounding the insanity defense and criminal responsibility evaluations, it is essential for the forensic evaluator to be familiar with the statues governing his or her practicing jurisdiction(s). In addition to which insanity standard is applied in the jurisdiction, it is important to be familiar with other key factors before beginning the criminal responsibility evaluation. Such factors include the legal standard of proof for determining insanity, the guidelines for how and to whom the criminal responsibility report will be distributed, and the rules for proffering testimony on the ultimate issue (Meyer & Weaver, 2006; Packer, 2009).

Best Practices

Criminal responsibility evaluations entail, at a minimum, clinical interviews and an extensive review of collateral data. Criminal responsibility, and all forensic evaluations for that matter, should be focused on testing alternative theories related to the criminal behavior. For example, in criminal responsibility evaluations, the two hypotheses to be tested involve whether the defendant is or is not criminally responsible. Thinking about forensic evaluations in a hypothesis-testing manner can be helpful in keeping an open mind about the case and preventing confirmatory biases from influencing professional opinions.

Collateral Information

In preparing for a criminal responsibility evaluation, it is important to gather all pertinent records and read the entire discovery of the case. A review of police reports can provide important information about the defendant's mental state at the time of arrest. For example, valuable data can be gleaned from police interviews, and this provides an opportunity to obtain a sense of the defendant's thought process. Any notable or bizarre statements made by the defendant at the time of arrest or during interviews with the police should be noted, and it may be beneficial to ask the defendant about these statements during the clinical interview. Additionally, if video is available of the defendant's police interview, this could provide critical information about mental status in close proximity to the alleged offense. For example, an evaluator watching the interview may be able to determine how organized the defendant was, as well as if and to what degree he responded to internal stimuli. It is also important to read police interviews of family members and witnesses to the alleged crime. These documents can provide information about whether or not the defendant was behaving peculiarly in the time period leading up to the alleged offense and may include information about statements the defendant made during the offense. For instance, if, during the clinical interview, a defendant claims that he did not sleep for four days prior to the instant offense and if the police report includes a contradictory statement from the defendant's wife claiming that her husband was observed frequently sleeping, this would be beneficial to include in the written report.

In addition to the case discovery, supplementary records should be requested. Although criminal responsibility is only concerned with the mental state at the time of the alleged offense, records can provide invaluable historical information to support or provide evidence against a hypothesis. Requested records should vary depending on the defendant's history. School records can provide information about a defendant's intelligence, the presence of learning disorders, early behavioral problems, and psychiatric history. Requesting all mental health records is also very important. Although a prior psychiatric history is not necessary to argue that a defendant is not criminally responsible, this fact has proven useful in differentiating individuals found not responsible from those found responsible. In fact, Packer (1987) found individuals meeting the criteria for insanity often had previous findings of being not competent to proceed to trial. These defendants also were less likely to have a previous felony conviction and were more likely to have prior psychiatric hospitalizations and psychotic disorder diagnoses.

As discussed in greater detail below, the mere presence of a mental illness is not enough to claim that an individual is not responsible for their crime. Records may reveal that a defendant was involuntarily hospitalized in the week prior to the instant offense or may show that a psychiatrist noted that he or she was not exhibiting any symptoms during the routine medication management appointment the previous week. A comprehensive review of records should also include substance use treatment records. Additionally, jail records should be reviewed to determine whether the defendant is currently being prescribed medication, whether symptoms are reported, and what his or her behavior has been like at the jail. All of this information can be used to support or contradict a hypothesis.

Interviews

After the evaluator reviews all collateral documents related to the case, the next step is to conduct clinical interviews with the defendant. A forensic notification outlining his or her rights concerning the evaluation should always be provided. In some cases, it may be beneficial and prudent to have the defendant sign a form confirming receipt and understanding of the notification of rights. This will vary by state, but a defendant should be made aware that an NGRI plea is an affirmative defense, and a defendant should understand the potential consequences of pleading NGRI. It should be explicitly noted that the evaluation is not confidential and that everything the defendant says and does during the evaluation could be described in a written report and in subsequent testimony. The defendant should also be told who will have access to the report (i.e., the prosecuting attorney). In the best case scenario, the defendant's attorney will have already informed the defendant of the circumstances of an NGRI plea, and the defendant is aware that an evaluation is to take place. It is more often the case that an attorney requested a competency to stand trial and criminal responsibility evaluation with no mention of that request to his or her client. In these situations, the defendant will be unaware that an evaluation was requested or what this type of evaluation entails. These situations require the evaluator to provide a more thorough explanation of the purpose of the evaluation and notification of the defendant's rights.

The interview should begin with a review of the defendant's history, which includes information regarding developmental, social, abuse, educational, employment, medical, psychological, substance use, and legal history. A mental status examination should be completed, and the defendant's appearance, behavior, cooperation, reliability, speech, thought process, thought content, mood, affect, insight, judgment, perception, and cognitive functioning should be described (Robinson, 2008). Diagnostic impressions should be considered, whether they are made using a structured diagnostic interview or asking about symptoms during the clinical interview. A diagnosis (or at the very least, specific symptoms) should be provided in the written report. The history of these symptoms and all previous treatment and hospitalizations should be described in detail in the mental health history section of the report, as this information could provide information about a defendant's mental illness (or lack thereof), which is necessary (but not sufficient by itself), for a criminal responsibility defense.

The next step in the evaluation process is to ask the defendant to provide his or her account of what happened at the time of the offense. Some defendants may provide a detailed description of the events, and others may need to be prompted. Whenever possible, it is best to start with open-ended questions and progress to more specific, close-ended questions as needed. It is important to gather information about the defendant's behaviors and functioning before, during, and after the alleged offense, as well as his or her understanding and explanation of these behaviors. This information can provide the evaluator with an idea of the defendant's mental status around the time of the alleged offense. Table 3.1 includes examples of questions that could help the evaluator elicit such information.

Melton and his colleagues (2007), as well as Packer (2009), also provide similar examples of questions that can be helpful to elicit information in these evaluations.

After the defendant provides his or her statement, it is recommended that the evaluator then ask questions about statements that were made during the arrest and question other data obtained from the police records. For instance, a defendant may make a bizarre statement that sounds delusional during the police interrogation. If given an opportunity to explain such statements, it may be discovered that the statement was, in fact, quite rational and that it makes sense once the context is known. Of course, forensic evaluators must be cognizant that evaluees often appear more rational during their interviews. As such, a close review of all collateral information is useful in parsing out symptoms of mental illness from atypical behaviors and odd statements.

Defendants Who Deny the Allegations

As a NGRI plea is an affirmative defense, a defendant must admit to committing the crime. Therefore, an evaluator may conclude that a criminal responsibility evaluation is not possible if the defendant denies the allegations; however, if the defendant is willing to answer more vague or hypothetical questions, the evaluation should still continue under these circumstances. Instead of asking the defendant for specific information regarding the alleged crime, it is recommended that the evaluator ask more general questions. Examples of such questions are provided in Table 3.2.

Additionally, asking the defendant to describe what was happening in his or her life and how he or she was feeling (psychologically and physically) around the time period of the arrest can reveal important information. Asking about symptoms, medications, illicit substance use, sleep patterns, and sleep disturbances is recommended, even for defendants who deny the allegations.

Testing

Psychological testing is not directly related to criminal responsibility evaluations, and the use of testing is indicated on a case-by-case basis (Packer, 2009). Packer reviewed studies that found 57% of forensic psychologists indicated they always incorporated psychological testing into criminal responsibility

TABLE 3.1 Examples of Questions for a Criminal Responsibility Interview

Possible Questions

Behavior Before the Alleged Offense

What was happening in the weeks leading to the crime?

Were you sleeping, eating, prescribed and taking medication?

Were you using alcohol in the weeks leading up to the alleged crime?

Behavior During the Alleged Offense

On what day and where did the alleged crime occur?

Begin with the morning of the alleged crime; tell me about your whole day.

Were you hearing voices, seeing visions?

Did you drink alcohol on this day?

Were you using drugs on that day of the alleged crime?

What happened during the crime?

What were you thinking?

Were there any problems with the way you were thinking?

What was it about that moment/why did you allegedly commit the crime at that time versus other times?

Behavior After the Alleged Offense

Tell me about what you did after the alleged offense?

Did you do anything to avoid being caught?

What did you think when you got arrested?

What did you tell the police?

Did you tell anyone else about the crime?

Reasoning and Understanding of Actions

What was your reason for doing that action during the alleged offense?

Did you know the victim?

Why did you choose this particular victim?

Have you ever done or considered doing this in the past? If so, where, when, to whom?

What did you expect to happen as a result of your actions?

Did you consider not taking these actions?

What could have prevented you from taking these actions?

Would you have done the same thing if there was a police officer nearby at the time of the crime?

Did you know you could get into trouble?

How did the police know that you did it?

How are you different now than you were at the time of the alleged crime?

TABLE 3.2   Examples of Questions for Defendant's Denying Criminal Allegations

How would someone go about engaging in these actions?

Why would someone do this?

What purpose would these actions serve?

How could a person benefit from doing this crime?

Would you ever engage in this type of behavior?

Is this crime wrong?

evaluations. Specifically, individuals being charged with a crime may be motivated to malinger or feign symptoms of a mental illness, cognitive deficits, or intellectual disability. It is recommended that malingering tests be used if there is any question regarding the genuineness of symptoms. For example, the Miller Forensic Assessment of Symptoms Test (M-FAST; Miller, 2001) is an empirically supported screening measure of feigned psychiatric symptoms. The M-FAST is one of several measures that assesses feigned symptoms, but this test is very commonly used as a brief assessment. For a more in-depth examination of feigning or after a positive M-FAST result, the Structured Interview of Reported Symptoms, Second Edition (SIRS-2; Rogers, Sewell, & Gillard, 2010) is recommended as it has been validated and supported by empirical research (Rogers, 2008b). To examine the feigning of memory deficits, the Test of Memory Malingering (TOMM; Tombaugh, 1996) could be used. Although the TOMM is frequently used, there are other measures that can assess feigned memory deficits (for a complete listing of these measures please refer to Sweet, Condit, & Nelson, 2008).

Other types of testing that may be warranted include standardized intelligence tests, such as the Wechsler Adult Intelligence Scale, Fourth Edition (WAIS-IV; Wechsler, 2008), or a personality assessment. The use of the Minnesota Multiphasic Personality Inventory-2-Restructured Form (MMPI-2-RF; Ben-Porath & Tellegen, 2008) or the Personality Assessment Inventory (PAI; Morey, 2007) would afford the evaluator an opportunity to examine the defendant's performance on validity scales that assess effort, exaggeration, and minimization, as well as to identify useful information about current symptoms from the clinical scales. Packer (2009) summarized studies that found that 94% of forensic psychologists studied reported they used the MMPI, and 78% reported using the WAIS in their evaluations. The use of psychological assessments can be instrumental in hypothesis testing during criminal responsibility evaluations, but some thought should be put into deciding which tests will be useful. Like all forensic reports, as the written product of the evaluation could be scrutinized in court, the use of any psychological test must be fully justified.

Writing the Report

The written product is arguably the most important aspect of any forensic evaluation and may be the only opportunity an evaluator has to clearly piece together the evidence and present his or her opinion. It is of utmost importance to include all relevant facts, even if a particular piece of information contradicts the evaluator's final conclusion. Including information that contradicts the opinion, even if it could confuse the clinical picture, contributes to the creation of an unbiased report.

The written product should begin with the defendant's identifying information, where and when the evaluation took place, and who ordered it. The fact that the defendant was informed and signed (or refused to sign) a notification of rights form should be clearly stated, and a list of all of the collateral sources reviewed should be included. It may be useful to include the statute for the state in which the criminal responsibility evaluation is taking place to clearly outline the framework that is being considered in the evaluation. Next, the relevant historical information should be described, the mental status examination outlined, the results of any psychological tests that were administered explained, and the diagnostic impressions provided. For the criminal responsibility section, a detailed account of the crime should be included based on the police report and other documents included in the discovery materials. This section would also be where the defendant's statement to the police is detailed and any available witness statements are summarized. The defendant's description of the offense obtained during the evaluation should follow the official description of the crime. The use of quotes can be a helpful way to illustrate how the defendant described his or her perception of the events of the crime. After the defendant's account of events is described, the questions regarding how he or she was functioning in the time period leading up to the crime should be outlined. Some evaluators then choose to offer their opinion on the ultimate issue (i.e., if the evaluator believes that the defendant was or was not criminally responsible at the time of the crime), whereas other evaluators simply describe their evaluation of the defendant and leave the ultimate issue decision to the trier of fact.

The decision to offer an opinion on the ultimate issue should be informed by one's practicing jurisdiction's stance on this issue. For example, for evaluations in federal courts, Rule 704(b) of the *Federal Rules of Evidence* (2013) states, "In a criminal case, an expert witness must not state an opinion about whether the defendant did or did not have a mental state or condition that constitutes an element of the crime charged or of a defense. Those matters are for the trier of fact alone" (pp. 15–16). Despite this prohibition on ultimate opinion testimony, there are no bans against providing an ultimate opinion in a report. Likewise, some state courts may not accept a report in which an ultimate opinion is not offered. Although we acknowledge the debate on the ultimate issue within the field of forensic mental health (Rogers & Ewing, 2003; Tillbrook, Mumley, & Grisso, 2003), we propose that reports should contain this information and allow the trier of fact to place appropriate weight on these opinions.

Regardless of whether or not an ultimate opinion is offered, the written report should contain enough information that a judge or jury can make an informed decision and for the reader to draw conclusions for each component of the insanity standard used in that area. For example, in order to assess the defendant's appreciation of the nature and quality of the actions (cognitive prong), it is important to include the defendant's perception of the crime as well as all collateral information regarding his or her actions during the alleged offense. To assess the defendant's appreciation of the wrongfulness of the offense, the evaluator should ask questions that could uncover a delusional thought process, as this might affect the perception of wrongfulness. In order to assess volition, the evaluator should inquire about any attempts to engage in alternative actions, as well as any previous feelings to compulsively engage in this (or similar) actions.

Case Vignette

The following case study is meant to highlight aspects of a criminal responsibility evaluation, which incorporates standards of best practice, as previously described. This case was created by the authors based on their professional experiences and any likenesses to an actual case are purely coincidental. This case is not meant to serve as a forensic report.

Reason for Referral

A criminal responsibility evaluation was requested for Mr. Doe by his defense attorney. Mr. Doe was a 29-year-old Caucasian male who was arrested for first-degree murder. He was being held at the county jail.

Sources of Information

Prior to evaluating Mr. Doe, available records were requested and reviewed, including prior medical and psychiatric records, school records, employment records, the police report and discovery materials for the crime, and records from the jail where Mr. Doe was being held. Requests also were made to speak with relevant family members who had regular contact with Mr. Doe.

Notification of Rights

Mr. Doe was evaluated by a forensic evaluator on two occasions for approximately 180 minutes, and again for an additional 60 minutes, at the county jail.

The case vignette has been redacted and all identifying information removed. It is not meant to serve as a forensic report. Any likeness to a case is purely coincidental.

Prior to the evaluation, Mr. Doe was informed about the purpose of the evaluation, the limits of confidentiality, who would be given copies of the report, and the voluntary nature of his participation. Mr. Doe also read and signed a consent form that reiterated this information. He agreed to proceed with this evaluation.

Relevant Background Information

The evaluation commenced with a brief clinical interview to glean pertinent information regarding Mr. Doe's history. Mr. Doe was considered to be a reliable but guarded historian. He described an average, unremarkable development and upbringing. His mother noted that he had difficulty making friends growing up and was "a loner." He also earned average grades in school and completed two years of college at a local university where he was studying geology. He explained that he was walking to class one day when he felt a gust of wind and knew he had "learned everything I would ever need to know." He stopped attending classes and eventually dropped out of college. According to records from the university, he had difficulty concentrating in classes, and he would hand in assignments and tests with bizarre responses. For example, he wrote illogical, tangential essays regarding "darkness and evil." Mr. Doe explained that when he dropped out of college, he obtained an apartment and performed odd jobs before being employed as a janitor at a movie theater. He described an unremarkable medical history and denied ever being married or fathering any children. Mr. Doe admitted drinking four beers every night for one year prior to the alleged offense but denied experimenting with illicit substances or requiring substance abuse treatment. With some reluctance, Mr. Doe reported receiving mental health treatment in the community at the encouragement of his parents after dropping out of school. He was prescribed psychiatric medications and diagnosed with a mental illness but was unable to recall the names of his medications or diagnosis. His mental health records support a diagnosis of Schizophrenia and prior medications include a variety of typical and atypical antipsychotics (e.g., Risperdal, Zyprexa, and Navane). Regarding a family history of mental illness, Mr. Doe reported that his uncle is "crazy" and his grandmother "had a nervous breakdown." Mr. Doe denied ever being arrested prior to this offense, which was confirmed by his criminal records.

Mental Status Examination

During the evaluation, Mr. Doe appeared his stated age of 29. He was slightly unkempt, as evidenced by his dirty fingernails and long, greasy hair; however, he was not malodorous. As previously noted, Mr. Doe was guarded, but he cooperated throughout the evaluation, and he was considered to be a fairly reliable historian. He made appropriate eye contact and seemed able to concentrate for the majority of the evaluation. His psychomotor movements were unremarkable, and he spoke at a normal rate and volume. There were times when Mr. Doe seemed to lose track of the question, and he exhibited some word-finding difficulties. At the outset of this evaluation, he described his mood as "fine." His affect presented as flat. While at the county jail, Mr. Doe was prescribed Haldol and Cogentin, which he took voluntarily; however, he lacked insight into why he was prescribed these medications and how they help him. As previously noted, Mr. Doe became noticeably more agitated and difficult to redirect when discussing the events surrounding the crime. His speech was rapid and pressured. He presented as agitated and intent on sharing his account of events. His responses also were more tangential and much more difficult to follow.

Mr. Doe had some limitations in his fund of general knowledge. He was able to identify the current president of the United States, but struggled to list any factual current events as he maintained the only events on the evening news were the newscasters telling him about his neighbor's evilness. Mr. Doe's immediate memory was intact, as he was able to immediately repeat back three unrelated words. He had some impairment in his delayed memory (i.e., the ability to recall information that was previously presented), as he was unable to recall any of the three words on his own. After being given categorical prompts, he was able to recall all three words. Mr. Doe was able to complete five serial seven subtractions, as well as correctly spell words forwards and backwards. These tasks were given to briefly assess his working memory abilities. His abstract reasoning abilities were concrete and limited. For example, when asked to interpret a common proverb ("the early bird gets the worm"), Mr. Doe stated, "The birds have to get up, and they eat worms." He demonstrated adequate problem solving abilities, as evidenced by his simple responses to commonplace problems. For example, he responded "yell and get help" to what he would do if he saw a building on fire.

Mr. Doe's Account of Events Related to the Alleged Offense

Approximately three months ago, Mr. Doe was working as a janitor at a movie theater and saw his neighbor enter the theater. Shortly afterwards, Mr. Doe's boss called him into his office, and Mr. Doe was fired. Records from his employer document a history of Mr. Doe coming to work late and missing shifts and his employer receiving complaints that Mr. Doe followed customers from the theater and into the parking lot. Mr. Doe reported that he had suspicions that his neighbor was "evil" for a while, and seeing him when he lost his job confirmed this belief in his mind.

Mr. Doe provided numerous examples of events and explanations for why he was certain his neighbor was evil. Mr. Doe admitted that he began watching his neighbor more carefully and documenting in his journal the negative events he believed his neighbor was responsible for. One commonly documented event was that whenever Mr. Doe saw his neighbor, he would have difficulty sleeping that night. Mr. Doe reported that he attributed his difficulty sleeping to some of his neighbor's evilness transferring to him whenever they would pass one another. Mr. Doe also described seeing his neighbor pull into the parking lot, get out of his car, and enter their apartment building. When Mr. Doe went to start his car after witnessing his neighbor coming home, his car would not start. Although Mr. Doe's car battery was dead, he again attributed this event to his neighbor's evilness. Mr. Doe also believed his neighbor was evil because he drove a red truck. He started going through his neighbor's mail and found letters from addresses that contained the number "6," which he interpreted as communications with the devil. Mr. Doe detailed a variety of other events and "signs" that were similar in nature.

Mr. Doe reported that this pattern of watching his neighbor and logging events went on for approximately two months until he felt unbearably distressed by the torture his neighbor was inflicting upon him. As he became more upset by the torture, his sleep impairments worsened. He also reported that the newscasters on television would tell him how worthless he was, how meaningless his life was, and how powerless he was to make his life better. He explained that hearing these messages agitated him further and prompted him to "take my life back."

On the day of the crime, Mr. Doe reported he was unable to find his television remote. He believed his evil neighbor was behind his missing television remote to prevent him from hearing the newscasters' messages to change his life. At that time, Mr. Doe walked across the hall to his neighbor's apartment and knocked on the door. When his neighbor answered the door, Mr. Doe repeatedly stabbed him while yelling for the "evil to end" and to "stop torturing me." He then moved the body inside his neighbor's apartment, shut the door, and returned to his own apartment. Mr. Doe proceeded to shower, change his clothes, and place his bloodied clothes and knife in the dumpster. According to police reports, neighbors heard Mr. Doe yelling while he stabbed the neighbor. They called the police and identified Mr. Doe as the assailant. He was arrested in his apartment. After a search warrant was executed for Mr. Doe's apartment, the journal in which he detailed every negative event he attributed to his neighbor was found.

Psychological Measures

Although Mr. Doe's presentation was consistent with genuine mental illness and malingering was not suspected, a Structured Interview of Reported Symptoms, Second Edition (SIRS-2; Rogers et al., 2010) was administered to ensure he was not feigning or over-exaggerating his symptoms. As previously explained, this measure is a structured interview designed to assess whether someone is feigning psychological symptoms in a variety of ways, such as exaggerating the severity of symptoms or endorsing very rare, uncommon symptoms that are inconsistent with genuine mental illness. On this measure, Mr. Doe responded selectively to symptomatic experiences. His results on each subscale fell within the "Genuine" range of responding, which further supported the hypothesis that Mr. Doe was not feigning symptoms of mental illness. There were no concerns regarding Mr. Doe's intellectual functioning based on his self-report, his presentation during the evaluation, his mother's report in a phone interview, and corroboration from educational records. Mr. Doe was administered the PAI, which is a self-report objective inventory of adult personality that assesses response style, personality, and psychopathology (Morey, 2007). He produced a valid PAI profile, which suggested he attended appropriately and consistently to the test items. Mr. Doe's responses on the PAI are consistent with individuals who have reported unusual perceptual experiences, such as hallucinations, confusion in their thinking, and delusional beliefs. He endorsed some questions associated with some alcohol use. These results are consistent with Mr. Doe's self-report and collateral sources (e.g., records, interview with family members).

Clinical Summary

Mr. Doe lives in a jurisdiction governed by the M'Naghten standard. This standard states that a defendant should be found not guilty by reason of insanity if, at the time of the alleged offense, he was suffering from a mental disease or defect that prevented him from knowing the nature and quality of his actions or, if he did have this knowledge, he was unaware that his actions were wrong. Based on his account of events, Mr. Doe knew that he was stabbing his neighbor with a knife (knowledge about the *nature* of his actions) and that stabbing his neighbor repeatedly would kill him (knowledge about the *quality* of his actions). Because he believed that killing his neighbor would stop the "torture" and suffering, he seemed to know the quality of his actions.

The issue in Mr. Doe's case centers around whether, as a result of a mental disease or defect, he was unable to appreciate that what he was doing was wrong. His actions of moving the body inside his neighbor's apartment and closing the apartment door, as well as showering and disposing of the bloodied clothes and knife, suggest that Mr. Doe knew his actions were wrong and made an effort to hide what he had done. His journal and some of his neighbor's stolen mail also were found in a drawer with a false bottom in Mr. Doe's nightstand.

There are also reasons to suggest that Mr. Doe did not understand that what he was doing was wrong because of his mental disease or defect. He has a well-documented history of schizophrenia, and although he was prescribed psychiatric medications, he had not taken them in more than four months. An interview with Mr. Doe's mother reported that over the last few months her son had become increasingly withdrawn and paranoid. He frequently spoke about the "evil all around him." Mr. Doe's journal also documented a long-standing belief that his neighbor was evil and torturing him. The journal contained rambling writings from Mr. Doe that he believed he would be killed by his neighbor if he did not do something to "get control" over his life soon. Based on his verbalizations during the murder, Mr. Doe believed that he was freeing himself from torture by killing his evil neighbor.

Questions to Consider When Formulating an Opinion

Because of the complex and challenging nature of criminal responsibility evaluations, the following questions in Table 3.3 can be helpful to consider when formulating an opinion. This is not meant to be an exhaustive list and questions will vary depending on the specific facts of the case.

In addition to these questions, Rogers (1987) has five points to be considered when evaluating volitional components of the insanity defense. These include a capacity to make choices, a capacity for delay, a regard for apprehension, foreseeability, and avoidability.[1]

Common Pitfalls and Considerations

A good criminal responsibility evaluation is one that avoids several common pitfalls. NGRI is not based on the presence of a mental illness alone. That is, simply having a psychotic spectrum diagnosis does not automatically suggest that the individual is NGRI (Miller, 2013). Indeed, one study reported that individuals who had been adjudicated sane and not NGRI obtained higher scores on the clinical scales of the MMPI-2 than did those adjudicated NGRI (Rogers & McKee, 1995). Rogers's (2008b) review of relevant literature led him to conclude that elevations on the MMPI family of instruments are not automatically more indicative of being NGRI. Of course, criminal responsibility evaluations in which an opinion of nonresponsibility is rendered must provide an explicit connection between the mental illness and the alleged criminal behavior. To that end, the MMPI-2 and other multiscale inventories are incapable of making this explicit connection.

Another pitfall to avoid is accepting the defendant's account of the alleged offense as complete and accurate and not requesting or reviewing collateral data that could be contradictory to the defendant's self-report. It is possible

TABLE 3.3   Examples of Questions to Consider When Formulating an Opinion

Possible Questions

Cognitive Prong

Was the defendant mentally ill at the time of the alleged offense?

What is the nature and severity of this individual's mental illness?

At the time of the alleged offense, was the defendant receiving treatment? If so, was he compliant with the treatment?

Is there evidence that treatment was effective or ineffective in managing symptoms of mental illness?

Was the defendant abusing substances at or around the time of the offense? If so, what substance(s)? How much? How frequently?

If the defendant was mentally ill at the time of the offense, how did the illness directly impact his ability or inability to differentiate right from wrong? Be specific and identify clear links (if any exist) between his mental illness and psycholegal deficits.

Was there planning and preparation involved in the act? If so, how much?

Were there steps taken to destroy or hide evidence? If so, what were they?

Were there measures taken to avoid apprehension? If so, what were they?

What is the defendant's history with the victim?

Was it a random victim or were they known to one another?

Is there a clearly identified motive for the crime?

What was the defendant's stated explanation for the alleged offense?

What is the defendant's current understanding of the wrongfulness of the alleged offense?

An evaluator should always consider potential issues regarding response style (e.g., malingering). Was there any evidence the defendant was malingering regarding clinical presentation related to the alleged offense?

Volitional Prong*

If the defendant was mentally ill at the time of the offense, how did the illness directly impact his ability or inability to conform his actions as required by the law? (Be specific and identify clear links [if any exist] between his mental illness and psycholegal deficits.)

What evidence is there for impulsivity?

What is the evidence for planning?

Why was the crime committed at this particular time? Why now?

Were there times when this impulse was successfully resisted?

Were there steps taken to destroy or hide evidence? If so, what were they?

Were there measures taken to avoid apprehension? If so, what were they?

*In jurisdictions that have a volitional prong, additional questions should be considered. There will be overlap between the questions considered, such as the need for assessing for the presence or absence of mental illness.

that defendants may attempt to feign or exaggerate symptoms or problems, while other defendants may minimize or deny problems in order to appear healthier than they were at the time of the alleged offense. Collateral records and interviews with other people can help to identify this discrepancy. Additionally, making an overreaching conclusion that goes beyond what the data is suggesting is to be avoided.

Finally, a good forensic report should be extremely thorough. As indicated above, criminal responsibility evaluations should consist of hypothesis testing and evaluators should have their clinical opinions firmly rooted in the data obtained. Moreover, the report should not reflect the evaluator's personal opinions but should include only professional opinions rooted in the scientific method. Including data in the written product, even data that contradicts the evaluator's opinion, is of the utmost importance.

Conclusion

As previously explained, when conducting a criminal responsibility evaluation, it is necessary to know what standard of insanity governs the jurisdiction in which the evaluation is being completed. The evaluation should clearly present the available evidence both supporting and refuting components of that standard used to evaluate an insanity defense. The report should present this information and clearly guide readers through the evaluators' thought process and reasoning. It is important for an evaluator to be aware of the legislative requirements and his or her own professional stance on providing an ultimate issue opinion in criminal responsibility evaluations. The final report should be in compliance with these standards.

Note

1. An ultimate opinion is not being provided in Mr. Doe's case to allow the reader an opportunity to independently think through the information provided, establish their own opinion, and identify how they reached that opinion and rejected the alternative hypothesis.

References

Bartol, C. R., & Bartol, A. M. (2015). *Psychology and law: Research and practice*. Thousand Oaks, CA: Sage.

Ben-Porath, Y., & Tellegen, A. (2008). *MMPI-2-RF (Minnesota Multiphasic Personality Inventory-2 Restructured Form): Manual for administration, scoring, and interpretation*. Minneapolis: University of Minnesota Press.

Clark v. Arizona, 548 U.S. 735, 126 S. Ct. 2709, 165 L. Ed. 2d 842 (2006).

Delling v. Idaho, 133 S. Ct. 504 (U.S. 2012).

Durham v. U.S., 214, F.2d 862 (1954).

Federal Rules of Evidence. (2013). Washington: DC: Lexis-Nexis Group.

Finger v. State, 27 P.3d 66, 117 Nev. 548 (2001).

Insanity Defense Reform Act of 1984, 18 U.S.C. §17.

Melton, G. B., Petrila, J., Poythress, N. G., & Slobogin, C. (2007). *Psychological evaluations for the courts: A handbook for mental health professionals and lawyers* (3rd ed.). New York, NY: Guilford Press.

Meyer, R. G., & Weaver, C. M. (2006). *Law and mental health: A case-based approach.* New York, NY: The Guilford Press.

Miller, H. (2001). *Miller Forensic Assessment of Symptoms Test manual.* Odessa, FL: Psychological Assessment Resources.

Miller, L. (2013). Psychological evaluations in the criminal justice system: Basic principles and best practices. *Aggression and Violent Behavior, 18,* 83–91.

M'Naghten case, 8 English Reporter 718 (1843).

Morey, L. C. (2007). *Professional manual for the Personality Assessment Inventory* (2nd ed.). Lutz, FL: Psychological Assessment Resources.

Packer, I. K. (1987). Homicide and the insanity defense. A comparison of sane and insane murderers. *Behavioral Sciences & the Law, 5,* 25–35.

Packer, I. K. (2009). *Evaluation of criminal responsibility.* New York, NY: Oxford University Press.

Rex v. Arnold, 16 Howell's State Trials 684 (1723).

Robinson, D. J. (2008). *The mental status exam explained* (2nd ed.). Port Huron, MI: Rapid Psychler Press.

Roesch, R., Zapf, P., & Hart, S. D. (2010). *Forensic psychology and law.* Hoboken, NJ: Wiley.

Rogers, R. (2003). The prohibition on ultimate opinions: A misguided enterprise. *The Journal of Forensic Psychology Practice, 3*(3), 65–75.

Rogers, R. (2008a). Insanity evaluations. In R. A. Jackson (Ed.), *Learning forensic assessment* (pp. 109–128). New York, NY: Taylor & Francis Group.

Rogers, R. (2008b). Structured interviews and dissimulation. In R. Rogers (Ed.), *Clinical assessment of malingering and deception* (pp. 301–322). New York, NY: The Guilford Press.

Rogers, R., & Ewing, C. P. (1987). The APA position on the insanity defense: Empiricism vs. emotionalism. *American Psychologist, 42,* 840–848.

Rogers, R., & McKee, G. R. (1995). Use of the MMPI-2 in the assessment of criminal responsibility. In Y. S. Ben-Porath, J. R. Graham, G. C. Hall, R. D. Hirschman, & M. S. Zaragoza (Eds.), *Forensic applications of the MMPI-2* (pp. 103–126). Newbury Park, CA: Sage.

Rogers, R., Sewell, K. W., & Gillard, N. D. (2010). *Structured Interview of Reported Symptoms,* (2nd ed.): *Professional manual.* Lutz, FL: Psychological Assessment Resources.

Sweet, J. J., Condit, D. C., & Nelson, N. W. (2008). Feigned amnesia and memory loss. In R. Rogers (Ed.), *Clinical assessment of malingering and deception* (pp. 218–236). New York, NY: The Guilford Press.

Tillbrook, C., Mumley, D., & Grisso, T. (2003). Avoiding expert opinions on the ultimate legal question: The case for integrity. *Journal of Forensic Psychology Practice, 3*(3), 77–87.

Tombaugh, T. (1996). *Test of Memory Malingering (TOMM).* New York, NY: Multi Health Systems.

United States v. Brawner, 471 F.2d 969 (D.C. Cir. 1972).

Wechsler, D. (2008). *Wechsler Adult Intelligence Scale, Fourth Edition.* San Antonio, TX: Pearson.

4

Capital Case Sentencing Evaluations

Samuel Witta Dworkin and Steve K. D. Eichel

In capital cases, a defendant faces criminal charges that could result in a death sentence (i.e., capital punishment). These are the most serious types of criminal cases in that the ultimate loss of one life rests in the outcome of a complex justice system. The defendant, defense counsel, prosecutors, judges, jurors, victims, experts, media, and others all have a role in this process. This chapter will focus on the role of the forensic evaluator in cases of capital sentencing, highlighting the work as part of an interdisciplinary team with mitigation specialists and defense counsel.

There are numerous types of evaluations that call for experienced and skilled forensic psychologists, clinicians, and practitioners in the realm of capital cases. *Atkins* evaluations, which are geared toward determining a defendant's level of intellectual disability (formerly mental retardation), are quite common. Evaluators conduct competency evaluations on defendants to ascertain their ability to understand the proceedings and assist their counsel or ascertain whether the defendants demonstrate the necessary competency to be executed. Violence risk assessments are also common in capital cases.

This chapter will focus on capital sentencing evaluations, which are conducted, not to determine why the defendant carried out the crime or the offense for which he or she has been charged but to provide the defense team with biopsychosocial life history evidence of the defendant that could demonstrate a lower level of moral culpability and support life imprisonment as an alternative to a death sentence. The question of "why" the crime occurred is often a guilt/innocence phase issue, whereas answering "how" the defendant got to be in this particular place in life is most applicable in the sentencing phase of trial. It is the forensic evaluator's responsibility to work with the defense team to craft a narrative that persuades the jury on how the defendant's history, character, and life circumstances affected the trajectory of his or her behavior. In capital sentencing, the forensic evaluator must develop a complete, nuanced, and intimate understanding of the defendant to assist the defense team in presenting the full picture of the defendant to the sentencer. In this chapter, we will discuss relevant case law, applicable literature, and guiding beliefs regarding best practices for conducting capital sentencing evaluations. We will also outline a case vignette to demonstrate in real-life terms how these evaluations are conducted.

Relevant Case Law

In order to understand the full scope and nature of the proceedings in a capital case, one must first understand the background and history of the death penalty in the United States. Capital punishment has roots in the United States dating back to its early colonization. As explained by Stuart Banner, early colonialists enacted capital punishment laws for a host of crimes, including blasphemy, property crimes, and others (Banner, 2002). Throughout the eighteenth and nineteenth centuries, capital punishment was used largely in racism and oppression, evolving in its scope of offense and offender, but taking full aim at the minority populations of the United States. In 1972, the United States Supreme Court struck down the death penalty in *Furman v. Georgia*, creating a moratorium on capital punishment. The court concluded that the imposition of the death penalty was in fact cruel and unusual punishment in that it violated the Eighth and Fourteenth Amendments. In a review of the arbitrariness of the state's statutes, the capital scheme on the whole was found unconstitutional. Justice Douglas stated, "These discretionary statutes are unconstitutional in their operation. They are pregnant with discrimination and discrimination is an ingredient not compatible with the idea of equal protection of the laws." *Furman v. Georgia* provided what might be the most guiding principle in capital case litigation and guidance: death is different. "Death is a unique punishment," "Death . . . is in a class by itself," the "penalty of death differs from all other forms of capital punishment, not in degree but in kind" (*Furman v. Georgia*, 1972).

In 1976, however, in *Gregg v. Georgia*, the U.S. Supreme Court reinstituted the imposition of the death penalty and "provided the states with clarification on the distinction between constitutional and unconstitutional death penalty statutory schemes" (DeMatteo, Murrie, Anumba, & Keesler, 2011). Since the moratorium on capital punishment has been lifted, though, there has been a continued reexamination of statutes and related issues. Efforts to narrow the imposition and application of the death penalty are seen in decisions like *Atkins v. Virginia* in 2002 (making it unconstitutional to execute the mentally retarded), *Roper v. Simmons* in 2005 (disallowing the imposition of death for juveniles under the age of 18 when the offense was committed), and *Kennedy v. Louisiana* in 2008 (barring the death penalty for the rape of a child in which the child did not die).

Notable case law exists for the purposes of capital sentencing evaluations, and this case law is illustrated in the emergence of opinions emphasizing individualized sentencing and the duty to investigate, uncover, and develop mitigation. In 1975, the U.S. Supreme Court struck down North Carolina's statutes of mandatory death sentences for all convicted first-degree murderers. It stated in a 5–4 decision:

> Death, in its finality, differs more from life imprisonment than a 100-year prison term differs from one of only a year or two. Because of that qualitative difference, there is a corresponding difference in the need for reliability in the determination that death is the appropriate punishment in a specific case.

Here we see two interesting points. The court uses language that recognizes not only the finality of death but also the "need for reliability in the determination" of the sentence. This is the beginning of the recognition of heightened scrutiny in sentencing determinations. While not directly stated, this opinion expounds on the importance of expert assistance and evaluations in sentencing. The second component to the decision is the notation of what is "the appropriate punishment in a *specific case.*" This is illustrative of the need for the *individualized* assessment model on which capital case forensic evaluations are based.

In 1978, The U.S. Supreme Court also held in *Lockett v. Ohio* that Ohio's capital sentencing scheme was unconstitutional:

> The Ohio death penalty statute does not permit the type of individualized consideration of mitigating factors we now hold to be required by the Eighth and Fourteenth Amendments in capital cases. . . . The limited range of mitigating circumstances which may be considered by the sentencer under the Ohio statute is incompatible with the Eighth and Fourteenth Amendments. To meet constitutional requirements, a death penalty statute must not preclude consideration of relevant mitigating factors.

Again, we are seeing the emergence of emphasis not only on mitigation in sentencing but also on individualized consideration. This sets up the basis for the need of forensic psychologists, psychiatrists, and practitioners to do capital sentencing evaluations.

In an ineffective assistance-of-counsel claim in 2003, the U.S. Supreme Court held that Wiggins's attorneys "fell short of the professional standards" and that "the scope of their investigation was also unreasonable" given that "the mitigating evidence counsel failed to discover and present in this case is powerful" (*Wiggins v. Smith*, 2003, p. 22). In *Rompilla v. Beard* (2005), the court also emphasized the importance of defense efforts in investigating mitigation, holding "that even when a capital defendant's family members and the defendant himself have suggested that no mitigating evidence is available, his lawyer is bound to make reasonable efforts to obtain and review material that counsel knows the prosecution will probably rely on as evidence of aggravation at the sentencing phase of trial" (p. 18).

Review of Literature

Given the variety of standards and regulations surrounding capital sentencing evaluations, and the complexities involved in death penalty litigation in general, it is essential for the forensic evaluator to be familiar with the statutes governing his or her practicing jurisdiction(s). Aside from the aforementioned case law, which outlines the necessity and constitutionality of individualized mental health and mitigation assessments for capital defendants, additional legal and nonlegal binding literature exists to support the need for, and importance of, these forensic evaluations.

State courts, federal jurisdictions, and military commissions all employ different language when outlining the complexity of the capital defense team and its roles. However, it is accepted that the defendant is entitled and required to have a mitigation investigation take place, and to have the assistance of a qualified and competent forensic evaluator to assist in the sentencing evaluation. For example, in Virginia, statute §19.2-264.3:1 outlines the defendant's statutory right to a forensic sentencing evaluator:

> Expert Assistance when defendant's mental condition relevant to capital sentencing: the court *shall* appoint one or more qualified mental health experts to evaluate the defendant and to assist the defense in the preparation and presentation of information concerning the defendant's history, character, or mental condition, including (i) whether the defendant acted under extreme mental or emotional disturbance at the time of the offense; (ii) whether the capacity of the defendant to appreciate the criminality of his conduct or to conform his conduct to the requirements of the law was significantly impaired at the time of the offense; and (iii) whether there are any other factors in mitigation relating to the history or character of the defendant or the defendant's mental condition at the time of the offense. (emphasis added)

The American Bar Association (ABA) also sets forth standards of care and competence for defense counsel in capital cases. Guidelines 4.1 and 10.4 of the 2003 ABA Guidelines lay out the minimum requirements for the defense team composition. It states that, among the qualified counsel, an investigator, and a mitigation specialist, there must also be "at least one member qualified by training and experience to screen individuals for the presence of mental or psychological disorders or impairments".

Just as the legal team is bound by guidelines and principles, so too is the forensic evaluator/examiner. Familiarization with the latest America Psychology Association (APA) guidelines is a must, specifically the 2013 "Specialty Guidelines for Forensic Psychology." Developed by the American Psychology-Law Society and the American Academy of Forensic Psychology, these guidelines lay out several areas of importance for the evaluator. Areas of particular importance in capital sentencing evaluations include, but are not limited to, Knowledge of the Scientific Foundation for Opinions and Testimony (Guideline 2.05), Appreciation of Individual and Group Differences (Guideline 2.08), Communication with Collateral Sources of Information (Guideline 6.04), Focus on Legally Relevant Factors (Guideline 10.01), and others.

Best Practices

The forensic evaluator's goal is not to do a results-oriented evaluation. This may be difficult when the defense team has identified the evaluator as the expert of choice and has had him or her appointed with an understanding of the specific hypothesis the defense wants confirmed. Although it is unethical to conduct a "defense team hypothesis-confirmation evaluation," it is completely reasonable to have those hypotheses on a short list. In fact, it would be unreasonable to discount and discard the defense team's thoughts completely. It is the role of the mitigation specialist and defense team to supply the practitioner with interviews, records, and data points that will be considered. These are the same data points that have led the defense team to its hypothesis (or hypotheses) as well. It is important for the evaluator to conduct the capital sentencing evaluation with an open mind but also be bound by the scope of the referral question, the applicable case law and statutes, and the confines and requirements of his or her appointment.

For example, in looking back at Virginia's statute authorizing appointment of a forensic sentencing evaluator in capital cases (§19.2-264.3:1), note the language "to evaluate the defendant *and to assist the defense* in the preparation and presentation of information concerning the defendant's history, character, or mental condition." Here it is clear that the evaluator is not just to do testing and an independent evaluation but is to work with the defense team, assisting in the preparation and presentation of mitigation and sentencing information. Again, this does not give the evaluator carte blanche to abandon principles of objectivity and independence. However, the language seeks to inform the evaluator that he or she is a member of the defense team, tasked with assisting them, working on behalf of the defendant and for the betterment of that defendant's sentencing.

It should also be noted that the forensic sentencing evaluator is to conduct a culturally competent evaluation. This means not only finding an evaluator who ideally speaks the same language as the defendant but also screening for culturally appropriate and applicable mental health disorders, as well as using appropriately normed tests and evaluation materials.

As noted previously, there are many types of forensic evaluations that can take place in a capital death penalty case. This chapter looks at what goes into conducting a capital sentencing evaluation and examines the interdisciplinary approach and skill sets required for this type of evaluation. The first half of the case vignette tracks the efforts and methods of the mitigation specialist in a capital case. The second half of the case vignette tracks the efforts of the forensic evaluator.

First, the mitigation specialist works to develop trust and rapport for the purposes of conducting a social history investigation. This involves gathering background information about the defendant that guides the investigation. The mitigation specialist is then informed where to go to collect records and collateral witness interviews. This process includes, but is not limited to, interviewing the defendant, friends, family, teachers, employers, medical personnel, and many others, as well as obtaining records of all aspects of the defendant's life (see the 2008 *ABA Supplementary Guidelines for the Mitigation Function of Defense Teams in Death Penalty Cases*). While utilizing his or her mental health training and knowledge, the mitigation specialist screens for potential disorders, symptoms of mental illness, neurological impairments, and other factors that would aid the defense team in making an appropriate selection of a forensic evaluator (see Guideline 10.11E of the 2008 *ABA Supplemental Guidelines*).

There can be several factors to consider when choosing a forensic capital sentencing evaluator. Most notable would be the local state statutory requirements and guiding principles outlined above by the ABA. Evaluators can have specialties such as a background in neuropsychology, a focus on adolescent development and attachment, some foundational work in pharmacology, or a focus on traumatic brain injuries (TBI). The capital sentencing evaluator works in consultation with the defense team, engaging in interviewing strategies, reviewing collateral source information received from the mitigation specialist and defense team, testing (intelligence, neuropsychology, etc.), report writing, and possible testimony. The evaluator will conduct mental status examinations, potential psychological tests and measures, and ultimately may be asked for his or her clinical summary and opinion.

Case Vignette

The following case narrative is not based on any one specific case on the whole; rather, it incorporates a combination of real-life scenarios and fact patterns not uncommon to capital defense.

The case vignette has been redacted and all identifying information removed. It is not meant to serve as a forensic report. Any likeness to a case is purely coincidental.

Reason for Referral

Jason Smith was a 21-year-old white male from rural Pennsylvania. He was the younger child, born to unwed parents who separated after his birth. Mr. Smith had an older half brother. He has lived in Pennsylvania all of his life, although never in one permanent residence for more than a couple of years. Mr. Smith had, at times, lived with his biological father, but he spent the majority of his time with his mother and stepfather. He did not complete high school, and at the time of the instant offense was working for a construction company as a laborer.

Mr. Smith allegedly murdered his girlfriend Clare, who was eight months pregnant at the time. Mr. Smith called the police himself, and he was apprehended presumably only hours after the victims' deaths. He was being held at the local county jail, and he has been appointed capital-qualified counsel and resources, including a mitigation specialist. He was facing the death penalty, as he had been charged capitally under Pennsylvania's Title 18, Part I, Ch. 11, Sec. 1102 and Title 42, Part VIII, Ch. 97, Sec. 9711(d) for the first-degree killing in which the victim was in her third trimester of pregnancy.

RE: Mitigation Specialist: Meeting Defendant and Developing Trust and Rapport. During the first meeting with Mr. Smith, the mitigation specialist's goal was to build trust and rapport. The defendant was asked whether he likes the name "Jason" or goes by any nickname. The instant offense was not discussed; rather Mr. Smith was engaged in conversation and dialogue about his well-being and status. Had he been able to call family? Was he eating? Are there any immediate problems (other than his current incarceration) that needed to be addressed? It was important that Mr. Smith understood and began to see, through the mitigation specialist's words and actions, that he or she cared given the circumstances. While it was not known for sure, it was a distinct possibility that Mr. Smith had not had consistent caring relationships throughout his life. It was necessary to model positive behaviors and thoughtfulness of action to Mr. Smith in order to develop trust and rapport.

In the first couple of meetings, the mitigation specialist spent a good deal of his time with Mr. Smith engaging in conversation, wherever it was to lead. It was important not to go into the meeting with a checklist of questions, a recorder, or laptop. It was thought that taking copious notes during the interview would break up the flow and authenticity of getting to know Mr. Smith, as well as prevent him from getting to know a valuable member of his legal defense team. A laptop or note pad creates a barrier that hinders conversation. It was likely Mr. Smith had already sat in a similar room at the police station upon arrest, with police officers questioning him—legal pads out and recorders on—and reviewing the alleged offense in great detail. The goal was for the mitigation specialist to distinguish himself from that experience with law enforcement in Mr. Smith's mind and allow him to appreciate the nature in which they would be working with him as part of his defense team. One must still type up notes from the conversation immediately after interviews and disseminate them to the defense team. Keeping an accurate record of conversations and interviews is extremely important, as well as keeping the entire defense team informed of progress throughout the course of the interviews. Rapport is a must, but equally important is document-ing the interviews and information gleaned from the defendant.

Relevant Background Information

RE: Mitigation Specialist. Trust and rapport did not happen overnight. Nor does it happen the next week. It was a constantly worked-on and sought-after goal, requiring honest and genuine dialogue with Mr. Smith. Along the way, and once established, the mitigation specialist can begin to obtain biographical and social history information. This information provides the building blocks for the miti-gation investigation. It helps the mitigation specialist determine whom to speak with, where to obtain records, and other avenues for investigation.

Mr. Smith revealed that he did not graduate high school and dropped out after his junior year. He did not do well overall academically, and he recalled being in special education classes for a period of years in one middle school leading into high school. Mr. Smith reported that he played football for his middle school and high school teams but still felt that he did not fit into any one particular peer group. He thought this may be due to the fact that he and his mother moved a significant number of times during his childhood. Mr. Smith attended two elementary schools, three middle schools, and two different high schools before he ultimately dropped out. While Mr. Smith did not disclose specific instances or recollections of bullying by his peers, he elu-sively stated he did not get along with his peer group in school and mentioned some "behavioral issues" on his part.

Mr. Smith could not recall all the various addresses at which he has lived over the years. He liked some areas better than others and stated that this was mainly due to availability of other kids his age. While he never made any long-lasting friendships, there were several individuals he recalled by name as hav-ing played with and enjoyed.

Growing up, Mr. Smith remembered not having a father figure. His bio-logical father was no longer with his mother and was living across the state. Mr. Smith stated that he did not know his father until the past five or six years. His mother had many boyfriends while he was growing up. He named two in particular, but said the majority of her boyfriends did not talk to or associate with him. He recalled that one of his mother's boyfriends was physically and emotionally abusive to her and him. This boyfriend locked Mr. Smith out of the house when angry. Mr. Smith would get back in after the boyfriend passed out. This boyfriend would beat Mr. Smith with a belt and extension cord, espe-cially when he was intoxicated. On several occasions, Mr. Smith watched as the boyfriend hit and punched his mother. Mr. Smith cried and shook as he recalled this information.

During visitations with the mitigation specialist, Mr. Smith was asked about any scars or tattoos on his body. He did not have any tattoos, but he had several scars. During these conversations, he did not address one scar, but the mitigation specialist noticed it on his left wrist and made a mental note to discuss it later and be aware of a possible suicide attempt in his past. Mr. Smith detailed other scars on his body, speaking about injuries he sustained in various levels of detail. He recalled some of the hospitals and clinics at which he was treated, but he did not remember all of them, let alone all of his scars' origins.

Mr. Smith stated that he had had several jobs over the years. He worked at a movie theater as an usher, which lasted six months until he quit "just because." He then worked at an ice cream store that was part of a chain with locations in the towns he moved to, so he was able to transfer employment during his relocations. Mr. Smith recalled really enjoying this work. "I liked the place. It was quiet and I could just be," he said. After dropping out of high school, there was a gap in his employment as he moved out of his mother's home to live with his father. He returned to the area though and obtained employment with a local construction company, helping as a runner and with trash removal.

Mr. Smith left to live with his father after an altercation with his mother that resulted in the police being called. Both parties were found to be at fault in the disturbance, and since they were family, the police did not charge either of them that night. Mr. Smith reported that he did not have a real relationship with his father prior to moving in with him, although they had written to each other occasionally over the years. He stated that his father was very guarded and seemed like a "loner." He was often inebriated. His father was not working, and Mr. Smith believed his father received a living income from military service due to disability, although Mr. Smith could not articulate the specifics of the disability. While he enjoyed the quiet at his father's residence, his often-odd behavior and mannerisms were reasons Mr. Smith decided to move back with his mother.

Upon arriving back at his mother's home, Mr. Smith found work at a construction company. There he met Clare, an administrative assistant with the company. The two interacted infrequently but started to develop an attraction and friendship. Mr. Smith reported that this turned into a romantic relationship very quickly and he became very close to her. As she was the victim in the case, Mr. Smith had a hard time talking, in general, about his feelings for Clare. It became clear that she meant a great deal to him, even if the allegations of the instant offense were true. He reported periods during which she attempted to end the relationship, but they always got back together. Clare became pregnant with Mr. Smith's child and, for the first few months of the pregnancy, they stayed together. After the third month of pregnancy, Clare decided she did not want to be with Mr. Smith and spent the next several months trying to end the relationship.

Relevant Records

Investigation of Collateral Sources   RE: Mitigation Specialist. During the months that the mitigation specialist and Mr. Smith were visiting and speaking, the mitigation specialist also attempted follow up with collateral sources. He tried to obtain all of the defendant's records (e.g., birth, medical, educational, employment, psychological, and financial) and to speak with everyone who crossed paths with Mr. Smith (e.g., teachers, coworkers, friends, family, therapists, doctors, neighbors, supervisors, counselors, and coaches). This parallel investigation was ongoing and multigenerational. Information obtained from Mr. Smith's parents, grandparents, extended family, and others were as crucial to the case as his records. It is widely known and accepted that that an individual's mental health problems and disorders can have genetic components, so delving into these avenues of exploration were also a critical aspect of the mitigation and sentencing investigation. A brief example of witness meetings and record gathering is illustrated below. These examples are provided as means of illustration but are in no way an exhaustive list of the types or number of interviews and records requested.

Mr. Smith's various and multiple school records indicated that he had an individualized education plan (IEP). Records revealed the reason he was referred, counselors he met with, courses he took, and teachers' names. It was imperative that the mitigation specialist meet and speak with all parties mentioned, not only to learn about Mr. Smith, gain insight, and more fully appreciate the complete contextual framework, but to also obtain any records those individuals might possess that were not included in the schools' files.

The school records included the name of a private psychologist to whom Mr. Smith was referred. The psychologist was contacted and provided with an authorization to release and disclose information. She then agreed to meet and gave the mitigation specialist access to her file, which contained handwritten notes from individual counseling and therapy sessions. The file revealed a potential diagnosis of Posttraumatic Stress Disorder (PTSD); notations included the psychologist's observations of intrusive thoughts and flashbacks, nervousness and concentration problems, efforts to block out thoughts by banging his head, and other symptomology consistent with PTSD criteria. She noted that Mr. Smith confided in her many of his thoughts and distresses due to the abuse he suffered and witnessed in his mother's home. It became evident that his behavioral problems at school were possibly due to Mr. Smith's underlying mental health problems.

After seeing a notation mentioning the name of one of Mr. Smith's high school football coaches, a meeting was scheduled. The coach recalled Mr. Smith, saying that "while football is a team sport, [Mr. Smith] just couldn't mesh with the rest of the guys." He explained that Mr. Smith played his position fairly well but did not interact much with the rest of his teammates on or off the field. The coach described Mr. Smith as a "loner." The coach also recalled that Mr. Smith seemed more prone to concussions, as he had approximately three his first year, and another two the following year.

A canvass was done at the various addresses where Mr. Smith lived while growing up. At one such address, a neighbor recalled that she was friends with Mr. Smith's mother. This was the address where his mother lived while pregnant with Mr. Smith until he was approximately 3 years of age. This neighbor liked Mr. Smith and his mother; however, the neighbor distinctly recalled seeing Mr. Smith's mother drinking alcohol and smoking marijuana while she was pregnant with Mr. Smith. The neighbor recalled mentioning the importance of not drinking or using drugs during pregnancy, but indicated that this did not deter Ms. Smith from drinking alcohol.

Records were requested from the hospitals and clinics that were in the vicinity of Mr. Smith's various home residences. Records from one such hospital revealed the nature and cause of the scar on Mr. Smith's wrist. Approximately two months prior to the instant offense, Mr. Smith was brought in to the hospital for a laceration to his left wrist. While he denied any homicidal or suicidal ideation at the time, the examining nurse practitioner noted "possible superficial suicide attempt" in the record. Medical records were also collected from other institutions, which revealed that Mr. Smith had been referred to child protective services for bruising.

A visit with Mr. Smith's older half brother, Mr. Tom Smith, provided additional insight and corroboration into a potential mitigation theory involving Fetal Alcohol Syndrome (FAS). Tom reported that he had an official diagnosis of FAS due to his mother's drinking during pregnancy and that he suspected she drank while pregnant with Mr. Smith as well. Tom did not grow up with his brother, as his biological father removed him from his mother's care and terminated her parental rights when he was an infant. Tom could not recall the specifics of his mother's care but believed that it was severely lacking, and he reported being thankful to have "escaped that situation when young."

Identification of Forensic Evaluator RE: Mitigation Specialist. After getting to know the defendant and starting to gather a good sense of themes and information that might be pertinent in the sentencing phase, it was time to obtain a forensic evaluator to be appointed to the team. As noted previously in the chapter, this practitioner must be well versed in forensic evaluations and have the ability to assist the defense team in developing mitigation and sentencing strategies. The use of testing should also be considered at this point. It is important that the factors specific to the client and case be discussed when choosing the appropriate evaluator. It is especially important to have discussions about what potential subspecialties (and types of, if any) might be required for your case. It is important to discuss whether testing is applicable as well and, if it appears to be beneficial, what types of testing might be needed.

Mental Status Examination

RE: Forensic Evaluator: Getting Started. After gathering records, speaking with witnesses, and engaging in the multigenerational mitigation investigation of Mr. Smith, it became apparent that he had some specific mental health problems and some areas of concern that might require the assistance of an expert. Although the mitigation investigation was not complete at this stage, the defense team agreed that it would be beneficial to have a forensic evaluation of Mr. Smith completed to assist in the sentencing phase of trial.

The team agreed that there was reason to believe that Mr. Smith may have symptoms of FAS as well as PTSD. Expert testing and evaluation in these areas was determined appropriate. Because of the coach's reports of multiple concussions, an expert screening for traumatic brain injuries and other potential neurological problems seemed appropriate. The team ultimately decided that forensic psychologists with pharmacology backgrounds were not necessary or applicable in Mr. Smith's case but identifying a practitioner with adolescent experience, and intelligence testing, and neuropsychological testing expertise was preferred.

The decision to use a mental health expert (MHE) as a forensic evaluator (FE) is not always straightforward. Psychologists and psychiatrists are trained to consider the complexities of the human psyche, and in terms of courtroom strategy, complexity can lead to confusion. Juries benefit from simple, clear, and concise answers. The worst moment in a forensic evaluator's career is when she looks at the jury box to find half the jurors looking utterly puzzled while the other half is yawning and trying to stay awake. While less is sometimes more when testifying, during the actual evaluation phase the opposite is often true. The MHE wants to be able to speak with confidence and psychological certainty; he needs to be convinced in order to be convincing. To do that, he wants to make sure his evaluation procedure involves data that can withstand being challenged by invoking the standard error of measurement (tests are not 100% accurate), or Type I (false positive) or Type II (false negative) errors.[1]

During the penalty phase of a capital case, it is not unusual for mitigation specialists and defense teams to use the MHE/FE to explain to a jury the convicted perpetrator's story. The goal is to gain the jurors' trust and explain details accurately. A respected psychiatrist or psychologist is best, but one of his or her most important characteristics is the ability to emotionally connect and touch the audience, the jury.

General Considerations

When a decision is made to involve a MHE/FE,[2] there are three possible general outcomes:

1. *The results of the forensic evaluation add data that round out and amplify the findings of the mitigation specialist and defense team.* Their initial hypothesis is confirmed and strengthened. For example, the defense team suspects neurological impairment from a childhood traumatic brain injury. The psychologist reviews childhood and educational testing and clinical data (which suggest neurological impairment), performs his or her own neuropsychological evaluation, and finds neurological impairment (specifically frontal lobe impairment) that affects impulse control and executive functioning. The psychologist can speak with great certainty and authority that a documented traumatic injury did indeed cause brain damage, that the brain damage is still evident, and that the damage occurred prior to the crime and was therefore at least partially to blame for the crime, lowering culpability.

2. *The results of the forensic evaluation add data that may not fully confirm the initial hypothesis but may instead alter it and lead to a modified but not fundamentally different hypothesis.* This is what essentially happened in a recent capital case in which a 19-year-old man was accused of murdering a 60-year-old man with whom he had become involved, presumably because the older man wanted sex. The initial hypothesis was based on a difficult-to-prove history of exposure to vicarious trauma (the family, originally from a South American country enveloped in a civil war, had been the victims of a rebel attack). Upon examination, the psychologist discovered (initially through testing and then subsequent interviewing) a history of ongoing and violent sexual abuse. Thus, a traumatic antecedent to the crime was indeed found—one that did not negate the initial hypothesis of traumatic sequelae but was a much stronger and more easily understood one.

3. *The results of the forensic evaluation contradict the initial hypothesis and in fact lead to the generation of a completely different hypothesis.* In the first example, let's imagine the defense team discovered the defendant had a history of having been routinely bullied throughout high school, and that became the initial hypothesis. However, on evaluation, the neurological impairment could be traced back to an injury prior to the bullying, so the psychologist might recommend forgoing a "bullying" mitigation (especially with certain juries) in favor of the competing hypothesis of neurological impairment.

Thus, the forensic evaluator is essentially involved in a dialectical process, one that usually begins with an evaluation of the defense team-generated hypothesis (*thesis*), then includes evaluating for the possibility of other competing and even contradictory hypotheses (*antithesis*), and finally, when supported by the data, concludes with an explanation that accounts for all hypotheses (*synthesis*). In some cases, the evaluator's findings will not be supportive of mitigation.

Psychological Measures Administered

RE: Forensic Evaluator: Testing and Evaluation. In the example of Mr. Smith, the strength of the background material uncovered by the mitigation specialist strongly suggested that the psychologist's findings would fall into the first or second categories; that is, the data would either (1) add to and confirm, or possibly (2) modify but still confirm the defense team's hypothesis. Given the information provided, the forensic psychologist began with a standardized Mental Status Examination and Quick Neurological Screening Test; both incorporate cognitive, sensorimotor, and memory tasks that are part of a standard neurological screen in addition to being age-normed and thus going beyond clinical judgment. A formal assessment of intellectual functioning, using the latest edition of the Wechsler Adult Intelligence Scale, Fourth Edition (WAIS-IV)[3] along with the Wechsler Memory Scale,[4] was also indicated. Both instruments are thoroughly researched, both provide an incredibly rich fund of information about specific cognitive skills as well as general intelligence, and both have repeatedly met *Daubert* admissibility standards (Flynn, 2009; Hagan, Drogin, & Guilmette, 2010). In addition to neurological screening, a standard drawing test such as the Bender Visual-Motor Gestalt Test or the Beery-Buktenica Developmental Test of Visual-Motor Integration was also suggested.

Given his educational and family backgrounds, it was surprising that Mr. Smith tested in the low average range of general intelligence, with a Full Scale IQ between 82 and 89 (90% confidence level). Based on the evidence obtained thus far, it was highly likely that Mr. Smith would demonstrate mild impairment in some areas of executive functioning, as evidenced by his performance on the following WAIS-IV subtests:

1. Borderline to low average-range score on the Similarities subtest, a test of verbal concept formation.
2. Borderline to low-average-range score on the Matrix Reasoning subtest, a test of nonverbal concept formation.
3. Borderline to low-average-range score on the Letter-Sequencing subtest, a test of visual-motor sequencing, attention, concentration, and memory.

4. Low-average-range score on the Digit Span subtest, a test of verbal attention and memory; it would be expected that his Digits Backward score would be significantly lower than his Digits Forward score.

His average-range scores on Block Design, Visual Puzzles, Symbol Search, and Coding were contraindicative of significant (but not "soft") neurological impairment. His low-average scores on Information, Vocabulary, and Comprehension were interpreted as primarily the result of poor school attendance and performance.

His performance on the Bender and/or Beery tests were consistent with his general intelligence and thus not in and of themselves significant indicators of visual-motor neurological impairment. This finding was also consistent with his WAIS-IV perceptual reasoning and processing speed index scores. Still, because his WAIS-IV performance provided some evidence of executive functioning impairment, a referral for full neuropsychological testing (assuming funding permitted it; the HRNB is costly to administer and interpret) was indicated.

Mr. Smith's scores on the Halstead-Reitan Neuropsychological Test Battery (HRNB; Reitan & Wolfson, 1993; Bigler, 2007) Category and Trail-Making tests provided strong corroborating evidence of executive functioning impairment, specifically in the frontal lobes. The remaining subtest scores were more diffuse, and the most parsimonious explanation was that they were consistent with his somewhat low general intelligence and thus not indicative of specific neurological damage. Because Mr. Smith's extended family background included some blood relatives who evidenced average-range or better intellectual functioning, it was reasonable to conclude that Mr. Smith's overall intellectual development was not genetic in etiology. Rather, his intellectual functioning was more likely impaired by a combination of his mother's suspected prenatal substance abuse combined with early environmental deprivation.[5] Thus, one of the defense team's initial hypotheses could be confirmed, albeit with a moderate degree of certainty.

The usefulness of personality assessment is not always evident and can be controversial. Many defense attorneys and forensic evaluators steer clear of formal psychological testing in general, and personality testing in particular (Melton, et. al., 2007). Personality is a complex construct—within different branches of psychology, there are differing ways of defining and measuring. Psychologists have frequently questioned the value in capital sentencing evaluations, typically noting that specific circumstances are almost always a more accurate predictor of behavior than personality traits (Epstein, 1983; Synder, 1983; Fleeson, 2004). In addition, there is the possibility of discovering that the defendant has a "personality disorder," which in most people's understanding refers to a characterologically intractable, incurable "mental disorder."

When a defendant clearly demonstrates impaired functioning below the 2nd percentile (mentally deficient range) on both intellectual and adaptive functioning measures or a brain injury that can be clearly demonstrated using both brain imaging technology and neuropsychological testing, thereby meeting Atkins (2002) criteria, personality testing will obfuscate rather than clarify and generally should not be employed. On the other hand, in some cases (especially when the issue of psychopathy or antisocial personality is raised), psychologists can sometimes be vulnerable during cross-examination to questions about why they did *not* look at personality factors with the same degree of scrutiny (e.g., with objective psychological tests) as they did other possible factors (e.g., intellectual functioning).

When utilizing personality assessment, the goal is not necessarily to arrive at a formal diagnosis using psychiatric nomenclature (e.g., the *Diagnostic and Statistical Manual of Mental Disorders*, or *DSM*[6]); ever since its third revision (*DSM-III*), the *DSM* has employed a categorical rather than a functional/process-oriented approach to diagnosing, and although often and erroneously cited in courts as the "bible" of psychiatry and psychology, it is nevertheless known for its lack of reliability and subsequent dubious validity. In testimony, it is better to rely on describing a psychological process as opposed to a diagnostic category, since the former is dynamic and therefore impermanent while the latter is static and implies that the defendant cannot change. For example, discussion of a defendant's emotional instability, great underlying rage, and tendency to love and then hate a romantic partner would be preferable to explaining how, depending on one's interpretation of a single criterion, he or she may or may not meet the diagnosis of borderline personality disorder. Such a diagnosis, once arrived at, would never leave her; a borderline may go into "remission" for decades but is rarely, if ever, cured. In Mr. Smith's case, given the less-than-clear neuropsychological findings, the use of empirical personality testing might also be advised. The evaluator might hypothesize that he will find indications of impulsivity and emotional/behavioral dysregulation as well as anxiety, depression, avoidance and traumatic flashbacks, all potential signs of the formal diagnosis of posttraumatic stress disorder. What the evaluator is *not* likely to find is equally important; objective personality tests like the MMPI-2-RF[7] and Personality Assessment Inventory (PAI) have well-researched scales that assess a range of specific factors that contribute to antisocial tendencies and/or behaviors. In addition to the overall Antisocial Behavior scale (derived from the "Pd" scale on the MMPI and MMPI-2) on the MMPI-2-RF, there are related scales that assess Anger Proneness, Juvenile Conduct Problems, Aggression, Activation and Disaffiliativeness, all of which are related to overall tendencies to engage in antisocial and/or criminal behavior. The PAI breaks down its general Antisocial Scale score into three components: Antisocial Behaviors, Egocentricity, and Stimulus-Seeking. Moderate elevations on some of these scales may be indicative of a tendency to bend or break social convention or may be related to abuse substances rather than engagement in behaviors that are intended to manipulate, abuse, or harm other people and thus suggest to a jury that the defendant is a hopeless and helpless psychopath. Taken together, the MMPI-2-RF and PAI assess antisocial behavior, impulsivity, aggression and dominance scales are moderately correlated with the Psychopathy Checklist, Revised (PCL-R) and thus provide valuable insight into the presence—or absence—of psychopathy (Walters & Duncan, 2005; Mufson, 2012).

Based on what was known about Mr. Smith, it was unsurprising when he scored relatively high on psychological test indices related to depression,[8] anxiety, and anger proneness. He also scored relatively high on the MMPI-2-RF's Juvenile Conduct Problems and PAI's Stimulus-Seeking subscales, but he did not score in the clinical range on either the MMPI-2-RF or the PAI scales that more generally measure antisocial traits and behaviors. The evaluator found elevated scores on scales related to addiction *potential*, although not in the clinical range on the PAI's Alcohol and Drug Abuse scales. It is the experience of this evaluator that test scores rarely fall nicely into a "clean" posttraumatic stress (PTSD) profile pattern. Rather, those who have experienced chronic and complex trauma (as appears to be the case with Mr. Smith) sometimes present with a profile that seems indecipherable on the surface and with scores that do not generally cluster together. Although not part of the "traditional" PTSD pattern, high scores are often seen on the MMPI-2-RF Aberrant Experiences or the PAI's Psychotic Experiences or Thought Disorder scales, for example, as well as various configurations indicating multiple cognitive and/or somatic complaints. The former often turn up as complaints about dissociative-like experiences or sensations. For over a decade, there has been a debate as to whether PTSD should be strictly classified under the broader categories of anxiety or dissociative disorders; the *DSM-5* attempted to resolve this debate by creating a third category, Trauma and Stressor-Related Disorders. Although not a forensic instrument, the Dissociative Experiences Scale (Carlson & Putnam, 1993), now in its second edition (DES-II), can provide structured information about an individual's experiences of dissociation; the Clinician-Administered PTSD Scale (CAPS; Weathers, et. al., 2004) or the Trauma Symptom Inventory (TSI; Briere, 1995, 1997) can quantify PTSD symptoms. It is advisable to wait until significant rapport and (whenever possible) trust has been established, a solid clinical history obtained, and as much information as possible elicited through standard clinical interviewing before administering structured psychological tests. Contrary to the popular belief that most defendants want to look "crazy" to either obtain a not guilty by reason of insanity (NGRI) verdict or a lesser sentence, many defendants in capital cases are loathe to admit to any psychological disturbance, which they consider a "weakness."

In Mr. Smith's case, there is considerably strong historical data, including interview data from his older half-brother, a previous psychologist, school personnel, and some family friends or neighbors. This is one reason, of many, why the mitigation specialist's investigation is vital. After establishing at least some degree of rapport, the evaluator worked this information into his clinical interview with Mr. Smith in the hope of obtaining further details and the expansion of information that would then potentially facilitate more forthright responses to the psychological tests administered.

The judicious employment of projective tests, especially the Rorschach Inkblot Technique, is sometimes appropriate. While most forensic specialists advise against using projective tests, others believe such a general admonition is akin to throwing the baby out with the bathwater. Hess (2006), for example, opined that "if an instrument is banned . . . [how] can we discover its uses? Moreover, it is the use of the [Rorschach] in the clinician's hands rather than the instrument that is central to validated use" (p. 823). In their analysis of the admissibility of psychological tests in courtroom testimony, Shook and Jackson (2014) reported Rorschach results were admitted slightly better than 50% of the time. Meloy (2008) noted that courts have largely upheld the validity of the Rorschach (as a *technique* rather than a "test") when it was used for the purposes of assessing what it is best at assessing: ego strength/maturity and disordered thinking. It is inappropriate to use the Rorschach as a stand-alone assessment tool or to base diagnoses like depression or anxiety on its results, since there is little data to support its efficacy in these situations, and there are far better tools available. Projective tests can add significant clinical information especially when the evaluator suspects disturbed thought processes that the defendant can mask from objective tests like the MMPI-2-RF; as a means of delineating neurological damage, the Rorschach can be invaluable (Erard, 2012). Rorschach responses are sometimes useful in combating the ubiquitous opinion rendered by most prosecution experts: that the defendant has Antisocial Personality Disorder. When combined with a history of relational capacity, clinical impressions, and objective personality test scores that do not indicate psychopathy, projective tests can add to the argument that the defendant is capable of some degree of warm interpersonal relationships.

In Mr. Smith's case, there was good reason to employ projective testing. Based on his history, the evaluator's clinical impressions and the client's objective tests results, both neurological signs and indicators of diminished executive functioning (planning and impulse control) were expected and obtained.

A basic principle of psychological investigation is that of hypothesis-generation and corroboration through multiple data sources (Hall & Sbordone, 1993; Achenbach, 2006; Weiner & Hess, 2006); forensic psychologist Kirk Heilbrun notes that this principle is especially important in forensic cases (Heilbrun et. al., 2008), and there is no case that impacts a defendant more than one that could invoke the death penalty. In Mr. Smith's case, conclusions were drawn with reasonable psychological certainty based on (a) a clinical history supported not only by self-report but through corroborating collaterals, (b) data derived through clinical interview and clinical assessment by the forensic psychologist, and (c) significant cross-validation between several empirical tests that assess both cognitive and personality functioning, both historically and in the present.

Forensic Summary and Opinion

RE: *Forensic Evaluator:* Historical, clinical and empirical data were consistent in painting a picture of a young man who was probably born with a vulnerable neurological system to begin with due to his mother's reported use of alcohol and drugs during pregnancy. It was evident from the client records, witness and evaluator interviews, and other materials reviewed that he exhibited signs of neurological problems from an early age. Moreover, the data reflected the expected traumatic sequelae of a history of family chaos, childhood neglect, and both direct and vicarious exposure to physical violence. These included (1) chronic and severe depression (as indicated by suicide attempts) that, based on test data, continued throughout his young life; (2) early onset of trauma-related dissociation, again as indicated by test results as well as intermittent amnesia for significant traumatic events; and (3) numerous trauma-based symptoms as a teenager (and therefore prior to the offense) as reported by his previous psychologist.

It is clear from myriad studies, but based most notably on results obtained from the large-scale and ongoing longitudinal Adverse Childhood Experiences study jointly sponsored by the Centers for Disease Control and Prevention and Kaiser Permanente (CDC, 2014; Chapman et al., 2007), that Mr. Smith had many strikes against him well before he became involved with the victim, Clare. His medical history and recent test data indicated neurological impairment, especially of his executive functions (most notably, impulse control, emotional/behavioral regulation and planning). Although it was not clear whether this impairment was caused pre- or postnatally, it was clear that it was present well before the offense, and it was reasonable to assume that early abuse and neglect either caused or exacerbated it if it existed prior to birth.

Thus, it was concluded that Mr. Smith, a convicted murderer who, by no choice of his own and therefore with limited responsibility, likely experienced delayed prenatal brain development, was made even more vulnerable to delayed brain development by his early childhood environment, grew up under conditions (e.g., ongoing chaos, poor attachment, neglect and abuse) known to retard cognitive development and make a school-aged child highly vulnerable to emotional and behavior dysregulation. Ultimately he did not receive adequate interventions despite early indications of all the above.

Common Pitfalls and Considerations

The potential impact of capital mitigation can quite literally mean the difference between life and death. It is therefore especially incumbent on the psychologist to be aware of potential pitfalls in evaluations of this type. In this evaluator's experience, and based on conversations with other forensic psychologists, these can be grouped under the broad categories of (1) under-reaching, (2) overreaching, (3) hubris, (4) brain-lock/overspecialization and (5) opinion-for-hire.

Psychologists who under-reach tend to focus on those areas with which they are most familiar (e.g., psychosis or mood disorders) and focus too heavily on exploring those facets of a case to the detriment of other possible, or even more likely, considerations. If they use tests, their choice of tests reflects this somewhat narrow focus of investigation. They might, for example, employ the Beck Inventories and find depression and anxiety without giving enough consideration to the examinee's background, which may include significant trauma that in fact subsumes the mood and anxiety disorders. In testimony, this psychologist may sound simplistic and scattered and, therefore, easy to dismiss; after all, who hasn't experienced depression and anxiety, so why should a jury give much weight to these symptoms in someone convicted of murder? Lack of experience with formal assessment can also result in under-reaching. Although formal testing is the one activity that most clearly delineates psychology from the other mental health professions, many psychologists receive relatively little ongoing training and supervision in formal assessment that includes psychological testing. This was not always the case; the advent of managed behavioral healthcare resulted in a sharp decline in (or in some cases the complete elimination of) reimbursement for testing by insurance plans. As a result, many agencies and hospitals that once utilized (and trained psychologists) tests as part of their formal assessment process no longer do so; lack of broad formal assessment knowledge and skill can be one cause of under-reaching.

Overreach can be problematic as well. Psychologists who use a shotgun approach to evaluation and basically "throw" tests and assessment procedures at an examinee may find themselves with a confusing and overwhelming array of data, both erroneous as well as potentially meaningful. How does she separate the wheat from the chaff? In testimony, the psychologist then risks sounding scattered and overly reliant on psychological testing jargon. Testimony that is overly complicated and too difficult to follow can sound condescending, obfuscating, irrelevant, and—perhaps worst of all—boring. When testifying about a defendant's psychological state, there are few experiences more professionally debilitating than noticing jurors yawning or even nodding off to sleep. Moreover, such testimony may bias a jury against taking a nuanced, psychologically sophisticated view of the defendant altogether.

Hubris—overconfidence in one's abilities and judgment—can be a major pitfall. In capital cases, it is extremely important to coordinate with and give weight to the opinions of other members of the defense team. Psychologists who are well trained in individual psychopathologies may fail to give appropriate weight to social and contextual factors, for example. Early in this evaluator's career, a particular defendant was once judged as psychotic when in fact his beliefs, thinking, behaviors, and perceptions were not unusual within the community in which he was raised (an extremely controversial religious "cult.") Imprisonment removed him from his community, and in a few months, he no longer met the criteria for schizophrenia. He was not "cured" of his psychosis; his unusual thinking and presentation were artifacts of his cult involvement. When testifying, there can be a thin line between inspiring confidence and appearing arrogant.

Both overreaching and hubris can contribute to a psychologist "promising too much." When reporting high success rates (as defined by favorable court decisions), it is misleading to claim that favorable outcomes are a direct result of (or even correlated with) the psychologist's testimony. In fact, a favorable decision may at times be made *despite* a psychologist's poorly received testimony. Fulero and Wrightsman (2009) similarly warn against the psychologist substituting advocacy for objectivity. Testifying about new "syndromes" may attract attention and even sway opinions, but they have little or no basis in scientific research and can in fact be boldly created to advocate for a specific belief or social/political position.

Brain-lock is an especially problematic pitfall. Expert witnesses are too often called into a case because of their strongly held a priori beliefs rather than their professional objectivity. For example, there are a myriad of controversial "syndromes" that psychologists have testified about, such as "false memory syndrome," "recovered memory syndrome," "battered woman syndrome," and "post-cult trauma syndrome" and, more recently, "affluenza" (the "rich kid syndrome" that some media claimed spared a wealthy Texas teenager from serving jail time after killing four people while driving drunk). Psychologists—and perhaps especially those engaged in research and academia—may take forensic cases in the hope that they will advance a specific professional and/or personal agenda. Other psychologists simply have strong beliefs or professional experiences for which they, consciously or unconsciously, desire vindication by a court. Sometimes, overreliance on a particular test's results can result in brain-lock; a more common pitfall is being overly trusting of one's own clinical judgment and experience, despite the plethora of studies that question clinical accuracy and a mental health professional's ability to discern when someone is being deceitful[9] (Ekman & O'Sullivan, 1991; Adelson, 2004). When combined with hubris, brain-lock can lead a psychologist down a path that bears little resemblance to objectivity or truth.

Overspecialization can also be a cause of brain-lock. This can be a problem for the psychologist who has considerable training in forensics but not in other areas of clinical practice (e.g., psychotherapy, consultation). For that reason, many forensic psychologists maintain at least a small clinical practice as well, which allows ongoing exposure to and experience with a broad range of concerns, from everyday "problems of living" to severe psychopathology (other than antisocial behavior or psychopathy).

Finally, and perhaps worst of all, mental health professionals generally don't want to admit to being potentially influenced by the potential for future work and, in a few cases, by fame and fortune. Psychologists can also become "pigeonholed" as either exclusively experts for the prosecution or the defense, which can potentially impinge on their objectivity. There is little evidence to support the feeling that psychologists are "above" being "bought." In her provocatively titled book, *Whores of the Court,* psychologist Margaret Hagen (1997) targets forensic mental health specialists for being "clinical charlatans and greedy frauds" (p. 73). While that may be an extreme judgment, if we are honest with ourselves, this author believes most forensic evaluators will admit to feeling seduced by those rare cases that garner significant media attention and/or might involve significant fees. On a more basic and common level, forensic evaluators can feel pressured to please the attorney, court, or agency that hired or retained them. There is no simple solution to this problem (although self-awareness is a necessary start); there are several ways to safeguard against, or at least mitigate the risk of, becoming a "hired gun." Without exception, the psychologist working for private attorneys should always utilize a signed contract that clearly identifies the client (the attorney, the defendant/ accused, the court, etc.) and the rights and obligations of all parties involved in the forensic evaluation. Personally, this evaluator will not work without a retainer and full reimbursement of fees before any opinion is communicated, in writing or otherwise, to anyone. If hired by the state (e.g., a court) or a state agency (e.g., division of family services) a retainer is not required, however acknowledgment of the terms of the evaluator involvement (financial and otherwise) in writing is required.

In addition to guarding against overspecialization and brain-lock, maintaining a practice that balances nonforensic against forensic work is another way of avoiding being seen as (and, in fact, becoming) a "hired gun." As everyone in the field knows, the intersection of law and psychology does not accurately reflect everyday people or situations; the court system and all its various players constitute a world unto itself, complete with its own highly idiosyncratic customs, rules, roles, and rituals. Teaching, consulting, and/or clinical practice can help keep the forensic clinician connected to the "real world" of real people, patients, and problems. Thus, in addition to providing another source of income, a broad and diverse professional practice can enhance the effectiveness of the forensic specialist's testimony; it also serves to minimize the appearance of being a "hired gun" who relies solely on being paid to evaluate and testify in court cases.

Notes

1. A "false positive" error occurs when, say, an expert finds a neurological impairment when in fact one does not exist; conversely, a "false negative" involves mistakenly missing an important characteristic or diagnosis.

2. For the remainder of this section, the mental health expert/forensic examiner will be assumed to be a psychologist.

3. As of this writing, in its fourth edition (WAIS-IV).

4. Also in its fourth edition as of this writing (WMS-IV).

5. Based on the fact that Mr. Smith had an IEP early in his academic career, it seems unlikely that any intellectual impairment would be the result of his concussions, which occurred when he was in high school.

6. The *Diagnostic and Statistical Manual of Mental Disorders*, published by the American Psychiatric Association and routinely referred to as the "*DSM*," is currently in its fifth edition (i.e., the *DSM-5*).

7. The MMPI-2-RF is psychometrically "cleaner" version with significantly better discriminant validity than its predecessors, the MMPI and MMPI-2. The MMPI and MMPI-2 employ a "Pd" (Psychopathic Deviance) scale that often has limited diagnostic utility, especially in forensic settings, as it could be just as indicative of a tendency to avoid, bend, or break social convention (think Steve Jobs or Andy Warhol) as it could of actual psychopathic behavior.

8. For example, Demoralization, Suicidal/Death Ideation, Malaise, Low Positive Emotions, Helplessness/Hopelessness on the MMPI-2-RF/.

9. Psychologists are not especially good at judging when an examinee is lying, for example.

References

Achenbach, T. M. (2006). As others see us: Clinical and research implications of cross-informant correlations for psychopathology. *Current Directions in Psychological Science 15*, 94–98.

Adelson, R. (2004, July/August). Detecting deception. *APA Monitor, 35,* 70.

Atkins v. Virginia, 536 U.S. 304, 260 Va. 375, 534 S. E. 2d 312 (2002).

Banner, S. (2002). *The death penalty: An American history.* Cambridge, MA: Harvard University Press.

Bigler, E. D. (2007). A motion to exclude and the "fixed" versus "flexible" battery in "forensic" neuropsychology: Challenges to the practice of clinical neuropsychology. *Archives of Clinical Neuropsychology, 22,* 45–51.

Briere, J. (1995). *Trauma Symptom Inventory professional manual.* Odessa, FL: Psychological Assessment Resources.

Briere, J. (1997). *Psychological assessment of adult posttraumatic states.* Washington, DC: American Psychological Association.

Carlson, E. B., & Putnam, F. W. (1993). An update on the Dissociative Experiences Scale. *Dissociation, 6,* 16–27.

Centers for Disease Control and Prevention. (2014). *Linking childhood trauma to long-term health and social consequences.* Retrieved from http://www.acestudy.org/

Chapman D. P., Dube, S. R., Anda, R. F. (2007). Adverse childhood events as risk factors for negative mental health outcomes. *Psychiatric Annals, 37,* 359–364.

Daubert v. Merrell Dow Pharmaceuticals, 509 U.S. 579, 589 (1993).

DeMatteo, D., Murrie, D. C., Anumba, N. M., & Keesler, M. E. (2011). *Forensic mental health assessments in death penalty cases.* Oxford, UK: Oxford University Press.

Ekman, P. & O'Sullivan, M. (1991). Who can catch a liar? *American Psychologist, 46,* 913–920.

Epstein, S. (1983). Aggregation and beyond: Some basic issues on the prediction of behavior. *Journal of Personality, 51,* 360–392.

Erard, R. E. (2012). Expert testimony using the Rorschach performance assessment system in psychological injury cases. *Psychological Injury and Law, 5*(2), 122–134.

Fleeson, W. (2004). Moving personality beyond the person-situation debate: The challenge and the opportunity of within-person variability. *Current Directions in Psychological Science, 13,* 83–87.

Flynn, J. R. (2009). The WAIS-III and WAIS-IV: Daubert motions favor the certainly false over the approximately true. *Applied Neuropsychology, 16,* 98–104.

Friedman, H., & Orgel, S. A. (1964). Rorschach developmental scores and intelligence level. *Journal of Projective Techniques and Personality Assessment, 28,* 425–428.

Fulero, S. M., & Wrightsman, L. S. (2009). *Forensic psychology.* Belmont, CA: Wadsworth.

Hagan, L. D., Drogin, E. Y., & Guilmette, T. J. (2010). Science rather than advocacy when reporting IQ scores. *Professional Psychology: Research and Practice, 41,* 420–423.

Hagen, M. (1997). *Whores of the court: The fraud of psychiatric testimony and the rape of American justice.* New York, NY: ReganBooks.

Hall, H. V., & Sbordone, R. J. (1993). *Disorders of executive functions: Civil and criminal law applications.* Boca Raton, FL: CRC Press.

Heilbrun, K., DeMatteo, D., Marczyk, G., & Goldstein, A. (2008). Standards of practice and care in forensic mental health assessment: Legal, professional, and principles- based consideration. *Psychology, Public Policy, and Law, 14,* 1–26.

Hertz, M. R. (1970). *Frequency tables for scoring Rorschach responses.* Berkeley, CA: University Press Books.

Hess, A. K. (2006). Practicing principled forensic psychology: Legal, ethical, and moral considerations. In I. B. Weiner & A. K. Hess (Eds.), *The handbook of forensic psychology.* Hoboken, NJ: Wiley.

Klopfer, B. (1962). *Rorschach Technique: An introductory manual.* New York, NY: Harcourt College.

Meloy, J. R. (2008). The authority of the Rorschach: An update. In C. B. Gacono, F. B. Evans, N. Kaser-Boyd, & L. A. Gacono (Eds.), *The handbook of forensic Rorschach assessment.* New York, NY: Routledge.

Melton, G. B., Petrila, J., Poythress, N. G., & Slobogin, C. (2007). *Psychological evaluations for the courts: A handbook for mental health professionals and lawyers.* New York, NY: Guilford Press.

Mufson, L. (2012). *Validity of MMPI-2-RF measures of psychopathy* (Doctoral dissertation). Pepperdine University. Retrieved from http://media.proquest.com/media/pq/classic/doc/2866947541/fmt/ai/rep/NPDF?_s=dd9o7Q%2B8zjWsNFgkQzIPsMadGu8%3D

Reitan, R. M., & Wolfson, D. (1993). *The Halstead-Reitan Neuropsychological Test Battery: Theory and clinical interpretation* (2nd ed.). Tucson, AZ: Neuropsychology Press.

Shook, J., & Jackson, M. (2014). Admissibility of psychological assessments in expert testimony: Assisting the trier of fact. Presentation at the 2014 annual meeting of the American Psychological Association: Washington, DC. Retrieved from http://dx.doi .org/10.1037/e551092014-001

Snyder, M. (1983). The influence of individuals on situations: Implications for understanding the links between personality and social behavior. *Journal of Personality, 51,* 497–516.

Wagner, E. E. (2001). *The logical Rorschach: A brief scoring method to screen for psychopathology.* Los Angeles, CA: Western Psychological Services.

Walker, L. E. A., & Shapiro, D. L. (2003). *Introduction to forensic psychology: Clinical and social psychological perspectives.* New York, NY: Plenum Press.

Walters, G. D., & Duncan, S. A. (2005). Use of the PCL-R and PAI to predict release outcome in inmates undergoing forensic evaluation. *Journal of Forensic Psychiatry and Psychology, 16,* 459–476.

Weathers, F. W., Newman, E., Blake, D. D., Nagy, L. M., Schnurr, P. P., Kaloupek, D. G., . . . Keane, T. M. (2004). *Clinician-Administered PTSD Scale (CAPS).* Torrance, CA: Western Psychological Services.

Weiner, I. B., & Hess, A. K. (2006). *The handbook of forensic psychology.* Hoboken, NJ: Wiley.

5

Conducting Mental Health Diversion Evaluations

Virginia Barber-Rioja, Merrill Rotter, and Faith Schombs

Diversion programs were created largely as a response to the overrepresentation of individuals with psychiatric disorders in the criminal justice system. The main goal of diversion programs is to identify individuals with mental illness in the criminal justice system and divert them to treatment programs in the community in lieu of incarceration (Steadman et al., 1999). Depending on the point of criminal justice contact at which diversion takes place, diversion programs can be classified into two categories: prebooking diversion, which occurs before the individual is arrested and formal charges have been filled, and postbooking diversion, which takes place after the arrest and formal charges have been filled (Broner, Borum, & Gawley, 2002). Diversion can take place through a special jurisdiction court, such as a mental health court (MHC; e.g., centralized diversion), or outside of the MHC through any trial part (e.g., decentralized diversion; Barber-Rioja & Amrhein, 2010).

Regardless of whether diversion takes place inside or outside of a special jurisdiction court, four key elements to postbooking diversion have been identified: (1) screening of individuals in contact with the criminal justice system for the presence of mental illness; (2) evaluation of defendants for treatment eligibility in lieu of incarceration by mental health professionals; (3) negotiation with prosecutors, defense attorneys, and community-based treatment providers to develop community-based treatment dispositions; and (4) linkage of individuals to treatment programs in the community (Steadman et al., 1999). We propose a fifth element, which is the clinical monitoring and supervision of the participants once released to the community. This chapter focuses on the second key element: the assessment of defendants for eligibility for diversion specifically in the context of postbooking diversion, a type of assessment that we will refer to as "diversion evaluations." A diversion evaluation is used to assess a defendant's eligibility for treatment in the community in lieu of incarceration. However, it is important to note that diversion evaluations also inform elements 3, 4 and 5.

The number of diversion programs is rapidly growing nationwide. Approximately 54 diversion programs were in existence in 1992 (Steadman, Morris, & Dennis, 1995), whereas over 300 of these programs were in operation by 2005 (Steadman & Naples, 2005). Similarly, since 1997, when the first MHC was established, the number of these courts has increased to over 300 today, with these programs found in almost every state (The Council of State Governments [CSG], 2014; http://csgjusticecenter.org/mental-health-court-project/). As diversion programs rapidly increase, so do the number of forensic mental health professionals needed to conduct diversion evaluations. Although no specific statistic on the number of diversion evaluations conducted nationally is available, diversion programs are increasing at such a rate that they have probably become one of the most common evaluations requested by the courts. For example, according the New York Queens District Attorney's Office, in a one-year period (October 2009 to October 2010), 1,610 defendants were referred for diversion in the borough of Queens (a jurisdiction with about 2.3 million residents).

While recommendations for standards governing diversion and MHCs have been promulgated (e.g., CGS 10 elements), each local jurisdiction implemented its program within a unique legal, clinical, and services context; consequently, these standards did not include a universally accepted definition of the eligibility criteria or an identification of the relevant forensic issues that should be addressed as part of diversion evaluations. The focus of the clinical needs within the diversion mission may make it seem that it is purely a clinical evaluation; however, to the extent that these evaluations are conducted "for the purpose of assisting the [legal] decision-maker or one of the litigants in using relevant clinical and scientific data" (Heilbrun, 2001, p. 3), they can be considered a type of forensic mental health assessment (FMHA; Heilbrun, 2001), and as such, should follow the general principles of FMHA. This chapter constitutes an initial attempt to provide mental health professionals with some procedures in forensic assessment that apply to diversion evaluations.

Review of the Literature

The Legal Context of Diversion

It is widely recognized that the prevalence of mental illness in jail and prison is significantly higher than that found in the general population. The numbers found in studies vary depending on instruments used and whether only severe psychiatric disorders are included versus a broader definition of mental illness. However, even the most restrictive studies have found that about 15% of individuals who are incarcerated in the jail system suffer from a mental illness (Steadman, Osher, Robbins, Case, & Samuels, 2009). The causes for the overrepresentation of individuals with mental illness in jails and prisons are likely multidimensional, including deinstitutionalization, more restrictive civil commitment criteria, limited resources in the community, and tougher sentencing guidelines for drug charges.

The historical origins of diversion can be traced back to the early 1960s and the bail reform movement. In *Brandy v. United States (1960)*, the Supreme Court held that a defendant without property who is thus denied bail is therefore denied "equal protection under the law." In 1961, the Manhattan Bail Project funded by the Vera Institute of Justice began interviewing arrestees and making recommendations to be considered at the bail hearing. They found that a very small percentage of individuals who had been released on recognizance failed to appear (Lotze et al., 1999). Two years later, the Supreme Court decided in *Robinson vs. California* (1962) that the mere fact of being addicted was not enough to warrant imprisonment. This case reframed addiction as an illness, which had deep implications for policy responses, including the perception that treatment was a better solution. Within this climate came the extension of the bail reform movement, which included enhanced conditions for release, such as clinical and social services. Pretrial diversion became the term to refer to cases where arrestees were offered the opportunity to have their charges dismissed in exchange for successful participation in social services (Amrhein & Barber-Rioja, 2011). In the 1970s, the National Coalition for Jail Reform recommended the establishment of diversion programs. Early diversion efforts concentrated on individuals with substance abuse disorders, and although many of these individuals likely had a co-occurring mental illness, programs that explicitly offered diversion opportunities for individuals with mental disorders did not develop until the 1990s (Barber-Rioja & Rotter, 2015). The rapid increase in jail diversion in the past decades results from multiple factors, including downsizing of state hospitals, increased sentences, increased prison population, the drug war, and the development of the problem-solving court movement (Amrhein & Barber-Rioja, 2011).

In addition to the belief that jails and prisons are not the appropriate places to treat individuals with psychiatric disabilities (Barr, 1999), assumption under which diversion programs were implemented, the creation of special jurisdiction courts for individuals with mental illness was affected by the principles of therapeutic jurisprudence (Winick, 2002). This concept proposes that the rules of law, legal procedures and legal actors can produce therapeutic or antitherapeutic consequences (Wexler & Winick, 1991) and advocates the use of treatment and rehabilitative services to address the offenders' underlying problems (Winick, 2002). Diversion programs were not necessarily created under the assumption that individuals to be diverted committed their offenses as a direct result of psychiatric symptoms. Therefore, finding a direct connection between the instant offense and symptoms of mental illness is not usually a prerequisite for diversion or the focus of the diversion evaluation.

Diversion programs and MHCs differ in a number of ways, such as whether a guilty plea is necessary prior to entry to the program and whether punishment should be used for noncompliance with treatment (Petrila, 2003). However, as MHCs and diversion programs become more open to diverting individuals with felony charges and violent offenses, they are also more likely to use post-plea adjudication models and to use jail as a sanction (Redlich, Steadman, Monahan, Petrila, & Griffin, 2005). Furthermore, some MHCs require that the participants meet the criteria for Serious Mental Illness (SMI), whereas others are less strict and require only "demonstrable mental health problems" (Redlich et al., 2005, p. 607). Some diversion programs would consider an individual who suffers from a personality disorder only, whereas others would use a broader definition of eligibility. The monitoring period also varies across jurisdictions and diversion programs. For example, in New York, the Queens Felony MHC requires a minimum of twelve months, whereas the Bronx Felony MHC requires eighteen to twenty-four months.

Despite the variations among programs, the following core features can be found in most mental health diversion programs that use a post-adjudication model: the presence of at least mental health difficulties; the requirement for defendants to enter a plea of guilty before enrolling in diversion (Redlich et al., 2005); the deferral of the sentence until successful completion of a treatment plan, at which time charges are either dropped or reduced or the initial conviction is vacated; and finally, the option of an alternative sentence, which is established at the time of the guilty plea and given to defendants who violate the conditions of their plea. Also common to all diversion programs is that candidates have the choice to be diverted or continue with regular criminal court proceedings. Therefore, participation is voluntary, and it requires the consent of all parties, including the mentally ill defendant (Redlich, Hoover, Summers, & Steadman, 2010). Although the compliance requirements of diversion programs also vary, in general, plea agreement conditions include compliance with mental health or substance abuse treatment, which may include taking medications and attending both regular meetings with a case manager and regular status hearings. The sanctions imposed for noncompliance with these conditions can include increased treatment, increased supervision, and reincarceration (Redlich et al., 2010).

Best Practices

There is no single definition of diversion or even a clear or simple description of what constitutes an MHC; furthermore, there is no legal standard for diversion as defined by case law. As such, legal standards for diversion can be considered "insufficiently specific" (Heilbrun, 2009, p. 42). Diversion evaluations should involve a thorough psychological evaluation including a clinical interview, a mental status exam, and on most occasions psychological testing, as well as a review of collateral information. However, since there is no legal standard for diversion to guide these evaluations, it is important for evaluators to understand the forensic issues involved within any given jurisdiction. Broadly speaking, the question facing the decision maker in the context of diversion could be broadly described as whether a defendant meets the eligibility criteria of a manageable mental disorder within a court-mandated context. If so, the individual will be diverted from incarceration into community-based mental health treatment and will be able to avoid jail (Redlich et al., 2010). Given the variety of eligibility standards and regulations surrounding diversion evaluations, it is essential for the forensic evaluator to be familiar with the eligibility regulations governing his/her practicing jurisdictions, diversion programs or special jurisdiction courts, as well as with the treatment resources available in the specific jurisdiction. In addition to which eligibility standard is applied in the jurisdiction, it is important to be familiar with the factors outlined below when conducting diversion evaluation.

Relevant Forensic Issues

Diversion evaluations can be conceptualized as a specific type of forensic assessment in that they are initiated specifically to provide information that would aid the court and/or prosecutor in making the ultimate legal diversion decision. Many of the relevant forensic issues involved in diversion evaluations (i.e., risk assessment and assessment of response style) are shared with those assessed when the legal question is competency, responsibility, or in the context of incarcerated defendants, "release decision making" (Heilbrun et al., 2002), which for example guides evaluations conducted for parole boards. The relevant forensic issues to be assessed in diversion evaluations include the presence of mental illness, malingering, competency to be diverted/voluntariness of the decision, risk for violence, criminogenic factors, and treatment/ management. In short, as per the general principles of FMHA, the focus of the diversion evaluation should be whether the defendant has certain "capacitates, abilities or behavioral tendencies that must be understood" (Heilbrun, Grisso, & Goldstein, 2009, p. 13) to help the legal decision maker determine whether a defendant should be diverted, and, if so, under what conditions.

Presence of Mental Illness   Before assessing the presence of mental illness, the forensic evaluator should be familiar with the clinical eligibility criteria for diversion for the specific jurisdiction or diversion program. Some diversion programs only require that candidates have identifiable mental health difficulties (Redlich et al., 2005). However, other diversion programs require evidence of a *Diagnostic and Statistical Manual of Mental Disorders* (*DSM*) diagnosis (American Psychiatric Association, 2013). Even if the general requirement includes the presence of identifiable mental health difficulties, the district attorney's office may only consent to diversion if the defendant meets criteria for a SMI other than a personality disorder. For example, it has been these writers' experience that it is not unusual for the prosecutor to require evidence of the presence of a SMI when the instant offense involved violence and a victim. Therefore, the forensic clinician should also be aware of the specific requirements of the case. From a clinical risk management perspective (see section below), SMI disorders are often the most amenable to treatment, so the forensic clinician may have more confidence in being able to address the violence risk.

Frequently, defendants are referred for diversion because they have been diagnosed with a mental disorder while incarcerated, because of a reported history of receiving mental health treatment, or because attorneys have observed what they believe to be symptoms of mental illness in their clients. We strongly advise against using these sources of information as proof of the clinical eligibility requirement, although they often serve an important screening and identification purpose. Instead, FMHA principles should be followed, and clinical characteristics should be assessed through valid and reliable methods (Heilbrun, 2009). The appropriate identification of mental health and substance abuse diagnoses is particularly relevant in the context of diversion, as it would guide the treatment plan that defendants will have to follow if they choose to participate in diversion. In addition, the complex interplay of mental illness and substance abuse and the confounding influences on their presentations governs the eligibility decision and monitoring considerations.

In order for forensic evaluators to reliably assess clinical eligibility, it is necessary to obtain relevant historical information (Heilbrun, 2001). Sometimes a thorough psychosocial history, clinical interview, and mental status examination are enough to determine the existence of mental illness. Other times, clinical assessment instruments (such as structured clinical diagnostic interviews or personality inventories) are necessary for diagnostic clarification.

The use of clinical assessment instruments in diversion evaluations can be particularly useful when assessing for the presence of personality disorders. Available studies suggest that the lifetime prevalence of any personality disorder in the forensic populations may be over 80% (Hart, 2002). Teplin (1994) found that, in a sample of 728 male inmates, 48% exhibited antisocial personality disorder, while Jordan, Schlenger, Fairbank, and Caddell (1996) found a high prevalence of borderline personality disorders among the female prison population. The assessment of personality disorders in the diverted population is of special importance due to the increased risk for future violence, the poor response to traditional psychological treatments observed in individuals diagnosed with a personality disorder (Hart. 2002), and the need for specialized treatment approaches. The presence of antisocial or borderline personality traits generally worsens the prognosis regarding diversion compliance, and therefore, treatment plans and court expectations need to be adjusted accordingly. Psychological testing may also be necessary when a cognitive limitation or intellectual disability is suspected, as this may inform the defendant's eligibility, as well as the treatment plan.

In addition, the assessment of clinical characteristics in diversion evaluations should include the use of archival and third-party information (Melton, Petrila, Poythress, & Slobogin, 2007). Melton et al. (2007) listed the following reasons using collateral information in both forensic evaluations and diversion evaluations: "greater need for accuracy, differences in response style between persons in therapeutic and forensic evaluation contexts, and the greater scrutiny that the evaluators' conclusions receive" (p. 53). In the context of diversion, accuracy of diagnosis sometimes determines the decision. It is also important not to rely solely on the examinee's self-report in making diagnostic decisions, given the external incentives afforded by being diverted and the increased knowledge that arrestees have of the existence of a diversion option. Such diagnoses are often questioned by defense attorneys, prosecutors, or prior treatment providers who may be invested in a particular diversion outcome.

Symptom Exaggeration   Given the incentives afforded by participation in mental health diversion programs, specifically the avoidance of incarceration and/or the dropping of criminal charges, jail detainees may attempt to feign or exaggerate the severity of psychiatric disorders in order to gain access to the diversion program. The *DSM-5* (American Psychiatric Association, 2013) states that one of the factors indicating that an individual may be malingering is a lack of treatment compliance (section V65). Conversely, Rogers (1990) has stated that there is no empirical evidence to conclude that individuals who malinger are less likely to comply with treatment. However, no further published studies have specifically examined this relationship. Because individuals who successfully feign psychiatric symptoms for an external incentive are sometimes found eligible for diversion and needlessly placed into mental health treatment programs, it stands to reason that they will be less likely to adhere to treatment attempts and or to comply with the rules and regulations of the diversion program. However, the lack of research in this area makes this prediction speculative.

No published data are available on the prevalence of malingering in individuals being referred to diversion. An unpublished dissertation that assessed 61 individuals being referred for diversion in New York City found that 54% of individuals scored above the cutoff recommended for suspecting malingering on the Miller Forensic Assessment of Symptoms Test (M-FAST; Miller, 2001), a brief structured interview created to screen for malingering by an assessment of an individual's general response style (Barber-Rioja, 2009). Although feigning does not preclude the presence of genuine mental illness, this finding suggests that further assessment of malingering should have been conducted in more than half of the sample. It is therefore recommended that standardized instruments to screen and/or assess for feigning and malingering of psychiatric disorders be administered as part of the diversion evaluation.

Competency and Voluntariness   One of the core features of diversion is that participation is voluntary (Redlich, 2005). In addition, all candidates of diversion are presumed to be competent when allowed to enter a guilty plea prior to being diverted (Redlich et al., 2010). However, the issue of whether defendants are actually competent to accept diversion and treatment and whether participation in diversion is truly voluntary has frequently been raised (Poythress, Petrila, McGaha, & Boothroyd, 2002; Redlich, 2005; Redlich et al., 2010; Seltzer, 2005; Stafford & Wygant, 2005). Most research or commentaries about this issue refer to competency to participate or be transferred to an MHC. It has been reported that the adoption of nontraditional roles by attorneys, prosecutors, and judges in MHCs makes participants more vulnerable to competency issues (Petrila, 2003; Redlich, 2005). This level of informality and the potentially paternalistic context in which MHCs process cases make courts more susceptible to violations of due process by adjudicating defendants who do not understand the voluntary nature of MHCs or do not "understand and appreciate the decision before them" (Redlich, 2005, p. 605). As in juvenile and mental hygiene courts, a focus on the defendant's best interest can, if unchecked, undermine the justice and fairness associated with the respect for his or her autonomy. Although this level of informality does not fully apply to diversions taking place outside of MHCs, the issues of voluntariness and competency are believed to be applicable not only to MHCs but also to decentralized diversion.

Some features inherent to diversion increase participants' likelihood to experience competency issues. By definition, participants of diversion programs are mentally ill. Frequently, these defendants are expected to make decisions about their involvement in diversion dispositions after they have been arrested and spent time in jail without receiving the appropriate treatment for their mental health needs (Bazelon Center for Mental Health Law, 2003). Such decisions are therefore made under significant stress and time pressure and often result in decisions that are not fully informed or voluntary (Erickson, Campbell, & Lamberti, 2006; Redlich et al., 2010; Seltzer, 2005).

Since MHC comprehension is related to other legal competencies (Redlich, 2005), it is expected that competency to participate in a MHC would be problematic in a high proportion of the referred cases. For example, according to Stafford and Wygant (2005), 77.5% of 80 defendants participating in an Ohio MHC who were referred for competency to stand trial evaluations were found incompetent, which led the authors to conclude that many of the participants did not present with the capacity to waive the constitutional rights and to make the informed decisions required to participate in these courts. A recent study used the MacArthur Competency Assessment Tool-Criminal Adjudication (MacCAT-CA; Poythress et al., 1999) to determine whether participants of two MHCs (Brooklyn MHC and Washoe MHC) experienced impairments in legal competency. The study found that 16% to 17% of Brooklyn and 9% to 13% of Washoe MHCs participants demonstrated clinically significant impairments in legal competency (Redlich et al., 2010).

The fact that most diversion programs require defendants to enter a plea of guilty makes competency a relevant forensic issue in diversion evaluations. The decision to participate in diversion and therefore to enter a plea of guilty must be "knowing, intelligent, and voluntary" (Melton et al., 2007). In order for a defendant to make an informed decision regarding his plea and diversion, he must understand all of the conditions of the plea agreement, including the particular requirements of the diversion program, the release of confidential information, the consequences of noncompliance including the alternative sentence, and the alternative courses of legal action (Redlich et al., 2010). It is also important for the defendant to understand the requirements of the treatment plan being designed, including whether he or she would be required to attend outpatient or residential treatment or to comply with psychiatric medications. In addition, defendants usually do not understand that the judge has discretion over the monitoring period and therefore can extend it if participants are not fully compliant with treatment and that the time completed in treatment does not count toward the alternative sentence.

Under *Godinez v. Moran* (1993), the United States Supreme Court decided that the legal standard for competency to plead guilty is not higher than competency to stand trial (CST) in general, although in practice the specific decisions and decision-making capacities may be different. Decision making associated with MHCs take into account elements of both general competency to stand trial and evaluation of a decision to plead guilty. Redlich (2005) has argued that the constructs of understanding, reasoning, and appreciation that define adjudicative competence and competence to make treatment decisions can also be used to define comprehension in the context of MHCs. She pointed to a number of diversion characteristics that participants need to comprehend, such as entering a guilty plea, agreeing to engage in treatment, and consenting to release confidential records to the court. In reference to reasoning, participants need to consider the repercussions of enrolling versus not enrolling. Participants also need to appreciate the consequences of dropping out, violating the conditions, or successfully graduating from the court.

Redlich et al. (2010) found that, although most participants of the Brooklyn and Washoe MHCs understood the basic components of the MHC, few fully understood more nuanced details. For example, more than half of the participants reported not knowing that the choice to enroll and therefore plead guilty was voluntary. It is important to note that frequently a defendant being considered for diversion does not meet with a mental health professional until he is being examined for diversion eligibility. Therefore, the clinician conducting the diversion evaluation may be the first mental health professional to come in contact with the defendant. As a result, as part of the diversion evaluation, forensic clinicians should assess whether the defendant understands the voluntary nature of his choice and "screen" for adjudicative competency. Examiners should fully explain to defendants the specific requirements of the diversion program including the treatment plan, and the voluntary nature of the decision, and should assess whether the presence of active psychiatric symptoms or cognitive disabilities may preclude examinees from making knowingly intelligent and voluntary decisions regarding diversion.

Although a diversion evaluation is clearly not a CST evaluation, forensic evaluators who have reasonable doubt about the defendant's competency to proceed should raise the competency question to the referral source and recommend that an adjudicative competency evaluation be ordered. Conversely, if the examiner does not believe that competency is an issue, this should clearly be stated in the report, as well as whether the examiner believes that the defendant understands the voluntary nature of their choice. Assessing these functional legal capacities as part of the diversion evaluation would hopefully decrease the chances of engaging in violations of defendants' due process by minimizing the number of incompetent participants who enter guilty pleas as a condition of diversion.

Finally, from a clinical perspective, voluntariness is also critical. The greater the understanding and perception of fairness, the better defendants do within diversion programs. It is recommended that, given different alternatives in terms of types of treatment modality, participants be given a choice. Feeling like they have a choice in the type of treatment that they are mandated to attend likely increases perceptions of procedural justice (e.g., the degree to which defendants feel like they have a voice and are heard; Lind & Tyler, 1988), which in turn is related to MHC graduation and reduced recidivism (Redlich & Han, 2014). Similarly, the better the insight into at least what treatment they are agreeing to and the need to comply with a court mandate (if applicable), the more likely defendants are to complete the program successfully.

Violence Risk   Individuals charged with violent offenses are increasingly being considered for participation in diversion programs. In fact a "second generation" of MHCs that accept more felonies has been identified (Redlich et al., 2005). These individuals typically face longer prison sentences if violated by the diversion program (Barber-Rioja, Dewey, Kopelovich, & Kucharski, 2012), and jail is more often used as a sanction for noncompliance (Relich, 2005). The goal of diverting individuals with mental illness from the criminal justice system should not take place at the expense of public safety (Barber-Rioja et al., 2012); therefore, evidence-based violence risk assessment should also be incorporated into diversion evaluations. In this context, the question is not one of violence prevention but violence management. The question faced by diversion evaluators is not only what is the level of risk of a given defendant but also whether that level of risk can be managed in the community with the resources available in that jurisdiction. Since the focus is more on risk management and therefore on dynamic risk factors, the use of Structured Professional Judgment (SPJ) tools like the HCR-20 is recommended (as opposed to actuarial tools). This tool has also been shown to be useful in predicting diversion compliance (Barber-Rioja et al., 2012).

Criminogenic Factors   Research has shown that MHCs are effective in reducing recidivism (Anestis & Carbonell, 2014; Burns, Hiday, & Ray, 2012; Hiday, Wales, & Ray, 2013; Linhorst & Linhorst, 2012; Ray, 2014), despite no consistent evidence that diversion programs lead to a significant reduction in psychiatric symptoms (Boothroyd, Mercado, Poythress, Christy, & Petrila, 2005; Cosden, Ellens, Schnell, Yamini-Diouf, & Wolfe, 2003; Steadman & Naples, 2005). This lack of symptom reduction suggests that decreases in reincarceration reported by diversion programs may be due to something other than mental health treatment. Research has suggested that offenders with mental illness share the same risk factors as those without mental illness (Epperson et al., 2011; Skeem & Louden, 2013). In fact, it has been argued that some negative recidivism outcomes found in interventions that target offenders with mental disorders may be a result of overreliance on clinical treatment (Wolff et al., 2013). It is now widely accepted that to attain rehabilitation for offenders with mental illness, diversion programs should focus their efforts not only on mental health needs but also on criminogenic risk factors that provide a range of psychosocial supports (Edgely, 2014). Probably the conceptual model most frequently used by programs designed to reduce recidivism that addresses criminogenic factors is the Risk-Needs-Responsivity model (RNR; Andrews, Bonta, & Wormith, 2011). Although not specifically developed for offenders with mental disorders (Morgan et al., 2011), its authors argue that since predictors of general recidivism are almost the same for offenders with and without mental disorders, RNR can be applied to both groups (Bonta, Law, & Hanson, 1998). There is evidence that the RNR model and associated needs are relevant for offenders with mental disorders (Bonta, Blais, & Wilson, 2014; Fass, Heilbrum, Dematteo, & Fretz, 2008; Skeem & Louden, 2013) and therefore should also be evaluated.

Treatment/Management Planning   If the forensic evaluator conducting the diversion evaluation decides that the defendant is eligible for diversion, a treatment/management plan that addresses psychiatric/substance abuse issues, as well as risk factors for violence and recidivism (e.g., criminogenic factors), should be clearly delineated. It is also important to note that diversion evaluations frequently have a different audience; although such reports are prepared primarily for the courts, they are also used to refer individuals to treatment in the community, making this part of the evaluation critical as it informs community providers and case managers about the expectations of the court mandate. The examiner should be knowledgeable about the treatment resources available in the community; recommending treatment modalities that are not feasible or not available in the community is not helpful to the courts.

It is recommended that the management plan be organized as suggested by the HCR-20 V3 manual, which includes delineating four basic types of activities: monitoring, supervision, treatment, and victim safety planning (Kroop, Hart, Lyon, & Lepard, 2002). Monitoring refers to using surveillance to evaluate changes in risk over time so that risk management strategies can be modified accordingly. Diversion monitoring strategies typically involve face-to-face meetings with case managers, regular urine toxicology exams, and regular court hearings. The MHC or diversion judge has been identified as an essential element that promotes the rehabilitation of the offender with mental illness through the establishment of a therapeutic alliance (Edgely, 2014). As a result, frequent supervisory status hearings should be included as a monitoring strategy.

Treatment refers to any rehabilitative services, such as substance abuse or mental health treatment, vocational services, psychiatric medications, or trauma-informed counseling. Supervision refers to any restrictions in movement that limit the opportunities for the individual to engage in violence or criminal activities. In the context of diversion, this can include a curfew and order of protection, admission into detox or drug rehabilitation programs, or psychiatric hospitalizations. Finally, victim safety planning should be delineated when the instant offense involved a victim, and it should include steps to be taken to protect the victim when management strategies have failed (Kroop et al., 2002).

Interview

Regardless of the referral source, prior to conducting a diversion evaluation, the defense attorney should always be informed that his or her client has been referred for a diversion evaluation and will be interviewed. Sometimes the attorney may not believe that diversion is in the client's best interest and may refuse to consent to the evaluation. For risk assessment purposes, diversion evaluations may elicit information about the instant offense that may be incriminating if the case is resolved through trial. A review of records, such as the defendant's criminal history, medical records, criminal complaint, and interview with collateral sources of information is necessary to corroborate the defendant's self-report and also to obtain information about his or her history of treatment compliance, the prior response to supervision or court-mandated treatment, and the presence or absence of social supports in the community.

Prior to the beginning of the evaluation, the defendant should be informed of the purpose of the interview (e.g., to decide eligibility for diversion), the voluntary nature of the decision to participate if found eligible, and the limits of confidentiality. Diversion evaluations often require more than one meeting. During the first meeting, the evaluator gathers the information that determines eligibility and, during the second meeting, a treatment/management plan is presented to the eligible client.

The interview requires collecting psychosocial background and a thorough developmental history, including history of abuse or trauma, school and employment, past and current relationships, psychiatric diagnoses and treatment, substance abuse involvement, and criminal activities. Risk assessment tools should be used to gather information that identifies violence and criminogenic risk factors. The interview should also include a thorough mental status examination, psychological testing for diagnostic clarification, assessment of cognitive limitations or intellectual disabilities, and screening for evidence of malingering.

During the interview the examiner should also gather information about the client's insight into his/her mental illness/substance use, triggers for criminal behavior, and motivation for treatment.

Report Writing

The written report should start with identifying and referral information, followed by the sources of information used, the purpose of the interview, and the limits of confidentiality. In this section the examiner may also include whether the client appears competent to proceed with the interview and whether he or she understands the voluntary nature of the decision to participate in diversion.

The sections that follow provide all relevant background information, an outline of the mental status examination, results of any psychological tests, diagnostic impressions needed to meet the requirement for diversion eligibility, a violence risk assessment, and an assessment of recidivism risk. It is the authors' experience that the risk information must be documented both honestly and carefully, taking into account the audience (e.g., courts and treatment providers).

If the risk information is not contextualized and associated immediately with the risk management strategy to mitigate the risk, readers will often become inappropriately concerned. The final sections should include an opinion regarding whether the client is eligible for diversion, based on all the prior sources of information reviewed, and a thorough delineation of the recommended treatment/ management plan that will be put into effect if a plea is entered.

Case Vignette

The following case study is meant to highlight aspects of a diversion evaluation, which incorporates recommendations for the best practices described previously. All identifying information has been changed.

Reason for Referral

Ms. Johnson was a 26-year-old Caucasian, single, incarcerated female, diagnosed with Schizophrenia and Alcohol Use Disorder by the County Jail's health services. She was currently charged with arson in the second degree. Ms. Johnson was referred by the district attorney's office for a psychological evaluation specifically with the purpose of determining her eligibility for diversion and providing treatment/monitoring recommendations accordingly. Prior to the interview, Ms. Johnson was informed that the purpose of the interview was to determine her eligibility for mandated treatment in the community in lieu of incarceration. She was also informed of the plea requirement and the voluntary nature of her decision to participate in a diversion option versus regular criminal proceedings. Ms. Johnson was also informed of the limits of confidentiality, specifically that the results of the evaluation would be reported to her defense attorney, prosecutor, judge, and, if deemed eligible for diversion, treatment providers in the community as well. Ms. Johnson appeared to understand the limits of confidentiality and the voluntary nature of a diversion option, and the interview proceeded on that basis.

Summary of Relevant Records

In addition to a clinical interview and testing session of about four hours conducted by a licensed psychologist, the following records were reviewed: medical records of three psychiatric hospitalizations at a city hospital, the criminal complaint, and the defendant's criminal record. Additional collateral information was also obtained from Ms. Johnson's mother over the telephone.

The case vignette has been redacted and all identifying information removed. It is not meant to serve as a forensic report. Any likeness to a case is purely coincidental.

Relevant Background Information

Background Information was obtained from Ms. Johnson's mother, a review of records and Ms. Johnson's self-report.

Ms. Johnson was born in San Jose, California, and raised by both parents until the age of 16. She has no siblings. Her father worked in construction and her mother was a homemaker. She described an upbringing significant for witnessing violence and being sexually abused. Ms. Johnson's father suffered from an addiction to alcohol and would frequently beat Ms. Johnson's mother. In addition, Ms. Johnson was sexually abused by her father's brother from ages 9 to about 12. Escaping from the abuse, Ms. Johnson moved with her mother to New York to reside with an aunt when Ms. Johnson was 16 years of age. She reported that her grandmother is diagnosed with Schizophrenia.

Ms. Johnson reported that she experienced learning problems in school and was placed in special education classes at an early age. However, she attended school and passed all her classes until the age of 14 when she began showing up to class intoxicated. Ms. Johnson began drinking alcohol with her father at the age of 14 and said that she became addicted shortly after. At the age of 15, while in the tenth grade, Ms. Johnson was expelled from school for cutting classes. Once in New York, Ms. Johnson had several odd jobs waiting tables and cleaning houses. However, she was fired from most jobs due to alcohol intoxication. At the age of 17, Ms. Johnson attended her first alcohol detoxification and rehabilitation programs at the request of her mother. However, her mother said that she relapsed within a week of completing the program. While in the rehabilitation program, Ms. Johnson met a man with whom she maintained a sexual relationship and became pregnant. She gave birth to her daughter at 18 years of age. Ms. Johnson's daughter was removed from her custody by social services shortly after her birth due to Ms. Johnson's continuous alcohol use.

Ms. Johnson was first admitted into a psychiatric hospital at 20 years of age after her mother called 911 because she was talking to herself and voicing paranoid ideation (e.g., believing that there were cameras in their house). She was admitted for one month and prescribed antipsychotic medications. Ms. Johnson did not follow up with medications or outpatient treatment and continued drinking once discharged. She was admitted four more times from 20 to 26 years of age in different local hospitals for periods ranging from one to six months. She has no significant medical conditions.

Ms. Johnson has a history of one prior arrest, also for arson in the second degree. This charge was eventually reduced to arson in the third degree, and she was sentenced to time served after ten months in the local jail. With respect to the instant offense, Ms. Johnson was accused of having placed papers under a neighbor's door after lighting them on fire. No injuries were reported but the building had to be evacuated. Ms. Johnson reported that she was intoxicated and began hearing voices telling her to set things on fire. Ms. Johnson related a similar account of the events that led to her prior arson charge. Since her arrest and incarceration nine months ago, Ms. Johnson was compliant with medication and free of acute psychopathology.

Ms. Johnson's mother reported that Ms. Johnson is a calm and sweet person when she is sober but that she becomes agitated when drunk. She also said Ms. Johnson hears voices at times and becomes paranoid that there are people out to hurt her and kill her and that people can hear her thoughts. Ms. Johnson's mother was not able to identify a significant period of time during which Ms. Johnson was sober except for her nine-month pregnancy. She stated that she never fully complies with the hospitals' discharge plans because she relapses on alcohol shortly after leaving the hospital. She denied that Ms. Johnson has ever engaged in any acts of physical aggression or antisocial behaviors. She denied that Ms. Johnson has ever engaged in any fire-setting behaviors or voiced any fascination with fire. She corroborated a family history of Schizophrenia.

A review of records from her hospitalizations indicated that Ms. Johnson was consistently intoxicated prior to admission into the hospital. However, it appears that symptoms of psychosis, such as auditory hallucinations and paranoid delusions, remained for significant periods of time after she had been detoxed from alcohol. For example, on one occasion Ms. Johnson endorsed psychotic symptoms for almost three months after admission to the hospital.

Mental Status Examination

During the interview Ms. Johnson presented as a white female of average height and weight who appeared her stated age. She was dressed in jail attire, and her hygiene and grooming were appropriate. She was cooperative and calm during the interview. She related oddly with her interviewers but maintained good eye contact. She was alert and oriented across all spheres. Psychomotor activity and speech were within normal limits. Her thought process was logical and goal-directed with no evidence of thought disorder. She reported her mood as "OK." Her observed affect was euthymic (neutral), constricted in range, and appropriate to the content of conversation. She denied any visual or auditory hallucinations, and no psychotic delusions were elicited. She reported that she was currently complying with psychiatric medications prescribed by the jail (Risperdal, an antipsychotic). She denied any suicidal or homicidal ideation. Ms. Johnson impressed as functioning at a below average range of intelligence. Her judgment and impulse control during the interview were grossly intact. She demonstrated adequate insight into her alcohol use disorder but poor insight into her auditory hallucinations, her paranoid delusions, and the symptom improvement that she experiences when complying with medications. She expressed adequate insight into the reasons for her arrest (e.g., connection between getting drunk and setting things on fire) but not into her difficulties remaining sober or complying with treatment.

Psychological Measures

Given Ms. Johnson's apparent cognitive limitations (e.g., concrete thinking), she was administered the Wechsler Adult Intelligence Scale, Fourth Edition (WAIS-IV), an individually administered test of a person's intellectual functioning and cognitive strengths and weaknesses. On this test, she obtained a Full Scale IQ (FSIQ) within the borderline range. Although no significant discrepancies were found among the four indices that composed the FSIQ, her performance was significantly low on measures of verbal abilities that required reasoning, comprehension, and conceptualization. To ensure that Ms. Johnson put forth adequate effort, prior to the administration of the WAIS-IV, she was administered the Test of Memory Malingering (TOMM), a forced-choice visual discrimination task designed to differentiate between feigned and genuine memory impairment that is also sensitive to motivation and effort. On this test, Ms. Johnson scored above the cutoff for suspected malingering, suggesting that the results of the WAIS-IV were a valid representation of her actual level of intellectual functioning.

Exaggeration of psychiatric symptoms was not suspected and, in fact, Ms. Johnson minimized some of her symptoms. As a result, no test for the assessment of malingering of psychiatric symptoms was considered necessary. In addition, a review of medical records provided ample evidence of Ms. Johnson's psychiatric symptoms and diagnoses. No further psychological testing was required.

Since Ms. Johnson's index offense was a violent felony, a violence risk assessment was indicated and conducted via use of the HCR-20 V3. In addition, to assess for criminogenic needs, the Level of Service/Case Management Inventory (LS/CMI; Andrews et al., 2004) was administered. The LS/CMI is a tool developed to assess criminogenic needs of offenders.

Clinical Summary and Opinions

Ms. Johnson was a 26-year-old Caucasian, incarcerated female with a history of Schizophrenia and Alcohol Use disorder, who was referred by the district attorney's office for a psychological evaluation to determine her eligibility for diversion. Based on a culmination of clinical interviews, behavioral observations, testing, and collateral information, the following conclusions were made:

Ms. Johnson was cooperative and forthcoming during the interview. There was no evidence that she attempted to exaggerate or grossly minimize her presentation. Despite her cognitive limitations, she appeared to understand the limits of confidentiality and the voluntary nature of her decision to participate in diversion. No acute psychiatric symptoms were observed that could interfere with her competency to enter a plea of guilty at this time.

Diagnostically, Ms. Johnson's primary problem was a long and severe history of alcohol use that probably originated as a result of both a biological predisposition (father's history of alcohol use) and environmental factors (drinking with his father and sexual abuse history). However, in addition to this, there was evidence that she suffered from symptoms consistent with a diagnosis of Schizophrenia (e.g., auditory hallucinations and paranoid delusions). A review of records provided some evidence that Ms. Johnson had experienced psychotic symptoms while the effects of intoxication had subsided, making it likely that she also suffered from a psychotic disorder that became exacerbated when intoxicated. In addition, her chronic symptoms are unusual for mere intoxication or alcohol-related psychosis, although they may be more intensely experienced or expressed behaviorally when intoxicated. Supporting this hypothesis is the fact that Ms. Johnson has a family history of Schizophrenia. Results of testing indicated that Ms. Johnson functioned within the Borderline level of intellectual functioning and demonstrated impairments in her ability to process ideas that involved complex concepts and to generalize information. Given her difficulties thinking beyond what was presented as concrete concepts, once a treatment/management plan was developed and a plea agreement is negotiated, it was recommended that verbal stimuli be presented to her in simpler terms and that complex concepts would be repeated several times until she demonstrated understanding.

Using the structure of the HCR20 V3, the following were identified as relevant violence risk factors for Ms. Johnson: a history of problems with violence (e.g., arson), traumatic experiences, substance abuse, mental illness, unemployment, and treatment compliance, as well as recent problems with insight. Given her fire-setting instant offense, programs may be reluctant to house her, and as such, she would likely experience problems securing structured community placement—the first of the Risk Management risk factors, that is, problems with professional services. In addition, her past history indicated she likely had experienced difficulty with treatment and supervision response and with coping with stress. On the other hand, Ms. Johnson had a limited repertoire of dangerous activity, within a very specific context. Her only acts of violence were setting things on fire and, on both occasions, she was intoxicated and likely experiencing an exacerbation of symptoms of Schizophrenia due to treatment noncompliance. Thus, while her risk for violence and in particular for fire-setting behavior was high in the context of noncompliance with treatment and intoxication, if she was sober and psychiatrically stable, the risk would be significantly diminished.

With respect to criminogenic risk, the LS/CMI was used to identify the following risk factors in need of intervention: lack of leisure and recreation, lack of achieving in education and employment, family problems (lack of custody of her daughter), and alcohol use. There was no evidence that Ms. Johnson had a procriminal attitude or orientation or an antisocial pattern.

Given the presence of a co-occurring psychiatric and substance use disorder, as well as a level of risk that was considered manageable in the community under appropriate treatment and supervision, the psychologist concluded that she is eligible for diversion, and the following management plan was recommended to address her needs:

Treatment   Ms. Johnson was primarily in need of substance abuse treatment. She was detoxed from alcohol while in jail and at this point had been sober in a controlled environment for a period of nine months. Ms. Johnson had attended several rehabilitation programs lasting between 28 to 30 days. At this time of the evaluation, given her charge, no residential treatment program would accept her in the jurisdiction where she resided. Therefore, intense outpatient treatment for substance abuse was recommended. Given her long and severe alcohol use disorder and unsuccessful attempts to quit, pharmacological treatments for substance-related disorders such as Naltrexone or Antabuse were considered. In addition, it was recommended that Ms. Johnson should be seen by a psychiatrist for medication reevaluation once she was discharged. Furthermore, her history of trauma suggested that she would benefit from trauma-informed care and individual counseling. To further address her criminogenic needs, Ms. Johnson expressed interest in vocational training. In addition, it was recommended that her counselor explore different options for leisure and recreation. Ms. Johnson expressed a desire to obtain rights to visit her daughter who was currently in foster care. Therefore, it was recommended that her case manager assist her in determining the expectations and if this was a feasible option.

Monitoring   Given the increased risk that Ms. Johnson posed if she relapsed back to abusing alcohol, it was recommended that she be tested initially twice a week and meet face-to-face with her case manager on a weekly basis to reassess her mental status and level of risk. Due to her difficulties with verbal comprehension and abstract thinking, it was recommended that her case manager provide specific written instructions listing all of her appointments and plea requirements. In addition, since this is the first time that Ms. Johnson would be in court-mandated treatment, frequent court hearings were recommended.

Supervision   According to the mother, Ms. Johnson tended to engage in drinking at night when she left the house at about 5:00 p.m. to go to bars or friends' houses and returned home at 2:00 or 3:00 a.m. intoxicated. As a result, a curfew is initially recommended until Ms. Johnson is able to remain sober for a significant period of time in the community.

Common Pitfalls and Considerations

One of the most common mistakes made by evaluators when conducting diversion evaluations is to not be familiar with the forensic issues or the eligibility for diversion within the specific jurisdiction. In this evaluation, the first relevant forensic issue that needed to be addressed was whether Ms. Johnson met clinical eligibility for mental health diversion. In the jurisdiction where this evaluation took place, a finding of mental illness by itself is not enough to be considered for mental health diversion; in addition, the individual needs to suffer from a psychiatric disorder (other than a substance use disorder) that meets criteria for a designation as Seriously Mentally Ill (SMI), meaning that the individual experiences significant impairment in functioning as a result of a psychiatric disorder (other than a personality disorder) and is not able to function in the community without psychosocial rehabilitation efforts. In this case, the fact that Ms. Johnson had been using alcohol for a prolonged period of time with no significant periods of sobriety, made it difficult to determine whether psychotic symptoms were always induced by alcohol or were a result of an independent psychotic disorder. This distinction is important in the context of diversion because it determines eligibility and informs treatment planning. If it were determined that her psychotic symptoms were all alcohol induced, transfer to a drug treatment court or a substance abuse diversion program could be recommended. Such programs typically manage cases differently, with more of an emphasis on sanctions and rewards (National Association of Drug Court Professionals, 1997) and less emphasis on medication compliance. Since Ms. Johnson does not have appropriate insight into her psychotic symptoms and was not a good historian when it came to her reasons for hospitalization (e.g., she only identified being drunk), a review of records was crucial when clarifying her diagnosis and the interplay between her mental illness and alcohol use disorder. Psychological testing was necessary to determine her actual level of cognitive functioning. Her borderline intellectual level made it difficult for her to understand and appropriately process the requirements of the plea agreement, and it was the opinion of the evaluator that it could interfere with her ability to follow all of the requirements of post-plea treatment and monitoring. As a result, potential noncompliance post-plea may be interpreted as resulting from a lack of interest and therefore leading to a violation of the plea conditions and potential incarceration, as opposed to understanding her noncompliance as an inability to comprehend instructions. Identifying her cognitive limitations may change the expectations of compliance for the courts and also inform the treatment providers so that they can adjust treatment accordingly. Failing to identify significant cognitive impairment throughout the diversion evaluation process can have significant negative consequences for individuals (e.g., violation and resulting incarceration).

It is also very important for evaluators to be familiar with the standards of competency within the jurisdiction so that they can screen for whether the detainee may need a competency evaluation prior to making decisions regarding a plea to diversion. Evaluators should also make sure that the clients understand the voluntary nature of the decision. In this case, despite her cognitive limitations, Ms. Johnson appeared to understand the limits of confidentiality, the purpose of the evaluation, the concept of diversion, and the fact that she had a choice not to participate. The assessment of cognitive limitations informed her defense attorney how to communicate with this client (e.g., repeat concepts several times and express them in simpler terms) as the plea negotiation proceeded and her choices became more complicated (e.g., learning the prison sentence that she would face in case of noncompliance [fifteen years in her case], or the period of time that she was expected to comply with court-mandated treatment).

Evaluators should recognize that public safety is a very important part of diversion, and as a result, providing a diagnostic evaluation may not be enough to aid the courts when making diversion decisions. Ms. Johnson did not provide much information in reference to her motivations for engaging in fire setting, other than that she was intoxicated and hearing voices. She also did not provide an explanation of why she chose to set something on fire versus any other behavior responding to auditory hallucinations. A review of the criminal complaints suggested that in both situations her behaviors appeared random in that she did not know the neighbor, did not appear to be targeting anyone in particular, and presented as intoxicated when interrogated by the police. A sole review of the criminal records would have revealed one arson conviction and a current arrest for arson, which would have provided no information about her actual level of risk or what steps, if any, could be taken to prevent her from engaging in this behavior again. In addition, without placing the behavior into context (e.g., a risk assessment), it is likely that no treatment provider in the community, including outpatient programs, would have agreed to accept her.

As previously noted, risk communication is particularly important in the context of diversion and, if the participant is found eligible, communication of levels of risk for violence should be directly linked to the management interventions. A challenge in this case was the fact that her charge made it impossible for her to be admitted into residential treatment, which may have been a good option given her long history of noncompliance with outpatient treatment. When determining whether her level of risk was manageable in the community given her long history of noncompliance, the evaluator considered whether any intervention that had not been tried before was available. Ms. Johnson had never been under any court-mandated treatment or judicial supervision. The court monitoring and supervision, as well as the knowledge of the jail time being faced, can motivate individuals to comply with treatment. In addition, Ms. Johnson had never tried any pharmaceutical interventions for the treatment of alcohol use, which was thus recommended as part of her treatment. Monitoring considerations, such as frequent face-to-face meetings with her case manager, urine toxicologies, and court hearings, were made based on her risk factors and the lack of appropriate resources in the community (e.g., residential treatment).

Finally, evaluators need to be able to communicate risk for recidivism as involving a different set of risk factors than those related to risk for violence. Evaluators must be able to identify areas for which targeted interventions can reduce rearrest. To this end, familiarity with the offender rehabilitation literature and identification of dynamic offender needs that are changeable with intervention are essential. In the case described above, Ms. Johnson's criminogenic needs were assessed through the use of the LS/CMI. She was not considered to be at high risk for recidivism as long as she remained sober and free of psychotic symptoms, but her criminogenic needs were incorporated into the management plan.

References

American Psychiatric Association. (2013). *Diagnostic and statistical manual of mental disorders* (5th ed.). Washington, DC: Author.

Amrhein, C., & Barber-Rioja, V. (2010). Jail diversion models. In S. A. Estrine, R. T. Hettenbach, H. Arthur, & M. Messina (Eds.), *Service delivery for vulnerable populations: New directions in behavioral health* (pp. 329–352). New York, NY: Springer.

Andrews, D. A., Bonta, J., & Wormith, J. S. (2011). The risk-need-responsivity (RNR) model: Does adding the good lives model contribute to effective crime prevention? *Criminal Justice and Behavior, 38,* 735–755. doi:10.1177/0093854811406356

Anestis, J. C., & Carbonell, J. L. (2014). Stopping the revolving door: Effectiveness of mental health court in reducing recidivism by mentally ill offenders. *Psychiatric Services, 65,* 1105–1112. doi:10.1176/appi.ps.201300305

Barber-Rioja, V. (2009). *An examination of predictive variables of success in mental health diversion programs* (Doctoral dissertation). Retrieved from ProQuest Dissertations & Theses Database. (3378542).

Barber-Rioja, V., Dewey, L., Kopelovich, S., & Kucharski, L. T. (2012). The utility of the HCR-20 and PCL:SV in the prediction of diversion noncompliance and reincarceration in diversion programs. *Criminal Justice and Behavior, 39,* 475–492. doi:10.1177/0093854811432609

Barber-Rioja, V., & Rotter, M. (2015). Diversion programs and alternatives to incarceration. In R. Trestman, K. Appelbaum, & J. Metzner (Eds.), *Oxford Textbooks in Psychiatry: Oxford Textbook of Correctional Psychiatry.* New York, NY: Oxford University Press.

Barr, H. (1999). *Prisons and jails, hospitals of last resort: The need for diversion and discharge planning for incarcerated people with mental illness in New York.* New York, NY: Correctional Association of New York and the Urban Justice Center.

Bonta, J., Law, M., & Hanson, K. (1998). The prediction of criminal and violent recidivism among mentally disordered offenders: A meta-analysis. *Psychological Bulletin, 123,* 123–142.

Boothroyd, R. A., Mercado, C. C., Poythress, N. G., Christy, A., & Petrila, J. (2005). Clinical outcomes of defendants in mental health court. *Psychiatric Services, 56,* 829–834.

Broner, N., Borum, R., & Gawley, K. (2002). Criminal justice diversion of individuals with co-occurring mental illness and substance use disorders: An overview. In G. Landsberg, M. Rock, L. Berg & A. Smiley (Eds.), *Serving mentally ill offenders: Challenges and opportunities for mental health professionals* (pp. 83–106). New York, NY: Springer.

Burns, P. J., Hiday, V. A., & Ray, B. (2012). Effectiveness 2 years postexit of a recently established mental health court. *American Behavioral Scientist, 57,* 189–208. doi:10.1177/0002764212465416

Cosden, M., Ellens, J. K., Schnell, J. L., Yamini-Diouf, Y., & Wolfe, M. M. (2003). Evaluation of a mental health treatment court with assertive community treatment. *Behavioral Sciences and the Law, 21,* 415–427. doi:10.1002/bsl.542

The Council of State Governments (CSG), Justice Center. (2014). Mental health courts. Retrieved from http://csgjusticecenter.org/mental-health-court-project/

Edgely, M. (2014). Why do mental health courts work? A confluence of treatment, support & adroit judicial supervision. *International Journal of Law and Psychiatry, 37,* 572–580. doi:10.1016/j.ijlp.2014.02.031

Epperson, M., Wolff, N., Morgan, R., Fisher W., Frueh, B. C., & Huening, J. (2011). *The next generation of behavioral health and criminal justice interventions: Improving outcomes by improving interventions.* New Brunswick, NJ: Center for Behavioral Health Services & Criminal Justice Research: Rutgers University.

Erickson, S. K., Campbell, A., & Lamberti, J. S. (2006). Variations in mental health courts: Challenges, opportunities, and a call for caution. *Community Mental Health Journal, 42,* 335–344. doi:10.1007/s10597-006-9046-7

Godinez v. Moran, 509 U.S. 389 (1993).

Hart, S. D. (2002). Commentary: The forensic relevance of personality disorder. *Journal of the American Academy of Psychiatry and the Law, 30,* 510–512.

Heilbrun, K. (2001). *Principles of forensic mental health assessment.* New York, NY: Kluwer Academic/Plenum.

Heilbrun, K. (2009). *Evaluation for risk of violence in adults.* New York, NY: Oxford University Press.

Heilbrun, K., Grisso, T., & Goldstein, A. M. (2009). *Foundations of forensic mental health assessment.* New York, NY: Oxford University Press.

Hiday, V. A., Wales, H. W., & Ray, B. (2013). Effectiveness of a short-term mental health court: Criminal recidivism one year postexit. *Law and Human Behavior, 37,* 401–411. doi:10.1037/lhb0000030

Jordan, B. K., Schlenger, W. E., Fairbank, J. A., & Caddell, J. M. (1996). Prevalence of psychiatric disorders among incarcerated women: Convicted felons entering prison. *Archives of General Psychiatry, 53,* 513–519.

Lind, E. A., & Tyler, T. R. (1988). *The social psychology of procedural justice.* New York, NY: Plenum Press.

Linhorst, P. A., & Linhorst, D. M. (2012). Recidivism outcomes for suburban mental health court defendants. *American Journal of Criminal Justice, 37,* 76–91. doi:10.1007/s12103-010-9092-0

Lotze, E., Clark, J., Henry, D. A., & Juzkiewicz, J. (1999). *The pretrial services reference book.* Washington, DC: Pretrial Services Resource Center.

Melton, G. B., Petrila, J., Poythress, N. G., & Slobogin, C. (2007). *Psychological evaluations for the courts: A handbook for mental health professionals and lawyers.* New York, NY: The Guilford Press.

Miller, H. A. (2001). M-FAST: *Miller Forensic Assessment of Symptoms Test and professional manual.* Odessa, FL: Psychological Assessment Resources.

Morgan, R. D., Flora, D. B., Kroner, D. G., Mills J. F., Varghese, F., & Steffan, J. S. (2012). Treating offenders with mental illness: A research synthesis. *Law and Human Behavior, 36,* 37–50. doi:10.1037/h0093964

Ogloff, J. R. P., & Davis, M. R. (2004). Advances in offender assessment and rehabilitation: Contributions of the risk-needs responsivity approach. *Psychology, Crime & Law, 10,* 229–242. doi:10.1080/10683160410001662735

Petrila, J. (2003). An introduction to special jurisdiction courts. *International Journal of Law and Psychiatry, 26,* 3–12.

Poythress, N. G., Nicholson, R., Otto, R. K., Edens, J. F., Bonnie, R. J., Monahan, J., & Hoge, S. K. (1999). *The MacArthur Competence Assessment Tool—Criminal Adjudication.* Odessa, FL: Psychological Assessment Resources.

Poythress, N. G., Petrila, J., McGaha, A., & Boothroyd, R. (2002). Perceived coercion and procedural justice in the Broward mental health court. *International Journal of Law and Psychiatry, 25,* 517–533. doi:10.1016/S0160-2527(01)00110-8

Ray, B. (2014). Long-term recidivism of mental health court defendants. *International Journal of Law and Psychiatry, 37,* 448–454. doi:10.1016/j.ijlp.2014.02.017

Redlich, A. D. (2005). Voluntary, but knowing and intelligent? Comprehension in mental health courts. *Psychology, Public Policy, and Law, 11,* 605–619. doi:10.1037/1076-8971.11.4.605

Redlich, A. D., & Han, W. (2014). Examining the links between therapeutic jurisprudence and mental health court completion. *Law and Human Behavior, 38,* 109–118. doi:10.1037/lhb0000041

Redlich, A. D., Hoover, S., Summers, A., & Steadman, H. J. (2010). Enrollment in mental health courts: Voluntariness, knowingness, and adjudicative competence. *Law and Human Behavior, 34,* 91–104. doi:10.1007/s10979-008-9170-8

Redlich, A. D., Steadman, H. J., Monahan, J., Petrila, J., & Griffin, P. A. (2005). The second generation of mental health courts. *Psychology, Public Policy, and Law, 11,* 527–538. doi:10.1037/1076-8971.11.4.527

Rogers, R. (1990). Models of feigned mental illness. *Professional Psychology: Research and Practice, 21,* 182–188.

Seltzer, T. (2005). Mental health courts: A misguided attempt to address the criminal justice system's unfair treatment of people with mental illnesses. *Psychology, Public Polity, and Law, 11,* 570–586. doi:10.1037/1076-8971.11.4.570

Stafford, K. P., & Wygant, D. B. (2005). The role of competency to stand trial in mental health courts. *Behavioral Sciences and the Law, 23,* 245–258. doi:10.1002/bsl.649

Steadman, H. J., Deane, M. W., Morrissey, J. P., Westcott, M. L., Salasin, S., & Shapiro, S. (1999). A SAMHSA research initiative assessing the effectiveness of jail diversion programs for mentally ill persons. *Psychiatric Services, 50,* 1620–1623.

Steadman, H. J., Morris, S. M., & Dennis, D. L. (1995). The diversion of mentally ill persons from jails to community-based services: A profile of programs. *American Journal
of Public Health, 85*, 1630–1635.

Steadman, H. J., & Naples, M. (2005). Assessing the effectiveness of jail diversion programs for persons with serious mental illness and co-occurring substance use disorders.
Behavioral Sciences and the Law, 23, 163–170. doi:10.1002/bsl.640.

Steadman, H. J., Osher, F., Robbins, P., Case, B., & Samuels, S. (2009). Prevalence of serious
mental illness among jail inmates. *Psychiatric Services, 60*, 761–765.

Teplin, L. A. (1994). Psychiatric and substance abuse disorders among male urban jail
detainees. *American Journal of Public Health, 84*, 290–293.

Wexler, D. B., & Winick, B. J. (1991). Therapeutic jurisprudence as a new approach to mental
health law policy analysis and research. *University of Miami Law Review, 45*, 979–1004.

Winick, B. J. (2002). Therapeutic jurisprudence and problem solving courts. *Fordham
Urban Law Journal, 30*, 1055–1090.

Wolff, N., Frueh, B. C., Huening, J., Shi, J., Epperson, M. W., Morgan, R., & Fisher, W.
(2013). Practice informs the next generation of behavioral health and criminal justice
interventions. *International Journal of Law and Psychiatry, 36*, 1–10. doi:10.1016/j.ijlp
.2012.11.001

6

Sex Offender Risk Assessment

Angel Daniels, Georgia M. Winters, and Elizabeth L. Jeglic

In the last two decades, there has been heightened public concern about the potential dangers of sex offenders within the community. Consequently, a series of laws have been enacted to monitor and contain sex offenders with the goal of improving community safety (Hanson, 2005). In order for these policies to be effective, evaluators must be able to assess risk and identify those sex offenders who would be at higher risk for future offending. Thus, a sex offender risk evaluation is used to assess the level of risk that an individual poses for committing additional sexual offenses. The risk assessment is derived from a variety of sources of data and actuarial information and ultimately provides information to members of the legal and criminal justice system to assist in their decisions about the best placement and environment for the offender. Therefore, a great deal of research and attention has focused on identifying empirically supported risk factors for sex offender recidivism and developing evidence-based risk assessment.

Relevant Case Law

As public concern about sex offenders has increased over the last two decades, the United States has responded with increasingly punitive legislation and sanctions against them (Edwards & Hensley, 2001; Lussier & Gress, 2013). Compared with those who commit nonsexual crimes, sex offenders are sentenced to longer periods of incarceration, and their sentences are increasing over time (Edwards, & Hensley, 2001; Langan & Levin, 2002). In fact, some states currently allow those convicted of first-degree sexual assault to be sentenced to life in prison without the possibility of parole, and others allow for sentencing guidelines to be doubled if the victim of the sexual offense was a child (Edwards & Hensley, 2001; Levenson, Brannon, Fortney, & Baker, 2007).

Once convicted of a sex offense, an individual may be subject to any number of special laws and policies that are directed at sex offenders specifically, and this individual may experience the impact of these laws and policies long after his or her incarceration terms have been served. The policies include, but are not limited to, community registration and notification programs, restrictions on where the individual may live and work, constant monitoring of an offender's whereabouts via global positioning systems, and sexually violent predator statutes (Calkins, Jeglic, Beattey, Ziedman, & Perillo, 2014; Lussier & Gress, 2013). The goal of these policies is to protect the public from sexual offenders by increasing community surveillance of those who have been released from prison and incapacitating those who are deemed too dangerous to live in the community (Lussier & Gress, 2013). It should be noted that these laws are not without their challenges and criticisms, as these laws have been considered by some to violate the rights of the offenders and have been blamed for the difficulties that many offenders experience with reintegration to the community (Tewksbury & Lees, 2006).

Community Registration and Notification

In response to several highly publicized cases of convicted sexual offenders recidivating violently against children, Congress passed the Jacob Wetterling Act and Megan's Law in the mid-1990s (Calkins et al., 2014; Tewksbury & Lees, 2006). Together, these laws were aimed at promoting the community's awareness of the sex offenders who live among them and preventing recidivism of sex offenders in the community. These laws initiated and formalized sex offender registration programs and made the information on the registries publicly available in the hopes that citizens might be empowered to proactively protect themselves and their children.

In 2006, Congress passed more expansive legislation to bring uniformity and stricter requirements to the sex offender registration system. The Adam Walsh Child Protection and Safety Act of 2006 included the Sex Offender Registration and Notification Act (SORNA), which established national standards for sex offender registries and included the development of a tiered registration requirement framework based upon risk and the type of crime comitted (Visgaitis, 2011). SORNA assigns offenders to one of three tiers, based on the type of crime that they committed. Tier III requires lifelong registration and is reserved for the offenders whose crimes were deemed to be most severe, including sexual contact with a child under the age of 13, kidnapping a minor (a person under the age of 18) in the course of a sexual offense, sexual assaults involving sexual acts, or almost any sex offense committed after previously committing a Tier II offense (Calkins et al., 2014; SORNA, 2006; Visgaitis, 2011). Tier II mandates registration for 25 years, and this tier is used for offenders who have committed certain felony crimes against minors, including abusive sexual conduct, coercion and enticement, sex trafficking, using a minor in a sexual performance (i.e., child pornography), soliciting a minor to engage in prostitution, or producing or distributing child pornography. Finally, Tier I requires registration for 15 years, and this tier is used for any offender who has committed a sexual crime that does not fit the criteria for Tiers II and III, namely, misdemeanor crimes that typically do not involve any sexual contact (e.g., registration violations, possession of child pornography, etc.; Calkins et al., 2014; SORNA, 2006; Visgaitis, 2011).

Residence and Employment Restrictions

In 1995, Florida became the first state to pass laws to place limitations on where convicted sex offenders may live (Galeste, Fradella, & Vogel, 2012). Since then, over thirty states have approved similar restrictions, which often identify areas in which convicted sex offenders are prohibited from living, working, or loitering (Meloy, Miller, & Curtis, 2008). Typically, the laws contain language that restrict sex offenders from spending significant time near or living or working within a specified distance from *places where children congregate*, including schools, child care centers, parks, churches, bus stops, and certain commercial businesses (Calkins et al., 2014; Dallas, 2009; Meloy et al., 2008). Some of these restrictions are so limiting that offenders have found it difficult, if not impossible, to find a place to live and a legitimate job to support themselves that complies with the contraints. Furthermore, research has strongly indicated that these restrictions serve to increase stress levels and negatively impact the social support of offenders in a way that could potentially elevate their risk of recidivism (Calkins et al., 2014; Levenson & Hern, 2007; Mercado, Alvarez, & Levenson, 2008).

GPS Monitoring

The use of GPS or other electronic devices to track and monitor sex offenders began in 1984 in New Mexico and has since been adopted by every other state (CalGaleste et al., 2012). This particular approach is based on the premise that offenders may be deterred from engaging in criminal activities or impulsive behavior if they are being monitored (Galeste et al., 2012). When this approach is used, certain offenders may be required to wear a GPS transmitter for the entire term of their supervised release or for a period deemed appropriate by their probation or parole officer. The transmitter relays information to the probation or parole officer about offenders' location, how long they remain in any given location, and whether they are venturing into locations that are restricted or off-limits to them (Calkins et al., 2014; Galeste et al., 2012).

Sexually Violent Predator Laws

When an offender is deemed too dangerous or high-risk to live in the community, he or she may be subject to Sexually Violent Predator (SVP) legislation. SVP legislation, generally, may be applied to convicted sex offenders who have committed offenses that are deemed to be "sexually violent" and who possess some sort of mental abnormality or personality disorder, present a high risk for sexually violent recidivism, and exhibit a likelihood of sexual recidivism that is directly related to their mental abnormality (Calkins et al., 2014). If an offender meets this criteria (or the specific criteria of the state in which he or she resides), the offender may be civilly committed (against his will) to a psychiatric facility after having served the prison sentence. The length of civil commitment is indefinite, and the individual can be held until he or she is determined to no longer be at risk of recidivism. There is no shortage of controversy surrounding SVP statutes, and some of the most pressing concerns include that the criteria for determining "mental abnormality" and risk of recidivism are vague (Jackson & Richards, 2007; Mercado, Schopp, & Bornstein, 2005; Schopp, Scalora, & Pearce, 1999) and that civil commitment after one has served his prison sentence may violate that individual's constitutional rights (Janus & Prentky, 2003).

Given that sex offenders are subject to such potentially restrictive policies and laws, and many of these policies depend on an evaluation of the level of risk that an individual sex offender poses, the importance of accurately estimating risk of sexual recidivism cannot be overstated. The roles of psychologists and forensic evaluators are also of key importance, as is their ability to understand and synthesize available literature and empirical data.

Review of the Literature

Risk assessment is broadly defined as the process of identifying the likelihood of future dangerousness (Association for the Treatment of Sexual Abusers, 2014). This commonly involves the use of empirically derived tools or instruments that are designed to estimate an offender's potential risk for future recidivism (i.e., sexual, violent, and/or general reoffending).

There are five main legal contexts for sex offender risk assessments: 1) pre-adjudication, 2) post-adjudication, 3) registration and community notification, 4) eligibility for civil commitment, and 5) and release from civil commitment (Witt & Conroy, 2009). Pre-adjudication evaluations can be conducted to inform decisions such as whether the offender should be released on bail or could be managed in outpatient treatment on probation. If a person is found guilty, the post-adjudication evaluations can be useful in determining whether the offender should receive special sentencing, which may require the completion of sex offender treatment or a more stringent process before being released to the community. Risk assessments are also used to inform decisions about the appropriate tier of community notification and registration on which the sex offender should be placed when released into the community. Lastly, sex offender risk assessments are used when deciding whether an offender should be civilly committed as a sexually violent predator. Evaluators will then use risk assessment when deciding whether the offender's risk has decreased after this commitment and whether it is safe for him or her to return to the community.

Although the accuracy of sex offender risk assessments has improved over the past decade, some general limitations should be noted. First, the majority of sexual offenses go undetected or unreported (Association for the Treatment of Sexual Abusers, 2014). Therefore, since risk assessments rely on information about rearrests and reconvictions, these assessments may underestimate risk for this population (Harris, 2006). Second, the probabilities gathered from risk assessments are dependent on the length of time the offenders were followed in the study. Meta-analyses suggest the average follow-up period is five years, though reoffenses may occur beyond this time frame (Hanson, Stey, & Gauthier, 1993). Third, sex offenders are a heterogeneous group, which raises questions about the universal applicability of these measures to all sex offenders (Harris, 2006). Not addressing differences between subgroups of sex offenders (e.g., child molesters, rapists, exhibitionists) leaves some to question the validity of these tools in predicting violence across the population. Furthermore, the current risk assessment measures fail to account for factors that would contribute to an escalation in an individual's offenses. In other words, there are no measures to track an increasing trajectory of offending that would allow us to predict more severe offenses in the future, such as noncontact sexual offenders who escalate to contact offenses. Finally, the majority of these risk assessment instruments were not normed on diverse populations, and thus, when conducting risk assessment of a nonwhite sex offender, the limitations of the tool must be noted.

Risk Factors

For risk assessments in general, there are four broad categories of factors that have been considered (Andrews & Bonta, 1998; McGuire, 2000). The first is dispositional factors, such as antisocial or psychopathic personality traits. Second, historical factors such as developmental events, history of criminal and violent behavior, and prior treatment compliance have been explored. Third, contextual components of violence are considered, including criminogenic needs, deviant peers, and lack of positive support systems. Fourth, clinical factors such as psychiatric and substance use disorders have been of interest. Evaluators should take into account a wide range of potential risk and protective factors when conducting risk assessments.

Across all offending populations, studies have identified several predictors of general criminal recidivism, including younger age at first encounter with the criminal justice system, prior criminal history, substance use, and antisocial personality traits (Seto, 2013). However, for sex offenders specifically, several studies have identified two major predictors of long-term sexual recidivism: 1) sexual deviancy, for example, paraphilia, sexual arousal to children, sexual arousal to violence, and victim characteristics, and 2) antisocial orientation, for example, poor interpersonal competence and failure in adult relationships (Hanson & Bussière, 1998). Sexual deviancy refers to an arousal to or interest in people, objects, or activities that are illegal, inappropriate, or highly unusual (Harris & Hanson, 2010). Sexual deviancy is typically measured using phallometric testing, self-report measures, and behavioral/criminal history. The second main factor, antisocial orientation, describes aspects of an unstable and criminal lifestyle, which may include substance use, a history of violating rules, employment difficulties, and impulsive behaviors. It has been found that antisocial lifestyle is highly associated not only with sexual recidivism but also with violent and general recidivism among sexual offenders (Hanson & Morton-Bourgon, 2004) and general recidivism among nonsexual offenders (Bonta, Law, & Hanson, 1998). Given that numerous risk factors for recidivism have been empirically identified, competent evaluators must take into account an array of risk factors in order to accurately evaluate risk level. In addition to the aforementioned risk variables, studies have also shown moderate predictive value for sexual recidivism for factors such as age, the number of prior offenses, being unmarried, prior treatment failure, sexual preoccupations, and intimacy deficits (Hanson & Bussière, 1998; Hanson & Morton-Bourgon, 2004). It is also important to be aware of factors that have not been empirically shown to increase risk, to avoid assumptions that these might contribute to increased levels of risk. Some examples include taking responsibility for the crime, showing empathy for the victim, verbalizing motivation to offend, and successfully completing treatment goals (Hanson & Bussière, 1998).

Sex offender risk assessments have typically focused broadly on static and dynamic factors related to recidivism. Static risk factors are primarily historical factors (e.g., criminal history) or those highly unlikely to change (e.g., pedophilia, psychopathy) and therefore are thought to be strong predictors of long-term recidivism (Lanterman, Boyle, & Raguse-Salerno, 2014). One advantage to static factors is that the information is typically available in records and requires little subjective judgment in identifying the presence or absence of the factors. In contrast, a dynamic risk factor is one that can change over time and may include cognitive distortions, substance abuse, and feelings of anger or depression. Dynamic risk factors are often associated with the predictions of short-term risk that can change over the course of days, weeks, months, or even years (Seto, 2013). Dynamic factors can further be divided into stable and acute factors. Stable dynamic factors can be amendable over time but typically do not fluctuate in the short term (e.g., cognitive distortions, insight, treatment compliance, criminogenic attitudes). On the other hand, acute dynamic factors may change over a short period of time and can include factors such as employment status, residence, relationship status, access to drugs or alcohol, or access to potential victims. Hanson and Harris (2000b) found that the dynamic factors most strongly related to recidivism were social adjustment, attitudes toward the victim, self-awareness of risk, access to victims, and compliance with supervision and treatment. A study by Knight and Thornton (2007) found that by adding dynamic risk factors to static information, the predictive power of risk assessment tools is increased. The major benefit of identifying dynamic risk factors is the potential to influence treatment and supervision, given that they may be amenable to change with intervention.

Approaches to Assessment

There are a multitude of methods to evaluate risk among sex offenders. Doren (2004) identified more than twenty instruments that can be utilized to assess risk among this population. Some of the measures target general risk for violence, while others focus on the risk for committing future sexual offenses. Risk assessments also vary in the level of clinical judgment utilized versus a purely actuarial tool that leaves no room for subjective decision making. Furthermore, instruments can also be designed to examine static variables, while others may utilize dynamic factors or both. In general, there are three broad strategies for assessing risk: unstructured judgment, structured judgment, and actuarial measures.

Unstructured judgment involves a clinician subjectively selecting and weighing risk factors, combining the information, and then forming an opinion about the risk for reoffense based upon his or her clinical judgment. This process involves interviewing the offender, reviewing file information, and forming a subjective opinion about the risk level. Research has consistently shown that unstructured judgments were no more accurate than chance predictions were, and therefore, the field has turned to the use of structured judgment and actuarial tools as alternative methods (Monahan, 1981). It has also been proposed that unstructured clinical judgment may be subject to various cognitive biases, such as primacy and recency effects, representative heuristics, and availability heuristics (Seto, 2013).

Structured judgment or clinically adjusted actuarial measures refer to the process by which the evaluator uses preselected items related to risk, but the overall determination of risk lies in the hands of the evaluator. Structured clinical judgments for sex offenders, such as the Sexual Violence Risk-20 (SVR-20; Boer, Hart, Kropp, & Webster, 1977), typically include dynamic risk factors that are amendable over time. Proponents of the structured judgment approach to risk assessment suggest that these types of assessments allow for clinical case formulation and have stronger predictive accuracy than unstructured approaches do (Hanson & Bussiere, 1998; Hanson & Morton-Bourgon, 2004). The advantages to clinical actuarial tools include that they are based on empirical research, that they are more comprehensive than actuarial tools because they include dynamic factors, and that the predictive validity appears to be comparable with actuarial measures. Some disadvantages include that these tools allow more room for errors because of their subjective nature (Hanson, 1998), that the factors assessed may be highly correlated, which would provide redundant information (Seto, 2013), and that these tools may not be applicable to populations not included in the development of the tools.

In the last several decades, actuarial risk assessments have become the gold standard in the field. Actuarial measures utilize an empirically derived set of risk factors that are weighted and summed to create a risk score and classification. Doren (2002) identified two characteristics of actuarial assessments: 1) the risk items are selected based on their ability to predict future offending, typically through meta-analytic studies using large samples of offenders; and 2) there are stringent rules for how to obtain the composite score, allowing little room for deviation. Proponents of actuarial measures argue that standardizing the scoring allows for more objective decision making compared with other methods. Additionally, these actuarial measures allow the evaluator to make probabilistic statements regarding the proportion of people with the same score who would be expected to reoffend (Seto, 2013). The actuarial tools have also been praised for containing items that are empirically supported and that these tools are easily scored using archival data. In the meta-analysis of 188 research studies examining actuarial tools, Hanson and Morton-Bourgon (2009) found the predictive accuracy of these tools ranged from low to moderate.

However, actuarial tools are not without their detractors. Actuarial tools have been criticized for not including dynamic factors, excluding items not yet validated in meta-analyses, ignoring contextual and situational aspects of offending behavior, neglecting unique risk factors for particular subgroups, and not capturing information in unusual cases (e.g., an offense committed when psychotic). Further, actuarial tools have been criticized for a lack of a standardization in the definition of recidivism (Stadtland et al., 2005), the atheoretical nature of the measures (Beech, Fischer, & Thornton, 2003), the limited length of the follow-up period for which recidivism was assessed (Harris, 2006), and the lack of validation with certain discrete populations such as juvenile sex offenders, female sex offenders, and racially and ethnically diverse sex offenders (Walters, Knight, & Thornton, 2009). Clinicians have argued that rigid scoring criteria limit the use of the clinical judgment and that clinically relevant information may be neglected because it does not fall within the instruments parameters. Additionally, actuarial tools classify offenders' risk based on a single composite score. However, this method fails to account for the fact that offenders who fall within the same risk category may display very different constellations of risk factors that would be important for treatment planning and supervision. It should also be noted that the base rates used to interpret risk scores may differ based on offense type and that the recidivism rates used to derive the measures may fluctuate over time and jurisdictions (Hanson & Morton-Bourgon, 2004).

The Association for the Treatment of Sexual Abusers (ATSA) recommends the use of structured or actuarial risk assessments in their best practice guidelines. This is largely due to the fact that studies have consistently demonstrated that actuarial and structured measures are superior in predicative ability compared with the unstructured judgments (Hanson & Bussiere, 1998; Hanson & Morton-Bourgon, 2004). When predicting general recidivism for sexual offenders, actuarial measures were found most accurate, followed by guided clinical judgment and unstructured clinical judgment. A meta-analysis conducted by Hanson and Morton-Bourgon (2004) found that the unstructured judgment was significantly less accurate than actuarial tools in predictive general, violent, and sexual recidivism. This is likely due to the fact that the unstructured judgments rely on subjectively chosen risk factors and clinical opinion, whereas actuarial and structured tools identify set variables, operationally define these variables, and have explicit rules for coding. This decreases the subjectivity, thereby increasing the reliability of the measures.

Risk Assessment Tools

Several tools have been developed to assess risk for recidivism in sex offenders. The most commonly used and best validated of these tools are presented below.

RRASOR The Rapid Risk Assessment for Sexual Offense Recidivism (RRASOR; Hanson, 1997) contains four variables (prior sexual offenses, extra-familial victim, offender under the age of 25, male child victims), all of which can be coded by record review. While the RRASOR is commended for the simplicity, short length, and moderate predictive ability, some argue it overlooks other important risk factors such as deviant sexual interest, antisocial orientation, and treatment compliance. Conveying the predictive accuracy of actuarial tools is typically done utilizing the area under the curve (AUC), which is "the extent to which a randomly selected sexual recidivist would be likely to have a higher score on the risk measure than a randomly selected non-recidivist" (Amenta, Guy, & Edens, 2014, p. 43). Hanson and Thornton (2000) reported the average AUC for the RRASOR was .68 for predicting sexual recidivism.

Static-99   The Static-99 (Hanson & Thornton, 1999) is currently the most commonly used measure of sex offender risk. It has been actuarially derived and includes ten static factors: current age, live-in intimate relationship for two or more years, index offense of nonsexual violence, prior offenses of nonsexual violence, prior charges or conviction for a sexual offense, prior sentence dates, convictions for noncontact sexual offenses, unrelated victims, stranger victims, and male victims. The scores from each item are summed to create a composite score that is associated with observed recidivism rates across the norm-referenced group. Hanson and Thornton (2000) found that the Static-99 added to the predictive accuracy of the RRASOR for long-term risk estimates and found the Static-99 has an average AUC of .71 for prediction sexual recidivism. The developers also released the Static-99R, which is a revised version of the Static-99 that includes a continuous scale for the item inquiring about offender's age rather than the previous dichotomous code. Hanson and Thornton (2003) developed the Static-2002 to include more theoretically meaningful factors that will contribute to risk. The measure includes fourteen items, with overlap from the Static-99, but organizes the items in five categories: age, persistence of sex offending, deviant sexual interests, relationship to victim, and general criminality.

SORAG   Another widely used, actuarially derived measure is the Sex Offender Risk Appraisal Guide (SORAG; Quinsey, Harris, Rice, & Cormier, 1998), which was adapted from a general violence risk assessment measure called the Violence Risk Appraisal Guide (VRAG; Harris, Rice, & Quinsey, 1993). The SORAG acknowledges psychological variables such as psychopathy and major mental illness, along with other factors similar to those in the Static-99. Hanson and Thornton (2000) found the SORAG and Static-99 similarly predict sexual recidivism, although the SORAG was stronger at predicting violent, nonsexual recidivism.

MnSOST-R   Another tool, the Minnesota Sex Offender Screening Tool-Revised (MnSOST-R), was developed by the Minnesota Department of Corrections (Epperson, Kaul, & Hesselton, 1998). The measure consists of sixteen items to assess prisoners, and it has been commended for utilizing a broader range of categories than do some of the other actuarial tools. The categories include information about the offender's criminal and antisocial history (e.g., number of sexual convictions, length of sexual offender history, whether the sexual offense was committed while under supervision, antisocial behavior as an adolescent, substance abuse, employment history), the offense itself (e.g., offense committed in a public location, use or threat of force, multiple acts on a single victim, different victim age groups, offenses against a victim 13 to 15 years of age, or that the offender is older than victim by five years, stranger victim), and the offender's current incarceration (e.g., discipline history while incarcerated, chemical dependency while incarcerated, sex offense treatment while incarcerated, and age at release). The MsSOST-R has been noted as being more difficult to score compared with the RRASOR and Static-99 and having variables that might not apply to other states, such as sex offender treatment and chemical dependency (Beech, Fisher, & Thornton, 2003). The AUC for the MnSOST-R has been found to range from .70 to .76 in its predictive accuracy (Epperson, 2000; Langton, Barbaree, Harkins, Seto, & Peacock, 2002).

Other Actuarial Measures

Risk Matrix 2000 (RM2000; Thornton et al., 2003) consists of three static items (i.e., current age, sexual crime history, and general crime history) and four aggravating factors (i.e., male victim, stranger victim, noncontact sexual offenses, and lack of long-term intimate relationships). The Sex Offender Needs Assessment Rating (SONAR; Hanson & Harris, 2000a) targets dynamic factors, but this measure is still in the nascent stage of research. It should also be noted that the Psychopathy Checklist-Revised (PCL-R; Hare, 1991) has been implemented in sex offender risk assessments, though it is not specific to sexual offending. The reasoning behind the use of a psychopathy measure is that research has consistently shown that psychopathy is correlated with various forms of recidivism.

Structured Clinical Decision Tools

The Sexual Violence Risk-20 (SVR-20; Boer et al., 1977) was developed by the authors after a thorough review of empirical literature and utilizing input from experts in clinical and forensic domains. The measure includes twenty items that target factors in three domains: psychosocial adjustment, nature of the offense, and future plans. Examples of items include past supervision failure, offending history, criminogenic thinking, psychopathy, mental illness, employment and relationship difficulties, lack of planning, and sexual deviancy. The measure also includes three dynamic factors: acute mental disorder, recent loss of social network, and frequent contact with potential victims. The SVR-20 does not include a procedure for computing an overall level of risk; rather the evaluator is instructed to use professional judgments to rate the risk level as low, moderate, or high. This measurement is praised for its ability to both assess risk and contribute to case management plans.

Actuarial Assessments for Noncontact Offenders

There is much concern over the likelihood that a noncontact or Internet-related sexual offender will escalate to contact offenses in the future. Therefore, risk assessments have been important to those evaluating the potential for reoffenses for this particular sex offender subtype.

There is evidence that the strong predictors of recidivism, antisocial orientation and sexual deviancy in particular, are applicable to both online and offline offenders (Seto, 2013). For example, the presence of antisocial characteristics in online sex offenders increases the risk for a future sex offense (Seto, 2003). However, some have proposed that other Internet-specific risk factors should be considered when determining level of risk for this subtype of sex offender, such as amount of child pornography or time spent online. However, it should be noted that to date these have yet to be empirically supported (Eke & Seto, 2012). Early research findings suggest that modifications to current risk tools would make the measures applicable to online sex offenders, but there is a question as to whether the probability estimates would generalize to that population (Wakeling, Howard, & Barnett, 2011). Seto (2013) concluded the preliminary research comparing online offenders with contact offenders shows support for common risk factors for both subtypes and that some modifications to current risk measure would likely result in adequate predictive accuracy for online sexual offenders. However, more research is needed in assessing risk for noncontact sexual offenders.

Other Sources of Information

Records   It has been suggested that the use of collateral information is a crucial element in risk assessment, and it has even been argued to be more important than the interview with the offender (Conroy & Murrie, 2007). Records can include rap sheets, criminal complaints, prison records, and medical and psychiatric records. Records gathered from various agencies often differ in quality and comprehensiveness, therefore making it crucial for the evaluator to identify potential limitations in the files and be open about the shortcomings in the report. When examining records regarding past convictions, evaluators should be aware that the reports might not fully encapsulate the offense history, given that prosecutors often drop or modify charges and that some offenses go undetected. This further stresses the importance of using a variety of sources in gathering information for the evaluation.

Collateral Contacts   Often, the evaluator can gather important information from those who have had contact with the offender such as friends, family, therapists, probation officers, and correctional officers, among others. These individuals may see the offender on a frequent basis and may have some insight into the offender's patterns of behaviors and psychological functioning that cannot be obtained from records or the offender's self-report.

Clinical Interview   Another element of the risk assessment involves the clinical interview of the sex offender, which should include a self-report on his or her criminal and psychological history. While such interviews lack the standardization and validity of the actuarial and psychological testing, they can provide useful biographical information, and information derived through behavioral observation can be used to identify cognitive distortions and maladaptive thinking patterns. It is also a useful opportunity to probe for inconsistencies between records and the offender report. The clinical interview should always be used as but one source of data in conjunction with a comprehensive risk assessment battery.

Self-Report Measures   Psychology testing can be used to assess a wide range of personality and cognitive functioning. Objective personality tests such as the Minnesota Multiphasic Personality Inventory-2 (MMPI-2; Butcher, Dahlstrom, Graham, Tellegen, & Kaemmer, 1989), the Millon Clinical Multiaxial Inventory-III (MCMI-III; Millon & Davis, 1997), and the Personality Assessment Inventory (PAI; Morey, 2007) can help inform decisions about mental health diagnoses. These scales all have validity indices that can be useful in determining whether an offender is misrepresenting his presentation. While such psychological measures of personality can provide additional corroborative information regarding psychological functioning, the evaluator cannot make a diagnosis or conclusions based solely on these tools and must integrate additional sources of information.

Measures of Sexual Preferences   Self-report measures of sexual interests have been developed as an inexpensive and efficient method of gathering information on the offender's deviant sexual interests; these include the Multiphasic Sex Inventory (MSI; Nichols & Molinder, 1996) and the Multidimensional Inventory of Development, Sex, and Aggression (MIDSA; Knight, 2008). However, the obvious limitation to these self-report measures is that offenders may minimize or deny deviant sexual interests or may lack insight into their sexual preferences.

Psychophysiological Assessment   There is much debate in the field about the use of psychophysiological assessment, though many of these measures are commonly used in assessing risk for future sexual offending.

Phallometric testing utilizes the penile plethysmograph on a male offender, which measures the volume or circumference of the individual's penis while viewing sexual stimuli. These tests are designed to identify deviant sexual arousal patterns depending on which stimuli the offender is sexually aroused to. A meta-analysis by Hanson and Bussiere (1998) found the phallometric testing correlated well with sexual recidivism for child molesters, though this pattern was not found for rapists. According to ATSA, phallometric testing can be useful as a *corroborating* measure to the offender's self-report. Penile plethysmographs have been criticized for their invasive nature and for ethical and practical concerns as well as the validity and reliability of the measure (Witt & Conroy, 2009).

Polygraphs are a second form of psychophysiological assessments that have the goal of detecting malingering based on observed physiological changes in response to questioning. ATSA suggests that polygraphs may be beneficial for two reasons: 1) they generate information beyond that obtained from self-reports, and 2) they increase compliance with treatment and supervision conditions (Association for Treatment of Sexual Abusers, 2014). Information from empirical studies has suggested that evaluators must be wary of polygraphs since there is a risk for false positives (Branaman & Gallagher, 2005). Given the questionable reliability and validity of these measures, it is not recommended they be utilized in decisions regarding civil commitment of sex offenders. However, polygraphs may be helpful in instances of post-conviction release when the offender is being monitored in the community to increase accountability.

More recently, several additional cognitively based measures of deviant arousal have been studied. The Abel Assessment of Sexual Interest (AASI; Abel, Huffman, Warberg, & Holland, 1998) is one of the most widely used of these types of tools. The AASI assesses the sex offenders' viewing time of sexual stimuli to make assumptions about sexual deviancy. The hypothesis is that people will view stimuli they find sexually arousing longer. However, there is great concern over the high error rate and lack of validity in these types of measures. In addition, some research has been done assessing response latencies to deviant word and picture stimuli using a modified version of the Emotional Stroop Task (EST). To date the research on ESTs remains inconclusive and such cognitive measures should not be utilized as part of standardized risk assessments.

Best Practices

Sex offender risk assessment is a high-stakes endeavor. Overestimating risk can deprive the sex offender of civil liberties while underestimating risk can put the community at significant risk. Therefore, it is imperative that those conducting risk assessments adhere to best practices guidelines. Such guidelines have been proposed by ATSA and stipulate that clinicians conducting sex offender risk assessments need to gather and verify information, interview the offender and collateral contacts, and utilize standardized and validated actuarial tools. Further, according to the American Psychological Association "Ethical Principles of Psychologists and Code of Conduct" (American Psychological Association, 2010) only those competent to administer and interpret such assessments should perform sex offender risk assessment. A competent clinician would be one who has appropriate education, training, supervised experience, consultation, or study with regard to the topic. Given the variety of standards and regulations surrounding sex offender risk evaluations, it is also essential, and ethically sound, for the forensic evaluator to be familiar with the statutes governing his or her jurisdictions of practice.

In terms of selecting a measure, ATSA notes that, due to the heterogeneous nature of the offending population, there is not one tool that is superior to the others. The appropriate measures should be selected based on the question proposed and the particular individual being assessed. Craig and Beech (2009) suggest that the evaluator must be aware of the methodology and limitations of the risk assessment tool in order to ensure appropriate application and interpretation of tools and that these limitations should be noted in reports. Competent evaluators should understand the concepts and factors that will influence the actuarial scores, such as base rates, age, gender, race and ethnicity, and downgrading of charges.

Furthermore, it has been proposed that the tools and their applications be continually monitored through supervision, mentorship, and peer reviewing processes. Evaluators should utilize multiple sources of data to corroborate findings including collateral information—such as records, collateral contacts, psychological assessments, and psychophysiological assessments—throughout the evaluation process. When possible, collateral information should ideally be reviewed prior to interviewing the offender in order to focus the interview and explore any inconsistencies.

Case Vignette

The case study presented in this chapter is based on a composite of clients who were seen in an outpatient forensic mental health clinic that specializes in the evaluation and treatment of sex offenders. Generally, a client may be referred to this particular clinic for a sex offender evaluation by the court or Department of Corrections at one of three different stages in the legal process, which were mentioned earlier in the chapter: 1) pre-adjudication, 2) post-adjudication, and 3) registration and community notification. These types of evaluations take slightly different forms, as the presentencing evaluations are generally time-limited, and rely primarily on brief clinical interviews and the synthesis of empirical

---

The case vignette has been redacted and all identifying information removed. It is not meant to serve as a forensic report. Any likeness to a case is purely coincidental.

evaluation measures. Conversely, a client who is ordered by the court or Department of Corrections to undergo evaluation at the onset of the probationary period typically enters into a treatment contract with this mental health clinic, in which he or she agrees to participate in an extended assessment period to determine whether this program is appropriate and whether the client is, indeed, amenable to outpatient treatment and community supervision. This assessment period may last for anywhere from several weeks to several months, as the client completes multiple assessment measures, completes psychoeducational and treatment-oriented homework assignments, and participates in a weekly group therapy process to gain a greater understanding of his or her ability and willingness to engage in the treatment process. Furthermore, this clinic utilizes a "team-based" approach, in which the evaluators, clinicians, and probation officers obtain consents from the client to freely exchange information among themselves in order to inform treatment and supervision and ultimately to maintain community safety.

As discussed earlier, regardless of when or why the sex offender evaluation is being conducted, best practices always involve the utilization of multiple sources of information, both empirical and clinical. Clinically, this means that, in addition to interviewing the client directly about his or her experiences and background, an evaluator should also make every effort to gather data from collateral contacts that can provide alternate perspectives on the client's history, functioning, and lifestyle. Typically, this will take the form of interviewing the client's spouse, family members, and any other mental health professionals who have worked with the client. Empirically, multiple forms of psychological assessments should be incorporated, including actuarial risk assessment tools, self-report measures, structured interview templates, legal records, and any other appropriate measures for assessing functioning. Given this approach, it is clear that even the briefer forms of sex offender evaluations require a significant amount of time and effort on the part of the evaluator and should never be conducted based on a single session with the client alone.

Reason for Referral

The client discussed herein was referred to the clinic by his probation officer, who requested a Psychosexual Risk Assessment to determine his amenability and appropriateness for outpatient sex offender treatment. The client had pled guilty to charges of possession and distribution of child pornography, a class six felony in the state in which he was convicted, which normally carries a five- to twenty-year sentence in a state correctional facility. However, due to the fact that this was his first offense, and in exchange for his guilty plea, this client was sentenced to five years of supervised release (i.e., probation under the supervision of the Department of Corrections), with the condition that he participate in, and complete, a sex offender treatment program.

This case is an example of a hybrid of a post-adjudication evaluation and a registration and community notification evaluation. The assessment process took place over a period of six months, while the offender simultaneously participated in individual and group therapy, which were useful not only in gathering additional clinical information and but also in providing him with basic behavioral management skills. This client also presented with a number of psychological assessment reports that had been conducted prior to his participation in this program, so his final evaluation report incorporated several forms of psychosexual evaluations—the conclusions drawn from the time-limited empirical evaluations conducted previously, and the data obtained from the more in-depth clinical and assessment process by the forensic evaluator.

As stated previously, the client discussed here, whom we will call Mr. Coe, presented for sex offender evaluation and treatment, following his guilty plea to charges of possession and distribution of child pornography. According to the police report, Mr. Coe had been exchanging videos of prepubescent females engaged in sexual acts with adult males with another man via e-mail. His Internet service provider intercepted these e-mail exchanges and reported them to the National Center for Missing & Exploited Children, which was able to trace the digital records back to Mr. Coe, and the center reported him to law enforcement. Initially, Mr. Coe reported to his treatment team (his clinicians and probation officer) that his referral offense represented the first time that he had viewed or tried to exchange any form of child pornography. Throughout the assessment period, however, he disclosed that he had actually been viewing child pornography in various forms for several years. He also reported several other offending behaviors, and sexually deviant behaviors and interests, for which he had not been caught and which will be discussed in greater detail later.

The purpose of the evaluation, the associated limits of confidentiality, and his rights throughout the process were explained to Mr. Coe when he was initially interviewed. He reported that he understood, signed all relevant releases of information and consent forms, and agreed to continue with the process. The evaluator spent a total of 27.5 hours conducting clinical interviews, observation, and testing of Mr. Coe.

Psychological Measures

Assessment Materials:

- Millon Clinical and Multi-Axial Inventory (MCMI-III)

Summary of Relevant Records

After obtaining Mr. Coe's informed consent for the evaluation process, the next step was to review his previous assessment and treatment records, which were extensive. Mr. Coe provided his treatment team with several documents including childhood medical records, psychological evaluations completed when he was 5 years of age and 9 years of age, a psychosexual evaluation conducted two months after his arrest, a psychological evaluation dated nine months after his arrest, and a treatment summary from another sex offender treatment provider ten months after his arrest.

Records Reviewed:

- Police Department Arrest Report
- District Attorney's Statement of Facts
- Medical Records: childhood through adolescence
- Psychological Evaluation (age 5)
- Speech, Language, & Hearing Evaluation (age 7)
- Psychological Evaluation (age 9)
- Pre-adjudication Psychosexual Evaluation (two months post-arrest)
- Psychological Report (nine months post-arrest)
- Sex Offender Treatment Summary (previous treatment provider; dated 10 months after his arrest)
- Collateral Contacts:
  o Consultation with Mr. Coe's court-ordered individual and group therapists (treating Mr. Coe during the time period of this evaluation) and review of their treatment records and clinical notes
  o Consultation with Mr. Coe's probation officer
  o Telephone interview with Mr. Coe's previous sex offender treatment provider
  o Telephone interview with the writer of Mr. Coe's previous psychological assessment
  o Telephone interview with Mr. Coe's adoptive mother
  o Telephone interview with another treatment provider that Mr. Coe sought consultation with during the assessment period

Mr. Coe's childhood medical records revealed that he had significant prenatal, perinatal, medical, and developmental issues in early childhood. According to his records, he was born several months premature, weighing less than four pounds at birth. His mother was a patient in an inpatient psychiatric hospital who reportedly received no prenatal care and who was suspected of drinking alcohol during her pregnancy. His birth was described as "traumatic," with no medical staff in attendance. Mr. Coe was hospitalized for the first five weeks of his life, after which he was adopted by a couple who had several biological children, and who later adopted another child.

Mr. Coe's early childhood was marked by significant health issues that required multiple treatments including respiratory, digestive, and mobility assistance. By the time he was attending elementary school, Mr. Coe was already exhibiting several problematic behaviors that warranted psychological evaluation and that raised concerns about his social and emotional development. For example, between the ages of 2 and 4 years of age, Mr. Coe was reported to have slept only a few hours per night, to have frequently roamed the house and destroyed items while his family slept, and to have even occasionally left the house entirely. His adopted mother also reported that until he was 5 years old, he never cried "real tears" or responded to any painful stimuli (including getting stitches on numerous occasions). In addition to exhibiting learning delays, Mr. Coe was reported to be hyperactive, inattentive, and emotionally dysregulated. Due to these and other concerns, Mr. Coe underwent two separate psychological evaluations at 5 years and 9 years of age, respectively. These evaluations included the use of the Wide Range Achievement Test-Revised (WRAT-R; Wilkinson & Robertson, 2006), Robert's Apperception Test (McArthur & Roberts, 1982), Projective Drawings, the Bender Gestalt Test (Pascal & Suttell, 1951), Conners's Ratings for Hyperactivity (Goyette, Conners, & Ulrich, 1978), the Personality Inventory for Children (PIC; Lachar, Klinedinst, & Seat, 1981), and the Child Behavior Checklist, Parent and Teacher Report (Achenbach & Edelbrock, 1983). The psychological reports indicated that Mr. Coe was in the average to above-average range of intelligence and was able to follow directions and concentrate on a task when interested. Academically, he performed at or above his expected grade level. The writers of his childhood psychological reports concluded that any learning delays that were exhibited were likely reflections of behavioral and emotional factors rather than deficits in information processing. Socially, Mr. Coe exhibited problematic relationships with his peers that included being subjected to intense teasing and bullying, as well as a tendency to act out his frustrations and anxieties behaviorally rather than processing them verbally. It was recommended that Mr. Coe participate in individual psychotherapy in order to help him understand and connect his emotions with his behavior. According to Mr. Coe, he stopped attending psychotherapy after two sessions for reasons that are unclear.

According to Mr. Coe's self-report, he was seen by several physicians and psychologists over the next several years, and he received diagnoses of Attention Deficit Hyperactivity Disorder (ADHD), Major Depressive Disorder, and Bipolar I Disorder. He was prescribed a variety of psychotropic medications to address these issues, but he did not feel as though any of them adequately addressed his symptoms.

He completed college, a master's degree, and a teaching credential before being hired as a middle school physical education teacher. Of course, given the nature of his charges, his decision to pursue this particular career and his behavior while performing his job duties warrant further investigation and will be explored shortly.

Upon his arrest and on the advice of his defense attorney, Mr. Coe opted to undergo a psychosexual evaluation in order to inform his legal defense (identified as *Pre-adjudication Psychosexual Evaluation [two months post-arrest]* in the list of Records Reviewed). He reported to the clinician providing this evaluation that he believed his Bipolar Disorder was responsible for his poor decision making and cited incidents of "getting in trouble" at work for the way that he spoke to his superiors during what he considered to be manic episodes. He also began to disclose his sexual interests in this report and indicated that he first noticed a sexual attraction to preschool children when he was approximately 7 years of age. He noted several other incidents during adolescence and young adulthood, during which he found himself attracted to female children between the ages of 2 and 12 years and reported that while babysitting he manipulated situations in order to have physical contact with the children, which resulted in erections. He maintained, however, that he had never sexually abused, nor inappropriately touched, a child. The results of this evaluation indicated that Mr. Coe was an individual who was emotionally labile and exhibited poor insight related to his own behaviors and limitations. It also concluded that Mr. Coe was most sexually aroused by prepubescent females, particularly preschool- and elementary-school-aged girls, and by fantasies and scenarios involving persuasion, coercion, and force. Based on the results of the assessments administered (MMPI-2 [Butcher et al., 1989] and penile plethysmograph examination) and a clinical interview, this report concluded that Mr. Coe warranted diagnoses of Bipolar I, Pedophilia, and ADHD (by history).

Following the completion of this psychological report, Mr. Coe and his attorney agreed that it would be in his best legal interest to proactively engage in sex offender treatment (prior to his trial and sentencing). He participated in weekly group therapy sessions with a sex offender treatment program for six months before deciding to seek another opinion about his psychological status. Eight months after his most recent psychosexual evaluation, Mr. Coe solicited an independent psychological evaluation by another psychologist. According to that report (identified as *Psychological Report [nine months post-arrest]* in the list of Records Reviewed), Mr. Coe indicated that he was seeking another assessment because he did not believe that the interventions he had received to that point had been helpful in improving his symptoms and the quality of his life. This evaluation included a clinical interview and administration of the MMPI-2 and Rorschach test (Rorschach, Lemkau, Kronenberg, & Morgenthaler, 1942). The Rorschach test is a projective inventory that provides clinicians with information about how a client is likely to perceive, process, and respond to information and the implications that may have on his functioning. Though many forensic evaluators choose to avoid the use of pro-jective inventories because of ongoing debates about their validity and empiri-cal value for predicting behavior, the clinician conducting the assessment in question was simply asked by Mr. Coe's attorney to provide a psychological assessment, not a forensic evaluation. Thus, it may explain her willingness to include this particular measure.

In the clinical interview portion of this evaluation, Mr. Coe indicated that he had experienced a number of disciplinary problems at work because his bosses didn't like him and were harder on him than other staff. One should note that this is a different view of his behavior than he provided in the previous assess-ment in which he asserted that his behavior was inappropriate due to symptoms of mania. The results of the assessment measures revealed that Mr. Coe was endorsing unusually high levels of emotional difficulties and severe psychiatric symptoms. The tests also indicated that Mr. Coe was obsessed with sex and had a heightened focus on the objectification of people. Additionally, he exhibited a disorganized thought process and often focused on less-relevant details while missing important information pertinent to everyday life. The clinical impres-sions of this evaluation concluded that Mr. Coe struggled to develop and main-tain empathy toward others and needs to understand that any poor treatment in his past does not justify acting out when he is angry. This evaluator diagnosed him with what would now be called an Autism Spectrum Disorder (at the time it was termed "Asperger's Disorder" by the *DSM–IV–TR*, but the *DSM-5* has since eliminated this particular terminology). The clinician providing this evaluation also concluded that these results suggested that Mr. Coe should be receiving consistent, intensive individual therapy, at the very least, or possibly a more intensive inpatient or partial hospitalization if outpatient therapy was deemed to be inadequate. Interestingly, collateral contact with this evaluator revealed that she was not made aware of Mr. Coe's sexual offense in any signifi-cant way, which explained why his sexual functioning was not incorporated into the analysis.

Shortly after this evaluation was completed, Mr. Coe's sex offender therapist provided his client's attorney with a summary of his progress in treatment thus far, which served to validate and highlight some of the issues that the previ-ous evaluations had raised. Namely, the treatment summary detailed that Mr. Coe's participation in treatment was marked by his hyperfocus on finding a mental illness that "made" him do what he did, by focusing on small details that he had found in books that supported his particular perspectives, and on repeated attempts at "attention-getting." According to this report, when chal-lenged to focus instead on learning to adjust his thinking and behaviors, Mr. Coe reportedly resorted to becoming argumentative, verbally combative, and enraged. This unwillingness to take responsibility for his choices, in their view, was reflected in what they saw as his "therapist shopping" and seeking multiple evaluations that could prove him right. In fact, throughout his participation in group therapy, he simultaneously began individual treatment with another provider, against his group therapist's wishes. In summary, his treatment report indicated that Mr. Coe's engagement in therapy was generally counterproductive and concluded that his prognosis was extremely guarded.

Relevant Background Information

Within six months of the treatment summary, Mr. Coe pled guilty to his charges and was ordered to begin the assessment and a court-ordered treatment process discussed herein. The wealth of information that was provided at the onset of this assessment phase allowed a preliminary clinical picture to be drawn, on which an initial treatment plan was developed by his treatment team. Generally, he was viewed as a client with significant dynamic and static risk factors including, but not limited to, labile emotions, poor boundaries, limited self-regulation skills, distorted cognitions, and an intense attraction to children. Though the treatment program is therapeutic in nature, the first responsibility is always to protect community safety, so it was deemed necessary to closely evaluate and monitor him throughout his entire treatment process.

For the purposes of the present evaluation, clinical interviews with Mr. Coe and collateral contacts produced much of the same background information as was provided in previous psychological assessments and evaluations. Mr. Coe had a limited recollection of his childhood, aside from several incidents of teasing and bullying by his peers, and memories of the few visits he had with his biological mother, which he described as "scary" and "upsetting." His portrayal of his interpersonal, professional, and behavioral problems in adulthood reflected his previous therapists' impression that he was unwilling to accept responsibility for many of his choices and behaviors. Instead, he unfailingly blamed his various mental health diagnoses or other people for his mistakes. In general, information gained from consultation and interviews with collateral contacts further supported previous assessment reports and conclusions.

During the time period that Mr. Coe was undergoing the current evaluation, he was also participating in court-ordered sex offender therapy. Consultation with Mr. Coe's court-ordered individual and group therapy treatment providers revealed even more information about Mr. Coe's current functioning. According to his therapists, Mr. Coe's participation in the therapy process further illuminated the role that his cognitions and emotion regulation played in his sexual fantasies and behaviors. These providers reported that Mr. Coe tended to approach therapeutic interventions as combative and stated on several occasions that he felt as though his treatment team members were "playing games" with him, "out to get him," and unwilling to address the true source of his problems, which he attributed to his various mental health conditions. He consistently spent individual sessions attempting to engage his therapist in arguments about how members of his treatment team have phrased different statements in ways that offended him and in attempting to educate his therapist about the nature of his disorders. For instance, he presented the therapist with books and articles that he requested she read between therapy sessions in order to better understand how his ADHD, Bipolar Disorder, and Asperger's Disorder have contributed to his sexual attractions and offense.

Another important aspect of sex offender treatment and evaluation is identifying any patterns of sexual fantasy and masturbation that may be connected to emotional, cognitive, or social stressors or processes. Mr. Coe reported that he found himself having many more sexually violent fantasies following therapy sessions and following any interactions that he found to be frustrating or distressing. For example, after a boundary was set by a therapist or his probation officer, Mr. Coe reported going home and masturbating to fantasies involving pain and humiliation of those individuals, as well as women and children in general. He would also perseverate on the specific words or tones that he perceived being used in conversations with others and would dwell on "getting back at" that individual for offending or hurting him. His sexual fantasies and masturbatory behaviors were so closely tied to his emotional distress that he began masturbating in his car immediately following interactions with his treatment team, which was concerning from an offending and public-safety standpoint. Due to the link between emotional distress, which was fed by his distorted cognitions about the intentions and role of his treatment team, and his increasing sexual acting-out behaviors, it was decided that Mr. Coe was in immediate need of coping skills to help him tolerate distress and regulate emotions without reverting to inappropriate fantasies and masturbation, or worse. Thus, individual therapy utilized techniques from dialectical behavior therapy (DBT; Linehan, 1993), which is designed for people who experience overwhelming emotions and cope with them in maladaptive ways. Traditionally, DBT has been used with individuals who have symptoms of Borderline Personality Disorder and has been especially helpful in reducing self-harming behaviors associated with the intense emotions experienced by those individuals. In their book, *The Dialectical Behavior Therapy Skills Workbook: Practical DBT Exercises for Learning Mindfulness, Interpersonal Effectiveness, Emotion Regulation & Distress Tolerance*, McKay, Wood, and Brantley (2007) explain:

> For some people, emotional and physical pain feels more intense and occurs more frequently than it does for other people. Their distress comes on more quickly and feels like an overwhelming tidal wave. Often, these situations never end and the people experiencing them don't know how to cope with the severity of their pain . . . people struggling with overwhelming emotions often deal with their pain in very unhealthy, very unsuccessful ways because they don't know what else to do. (p. 5–6)

Conceptually, Mr. Coe's sexual fantasies and behaviors, which were triggered by extreme anger and distress, could be viewed in the same way that self-harming behaviors are. Thus, the same techniques used to address those behaviors were applied to reducing and eliminating Mr. Coe's use of sexual fantasy and masturbation as a way to cope with intense emotional distress. Eventually, as Mr. Coe was taught more coping skills, he was prohibited from engaging in any sexual fantasies that were deemed inappropriate (i.e., those involving force, coercion, violence, humiliation, degradation, dehumanization, and children). He was also not allowed to masturbate when feeling emotionally distressed, as he was required to utilize more appropriate coping skills instead. Mr. Coe was not willing or able to adhere to these limits. It was at this point in treatment that Mr. Coe's acting-out behaviors intensified dramatically. He began texting his individual therapist on her personal mobile phone (which was to be used strictly for scheduling purposes) at all hours of the day and night to communicate clinically relevant information and express his emotions. Despite a boundary being set (and recommunicated three weeks in a row) about the appropriate use of this phone number and of text messaging, Mr. Coe sent a total of eighteen text messages to his therapist over a four-day period, which ranged in tone from solicitous, to antagonistic, to accusatory. During this period, he also made appointments with two different mental health professionals in which he complained about the techniques and approaches used by his treatment team and requested that they provide documentation supporting his belief that he was being treated unfairly. He reportedly also made contact with a human rights group to report that his basic human rights were being violated in treatment. Finally, late one evening, Mr. Coe texted his individual therapist to report that he had seen two attractive female children at a retail store earlier that day and had purposely lingered in the store to watch them.

Mental Status Examination

When initially meeting with a client to begin a psychological evaluation, the first objective is to gather basic data to determine whether the client possesses any cognitive or intellectual deficits or psychological impairments that may impact his or her ability to participate meaningfully in the evaluation and to assess overall functioning. Mr. Coe was a 36-year-old Caucasian male who had never been married and had no children. He owned his own home, he had obtained a master's-level education, and until his arrest, he was gainfully employed as a middle school physical education teacher. Based on the fact that he was able to complete a graduate degree, obtain employment, and manage his finances, it was assumed that his cognitive capacities were intact and that he was able to function professionally and financially. Mr. Coe had no prior criminal charges or arrests and reported that he was actively involved with his church and had an adequate social support network. In each of his meetings with the evaluator, Mr. Coe's affect was agitated and defensive, and he usually described his mood as "fine" or "frustrated" (the frustration was usually attributed to various aspects of treatment or probation). In line with his overall functioning prior to his arrest, he presented as having average to above-average intelligence. He exhibited no signs of thought disturbance, hallucinations, or delusions. He did have somewhat paranoid and distrustful views of his treatment team, but those views were comparable with those of many forensic clients and did not reach the threshold for delusional beliefs. Throughout the entire evaluation process, he denied current suicidal, homicidal, or self-harming ideation, but he did endorse ongoing sexually deviant fantasies and urges. In summary, it was determined that he was competent to proceed with the evaluation and treatment process.

Actuarial Tools Most clients convicted of sexual offenses are assessed for their estimated risk of recidivism using one or more of the actuarial risk assessments discussed earlier (such as the Static-99 or Static-2002, RRASOR, and SVR-20), which are the most commonly implemented tools. Unfortunately, at this time, several of these tools explicitly state that they are not to be used for the risk assessment of online sex offenders who have not committed a contact-offense against a victim (Phenix, Doren, Helmus, Hanson, & Thornton, 2008), and others have not been normed on Internet only offenders. So, despite the best-practices inclusion of actuarial data, there were no such tools available that were appropriate for this particular case (Hanson, Helmus, & Thornton, 2009). However, it is possible to note, and include, any empirically supported indicators of risk of recidivism in one's clinical assessment. In Mr. Coe's case, he exhibited characteristics that were associated with both indicators of long-term recidivism (sexual deviancy and antisocial orientation), which will be discussed later.

Self-Report Measures An empirical assessment of Mr. Coe's personality characteristics were warranted at the time of this evaluation, but due to the fact that he had already completed the MMPI-2 twice in the past year, it was determined that an alternate measure should be used. Thus, Mr. Coe was administered the Millon Clinical and Multi-Axial Inventory (MCMI-III; Millon & Davis, 1997), which, similar to the MMPI-2, is a standardized personality inventory used to assess for a number of psychological problems and to identify maladaptive personality characteristics that may impact a person's functioning. It contains 175 true-false questions that ask the test-taker to indicate his or her behavioral and emotional patterns within the past six to twelve months. It also contains validity scales to detect any attempts on the part of the test-taker to manipulate the results or misrepresent his functioning, as well as clinical scales.

According to the validity scales, Mr. Coe did not appear to try to misrepresent himself on the test, and his results were deemed valid for interpretation. On the clinical scales, Mr. Coe exhibited extremely high levels of depressive symptoms, anxiety, mood fluctuation, thought problems, suicidal ideation, and posttraumatic stress. All of these scales were elevated to at least two standard deviations above the mean, and these deviations are representative of a significant amount of emotional distress. However, it should also be noted that scores of this severity are unusual for someone who is not in intensive or inpatient mental health treatment, so the possibility of him exaggerating his symptomology must be considered.

His response pattern also indicated some personality characteristics that may be intrusive in his ability to form and sustain relationships, as he seemed to approach relationships from a very black-and-white perspective. His responses suggested that he tended to idealize some people at times, while demonizing them at other points. He also appeared to approach conflict quite readily and become emotionally intense very quickly. When someone offended or betrayed him, in his opinion, he quickly dismissed their perspective, disengaged, and might even have become inclined to retaliate. It appeared as though he lacked the coping skills to stay more balanced in his perspective and to be able to problem solve. To some extent, this pattern may have been exacerbated by a lack of insight into others and the misinterpretation of social cues.

Sexual History It was determined that, in addition to immediately participating in group therapy sessions with other offenders with pedophilia, Mr. Coe should also complete a thorough sexual history interview to gather as much information as possible about his sexual attractions, sexual relationships, sexual fantasies, pornography use, and any undisclosed sexual offenses. The gathering of all of Mr. Coe's sexual history information took longer than usual, as he fell into a pattern of initially reporting limited information and then returning the next week to clarify or add new information that he had intentionally withheld previously. Thus, at any given point, his clinicians and evaluator were unsure if he was fully reporting all of his sexual interests and behaviors, which, from a safety management standpoint, was concerning. Over time, in addition to his attraction to prepubescent children and several incidents of arousal in the presence of children in his early adulthood, Mr. Coe disclosed a great deal of new information regarding his behaviors, attractions, and fantasies.

Mr. Coe claimed that his sexual attraction to minors was not the reason that he chose to enter teaching profession and maintained that he never inappropriately touched any children or students. However, he did report many incidents of engaging with his physical education students in ways that provided him with sexual pleasure or gratification. These incidents included touching them unnecessarily to provide "instruction" on various activities, purposely brushing his hands against their breasts, volunteering to teach sex education because he found it arousing to talk to them about sex, asking them personal questions about their relationships, wearing shorts that revealed his genitals, and purposely holding students after class to talk to them. There is no indication that any students ever reported his behaviors or were aware of his intentions. He also reported masturbating to fantasies about scenarios involving coercing or forcing his female students into sexual activity with him.

Sexual Fantasy and Masturbation Log Throughout the sexual-history gathering process, Mr. Coe was also asked to maintain a log of the sexual fantasies that he engaged in and masturbated to. Mr. Coe's log revealed that, in addition to having pedophilic attractions, he was strongly aroused by fantasies with sexually sadistic elements. Namely, he claimed that his "most arousing" fantasies incorporated verbal and physical humiliation of women and girls, abduction, violent rape, forcing young females to perform sexual acts on one another, physical abuse, buying a young female child as a sex slave, and sexual torture involving weapons. To satisfy these attractions, Mr. Coe frequently viewed and masturbated to violent pornography and fantasies and used phone sex and web-camera services to pay women to be verbally degraded by him or to harm themselves while he watched. He recalled two specific incidents in which he paid young women on a web camera to role-play as young children, cut themselves with knives, defecate, and eat their own feces. He reported paying for sex with women in prostitution approximately fifty times in his life, though he denied incorporating any of his sadistic fantasies into those encounters.

Mr. Coe also reported a history of using nonexplicit stimuli for sexual purposes. For example, he recalled visiting nudist resorts on several occasions to watch the nude children, viewing mainstream media for sexual gratification (e.g., he enjoyed watching television shows and movies depicting rape while imagined himself in the role of the perpetrators), and even calling a suicide hotline and masturbating to the operator's voice on multiple occasions.

Clinical Summary and Opinion

It was determined that, due to the combination of his mental health issues, deviant sexual interests, and compulsivity, Mr. Coe was both a high-need and a high-risk client. This impression was supported by several dynamic and static risk factors that are associated with long-term risk for recidivism: deficits in sexual self-regulation (being overwhelmed by sexual thoughts and urges), deviant sexual interests, socioaffective deficits (e.g., difficulties developing healthy, respectful, and intimate relationships), self-regulation deficits (including problems controlling negative emotions), and noncooperation with community supervision (Lussier & Gress, 2013). Mr. Coe clearly exhibited deficits in sexual self-regulation, as well as emotional self-regulation problems, when he repeatedly masturbated to inappropriate fantasies and in inappropriate situations when feeling emotionally triggered. He also repeatedly became verbally combative and aggressive with members of his treatment team in reaction to stress or frustration. In terms of sexual deviancy, Mr. Coe reported sexual interests that are reflective of both a sexual arousal to violence and a sexual attraction to children (and a combination thereof). His socioaffective deficits were represented by his having few friends, a history of conflict with authority, and an absence of romantic relationships in his history. His noncooperation with community supervision was reflected in his problems adhering to treatment expectations and the rules of probation, refusal to take responsibility for his own behaviors, assertion that he was being treated unfairly, and belief that his treatment team was out to get him.

His mental health issues were recognized and accommodated for by his treatment team. He had been diagnosed by previous clinicians as having Bipolar Disorder, ADHD, and Pedophilia. In addition, in the course of his disclosures to his treatment team, he also exhibited attractions and fantasies involving inflicting pain, humiliation, and degradation on others, which warranted an additional diagnosis of Paraphilic Disorder, Sexually Sadistic Type. Due to his intense emotional dysregulation, maladaptive and potentially harmful coping mechanisms, and pattern of unstable interpersonal relationships and interaction styles, it is also likely that Mr. Coe qualified for a diagnosis of Borderline Personality Disorder. Mr. Coe often reverted to claiming that he was incapable of behaving as required because of these diagnoses (e.g., he claimed that he was not able to follow directions and respond appropriately to feedback because of his ADHD). However, his treatment providers were experienced with treating individuals with those issues and made reasonable accommodations for those types of needs by providing feedback and instructions multiple times and in several different formats and approaches, and Mr. Coe's lack of compliance appeared to be due to factors beyond those explained by those conditions.

Throughout his assessment and treatment, Mr. Coe displayed a pattern of behaviors that is representative of resistance to and fighting against the treatment process. Although he expressed a desire to understand and manage his sexual interests and attractions, his behaviors did not reflect that claim. In the group therapy process, he repeatedly received feedback from group facilitators and his peers that he seemed to be more interested in arguing and blaming his behaviors on others, or on forces beyond his control than in learning how to change and manage them. In individual therapy, he failed to complete homework assignments, primarily by being unwilling to practice and apply the coping skills that he had been taught to regulate his emotions, tolerate distress, accept reality, and refrain from engaging in sexually deviant fantasies.

He also displayed a tendency to react to boundaries by becoming emotionally escalated and verbally reactive and combative.

Because of his deviant sexual interests involving the use of force, inflicting pain, and offending against children, it was concluded that Mr. Coe should optimally be placed in a contained environment that offers a high level of supervision and restriction. However, due to a significant gap in available resources, this was not an option for him. For individuals who require inpatient treatment or a contained environment, there are four general options: 1) publicly funded inpatient/residential mental health facilities, 2) privately funded inpatient/residential mental health facilities, 3) civil commitment to a state forensic psychiatric facility for sexually violent predators, or 4) incarceration.

Option 1, **publicly funded inpatient/residential mental health facilities**, relies on government and social services funds to cover the costs of treatment and care for facility patients. Because of the severe limitations of these funds across the country, these facilities are usually only able to offer treatment to individuals who are at imminent risk of harming themselves or others and are believed to be incapable of controlling their own behavior. Because Mr. Coe was not reporting active suicidal or homicidal intentions, he did not meet the criteria for admission to one of these facilities. Option 2, **privately funded inpatient/residential mental health facilities**, requires that patients be able to pay for their own care. Mr. Coe's financial situation prohibited him from being able to do so. A thorough discussion of the nuances of option 3, **civil commitment of sexually violent predators to a state forensic psychiatric facility**, is beyond the scope of this chapter, but essentially Mr. Coe did not qualify for the label of a sexually violent predator because he had not been convicted of an offense involving actual physical sexual contact or violence against a victim. Many forensic psychology professionals find this particular limitation frustrating as it represents our legal system's tendency to be *reactive* rather than *proactive*. In other words, regardless of what clients disclose to us about their desires and urges to hurt someone, we have to wait for Mr. Coe (or individuals like him) to actually physically sexually assault a victim before we have the option of placing them in the contained environment they may warrant. Finally, option 4, **incarceration,** is clearly a matter decided by the courts, and in this case this option would require that Mr. Coe commit an additional offense or be found to be in violation of his terms of probation in order to be confined to a correctional facility.

Given that Mr. Coe did not qualify for any of the four options discussed above for placement in a restricted environment, in order to ensure community safety and amenability to treatment he needed to exhibit an ability to contain himself within the confines of an outpatient treatment program. His treatment team provided him with the highest available level of treatment (a combination of weekly group therapy and weekly individual treatment), but Mr. Coe was apparently unwilling to internalize and utilize the treatment tools that he had been given. Though his treatment team expressed concerns about his ongoing resistance to the treatment process and his approach to engaging in therapy, he continued to exhibit a preference for utilizing therapy time for debating and seeking justifications for various elements of the treatment program and for placing blame on various people for his behavioral violations. When challenged on this type of behavior, Mr. Coe almost unfailingly reverted to claiming that he is incapable of learning or applying coping skills or other elements of therapy due to his various mental health diagnoses. It is important to note, however, that there was clear indication that Mr. Coe's cognitive and learning abilities were intact, as he exhibited no difficulty in recalling information and even recalled the precise wording that served to confirm his preexisting ideas or the point he was trying to argue. This same ability, however, was not applied when receiving information that challenged or contradicted what he wanted to believe.

An example of this tendency was the incident he reported in which he watched two young girls in a retail store. His treatment program's consistent stance on incidents such as these is that the client should immediately leave a location in which he notices an attraction to a minor. His choice to not only remain in the proximity of the children but also to continue to look at them (for his own sexual gratification) was highly concerning in itself, particularly given that his history indicated a willingness to manipulate situations in which he has access to children for his own sexual gratification. In the context of his ongoing failure to control and contain himself and his urges in various situations, this particular incident became an example of a high-risk behavior.

Ultimately, it was clear to this treatment team that Mr. Coe's pattern of inappropriate behavior was not reflective of disability but was instead an indicator that he chose to engage in ongoing behaviors that were both in violation of his treatment contract and representative of a failure to internalize treatment concepts. This pattern included, but was not limited to, ongoing masturbation to inappropriate fantasies (involving force and coercion, inflicting pain and humiliation, and children), choices that represent poor judgment (renting movies and watching television programs involving sexual violence and masturbating to them, remaining in the presence of children in public), misuse of mental health resources (calling the suicide hotline for sexual gratification, going to the psychiatric emergency room to complain about his current treatment team), and boundary violations (being verbally combative and insulting to members of the treatment team, misuse of text messaging, and demanding extra time outside of treatment sessions).

In order for Mr. Coe to participate in and benefit from the outpatient treatment that was available, and to remain safely in the community, he had to be willing to use basic risk management strategies. His participation in the treatment program and the reports provided by previous treatment providers indicated that he was unwilling to do so at that time.

Clinical Summary and Opinion

As indicated thus far, Mr. Coe was a resistant participant who was unwilling to conform his behavior to the confines of an outpatient treatment program and basic risk management procedures. Mr. Coe was diagnosed with Pedophilia and Sexual Sadism, and admitted to being sexually attracted to pre-pubescent girls. By nature, these disorders tend to run a fairly chronic, intense, and persistent course. Individuals who suffer from Pedophilia often struggle with the compulsive nature of the disorder and have difficulty gaining mastery over the accompanying urges, which is why accountability and risk management practices are such important components of treatment. In addition, these disorders represent a lifelong management problem that does not go away, as the interest will likely always be present (American Psychiatric Association, 2013; Briken, Fedoroff, & Bradford, 2014; Frances & Sreenivasan, 2008). Currently, there are no known therapeutic approaches that have been able to successfully alter one's sexual orientations or interests, though the intensity of one's attractions may fluctuate over time (American Psychiatric Association, 2013; American Psychological Association, 2009; Chenier, 2012). Mr. Coe had been in treatment for some time and had been given quite a bit of latitude in an attempt to engage him in the therapeutic process and to accommodate some of his mental health issues. However, his continued resistance to the process, failure to take responsibility for his choices, unwillingness to make needed changes, and unwillingness to put in place adequate protective factors such as avoiding inappropriate situations and materials, indicated that he was not a good candidate for community containment at that time. Additionally, based on the behavior described above, it appeared that Mr. Coe was engaging in high-risk behaviors with few, if any, safety nets in place. As such, he was terminated from the treatment program for being too high risk for outpatient treatment, exhibiting a continuing pattern of resistance, refusing to take responsibility for his behaviors, and failing to make adequate progress in treatment.

Additional Information

Because participation in, cooperation with, and completion of a sex offender treatment program was a required condition of his probation and because he was engaging in high-risk behaviors, Mr. Coe was arrested for violating his probation terms following his termination from treatment. He appeared before a judge who, given the sex offender risk evaluation discussed above, revoked his probation and ordered him to serve an additional five years in prison with three of those years suspended. This means that after two years of incarceration, Mr. Coe will once again be placed on probation and ordered to repeat the evaluation and treatment process.

Common Pitfalls and Considerations

Working with forensic clients can present many challenges for clinicians and evaluators, even beyond those that are inherent in general clinical practice. This is especially true for professionals who may have started their careers or training with nonforensic populations and who then try to adjust to working with forensic clients.

Emotional Reactions

In order to work with sex offenders in a clinical setting, an evaluator or clinician must be willing to listen to the potentially disturbing details of the crimes committed, as well as any trauma the client may have been subjected to themselves. As is true for working with any trauma survivor, it can be emotionally trying to hear about, and sit with, the pain and horror that some individuals have had to experience in their lives. It can make one feel sad, angry, and powerless. But it can be equally as distressing, and even more confusing, to hear the stories from the offender's perspective. In fact, it may produce conflicting feelings of sadness and anger on the victim's behalf and compassion, grief, and regret for the offender. The experience of aligning with an offender's perspective itself, even minimally, can feel like a betrayal of the victim and can produce guilt and ambivalence within the clinician. An additional challenge for the clinician is appearing neutral, or at least not horrified or distressed, in the midst of this emotional confusion.

Another struggle for a forensic practitioner can be striking the right balance between genuine emotional self-disclosure (which facilitates an alliance with the client and can help them to understand the impact of their offenses) and professional neutrality (that enables a clinician to remain objective). To further complicate matters, the point on that spectrum that is most likely to elicit a favorable response will vary with each individual client. So, learning to continually assess where to find that delicate balance may be a career-long learning curve.

Though the role of a forensic evaluator is not to determine guilt or punishment for an offender, the outcomes of a sex offender evaluation may result in severe consequences for the client. This reality can produce feelings of responsibility, and even guilt, for an evaluator who has developed an alliance with or compassion for a client. Accepting that as a forensic practitioner you may simultaneously care about a client's well-being *and* play a role in them being sent to prison or experiencing negative consequences can be difficult. It is important to remind oneself that the only truly responsible parties for any consequences are the offenders themselves and that your role is simply to use the tools of psychology to elicit as much information as possible about the offender's functioning, needs, and risk level.

Over-Empathizing and Under-Empathizing

When developing a therapeutic or clinical relationship with a client, the clinician's ability to empathize appropriately can be crucial to ensuring that a secure alliance is formed. This alliance allows the clinician to accurately perceive and understand the client's emotional experience and enables the client to feel understood, accepted, and safe to lower their defenses. However, as with trying to strike an emotional balance in forensic work, it can be difficult to maintain empathy without going to either extreme of over-empathizing or under-empathizing. Over-empathizing with a client may lead a practitioner to be less critical of a client's version of their offenses, and less adept at challenging them when needed. In essence, a practitioner must be sure that empathy does not lead to them becoming unquestioning or gullible. On the other hand, under-empathizing with a client can create an adversarial relationship that inhibits a client's trust, openness, and cooperation. Unfortunately, it can also lead to cynicism and a generalized distrust and dislike of the clients that we are working with. It can be a complicated process for a forensic practitioner to find a way to abhor sex offenses without dehumanizing and demonizing the offender. At the end of the day, if mental health professionals are unable or unwilling to view their clients (regardless of the population they work with) as human beings, they have very little hope of facilitating positive change in their clients' lives (and ultimately, preventing future offenses and victimization).

Boundaries

Identifying, setting, and maintaining appropriate professional boundaries are common foci of clinical training and supervision. However, forensic clients in general, and sex offenders particularly, present with a heightened need for strong boundaries on the part of their clinician. The very nature of sex offending indicates a disregard for, or ignorance of, the boundaries and needs of others, so it is not surprising that sex offenders may model similar boundary issues with their clinician or evaluator. Furthermore, they have often become adept at using charm and manipulation to gain the trust of others or to influence others into relaxing their boundaries. Therefore, it is common for a provider, especially one who is new to working with forensic populations, to rely on the types of boundaries that they typically set with clients from the general population and to find that they have quickly become involved in a dynamic with their forensic client that has crossed their emotional or interpersonal boundaries. It is prudent, then, for practitioners to approach interactions with forensic clients with a heightened awareness of their boundaries and stricter guarding of them than they might typically apply. It is always much more difficult to assert or attempt to reassert a boundary that has already been crossed than to identify and maintain a clear boundary from the onset of treatment. However, even if a clinician experiences a boundary violation in treatment, it can be a useful learning experience for both the clinician and client, if communicated and discussed appropriately in the clinical setting.

Ethical Considerations

One ethical concern that runs through many elements of the practice of forensic psychology is that of the clinician serving a dual role. Though it is mandated that clinicians inform any forensic clients about the limits of confidentiality and who may receive copies of treatment reports or evaluations, the nature of a clinician's work with individuals from forensic populations may still pose opportunities for ethical opacity. In the case of sex offender treatment and evaluation, a forensic evaluator employs clinical approaches throughout the evaluation process (while working with the client and attempting to gather as much information as possible) and simultaneously answers to the legal system (serving the courts, probation, or parole) regarding any factors that may constitute risk to the community. Additionally, an evaluator who works in tandem with, or obtains treatment records from, a court-ordered treatment provider may (and should) utilize information that is disclosed in therapy as part of the risk evaluation. Therefore, while it is necessary for the client to be completely honest and open about his or her sexual interests, attractions, fantasies, and behaviors from a therapeutic and risk-management standpoint, it also places the client in a position in which he or she may face legal consequences for therapeutic disclosures.

Given the team approach used in Mr. Coe's case, many of his disclosures in therapy that could have represented an increased risk to the community were shared with his evaluator and probation officer. In the interest of protecting potential victims and reducing the likelihood of recidivism, the probation officer decided to impose additional restrictions or limitations on the client's freedoms. While the community's safety is of primary concern in cases such as these, it also served to essentially punish Mr. Coe (and clients like him) for being honest in the assessment process and/or therapy. Great effort was made to connect the importance of Mr. Coe's honesty with the purpose of requiring it; namely, that in order for him to gain control and mastery over his own behaviors and choices, he had to be fully open about them. Ultimately, his ability to manage his behaviors has a direct relationship with the level of risk he poses to the community. Therapeutically, this honesty and subsequent self-management is the goal of treatment. However, the goals of other treatment team members (i.e., probation) are centered on protecting the public from offenders first and foremost, and the same clinical information could be interpreted and used in ways that can feel antitherapeutic to the client. Thus, maintaining open communication and trust between clinician and client is often even more challenging than it would be normally. Ideally, a client would be as committed to the therapeutic process and the ultimate goal of protecting the public as his treatment team would be, but often clients perceive this dynamic as punishing and inhibiting.

In Mr. Coe's case, and in cases like his, another concern arises regarding the potential of limiting an individual's freedom not purely based on what they *have* done, but in light of what we believe they *might* do. Though concerns about potential behavior alone are not grounds for incarceration, they may be used to revoke the client's supervised release and ultimately force him to serve the remainder of his original sentence in a correctional facility. Though a client's supervised release is considered a privilege, rather than a right (since the original sentence was for a full term in a correctional facility), the revocation of it based on an *estimated* level of risk can walk the ethical fine line. There is always the chance that a clinician's guided risk assessment, based on clinical judgment and formalized assessments, indicates that an individual is at a high risk of reoffending, yet that client may never commit another sexual offense. Most often, though, forensic professionals operate on the principle that it is preferable to have a false positive (i.e., predict a high chance of recidivism when none actually occurs) than a false negative (i.e., predict a low chance of recidivism and then a reoffense occurs), because the stakes are so high; "recidivism" and "reoffense," when talking about sexual offending, is equal to one or more human beings being sexually violated.

References

Abel, G. G., Huffman, J., Warberg, B., & Holland, C. L. (1998). Visual reaction time and plethysmography as measures of sexual interest in child molesters. *Sexual Abuse: A Journal of Research and Treatment, 10*, 81–95. doi:10.1177/107906329801000202

Adam Walsh Child Protection and Safety Act, Pub. L. No. 109–248, 120 Stat. 587 (2006).

Amenta, A. E., Guy, L. S., & Edens, J. F. (2003). Sex offender risk assessment: A cautionary note regarding measures attempting to quantify violence risk. *Journal of Forensic Psychology Practice, 3*(1), 39–50. doi:10.1300/J158v03n01_04

American Psychiatric Association. (2013). *Diagnostic and statistical manual of mental disorders* (5th ed.). Washington, DC: Author.

American Psychological Association. (2009). *Report of the American Psychological Association Task Force on appropriate therapeutic responses to sexual orientation.* Washington, DC: Author.

American Psychological Association. (2010). *Ethical principles of psychologists and code of conduct.* Washington, DC: Author. Retrieved November 10, 2014, from http://www.apa.org/ethics/code/index.aspx

Andrews, D. A., & Bonta, J. L. (1998). *The psychological of criminal conduct* (2nd ed.). Cincinnati, OH: Anderson.

Association for the Treatment of Sexual Abusers. (2014). Risk Assessment | ATSA. Retrieved November 10, 2014, from http://www.atsa.com/risk-assessment

Bartosh, D. L., Garby, T., Lewis, D., & Gray, S. (2003). Differences in predictive validity of actuarial risk assessments in relation to sex offender type. *International Journal of Offender Therapy and Comparative Criminology, 47*(4), 422–438.

Beech, A. R., Fisher, D. D., & Thornton, D. (2003). Risk assessment of sex offenders. *Professional Psychology: Research and Practice, 34*(4), 339–352. doi:10.1037/0735-7028.34.4.339

Boer, D. P., Hart, S. D., Kropp, P. R., & Webster, C. D. (1997). *Manual for the Sexual Violence Risk-20. Professional guidelines for assessing risk of sexual violence.* Vancouver, British Columbia, Canada: Institute Against Family Violence.

Bonta, J., Law, M., & Hanson, R. K. (1998). The prediction of criminal and violent recidivism among mentally disordered offenders: A meta-analysis. *Psychological Bulletin 123*, 123–142.

Branaman, T. F., & Gallagher S. N. (2005). Polygraph testing in sex offender treatment: A review of the limitations. *American Journal of Forensic Psychology, 23*, 45–64.

Briken, P., Fedoroff, J. P., & Bradford, J. W. (2014). Why can't pedophilic disorder remit? *Archives of Sexual Behavior, 43*(7), 1237–1239. doi:10.1007/s10508-014-0323-1

Butcher, J. N., Dahlstrom, W. G., Graham, J. R., Tellegen, A., & Kaemmer, B. (1989). *The Minnesota Multiphasic Personality Inventory-2 (MMPI-2): Manual for administration and scoring.* Minneapolis, MN: University of Minnesota Press.

Calkins, C., Jeglic, E., Beattey, R. A., Ziedman, S., & Perillo, A. D. (2014). Sexual violence legislation: A review of case law and empirical research. *Psychology, Public Policy, and Law, 20*(4), 443–462.

Chenier, E. (2012). The natural order of disorder: Pedophilia, stranger danger and the normalising family. *Sexuality & Culture, 16*(2), 172–186.

Conroy, M. A., & Murrie, D. DC. (2007). *Forensic assessment in violence risk: A guide for risk assessment and management.* Hoboken, NJ: Wiley.

Craig, L. A., & Beech, A. R. (2010). Towards a guide to best practice in conducting actuarial risk assessments with sex offenders. *Aggression and Violent Behavior, 15*(4), 278–293. doi:10.1016/j.avb.2010.01.007

Dallas, C. (2009). Not in my backyard: The implications of sex offender residency ordinances in Texas and beyond. *Texas Tech Law Review, 41*, 1235–1244.

Doren, D. M. (2004). *Bibliography of published works relative to risk assessment for sexual offenders.* Retrieved November 10, 2014, from http://www.atsa.com/pdfs/riskAssessment Biblio.pdf

Edwards, W., & Hensley, C. (2001). Contextualizing sex offender management legislation and policy: Evaluating the problem of latent consequences in community notification laws. *International Journal of Offender Therapy and Comparative Criminology, 45*(1), 83–101.

Eke, A. W., & Seto, M. C. (2012). Risk assessment of online offenders for law enforcement. In K. Ribisl & E. Quayle (Eds.), *Internet child pornography: Understanding and preventing on-line child abuse.* Devon, U.K.: Willan.

Epperson, D. L. (2000, March). *Minnesota Sex Offender Screening Tool–Revised.* Paper presented at the Sinclair Seminars Conference of Sex Offender Re-Offense Risk prediction, Madison, WI. (Videotape available from www.sinclairseminar.com.)

Epperson, D. L., Kaul, J. D., & Hesselton, D. (1998). *Final report on the development of the Minnesota Sex Offender Screening Tool-Revised (MnSOST-R).* Paper presented at the 17th Annual Conference of the Association for the Treatment of Sexual Abusers, Vancouver, British Columbia, Canada.

Frances, A., & Sreenivasan, S. (2008). Sexually violent predator statutes: The Clinical/Legal interface. *Psychiatric Times, 25*(14), 49.

Galeste, M. A., Fradella, H. F., & Vogel, B. (2012). Sex offender myths in print media: Separating fact from fiction in U.S. newspapers. *Western Criminology Review, 13*(2), 4–24.

Goyette, C. H., Conners, C. K., & Ulrich, R. F. (1978). Normative data on revised Conners parent and teacher rating scales. *Journal of Abnormal Child Psychology, 6*(2), 221–236.

Hanson, R. K. (1997). *The development of a brief actuarial scale for sex offender recidivism* (User Report No. 1997–04). Ottawa, Ontario, Canada: Department of the Solicitor General of Canada.

Hanson, R. K. (1998). What do we know about sex offender risk assessment? *Psychology, Public Policy, and Law, 4*(1–2), 50–72. doi:10.1037/1076-8971.4.1-2.50

Hanson, R. K., & Bussiere, M. T. (1998). Predicting relapse: a meta-analysis of sexual offender recidivism studies. *Journal of Consulting and Clinical Psychology, 66*, 348–362.

Hanson, R. K., & Harris, A. J. R. (2000a). *The Sex offender needs assessment rating (SONAR): A method for measuring change in risk levels.* Canada: Department of the Solicitor General of Canada. Retrieved November 10, 2014, from http://ww2.psepc-sppcc.gc.ca/publications/corrections/pdf/200001b_e.pdf

Hanson, R. K., & Harris, A. J. R. (2000b). Where should we intervene? Dynamic predictors of sex offense recidivism. *Criminal Justice and Behavior, 27*, 6–35.

Hanson, R. K., Helmus, L., & Thornton, D. (2010). Predicting recidivism amongst sexual offenders: A multi-site study of Static-2002. *Journal of Law and Human Behavior, 34*, 198–211.

Hanson, R. K., & Morton-Bourgon, K. (2004). *Predictors of Sexual Recidivism: An Updated Meta-Analysis.* Ottawa, Ontario Canada: Public Safety and Emergency Preparedness Canada.

Hanson, R. K., Stey, R. A., & Gauthier, R. (1993). Long-term recidivism of child molesters. *Journal of Consulting and Clinical Psychology, 61*, 646–652.

Hanson, R. K. (2005). Twenty years of progress in violence risk assessment. *Journal of Interpersonal Violence, 20*(2), 212–217.

Hanson, R. K., & Thornton, D. (1999). *Static-99: Improving actuarial risk assessments for sex offenders* (User Report No. 99–02). Ottawa, Ontario, Canada: Department of the Solicitor General of Canada.

Hanson, R. K., & Thornton, D. (2000). Improving risk assessments for sex offenders: A comparison of three actuarial scales. *Law and Human Behavior, 24*(1), 119–136.

Hare, R. D. (1991). *The Hare Psychopathy Checklist-revised.* Toronto, ON: Multi-Health Systems.

Harris, A. J. (2006). Risk assessment and sex offender community supervision: A context-specific framework. *Federal Probation, 70*(2), 36–43.

Harris, A. J., & Hanson, R. K. (2010). Clinical, actuarial and dynamic risk assessment of sexual offenders: Why do things keep changing? *Journal of Sexual Aggression, 16*, 296–310. doi:10.1080/13552600.2010.494772

Harris, G. T., Rice, M. E., & Quinsey, V. L. (1993). Violent recidivism of mentally disordered offenders: The development of a statistical prediction instrument. *Criminal Justice and Behavior, 20*, 315–335. doi:10.1177/0093854893020004001

Jackson, R. L., & Richards, H. J. (2007). Diagnostic and risk profiles among civilly committed sex offenders in Washington State. *International Journal of Offender Therapy and Comparative Criminology, 51*, 313–323.

Jacob Wetterling Crimes Against Children and Sexually Violent Offenders Registration Act, Pub. L. No. 103–322, 108 Stat. 1796 (1994).

Janus, E. S., & Prentky, R. A. (2003). Forensic use of actuarial risk assessment with sex offenders: Accuracy, admissibility and accountability. *The American Criminal Law Review, 40*, 1443–1499.

Knight, R. A. (2008). *MIDSA clinical manual.* Bend, OR: Augur Enterprises. Retrieved November 10, 2014, from www.midsa.us

Knight, R. A., & Thornton, D. (2007). Evaluating and improving risk assessment schemes for sexual recidivism: A long-term follow-up of convicted sexual offenders. Retrieved November 10, 2014, from https://www.ncjrs.gov/pdffiles1/nij/grants/217618.pdf

Lachar, D., Klinedinst, J. K., & Seat, P. D. (1981). *Multidimensional description of child personality: A manual for the Personality Inventory for Children.* Los Angeles, CA: Western Psychological Services.

Langan, P., & Levin, D. (2002). *Recidivism of prisoners released in 1994.* Washington, DC: U.S. Department of Justice, Office of Justice Programs, Bureau of Justice Statistics.

Langton, C. M., Barbaree, H. E., Harkins, L., Seto, M. S., & Peacock, E. J. (2002). *Evaluating the prediction validity of seven risk assessment instruments for sex offenders.* Paper presented at the Annual Research and Treatment Conference for the Association for the Treatment of Sexual Abusers. Montreal, Ontario, Canada.

Lanterman, J. L., Boyle, D. J., & Ragusa-Salerno, L. M. (2014). Sex offender risk assessment, sources of variation, and the implications of misuse. *Criminal Justice and Behavior, 41*(7), 822–843. doi:10.1177/0093854813515237

Levenson, J. S., Brannon, Y. N., Fortney, T., & Baker, J. (2007). Public perceptions about sex offenders and community protection policies. *Analysis of Social Issues and Public Policy, 7*, 137–161.

Levenson, J. S., & Hern, A. (2007). Sex offender residence restrictions: Unintended consequences and community re-entry. *Justice Research and Policy, 9*, 59–74. doi:10.3818/JRP.9.1.2007.59

Linehan, M. M. (1993). *Cognitive-behavioral treatment for Borderline Personality Disorder.* New York, NY: Guilford Press.

Lussier, P., & Gress, C. L. Z. (2014). Community re-entry and the path toward desistance: A quasi-experimental longitudinal study of dynamic factors and community risk management of adult sex offenders. *Journal of Criminal Justice, 42*(2), 111–122.

McArthur, D. S., & Roberts, G. E. (1982). *Roberts Apperception Test for Children.* Western Psychological Services.

McGuire, J. (2000). Explanation of criminal behavior. In J. McGuire, T. Mason, & A. O'Kane (Eds.), *Behavior, crime and legal processes: A guide for legal practitioners* (pp. 135–159). Chichester, England: Wiley.

McKay, M., Wood, J. C., & Brantley, J. (2007). *The dialectical behavior therapy skills workbook: Practical DBT exercises for learning mindfulness, interpersonal effectiveness, emotion regulation & distress tolerance.* Oakland, CA: New Harbinger.

Meloy, M. L., Miller, S. L., & Curtis, K. M. (2008). Making sense out of nonsense: The deconstruction of state-level sex offender residence restrictions. *American Journal of Criminal Justice, 33*, 209–222.

Mercado, C. C., Alvarez, S., & Levenson, J. (2008). The impact of specialized sex offender legislation on community reentry. *Sexual Abuse: Journal of Research and Treatment, 20*, 188–205.

Mercado, C. C., Schopp, R. F., & Bornstein, B. H. (2005). Evaluating sex offenders under sexually violent predator laws: How might mental health professionals conceptualize the notion of volitional impairment? *Aggression and Violent Behavior, 10*, 289–309.

Millon, T., & Davis, R. D. (1997). The MCMI-III: Present and future directions. *Journal of Personality Assessment, 68*(1), 69–85.

Monahan, J. (1981). *The clinical prediction of violent behavior.* Washington, DC: Government Printing House.

Morey, L. C. (2007). *Personality Assessment Inventory professional manual* (2nd ed.). Lutz, FL: Psychological Assessment Resources.

Nichols, H. R., & Molinder, L. (1996). *Multiphasic Sexual Inventory II handbook.* Tacoma, WA: Nichols & Molinder.

Pascal, G. R., & Suttell, B. J. (1951). *Bender-Gestalt Test.*

Phenix, A., Doren, D., Helmus, L., Hanson, R. K., & Thornton, D. (2008). *Coding rules for Static-2002.* Retrieved November 13, 2014, from http://www.static99.org/pdfdocs/static 2002codingrules.pdf

Quinsey, V. L., Harris, G. T., Rice, M. E., & Cormier, C. A. (1998). *Violent offenders: Appraising and managing risk.* Washington, DC: American Psychological Association.

Rorschach, H., Lemkau, P. T., Kronenberg, B. T., & Morgenthaler, W. (1942). *Psychodiagnostics: A diagnostic test based on perception (rev. and enlarged), including the application of the form interpretation test.* Bern, Switzerland: Verlag.

Schopp, R. F., Scalora, M. J., & Pearce, M. (1999). Expert testimony and professional judgment: Psychological expertise and commitment as a sexual predator after *Hendricks. Psychology, Public Policy, and Law, 5,* 120–174.

Seto, M. C. (2013). Risk assessment. In M. C. Seto, *Internet sex offenders* (pp. 193–223). Washington, DC: American Psychological Association. doi:10.1037/14191-008

Sex Offender Registration and Notification Act, 72 Fed. Reg. 8896, cod. (SORNA). At 28 C. F. R. § 72.3 (2006).

Stadtland, C., Hollweg, M., Kleindienst, N., Dietl, J., Reich, U., & Nedopil, N. (2005). Risk assessment and prediction of violent and sexual recidivism in sex offenders: Long-term predictive validity of four risk assessment instruments. *Journal of Forensic Psychiatry & Psychology, 16*(1), 92–108. doi:10.1080/1478994042000270247

Tewskbury, R., & Lees, M. (2006). Perceptions of sex offender registration: Collateral consequences and community experiences. *Sociological Spectrum, 26*(3), 309–334.

Thornton, D., Mann, R., Webster, S., Blud, L., Travers, R., Friendship, C., & Erikson, M. (2003). Distinguishing and combining risks for sexual and violent recidivism. In R. Prentky, E. Janus, M. Seto, & A. W. Burgess (Eds.), *Annals of the New York Academy of Sciences: Vol. 989. Sexually coercive behavior: Understanding and management* (pp. 225–235). New York, NY: New York Academy of Sciences.

Visgaitis, R. L. (2011). Retroactive application of the sex offender registration and notification act: A modern encroachment on judicial power. *Columbia Journal of Law and Social Problems, 45*(2), 273–302.

Wakeling, H. C., Howard, P., & Barnett, G. (2011). Comparing the validity of the RM2000 scales and OGRS3 for predicting recidivism by Internet sexual offenders. *Sexual Abuse: Journal of Research and Treatment, 23*(1), 146–168. doi:10.1177/1079063210375974

Walters, G. D., Knight, R. A., & Thornton, D. (2009). The latent structure of sexual violence risk: A taxometric analysis of widely used sex offender actuarial risk measures. *Criminal Justice and Behavior, 36*(3), 290–306. doi:10.1177/0093854808330341

Wilkinson, G. S., & Robertson, G. J. (2006). *WRAT 4: Wide Range Achievement Test.* Psychological Assessment Resources.

Witt, P. H., & Conroy, M. A. (2009). *Evaluation of sexually violent predators. Guides to best practices for forensic mental health assessments.* New York, NY: Oxford University Press.

7

Civil Commitment: Examining Mental Illness, Differential Diagnosis, Attributes of Risk, and Application to Case Law

Casey Sharpe and Anna Florek

Civil commitment is a state-sanctioned legal process through which individuals are deprived of their liberty via involuntary hospitalization. Generally, civil commitment proceedings occur when an individual presents with a mental disorder and has acted in a manner that warrants the need for care and treatment due to potential harm to self or others (Pinals & Mossman, 2012; Melton, Petrila, Poythress, & Slobogin, 2007). In some states, an individual may also be civilly committed if he or she is gravely disabled or presents with a very substantial risk to oneself. Such an individual would be considered unable to take care of his or her own basic, physical needs without the assistance of others (Menninger, 2001). Depending on the state, an individual may be eligible for civil commitment if considered acutely or persistently disabled, in that an individual is highly likely to suffer severe physical or mental harm because of impaired judgment due to a mental health condition (Menninger, 2001; Erickson, Vitacco, & Rybroek, 2005). The objective of civil commitment has traditionally been confined rehabilitation. Its purpose is not punishment; however, institutionalization is, in fact, a "deprivation of liberty" (Melton et al., 2007, p. 38) and as a result has been controversial (Melton et al., 2007; Erickson et al., 2005). Despite the intentions to be a rehabilitative process, civil commitment often historically occurred informally and for a wide variety of reasons. Consequently, civil commitment laws were challenged in the courts of the 1960s and 1970s, suggesting that the process and previously existing laws were potentially more harmful than helpful (Melton et al., 2007) to the confined individual.

Today, civil commitment evaluations are among the most common for forensic evaluators. Civil commitment laws are present in all 50 states, as well as the District of Columbia (Pinals & Mossman, 2012). While the total number of yearly civil commitment referrals is unknown, it is safe to reason that thousands are conducted annually nationwide. For instance, New York's "Kendra's Law," which dictates assisted outpatient civil commitment laws, yielded the need for over 10,000 evaluations after its implementation in 1999 (New York State Office of Mental Health, 2005). These numbers only reflect outpatient civil commitment referrals in one state. By amplifying these numbers nationwide, combining the inpatient and outpatient referrals made federally and in all 50 states and Washington, DC, we find there are likely upward of tens of thousands civil commitment referrals made each year.

Navigating the intricacies of civil commitment laws and best practices in actuarial measurements and psychological testing can be problematic for evaluators, as the concept of risk inevitably invites a greater level of complexity to the evaluation (Pinals & Mossman, 2012). Evaluators are expected to make rational, well-founded decisions amid a myriad of complicated factors. This chapter will review relevant mental health case law addressing the evolution of civil commitment laws in greater depth and briefly explain related best practices. A case vignette will allow readers to follow the rationale and guidance of how to formulate opinions in a civil commitment evaluation using best practices and keeping relevant legal issues in mind.

Relevant Case Law and Common Statutory Considerations

Evaluators need to be familiar with the civil commitment statutes and case law for the jurisdiction in which they practice. Currently, every state requires that an individual present with evidence of a mental illness as a predicate to involuntary commitment (Slobogin, Hafemeister, Mossman, & Reisner, 2014). However, mental illness may be defined differently depending on the jurisdiction. For the case included in this chapter, mental illness was defined by administrative code as a mental or emotional disorder that substantially impairs a person's thought, perception of reality, emotional process, judgment, behavior, or ability to cope with the ordinary demands of life but does not include a developmental disability, dementia or Alzheimer's disease absent psychosis, a substance abuse disorder, or an abnormality manifested only by repeated criminal or otherwise antisocial conduct (405 ILCS 5/1–129). Many states specifically exclude behaviors that would fall under the description of Antisocial Personality Disorder or Psychopathy, or drug or alcohol abuse, and these are important distinctions for the evaluator to consider. However, it has also been suggested that some personality disorders (e.g., Borderline Personality Disorder) might meet the statutory definition of a mental disorder

(Pinals & Mossman, 2012). It is not always clear when violent behavior may be attributable to symptoms of a mental illness, a personality disorder, or the context of the situation, and the same individual may meet criteria for involuntary commitment in one jurisdiction but not another, or at one time but not another. Many times it is a confluence of various factors that contributes to an individual's risk for violence. While it is ultimately the trier of fact who determines whether an individual meets criteria for civil commitment, the evaluator must evaluate how these various factors relate to a specific civil commitment statute or law and how an individual may or may not meet criteria for civil commitment.

Second, most state statutes require evidence that a person's violent behavior or risk for violent behavior is caused by or the direct result of mental illness in order to meet the criteria for civil commitment (Slobogin et al., 2014). Mental illness alone is not sufficient to deprive an individual of his or her civil liberty. In the landmark case, *O'Connor v. Donaldson* (1975), the Supreme Court of the United States held that a state could not confine an individual who is mentally ill and nondangerous and who is capable of residing safely in the community either alone or with the assistance of responsible family or friends. However, the terms dangerousness, dangerous conduct, violent behavior, or risk of serious harm may have different definitions depending on the jurisdiction, and even then, these terms may not be clear. In all civil commitment decisions, courts must determine whether the level of potential threat a person poses exceeds that individual's civil liberty interests (Slobogin et al., 2014). Given this fundamental aspect of the process, clarity of these terms is important, and the evaluator must also be familiar with statutory definitions of such, as well as any changes or updates in the law.

For example, the Supreme Court of Illinois recently recognized that Illinois legislative language related to the term "dangerous conduct" was unconstitutionally vague (In re Torski, 2009). In order to be civilly committed in Illinois, an individual must first meet a threshold of diminished capacity to make treatment decisions due to mental illness and must pose a threat to others by way of or because of his or her mental illness. Also according to this ruling, an evaluator must assess both the "magnitude" and "probability" of harm, according to state statute. The court found that the statutory term "dangerous conduct," defined as "threatening behavior or conduct that places another individual in reasonable expectation of being harmed," as impermissibly vague, elaborating that under this language, an individual may be committed for shouting a racial slur or otherwise causing psychological, emotional, or even financial harm to someone (*In re Torski*, 2009). The updated statute now specifies that dangerous conduct must include a reasonable expectation of being physically harmed (IL 405 5/1–119). This is important for evaluators to take into account, as evidence of an "overt act" is required in many jurisdictions to answer the question as to whether or not an individual poses a risk to himself or herself or others (Pinals & Mossman, 2012).

Third, many state statutes also suggest that individuals with mental illness who require treatment also must be provided this treatment in the least restrictive environment or setting (*Lake v. Cameron*, 1966). This means that, if there exists a setting that is less restrictive to civil liberty compared with an inpatient facility, the individual should receive treatment in that environment. The basis for such was established in *Lake v. Cameron* (1966), in which the U.S. Court of Appeals for the District of Columbia decided that an individual cannot constitutionally be confined against his or her will if there is a less restrictive way to safely manage and treat the individual within the community. Less restrictive options can include residential programs, family support, outpatient treatment as described earlier, or other alternative methods of treatment outside of a hospital setting (Conroy & Murrie, 2007). This aligns with best practices related to violence risk assessment, which suggest that an evaluator not only provide an opinion related to risk but also focus on risk management strategies and reduction solutions. In this manner, the evaluator must also consider what type of setting is best suited to reduce an individual's risk for violence in addition to the dynamic or potentially protective factors present. *Lessard v. Schmidt* (1972) reaffirmed the least-restrictive-setting requirement for civil commitment. While this case was specific to the state of Wisconsin, it is considered a landmark decision that highlighted other rights and processes due to individuals facing civil commitment. The *Lessard* decision outlined a set of specific procedural safeguards for the civil commitment process, and these closely mirrored those of criminal procedures, which indicated how seriously the court took the significant restriction of civil liberties. These included an adequate notice of rights, timely notice of the intent to detain the individual, a full court hearing, right to counsel, right to a jury trial, notice of privilege against self-incrimination, and proof beyond a reasonable doubt that a person is both mentally ill and dangerous.

In *Addington v. Texas* (1979), the Supreme Court held that, in order to appropriately balance both personal civil liberty and state public protection interests, the burden of proof in civil commitment proceedings needed to be clear and convincing (as opposed to the more strict "beyond a reasonable doubt" standard as outlined in *Lessard*). This means that, for an individual to be involuntarily committed against his or her wishes, the petitioner must demonstrate with clear and convincing evidence that the individual is mentally ill and also poses a danger to himself or others. This raised the burden of proof from the lower "preponderance of the evidence" standard for many states. However, this decision established only the minimum burden of proof and, as noted in the *Lessard* decision, some states have an even higher standard of beyond a reasonable doubt. While evaluators should follow best practices related to data collection and information gathering for civil commitment evaluations, it is important to recognize that the burden of proof standards may require more or less data in support of a particular opinion. While this tends to be more of a concern for attorneys, it is an important aspect of the evaluative and legal process, which evaluators need to understand.

Another consideration for evaluators involves self-incrimination, as many times the need for civil commitment may be evaluated in the context of criminal proceedings, such as competence to stand trial or criminal responsibility (sometimes referred to as quasi-criminal commitment). While the *Lessard* court stopped short of ruling that an attorney should be present for psychiatric interviews pertaining to civil commitment, it did state that an individual must be informed that his or her statements could be used in an effort to have the individual committed to a hospital, and as a result, he or she need not speak to an evaluator. Many states require that individuals be notified that they may refuse to speak to an evaluator, and statements made during a commitment evaluation may not be used against the individual in a criminal proceeding. This is important for evaluators to recognize, as it may impact what type of information or data is included in a report.

Lastly, evaluators often rely on many sources of information when conducting an evaluation related to civil commitment. In addition to an interview with the respondent, other sources of information can include police or arrest records, records related to past hospitalizations, and interviews with collateral sources such as friends and family members. Typically, if a clinician or other individual were to testify in court about information not personally observed, this would constitute hearsay and thus not be admissible. However, many jurisdictions have hearsay exceptions for civil commitment hearings so that an evaluator may testify to information that is relevant for commitment (Pinals & Mossman, 2012). Pinals and Mossman (2012) stress the importance of evaluators being aware of admissibility standards for the area in which they practice, as this will have an impact on the methods of data collection as well as the type of information gathered. For example, while Federal Rule of Evidence 703 allows for the admission of expert opinion based on data not personally observed but "reasonably relied upon" by experts in a specific field, not all states have this provision (Fed. R. Evid. 703; Pinals & Mossman, 2012). If data gathered is likely considered inadmissible in court, this will impact the utility of the evaluation and subsequent testimony.

Review of the Literature

In order to understand the process of civil commitment, it is essential that forensic evaluators be mindful of the jurisprudential basis for civil commitment. Civil commitment is not a criminal proceeding; however, it is useful to know that some aspects of the criminal justice system play a role in civil commitment laws. The foundation of civil commitment is best understood as a hybrid system that encompasses the legal contexts known as police power and parens patriae, respectively. Police power provides the jurisprudential basis of criminal law and gives authority to the state to protect the community (*Jacobson v. Massachusetts*, 1905; Melton et al., 2007; Pinals & Mossman, 2012). *Jacobson v. Massachusetts* (1905) explained that police power is justified because although freedom is a right, it does not grant citizens permission to act however they wish. There are reasonable restrictions to liberty, which are subject for monitoring and enforcement by the governing body. Essentially, police power provides the state with authority to protect the community (Melton et al., 2007), address the concept of future dangerousness, and empower the state to act in the best interest of itself.

Alternatively, civil commitment utilizes parens patriae authority for its primary justification for action (Melton et al., 2007). Parens patriae means that it is the role of the state to act in the best interest of the *individual*, not the community, as is the case when utilizing police power for public safety. This concept authorizes the state to care for those who are unable to do so for themselves, be it due to a mental disorder, grave disability, or persistent or acute disability. In the circumstances of civil commitment, it allows the state to make appropriate treatment decisions for those who are unable to do so for themselves (Janus, 1998; Melton et al., 2007; Pinals & Mossman, 2012; Moran, Robins, & Kurzban, 2000). Although the individual is restrained and deprived of liberty for what is generally thought of as the overall good of the public, the court in *Prochaska v. Brinegar* (1960) explained that it is done at the behest of the governing body for the individual's "own protection and welfare as well as for the benefit of society" (as cited in Melton et al., 2007, p. 328). Ultimately, the general basis for civil commitment legislation relies on both police power and parens patriae to protect the citizens of the country and rehabilitate those unable to care or act for themselves who have posed or may pose a potential threat to others.

Applications and Uses

The process of civil commitment, while widely varied among states, generally follows the same basic principles. According to the Moran, Robins, and Kurzban (2000), an initial petition is filed under the premise that an individual presents as an imminent danger to him- or herself or is in need of immediate treatment. The petition can be filed by any number of individuals; however, it is most likely to be filed by a hospital administrator or by hospital personnel (Erickson et al., 2005). Anyone can raise the issue or concern; however, a treating therapist, police officer, or family member would likely take the individual to a hospital for safety, rather than doing the actual filing.

Inpatient Commitment   The use of civil commitment can vary in that it is reliant on the circumstances of the situation (e.g., emergency hospitalization or extended stays of treatment). States are permitted to involuntarily hospitalize patients, but only for a brief time that has been predetermined (Testa & West, 2010, Moran, et al., 2000). Due to the progression and advancement of commitment statutes and standards through case law, patients are protected from indefinite, involuntary hospitalization (Melton et al., 2007; Testa & West, 2010; Pinals & Mossman, 2012; *O'Connor v. Donaldson*, 1975). Timeframes vary by state, but generally, patients can only be hospitalized against their will for periods ranging from two days to two weeks; however, these stays can be extended by the court (Testa & West, 2010; Moran et al., 2000). If after the predetermined length of commitment has elapsed and doctors continue to express concerns of imminent risk, a recommendation for continued involuntary commitment can be proposed (Testa & West, 2010; Moran et al., 2000; Pinals & Mossman, 2012). Patients are entitled to a court hearing with legal representation regarding the continuation of their commitment at these hearings (Testa & West, 2010). Regarding the evaluation for extended commitment, certain states may allow the current treating clinician or psychiatrist where the emergency hospitalization has occurred to conduct the evaluation; however, some states may require an independent, court-appointed evaluator to proceed. It is important to note that psychiatric providers are responsible for treating the individual using the "least restrictive alternative" method available (*Lake v. Cameron*, 1966).

Outpatient Commitment   While inpatient commitment is the predominant form of civil commitment, outpatient civil commitment has become another option in recent years as a means to satisfy the least restrictive alternative standards (Conroy & Murrie, 2007). According to Schopp (2003), outpatient civil commitment is utilized in one of three circumstances. First, an individual may be released from an inpatient psychiatric setting on a conditional basis, otherwise known as conditional release. This applies to patients who have been involuntarily committed to an inpatient facility under the state's general civil commitment statute because they have a mental illness and because they demonstrated an imminent degree of dangerousness or future risk (Schopp, 2003). Such patients are discharged from the hospital on the condition that they will comply with their treatment plan while in the community. However, failure to comply with the outpatient treatment plan can result in the return to an inpatient facility (Schopp, 2003). Second, outpatient civil commitment serves as an alternative to inpatient placement during civil commitment proceedings, but it requires strict monitoring as a least restrictive alternative to involuntary placement while the hearing is in progress (Schopp, 2003). Third, individuals who do not currently meet the criteria of mental illness and dangerousness but are soon expected to deteriorate to the point of likely meeting the involuntary commitment standards in the foreseeable future may be recommended for outpatient commitment in order to prevent more restrictive inpatient treatment (Schopp, 2003). Some states do not have provisions for outpatient commitment, and as a result, inpatient civil commitment may be the only available option for evaluators to consider.

Best Practices

Civil commitment cannot be divorced from violence risk assessment, as discussion of one necessitates the other. A thorough overview of best practices related to violence risk assessment can be found elsewhere in this book, as well as in other sources (Conroy & Murrie, 2007; Heilbrun, 2009). Additionally, best practices related specifically to the evaluation for civil commitment also exist (Pinals & Mossman, 2012). Consequently, this section will focus only briefly on the steps involved in violence risk assessment and civil commitment.

The actual process of evaluating an individual for civil commitment will often follow that which is suggested for violence risk assessment. According to Heilbrun (2009), there are broadly six steps related to violence risk assessment: 1) referral and identification of violence risk as an element; 2) selection of data sources; 3) interviews, administration of measures, and review of records; 4) interpretation of results; 5) communication of findings; and 6) a judicial finding. Given the nature of civil commitment, violence risk is naturally an element of the evaluative process. However, evaluators need to go beyond this and assess the nexus between an individual's risk for violence and his symptoms of mental illness.

The first step in an evaluation for civil commitment is for the clinician to determine whether or not a person presents with a mental illness. In doing so, Pinals and Mossman (2012) recommend that evaluators determine overt, behavioral manifestations of an illness or mental disorder. Rather than generally describing an individual as psychotic, it is more useful to be specific about that person's symptom presentation (e.g., the respondent believes that the FBI is bugging his home and inserting thoughts into his brain). This often requires at least one interview and a careful examination of a person's mental status, as well as, collateral interviews and a review of relevant mental health records. It is important to note that an evaluator can offer an opinion regarding civil commitment using other available data if a respondent declines participation or cannot participate in the evaluation; however, the opinion should be qualified (Pinals & Mossman, 2012). At the outset of the evaluation, individuals should be informed about the limits of confidentiality, the uses of information that the individual provides (i.e., involuntary hospitalization), and the possibility that the evaluator may be required to testify to such information in court (Pinals &

Mossman, 2012). At times, individuals may refuse to participate or decline to provide the appropriate releases of information to obtain protected health information. Pinals and Mossman (2012) state that a court order authorizing the evaluation and access to relevant records is sufficient for a clinician to do so and that some states have statutes providing permission to share clinical information in civil commitment evaluations. These statutes "constitute legitimate bases for releasing protected health information under HIPAA," (Pinals & Mossman, 2012, p. 185). Noting the above, it is also important for an evaluator to include only relevant information as part of the evaluation, keeping in mind a respect for an individual's privacy. Muting language or descriptions of events may be necessary at times, particularly if there is an ongoing criminal investigation or if there is information that could be potentially embarrassing to the evaluated individual. Clinicians need to balance respect for privacy with ensuring the clarity of relevant data (Pinals & Mossman, 2012).

Lastly, collateral sources should also be informed of the nature and purpose of the evaluation, as well as the limits of confidentiality as described above. Pinals and Mossman (2012) recommend being thoughtful about contacting individuals not already identified in legal documents or who are otherwise unaware of the individual's current situation. They offer two main reasons to contact collaterals in civil commitment evaluations, one being to determine the presence and significance of symptoms of mental illness and the other being to identify or verify the presence of violent or dangerous behaviors. In an effort to balance privacy with a comprehensive assessment, they recommend revealing as little as possible to any collateral source, particularly if the individual in question has not provided consent to release information. They also suggest that an evaluator consider the sources of information and reliability of those sources. For example, a family member may have motivation to distort the facts of the situation, and it is up to the evaluator to discern how reliable these informants may be in contributing relevant data.

Although psychological testing is a common tool for clinicians to use in diagnosing mental illness, Pinals and Mossman (2012) suggest that the use of such testing is irrelevant to most civil commitment decisions due to the fact that individuals presenting for civil commitment will likely demonstrate fairly significant and obvious symptoms of a mental illness. Additionally, only a few jurisdictions require a formal diagnosis from the *Diagnostic and Statistical Manual of Mental Disorders* as part of the evaluation for civil commitment (Pinals & Mossman, 2012). Most often, evaluators are only required to demonstrate how a respondent meets the statutory criteria for mental disorder, and most major *DSM-5* diagnoses (e.g., Schizophrenia) will align with these. However, Pinals and Mossman (2012) also acknowledge there are times when testing may be important with regard to clarification and differential diagnosis. That said, the use of psychological testing in civil commitment evaluations is not always considered necessary.

Currently, there are no forensic assessment instruments designed specifically for use in civil commitment, and Pinals and Mossman (2012) suggest that such instruments are unlikely to be created in the future for a variety of reasons. For example, the main tasks in civil commitment decisions involve diagnosis and choosing an appropriate setting for treatment. These are issues that involve the use of standard clinical skills most psychologists and psychiatrists should possess; additionally, commitment standards vary by jurisdiction, and it would be impossible to design an instrument that incorporates the myriad nuances of these standards. However, given that civil commitment decisions typically involve an assessment of risk, structured professional judgment instruments used in the area of violence risk assessment may prove useful. To this end, it is important for the evaluator to be familiar with these tools as well as their utility and limitations (see Heilbrun, 2009; Pinals & Mossman, 2012). Different groups of individuals will demonstrate different base rates of violence, and different risk assessment tools have been normed on specific populations. The Classification of Violence Risk (COVR) was designed specifically for the assessment of violence in individuals who had been psychiatrically hospitalized and discharged to the community, and the COVR has demonstrated very good predictive validity (Monahan, Steadman, Appelbaum, Grisso, Mulvey, Roth, Robbins, Banks, & Silver, 2006). The HCR-20 (Historic, Clinical, Risk Management) is another tool that was initially developed and validated with a civilly committed population and has similarly demonstrated strong predictive validity (Douglas & Skeem, 2005). It is important to consider the group to which the individual being assessed belongs (e.g., mentally ill, sex offender, civil). There may be times in which a risk assessment tool does not exist for the individual being evaluated, as there tends to be a considerable lack of risk assessment tools that are appropriate for individuals from diverse backgrounds. Additionally, no tools measure other aspects of civil commitment, such as suicide risk specifically or a very substantial or grave likelihood of harm to self due to mental illness (Pinals & Mossman, 2012). Lastly, courts tend to be more accepting of idiographic, as opposed to nomothetic, data (Conroy & Murrie, 2007). In this sense, an anamnestic approach may prove to be a useful adjunct or complement to structured professional judgment or actuarial violence risk tools (Heilbrun, 2009). This approach involves gathering very specific and detailed information regarding past episodes of violence in an effort to identify patterns or themes in an individual's violence history.

Once the predicate mental illness or disorder has been established (or ruled out), the evaluator must consider whether those existing symptoms cause gross impairment. If such is the case, it must be decided in what areas related to the statute (e.g., thought, behavior, judgment) are relevant and which specific behavioral manifestations of that impairment should be sought and described. As previously noted, it is not enough that a person presents with a mental illness and demonstrates aggressive or potentially violent behavior; the evaluator is tasked with demonstrating the nexus between the individual's symptoms of mental illness and precisely how those symptoms impact a person's behavior (i.e., may be contributory to violent behavior). Pinals and Mossman (2012) outline best practices regarding the above and suggest that an evaluator ask the following questions: a) How do I know that the respondent has a substantial mental disorder? b) Does that disorder cause gross impairment? c) How do I know that the respondent poses a risk to self or others due to that mental disorder? These questions are best illustrated by way of case example and will be elucidated later in the chapter.

One factor in violence risk assessment and civil commitment that tends to receive minimal attention in practice is that of base rates related to violence. Broadly speaking, base rates for violence tend to vary considerably, depending on the community, population, and type of violence (Conroy & Murrie, 2007), and it has been suggested that clinicians tend to overestimate risk and thus overcommit individuals (Monahan, 1981, 1992; Eccleston & Ward, 2004). Anecdotally, it seems that base rates tend to be referred to more often in sex offender evaluations, given that the actuarial assessment tools designed to assess risk for recidivism provide results in terms of such. However, it seems that the use of base rates and, in particular, local base rate data may useful for a violence risk assessment as courts may be more accepting of local statistics (Conroy & Murrie, 2007). Conroy and Murrie describe local base rate data as "data from a specific, narrowly defined population, such as the population from one large facility, statewide system, or other circumscribed population" (p. 60). Clinicians should consider seeking out this information if possible, although it may not always be easy to find, and evaluators may question which statistics may be most relevant and reliable.

Lastly, clinicians are required to offer an opinion regarding the most appropriate setting for an individual's treatment. There is a growing body of research that focuses on dynamic risk factors in the assessment process (Douglas & Skeem, 2005). Both protective and dynamic risk factors as they relate to an individual's risk for violence are far less researched than are historical or static factors. It is important to note that the focus of a risk assessment should include not violence alone but situations and behaviors that did not result in violence (Heilbrun, 2009). Pinals and Mossman suggest that an evaluator ask whether the option for voluntary inpatient treatment had been explored, whether outpatient treatment would work and, if outpatient treatment had previously been attempted, delineate why or why not it did not work. It is important here to emphasize the question of timeframe as an aspect of violence risk assessment. While not all jurisdictions require imminence as part of their civil commitment criteria, the question of when a particular danger may occur is important to consider in recommending treatment placement. A particular treatment or placement may have "worked" briefly; however, a person's condition may have decompensated via a series of events or exposure to destabilizers posttreatment. An evaluator must consider a person's historical response to treatment in addition to his or her current mental state and amenability or willingness to engage in less restrictive alternatives.

Not only is it important for the evaluator to describe the nexus between symptoms of a mental disorder and violence risk in civil commitment evaluations but it is also similarly important to describe a lack of this connection where there is none. Much forensic literature cautions against an evaluator giving an opinion on the ultimate legal question (Tillbrook, Mumley, & Grisso, 2003) as this decision is up to the court. This is somewhat different from other forensic questions in that the basis for civil commitment is the presence of mental illness and need for hospitalization for care and treatment, which are decidedly clinical issues (Pinals & Mossman, 2012). Due to the fact that the state is involved in restricting an individual's liberty, the ultimate legal decision falls with the trier of fact, and there is a lack of consensus among clinicians about providing the ultimate opinion (Pinals & Mossman, 2012). Pinals and Mossman (2012) suggest it may be appropriate for evaluators to provide something of a penultimate opinion, whereby symptoms are described and statutory language is used. For example, an evaluator could describe how delusions and hallucinations represent a significant "mental disorder" and how individuals' suicide attempts place them at a "substantial risk for harm to themselves" as outlined by the jurisdictions statute.

Case Vignette

Mr. Anderson was a 32-year-old Caucasian man, who was court ordered to undergo an evaluation of his fitness to stand trial and his need for treatment in an inpatient hospital setting. At the time of the evaluation, Mr. Anderson was facing a charge of assault and battery. This evaluator had opined that Mr. Anderson was fit to stand trial, and thus the question of whether or not he met criteria for involuntary hospitalization was separate from that particular legal question.

Reason for Referral

This case was part of a court-ordered evaluation following an arrest on a charge of assault and battery. It was alleged that Mr. Anderson punched his roommate in the head during the course of an argument, rendering him unconscious. This was his first admission to a state hospital. At the beginning of his evaluation, Mr. Anderson was informed of the limits to confidentiality that would relate to statements he made. He acknowledged that he understood that any

---

The case vignette has been redacted and all identifying information removed. It is not meant to serve as a forensic report. Any likeness to a case is purely coincidental.

information he provided could be included in a written report and/or oral testimony provided to the court and that he had the right to choose not to participate in the evaluation, to answer questions selectively, and/or to stop the interviews at any time. He was able to repeat this information in his own words and agreed to participate.

According to the statute under which this evaluation was conducted, a person may not be committed to a mental health facility unless it is shown by clear and convincing evidence that the individual has a mental illness, that failure to hospitalize the individual would create a reasonable expectation of physical harm to that person or others because of the *mental illness* (emphasis added), and that there is not a less restrictive treatment alternative to hospitalization by which the individual may receive care. Additionally, in this particular jurisdiction, an individual with a dual diagnosis (including alcohol or drug abuse) may only be committed if the likelihood of serious harm results from the respondent's mental illness (which is not to include a substance abuse disorder, as outlined via statute). All of these aspects were considered during the course of this evaluation.

Summary of Relevant Records

For this evaluation, the police report related to the index offense, and records from four past hospitalizations and rehabilitation centers were reviewed. Additionally, relevant progress notes related to his behavior and progress while hospitalized were reviewed.

Although records from three other hospitals were requested, they were not received prior to the statutorily designated end of the evaluation period. The evaluator also requested an interview with the alleged victim in this case; however, Mr. Anderson stated he did not want this interview to take place. Given this evaluation was court ordered, contacting the victim despite Mr. Anderson's request to not speak with him was considered; however, legal counsel advised the alleged victim that it would be best to refrain from participating in the interview since the case was an ongoing potential criminal investigation. Contact with the police officers who were noted in the official police report as present at the scene was also attempted; however, they were not available prior to the end of the evaluation period. Although Mr. Anderson was asked to participate in psychological testing, he declined to so.

Records from a rehabilitation facility indicated that Mr. Anderson experienced problems in school while growing up. Specifically, he was described as "a class clown" who was often sent to the principal's office during grammar and middle school. These records also stated that Mr. Anderson "always did poorly in school," which was later attributed to a diagnosis of Attention Deficit Hyperactivity Disorder (ADHD).[1]

Mr. Anderson attended his first drug treatment program at the behest of his parents. Records from this program indicated that Mr. Anderson was admitted when 22 years of age. His treatment areas included lack of understanding of the disease model of chemical dependency, low self-esteem, difficulty trusting others, anger, and relapse prevention. These records indicated that Mr. Anderson struggled with compliance of unit expectations and impulsive behaviors. A little more than a week after his admission, he was discharged for various rule violations

While at this drug treatment program, Mr. Anderson participated in psychological testing, which included intellectual, achievement, and personality testing. He was found to be in the above-average range on intelligence testing, and he obtained scores that were within normal limits on achievement testing for reading and spelling. Testing indicated depressive symptoms, including suicidal ideation without intent. Results also suggested he might have exaggerated symptoms, perhaps as a "cry for help." It was reported that Mr. Anderson responded to the test in a manner similar to that of individuals who experience psychotic symptoms, including visual hallucinations and delusions, as well as, a degree of social alienation and isolation. He appeared to be an individual who was interpersonally suspicious, hostile toward others, and paranoid. Mr. Anderson was also described as having a high degree of anxiety and did not appreciate situations involving rules and authority figures.

Mr. Anderson was subsequently admitted to various rehabilitation facilities between the ages of 24 and 26 years. Records indicated that he was typically voluntarily admitted at the urging of his parents due to suspected drug and alcohol abuse. The psychologist reported that he appeared to demonstrate symptoms consistent with ADHD, including impulsivity. Additionally, Mr. Anderson displayed suicidal and paranoid ideation. He expressed beliefs that there was a conspiracy against him and that there were cameras in his room and he was being watched. He was transferred to a dual-diagnosis (for mental illness and substance abuse) program for thirty days, where he was diagnosed with Bipolar I Disorder, Most Recent Episode Mixed.[2]

He reportedly responded well to a medication regimen and no longer presented with paranoid delusions. He reported feelings of anxiety and mood swings, and his affect was observed to be expansive and irritable. It was reported that Mr. Anderson participated minimally in the treatment. He avoided being around other patients in social situations. He was discharged after thirty days of treatment, though it was noted that his motivation to participate in treatment was unclear and that his insight into his addiction was minimal.

Mr. Anderson was first admitted to a psychiatric hospital voluntarily when he was 25 years of age. He was residing at home with his parents and sister at the time. Mr. Anderson believed that people were inserting thoughts into his brain and controlling his brain. The discharge summary from the hospital indicated that he had recently experienced thoughts that someone would kill him just prior to admission. It was noted that Mr. Anderson improved rapidly with medication and that his delusional thoughts ceased as a result. There was no toxicology report available from this hospitalization, although Mr. Anderson reported upon admission that he had last used cocaine and alcohol three to five months prior to admission. He was diagnosed with Psychotic Disorder, Not Otherwise Specified,[3] Cocaine Dependence,[4] and Alcohol Dependence.[5]

He was subsequently admitted to a twelve-step residential program. Records described him as withdrawn and suspicious of others. Psychological testing indicated that Mr. Anderson presented with evidence of a psychotic disorder and depressive symptoms, and he was considered at risk for suicide. He reported past experiences of auditory hallucinations and periodic paranoid delusions including the belief that people were following him, including members of the federal government. Mr. Anderson's father reported he received a phone call from staff stating that his son had stolen items from other residents in the program. He was discharged after he displayed aggression, striking a peer after an argument over theft.

Mr. Anderson's second psychiatric hospitalization followed his discharge from rehabilitation, where he reportedly struck a peer in the face during group, in the midst of an argument over seating. It was reported that Mr. Anderson minimized the significance of the event and reportedly justified his behavior stating that the individual had taken his usual seat during group. Mr. Anderson was subsequently transferred to a dual-diagnosis program after one week. He displayed an increase in irritability, reported auditory hallucinations, and anxiety symptoms. He was transferred to a more acute unit where he was reported to be threatening and agitated, and he required restraint and seclusion to prevent harm to himself and others. He was discharged to a transitional living program three weeks later, with a follow-up appointment at an intensive outpatient program. He received a diagnosis of Schizoaffective Disorder.[6]

During his initial two weeks at the transitional living program, Mr. Anderson was described as compliant with the program. His compliance deteriorated after being informed that he was no longer able to return home upon completion of the program, due to the fact that his parents were conducting home renovations at the time. At that point, Mr. Anderson began refusing groups, chose to stay in bed, and refused medications at times, stating that he wanted to return home to his parents' house. Mr. Anderson reported that he felt hopeless, reported that he was hearing derogatory voices, and reported a belief that others could read his thoughts. He improved with medication adjustments and upon learning that his father might be preparing a space for him at home, Mr. Anderson displayed increased participation at meetings and showed improvement with anger management, problem solving, interpersonal skills, and coping skills, among other things. Mr. Anderson was discharged to a residential community program.

According to the police report, Mr. Anderson reportedly yelled, "He [his roommate] accused me of stealing from him and threatened to hit me, so I was forced to protect myself!" Mr. Anderson relayed that his roommate "barged" into their room and demanded that Mr. Anderson give the roommate his ATM card back. Mr. Anderson stated that he thought his roommate was going to hit him, and Mr. Anderson allegedly hit his roommate over the side of the head. Mr. Anderson allegedly told police that his roommate was at fault. The two employees on the scene offered their account to the officers. The employees both reported that they were in living room when they heard "yelling over money," and that when the employees walked into the dorm room, they saw Mr. Anderson's roommate on the floor. The employees stated the roommate was unconscious at the time. The employees stated that the two roommates argued often over money, missing items from their respective rooms, and expectations for living together.

The officer interviewed Mr. Anderson's roommate who was transported to the hospital. He stated that he went into the community room where Mr. Anderson was playing loud music and he asked him to turn it down. Evidently this had been an ongoing violation from which Mr. Anderson was continually requested to refrain. The roommate stated that Mr. Anderson said he did not care, and Mr. Anderson continued to turn the music up louder. A few minutes later the alleged victim noticed that his ATM card was missing, and went to confront Mr. Anderson. Mr. Anderson reportedly said, "You owe me money anyway," and punched him in the face. Mr. Anderson reportedly noted that he felt there was hostility brewing between him and the alleged victim for some time prior to the incident. He reported that he had asked staff to intervene on his behalf so that his roommate would "stop complaining" and "back off" of him.

Relevant Background Information

The following history was obtained from an interview with Mr. Anderson on three different days for a total of approximately five-and-a-half hours, as well as multiple phone interviews with his father for a total of approximately three hours. Mr. Anderson did not appear to be a reliable reporter, as he was often vague and inconsistent with other sources. While his father was considered a generally reliable historian, there was some information he provided that was inconsistent with other sources, and he seemed vague when questioned about particular details of his son's history and upbringing. The forensic evaluator also interviewed Mr. Anderson's psychiatrist at the time of his arrest, as well as his social worker. Although the evaluator attempted to interview his step-mother, she declined to be interviewed. Mr. Anderson's treatment team at the state hospital was also engaged in a clinical consultation.

Mr. Anderson was born and raised in a relatively small town as the oldest child of three. Mr. Anderson was raised by his biological father and stepmother, as his mother passed away when he was 4 years of age, and his father remarried when he was 6 years of age. Mr. Anderson's father described his son as "a great kid" growing up. The father reported that his son was pleasant and often helped around the house. Mr. Anderson's father reported no problems with developmental milestones, childhood illnesses, or childhood injury. Mr. Anderson reportedly grew up in an upper middle class neighborhood with highly educated parents.

Mr. Anderson's father reported that his son attended private schools and obtained mostly Bs and Cs throughout his education. Mr. Anderson's father denied that his son was ever held back a grade, although the father reported that his son had to attend at least one semester of summer school for unknown reasons. Mr. Anderson's father reported that his son was diagnosed with ADHD and prescribed Adderall at 10 years of age, stating that his son's behavior was impulsive and that his son was "getting in trouble" at school.

Mr. Anderson graduated high school and attended one year of college at a university out of state. Although he reportedly did well, he became drug involved while at school and eventually dropped out. Mr. Anderson also had a lengthy history of multiple inpatient rehabilitation stays, dual-diagnosis programs, residential/transitional living programs, and psychiatric hospitalizations. Mr. Anderson's father indicated that they had tried a variety of different treatment programs and that his son displayed difficulty understanding that he needed treatment. While he always complied with his parents' directives to participate in treatment programs, Mr. Anderson's father reported that his son consistently expressed a desire to remain at home with his parents. Since college, Mr. Anderson had reportedly lived at home for brief (two-to-three-month) periods of time without incident. Mr. Anderson's father stated that he sent his son to various treatment settings because his parents could not properly monitor him at home as a result of their jobs and had concerns about the possibility of his using drugs in the home. Mr. Anderson denied use of or access to drugs while residing with his parents. Mr. Anderson's father stated that he called the police on one occasion, due to his son "complaining of his old college roommate monitoring his thoughts." His father thought this was drug related, which is why he contacted the police at the time.

Mr. Anderson's father reported that they placed his son in residential treatment when he was 26 years of age. Mr. Anderson's case manager reported that Mr. Anderson was viewed as not appropriate for that particular program due to "bullying" behaviors, such as "intimidating" other residents to give him money, pilfering items from others, and striking another resident in the face after an argument. Mr. Anderson was then transferred to another independent living program, which is where he resided at the time of his arrest.

Mr. Anderson's case manager reported that Mr. Anderson displayed highly impulsive behavior related to peer interactions (such as picking up someone and holding him over his head). His psychiatrist described Mr. Anderson as rigid and as having low empathy. Mr. Anderson reportedly had difficulty adjusting his plans, such that he continued to hold onto the idea that he could simply return to live with his parents, despite lacking insight into drug addiction and independent living skills.

Mr. Anderson was vague about his overall drug use. He reported that he did not remember the first time he tried drinking alcohol but stated that he began using both cocaine and marijuana around the age of 18. He reported that he used to smoke approximately three to four "blunts" per day, for approximately four years. He stated that he typically used cocaine anywhere from once a month to once a week. Mr. Anderson initially denied that his drug use ever negatively interfered with his school performance or other aspects of his life. He later acknowledged that it had negatively impacted his school performance; however, he felt that it was worth it because it was "fun." He reported that he would "binge" on cocaine for days at a time. Mr. Anderson reported withdrawal symptoms from cocaine use including "a severe depression" where he withdrew from others and felt he could not get out of bed. He also stated he abused his Adderall while in high school, but he denied other drug use. He reported that cocaine is his drug of choice and that he typically used money received from his parents or money stolen from others to buy drugs. Mr. Anderson reported that his longest period of sobriety was for approximately one year while he was in a locked unit facility, two years prior to the evaluation. He also reported that he typically refrained from drug use while living with his parents. When asked about this, he stated, "They would kick me out if I used at home and I got it good there." Available records indicated that Mr. Anderson had consistently received diagnoses of both Cocaine Dependence and Alcohol Dependence. According to staff at his residential program at the time of his arrest, Mr. Anderson's last relapse with the use of cocaine was approximately two months prior to the alleged incident.

With regard to relationships, Mr. Anderson reported several short-term relationships that he described as insignificant. Mr. Anderson had no significant work history. He reportedly obtained a few low level positions, but he was fired either due to substance abuse or chronic absenteeism. Mr. Anderson reported that he would like to own a restaurant, although recognized that he had no experience in this area.

With regard to symptoms of mental illness, Mr. Anderson described feeling that people were following him and that he was being watched. He reported feelings of paranoia, including beliefs that people could read his mind. He also reported hearing voices in the past, which say disparaging things to him. Mr. Anderson reported that he initially heard voices the first time he used cocaine, although stated that he also heard them when he is not under the influence of drugs. Mr. Anderson stated that he first heard voices in the absence of drug use when he was approximately 20 years of age. He indicated the last time he experienced auditory hallucinations was approximately one month prior to the evaluation. He described the voices as "off and on" and not constant. He denied the use of any coping skills that helped alleviate the voices when they occurred and stated that they tend to dissipate on their own.

Mr. Anderson reported no history of suicide attempts, although he reported transient suicidal thoughts in the past. Mr. Anderson said he first thought about killing himself his sophomore year of college. He reported feeling as though his family did not love him, and he was dwelling on negative thoughts related to feeling as though he had no friends or girlfriends. He denied a concrete pattern of occurrences, stating that these episodes typically occurred upon withdrawals from cocaine, and he stated he had not felt suicidal in approximately five years.

Aside from the index offense, Mr. Anderson had no prior legal history, and he had never been arrested. However, according to records from previous facilities, Mr. Anderson had reportedly engaged in a number of illegal activities throughout his life. When asked for clarification, his father stated that Mr. Anderson used to steal "insignificant" items from family members, like small amounts of money from his parents. He also reportedly got into trouble at school for stealing from classmates and for fighting, although these behaviors were never brought to the attention of greater authorities. He was detained by police on one occasion for possession of drugs (cocaine) while in college; however, he was reportedly released and charges were never filed.

Just prior to his arrest, Mr. Anderson was residing at an assisted living program in his own apartment. He had lived there for approximately six months before the alleged incident occurred. It appeared as though Mr. Anderson continued to display problems with independent living skills, in that his living quarters were reportedly unkempt; however, he was otherwise described as doing well. He was prescribed an antipsychotic medication, and he was reportedly medication compliant. According to his treatment team, Mr. Anderson had not displayed symptoms of mania or psychosis, and he had been abstinent from drugs or alcohol for approximately two months. Mr. Anderson similarly denied any drug or alcohol use.

Mr. Anderson's father reported that he and his wife hoped to have Mr. Anderson discharged to their home following the evaluation period. He stated that they had recently retired from their jobs and, as a result, felt they could provide the care and monitoring their son required. They set up an appointment with a psychiatrist in the community, who had previously treated Mr. Anderson, and scheduled an intake appointment for a day treatment program, which Mr. Anderson agreed to attend. Mr. Anderson reported a willingness to follow his parent's advice (e.g., meet regularly with the psychiatrist, refrain from substance use), and he stated that he preferred to live at home rather than with other people who were "strangers" to him and whom he did not trust. He reported that he liked the idea of a day treatment program because he could return home to his parents' house when the day was over.

Mental Status Examination

Mr. Anderson was a biracial (African American and Caucasian) man who appeared his stated age. He was oriented as to the date, time, place, and situation. Mr. Anderson demonstrated various restless and purposeless actions (psychomotor agitation), as he often fidgeted in his chair and leaned his chair back from the table causing it to become imbalanced. He appeared to have a nonchalant, light-hearted approach to the interview; laughing often in response to serious topics. He was generally cooperative with questions although appeared guarded and somewhat evasive with regard to his history.

His affect was both affable and irritable at times and not appropriate to the situation. He initially reported that his mood was "happy" but then later stated that he was "depressed." He had a smile on his face for most of the interview, regardless of topic. He casually called this evaluator by her first name on several occasions during the interview and did not always answer questions seriously. At times, Mr. Anderson would answer questions in French or provide an answer meant as a joke. For example, when asked what type of job he would want if he could have any job in the world, Mr. Anderson answered, "The President of Russia." While his observable mood was one that did not match his circumstance or situation, he commented on a few occasions that he did not want to be in jail and believed the situation was "terrible." Mr. Anderson displayed a lack of awareness around social cues, both direct and nonverbal. For example, when again commenting on his apparent lack of seriousness related to his hospitalization and arrest, Mr. Anderson reported that this evaluator had no sense of humor. He was able to self-redirect his attention back to the evaluation after a brief period of time.

He displayed behavior that appeared intrusive for the setting. For example, when discussing his past substance abuse, he asked this evaluator about past personal drug use. He endorsed feelings of confusion at times and reported that the past few years have "been a big blur" due to the fact that he has been "in and out of rehabs." His speech was pressured at times, and, at other times, Mr. Anderson provided brief, one-or few-word answers without much elaboration, often stating, "I don't know." He denied problems with sleeping or eating, although hospital observations indicated that he slept a few hours per night. Mr. Anderson stated that he was not currently suicidal. He also stated that he was not having homicidal thoughts or thoughts of hurting other people.

He endorsed current feelings of paranoia, discussed feeling as though people could read his mind, and said that he felt threatened. When asked what made him feel threatened, he stated it was a feeling he had. He denied that he would respond aggressively when feeling threatened due to a desire to be discharged. He denied current auditory hallucinations or other perceptual disturbances. He reported feelings of anxiety around people or crowds of people at times. His insight was poor. He denied being diagnosed with a mental illness. He displayed poor judgment throughout the interview, as evidenced by his asking the evaluator intrusive questions and consistently asking a corrections officer outside of the interview room to "join in the conversation."

Mr. Anderson was able to sustain attention on topics through lengthy interviews. He presented with average skills for abstraction (could appropriate provide meanings for common proverbs, and apply it to a real-life situation) and orientation/memory (could correctly state the past four presidents, was able to retain aspects of the limits of confidentiality warning between interviews without prompting), and he was able to provide socially appropriate answers to common dilemmas. Mr. Anderson was asked whether he was experiencing any psychiatric symptoms at the time of his arrest, such as those he had reported experiencing in the past (auditory hallucinations, feelings of paranoia). He reported hearing voices occasionally (once to twice a month) and thoughts of people reading his mind. He denied that he thought his roommate could read his mind and stated, "It's irrelevant, and a waste of my time."

Mr. Anderson was admitted to the state hospital following his arrest. He agreed to take medication upon admission. Mr. Anderson was described as alert, calm, and cooperative. His affect was noted to be appropriate, and his thought processes appeared clear and logical, although he was reported to lack insight into his mental illness and demonstrated problems following staff direction while in the hospital.

Mr. Anderson was transferred to a more restrictive unit one time during his period of evaluation, after reportedly pushing another patient. However, he also reportedly engaged in other types of negative behavior, such as taking other patients' food and leaving groups without authorization. When asked about these situations by the evaluator, Mr. Anderson reported that he pushed the other patient because the patient "cut" him in line. While he could state that pushing the other patient was "wrong," he could not provide reasons for why taking food from a patient or leaving a group abruptly would be considered problematic. He justified his decision to push the patient by stating, "He had no manners and it was disrespectful to me." He was transferred back to the less restrictive evaluation unit the following day. Mr. Anderson was prescribed Haldol (antipsychotic). He was compliant with his medication while hospitalized.

Psychological Testing/Measures Used

Mr. Anderson was asked to participate in psychological testing, but he declined. An objective measure of personality assessment would have been helpful in gaining diagnostic clarification regarding his symptoms; however, in situations such as this, data are not always available. Given that personality testing was not completed, a reliance on self-report, collateral interviews with his father, treatment records, and behavioral and clinical observations were necessary. Despite the lack of personality testing for diagnostic clarification, violence risk measures can often be completed without the evaluee's participation, as they are based on historical and dynamic factors such as those found in the evaluee's records and interview responses. The results of these measures can greatly contribute to a decision regarding the participant's future dangerousness.

For this case, the Historical, Clinical, Risk-20 (HCR-20), and the Psychopathy Checklist-Screening Version (PCL-SV) were selected (Webster, Douglas, Eaves, & Hart, 1997; Hart, Cox, & Hare, 2003). These instruments were chosen given his history of violent behavior and the referral issue, as well as for these instruments' utility with psychiatric inpatient, civil, and community populations. Additionally, past studies indicated that the HCR-20 added incremental validity to the PCL-SV when predicting risk for violence in an inpatient psychiatric population (Douglas, Ogloff, Nicholls, & Grant, 1999), although later studies have suggested that the HCR-20 used independently of the PCL-R is uniquely predictive of violence (Guy, Douglas, Hendry, 2010). The PCL-SV can be used in forensic settings to screen for psychopathic traits or for diagnosis of individuals undergoing civil psychiatric evaluations (Hart, Cox, & Hare, 2003). Given the limited evaluation period based on state statute, the instruments chosen needed to be fairly brief but still able to provide a structured method to assess risk factors related to violence. The PCL-SV was used to assess for traits of psychopathy, given that Mr. Anderson appeared to present with numerous antisocial characteristics, including low empathy and impulsivity.

Results from the HCR-20 indicated that Mr. Anderson presented with a number of historical and clinical risk factors for violence. Definite historical factors included a history of previous violence (including the index offense), relationship instability (which included a lack of significant intimate relationships with others), employment problems (no history of stable employment), substance use problems, previous diagnosis of a major mental illness (Bipolar Disorder, Psychosis NOS), the presence of traits of Psychopathy (score of 19 on the PCL-SV), and prior supervision failure (eloping from previous treatment facility). Another historical factor included the possible presence of a personality disorder; however, there did not appear to be substantive evidence to reach a conclusion. Given Mr. Anderson's history, it was suspected that there might have been more indicators of early maladjustment; however, the information given by his father indicated only possible or less serious indicators, such as some behavioral problems in school. His first reported act of violence based on the available information occurred when he was between the ages of 20 and 39 years, and therefore the item, "Young Age at First Violent Incident," was given a score of 1.

Definite clinical factors that were present included a lack of insight into his mental disorder, the impact and consequences of his symptoms, negative attitudes, and affective impulsivity/instability. Possible clinical issues present included potential unresponsiveness to treatment (he was accepting prescribed medication in the hospital; however, he appeared to demonstrate low motivation with regard to attending groups, etc.) and active symptoms of mental illness (he was demonstrating some symptoms, such as a belief that others could read his mind; however, they appeared mild at the time of the evaluation). Finally, with regard to risk management, Mr. Anderson presented with considerable personal support (his parents) and little likelihood of exposure to stress (some), but not a strong likelihood of exposure to destabilizers (drugs or alcohol). His plan for discharge while residing in the community appeared feasible, given that his parents were able and willing to accept him into their home and had the time and resources available to monitor him. The final risk rating based on this information was moderate.

To screen for traits related to psychopathy, the PCL-SV was used. Mr. Anderson was given a total score of 19 (a score of 18 is indicative of "definite" psychopathy according to the PCL-SV manual). Most salient to his case were lack of remorse, lack of empathy, not accepting responsibility for his behaviors, impulsivity, poor behavioral controls, lack of realistic goals, and irresponsibility. His adolescent antisocial behavior was questionable in that the details around this topic were unclear, and he demonstrated some (but not definite) problems related to superficiality, grandiosity, and deceitfulness.

Clinical Summary and Opinion

Based on available data, it was opined that Mr. Anderson had a mental illness as defined in relevant regulations of the Department of Mental Health in the jurisdiction where the evaluation took place. While in the acute phase of this disorder, Mr. Anderson experienced paranoid ideation (believing others can read his thoughts, that someone might kill him, or that people follow him), auditory hallucinations, thought insertion (believing that people were inserting thoughts into his brain), difficulty with reality testing, and agitation. Mr. Anderson had experienced these symptoms for many years, including those times in which he was not abusing substances. Mr. Anderson had also experienced mood-related symptoms including hopelessness, irritability, decreased energy, and lack of interest in activities, and he was overly expressive and energetic at times. Additionally, Mr. Anderson had a lengthy history of substance abuse and dependence problems, and these continued to be ongoing problems for him. His substance abuse and symptoms of psychosis, coupled with frequent rehabilitation admissions and hospitalizations, interfered with his ability to successfully complete college or to hold sustained, meaningful employment. He had endorsed feelings of hopelessness and melancholy, in addition to feelings of anxiety, although these symptoms did not appear to significantly impact his presentation or behavior at the time of the evaluation. Mr. Anderson's symptom presentation seemed to be best categorized as Schizoaffective Disorder, Depressive Type.

In addition, Mr. Anderson presented with attributes that were not clear diagnostically. He seemed unaffected by his situation, despite the fact that he was facing serious legal charges and could have served time if convicted and incarcerated. He displayed difficulty understanding why others may have been concerned about his behaviors (aggression toward others, potentially hurting others) and described what would usually be considered troubling symptoms, thoughts, and situations with an observable appearance that appeared flip and unconcerned. He displayed a casual attitude toward the overall evaluation, and he appeared unresponsive to social cues and frank discussions regarding the serious nature of his situation. He displayed impulsive behavior related to institutional protocols while at the state hospital and within peer relationships, as well as evidence of misinterpreting social cues in social situations. It was not clear to the evaluator at the time whether these aspects of Mr. Anderson's presentation were the result of symptoms of a mental illness or simply poor judgment and impulsivity, which could have been characterological in nature or of some other unknown etiology. Mr. Anderson had a long-standing history of impulsivity, problems following staff and program directives, provoking other patients, and being aggressive toward other patients at various programs. Based on a review of his past aggressive behaviors and presentation while hospitalized, there was no evidence that his suspiciousness, mood issues, delusions that others could read his mind, or auditory hallucinations were a risk for violence for him specifically. Rather, due to the long-standing nature of these issues, it appeared more likely that these behaviors were attributable to personality issues, rather than his symptoms of mental illness, although they could have been exacerbated by such symptoms.

How was the opinion reached? Given that Mr. Anderson had never displayed aggression or violent behavior toward his family and, in fact, demonstrated evidence of more controlled and less impulsive behavior while at least in the presence of his father, there were indications that this plan for discharge was adequate should the court decide to allow him to await trial in the community. His parents were both willing and seemingly capable of providing him with a supportive environment, and with appropriate supervision, given that his father and stepmother were retired at the time of the evaluation and able to provide increased supervision (something that was absent when he previously resided at home). Mr. Anderson indicated a desire to reside at home with his parents, and he did not have a history of substance use while residing with them. He demonstrated a history of cooperating with treatment directives suggested by his parents should the need arise or should his circumstances change, and he indicated an increased risk for violence due to mental illness. His parents had also previously demonstrated a willingness and ability to seek out more restrictive services if needed or seen as necessary.

Best practices suggest that evaluators must take into account not only static risk factors but also current presentation and risk management factors, when forming opinions related to violence risk assessment and civil commitment (Heilbrun, 2009). Additionally, an evaluator must be familiar with the statutory language under which he or she is working, as civil commitment laws vary in their wording related to definitions of mental illness, their impact on dangerousness and the imminence of potential violent behavior. This case highlights the importance of mitigating factors related to violence risk in relation to a risk management plan, keeping in mind the guideline of a least restrictive environment.

Common Pitfalls and Considerations

This case was complex for a variety of reasons. First, this individual presented with a long history of drug abuse, and thus issues related to dual diagnosis needed to be considered. According to the state statute under which this evaluation was conducted, a mental illness was defined as a substantial disorder of mood, thought, and perception that grossly impairs his behavior, judgment, ability to recognize reality, or ability to meet the ordinary demands of life. The statutes also explicitly excluded alcoholism or substance abuse, and thus drug or alcohol abuse problems, while important to consider, would not necessarily be classified as a mental illness according to this definition. Second, Mr. Anderson presented with a history of significant symptoms of mental illness, seemingly while not under the influence of drugs. Third, Mr. Anderson presented with some significant personality or characterological issues that appeared to impact the clinical picture. As a result, it was difficult to tease apart which symptoms or problems were impacting his risk for violence— drug use, symptoms of mental illness, a possible personality disorder, or the confluence of all of the above.

While the aforementioned provisions were thought to be crucial to Mr. Anderson's ongoing treatment, there were continued concerns regarding his mental health and substance abusing behaviors. The evaluator struggled with these issues in considering how they could impact his future risk for violent behavior. Mr. Anderson exhibited minimal insight into his mental illness, impulsive behavior, poor judgment, or related consequences. He had last used illicit substances approximately five weeks prior to the alleged offense, and he admittedly used alcohol (albeit in minimal amounts) while residing in the community. Mr. Anderson was generally compliant with medication while residing in the community, although had demonstrated periods of decompensation. He endorsed auditory hallucinations associated with his medication noncompliance in the past. Aside from the index offense, Mr. Anderson had reportedly not displayed any violent or aggressive behavior while residing in the community. Mr. Anderson's impulsivity with regard to substance abuse coupled with his existing symptoms of mental illness created an increased risk for aggressive and violent behavior. Mr. Anderson had a history of failed placements in rehabilitation centers and with other psychiatric residential placements. He left one program and returned home to his parents' house without staff permission. He displayed difficulty following staff directives, and he has demonstrated aggressive behavior toward other patients, both of which resulted in his discharge from certain placements. Further, Mr. Anderson had displayed a history of psychiatric decompensation within less structured settings requiring transfers to places that are better equipped to deal with more acute symptoms of mental illness.

In evaluations for civil commitment, a common pitfall occurs when evaluators view a person who presents with mental illness and risk factors for violence as meeting criteria for involuntary hospitalization, when the two may be unrelated to one another. In this example, while Mr. Anderson presented with a mental illness as defined by relevant regulations, he did not appear to meet criteria for involuntary hospitalization at the time of the evaluation, as his risk for violence appeared unrelated to his symptoms. The guiding statute under which this evaluation took place indicated that an individual is reasonably expected, because of his mental illness and unless treated on an inpatient basis, to engage in conduct placing such person or another in physical harm or in reasonable expectation of being physically harmed (405 ILCS 5/1–119). It was opined that Mr. Anderson was reasonably expected to engage in conduct placing other persons or possibly himself at risk of physical harm; however, this risk appeared attributable to Mr. Anderson's aforementioned immaturity, impulsivity, poor judgment, and propensity for substance abuse rather than his symptoms of mental illness. In essence, while Mr. Anderson presented with a mental illness and with risk factors related to possible violence, it appeared that his risk for violence was unrelated to his mental illness, and as a result, he did not meet criteria for involuntary hospitalization. This is not to say that he may not have met criteria in other jurisdictions, depending on the wording of the statutes, or that he might not have met criteria if he were more symptomatic at the time of the evaluation.

At times, recommendations against involuntary hospitalization may not carry the risk for violence. It is up to the evaluator to consider all of the factors that contribute to a risk for violence and compare this with statutory guidelines.

Another common pitfall occurs when evaluators do not take into account dynamic risk factors that counter the risk of violence. Such an error can lead to prematurely dismissing the least restrictive alternative setting for treatment. For example, Mr. Anderson was not complaining of mood-related symptoms at the time of the evaluation and denied current suicidal or homicidal intent. He had been medication compliant while at the state hospital, and his psychotic symptoms had also been largely controlled via Haldol, an antipsychotic medication. He did not endorse auditory hallucinations while at the hospital, nor did he present as responsive to internal stimuli. He presented with residual symptoms of paranoia and, in particular, reported a belief that others could read his thoughts, although this did not appear to be interfering with his ability to control his behavior. Further, Mr. Anderson could have potentially returned home on bail, as he had no known history of violence against his family members or against others in the community where his family resided. He had family support, in that they created what was believed to be reasonable provisions for him in the community. These provisional requirements allowed him to receive follow-up medication monitoring and day treatment care with the local community agency. An integrated support system such as this would contribute to a greater likelihood of success living in the community. Overall, the combination of factors that both increase and decrease risk play a significant role when making decisions regarding civil commitment.

Notes

1. According to the *Diagnostic and Statistical Manual* (4th ed., text revision; *DSM-IV-TR*), ADHD is characterized by six or more symptoms of inattention or hyperactivity/impulsivity, with some symptoms present prior to age 7 and causing impairment in at least two settings (e.g., school/home). *DSM-IV-TR diagnoses are included here, as the diagnoses were made using this version.

2. According to the *DSM-IV-TR*, Bipolar I Disorder, Most Recent Episode Mixed, is characterized by symptoms of both mania and depression.

3. According to the *DSM-IV-TR*, Psychotic Disorder, Not Otherwise Specified, includes psychotic symptoms (i.e., delusions, hallucinations, disorganized speech, disorganized behavior) about which there is inadequate information to make a specific diagnosis.

4. According to the *DSM-IV-TR*, Cocaine Dependence involves a maladaptive pattern of cocaine use, leading to clinically significant impairment or distress, as manifested

by three (or more) symptoms related to tolerance for the drug, withdrawal symptoms, increased use, unsuccessful attempts to control use, continued use despite recurrent physical or psychological problems, a great deal of time spent in efforts to obtain or recover from the drug, or interference in occupational or recreational activities.

5. According to the *DSM-IV-TR*, Alcohol Dependence involves a maladaptive pattern of cocaine use, leading to clinically significant impairment or distress, as manifested by three (or more) symptoms related to tolerance for the drug, withdrawal symptoms, increased use, unsuccessful attempts to control use, continued use despite recurrent physical or psychological problems, a great deal of time spent in efforts to obtain or recover from the drug, or interference in occupational or recreational activities.

6. According to the *DSM-IV-TR*, Schizoaffective Disorder is described as an uninterrupted period of illness during which there is either a Major Depressive Episode, a Manic Episode, or a Mixed Episode concurrent with symptoms of Schizophrenia (e.g., delusions, hallucinations, disorganized speech/behavior, and/or negative symptoms (e.g., flat emotional expression).

References

Addington v. Texas, 441 U.S. 418 (1979).

Conroy, M. A., & Murrie, D. C. (2007). *Forensic assessment of violence risk: A guide for risk assessment and risk management.* Hoboken, NJ: Wiley.

Douglas, K., Ogloff, J., Nicholls, T., & Grant, I. (1999). Assessing risk for violence among-psychiatric patients: The HCR-20 violence risk assessment scheme and the Psychopathy Checklist: Screening Version. *Journal of Consulting and Clinical Psychology, 67,* 917–930.

Douglas, K. S., & Skeem, J. L. (2005). Violence risk assessment: Getting specific about being dynamic. *Psychology, Public Policy, and Law, 11*(3), 347–383.

Eccleston, L., & Ward, T. (2004). Assessment of dangerous and criminal responsibility. In W. T. O'Donohue & E. R. Levensky (Eds.), *Handbook of forensic psychology: Resource for mental health and legal professionals* (pp. 85–101). New York, NY: Elsevier Science.

Erickson, S. K., Vitacco, M. J., & Van RyBroek, G. J. (2005). Beyond overt violence: Wisconsin's progressive civil commitment statute as a marker of a new era in mental health law. *Marquette Law Review, 89*(2), 359–405.

Federal Rules of Evidence § 703 (2011). Bases of an expert witness.

Guy, L. S., Douglas, K. S., & Hendry, M. C. (2010). The role of psychopathic personality disorder in violence risk assessment using the HCR-20. *Journal of Personality Disorders, 24*(5), 551–580.

Hart, S. D., Cox, D. N., & Hare, R. D. (2003). Hare PCL: SV. Psychopathy Checklist: Screening Version. New York, NY: Multihealth Systems.

Heilbrun, K. (2009). *Evaluation for risk of violence in adults.* New York, NY: Oxford University Press.

Illinois Compiled Statutes Mental Health and Developmental Disabilities Code IL 405 5/1–119.

In re Torski, 395 Ill. App. 3d 1010, 918 N.E. 2d 1218, 335, Ill. Dec. 405 (4th Dist. 2009).

Jacobson v. Massachusetts, 197 U.S. 11, 26 (1905).

Janus, E. S. (1998). Hendricks and the moral terrain of police power civil commitment. *Journal of Psychology, Public Policy, and Law, 4*(1/2), 297–322.

Lake v. Cameron, 364 F.2d 657 (1966).

Lessard v. Schmidt, 414 U.S. 473 (1974).

Melton, G. B., Petrila, J., Poythress, N. G., & Slobogin, C. (2007). Psychological evaluations for the courts: A handbook for mental health professionals and lawyers (3rd ed.). New York, NY: Guilford Press.

Menninger, J. A. (2001). Involuntary treatment: Hospitalisation and medications. In Jacobson, James L., and Jacobson, Alan M. (Eds.), *Psychiatric Secrets* (2nd ed., pp. 477–484). Philadelphia, PA: Hanley & Belfus.

Monahan, J. (1981). *The clinical prediction of violent behavior.* Washington, DC: Government Printing Office.

Monahan, J. (1992). Major mental disorder and violent behavior: Perceptions and evidence. *American Psychologist, 47*(4), 511–512.

Monahan, J., Steadman, H. J., Appelbaum, P. S., Grisso, T., Mulvey, E .P., Roth, L. H., Robbins, P. C., Banks, S., & Silver, E. (2006). The classification of violence risk. *Behavioral Sciences & the Law, 24*(6), 721–730.

Moran, G. E., Robins, C., & Kurzban, S. (2000). *Civil commitment under Medicaid managed care.* Rockville, MD: Center for Mental Health Services, Substance Abuse and Mental Health Services Administration.

New York State Office of Mental Health (2005). Kendra's Law: Final report on the status of assisted outpatient treatment. Albany, NY: New York State Office of Mental Health.

O'Connor v. Donaldson, 422 U.S. 563 (1975).

Pinals, D. A., & Mossman, D. (2012). *Evaluation for civil commitment.* New York, NY: Oxford University Press.

Prochaska v. Brinegar, 251 Iowa 834, 102 N.W. 2d 870, 872 (1960).

Schopp, R. F. (2003). Outpatient civil commitment: A dangerous charade or a component of a comprehensive institution of civil commitment? *Journal of Psychology, Public Policy, and Law, 9*(1/2), 33–69.

Slobogin, C., Hafemeister, T. L., Mossman, D., & Reisner, R. (2014). *Law and the mental health system: Civil and criminal aspects* (6th ed.). St Paul, MN: West Publishing Company.

Testa, M., & West, S. G. (2010). Civil commitment in the United States. *Journal of Psychiatry, 7*(10), 30–40.

Tillbrook, C., Mumley, D., & Grisso, T. (2003). Avoiding expert opinions on the ultimate legal question: The case for integrity. *Journal of Forensic Psychology Practice, 3*, 77–87.

Webster, C. D., Douglas, K. S., Eaves, D., & Hart, S. D. (1997). *HCR-20 Assessing Risk for Violence Manual.* Burnaby, British Columbia, Canada: Simon Fraser University, Mental Health Law and Policy Institute.

8

The Psychological Assessment of Personal Injury Claims

Eric G. Mart

The psychological assessment of personal injury claims is a complex area of forensic practice. Such cases are part of the civil rather than the criminal justice system of the judiciary. In the criminal system, persons accused of committing a serious crime such as a felony are charged in a formal accusation referred to as an indictment, while less serious crimes are charged upon information. Criminal law deals with acts of intentional harm to individuals such as assault, breaking and entering, or murder. However, these criminal acts are considered to be offenses against not only the individuals who have been harmed but also the broader society as a whole. For example, the victim of a home invasion may be psychologically traumatized and physically harmed, but the commission of this type of crime affects all of us by making us feel less secure in our homes. Contrary to popular belief, it is not the responsibility of the victim to "press charges"; charges are brought by prosecutors on behalf of the government, and the victim is not a party to the legal action. In order to be convicted of a criminal offense, the prosecution must prove beyond a reasonable doubt that the criminal defendant committed a particular act and meant to cause the harm that ensued. The action itself is referred to as the actus reus or "guilty act" and the intentional element is referred to as "mens rea" or "guilty mind." There are exceptions to the necessity for mens rea and criminal law in cases that are referred to as strict liability cases. These are crimes in which there was no conscious intent to cause harm, but harm occurred through the defendant's reckless or inattentive behavior coupled with the knowledge that others could be hurt by such behavior (Cornell University Law School, n.d.; Gifis, 2010, p. 520).

Relevant Case Law

Persons convicted of criminal offenses are punished for a number of reasons including deterring the convicted individual from committing the crime again and deterring other individuals from acting in a similar manner. Another purpose of sentencing is incapacitation, which means that an incarcerated individual cannot commit crimes against members of the general population while behind bars. Retribution or "just desserts" is another goal of sentencing, as is the rehabilitation of the criminal (Barton, 2012, p. 504). The civil justice system has very different goals and somewhat different rules from the criminal justice system. A civil case is brought to court when an individual or other entity—such as a corporation (referred to as the plaintiff)—alleges that another person or entity (the defendant) has failed to carry out a duty or obligation owed to the plaintiff (The Law Dictionary, n.d.; Gifis, 2010, p. 174). In some cases this is contractual. For example, a contractor might sue a homeowner if the contractor is not paid the agreed-on amount he or she was promised for the home repairs performed. In other cases, an individual who was injured through the negligence of the hospital that performed surgery on him or her could sue the hospital for damages.

Cases in which harm to an individual or entity occurs are sometimes referred to as *torts*; the term is derived from Old French and means "twisted" or "wrong" (The Law Dictionary, n.d.; Gifis, 2010, p. 174). Tortious conduct involves four elements, which must be established before the court. The first of these is the existence of duty owed to another. There are many definitions of what constitutes a duty, but it is generally considered to be a responsibility to another. Examples of such responsibilities include keeping one's premises safe and paying adequate attention when driving. Such cases also arise when a medical, legal, or other type of professional does not act in accordance with the generally accepted standards of his or her profession (Moffett & Moore, 2011).

The second element of a tort is a breach of the as-defined-above duty owed to another. For example, a surgeon who leaves forceps in the abdominal cavity of a surgical patient, a psychologist who does not assess a depressed patient for suicide potential, or a lawyer who produces a flawed contract that causes monetary damages for a client would all be considered to be breaching their duty toward the patient or client (Moffett & Moore, 2011). Such a breach of duty can be intentional or unintentional, but in either case the behavior of the defendant toward the plaintiff must be shown to fall below the standards of his or her profession or constitute negligence when compared with what a "reasonable person" has a right to expect from another (Moffett & Moore, 2011). When applying the reasonable person standard to a case, the behavior of the defendant is compared with that of a person exercising average care, skill, and judgment in a particular situation. However, an individual acting in a professional capacity will be held to the higher standard of average performance in his or her area of practice (Hunt v. Bradshaw, 1955).

The third element of a tort is what is known as "proximate cause." *Barron's Law Dictionary* (Gifis, 2010, p. 75) defines proximate cause as "that which in natural and continuous sequence unbroken by any new independent cause produces an event, and without which the injury would not have occurred." This is also sometimes referred to as the "but for" test (Cornell University Law School, n.d.). For example, it might be the case that "but for" the plaintiff having left the gate to his yard unlocked, the neighbor child would not have fallen into his swimming pool and drowned. However, the law recognizes that the actions of the defendant need not be the sole cause of an injury or harm to the plaintiff but may significantly exacerbate a preexisting condition. This is sometimes referred to as the "thin-skull rule," which states that the defendant is liable for all harm resulting from his or her behavior, even if the victim was unusually vulnerable (e.g., had a congenitally thin skull that shattered as a result of the defendant's negligence, even though a healthy individual would have been unharmed).

The last element of a tort is the presence of compensable damages. Courts recognize that while certain harms may occur due to the conduct of another, these harms must be significant. Not all harms meet this test. For example, having one's arm broken due to the negligence of another is likely to be compensable, while receiving a bad haircut or having one's feelings hurt would generally not be. There is recognition by the legal system that people will sometimes act rudely or irresponsibly, but the impact of their behavior is simply not severe enough to make monetary compensation necessary.

When evaluators are brought into personal injury cases, it is generally to establish that the plaintiff has suffered psychological damage, harm, or distress as a result of the tortious conduct of another. All of the elements of a tort apply to psychological damages.

Before undertaking a forensic assessment related to a personal injury case, there are a number of ethical issues that must be addressed. The first and most obvious is whether the forensic evaluator has the required competence to perform such an evaluation. After looking at the fact pattern of the case and determining the psycholegal issues involved, the evaluator must ask him or herself whether he or she has the competence to address the specific issues involved. For example, if the case requires the assessment of possible posttraumatic stress disorder or cognitive deficits brought about by a traumatic brain injury, does the forensic practitioner have the requisite education, training, and experience to perform such an evaluation? Section 2 of the "Ethical Principles of Psychologists and Code of Conduct" (APA, 2002) addresses this directly.

Boundaries of Competence

"Psychologists provide services, teach, and conduct research with populations and in areas only within the boundaries of their competence, based on their education, training, supervised experience, consultation, study, or professional experience" (APA, 2002, p. 4).

Bases for Scientific and Professional Judgments

"Psychologists' work is based upon established scientific and professional knowledge of the discipline" (APA, 2002, p. 5). It should be noted that there is an enhanced standard of competence when undertaking forensic assessments above and beyond what may be expected in a clinical setting. This is because an evaluator can reasonably expect that his or her training, experience, and work product will be subjected to the intense scrutiny of the adversarial legal system. Further, since forensic psychology operates at the intersection of clinical psychology and the law, there is an expectation that the evaluator will have a reasonable understanding of the legal issues that inform their assessments. The "Specialty Guidelines for Forensic Psychology" (APA, 2013) note that:

Scope of Competence   When determining one's competence to provide services in a particular matter, forensic practitioners may consider a variety of factors, including the relative complexity and specialized nature of the service, the relevant training and experience, the preparation and study they are able to devote to the matter, and the opportunity for consultation with a professional of established competence in the subject matter in question. Even with regard to subjects in which they are expert, forensic practitioners may choose to consult with colleagues.

Knowledge of the Legal System and the Legal Rights of Individuals
Forensic practitioners recognize the importance of obtaining a fundamental and reasonable level of knowledge and understanding of the legal and professional standards, laws, rules, and precedents that govern their participation in legal proceedings and that guide the impact of their services on service recipients.

Forensic practitioners aspire to manage their professional conduct in a manner that does not threaten or impair the rights of affected individuals. They may consult with, and refer others to, legal counsel on matters of law. Although they do not provide formal legal advice or opinions, forensic practitioners may provide information about the legal process to others based on their knowledge and experience. They strive to distinguish this from legal opinions, however, and encourage consultation with attorneys as appropriate (APA, 2013, p. 9).

Knowledge of the Scientific Foundation for Opinions and Testimony
Forensic practitioners seek to provide opinions and testimony that are sufficiently based on an adequate scientific foundation and on reliable and valid principles and methods that have been applied appropriately to the facts of the case. When providing opinions and testimony that are based on novel or emerging principles and methods, forensic practitioners seek to make known the status and limitations of these principles and methods (APA, 2013, p. 9).

A special issue related to the guidelines noted above is the fact that forensic psychologists conducting personal injury assessments need to make sure that the techniques and tests they utilize will be admissible in court. There is some variation in jurisdictions regarding the admissibility of expert testimony. Initially, all states and jurisdictions utilized the *Frye* standard (*Frye v. United States*, 1923) in determining admissibility. The *Frye* standard states that for expert testimony to be admissible, "The thing from which the deduction is made must be sufficiently established to gain general acceptance in the particular field in which it belongs" (*Frye v. United States*, 1923, p. 1). However, in 1993 this general acceptance standard was superseded in many jurisdictions and in the federal court system by standards put forth in the case of *Daubert v. Merrill-Dow Pharmaceuticals* (1993). The Daubert test was more complex and puts forth a multifactor test to determine the admissibility of expert testimony. These factors are as follows:

- The testimony must be relevant to the facts at issue
- The theory or technique can be (and has been) tested
- The theory or technique has been subjected to peer review and publication
- The theory or technique has known or potentially knowable error rates
- The theory or technique has attracted widespread acceptance within the relevant scientific community

The decision goes on to state that the standards mentioned above should be applied in a flexible manner to the principles and methods used as opposed to the conclusions arising from those principles and methods. In practical terms this means that experts in personal injury cases should not rely on novel scientific techniques that have not been closely scrutinized and peer-reviewed. Certain tests in wide usage such as the Wechsler IQ tests or the MMPI-2 would easily meet this standard. Other tests such as the Thematic Apperception Test or projective drawings might not be admitted, since these tests lack established reliability and validity, and the error rate of conclusions drawn from their use could not be easily established (Lillienfeld, James, & Howard, 2000; Wechsler Adult intelligence Scale, Fourth Edition, 2003; Butcher et al., 1989; Murray, 1943). Consequently, forensic evaluators performing personal injury assessments should rely on well-established tests that are widely used in these types of evaluations.

Case Vignette

Reason for Referral

The following case study details a personal injury evaluation performed several years ago. It should be noted that all names of individuals, treatment

---

The case vignette has been redacted and all identifying information removed. It is not meant to serve as a forensic report. Any likeness to a case is purely coincidental.

providers, and institutions have been changed and to some extent hybridized to protect the identities of these entities. Approximately twenty-two months before this request was made, Anna Cohen, who was 18 years of age at the time she was evaluated, was riding her bicycle with several friends along a busy road at sunset. An inattentive driver drifted off the road and struck Ms. Cohen; her friends were not injured.

Summary of Relevant Records

As part of the assessment, documentation detailing the accident, as well as educational records from before and after the accident, was reviewed. Pertinent documents included records from law enforcement and EMTs at the time of the accident as well as medical records detailing the initial diagnostic findings related to the injuries Ms. Cohen received as a result of the accident. These records are important because the severity of a brain injury and the likely prognosis can to some extent be determined by a number of factors, as well as scores on rating scales. For example, the Glasgow Coma Scale (GCS; Teasdale & Jennett, 1974) can be used to rate patients in terms of whether they can open their eyes normally in response to speech when questioned loudly or in response to pain such as a pinch. Patients are also rated with regard to the intelligibility of speech and their ability to follow simple commands. Lower GCS scores are associated with more severe damage. Other methods of assessing the severity of traumatic brain injury include the duration of post-traumatic amnesia, which generally begins at the moment of the injury and can extend from a few minutes to more than four weeks. The length of post-traumatic amnesia is generally more accurate than GCS scores in predicting the victim's long-term cognitive status (Bishara, Partridge, Godfrey, & Knight, 1992). Initial medical records provide information regarding the nature of the injury and subsequent cognitive status.

In this case, the police officer who initially responded to the scene of the accident reported that he immediately called an ambulance and spoke to the driver of the car who had stopped further up the road. The driver appeared to be stunned but was able to tell the officer that he had been distracted when he had spilled his coffee and that his car had crossed onto the berm of the road. He looked up and saw the bicyclists, but he was unable to stop or maneuver back onto the road because of the speed he was traveling and the short time he had to respond. The officer noted that Ms. Cohen had been thrown approximately fifty feet from the point of impact and had sustained injuries to her head and back.

The report of the paramedic who initially attended Ms. Cohen noted that Ms. Cohen had been struck in the back by the automobile and had been thrown a considerable distance. One of Ms. Cohen's friends had gone to her aid immediately and found Ms. Cohen lying on her back, unresponsive and not breathing. The friend attempted to revive Ms. Cohen without immediate success, but after a few moments, Ms. Cohen gasped and began breathing again. The same friend reported that, while she waited for assistance, Ms. Cohen continued in an unconscious state with her eyes rolled back in her head. The paramedics described Ms. Cohen as having an altered mental status, confused speech, and right-sided weakness. Additionally, she was described as having a deep laceration on the right side of her forehead and significant abrasions on her elbows and knees. She was described as conscious but not oriented and unaware of what was happening. She was later described as able to speak and answer certain questions but to be perseverative and distraught. She attempted to rise but was placed on a backboard and restrained, and she continued to ask why she was not allowed to go home. Ms. Cohen was initially taken to a local hospital but was almost immediately taken by helicopter to a larger regional hospital.

Notes from her immediate treatment were unavailable, but a report of a follow-up examination by a neurologist who had treated Ms. Cohen had been obtained. The report indicated that at the regional hospital, Ms. Cohen received several CT scans of her brain, which revealed a subdural hematoma that did not require surgical correction. She subsequently developed serious headaches as well as problems with sleep. The doctor noted that after the accident, Ms. Cohen had posttraumatic amnesia, which lasted several days after her injury, along with a relatively brief period of retrograde amnesia. This suggested that she had experienced a moderately severe traumatic brain injury. It was also reported that she was experiencing significant memory problems and mood swings and that she had difficulty focusing her right eye. Also noted were episodes of chest pain that the doctor thought were related to palpitations. The neurologist performed an examination of Ms. Cohen. Her language was fluent and coherent and her speech was clear with normal prosody. Memory deficits were apparent as well as difficulties with directional skills. The neurologist noted that her cognitive status was improved but that she was still suffering significant symptoms of postconcussive syndrome.

The forensic evaluator was also able to review Ms. Cohen's educational records both from before the accident occurred and subsequently. The records from before her accident indicated that her scores on standardized reading, mathematics, and writing tests, which were given routinely in her school district, were all average to above average. Additionally, her grades were all above average, and she received no special education or other academic accommodations. This strongly suggested that her cognitive abilities prior to the accident were at least in the average range.

Several teachers at Ms. Cohen's high school who had worked with her both before and after the accident were also interviewed. These conversations made it clear that, prior to the accident, Ms. Cohen had good to excellent grades and no difficulty with comprehension, concentration, attention, or organization. When she was able to return to school, she had much more difficulty in these areas. She had difficulty focusing in the classroom due to noise and distractions and her work left her very fatigued. She required special modifications that allowed her more time to complete assignments and to take tests without time limits in a separate, quiet environment. She was also noted to be more anxious and easily startled, and she also had more difficulties relating to her fellow students and teachers. While these problems gradually improved as the months went by, and her acute symptoms abated to some extent, she still had difficulty during the entirety of the following academic year. In performing the assessment of Ms. Cohen, the evaluator employed the following tests and techniques:

- Record Review
- Collateral Interviews
- Mental Status Examination
- Clinical Interview
- Reynolds Intellectual Assessment Scales (RIAS)
- Neuropsychological Assessment Battery (NAB)
- Behavior Rating Inventory of Executive Function-Adult Version
    o   Self and Other Rater Forms
- Validity Indicator Profile (VIP)
- Personality Assessment Inventory (PAI)
- Mayo-Portland Adaptability Inventory-4
- Posttraumatic Stress Diagnostic Scale (PDS)

Mental Status Examination

All forensic psychological evaluations should include a formal mental status examination (MSE). While this component of an assessment is often neglected, virtually all authorities on the subject of forensic assessment agree that a good mental status examination is an essential component of such an examination. For example, in the fifth edition of *Neuropsychological Assessment* (Lezak et al., 2012, p. 761) the authors note that "by beginning the examination with the brief review of cognitive and social behavior afforded by the mental status examination, the psychologist may be alerted to problem areas that will need more detailed inquiry; the MSE will usually indicate whether the patient's general level of functioning is too low for standard adult assessment techniques. It is also likely to draw out personal idiosyncrasies or emotional problems that may interfere with the examination or require special attention of procedural changes." While there are many definitions of what constitutes mental status examination, is generally considered to be a series of systematic observations of a subject's mental state at the time of assessment and is generally based on the observations of the mental health professional rather than the statements and symptom reports of the individual. Some practitioners utilize checklists for these observations while others perform the examination while simultaneously conducting the clinical interview. Most authorities agree that the mental status examination should cover the following areas:

- Level of consciousness (alert, drowsy, lethargic)
- Attitude and interpersonal behavior (interested and engaged, distractible, preoccupied, hostile)
- Appearance (posture, attire, grooming, hygiene, eye contact, facial expression)
- Activity level and movement (slowed movements, restlessness, psychomotor agitation, tremor)
- Mood and affect (calm, apathetic, labile, flat, or inappropriate emotional reaction)
- Speech and language (fluency, signs aphasia, amount, and tone)
- Thought processes (logical and coherent, circumstantial, perseverative)
- Thought content (paranoid, ideas of reference, hallucinations, delusions)
- Cognition (fully oriented, memory deficits problems with attention or abstract reasoning)
- Insight (understanding of his or her deficits or condition)
- Judgment (presence or absence of realistic plans, ability to make good choices)

When Ms. Cohen was seen for evaluation, her mental status examination was for the most part unremarkable. She was cooperative and engaged and appeared to put forth good effort. She did appear anxious at times. Her affect was appropriate to the content of the interview, although this evaluator did note that it was slightly flattened and mildly restricted in range. Her speech was fluent with a mildly slow cadence and low volume. Some difficulties with verbal abstraction were noted, and her insight into her condition was fair in that she did not appear to understand some of her current cognitive limitations and their impact on her daily functioning.

The clinical interview provided the subject the opportunity to tell the evaluator his or her story with special regard to the events that have led to the personal injury case. It is also important to take a thorough history in order to help determine whether the symptoms began with the individual's injury, were preexisting but exacerbated by events, or were present before the alleged injury. The clinical interview of Ms. Cohen revealed that she had been raised by both biological parents, and she characterized her relationship with them in positive terms. This evaluator asked her about her adjustment to elementary school and middle school, and she told me that she did not remember much about that period of her life and could not recall whether she had been involved in any extracurricular activities. She had graduated from high school but had not attempted any college classes. Ms. Cohen did not recall having experienced any traumatic experiences as a child or adolescent other than her motor vehicle accident. Her medical history was unremarkable, and she denied any present or past use of alcohol or illegal drugs. She was not taking any prescription medications the time of the evaluation. Ms. Cohen had no history of arrests as a juvenile or adult.

Relevant Background Information

The forensic evaluator questioned Ms. Cohen about any psychiatric history she might have, and the evaluator was told that Ms. Cohen might have seen a therapist for one or two sessions after her injury but could not give any details. Ms. Cohen reported occasional moderate symptoms of depression that included sleep problems and fatigue but denied any thoughts of self-harm. She noted that she had problems with anxiety and experienced occasional panic attacks. She gave no indications of delusional thinking and reported no instances of hallucinations.

When asked about her accident, Ms. Cohen said that she recalled riding her bicycle with several friends, but she did not recall much about the next several days; she was unable to estimate how long her anterograde amnesia persisted. She reported that she experienced debilitating headaches several times a week and that she had pain in her ankle related to her injuries. The evaluator asked her about any cognitive changes and was told that, since the accident, she had been feeling more anxious and self-doubting and worried a great deal about the future. Ms. Cohen also thought that she was having more difficulty relating to people and it took her much longer to perform tasks than it had in the past.

Psychological Measures

After completing the clinical interview, the evaluator administered the Reynolds Intellectual Assessment Scales (RIAS), which is an IQ test made up of two verbal subtests and two nonverbal subtests. IQ testing is used in these types of examinations for a number of reasons. They provide a snapshot of the subject's current overall intellectual ability, and they can also be used in some cases to screen for poor effort or malingering. The RIAS was chosen for several reasons. It is relatively shorter than the Wechsler instruments, although highly correlated with that instrument. It is also co-normed with the Neuropsychological Assessment Battery (NAB), which was also utilized in her assessment. Ms. Cohen's scores on the verbal, nonverbal, and composite indexes all fell in the Borderline to Below Average range. It was the evaluator's impression that her scores may have been lowered to some extent by attentional problems.

Since the basis of Ms. Cohen's personal injury suit was in large part her claim that she had developed cognitive deficits as a result of her traumatic brain injury, neuropsychological assessment was required to document the presence or absence of these problems. There are a number of approaches to this type of assessment. Some psychologists assemble a battery of individual test instruments designed to measure cognitive functions such as attention, memory, language, spatial ability, and executive function. The examiner's choice of instruments tends to be based on the professional's training and experience. Clearly, any instruments chosen should be normed on populations with demographic characteristics similar to those of the plaintiff and should have adequate reliability and validity. Additionally, the instruments should be sufficiently well developed to be admissible under the relevant legal standards (e.g., Daubert or Frye). Other practitioners utilize fixed batteries such as the Halstead-Reitan or Luria Nebraska batteries. In Ms. Cohen's case, the evaluator utilized the Neuropsychological Assessment Battery (NAB), which is a relatively new instrument made up of subtests similar to many traditional freestanding tests used to assess different domains of cognitive functioning. The NAB has many advantages for this type of assessment. One major vantage of this instrument is that it includes a screening module (NAB-SM). The NAB-SM can be given to an individual prior to administering the full battery. Very elevated or depressed scores on the screening modules indicate that the subject is not likely to do any better or worse on the full modules, and these need not be administered. In some cases, the decision can be made to simply skip the screening module and simply administer the full battery. In this case, the screening battery was used because Ms. Cohen did not complain of any difficulties in certain cognitive domains. Ms. Cohen had very depressed scores (below the 2nd percentile) on the attention, memory and executive function screening modules and a well above average score on the language module; therefore, the full modules in these domains were not administered. Her spatial domain score fell in the average range, and the full module was administered. She had extremely low scores in the area of visual discrimination and also did very poorly on a task that required her to use a map to follow directions. However, she did very well on a task that required her to copy a complex geometric figure. Overall, problems with auditory attention and auditory working memory were observed, as well as slow processing of information, memory problems, and deficits in executive function. Her overall score on the NAB was strongly indicative of compromised cognitive functioning.

All assessments of cognitive functioning that occur in the context of a personal injury case should include a number of tests of effort. This is because many studies have shown that there is a high rate of feigning and malingering in these situations. As noted by Bush et al. (2005), "There are many potential threats to the validity of the information and test data obtained in the course of a neuropsychological evaluation. Examples of such threats include the potential for personal gain (malingering), a factitious disorder, opposition to the evaluation, and the presence of clinical factors that may interfere with successful participation in a neuropsychological evaluation. In order to place maximal confidence in the ability to interpret accurately results from cognitive measures and/or tests of personality or mood, a determination must be made that the examinee put forth appropriate effort on tasks and responded honestly to questions. Symptom validity assessment is the process through which such determinations are made." These authors go on to note that the potential for symptom fabrication or exaggeration is higher in forensic contexts than in many clinical contexts (Larrabee, 2003; Mittenberg, Patton, Canyock, & Condit, 2002). As a result of the client's increased incentive to mislead the examiner, neuropsychologists have a responsibility to conduct a more extensive assessment of symptom validity. Although there may be instances in which the use of specific symptom validity tests would not be indicated in forensic contexts, failure to administer at least one symptom validity test and/or administer tests with internal symptom validity indicators would need to be justified. As Iverson (2003) stated in the context of forensic practice, "Any neuropsychological evaluation that does not include careful consideration of the patient's motivation to give their best effort should be considered incomplete" (p. 138). Methods of assessing effort include the use of embedded measures in standard instruments and the use of tests specifically designed to assess effort. In this case, I relied upon embedded measures in the NAB as well as the Validity Indicator Profile (VIP). The VIP is a computer-administered test of effort and malingering. It consists of two subtests (verbal and nonverbal) that can be used together or separately. The subject is not aware of the nature of the test, which appears to be a measure of cognitive ability. There are a number of instruments that can be used in this manner including the Test of Memory Malingering, the Word Memory Test, and the Portland Digital Recognition Test. The VIP is well regarded and has advantages over the other instruments mentioned as it both measures intentional efforts to perform poorly and detects individuals who are simply not trying very hard on tests of cognitive ability. Both VIP subtests were administered to Ms. Cohen, and her scores indicated that she put forth reasonable effort on the tasks. Additionally, the embedded measures in the NAB indicated that she put forth reasonable effort. As a consequence, the forensic evaluator felt confident that her overall results on cognitive testing were likely to be an accurate reflection of her actual ability.

Both Ms. Cohen and her father completed the Behavior Rating Inventory of Executive Function-Adult Version (BRIEF-A). The BRIEF-A is a questionnaire designed to assist in the assessment of executive function, which is the ability to engage in purposeful, goal-directed problem-solving behavior. There have been concerns raised in the neuropsychological literature that more traditional psychometric tests of executive function lack ecological validity. Lezak (2012) notes that "Ecological validity is the degree to which a measure predicts behavior in everyday situations, such as ability to return to work or school, benefit from rehabilitation, live independently, or manage finances. Tests and techniques used for neuropsychological assessment are meant to have real-world validity, but there are many obstacles that limit the degree to which this can be accomplished. For example, testing in a quiet environment may not reveal the problems that patients have with concentration and memory as compared to natural work or home environment with her numerous distractions." There is mounting evidence that many traditional neuropsychological tests do a poor job of predicting an individual's real-world performance as related to executive function. Consequently, it is prudent to use both traditional instruments such as the executive function domain tests of the NAB and behavior rating forms such as the BRIEF-A in assessing this domain. Ratings by individuals who know the subject well are also quite helpful. Ms. Cohen saw herself as functioning normally in most areas measured by the BRIEF-A with the exception of problems in the area of working memory. The results of the BRIEF-A completed by her father demonstrated a much higher level of difficulty in executive functioning, including problems in shifting from one activity to another, planning and organizing, and monitoring task performance, as well as working memory. The difference between the self and other scores on the BRIEF-A suggested that Ms. Cohen appeared to lack insight into the extent of her problems in this area, which is not uncommon among individuals who have experienced a traumatic brain injury.

To gather more information about her actual functional capacity, the forensic evaluator had Ms. Cohen's parents complete the Mayo-Portland Adaptability Inventory-4, which is a rating scale designed to measure the most common sequelii of traumatic brain injury. The use of this type of instrument, which is completed by others, can be very helpful in assessing personal injury cases. As noted in the description of the BRIEF-A, the use of this form can give the evaluator a better sense of the individual's functional abilities. This instrument can be completed by a treating professional or by individuals who know the patient well. The results indicated that Ms. Cohen's parents viewed their daughter as having moderately severe impairments in abilities such as attention and concentration, fund of information, and problem-solving ability. She was also viewed as having moderately severe difficulties in personal adjustment, including high levels of anxiety, fatigue, and headache. Problems with leisure skills, money management, and employment were also noted.

It has long been recognized that all personal injury is accompanied by emotional distress, and in recent years this distress has been recognized as compensable in a personal injury lawsuit. Consequently, this aspect of personal injury should be assessed in these types of evaluations. Psychologists evaluating the presence and degree of emotional distress should rely on multiple sources of data. These sources can include the client's self-report, which should be corroborated by other sources to the extent possible, record review, and the use of objective tests. Tests commonly used for this type of assessment include the MMPI-2, the Personality Assessment Inventory and specific tests designed to assess the impact of traumatic events. Ms. Cohen completed the Personality Assessment Inventory (PAI), which is an objective test of personality functioning, as part of her assessment. This test was chosen because it is well validated and reviewed and also because it contains validity scales. Scores of personality measures on the validity scales are useful in determining whether an individual is either being defensive about problems and underreporting them or is likely to be exaggerating difficulties. The use of these instruments can be helpful in determining the extent to which the individual is suffering from depression, anxiety or posttraumatic stress as a result of the injury, and both tests can reveal somatizing tendencies that may contribute to the persistence of reported symptoms. Ms. Cohen showed notable defensiveness on the validity scales, which is unusual in the context of personal injury assessment. Ms. Cohen was somewhat defensive in her approach to the instrument, which is unusual in personal injury cases in which people are seeking compensation for their distress. A closer examination of her scores on the PAI validity scales appeared to stem a general tendency to deny problems in combination with a lack of insight into the actual severity of her difficulties. Despite this, Ms. Cohen had elevations on a number of PAI clinical scales. The scores indicated a tendency to develop physical symptoms under stress, although this can also be seen in individuals who have actual problems caused by conditions such as traumatic brain injury. Ms. Cohen also had elevations on scores that measure traumatic stress and indications that she was having difficulty with concentration, decision making, and memory.

Because the presence of trauma-related symptoms was indicated, the evaluator administered the Posttraumatic Stress Diagnostic Scale (PDS). Ms. Cohen's responses indicated that she was experiencing symptoms of avoidance, hyperarousal, and re-experiencing her motor vehicle accident. There are indications that she was having intrusive thoughts related to the accident as well as emotional upset when she was reminded of that experience. She also felt cut off and distant from others in close relationships. Overall, the results of the PDS indicated that she was experiencing moderate to severe symptoms of posttraumatic stress, which were causing significant impairment in her day-to-day functioning. Interestingly, her results on the PDS differed from her self-report in the clinical interview in that she did not explicitly endorse symptoms associated with posttraumatic stress disorder when asked about her general emotional state.

Clinical Summary and Opinion

Based on all the available information, the evaluator concluded that Ms. Cohen was continuing to experience a broad range of both cognitive and emotional problems since her motor vehicle accident. While her IQ was somewhat lower than what would be expected based on her school achievement prior to the accident, given the confidence interval of the RIAS and the magnitude of the differences between her current IQ scores and her scores on academic tests, this difference could not be reliably attributed to her traumatic brain injury. However, her scores on neuropsychological tests were indicative of significant cognitive deficits. While her overall language skills were above average, it was clear that she was experiencing problems in attention and concentration, memory, visual/spatial skills, and executive function that did not appear to be present prior to her injury. Her ability to plan, organize daily tasks, and sustain effort were all significantly compromised. Further, there were elements of anosognosia, a common problem in individuals with traumatic brain injury that refers to a lack of insight into their current condition and limitations. This is often problematic since these individuals often do not feel the need to participate in ongoing treatment or neurocognitive rehabilitation. They may also become frustrated when their efforts to accomplish tasks or continue their education do not meet with success.

In addition to symptoms directly caused by her brain injury, Ms. Cohen was also experiencing emotional problems that stemmed from her injury. She was experiencing hyperarousal and hypervigilance, avoidance of stimuli associated with the accident and intrusive, unpleasant thoughts related to her experience. She also had a foreshortened sense of her future, and she felt distant and cut off from people with whom she had previously been close. These classic signs of posttraumatic stress disorder had gone unnoticed both by those working with Ms. Cohen and by Ms. Cohen herself. There were also indications that she tended to be preoccupied with her physical condition and experienced medical conditions such as headaches and generalized pain exacerbated by her emotional distress. Based on the available information, Ms. Cohen was diagnosed (DSM-IV-TR under use at time of evaluation) as follows:

Axis I: Cognitive Disorder Not Otherwise Specified

Posttraumatic Stress Disorder, Chronic

Axis II: No Diagnosis

Axis III: Traumatic Brain Injury

Axis IV: Problems Related to Interaction with the Legal System–Litigation

Axis V: Global Assessment of Functioning-61 (Mild to Moderate Symptoms and Functional Impairment)

Because of the clear change in Ms. Cohen's cognitive and emotional status subsequent to the accident and the absence of any other intervening physical or emotional traumatic events, the evaluator had no difficulty concluding that the accident and the resulting traumatic brain injury was the proximate cause of her current cognitive and functional limitations as well as her posttraumatic stress disorder.

One of the issues to be addressed in personal injury assessments is the subject's prognosis and the likely impact of any observed deficits on the subject's future functional status. Individuals in Ms. Cohen's age group who were seen for assessment almost two years after a traumatic brain injury had likely reached an endpoint for improvement. However, the record review and clinical interview of Ms. Cohen made it clear that she had not received any neurocognitive rehabilitation treatment, nor had she received psychotherapy or psychiatric consultation. It should be understood that in civil cases, individuals who are injured by the tortious behavior of another are required to attempt to mitigate those damages. For example, if a litigant received a disfiguring facial injury due to the negligence of another that could be corrected with plastic surgery, the court may refuse to compensate that individual for certain effects of the disfigurement that could be avoided. In the case of Ms. Cohen, it was the opinion of the evaluator that it was possible that her functional status could improve if she received neurocognitive rehabilitation and psychiatric intervention, but it was not clear what degree of improvement might result. However, her lack of insight into her limitations was a direct consequence of the traumatic brain injury caused by the accident.

Often, when there are clear injuries associated with obvious negligence as there was in this case, and the expert opinions are clear, an out-of-court monetary settlement is reached. After the forensic evaluator's report was received by the parties in this case, such a settlement was reached, and the evaluator was not deposed, nor was he asked to provide expert testimony in court. Ms. Cohen did follow recommendations for rehabilitation and psychiatric consultation, and her condition improved, although she never returned to her premorbid status.

Common Pitfalls and Considerations

There are a number of problems that commonly occur when performing psychological assessments in cases of personal injury. Most of them come under the general heading of bias, whether conscious or unconscious. To understand this, it is important to understand the context in which these assessments take place.

Legal claims of personal injury take place within an adversarial system. Our civil legal process is predicated on the idea that the true state of affairs in a personal injury claim will be revealed through vigorous argument and advocacy between the attorneys for the plaintiff and the defendant. Forensic evaluators become involved in these cases when the attorney for one of the parties retains his or her services. Subtle and not-so-subtle pressures that can create bias in psychological assessments may be in with the very first phone call with the attorney who wishes to retain a forensic evaluator. Typically, the attorney will inquire as to whether there is any reason why the evaluator cannot perform the evaluation. These may include the evaluator having had previous contact with one of the parties in a treatment or consultative role or any other kind of prior relationship. After having ascertained that no conflict exists, the attorney will provide a brief outline of the case. This outline will almost invariably present the case in a manner that supports the position of the attorney's client, whether their representing the plaintiff or the defendant. This is perfectly appropriate for the attorney, since he or she is an advocacy role with the client. However, the forensic evaluator has an ethical obligation to be as objective and impartial as possible. The problem is that once this potentially slanted account of the case is heard by the evaluator, it can never be unheard. This can lead to the type of bias that is sometimes referred to as the anchoring effect. Anchoring effects refer to the unconscious tendency to place more weight on information that is first encountered than on data that is subsequently elicited. There is also an associated tendency to neglect to give new, disconfirming information appropriate weight.

Another related problem in performing these types of assessments is confirmatory bias, which is a normal human tendency. In forensic situations involving confirmatory bias, the evaluator prematurely arrives at conclusions about the case then unconsciously gives a good deal of weight to subsequent facts and findings that confirm the initial conclusion while neglecting data that do not. For example, a forensic evaluator may conclude that the depressive symptoms that a plaintiff develops after traumatic event are causally related to that event while neglecting the fact that the same individual had a past history of developing depressive symptoms when there was no obvious stressor.

Some of the factors that can cause bias in the evaluation reports of forensic evaluators seem obvious but are sometimes not recognized at the time. One of these is the fact that the evaluator has been hired by one side or the other and is being paid by the party by whom they were retained. It can be surprisingly difficult to accept payment and then come to conclusions that are not favorable to the retaining party. One way to guard against this is for the forensic evaluator to take a look at his or her work over a period of years. If he or she finds that they nearly always provide an opinion that is supportive of the retaining party, it is likely that he or she is being influenced by a sense of affiliation and obligation, and the evaluator needs to take steps to guard against this tendency. In the same way, many forensic evaluators can get caught up with the idea of winning or losing a case, which can affect objectivity.

In general, the best way to try to minimize bias is to employ strategies to avoid some of these patterns. One of the best ways of doing this is to use multiple sources of data in performing personal injury assessments. If the forensic evaluator performs a comprehensive assessment, they will be able to draw on their clinical impressions of the subject, information from self-report, data from document review, and other collateral sources as well as the results of objective tests. If the data from these different sources line up well, the forensic evaluator is likely to be on firm ground in his or her conclusions, while divergent results strongly suggest the need for more assessment. Finally, it is important that forensic assessments and testimony be transparent in the sense that they allow the court to follow the evaluator's reasoning and be able to draw independent conclusions about the information being presented. Developing an awareness of potential sources of bias and utilizing debiasing strategies will assist evaluators performing personal injury evaluations in minimizing these problematic tendencies and will increase the usefulness of reports and testimony.

References

American Psychological Association. (2002). Ethical principles of psychologists and code of conduct. *American Psychologist, 57*(12), 1060–1073. doi:10.1037/0003-066X.57.12.1060

American Psychological Association. (2013). Specialty guidelines for forensic psychology. *American Psychologist, 68*(1), 7–19. doi:10.1037/a002988

Barton, A. (2004). Just deserts theory. In *Encyclopedia of Prisons & Correctional Facilities* (pp. 504–507). Thousand Oaks, CA: Sage.

Bishara, S. N., Partridge, F. M., Godfrey, H. P., & Knight, R. G. (1992). Post-traumatic amnesia and Glasgow Coma Scale related to outcome in survivors in a consecutive series of patients with severe closed-head injury. *Brain Injury, 6*(4), 373–380.

Bush, S. S., Ruff, R. M., Tröster, A. I., Barth, J. T., Koffler, S. P., Pliskin, N. H., . . . Silver, C. H. (2005). Symptom validity assessment: Practice issues and medical necessity NAN policy & planning committee. *Archives of Clinical Neuropsychology: The Official Journal of the National Academy of Neuropsychologists, 20*(4), 419–426. doi:10.1016/j.acn.2005.02.002

Butcher, J. N., Dahlstrom, W. G., Graham, J. R., Tellegen, A, & Kaemmer, B. (1989). *The Minnesota Multiphasic Personality Inventory-2 (MMPI-2): Manual for administration and scoring.* Minneapolis, MN: University of Minnesota Press.

Cornell University Law School. (n.d.) But-for test. *Legal Information Institute.* Retrieved from http://www.law.cornell.edu/wex/but-for_test

Cornell University Law School. (n.d.) Strict Liability. *Legal Information Institute.* Retrieved from http://www.law.cornell.edu/wex/strict_liability

Daubert v. Merrill Dow Pharmaceuticals, 509 U.S., 113 S.Ct 2786, 125 L.Ed.2d 469 (9th Circuit 1993).

Frye v. United States, 293 F.3d F.1013, 34 ALR 145 (DC Cir. 1923).

Gifis, S. H. (2010). *Law Dictionary* (6th ed.). Hauppauge, NY: Barron's Educational Series.

Hunt v. Bradshaw, 746 88 SE 2d 762 (N.Carol. 1955).

Lezak, M. D. (Ed.). (2012). *Neuropsychological assessment* (5th ed.). Oxford, U.K.: Oxford University Press.

Lillienfeld, S., James, W., & Howard, G. (2000). The scientific status of projective techniques. *American Psychological Society,* 1(2): 27–66.

Moffett, P., & Moore, G. (2011). The standard of care: Legal history and definitions: The bad and good news. *Western Journal of Emergency Medicine, 12*(1), 109–112.

Murray, H. (1943). *Thematic Apperception Test manual.* Cambridge, MA: Harvard University Press.

Spooner, D. M., & Pachana, N. A. (2006). Ecological validity in neuropsychological assessment: A case for greater consideration in research with neurologically intact populations. *Archives of Clinical Neuropsychology: The Official Journal of the National Academy of Neuropsychologists, 21*(4), 327–337. doi:10.1016/j.acn.2006.04.004

Teasdale, G., & Jennett, B. (1974). Assessment of coma and impaired consciousness. A practical scale. *Lancet, 2*(7872), 81–84.

Wechsler Adult Intelligence Scale, Fourth Edition. (2003). San Antonio, TX: Psychological Corporation.

Part II

Cases, Approaches, and Practices with Specialized Populations

9

Psychological Evaluations to Determine Competency to Parent

Anthony J. Urquiza, Anna M. L. Westin,
and Dawn M. Blacker

No man really knows about other human beings.
The best he can do is to suppose that they are like himself.
—John Steinbeck, *The Winter of Our Discontent*

Review of the Literature

When one considers that psychologists conduct extensive research on so many important and relevant events, characteristics, behaviors, attitudes, and traits in humans—it is puzzling that empirical research related to psychological evaluations of parents involved in child welfare systems has received so little attention. The psychological literature on how to conduct such evaluations is sparse. While the American Psychological Association (APA) provides general guidelines about conducting psychological evaluations in child protection matters, they focus on basic principles and speak little to the actual process of conducting evaluations (American Psychological Association, 2013). This chapter will describe the process of determining the competency to parent using available best practices for psychological evaluations.

Most case law is specific to the termination of parental right rather than parental capacity. Guidelines specifying the determination of parental capacity as well as the termination of parental rights vary from state to state. Generally, these guidelines contain definitions of child maltreatment, factors that should be considered by the court prior to returning a child to the custody of the parent, and factors related to the parent's involvement in and response to intervention (Condie & Condie, 2007). Following the Adoption and Safe

Families Act (ASFA) of 1997, many statutes also specify time frames for successful reunification, as states are offered financial incentives for achieving permanency (i.e. moving children from foster care to long-term placement, guardianship, and/or adoption).

While there are many reasons for children to enter the child welfare system, most of the reasons have little to do with the children themselves—usually, petitions for placement of a child in protective custody are related to parent competencies. On this point, most parents who have their children removed from their care have problems with drugs and alcohol, serious mental health problems (e.g., intellectual disability, thought disorder), and/or problems (especially posttraumatic stress disorder and depression) related to their own childhood (a history of sexual abuse, neglect, or physical abuse that has resulted in severe long-term problems in functioning) or adult victimization (e.g., domestic violence, sexual assault; Dubowitz, Kim, Black, Weisbart, Semiatin, & Magder, 2011; Friesen, Katz-Leavy, & Nicholson, 2011; Traube, 2012). As a result of these difficulties, some parents are unable to safely and adequately care for their children.

In situations where the court is required to make a decision about whether parents can safely and adequately care for their child or children, they often seek out expert opinion about capabilities, mental health status, quality of the parent-child relationship, engagement and benefits related to mental health treatment, and recovery from substance abuse. Psychologists have unique competencies to evaluate parental competencies. In some cases, parents have limited abilities to care for their child safely and adequately, which are unlikely to improve over time with services. However, in many cases, psychologists can provide recommendations to improve parenting competency in order to increase the likelihood of successful reunification (Benjet, Azar, & Kuersten-Hogan, 2003; Melton, Petrila, Poythress, & Slobogin, 1997).

Best Practices

This chapter will describe the process of psychological evaluations to determine the competency to parent. In contrast to more traditional evaluations, this type of evaluation is dyadic in focus and requires specialized knowledge relevant to child welfare. Furthermore, the evaluator needs to carefully consider parent-child fit, issues of timing, and the veracity of the parent report. Gold standard components of such evaluations include use of standardized measures, clinical interviews, parent-child observations, review of records, and consultation with collateral sources. We will start at the beginning of the evaluation (i.e., referral for an evaluation) and will end with a case example to illustrate the main points.

What Is the Referral Question?

An essential element in undertaking an evaluation is having a clear understanding of the referral question. Typically, the referral question is related to determining whether the parents possess the skills and abilities to safely and adequately care for their child, and if not, what services would enable them to be able to care for their child. While there may be additional types of questions (e.g., has the parent successfully completed substance abuse counseling, can the parent safely manage the behavioral problems exhibited by the child?), the issues are usually at least indirectly related to the parent's ability to care for the child.

Timing of Referral and Evaluation

An additional issue concerning the referral question involves timing. It is necessary for evaluators to have a full understanding of the child welfare and institutional statutes related to reunification. Referral of a parent two months after his or her child enters dependency may be a substantially different circumstance than a parent with similar issues referred at nineteen months after a child enters dependency. That is, two months after dependency, the parent has the right to eighteen months of services to enable him/her to care for the child, and the referral may be made to assist in the development of a case plan, especially if the parent has some type of unique mental health concern (e.g., limited intellectual ability, severe depression). In contrast, the county has no mandated requirement to provide reunification services to a parent referred for an evaluation at nineteen months after the child has entered dependency. As a result, an evaluation of a parent referred later in the process may be more related to termination of reunification services or termination of parental rights (i.e., if the child was returned to the care of the parent at this time, would the parent be able to safely and adequately care for them?). Timing is important to consider when clarifying the referral question, as well as when completing the evaluation. An evaluator must determine not only whether or not a parent is competent at the time of the evaluation but also whether he or she has the potential to become competent, and if so, how long it would take the parent to be able to care for the children safely and adequately. In some cases, it may be likely that the parent can become competent, but not within the time frame provided by state statutes.

Focus of the Evaluation as a Parent-Child Dyad

While many traditional psychological evaluations focus on the individual, psychological evaluations to determine competency to parent should be framed from a dyadic (i.e., parent-child) perspective. Both the parent and child have to be acknowledged and assessed for a competent evaluation of parenting capacity. The relative strengths or weaknesses of both the parent and child should be considered. For example, it is important to understand that greater child psychopathology is likely to lead to a need for greater parenting capacities (e.g., a child with severe aggression and noncompliance requires greater parental skills and abilities to manage these behaviors). A child with special medical needs, who requires consistent medication, monitoring, or parent-administered medical procedures demands a parent who is knowledgeable and aware of the severity of the medical problem and who can reliably meet the child's medical needs. Conversely, a child with relatively few behavioral or emotional problems may be fairly easy to parent. Additionally, a child's age or developmental level is relevant, as children at different stages of development have different needs (e.g., a typically developing infant has different needs, and requires different parenting, than a typically developing teenager). Thus, the intersection of a child's age, special needs, and mental health/behavioral needs requires different parenting abilities. Therefore, it is best practice that a parent evaluation includes the child (ideally a face-to-face assessment of the child and, at a minimum, an understanding of the child through collateral sources and record review). While there may be some instances where a parent can be evaluated apart from the child, this should be uncommon and related to situations in which the dominant factor is parent capacity (e.g., parent and a healthy newborn infant), a solitary dimension of a parent's capacity (e.g., failure of a parent to sustain in a drug treatment program), and/or problems inherent in the parent-child relationship that may destabilize the child's placement (e.g., a significant increase in trauma symptoms due to contact with the parent).

Conducting an Evaluation

From Basics to Understanding the Story of the Parent   Parental competency includes a basic understanding of child development and the ability to learn and apply basic to complex caretaking skills depending on the child's needs. For example, at the most basic level, a parent must be able to consistently recognize the signs that an infant is hungry and must be able to provide the right type and amount of food. However, the assessment of parenting competencies is not simply the verbal recounting of steps necessary to parent, but a description of the pattern of events that have led to the child being placed in dependency and the actions toward reunification. This includes the parents providing information not just about their skills, knowledge, and abilities— but the entire story that they tell about their life, the roles of significant people in their life (e.g., children, grandparents, partners), and their past and current capacities to sustain healthy relationships. While a description of relationship history is not always a predictor of how parents will engage in future relationships (i.e., parents will always have the capacity to change the way in which they live their lives), the pattern of past relationship problems and their awareness of these problems provide guidance about their ability to have a safe and healthy relationship with their child. From this viewpoint, it is incumbent on the evaluator to allow the parents to tell their story about their history of relationships and, especially, the history of their relationship with their child that led to their child's entry into dependency.

As part of the telling of this story, it is essential to hear the content of what happened and why it happened, to understand the consequences, and to acquire information about lessons learned. However, because of a parent's propensity to present an overly positive façade during the evaluation, it is also essential to understand the process by which the story is told (Benjamin, 1993). Attachment is one of the most meaningful elements of human development, mental health, and safe and healthy families. An individual's relationship history is a reflection of his or her self-image and a predictor for the future. For example, a young woman neglected in early childhood and removed and placed in foster care at age three, with more than twenty-five subsequent foster and group home placements throughout the course of her life, is likely to struggle with understanding and consistently engaging in the give and take of meaningful relationships as a parent. That is, limited exposure to the many behaviors and actions of good parenting leaves that child with limited parenting capacities as she grows older. To modify a position asserted by Fogel and colleagues (Fogel, Garvey, Hsu, & West-Stroming, 2006), relationships are the architecture through which we learn to live our lives and to live in the lives of others. Is it possible that a person with a pattern of adverse relationship experiences that include events such as multiple foster placements, domestic violence, and absence of a trusted confidant could derive and develop the qualities of good parenting? Certainly. Is it likely? It would be difficult and uncommon. This is because the story of healthy parenting capacities lies in the hundreds of thousands of positive affiliative interactions experienced by a parent throughout the course of his or her own infancy, childhood, adolescence, and adulthood. Is this an assertion that being born of a "good" family leads to good parenting or that being born of a troubled family leads to poor parenting? We know that there are many factors that contribute to an overall sense of resiliency—an improvement in one's capacities, even in light of multiple and sometimes significant adversities.

But everyone has a story—and careful listening to the content and process of the story can lead to a better understanding of the overall context in which the parents had their child removed from their care, the potential for them to be able to successfully reunify with the child, and the steps necessary to support a healthy parent-child relationship. An essential element of an evaluator is to listen carefully enough to the parent's story and to see clearly enough to provide an opinion that is fair to both the parent's right to reasonable services and the best interests of the child.

The Broad Range of Common Child Welfare Knowledge   It is necessary for an evaluator to have a solid understanding of common problems encountered in the child welfare system (e.g., substance abuse, domestic violence, personality disorders, limited intellectual abilities, trauma, parent-child relationship qualities, early childhood attachment). Important and difficult questions arise that demand an informed clinician:

- What is the effect of methamphetamines on a fetus?
- How does trauma and depression interact to impair awareness of oneself and the child?
- What is the effect of antidepressants on parental functioning?
- How does one differentiate between Posttraumatic Stress Disorder and Attention Deficit Hyperactivity Disorder in a young child?
- What are effective treatments for substance abuse?

Additionally, it is important for an evaluator to appreciate the distinctions of mental health and human development that may be immutable or can be ameliorated by social services and/or mental health interventions. For example, certain conditions (e.g., Down's syndrome) are likely to limit a parent's potential for acquiring increased parenting capacities through interventions, while other conditions (e.g., depression) may have multiple interventions that can significantly improve parental functioning. While it is not reasonable for an evaluator to understand all elements of parenting and child welfare systems, the level of knowledge to competently conduct such evaluations is typically well beyond that taught in graduate school. In order to provide quality services, evaluators may need specialized training in child welfare evaluations following the completion of their degree.

A Comment about Attachment   Without question, research conducted over the last several decades has identified attachment as the hallmark of psychological health throughout the lifespan and problems with attachment as a clear indicator of a range of psychopathologies. While the wide range of attachment research with children and adults (Cassidy & Shaver, 2008) has focused on a unifying theme of health throughout life; others have recognized that child maltreatment (Crittenden & Ainsworth, 1989) and exposure to violence (Gewirtz & Edleson, 2004) are strongly associated with disrupted attachment relationships. An extensive discussion of the roles of attachment and child maltreatment are beyond the scope of this chapter. (For a review, see Toth & Cicchetti, 2013). However, it is important to highlight that children may be connected to their parents in a manner that is not healthy and/or that contributes to their psychopathology.

The important element in the 2 × 2 table (Table 9.1) is to demonstrate that examining the quality of a parent-child relationship is more complex than the presence or absence of an attachment relationship. While it should be understood that parent-child attachment is a complex phenomenon (hence, the oft-used phrase of attachment being an "internal framework"), description of a parent-child relationship within the dimensions of positive/negative and strong/weak *at least* presents the notion that a child may have a strong relationship with the parent (and—possibly vice-versa), yet the relationship may be harmful and damaging to the child. For example, a child may be raised by a parent who has a chronic problem with alcohol and is physically and emotionally abusive. Due to caregiver difficulties, multiple substitute caregivers may also be present in the life of the child (e.g., grandparents, foster parents, aunts/uncles). This may lead to the child having an inconsistent relationship with their parent that includes frequent anger and hostility.

Veracity—Sometimes Parents Fail to Tell the Truth   While it is essential to listen carefully to the life story of the client, it is also important to understand that not everything the client shares is truthful or accurate. Sometimes parents lie about past events in an effort to hide events and characteristics that they might perceive as damaging to their effort to reunify with their child. Other times, parents may fail to provide an accurate account of past events, not because they are overtly lying, but because they have distorted perceptions of themselves and the world (e.g., poor insight, delusions). For example, a parent being evaluated asserted a career choice as being an emergency medical technician (EMT) because she thought her prior history of speeding and reckless driving would be perceived as a testament to her "exceptional driving skills." While this would be an unlikely scenario (and clearly an important statement concerning her judgment), it appeared to reflect a genuine position

TABLE 9.1   Attachment Strength and Quality

	Strong	Weak
POSITIVE	Positive affiliative parent-child relationship, with continuity and consistency	A positive relationship, although with infrequent or inconsistent contact
NEGATIVE	A stable relationship, with frequent anger, frustration, and hostility	An inconsistent relationship with anger, frustration, and hostility

by this parent. Finally, although not directly related to veracity, sometimes parents possess serious limitations in their intellectual and developmental abilities that result in failure to appreciate the importance of significant events in their life. A common example would be a mother who repeatedly becomes involved in intimate relationships with aggressive men, which often results in domestic violence. Although responsibility for aggression always lies with the aggressor, a mother's failure to recognize a pattern of placing herself and her children at risk through a series of dangerous partners is a level of self-distortion that weighs on parental capacity.

While it can be frustrating to not obtain a complete or accurate account or understanding of events, parents' partial, incorrect, or delusional stories are still helpful to inform decisions about their parenting competencies. The way a parent processes information, makes meaning of the world, and chooses to share it are all significant aspects related to their ability to care for their child safely and adequately. Nonetheless, issues of poor reporting or overt lying also highlight the importance of record review and consultation with multiple collateral sources to support facts (e.g., did the parent successfully complete his drug program?) and gain alternative perspectives.

Observation of the Parent-Child Relationship   As stated earlier, parenting assessment usually requires assessment of the parent, the child, and the dyad. Typically, dyadic assessment involves some type of observational session, where the evaluator can observe specific parent-child behaviors and interactions that cannot readily be conveyed by collateral sources (e.g., in conversation with a social worker, a therapist, a teacher). Although some benefit can be gained through an informal observational session of an interaction between a parent and a child (e.g., observing a mother care for a newborn infant, change a diaper, feeding), the use of some type of formal behavioral observation system is recommended.

There are several formal observational coding schemes that can provide valuable information about parenting capacity and parent-child relationship quality (Cerezo, Keesler, Dunn, & Wahler, 1986; Eyberg, Nelson, Duke, & Boggs, 2005; Biringen, 2008). While no specific behavioral observation coding scheme is recommended, it is strongly suggested that an evaluator have a good working knowledge of at least one observational protocol and an awareness of specific types of parenting or child behaviors that reflect positive relationships. Being familiar with a behavioral coding scheme can aid the evaluator in seeing patterns of behavior and understanding parent-child interactional dynamics rather than solely relying on parental verbal reports or reports from others (e.g., teacher, social worker, visit supervisor).

As a final note, it is important to understand the limits of behavioral observations, including that they may provide an artificial snapshot of the parent-child relationship, depending on a number of factors that may detract or enhance the extant situation (e.g., child is sick, parent is nervous, observation takes place in a novel setting, parent brings food/treats to the session). For example, a parent who has very limited opportunity to visit with his or her child (e.g., one hour of supervised visitation per week) may not have sufficient contact to maintain a consistent relationship. Thus, conducting an observation of a parent-child dyad with limited contact may distort the natural processes of the parent-child dyad and may lead to faulty conceptualizations about the relationship.

Understanding the Use and Application of Standardized Assessment Measures   There is no single standardized assessment or measure (nor set of measures) that can definitively determine whether an individual can safely parent. However, conducting psychological evaluations within a child welfare setting can result in the need to assess a variety of both parent and child domains. Because of this, the evaluator will need to be familiar with many different types of standardized assessments and their appropriate uses. A portion of this issue is the *strong* assertion that only measures with demonstrated validity and reliability be used in child welfare settings. While it may be argued that certain psychological qualities or concepts can only be captured with a projective test, others have clearly articulated that there are many inherent flaws in the development and use of projective tests (Lillienfield, Wood, & Garb, 2000).

It is also important to note that many standardized assessments have not been developed with discrete versions for different cultural groups. Issues of language use and language comprehension may distort a parent's response to standardized questionnaires. Parents with intellectual disabilities or poor academic achievement may not be able to complete standardized questionnaires. Additionally, misuse of standardized questionnaires based on limited research into cultural differences may increase the likelihood that a parent responds to a test "differently" and is therefore perceived as possessing greater psychopathology (Urquiza, & Wyatt, 1993). Thus, a careful review of norms and test development is needed to reduce bias. For example, the Comprehensive Test of Nonverbal Intelligence (CTONI) may be a better measure of cognitive abilities than the WISC-IV when there are concerns about bias due to language, hearing, or culture. When standardized measures are not appropriate, and less-biased alternatives are not available, the evaluator will have to rely more heavily on other sources of data (e.g., interview, collaterals).

Use of Collateral Contacts   While it is important to acquire evaluation data through clinical interviews, direct informal observation, structured observations, and use of standardized assessments, contacting collateral information sources is often vital to a clear understanding of the parent-child relationship. Often, parents under evaluation may alter their presentation while participating in an evaluation; they may attempt to present themselves in the best possible light. By contacting relevant people in the life of the parent and/or child, an evaluator can gain a better understanding of the functioning of the parent in his or her role as a caregiver, his or her response to mental health or social service interventions, and his or her use of informal social support systems. For example, teachers can provide information about whether a child arrived at school wearing appropriate clothes and well fed. A therapist can provide information about a parent's consistent attendance in treatment sessions and willingness to address mental health problems. Finally, grandparents can speak to their ability and willingness to be a support to the parent and their grandchild.

Culture and Child Welfare Evaluations   Culture can be considered a pattern of beliefs, thoughts, ideas, and traditions commonly held by a group of people. While many people consider culture synonymous with race or ethnicity, there is great cultural heterogeneity within racial groups, and many other group variables are associated with culture (e.g., language, disability status, socioeconomic status). A review of culture and child maltreatment is beyond the scope of this chapter (for a comprehensive review, see Fontes, 2005), but it is important to note that culture influences attitudes about parenting, definitions of child maltreatment, and system responses to families. For example, African American families are overrepresented in child welfare investigations, enter the foster care system at disproportionate rates, and are less likely to be reunified or adopted than their Caucasian peers (Fluke, Yuan, Hedderson, & Curtis, 2003; Fox, 2005). Multiple factors impact the rate of child maltreatment, as well as response of child welfare systems to families, in different cultural groups.

It is important that the evaluator have knowledge of the literature on culture and child welfare, along with an awareness of his or her own biases. Different cultures may have different definitions of child maltreatment; however, child maltreatment is likely clearly defined by law in the location where the evaluator operates. Nonetheless, having knowledge of other definitions will provide a context for the evaluator to better understand the family. For example, instances of leaving a child unattended that would qualify as neglect in the United States would not be unusual in Sweden, and while female genital mutilation is accepted in some parts of the world, it is considered abuse in the United States. More commonly, American families will present with varying attitudes about family life, parenting, and punishment. For example, African American families, and families whom live in more dangerous neighborhoods (regardless of race), tend to endorse harsher punishment (e.g., Barajas-Gonzalez & Brooks-Gunn, 2014).

Having a thorough understanding of the presenting family's culture is essential in conceptualizing how the family came to the attention of child welfare and will also influence prognosis and treatment recommendations. A parent with a belief in harsh physical punishment, who consistently punishes his or her child (too harshly, by child welfare standards) for not following rules will be viewed differently than will a parent who does not believe in physical punishment but who has poor emotion regulation and beats a child in anger when having a bad day, noncontingent on the child's behavior. The first parent may live in a community where the majority of members share their beliefs, while the second is shamed by peers for unacceptable behavior. While the second parent would likely benefit from learning coping skills, this may be irrelevant for the first parent. Thus, an understanding of the parent's story includes meaning making, which is embedded in a larger cultural context.

Family culture and experiences with the child welfare system may also influence an individual's level of trust, cooperation, and level of honesty when completing an evaluation about parenting competency. It is the role of the evaluator to assess these attitudes, expectancies, and experiences to create a culturally informed conceptualization of the family. In order to be sensitive to the influence of culture, an evaluator must carefully explain his or her role and the purpose of the evaluation, select appropriate measures, critically evaluate information from service providers who may have a biased view of the family, and include collateral sources the parent would like the evaluator to contact (e.g., family friends, pastor, employer).

While some cultural attitudes may conflict with safe parenting and healthy relationships (Terao, Borrego, & Urquiza, 2000; 2001), culture can also represent a family strength. Such strengths can be used to inform treatment planning, to motivate change and reunification efforts, and to prevent future child maltreatment. For many families, culture may be a strong and important dynamic in strengthening family ties, involving extended family members in child care, and keeping children safe. Positive valuing of children, parenting, child caregiving, and family ties are all positive aspects of a parent's belief system that should be assessed. When beliefs contradict safe parenting, psychoeducation and parenting skills may help teach parents alternative behavior management strategies that are still consistent with their cultural beliefs (e.g., how can I get my child to respect his elders without using physical punishment?).

Making Meaning   The role of the evaluator is not to simply tally the pros and cons of a parent's functioning but to offer an opinion based on the results of information gathered in the evaluation. There is no clearly identified guideline, protocol, or log-linear process that can pinpoint—with any scientific accuracy—the direction the evaluator's opinion might take. Instead, it is necessary for the evaluator to utilize and integrate all of the tools at his or her disposal and then present the most well-reasoned and supported position to each referral question. In many instances, generating an opinion for the referral question requires development of a case conceptualization where none previously existed (Kegan, 1983). It is the responsibility of the evaluator to provide the court with a coherent understanding of the parent, within the immediate context of the specific referral questions (and the more distal context of the child welfare and institution statutes), which results in a better view of the parent and parent-child relationship. Such a view can serve to describe both the qualities of the relationship and the strengths and weaknesses of the parent, with the weaknesses being the focus of interventions that may reasonably lead to safe and adequate parenting capacities.

Specific and Focused Treatment Recommendations   After completing all aspects of an evaluation, an evaluator addresses each of the referral questions, often offering recommendations for treatment. Given that the evaluator may have developed the most thoughtful view of the parent and child, it is therefore incumbent on him or her to provide a concise, clear, and well-reasoned treatment plan. The treatment plan should be tailored to the child and parent, and the evaluator should recommend empirically supported treatments when available. It is helpful for the evaluator to be familiar with local resources and available treatments. In general, recommendations should be sufficiently detailed that the parent's social worker would be able to review the report and then make the appropriate referrals that would result in reasonable services to address the parent's problems.

Case Vignette

The following case vignette illustrates what is often required in completing evaluations to determine the ability to parent safely and adequately and what is considered a best-practice approach. Consider the following case example in light of the APA evaluation guidelines and general standards most courts must consider when making decisions about parenting competency matters. This case highlights many of the challenges that evaluators face during the evaluation process (i.e., caregiver axis I and axis II mental health problems, understanding the client's story and meaning making, concerns about veracity, and assessing strength, valence, and continuity of attachment).

Reason for Referral

Ms. Jones was referred for a court ordered evaluation by the County Deputy Public Defender, who was acting as her counsel in the child welfare action. The reasons for the evaluation are 1) to provide an opinion of Ms. Jones's current

---

The case vignette has been redacted and all identifying information removed. It is not meant to serve as a forensic report. Any likeness to a case is purely coincidental.

mental health status, 2) to provide an assessment of the bond/attachment between Ms. Jones and her son, David, and 3) to provide recommendations for reunification services.

Summary of Relevant Records and Relevant Background Information

Ms. Jones's biological parents separated when she was 5 years of age, and she lived with her mother and stepfather for the majority of her life. She grew up in a small town in California where she remains. Ms. Jones reported ongoing sexual abuse by several family members (i.e., her biological mother, biological father, and stepfather) between the ages of 6 to 17. She does not currently have contact with her family members and does not have any friends. She graduated from high school but described ongoing academic and behavioral difficulties starting in middle school (e.g., special education status, suspensions, truancy, fighting), which were supported by school records. As a result of her difficulties, she transferred schools multiple times. Ms. Jones was unemployed, although she has previously been employed in the fast food service industry.

With regard to romantic relationships, Ms. Jones started dating Mr. Martinez at age 16, and the couple separated when she was 19 years of age, approximately a year after the birth of their son, David. The pregnancy and delivery were unremarkable, and David met developmental milestones on time. Ms. Jones reports ongoing domestic violence in the relationship with Mr. Martinez and reports that she ultimately left him, fearing for her own life. She required medical attention on a number of occasions as a result of violence by Mr. Martinez. She started dating Mr. Brown immediately following the separation from Mr. Martinez, and the couple is currently engaged to be married and cohabitating. There have also been a few instances of violence perpetrated by Mr. Martinez following the termination of the relationship between Ms. Jones and Mr. Martinez, including Mr. Martinez threatening Ms. Jones with a gun, which was witnessed by Mr. Brown. Ms. Jones noted that she did not believe that she could have successfully sustained her separation from Mr. Martinez if she had not been supported throughout the process of separation by Mr. Brown. She described Mr. Brown as "always being there" for her and explained that the couple "do[es] everything" together. For example, she cited only a very few instances of their being apart over the last two years. Ms. Jones has never been single since she started dating at 16 years of age and expressed fears about being alone.

When asked about mental health symptoms, Ms. Jones endorsed significant trauma symptoms (e.g., re-experiencing, avoidance, and increased arousal) with an onset in childhood. She described dissociation associated with trauma triggers ("I become silent . . . I'm in Lala land") which was also confirmed by

Mr. Brown ("She becomes spaced out, has no emotion"). She also endorsed ongoing struggles with depression since adolescence (i.e., depressed mood, increased sleep need, anhedonia, difficulty concentrating, suicidal ideation). She described poor self-esteem, low self-efficacy, a passive personality style, and difficulty making decisions on her own. She was unsure about her own life goals. She described ongoing fears about Mr. Brown leaving her, despite reassurance from Mr. Brown that he was happy. Ms. Jones also acknowledged nine months of illegal drug use (methamphetamines) shortly after her son was born. She recalled that she felt her drug use was a problem that was impacting her parenting, so she decided to stop using any type of drug. She denied any drug use since that time. Ms. Jones denied other mental health symptoms. Further, she denied receiving mental health services but was open to therapy and medication management, if appropriate. Ms. Jones currently takes pain medications, following injuries from a car accident last year.

Ms. Jones made allegations to child welfare that her son, David, had been sexually abused by herself and several other family members (i.e., David's father, Mr. Martinez, David's maternal grandmother, and David's maternal step grandfather). Ms. Jones later denied abusing her son and denied knowing any information about anyone else abusing her son. The allegations of sexual abuse were unsubstantiated by child welfare services, but David was nevertheless removed from his mother's care due to concerns about Ms. Jones's mental health and her ability to parent David safely and adequately given false claims of sexual abuse. There was no additional child welfare history or any reports that David had suffered child maltreatment. At the time of this evaluation, David was placed with his paternal grandmother (where Mr. Martinez was also living). He had been removed from his mother's care for approximately five months, and had supervised visits with Ms. Jones for one hour in a child welfare clinic twice weekly.

When asked during the evaluation about her allegations of sexual abuse, Ms. Jones explained that she had started lying about a number of things (e.g., past and current problems) in an attempt to be close to her fiancé. Mr. Brown had a history of abuse in his childhood, prior drug use, and behavioral problems in his youth. He reported that he learned that acknowledging past abuse and any current problems is a necessary part of treatment and recovery, and he had encouraged Ms. Jones to do the same. Ms. Jones stated that she believed Mr. Brown might leave her if she did not share similar experiences so she reported that she had been sexually abused during her own childhood. She further reported that she had sexually abused her son (and that he also had been abused by her parents and Mr. Martinez) in an effort to develop a closer relationship with Mr. Brown. Additionally, Ms. Jones explained that part of her reasoning to make false allegations were fears related to her family members having requested more contact with her son. It should be noted that throughout the interviews, Ms. Jones cried extensively and said she felt "disgusted" with herself. Ms. Jones had difficulty articulating her reasoning clearly but continued to provide responses related to a strong desire to sustain her relationship with Mr. Brown. Conversely, Mr. Brown expressed regret related to unintentionally pressuring Ms. Jones to share past abuse information.

Evaluation Process

At the beginning of the initial interview, Ms. Jones was provided with a full explanation of her rights and the reason for the evaluation (i.e., informed consent), and she agreed to sign a document asserting her understanding of these rights. In order to complete an evaluation of Ms. Jones, David, and their relationship, a number of procedures were conducted, including

Document Review
- Social services/court reports
- Ms. Jones's school records

Clinical Interviews/Observations
- Interview with Ms. Jones
- Conjoint interview with Ms. Jones and Mr. Brown
- Observation of Ms. Jones and David

Psychological Testing for Ms. Jones
- Kaufman Brief Intelligence Test, Second Edition (K-BIT-2; Kaufman & Kaufman, 2004)
- Personality Assessment Inventory (PAI; Morey, 2007)
- Brief Symptom Inventory (BSI; Derogatis, 1993)

Psychological Testing for David
- Behavior Assessment System for Children—Parent Report (BASC-2; Reynolds & Kamphus, 2006)

Collateral Contacts
- Mr. Brown, fiancé
- Mr. Scott, county deputy public defender

Typically, evaluations take approximately 8–12 hours to complete (i.e., clinical interviewing, administering/scoring psychological tests, collateral contacts, report writing). This evaluation was slightly longer because the client lived in a different city—making the overall time to complete this evaluation slightly longer due to travel time for the clinical observation of the client and her son.

Mental Status Examination

Ms. Jones was a 21-year-old Caucasian woman of average build who was monolingual in English. She presented at both visits dressed and groomed appropriately for her age and the weather. She was interviewed alone and with her fiancé, Mr. Brown.

During the course of the evaluation, Ms. Jones was interviewed on three occasions. The first two interviews were conducted at the clinic (lasting about 2–3 hours each), with Mr. Brown in attendance (she indicated that she and Mr. Brown were always together, did all errands together, and went to all appointments together). Ms. Jones was interviewed by herself on one occasion and together with Mr. Brown on another occasion. A third clinical interview and behavioral observation (lasting about 2 hours) was conducted with her son at the county visitation center. Because Ms. Jones was required to have supervised visitation, the evaluator was allowed to be the supervisor for the visit. Mr. Brown was not allowed in the visitation center, so he was not present.

During the clinical interviews, Ms. Jones often started the conversation with a calm demeanor, and she was attentive and focused on responding to the questions presented to her. However, when asked more difficult questions, she cried extensively and sometimes appeared to be disconnected from the interview process (i.e., detached, staring, unfocused). When she was not distraught and crying, Ms. Jones had insight into her behavior when asked about it. Despite crying, she continued responding to questions and remained cooperative throughout the evaluation. Ms. Jones was oriented to time, place, and situation. No delusions, thought problems, or hallucinations were reported or observed. She denied current suicidal and homicidal ideation.

When Ms. Jones was interviewed and she became upset, she made repeated self-deprecating statements. For example, when describing the reasons for her decision to stop taking drugs, she said:

I was losing myself. I felt I was a horrible mother. I was like 90 pounds. I was disgusting—a person I did not like.

When later asked questions about why she had previously gotten in trouble for lying, she stated:

I was disgusting. I was lying so much, I was not good. I was lying about a lot of things. I was a big lie. I was afraid I was gonna lose him (Mr. Brown) so I just started lying and it kept on happening. I am such a disgusting person.

When interviewed with Mr. Brown, Ms. Jones tended to be more passive. Mr. Brown often answered questions for Ms. Jones. On a couple of occasions, he needed to be reminded that a question was presented to Ms. Jones, not to him. He appeared to easily understand that speaking for Ms. Jones was a concern and commented that he had a strong personality and that he often spoke for her. After some prompting, he was able to be less responsive to questions, allowing Ms. Jones to answer the questions. Ms. Jones frequently became stuck on questions when Mr. Brown was asked to let her respond. She had difficulty articulating responses and appeared uncomfortable speaking for herself.

David was a three-year-old Caucasian and Hispanic boy who appeared his stated age. He was appropriately dressed and groomed for his age and the weather during the parent-child observation. His speech tone, pitch, and production were within normal limits. His gait and motor skills were unremarkable. He provided developmentally appropriate responses to questions. His activity level was above average.

Psychological Measures

Summaries from psychological testing are provided below. Results from any one test were not used to form diagnostic or treatment conclusions. Rather, each test was used in conjunction with evaluative data from additional sources such as interviews, case history, direct observations, and other test data. Results below were considered valid unless otherwise noted.

Standardized Assessment Information on Ms. Jones

Kaufman Brief Intelligence Test, Second Edition (KBIT-2)   The Kaufman Brief Intelligence Test, Second Edition (KBIT-2) is a brief measure of intellectual ability. The KBIT-2 comprises two main subtest scores, Verbal and Nonverbal. In addition, there is an overall score, a KBIT-2 IQ Composite score.

Ms. Jones obtained an overall IQ Composite score (SS = 90) that falls in the "Average" range. Ms. Jones obtained a "Below Average" standard score of 82 on the Verbal subscale and an "Average" standard score of 100 on the Nonverbal subscale. There is a significant difference between her Verbal and Nonverbal subscale scores, suggesting that additional intellectual assessment is indicated to more accurately understand her cognitive strengths and weaknesses. However, her performance, along with data from other sources, does not suggest concern with regard to cognitive limitations impacting parenting ability. It is likely that Ms. Jones's below-average abilities on the Verbal subscale reflect her inconsistent involvement in school (i.e., school-based learning tends to be reflected in the Verbal subtests).

Brief Symptom Inventory (BSI)   The Brief Symptom Inventory (BSI) is a 53-item standardized self-report measure used to assess an individual's current psychological functioning. Two global indices provided information regarding overall symptom severity currently experienced by the respondent. Nine primary symptom dimensions provided more specific information about possible areas of concern.

On the BSI, Ms. Jones was clinically elevated on all (i.e., Anxiety, Depression, Interpersonal Sensitivity, Obsessive-Compulsive, Somatization, Paranoid Ideation, Phobic Anxiety, and Psychoticism) but one scale (i.e., Hostility). Her overall symptoms and severity index were also clinically significant. This suggests that Ms. Jones was currently experiencing severe and intense mental health symptoms across a range of areas.

Personality Assessment Inventory (PAI)   The Personality Assessment Inventory (PAI) is a self-administered, objective inventory of adult personality. The PAI contains 344 items that comprise 22 nonoverlapping scales. As a clinical instrument, the PAI provides information relevant to clinical diagnosis, treatment planning, and screening for psychopathology. On the validity scales of the PAI, Ms. Jones was significantly elevated on Negative Impression Management, indicating that she may have overrepresented the frequency and severity of mental health symptoms. The test developers suggest that some individuals who possess severe and unremitting mental health symptoms may be elevated on this specific validity scale and that it may represent an accurate reflection of the severity of problems they are experiencing. It is suggested in Ms. Jones's case that the experience of having her child removed from her care because of her false allegations and her consistent fears that her partner would leave her, combined with chronic depressed and anxious affect, together reflect her severe problems. This is further supported by observations during the clinical interview, where she cried consistently and made many self-deprecating statements ("I am so disgusting"). Nevertheless, the PAI can be interpreted only to the degree that it reflects the client's self-perception.

Based on Ms. Jones's self-perception, she indicated that she experienced problems with thinking clearly; currently had (or may have had) a problem with illegal drugs; experienced cognitive, affective, and physiological symptoms of depression; experienced significant stress; did not perceive much support in her environment; was passive in interactions with others; and was emotionally detached from others. Finally, Ms. Jones reported severe and unremitting trauma symptoms. The PAI profile indicated high likelihood for Dependent Personality Disorder, Posttraumatic Stress Disorder, Major Depressive Disorder, and (past) Substance Use. The treatment response scale suggested a positive prognosis should Ms. Jones enter mental health services.

Summary of Psychological Measures for Ms. Jones   According to standardized testing, Ms. Jones's intelligence was within the average range of functioning, and thus it did not appear that cognitive limitations were affecting her ability to parent. Additional testing for Ms. Jones confirmed information shared during clinical interviews and document review. She endorsed a significant trauma history and significant symptoms of re-experiencing, increased arousal, and avoidance. She acknowledged a history of substance abuse, but she denied current use. She also endorsed interpersonal sensitivity, a passive interpersonal style, and some difficulty related to staying on task, communicating clearly, and making decisions. Finally, she endorsed clinically significant symptoms of depression and anxiety.

Standardized Assessment Information on David

Behavior Assessment System for Children, Second Edition (BASC-2)   The Behavior Assessment System for Children (BASC-2) is an integrated system designed to facilitate the differential diagnosis and classification of a variety of emotional and behavioral disorders of children and to aid in the design of a treatment plan. There are multiple Clinical Scales and Adaptive Scales that form composite scores, including Internalizing, Externalizing, Adaptive, and Behavioral Composites. Scale scores in the "clinically significant" range suggest a high level of maladjustment. Scores in the "at-risk" range identify either a significant problem that may not be severe enough to require formal treatment or a potential of developing a problem that needs careful monitoring.

Parent Report. Ms. Jones completed the parent form of the BASC-2   She endorsed few concerns about David, only noting "at risk" concerns for hyperactivity (e.g., David is *Often* or *Almost Always* overly active, fidgeting, interrupting, and throws tantrums).

Summary of Psychological Measures for David   Results from David's testing were consistent with records, observation, and clinical interview. David generally functioned well and there were no reported concerns related to development or behavior. However, his activity level was above average, which combined with some concerns about frequent whining and tantrums, placed him at risk for behavioral problems in the future.

Observation of Ms. Jones with David   During the clinical observation of Ms. Jones and David, they were observed in several play scenarios. In the first scenario, Ms. Jones was asked to allow David to choose what to play and follow his lead. In the second scenario, Ms. Jones was asked to inform David that she would pick an activity and get him to play according to her rules. Finally, Ms. Jones was asked to get David to clean up the toys. The purpose of these scenarios was to observe the quality of their interactions and to observe how David responded to Ms. Jones's instructions/commands.

When David first saw Ms. Jones, he was excited, happy, and immediately moved to give her a hug. Throughout the observation, he referred to her as "Mommy" and often sought her out for affection, to share something with her, or to sit on her lap. Consistently throughout the interaction, Ms. Jones responded to David by praising his appropriate behavior. They played cooperatively throughout the observation, with frequent changes in activity. Because David had difficulty sustaining his attention on the same activity for longer periods of time, Ms. Jones and David often moved around the play area. David tended to be mildly demanding and whiny. Although the whiny behavior persisted throughout the observation, when Ms. Jones set a specific limit on David's behavior (e.g., cleaning up some toys), he was responsive to her. Toward the end of the observation, David became very whiny and Ms. Jones asked him whether he was tired. David stated that he was tired and then crawled onto his mother's lap and put his head on her shoulder. Ms. Jones explained that this was about the time that David would take a nap and that he often gets tired around this time of day.

During a portion of the clinical interview with Ms. Jones and David, they were coded using the Dyadic Parent-Child Interaction Coding System (DPICS). The selected portion below reflects a parent who might struggle with acquiring and sustaining child compliance (DPICS codes are bracketed below):

Parent and child playing with Legos, when parent is asked by the examiner to get the child to clean up the toys:

P: It's time to clean up now. [Information; Indirect Command/No Comply]

C: I want to play with the Space Legos!

P: Let's put the Legos in this box. [Indirect Command/No Comply]

C: Not yet. Not yet. I have to make a Space Lego man.

P: No, it's time to clean up. [Negative Talk; Indirect Command/No Comply]

(*Child ignores the command and continues to play with Legos*)

P: C'mon, let's clean up the toys. [Indirect Command; No Opportunity to Comply]

(*Child ignores the command and continues to play with Legos*)

P: *(With mild frustration)* I said, it's time for you to clean up the Legos! [Indirect Command/No Comply]

C: I'm putting all of these together, then I'm gonna make a car.

P: *(Increasingly frustrated)* No. It's time to clean up. Put them away or [Negative Talk; Information; Direct Command]

(Child responds by grabbing some of the Legos and moving away from the parent)

P: *(Raises voice with a forced angry tone)* If you don't starting putting them away . . . Now . . . You're gonna be sorry. [Negative Talk]

C: *(Whining, while continuing to play with the Legos)* But, I still gotta put together the Space man.

From this observation, it was apparent that the parent provided inconsistent or weak commands, to which the child did not comply. This may reflect a parent with limited parenting skills, who may struggle in providing a firm, clear, and consistent parenting relationship. Additionally, a pattern of child noncompliance is one signal of greater problems at school and more severe problems with relationship security. At a minimum, this interaction suggested that this parent-child dyad is in need of intervention to avoid more serious problems with child functioning. A pattern of such parental ineffectiveness and child noncompliance had been identified as one underlying foundation to child maltreatment (Urquiza & McNeil, 1996), and this pattern may signal an ongoing problem in both parenting capacities and child management.

Collateral Information

Ms. Jones had never received mental health services, and there were therefore no service providers available for collateral interviews. Ms. Jones further did not have any friends and felt uncomfortable with the evaluator contacting her biological family for collateral information (i.e., family members she reported had abused her in childhood whom she no longer kept in touch with). However, the evaluator was able to consult with Ms. Jones's public defender, her fiancé Mr. Brown, and previous records. These collaterals generally supported facts shared by Ms. Jones.

As a result of repeated conversations with Ms. Jones's attorney, Mr. Scott, it became clear that Ms. Jones had sought out her attorney as a confidant and source of support. Ms. Jones's attorney expressed concern that he did not possess the skills to be a counselor and provide the emotional support requested of him, and he did not think he should function in this quasi-mental health capacity. During the evaluation, the attorney was strongly encouraged to coordinate mental health services for Ms. Jones.

Clinical Summary and Opinion

Ms. Jones was referred for a psychological evaluation 1) to provide an opinion of Ms. Jones's current mental health status, 2) to provide an assessment of the bond/attachment between Ms. Jones and her son, David; and 3) to provide recommendations for reunification services.

Ms. Jones's Current Mental Health Status   After clinical interviews, formal standardized assessments, a clinical observation (Ms. Jones and her son, Ms. Jones and her fiancé), and a review of records, this evaluator determined that Ms. Jones met criteria for three *DSM-5* mental health diagnoses. These include Persistent Depressive Disorder, Posttraumatic Stress Disorder, and Dependent Personality Disorder. These are described below:

The diagnosis of Persistent Depressive Disorder is characterized by an individual with depressed mood during most of all of the day, problems with sleep, an appetite disturbance, low energy or fatigue, low self-esteem, poor concentration, and feelings of hopelessness. During clinical interviews, Ms. Jones reported problems with depressed mood, problems with sleeping (sleeping too much), fatigue, and problems with concentration and demonstrated a negative self-image/low self-esteem. Her mood problems emerged during adolescence and have been ongoing since that time. Depressive symptoms were also supported by the BSI and PAI results.

The diagnosis of Posttraumatic Stress Disorder (PTSD) is characterized by experiencing some type of traumatic event, followed by exhibiting symptoms of recurring intrusive symptoms (e.g., recurring intrusive memories of a past traumatic event, recurring distressing dreams, dissociative reactions), avoidance of stimuli associated with the trauma (e.g., avoiding stressful memories, avoiding events/places/people that trigger traumatic memories), and marked alterations in arousal (e.g., easily agitated, irritable, hypervigilance, problems in concentration). Although she reported sufficient symptoms to be diagnosed with PTSD, the nature of this case (Ms. Jones making false allegations about at least some specific instances of abuse) made the specific trauma she experienced difficult to discern. She reported an extensive history of sexual victimization by her mother, father, and stepfather—although it was not clear if these abusive events really occurred. In addition, she described repeated instances of violence by Mr. Martinez, for which there was corroborating evidence (i.e., at least one incident resulted in her hospitalization, and one incident was experienced/observed by Mr. Brown). A PTSD diagnosis was further supported by Ms. Jones's PAI profile.

It should be noted that it was not the position of this evaluator to make a determination regarding the veracity of allegations regarding her prior sexual victimization, the allegations that she sexually abused her son, and/or the allegations of domestic violence by Mr. Martinez. However, Ms. Jones possessed mental health symptoms (especially trauma symptoms) consistent with many victims of domestic violence and sexual victimization.

The diagnosis of Dependent Personality Disorder (DPD) is characterized by someone who has pervasive and excessive concerns about being taken care of that leads to submissive and clinging behavior and fears of separation. This was demonstrated by observing the interactions between Ms. Jones and Mr. Brown and reviewing Ms. Jones's history. Additionally, Ms. Jones explained that she was often more passive in decision making with Mr. Brown, and she expressed a strong fear of being abandoned. Ms. Jones displayed a similarly passive style in her relationship with Mr. Martinez, noted that she would not have been able to leave the relationship if Mr. Brown had not supported this process and that she never had been, and would not feel comfortable being, single. A passive interpersonal style and a DPD diagnosis are further supported by her PAI profile.

Ms. Jones's Allegations of Sexual Victimization Involving David   It should be understood that the pattern of making a false allegation of sexual abuse of others and including oneself is fairly atypical. Ms. Jones's explanation for this disclosure was that she strongly wanted to sustain a relationship with her current fiancé and felt that continuing to disclose past problems in her life was one way to sustain his support and attention. While this may seem like an unusual action to take, it reflects the degree to which Ms. Jones fears the possible abandonment by Mr. Brown. For many individuals who meet diagnostic criteria for Dependent Personality Disorder, the fear of abandonment from a loved one is terrifying and may lead to irrational thoughts and behaviors.

Combined with Ms. Jones's symptoms of depression (Persistent Depressive Disorder) and trauma (Posttraumatic Stress Disorder), she may have felt unable to successfully manage her life without the support of Mr. Brown. She reported feeling little to no support from family or friends and recognized that seeking symptom relief through illegal drugs (i.e., methamphetamines) was not safe for her or her son. Given the situation involving her fears of abandonment, her depressive and trauma symptoms, and the perception that both her mother and Mr. Martinez were also seeking access to her son, Ms. Jones's decision-making abilities were clearly compromised. By her report, these factors led to her allegation of sexual abuse that was false. When asked why she would make a false allegation of sexual abuse *that included herself*—she had no clear answer, other than to make self-deprecating comments ("I am so disgusting"). As a result, it is clear that Ms. Jones possessed three areas in need of mental health services—addressing depressive symptoms, addressing trauma symptoms, and working to improve her self-esteem, independence, and assertiveness. If these symptoms can be lessened, then it is reasonable to assume that Ms. Jones can safely care for her son. This opinion is supported by the fact that there appears to be a close, positive, and strong relationship between Ms. Jones and her son and that David exhibits relatively few behavioral problems.

Bond/Attachment between Ms. Jones and David   After an observation of Ms. Jones and David, as well as a review of this case, it appears that there is a close emotional relationship/attachment between them. Ms. Jones had been the primary caregiver throughout David's life. As a result of the quantity/stability and quality of their interactions, their relationship was considered strong and positive. Ms. Jones was attentive and responsive to David's needs, as evidenced by the pattern of her behavior toward her son—and his complementary response toward her. Additionally, when distressed/fatigued during the interview, David readily sought out Ms. Jones for comfort.

It was not known how David was managing his day-to-day life in the home of his biological father and paternal grandmother. Given the situation that had occurred over the last few months, David had experienced a partial loss of Ms. Jones by having only limited contact with her. Given that Ms. Jones is likely David's primary attachment figure, every effort was made to ensure that he understood she will continue to be a reliable part of his life and that eventually he will have his primary attachment relationship with his mother restored.

Recommendations for Reunification Services   At the current time, Ms. Jones was experiencing several mental health problems. During the evaluation, she was asked whether she would be willing to participate in mental health services if directed by the court. In response, she stated that she would be willing to comply with any court directive. Therefore, the following recommendations were made for Ms. Jones and her son.

Mental Health Treatment Recommendations   Individual therapy was recommended for Ms. Jones to address problems related to trauma and depression. She would most likely benefit from a cognitive-behavioral intervention to address these problems, as well as a component of prolonged exposure for the trauma she experienced. Ms. Jones appeared receptive to therapy and motivated to make progress. As therapy progresses, therapeutic efforts should focus on teaching and supporting Ms. Jones in improving her self-esteem, changing negative self-attributions, acquiring assertiveness skills, and developing her independent thinking in light of her significant dependent characteristics (e.g., fear of abandonment, needing to be involved in a relationship with another person, seeking advice and reassurance from others). This may also—eventually—require the involvement of Mr. Brown to support Ms. Jones in developing these personality characteristics. Continuing in a treatment relationship that confronts her about these issues can improve Ms. Jones's ability to tolerate conflict and disapproval, so that she can form healthy, honest, and trusting relationships. Treatment should aim to decrease her overreliance on others, identify the negative consequences of her doing so, and set appropriate interpersonal boundaries. Ms. Jones could use her coping skills and emotion regulation strategies to manage disruptive emotions when she feels threatened by interpersonal rejection, loss, or abandonment.

Psychiatric Assessment and Treatment   Ms. Jones has reported a serious problem with depressed mood. It was likely that she would experience significant improvement in functioning if she were assessed and prescribed antidepressant medication. During the course of the evaluation, she was asked if she would be willing to take antidepressant medication if this was prescribed to her by a psychiatrist. She acknowledged that she would be willing to do anything if it would help return her son to her care. Therefore, it was recommended that Ms. Jones be referred for a psychiatric assessment and comply with any recommendations resulting from this evaluation.

Parent-Child Interaction Therapy   Through informal and structured observation of David with his mother, and Ms. Jones's reports on a standardized assessment, it appears that Ms. Jones had difficulty setting firm limits with David and acquiring his compliance. Although there appeared to be a positive relationship between the two of them, when presented with a direct command, David consistently failed to comply. Therefore, it is recommended that Ms. Jones and David be referred to Parent-Child Interaction Therapy (PCIT) to provide her with skills to effectively manage David's problem behaviors. PCIT should include the following:

A. Coaching to increase the use of PRIDE skills (i.e., Praises, Reflections, Imitation, Descriptions, Enthusiasm).
B. Coaching to strategically use labeled praises to increase his prosocial behaviors (i.e., following directions, keeping his hands to himself, behaving calmly, sitting still, concentrating, using appropriate language, expressing positive affect, and other prosocial behaviors).
C. Training to use active ignoring techniques (i.e., silence, redirections, turn away, and walk away) to reduce negative/inappropriate behaviors.
D. Training to use BE DIRECT strategies and strategic consequences (i.e., time out procedure and removal of privileges) to further increase compliance.

Further, although no formal assessment or observation was made of Mr. Brown and David, it was recommended that Mr. Brown be allowed to participate in PCIT along with Ms. Jones. From information provided by

Ms. Jones and Mr. Brown, they expect to continue their relationship and hope to be married in the future. This suggested that Mr. Brown would assume a parenting role in David's life, which would lead to Mr. Brown benefiting from PCIT. This would also encourage Ms. Jones and Mr. Brown to have continuity in their parenting strategies.

Evaluation for Substance Abuse Problem   During this evaluation, Ms. Jones denied currently taking any type of illegal drugs. However, Ms. Jones reported that she had previously been involved in taking amphetamines and that this was a problem for her. She further acknowledged that she understood her drug problem was getting out of control, so she voluntarily stopped taking illegal drugs. Additionally, she reported currently taking pain medication—resulting from a car accident in which she hurt her back. Because of her history of illegal drug use and her current use of legally prescribed pain medication, it was recommended that she be evaluated for any substance abuse problem.

Visitation between David and Ms. Jones/Mr. Brown   It is important to note that Ms. Jones had been the primary caregiver for her son for nearly all of his life, which has resulted in her becoming his primary attachment figure. Further, David was placed in dependency due to allegations and questions regarding Ms. Jones's mental health, *not* because she was actually sexually or physically abusive to him. There weren't any concerns about neglect or failure to protect her son, and Ms. Jones is currently in a healthy relationship that does not pose a risk to David. Addressing Ms. Jones's mental health problems should render her fully able to care for her son. Given the fact that David and Ms. Jones have a strong, consistent, and positive relationship, a relatively rapid plan for increasing the amount of time David is in Ms. Jones's care is strongly recommended. Therefore, it was suggested that Ms. Jones be provided the ability to visit with her son outside of the confines of a visitation center so that they may begin to reestablish their mother-son relationship in a more natural setting. Further, it was recommended that, as soon as Ms. Jones has established a relationship with a psychotherapist and becomes stable on psychiatric medication (typically within 6–8 weeks after starting medication), she should be provided the opportunity to have extended visitation and to further rehabilitate the relationship with her son.

Common Pitfalls and Considerations

Evaluators conducting evaluations of parenting capacity are commonly trained to conduct more traditional diagnostic evaluations. The shift to conducting child welfare evaluations can be challenging, and new evaluators commonly experience some anxiety and confusion. As in most evaluations, the evaluator needs to have an open mind and integrate information from multiple measures and interviews to inform an opinion. In addition, the evaluator needs to focus on dyadic relationships, rather than individual functioning alone. The parents' mental health diagnosis matters, but is not sufficient to determine whether they can parent a child adequately or safely. For example, as many as 10% of mothers in the United States meet diagnostic criteria for a major depressive disorder (Ertel, Rich-Edwards, & Koenen, 2010). While there may be concern about these mothers' ability to care for children (especially young children), it is suggested that few of them possess incapacities that meet the level of requiring involvement in the child welfare system. The evaluator needs to conceptualize not only the parents' functioning but also their relationship with their child and their ability to meet the child's needs. Evaluators need to learn to tolerate that there will not always be a clear conclusion. Some parents are clearly competent or incompetent, but many referrals will be for parents that are in the middle, "maybe" being competent enough with some type of intervention. For example, Ms. Jones clearly had some areas of concern, yet she also had areas predicting a positive prognosis. Evaluators further need to become comfortable using some confrontation during interviews, which is uncommon in traditional evaluation and therapy (e.g., why did you not leave your boyfriend after you found out he was sexually abusing your daughter?). The process can become even more difficult when evaluators empathize with parents, whom themselves may be victims (e.g., feeling bad for Ms. Jones who herself had a terrible childhood). In contrast, other parents may be more difficult to relate to or can be quite challenging to work with interpersonally. Related to this point, evaluators need to establish rapport with clients and conduct evaluations in a respectful manner, while simultaneously engaging in some fact checking through record review and collateral contacts. Evaluators need to be aware of their own biases and values and need to keep in mind the best interest of the child, regardless of their own feelings about the parent.

Conclusions

Few aspects of clinical psychology require a greater range of competencies than conducting psychological evaluations within child welfare systems. Evaluators require a broad and ever-changing body of knowledge to perform these evaluations, a unique set of skills to conduct interviews, and the ability to conceptualize cases that bring together diverse information. Psychologists must balance parents' right to reasonable services with the best interests of the child at times when these rights are in direct opposition with one another.

It is challenging to complete these types of evaluations, both intellectually and emotionally. There is rarely a clear right or wrong position, and both parents and children may show distress during the evaluation, as well as after hearing the result of the evaluation recommendations. Evaluators must be internally motivated to provide a quality evaluation, do their best to understand their limits and biases, and stay up to date on literature and case law. Sometimes, important interpersonal and statutory priorities conflict, making the development of an opinion extremely difficult. In such situations, it is important to remember that all aspects of the evaluation take place within the context of the legal system, leading the evaluator to understand and comply with the statutes in their jurisdiction and, to the best of their ability, serve both the parents' right to reunify with their child and the best interests of their child.

After completing a large number of evaluations, it is not uncommon to question the place of evaluators to assert such life-changing opinions related to parents and children being able to live together. Is it fair to make judgments that result in such severe outcomes that a parent may not be able to raise their child? Is it fair that a child is not able to be raised in the same family as his biological siblings? Is it fair that grandmothers and grandfathers be prevented from seeing their grandchildren? What special insights or knowledge or abilities do evaluators have that enable them to answer these questions and permanently alter the lives of families? The first response to this question is that situations arise in which children are placed in danger, where parents cannot safely and adequately care for their children and/or where parental incapacities—due to mental illness, drugs, or other problems—prevent them from maintaining the integrity and safety of their child. It is because of the risk to children that the courts have decided that circumstances exist where it is permissible to remove children from the care of their parents, followed by termination of parents' rights if parents are unable to demonstrate their ability to safely care for their child. Because the answers to these questions involve psychological processes and development, the answers fall to psychologists (and, in some cases, psychiatrists). Therefore, it is essential that those who undertake these types of evaluations appreciate the gravity their opinions have on the lives of others and, of course, the limitations and flaws inherent in our opinions.

At best, we can provide reasonable opinions that are influenced by our academic training but are fundamentally grounded in our knowledge of families, derived from the families we know best. Few of us have been raised in households like those of the people we interview, assess, and evaluate. We may understand theories, testing, and psychological concepts, but few of us can really appreciate the chronicity of a violence or fear-filled household or parents who place illegal drugs as the priority in their life. It should be from this perspective that evaluators should regularly assess and reassess their judgments so that they can provide the most fair, accurate, and constructive evaluation possible. This is especially important since much of the territory of conducting psychological evaluations for child welfare systems treads new ground.

References

American Psychological Association. (2013). Guidelines for psychological evaluations in child protection matters. *American Psychologist, 68*(1), 20–31.

Barajas-Gonzalez, R. G., & Brooks-Gunn, J. (2014). Income, neighborhood stressors, and harsh parenting: Test of moderation by ethnicity, age, and gender. *Journal of Family Psychology, 28*(6), 855–866. doi:http://dx.doi.org/10.1037/a0038242

Barone, N. M., Weitz, E. I., & Witt, P. H. (2005). Psychological bonding evaluations in termination of parental rights cases. *Journal of Psychiatry & Law, 33,* 387–411.

Benjamin, L. S. (1993). Every psychopathology is a gift of love. *Psychotherapy Research, 3*(1), 1–24.

Benjet, C., Azar, S. T., & Kuersten-Hogan, R. (2003). Evaluating the parental fitness of psychiatrically diagnosed individuals: Advocating a functional-contextual analysis of parenting. *Journal of Family Psychology, 17,* 238–251.

Biringen, Z. (2008). *Emotional Availability Scales* (4th ed.). Colorado State University.

Brodzinsky, D. (1993). On the use and misuse of psychological testing in child custody evaluations. *Professional Psychology Research and Practice, 2,* 213–219.

Cassidy, J., & Shaver, P. R. (2008). *Handbook of attachment: Theory, research, and clinical applications.* New York, NY: Guilford Press.

Cerezo, M. A., Keesler, T. Y., Dunn, E., & Wahler, R. G. (1986). *Standardized observation codes III.* Unpublished manuscript, Child Behavior Institute, University of Tennessee.

Crittenden, P. M., & Ainsworth, M. D. S. (1989). Child maltreatment and attachment theory. In D. Cicchetti & V. Carlson (Eds.), *Child maltreatment: Theory and research on the causes and consequences of child abuse and neglect.* Cambridge University Press.

Derogatis, L. R. (1993). *BSI brief symptom inventory: Administration, scoring, and procedures manual* (4th ed.). Minneapolis, MN: National Computer Systems.

Dubowitz, H., Kim, J., Black, M., Weisbart, C., Semiatin, J., & Magder, L. (2011). Identifying children at high risk for a child maltreatment report. *Child Abuse & Neglect, 35*(2), 96–104.

Ertel, K. A., Rich-Edwards, J. W., & Koenen, K. C. (2010). Maternal depression in the United States: Nationally representative rates and risks. *Journal of Women's Health, 20*(11), 1609–1617.

Eyberg, S. M., Nelson, M. M., Duke, M., & Boggs, S. R. (2005). *Manual for the Dyadic Parent-Child Interaction Coding System* (3rd ed.). Gainesville, FL: University of Florida.

Fluke, J. D., Yuan, Y. Y. T., Hedderson, J., & Curtis, P. A. (2003). Disproportionate Representation of Race and Ethnicity in Child Maltreatment: Investigation and Victimization. *Children and Youth Services Review, 25,* 359–373.

Fogel, A., Garvey, A., Hsu, H., & West-Stroming, D. (2006). Change processes in relationships: A relational—historical research approach. Cambridge, UK: Cambridge University Press.

Fontes, L. A. (2005). *Child abuse and culture: working with diverse families.* New York, NY: Guilford Press.

Fox, K. (2005). Cultural aspects. In A. E. Brodeur & J. A. Monteleone (Eds.), *Child maltreatment: A clinical guide and reference* (3rd ed.). St. Louis, MO: G.W. Medical.

Friesen, B., Katz-Leavy, J., & Nicholson, J. (2011). *Supporting parents with mental health needs in systems of care.* Washington, DC: Technical Assistance Partnership for Child and Family Mental Health.

Gewirtz, A., & Edleson, J. L. (2004). *Young children's exposure to adult domestic violence: Toward a developmental risk and resilience framework for research and intervention.* Packard Foundation, University of Iowa Press.

Kalich, L., Carmichael, B., Masson, T., & Blacker, D. (2007). Evaluating the evaluator: Guidelines for legal professionals in assessing the competency of evaluations in termination of parental cases. *The Journal of Psychiatry and the Law.*

Kaufman, A. S., & Kaufman, N. L. (2004). *Kaufman Brief Intelligence Test* (2nd ed.). Bloomington, MN: Pearson.

Lillienfeld, S. O., Wood, J. M., & Garb, H. N. (2000). The scientific status of projective techniques. *Psychological Science in the Public Interest, 1*(2), 27–66.

Melton, G. B., Petrila, J., Poythress, N. G., & Slobogin, C. (1997). *Psychological evaluations for the Courts: A handbook for mental health professionals and lawyers* (2nd ed.). New York, NY: Guilford Press.

Morey, L. C. (2007). *Personality Assessment Inventory Professional Manual* (2nd ed.). Odessa, FL: Psychological Assessment Resources.

Reynolds, C. R., & Kamphaus, R. W. (2006). *BASC-2: Behavior Assessment System for Children* (2nd ed.). Upper Saddle River, NJ: Pearson Education.

Stokes, J. C., & Strothman, L. J. (1996). The use of bonding studies in child welfare permanency planning. *Child and Adolescent Social Work Journal, 13,* 347–367.

Terao, S. Y., Borrego, J., & Urquiza, A. J. (2000). How do I differentiate culturally based parenting practices from child maltreatment. In H. Dubowitz & D. DePanfilis (Eds.), *Handbook for child protection practice,* Thousand Oaks, CA: Sage.

Terao, S. Y., Borrego, J., & Urquiza, A. J. (2001). A reporting and response model for culture and child maltreatment. *Child Maltreatment, 6*(2), 158–168.

Toth, S. L., & Cicchetti, D. (Eds.). (2013). A developmental psychopathology perspective on child maltreatment [Special Issue]. *Child Maltreatment, 18,* 135–204.

Traube, D. (2012). The missing link to child safety, permanency, and well-being: Addressing substance misuse in child welfare. *Social Work Research, 36*(2), 83–87.

Urquiza, A., & Blacker, D. (2005). Psychological evaluations and the child welfare system. In P. F. Talley (Ed.), *Handbook for the treatment of abused and neglected children* (pp. 83–119). New York, NY: Haworth Press.

Urquiza, A. J., & McNeil, C. B. (1996). Parent-child interaction therapy: An intensive dyadic intervention for physically abusive families. *Child Maltreatment, 1*(2), 132–141.

Urquiza, A. J., & Wyatt, G. E. (1993). Culturally relevant research with children of color. *The APSAC Advisor, 7*(3), 1–20.

10

Termination of Parental Rights

Dawn M. Blacker, Anthony J. Urquiza,
Lisa Kalich, and Blake D. Carmichael

Termination of parental rights (TPR) is one of the most extreme and devastating actions undertaken by the courts. *In re Smith* (1991) likened the dissolution of parental rights to a sentence of death, underscoring the finality and significance of this legal decision. According to the United States Supreme Court, the termination of parental rights denies parents "physical custody, as well as the rights ever to visit, communicate with, or regain custody of the child" (*Santosky v. Kramer*, 1982, p. 749). As a result of the far-reaching consequences that accompany severing the parental relationship, the state is held to a higher standard of proof, and parents are afforded additional due process protections beyond those required in other child protection matters (Condie & Condie, 2007). Typically, the state is required to demonstrate a finding of abuse or neglect as well as a parent's unfitness, even after the provision of relevant, rehabilitative services.

Relevant Case Law

Guidelines specifying the grounds for termination of parental rights vary significantly from state to state. Generally, these guidelines contain definitions of child maltreatment, factors that should be considered by the court prior to returning a child to the custody of the parent, and factors related to the parent's involvement in and response to intervention (Condie & Condie, 2007). Following the Adoption and Safe Families Act (ASFA) of 1997, many statutes also specify time frames for successful reunification, as states are offered financial incentives for achieving permanency (i.e. moving children from foster care to long-term placement, guardianship, and/or adoption). According to Vesneski (2011), as a whole, most state statutes include far more criteria for termination of parental rights than the eight provided for by ASFA, with numbers ranging from seven criteria (Indiana) to twenty two (Kansas).

Grounds for termination may include parental incapacity to care for the child due to mental illness or substance abuse, extreme or repeated abuse or neglect, conviction of a crime carrying a long-term sentence, failure of the parent to improve in response to intervention, and limitations on the length of time a child may remain in state placement (Condie & Condie, 2007). According to Kundra and Alexander (2009), a considerable number of state statues also include "disability language" as a condition for the termination of parental rights, leaving those with mental illness, substance use, and developmental disability vulnerable to custody loss. Many of the grounds identified above, specifically those relating to neglect, substance abuse, and parental failure, are poorly defined in state law (Vesneski, 2011). While the overwhelming majority of states use the "clear and convincing" standard to terminate parental rights, recently, the California Supreme Court upheld a lower burden of proof (i.e., preponderance of the evidence) for findings of fact in that state (Kundra & Alexander, 2009).

Using the prevailing *best interest* standard (Condie & Condie, 2007), the court takes into consideration the child's relationships with parents, siblings, foster parents, and potential adoptive parents. Parental rights may be terminated even when a caregiver has made progress in addressing areas of concern, based on the quality and strength of the child's relationship to substitute caregivers and the length of time the child has spent in alternative placements. In some cases, the advantages associated with a permanent placement may outweigh the benefits of a continued relationship with a biological parent, even if that relationship is positive. For example, *In re Casey D.* affirmed that the "parent-child relationship (must) promote the well-being of the child to such a degree that it outweighs the well-being the child would gain in a permanent home with new, adoptive parents." Case law has also established that the "interaction between natural parent and child will always confer some incidental benefit to the child" (*In re Autumn H.*, 32 Cal. Rpter. 2d 535; Ct. App. 4 Dist. 1994) but that this "incidental benefit" alone was not sufficient to prevent TPR.

To adequately address questions of parental fitness, the court has begun to rely on the expertise of mental health professionals. Though the decision to terminate parental rights is ultimately left to the trier of fact, evaluators are often asked to evaluate the relationship between parent and child (or between a child and a substitute caregiver or siblings) in order to assist in making this determination. Given the significance of this determination for both parent and child, the need for competent and comprehensive evaluations is paramount; however, to date, forensic evaluators vary widely in their approach and execution of the termination of parental rights evaluations. In part, the varying approaches to TPR may result from the limitations in scientific knowledge regarding parenting capacity. While the literature may inform psychologists of the qualities of an optimal parent, determining whether a parent is "good enough" is slightly more elusive.

Review of the Literature

Identifying Functional Capacities

Because statutes governing TPR vary widely across states and are often vague and inconsistent in their applications of AFSA, there is a need for objective criteria to determine parental capacity. Over the past ten years, researchers have begun to emphasize the importance of a functional analysis of parenting abilities. Azar's (1998) widely cited functional-contextual model closely parallels Grisso's criteria (2003) for establishing a legal competency, offering five broad domains of parenting skill: a) child management skills, b) perceptual and observational skills, c) self-control, d) planning and coping skills, and e) social relationship skills. Building from the work of Grisso and Azar, Donald and Jureidini (2004) proposed a model that evaluates parental functioning based on the relationship between parenting capacity, a specific child's parentability, and mitigating circumstances that affect parenting. These models provide an overall framework for evaluators to approach TPR cases.

Reviewing the New APA Guidelines

Despite the progress in developing functional-contextual models of parenting capacity, according to Kalich et al. (2007), evaluators operate within a considerable area of ambiguity when undertaking TPR evaluations, as the profession is governed by forensic standards that are "vague and open to considerable interpretation" (p. 367). In this regard, the 1994 and 1999 Guidelines for Psychological Evaluations in Child Protection Matters provided a general framework for evaluators; however, these documents did little to inform psychologists as to specific best standards of practice.

In 2013, the American Psychological Association (APA) released the latest revision of the Guidelines for Psychological Evaluations in Child Protection Matters. The spirit of the guidelines remains similar to that of its predecessors, with few changes in the guidelines themselves. As with prior iterations, the guidelines are considered "aspirational" but, nonetheless, are intended to help "facilitate a high level of practice by psychologists" (p. 20). The guidelines are divided into three main areas: Orienting Guidelines, General Guidelines, and Procedural Guidelines. The Orienting Guidelines advise psychologists of the overarching principles that should govern their decision making in child protection matters. In contrast to the 1999 Orienting Guidelines, which emphasize "the child's interest and well-being" as "paramount" (APA, 1999, p. 3), the

2013 guidelines assumed a more neutral stance, instructing psychologists to be aware that the different interests represented in child protection matters (i.e., the interests of the child, the parent, and the state) may not always coincide. Nonetheless, evaluators are encouraged to consider the "developmental and functional impact" (p. 22) of child abuse and neglect, as well as potential future risk to the child's well-being brought about by parental maltreatment or lack of adequate care or protection. Evaluators are also tasked to examine a broad range of other risks to the child that may occur as the result of prolonged state intervention, including multiple out-of-home placements; maltreatment while in substitute care; inadequate supports due to the limited resources of the child welfare system; prolonged separation from parents, relatives, and other potentially adequate caregivers; and unwarranted institutional placement.

Another significant difference between the 1999 and 2013 Orienting Guidelines is the newfound emphasis on the "resulting fit" between the parent's capabilities and the child's developmental and psychological needs (p. 22). In addressing questions of "fit," it is suggested that evaluators consider both the adult's capabilities for parenting with a specific emphasis on maltreatment concerns, as well as the child's needs, including the strength of the child's attachment to the parent and the possible deleterious effects of separation. Rather than overemphasizing potentially problematic characteristics of the parent (i.e., mental illness, substance use, mental retardation), it is the match or "fit" between the child's needs and the parent's capacities to meet those needs that serves as the primary focus of TPR evaluations, an idea that has been long been championed by proponents of the contextual and functional analyses of parenting ability described above (Donald & Jureidini, 2004; Azar & Hogan, 2003; Azar et al., 1998). The importance of this issue cannot be overstated, as individuals with disabilities, including mental illness, are at high risk for discrimination in termination of parental rights proceedings (Kundra & Alexander, 2009). In fact, studies suggest that as many as 70% to 80% of mentally ill parents lose custody of their children (Kundra & Alexander, 2009), despite substantial research indicating that with effective supports, most parents with mental illness can parent adequately (Nicholson et al. as cited in Kundra & Alexander, 2009).

Despite these few notable changes to the Orienting Guidelines, the Procedural Guidelines—the practical and conceptual methods utilized by the evaluator to reach an opinion—remain largely unchanged from 1999, leaving evaluators with a relatively vague map with which to navigate this complex forensic area of practice.

Best Practices

Kalich et al. (2007) provide a useful accompaniment to the guidelines, detailing best practice standards for TPR evaluations. Initially, before proceeding with a TPR evaluation, the evaluator must develop a clear understanding of the specific information requested by the referring party. The referral question(s) will provide a framework for the evaluation and will assist the evaluator in identifying appropriate methods of data gathering. The evaluator's ability to provide a competent and useful evaluation is directly related to the quality and appropriateness of the referral questions. In this area, it is critical for evaluators to possess a thorough knowledge of the TPR statutes in their jurisdiction in order to ensure that the information provided will be useful to the court. Evaluators should be particularly aware of being urged to answer questions which are beyond the scope of their practice or expertise, including "Was the child abused" or "Who abused the child?" The evaluator should work collaboratively with the referring party to reframe or reword these types of inappropriate referral questions.

Consistent with the 2013 Guidelines, Kalich et al. (2007) emphasize the importance of relying on multiple methods of data gathering in forming opinions in TPR cases. Sources of data include multiple clinical interviews; collateral contacts with extended family members, clinical and social service providers, and teachers; psychological testing; parent-child observation; and record review. Given the adversarial context of child welfare evaluations, it is expected that parents may present with a distorted response style. By relying on numerous methods of gathering information, including more than one clinical interview, the effect of these situational variables is mitigated. It is also essential for the evaluator to consider the veracity and usefulness of collateral contacts. For example, therapists may have limited information about a client's functioning and are likely subject to the same distortions by the parent as the evaluator. With regard to parent-child observations, another critical piece of data in TPR cases, Kalich et al. (2007) recommend the use of a semistructured tool, such as the Dyadic Parent Child Interaction Coding System (DPICS; Robinson & Eyberg, 1981). The DPICS assesses three scenarios of parent-child interaction and enables the evaluator to qualitatively and quantitatively assess the ways in which parent and child engage. Evaluators must also remain cognizant of situations in which parent-child observations are contraindicated (i.e., if the parent and child have not had contact in a lengthy period of time and such contact is judged to be detrimental to the child).

A number of authors (Melton et al., 2007; Kalich et al., 2007, Brodzinsky, 1993) have expressed caution about the overreliance on psychological testing to answer forensic questions, including those related to parenting capacity, abuse potential, and termination of parental rights. Most psychological tests were developed to assist in diagnosis and treatment and have not been normed with a forensic population. To date, there are few tests designed to provide information regarding parenting capacity, and many evaluators continue to rely on measures that are only loosely correlated with parental fitness. In selecting appropriate and useful psychological tests in a forensic context, Melton et al. (2007) advises evaluators to consider a number of factors including, What is the nature of the construct being assessed? How directly does the test instrument measure that construct? Are there alternative means of assessing the construct more directly? Does the use of this instrument require an unacceptable degree of inference between the construct and the psycholegal issue? Does the instrument contain a measure of response style? As with other methods of gathering data, evaluators should never rely solely on psychological testing to answer referral questions related to the termination of parental rights.

The 2013 Guidelines also note the importance of properly interpreting data and providing opinions only when they are sufficiently supported by the data. Opinions rendered without sufficient support are likely to be the product of bias that would significantly compromise the utility and objectivity of a TPR evaluation. Kalich et al. (2007) encourage evaluators to conceptualize the client's functioning in a "meaningful way, acknowledging limitations, and providing alternate hypotheses for contradictory information are essential in order for an evaluator to sufficiently support his or her conclusions" (p. 385). The evaluator's conceptualization should articulate (in jargon-free language) the evaluator's understanding of the parent's mental health or emotional functioning. Condie and Condie (2007) suggest that the most useful reports include interpretations that are "made within a theoretical and developmental context" (p. 318). Points for explication include the caregiver's functioning, the child's functioning and developmental level, the parent-child relationship, risk and protective factors related to maltreatment, and amenability to treatment (p. 319). The child's age at time of the evaluation is also important to consider (e.g., a 3-month-old compared to a 13-year-old). Pitfalls common in this domain include a failure to acknowledge alternate hypotheses or to make clear any limitations on the reliability or validity of the conclusions. Evaluators should alert the reader to areas that may not have been fully explored by the evaluator or aspects of the report that may be misinterpreted by readers.

If offered, recommendations should directly address the referral questions and should be consistent with the data obtained during the course of the evaluation. Recommendations may include, but are not limited to, psychological/psychosocial treatment for the child, psychological/psychosocial treatment for the parent, and/or suggestions for parental rehabilitation.

Case Vignette

The following case vignette illustrates what is often required in completing TPR evaluations and what is considered a best-practice approach. Consider the following case example in light of the APA evaluation guidelines and general

The case vignette has been redacted and all identifying information removed. It is not meant to serve as a forensic report. Any likeness to a case is purely coincidental.

standards most courts must consider when making decisions about TPR matters. This case highlights many of the challenges that evaluators face during
the evaluation process (e.g., vague referral questions, discrepancies found in
reports/interviews, and conflicting results from psychological measures).

Reason for the Referral

A 40-year-old woman, Ms. Smith, and her 9-year-old son, John, presented for
a court-ordered evaluation. The referring party asked for a "bonding assessment" but did not provide clarification as to the specific matter before the
court. At the time of the referral, John had been in protective custody for
approximately fourteen months. Upon follow-up, the referring party clarified that there was a court order to determine 1) whether Ms. Smith had a
mental health condition that prevented her from safely and adequately parenting John, 2) whether there was a reasonable expectation that Ms. Smith could
successfully address mental health problems within a prescribed period (i.e.,
four to eight months) so that she could become a safe and adequate parent (in
this particular case, statutes dictated that Ms. Smith had eighteen months to
reunify with John), and 3) whether discontinuing the relationship between
Ms. Smith and John would lead to long-term emotional detriment for John
and prevent him from establishing permanency.

Relevant Records and Background

To gather background for this case, the forensic evaluator conducted interviews
and observations:

- Two meetings with Ms. Smith
- Two meetings with John
- One conjoint interview with Ms. Smith and John
- One structured behavioral observation of Ms. Smith and John (using DPICS)
- Phone interview with the social worker
- Phone interviews with treatment providers for Ms. Smith
  o Parenting instructor
  o Individual and group substance abuse counselors
  o Psychiatrist
- Phone interviews with treatment providers for John
  o Individual therapist
  o Behavioral specialist
- Phone interview with Ms. Smith's family friend
- Phone interview with John's foster mother

The evaluator also reviewed the following relevant records:

- Social services reports
- John's academic records
- Ms. Smith's treatment summaries
- John's treatment summaries

Ms. Smith and six siblings were raised by her biological mother and a stepfather, Mr. Jones. General family interactions were enjoyable and supportive, though Ms. Smith was sexually abused by her older stepbrother at 13 years of age. Ms. Smith disclosed the abuse to her parents one year after the abuse started, but they did not believe the abuse occurred. She elected to leave the home with friends at 14 years of age. Over the next ten years, Ms. Smith moved among different states and pursued various occupational endeavors (e.g., singing in a band, working in restaurants, and attending cosmetology school).

In her late teens, Ms. Smith entered her first romantic relationship. She and her boyfriend abused drugs and alcohol. By 20 years of age, her drug of choice was methamphetamine, and, at 25 years of age, she started using heroin. Ms. Smith "realized (she) would die" if her drug-related lifestyle continued, and she left her partner. She voluntarily entered substance abuse treatment, but stopped the program because "they were too confrontational." Shortly thereafter, Ms. Smith entered another relationship where she regularly used methamphetamines (up to daily use continued for approximately five years).

Ms. Smith became pregnant with John at 30 years of age. She stopped using methamphetamine when she discovered she was pregnant. John's father left Ms. Smith while she was pregnant, and no contact was ever reestablished with him. John was born without drugs in his system, and the birth had no complications. He met all early childhood developmental milestones on time. John did well academically, and there were no significant behavioral problems as a toddler. However, by 5 years of age John exhibited a number of oppositional and disruptive behaviors at home (e.g., talking back, refusing to comply, becoming destructive and aggressive). Ms. Smith resumed her use of methamphetamines when John became school-aged. She had significant difficulty getting him to complete basic age-appropriate activities of daily living (e.g., getting dressed, leaving for school, and brushing his teeth). This resulted in school tardiness/absences and hygiene problems (i.e., tooth decay, inadequately dressed for school).

When John was 6 years of age, Ms. Smith was arrested for being under the influence of methamphetamines. A referral was made to child welfare services (CWS), and their investigation found the home to be unsafe and unsanitary. It was discovered that John had stepped on a blood-filled hypodermic needle, but Ms. Smith had not sought medical treatment. John was placed in a foster home while Ms. Smith completed twelve months of drug treatment and parenting services. Ms. Smith described the programs as "wonderful." Staff encouraged her "to go to school and to have a life." John was returned to Ms. Smith after twelve months, and the case was dismissed. Ms. Smith maintained her sobriety for the next three years. During that time, CWS investigated three reports of general neglect, but they were inconclusive.

When John returned to Ms. Smith, she was living with her stepfather, Mr. Jones, so that she could provide him with daily living assistance (due to his advanced age). In addition to these demands, Ms. Smith had difficulty managing John's behaviors. It was particularly difficult when Mr. Jones undermined her directives (i.e., giving John special privileges after she attempted to remove them). Over time, John became more irritable and his moods changed quickly. He often asked Ms. Smith for help such as "mommy, use your calming voice" or "mommy hold me," but the symptoms persisted.

John eventually disclosed to Ms. Smith that he had been sexually abused by Mr. Jones for approximately twelve months (e.g., sitting naked on Mr. Jones's lap while he was touched on his bare chest, stomach, and penis). This was John's first disclosure of the abuse. During an unrelated CWS investigation for general neglect, John disclosed the abuse to the social worker, and Ms. Smith admitted that John had previously told her of the abuse. She explained that she did not make efforts to keep John from Mr. Jones because she did not believe the abuse had occurred. She later acknowledged it was "too much" to think about her son being abused, and that it triggered her to experience anxiety symptoms (i.e., racing heart, shortness of breath) as well as "flashbacks" to her own sexual abuse victimization. As a result of Ms. Smith's failure to protect John, he was taken into protective custody at 7-and-a-half years of age. Because no immediate or extended family was available to take placement of John, he was placed with a licensed foster family.

After John's removal, Ms. Smith experienced a significant increase in anxiety and "flashbacks." She also used methamphetamines on one occasion, after which she called her sponsor and John's social worker. Approximately six months after John's removal, Ms. Smith acknowledged that John had been sexually abused, discontinued contact with Mr. Jones, and found her own apartment. Ms. Smith's extended family "did not believe the abuse occurred" so she became estranged from them.

At the time of evaluation, John had been in the same foster placement for twelve months. Behavioral functioning was normative, and he was doing well in school. Ms. Smith had become more active in her twelve-step groups, and she enrolled in parenting classes and a group substance abuse treatment program. Visitations were attended regularly with no reported problems.

Mental Status Examination

Ms. Smith promptly attended her appointments, well-groomed and appropriately dressed. Her mood and affect were generally euthymic and appropriate to the situation. She was admittedly anxious about the outcome of the evaluation, but she presented as calm and confident. Her speech tone and production were adequate. She sometimes minimized problems (e.g., John's tooth decay) and became defensive (e.g., blaming others for her family circumstances). However, when challenged, she appropriately acknowledged past failures (e.g., parenting "out of guilt" and giving in quickly). Ms. Smith was oriented to person, place, time, and circumstance. She denied any homicidal or suicidal ideation. No hallucinations or delusions were noted.

John was appropriately dressed and groomed for age and weather. At the first appointment (interviewed alone), John was anxious and overactive. He had difficulty staying on task and responding to questions. He avoided questions related to emotions or his history of maltreatment. By contrast, his demeanor was more cooperative, calm, and friendly during the second visit (when his mother was present). He alluded to "bad things" that happened with Mr. Jones and endorsed sexual abuse victimization when responding to questions on the UCLA PTSD Index, but he declined to discuss specifics of the incident. John's speech tone, pitch, and production were within normal limits. He was oriented to person, place, time, and circumstance. He denied homicidal or suicidal ideation.

Psychological Measures

Summaries from psychological testing are provided below. Results from any one test were not used to form diagnostic or treatment conclusions. Rather, each test was used in conjunction with evaluative data from additional sources such as interviews, case history, direct observations, and other test data. Results below were considered valid unless otherwise noted.

Ms. Smith

Wechsler Abbreviated Scale of Intelligence, Second Edition (WASI-2) The Wechsler Abbreviated Scale of Intelligence, Second Edition (WASI-2) is a standardized measure that provides a quick and reliable estimate of IQ based on four subtests (Vocabulary, Block Design, Similarities, and Matrix Reasoning). The four subtests comprise the Full-Scale IQ. The Vocabulary and Similarities subtests comprise the Verbal Comprehension Index (VCI). The Block Design and Matrix Reasoning subtests comprise the Perceptual Reasoning Index (PRI).

Ms. Smith obtained a Full-Scale IQ in the "average" range. There was no significant discrepancy between the VCI and PRI; both were in the "average" range. Results suggested that her cognitive abilities developed evenly across domains. It was determined that Ms. Smith could understand/process verbal information in an age-appropriate manner and that she had the capacity to use logical and abstract reasoning skills.

Personality Assessment Inventory (PAI)   The Personality Assessment Inventory (PAI) is a self-administered, objective inventory of adult personality. It is comprised of four validity scales, eleven clinical scales, five treatment scales, and two interpersonal scales. Scales are nonoverlapping, which helps reduce scale contamination. As a clinical instrument, the PAI provides information relevant to clinical diagnosis, treatment planning, and screening for psychopathology.

On the PAI, Ms. Smith underreported problems to which people typically admit (Positive Impression Management Scale was elevated). Consistent with her defensive responding, Ms. Smith had no marked elevations on the clinical scales, and her general stress levels were within normal limits. She reported having an available support network that likely buffered her negative response to such stressors. Interpersonal indicators were that Ms. Smith maintained a balance of warmth, friendliness, autonomy, and assertiveness in her relationships (Dominance and Warmth Scales).

Ms. Smith did acknowledge a history of drug use and dependence (Drug Scale). There was also an elevation on the Antisocial scale (e.g., having a history of rule-breaking behavior, problems with authority, stimulus-seeking, and limited empathy). These scores were consistent with Ms. Smith's clinical interview, in which she acknowledged her drug use, and maintaining sobriety was a primary focus. The combination of an optimistic outlook, a sense of purpose, and the presence of a support system were indicative of a positive prognosis, should she commit to treatment (Treatment Rejection Scale).

Trauma Symptom Index, Second Edition (TSI-2)   The Trauma Symptom Inventory, Second Edition (TSI-2) is used to identify trauma-related symptoms and behaviors. It consists of two validity scales, twelve clinical scales, twelve subscales, and four general factors. It evaluates current symptomatology associated with trauma from any point in the respondent's lifespan, but it does not link symptoms to a single stressor or specific point in time.

Ms. Smith's overall posttraumatic stress factor was within normal limits, and all clinical scales were lower than clinical thresholds. Essentially, Ms. Smith's TSI-2 profile was not indicative of significant PTSD symptoms.

Child Abuse Potential Index (CAPI)   The Child Abuse Potential Inventory (CAPI) is a standardized measure used to assess an individual's characteristic similarity to known, active physical child abusers. The abuse scale is comprised of three factor scales related to psychological difficulties (i.e., distress, rigidity, unhappiness) and three factor scales related to interactional problems (i.e., problems with child and self, problems with family, and problems from others). There are also three validity scales.

Ms. Smith's responses led to an elevation on the "Lie" validity scale, which resulted in a "Faking Good" profile. Although it is not clear if Ms. Smith intentionally portrayed herself in an overly positive light, her response pattern was consistent with her tendency to minimize her role in parenting problems with John.

Parenting Stress Index/Short Form (PSI/SF)   The Parenting Stress Index/ Short Form (PSI/SF) is a standardized measure that uses thirty-six items to identify parent-child dyads that are experiencing stress or that may be at risk to develop dysfunctional parenting and child behaviors. The index consists of scales for Parental Distress, Parent-Child Dysfunctional Interaction, and Difficult Child.

Ms. Smith reported a total level of parenting stress within the normative range. Her interactions with John were largely reinforcing, and she did not portray John's behaviors as significantly disrupting her relationship with him. She also did not identify John's behaviors as difficult to manage. This finding was particularly discrepant from Ms. Smith's verbal report. However, Ms. Smith's perceptions on the PSI may have been altered because John had not lived with her for the past fourteen months, and there were no reports of disruptive behaviors during visitation. Therefore, her view of not currently experiencing John as a difficult child may have been influenced by her limited time with him.

Substance Abuse Subtle Screening Inventory, Third Edition (SASSI-3)
The SASSI-3 was designed as a substance-abuse-screening measure composed primarily of "subtle items" that appear to be unrelated to substance abuse, thus enabling the instrument to identify some individuals with substance-related disorders even if they are unable to acknowledge relevant symptoms. The SASSI-3 also provides clinical information that can be useful in helping identify problem areas, setting treatment goals, and developing treatment plans. The inventory can be completed according to a prescribed time period. However, because Ms. Smith was actively involved in drug treatment services and had maintained three years of sobriety prior to her recent lapse, she was asked to complete the SASSI-3 with regard to her lifetime.

Ms. Smith endorsed a number of thoughts, feelings, and behaviors commonly experienced by clients with substance abuse histories (Symptoms Scale). An elevation on the Face Valid Other Drugs Index suggested that Ms. Smith was aware of her substance abuse problem. Given her constellation of scores, it was likely that Ms. Smith suffered from a substance dependence disorder. Although such a result did not suggest that Ms. Smith was actively using illegal drugs, given her history of use she remained at moderate-to-high risk for abusing drugs unless she maintained significant structure and treatment compliance to support her sobriety.

Summary of Psychological Measures for Ms. Smith   According to standardized testing, Ms. Smith was well within the "average range" of intelligence, and thus it did not appear that cognitive limitations were affecting her functioning or ability to parent. Additional testing confirmed much of what she divulged during her clinical interviews and document review. She acknowledged a history of substance abuse, including her recent lapse after three years of sobriety. She was confident in herself and showed a balance of friendliness, autonomy, and assertiveness, reflecting a generally healthy interpersonal style. She did not endorse specific symptoms of trauma that would require clinical intervention, though reports of general stress were variable. This was not atypical given the current family disruption, and it appeared that she was engaging an adequate support network that served as a buffer for many of her stressors.

John

Behavior Assessment System for Children, Second Edition (BASC-2)   The Behavior Assessment System for Children (BASC-2) is an integrated system designed to facilitate the differential diagnosis and classification of a variety of emotional and behavioral disorders of children and to aid in the design of a treatment plan. There are multiple Clinical Scales and Adaptive Scales that form composite scores, including Internalizing, Externalizing, Adaptive, and Behavioral Composites). Scale scores in the "clinically significant" range suggest a high level of maladjustment. Scores in the "at-risk" range identify either a significant problem that may not be severe enough to require formal treatment or a potential of developing a problem that needs careful monitoring.

Self-Report   John achieved an elevated Atypicality scale, along with other at-risk concerns. He endorsed behaviors that are often considered odd, many of which are commonly associated with psychosis (e.g., hearing voices). However, the scale also captures symptoms of dissociation and inattentiveness, commonly associated with Posttraumatic Stress Disorder (PTSD) and/or

Attention-Deficit/Hyperactivity Disorder (ADHD). An "at risk" score for Hyperactivity reflected John's difficulty sitting still, excessive talking, and related impulsivity. A similar elevation was found for Attention Problems; John could be easily distracted and find it hard to concentrate. These symptoms are also commonly associated with ADHD but can also reflect PTSD. With accompanying "at-risk" concerns for low self-esteem and poor self-reliance, John did not feel adequately capable of managing distress. However, he did not have concerns about his relationship with Ms. Smith, a likely source of strength for him.

Parent Report   Both Ms. Smith and John's foster mother completed the parent form of the BASC-2. Both parties endorsed few concerns about John, though they each indicated "at risk" concerns for depressive symptoms. They also observed John to be easily distracted (Attention Problems Scale). Ms. Smith's responses further indicated concern about John's ability to complete daily living skills in an age appropriate manner (i.e., needing help to get out of bed in the morning and reminders to brush his teeth).

UCLA Post-Traumatic Stress Disorder Index (UCLA PTSD Index)   The UCLA PTSD Index for *DSM-IV* is a self-report paper-and-pencil screening instrument for the assessment of trauma exposure and posttraumatic stress symptoms among children and adolescents. At the time of the evaluation, there was not a published version for the *DSM-5*. However, symptom clusters on the current UCLA PTSD Index closely approximate diagnostic criteria in the *DSM-5*, including items that directly correspond with trauma symptoms such as Re-experiencing, Avoidance, and Increased Arousal.

John completed the UCLA PTSD Index with regard to sexual abuse. The PTSD Severity Score was well above cutoff scores indicative of significant trauma. He endorsed clinically significant symptoms across domains of increased arousal (e.g., hypervigilance, sleep problems, difficulty concentrating), avoidance (e.g., restricted affect, avoidance of thoughts), and re-experiencing (e.g., physiological reactivity to trauma reminders). As such, John's symptom severity likely warranted trauma specific interventions.

Summary of Psychological Measures for John   Results from John's testing revealed that he acknowledged having trouble with various mental health symptoms that are often associated with attention deficit (i.e., impulsivity and poor concentration). However, a number of these same symptoms are found in children with PTSD. John avoided discussions about being sexually abused, but on various measures he endorsed having significant symptoms of increased arousal (e.g., hypervigilance, sleep problems, difficulty concentrating), avoidance (e.g., restricted affect, avoidance of thoughts), and intrusion (e.g., physiological reactivity to trauma reminders).

DPICS Observation of Ms. Smith with John   During the clinical observation of Ms. Smith and John, they were observed in several play scenarios. In the first scenario, Ms. Smith was asked to allow John to choose what to play and follow his lead. In the second scenario, Ms. Smith was asked to inform John that she would pick an activity and get him to play according to her rules. Finally, Ms. Smith was asked to get John to pick up the room without her direct assistance. The purpose of these scenarios was to observe the quality of their interactions and to observe how John responded to Ms. Smith's instructions/commands.

Throughout the play, John was observed to smile and laugh. He easily took turns during game play and in conversations. Most of Ms. Smith's commands were indirect or phrased as questions (e.g., "How about we do it one more time? Let's put the Legos away"), which allowed him to respond with stalling and noncompliance. When John did not quickly comply, Ms. Smith repeated the command until it was completed; no other consequences were provided. Ms. Smith regularly provided praise, but it was generally unrelated to compliance (e.g., "You are so smart!"). At the conclusion of the appointment, John expressed disappointment and asked questions about when he would see his mother again. He was reassured when Ms. Smith informed him they had a visit the next day, at their regular location. When leaving the clinic, they shared terms of affection and separated easily after making plans for their next visit.

Collateral Information

Collateral sources showed general agreement that Ms. Smith actively and appropriately participated in treatment services. Her current individual and group counselors found that Ms. Smith "followed through on recommendations." After being gone from her twelve-step program for the previous year, she was "quickly getting back into twelve-step meetings and connecting with a new sponsor." In meetings, she was routinely "aware of her triggers" and avoided situations/relationships that prompted prior use. She was respectful and collaborative during group sessions, as well as "independent and motivated," which helped her with "setting goals for herself."

A psychiatrist had been working with both Ms. Smith and John for seven months and two months, respectively, prior to John's removal. Ms. Smith was prescribed antianxiety medications for the past eighteen months. Although she presented with general feelings of anxiety after being separated from John, the psychiatrist had no significant concerns about her current functioning. During treatment, there were no indications that she was using illegal drugs or that she desired to do so. She attended appointments and showed consistent medication compliance. The psychiatrist diagnosed Ms. Smith with Anxiety Disorder, PTSD (by history), and Opiate Dependence (by history). At the time of John's intake, the psychiatrist quickly had concerns about John's functioning and Ms. Smith's ability to tolerate stress resulting from John's "daily tantrums." John and Ms. Smith both initially denied occurrence of abuse, but the psychiatrist was concerned about a possible history of "abuse or trauma" given John's presentation (i.e., refused to be alone in the bathroom, complained of nightmares). John also complained of "hearing unspecified, non-command voices" for which he was prescribed an antipsychotic medication. Medication was discontinued after John had been in foster care for approximately six months, and there was no recurrence of auditory hallucinations.

The family's former parenting/behavior management service provider worked with the family after John's initial removal (at 6 years of age). The provider had last seen Ms. Smith and John three years prior to the current evaluation. John was described as "entitled" and clearly was "in complete control of the house" at the time. In treatment, Ms. Smith acknowledged her struggles, and learned to recognize and praise positive behaviors, as well as to remove privileges for negative behaviors. However, Ms. Smith continued to have difficulty remaining firm when removing favorite privileges. A major barrier to progress was that Mr. Jones undermined Ms. Smith's parenting because he gave John rewards when they were not earned. Mr. Jones was integrated into treatment, but he continued to undermine Ms. Smith's efforts.

A close family friend of ten years made similar observations about Ms. Smith's "largely passive parenting." However, the friend also noted that, "despite all of John's tantrums, meltdowns, and aggression," Ms. Smith "always took John to the library, and read with him, or did art at home. He loved it." Ms. Smith also routinely "spoke to him softly, and never yelled." Having known Ms. Smith for the duration of John's life, the friend stated, "I knew that she loved him dearly, and was trying to be the best she could be. She was staying away from Mr. Jones, and she needed to learn how to say no to John."

John's therapist had been working with him four months prior to the disclosure of the sexual abuse. At the time of intake, John presented with severe anger outbursts, mood swings, impulsivity, and difficulty respecting authority. He was diagnosed with Mood Disorder NOS, Anxiety Disorder NOS, and ADHD, Combined Type. Attempts to discuss sexual abuse (after it was disclosed) were met with John "throwing a fit and demanding to leave the session." During collateral contacts, Ms. Smith was "cooperative" in that she "listened" to the therapist and she tried to implement suggestions. Shortly after John was removed, Ms. Smith struggled to acknowledge the abuse had occurred, but shortly after moving away from Mr. Jones, she expressed feeling "guilty because the abuse took place under her nose." Ms. Smith appeared "open about her parenting struggles after John was removed," and it was clear that "she wanted her son back."

When John first arrived in foster care, he exhibited problems with defiance; he was "getting physically aggressive" with similar-aged children. Over time, it was determined that John was mostly "trying to defend himself" from a more aggressive child. After the more offensive child was removed from the home, John's behavior was largely appropriate, and he was compliant with house rules. The foster parent explained that John was a "typical kid, not wanting to clean up" or complete other chores, but when told he has to do something, he followed through without resistance. Overall John was the "best boy in the house. He stays calm, quiet, and he does not talk back."

Clinical Summary and Opinion

Prior to making the ultimate recommendation about the potential impact that TPR would have on John and Ms. Smith, the evaluator had to first determine 1) whether there were any mental health concerns for Ms. Smith that prevented her from safely and adequately parenting John, and 2) if concerns did exist, whether she could address those concerns within a prescribed period of time (four to eight months) in order to become a safe and adequate parent (understanding that by statute Ms. Smith had approximately four months left to reunify with John).

In evaluating someone's need for mental health services and an ability to benefit from them, it is important to consider the person's socioemotional functioning. A person's prospects for addressing concerns (if present) must also be considered when determining whether she has the ability to care for a child in a responsive and reliable manner. In the event that a parent is not able to manage her own personal, occupational, and interpersonal affairs, it becomes more unlikely that the parent would be able to adequately secure for the needs of a child.

Mental Health Functioning   Ms. Smith chronically abused alcohol, methamphetamines, heroin, and cocaine. She had a history of persistent desire to use and had unsuccessfully tried to control her use. Her recurrent use resulted in her failure to fulfill major role obligations at home, and she continued to use despite having significant negative impacts. Indeed, Ms. Smith exhibited symptoms of a Substance Use Disorder for many substances, though her most recent and prominent use had been with methamphetamine. Therefore, a primary diagnosis of Substance Use Disorder, In Early Remission, was offered. Ms. Smith also had a history of anxiety attacks for which she was prescribed medications. She acknowledged having moderate levels of anxiety associated with her life circumstances (e.g., worrying about reunification status). Ms. Smith's history of sexual abuse had also resulted in disruptive symptoms, though she denied that they were pervasive or persistent at the time of evaluation. It was determined that Ms. Smith did not meet full criteria for Posttraumatic Stress Disorder (PTSD), though associated anxiety symptoms were likely reduced given that she regularly took antianxiety medication. In the event that she discontinued the medication, it was anticipated that she would experience increased anxiety symptoms. It was also notable that Ms. Smith's feelings of being overwhelmed after discovering her son's sexual abuse initially prevented her from acting in a protective manner and triggered her lapse in sobriety. Therefore, her difficulty managing anxiety not only caused her distress but also placed her at risk for relapse. On this basis, a secondary diagnosis with Unspecified Anxiety Disorder was given.

Despite Ms. Smith's mental health diagnoses, it was determined that **her mental health condition did not preclude her from becoming a safe and adequate parent**. Individuals who have these diagnoses can learn to use coping skills in order to address symptoms and maintain medication compliance. It was anticipated that treating Ms. Smith's anxiety was likely to improve her quality of life, her ability to manage difficult child behaviors, and her success in maintaining sobriety.

Ability to Benefit from Services   The evaluator opined that Ms. Smith did not suffer from a mental health condition that precluded her from safely and adequately parenting her son. There were positive prognostic signs that Ms. Smith could improve her mental health functioning, but the evaluator also expressed significant concerns about Ms. Smith's present parenting ability.

It was remarkable that Ms. Smith made gains in prior services that helped her maintain sobriety for an extended period of time. Her continued efforts and participation in services also spoke to her willingness to enhance her insight into how her mental health impacts her daily and interpersonal functioning, as well as her child.

Another encouraging sign was that during the evaluation (within a structured and controlled environment) Ms. Smith displayed an ability to interact with and parent John in an appropriate manner. However, when Ms. Smith and John had been in a more natural setting, with multiple other demands placed on them (e.g., co-parenting with stepfather, getting John to complete less desirable daily activities), she struggled to manage John's behaviors. Service providers and family friends both observed Ms. Smith to have poor follow-through with setting limits, and they observed that Ms. Smith was generally "passive" or "parented out of guilt," something that would likely continue without structured intervention.

It was further acknowledged that Ms. Smith previously completed parenting services (i.e., classes and in-home support). However, she continued to have difficulty following through with effective commands, providing appropriate consequences, establishing appropriate daily/hygiene routines, and ensuring John's physical/sexual safety. It was believed that Ms. Smith's parenting limitations could be addressed in treatment more effectively at the present time, particularly now that some of the primary family stressors were no longer present (i.e., the stepfather no longer undermining Ms. Smith's parenting efforts; John was no longer being sexually abused).

Taken together, the evaluator concluded that treatment services would need to be in place to address Ms. Smith's ongoing mental health symptoms (i.e., anxiety) and parenting deficits. Given the extent of her symptoms and the proven benefit she received from prior substance abuse services, it was anticipated that Ms. Smith had the ability to become a safe and adequate parent within four to eight months if she adequately participated in an appropriate course of treatment (outlined below).

Quality of Ms. Smith and John's Relationship   After determining that Ms. Smith would be capable of addressing her mental health concerns, the evaluator addressed the main question for the evaluation: whether discontinuing the relationship between John and Ms. Smith would lead to long-term emotional detriment for John and prevent him from establishing permanency.

An underlying assumption for answering questions for TPR is that a significant developmental need for children is forming appropriate and stable relationships. Predictable and consistent care from a caregiver helps children develop security and trust and increases the likelihood that children can effectively negotiate future developmental and interpersonal growth/challenges. The early formation of a stable relationship between a parent and a child (e.g., typically the first three years of a child's life) is essential for promoting a child's healthy psychosocial development.

A useful way of evaluating parent-child relationships is by considering the strength (i.e., strong vs. weak) and the quality (i.e., positive vs. negative) of the relationship. When evaluating the strength and quality of relationships, it is also important to consider the timing, duration, and consistency of the relationship (e.g., How long has the child and caregiver been together? Were there significant disruptions in infancy or early childhood?). The early formation of a stable relationship between a parent and a child (e.g., typically the first three years of a child's life) is essential for promoting a child's healthy psychosocial development. Predictable and consistent care from a parent helps children develop security and trust with parents and increases the likelihood that children will be able to effectively negotiate future developmental and interpersonal growth/challenges.

As the evaluator considered the strength and quality of Ms. Smith and John's relationship, it was noted that John was in Ms. Smith's exclusive care for the first five years of his life, which spans beyond the critical time period when attachments are initially being formed between a child and a parent. John had been separated from Ms. Smith for a year at 6 years of age. Despite this, collateral sources and clinical observations indicated that Ms. Smith consistently expressed appropriate affection. She was also attentive and responsive to many of his needs. Additionally, during the current evaluation, John and his mother expressed shared affect and enjoyment. Ms. Smith also proved capable of attending to John's preferences and used many positive parenting skills (e.g., praise, physical affection, and reflections).

Although John acknowledged having positive affiliation with various parties, including his stepgrandfather and foster parents, he endorsed having a preferred attachment and desire for Ms. Smith over other people. He was significantly distressed about his removal from Ms. Smith. Taken together, the evaluator concluded that Ms. Smith and John had a strong and generally positive bond with one another in spite of the year-long separation. The stability of this relationship, in part helped sustain John's ability to tolerate the distress related to being separated from Ms. Smith and to function well in multiple settings (i.e., community, school, and foster homes). As such, it was believed that discontinuing John's relationship with Ms. Smith would negatively impact his long-term emotional and behavioral functioning, such that his prospects for permanency would be compromised.

Treatment Recommendations

Ms. Smith   It was recommended Ms. Smith continue working with her psychiatrist, and remain active in substance abuse specific support services. Such efforts would be particularly important when there were increased parenting stressors as John returned home and progressed into adolescence.

It was also recommended that Ms. Smith start her own individual treatment. During the current evaluation, Ms. Smith denied significant trauma symptoms associated with her own sexual abuse victimization. However, the recent revelation of John's sexual abuse triggered memories of her childhood sexual victimization. Ms. Smith's therapist was encouraged to assess further and determine whether specific trauma work was indicated. Regardless, Ms. Smith would benefit from cognitive-behavioral therapy that directly targets her anxiety symptoms and maladaptive coping strategies (i.e., avoidance, withdrawal, denial). Increasing more appropriate coping skills would also help support her drug recovery.

John Because John was experiencing multiple intrusive, arousal, and avoidance symptoms consistent with PTSD, it was strongly recommended that he participate in weekly individual therapy designed to directly address his trauma/maltreatment history. Trauma-Focused Cognitive Behavioral Therapy (TF-CBT) was specifically recommended because it is an empirically supported treatment for trauma and sexual abuse that can be used for children John's age. It was also highly recommended because it includes parent participation and safety planning that helps facilitate a positive, supportive, and protective parent-child relationship.

Parenting/In-Home Behavior Management Services Ms. Smith previously completed parenting classes but was doing so while Mr. Jones was in the home. It was likely that she would benefit from an updated parenting plan where she was the sole parent in the home. It was recommended that specific parenting components to address and master would include 1) sustaining a positive relationship, 2) providing effective commands, 3) using positive reinforcement for compliance, 4) implementing appropriate consequences, 5) ignoring negative behaviors (that did not pose a safety risk), and 6) establishing routines for hygiene and sleep. Effective treatment would require psychoeducation as well as coaching, role-plays, or modeling of skills.

Common Pitfalls and Considerations

Consistent with standards detailed by 2013 Guidelines and best practices for TPR evaluations, the psychologist who evaluated Ms. Smith and John relied on multiple methods and sources. Review of records, clinical interviews of Ms. Smith and John, administration of standardized psychological measures, and collateral contacts were conducted. Although there were concerns about Ms. Smith's history of substance abuse, her mental health symptoms, and her difficulty in managing John's behaviors, ultimately the evaluator determined that Ms. Smith did not have a mental health condition at the time that precluded her from benefiting from reunification services or becoming able to parent her child safely and adequately. There were barriers that impeded her ability to safely and adequately parent John at the time of the evaluation; however it was expected that Ms. Smith had the ability to become a safe and adequate parent within a four-to-eight-month timeframe. Moreover, given the strength and quality of the parent-child relationship, even without parenting improvements, discontinuing John's relationship with Ms. Smith would likely negatively impact his long-term emotional and behavioral functioning, such that his prospects for permanency would be disrupted.

As demonstrated with this case, conducting a psychological evaluation related to the termination of parental rights is a painstaking and difficult endeavor. Ethical and responsible psychologists and/or forensic evaluators should undertake such evaluations with a full understanding of child development, parent-child relationships, both adult and child psychopathology, and the role of an evaluation within the context of the child welfare system. It is the responsibility of the informed psychologist to meld multiple sources of information into a coherent conceptualization that serves as the foundation for their opinions. This opinion should fulfill the standards of the American Psychological Association, the statutes of the local jurisdiction, and most importantly, fairness to the best interests of the child.

References

American Psychological Association, Practice Directorate, Board of Professional Affairs Committee on Professional Practice & Standards. (1999). Guidelines for psychological evaluations in child protection matters. *American Psychologist, 54,* 586–593.

American Psychological Association, Practice Directorate, Board of Professional Affairs Committee on Professional Practice & Standards. (2013). Guidelines for psychological evaluations in child protection matters. *American Psychologist, 68,* 20–31.

Azar, S., Lauretti, A., & Loding, B. (1998). The evaluation of parental fitness in termination of parental rights cases: A functional-contextual perspective. *Clinical Child and Family Psychology Review, 1,* 77–100.

Benjet, C., Azar, S. T., & Kuersten-Hogan, R. (2003). Evaluating the parental fitness of psychiatrically diagnosed individuals: Advocating a functional-contextual analysis of parenting. *Journal of Family Psychology, 17,* 238–251.

Brodzinsky, D. (1993). On the use and misuse of psychological testing in child custody evaluations. *Professional Psychology Research and Practice, 2,* 213–219.

Child Welfare Information Gateway (2007). State Statutes Search. Available at www.childwelfare.gov

Condie, L., & Condie, D. (2007). Termination of parental rights. In A. Goldstein (Ed.), *Forensic psychology: Emerging topics and expanding roles* (pp. 294–330). Hoboken, NJ: Wiley.

Donald, T., & Jureidini, J. (2004). Parenting capacity. *Child Abuse Review, 13,* 5–17.

Eyberg, S., & Pincus, T. (2000). *Eyberg Child Behavior Inventory & Sutter-Eyberg Student Behavior Inventory—revised professional manual.* Odessa, FL: Psychological Assessment Resources.

Grisso, T. (2003). *Evaluating competencies: Forensic assessments and instruments* (2nd ed.) New York, NY: Kluwer Academics/Plenum.

In re Autumn H., 32 Cal. Rpter. 2d 535; Ct. App. 4 Dist. 1994.

In re Casey D., Court of Appeal, Fourth District, Division 1, California. 1999.

In re Smith, 77 Ohio App.3d 1, 16, 601 N.E.2d 45, 54. 1991.

Kalich, L., Carmichael, B., Masson, T., and Blacker, D. (2007). Evaluating the evaluator: Guidelines for legal professionals in assessing the competency of evaluations in termination of parental cases. *The Journal of Psychiatry and the Law, 35,* 365–397.

Kundra, L., & Alexander, L. (2009). Termination of parental rights proceedings: Legal considerations and practical strategies for parents with psychiatric disabilities and the practitioners who serve them. *Psychiatric Rehabilitation Journal, 33,* 142–149.

McVey, L., Henderson, T., and Burroughs Alexander, J. (2008). Parental rights and the foster care system: A glimpse of decision making in Virginia. *Journal of Family Issues, 29,* 1031–1050.

Melton, G. B., Petrila, J., Poythress, N. G., & Slobogin, C. (1997). *Psychological evaluations for the courts: A handbook for mental health professionals and lawyers* (2nd ed.). New York, NY: Guilford Press.

Milner, J. S. (1986). *The Child Abuse Potential Inventory manual* (2nd ed.). Webster, NC: Psytec.

O'Donnell, R. (2010). A second chance for children and families: A model statute to reinstate parental rights after termination. *Family Court Review, 48,* 362–379.

Santosky v. Kramer, 455 U.S. 745 (1982).

Urquiza, A., & Blacker, D. (2005). Psychological evaluations and the child welfare system. In P. F. Talley (Ed.), *Handbook for the treatment of abused and neglected children* (pp. 83–119). New York, NY: Haworth Press.

Vesneski, W. (2011). State law and the termination of parental rights. *Family Court Review, 49,* 364–378.

11

Child Custody and Parenting Plan Evaluations

Robert L. Kaufman and Daniel B. Pickar

Forensic mental health professionals (FMHPs) have been venturing farther and more broadly into areas of disputed child custody for more than three decades. Few, if any, areas of practice in psychology require professionals to have as many well developed skills in as broad a range of diverse content and process areas. Practitioners must be well versed in child development, individual psychopathology, family systems, parent-child attachment, and the particulars of family law, as well as an array of special issues that are specific to child custody work. It is a demanding field and, in many ways, a high-risk venture for the forensic mental health professional (Kirkland & Kirkland, 2001). However, child custody evaluations (CCEs) also can be enormously rewarding, as professionals have the opportunity to offer valuable insight and guidance for children and families at very troubling junctures in their lives.

The field of child custody has greatly evolved and expanded over the last few decades. FMHPs find themselves in various roles, offering an array of services associated with separating and divorcing couples and their interaction with the family law system. Such roles include court-appointed child custody evaluators, mediators, co-parenting counselors, parenting coordinators, and consultants. Each role is defined by the service offered by the professional, as well as by whether or not the relationship between FMHP and client(s) is privileged and confidential. This chapter will focus specifically on conducting child custody evaluations (CCE). The preparation of a child custody report is the culmination of a lengthy, often-intense, stressful, and intrusive process for parents and children. The CCE report is the evaluator's work product that presents not only a summary of the information collected but also the scrutiny and synthesis of all data into a cogent analysis of the case. Opinions and recommendations are offered to address the legal questions at hand, namely, a parenting plan to serve the best interests of the children.

The field is also complex and diverse. Families present with unique histories and circumstances, and because families enter into these evaluations after other means of resolving conflicts have failed, there are often very serious allegations to be addressed. Such special issues will only be briefly highlighted, as primarily this chapter will outline and describe the foundational issues in parenting plan evaluations, followed by a case presentation.

Relevant Case Law

It was not until the latter third of the twentieth century that case law in matters of child custody recognized that parents could provide nurturance and quality care of their children regardless of gender. By the 1970s and 1980s, courts started to move towards acknowledging the benefits of shared parenting or joint custody over awarding custody to one parent based on either rights or dominion (ex. 18th and 19th century assumptions of English courts) or gender-specific instincts (the "tender years doctrine"). As of 2013, thirty-six states have supported joint custody via presumption, by stated preference, or by statutory language in support of cooperative parenting (DiFonzo, 2014). Furthermore, there has been a trend towards conceptualizing legal custody and physical custody as *decision making* and *parenting time* respectively. *Shared parenting*, previously labeled joint custody, indicates that the parents share the authority to make decisions regarding the children and that each parent spends at least 30%–35% of his or her time with the children (Pruett & DiFonzo, 2014).

The legal standard that governs decision making in child custody matters is the *best interests of the children (BIC)*, and many of the principles were first outlined in the Uniform Marriage and Divorce Act of 1970 (UMDA). This act mandated that courts take into account a variety of factors when judicial officers determine BIC in custody cases. These generally include:

- The wishes of the parents;
- The wishes of the child;
- The interaction between the child and his/her parents, siblings, or other person who might significantly affect the child's best interests;
- The child's adjustment to its home, school, and community;
- The mental and physical health of all individuals involved (Uniform Law Commission, 1975).

Over the years, these factors have been further honed to include individual parenting strengths and weaknesses; each parent's willingness to support the child's relationship with the other parent; aspects of the co-parenting relationship; the age, adjustment, and developmental stage of the child; and the stability of proposed living arrangements. Several additional factors, if present, must also be considered. These possible factors include domestic violence; substance abuse; allegations of sexual, physical, or emotional abuse; serious mental health issues; and whether the child has special needs. In states like California, there has also been a strong trend toward considering the stated preferences of a child old enough and mature enough to offer a meaningful preference. What the BIC standard does not state explicitly is the relative weight that should be given to each factor. This is left to the discretion of the judge. This is one area in which custody evaluators may offer significant input and assistance to the court.

There has been criticism of the BIC standard as being ambiguous, difficult to operationalize, and varying across different jurisdictions (Emery, Otto, & O'Donohue, 2005). In turn, critics say that these shortcomings have led to too much judicial subjectivity regarding application of the BIC standard for custody determinations (Shuman & Berk, 2012). Nonetheless, it is clear that judges require information on a range of specific areas regarding the fit between parental competence and the child's needs to assist the court. In California, for example, the information that the court needs from custody evaluators, as well as the procedures for acquiring that information, is spelled out in the state's Family Code as well as the California Rules of Court.

Review of the Literature: Research on Special Issues in Child Custody Evaluations

More than in any other area of forensic psychology, child custody evaluators must be familiar with the available scientific research in the broad range of areas typically encountered in these assessments. Kuehnle and Drozd (2012) have noted that social science research is the foundation of the mental health experts' conclusions and opinions about parents and children in litigated child custody cases. First and foremost, evaluators must be aware of the ever-evolving research base regarding risk and protective factors associated with child and adolescent adjustment following separation and divorce (Kelly, 2012). Important volumes such as *Parenting Plan Evaluations: Applied Research for the Family* (Kuehnle & Drozd, 2012) offer an analysis of the research associated with many of the most important topics within the family court, describing the studies and methods utilized in examining such issues and summarizing the strengths and limitations of each research study. The authors offer an important caution, namely that "not all research is created equal." Thus evaluators must also critically examine the research literature to identify studies that have been well designed and executed and that are truly pertinent to their particular case (Drozd, Olesen, & Saini, 2013).

The court frequently orders child custody evaluations involving a number of special circumstances or populations. Examples include allegations of domestic violence or child sexual abuse, claims of parental alienation, or cases of a parent requesting to move to a different geographic location with children, over the objection of the other parent. The AFCC standards for custody evaluations (2006) specifically note (Standard 5.11) that evaluators must have the professional knowledge and training needed to conduct evaluations involving special and complex issues. Therefore, the evaluator must be familiar with not only the legal statutes and relevant case law regarding these complex areas but also the empirical research and current thinking regarding the assessment and analysis of such issues in a CCE. There are a substantial number of publications on each of these frequently encountered topics, but some key considerations will be highlighted.

Infants and Very Young Children

Parenting plans are responsibly informed by the cognitive, social, and psychological characteristics of children across a wide span of ages and developmental phases. Familiarity with research regarding attachment and overnight time sharing for infants and very young children is a necessity for working with this unique age group (Lamb, 2012; McIntosh, Pruett, & Kelly, 2014; Pruett, McIntosh, & Kelly, 2014). This has also been an area of emerging research and controversy within the custody field. The debate centers on such questions as, at what point can infants, toddlers, and very young children benefit from overnight visitation with the noncustodial parent without experiencing undue distress?

Relocation   In our increasingly mobile society, there are times when one parent in a divorced family seeks to relocate with the children to a geographic location that makes continued shared parenting impossible. These cases are frequently referred for child custody evaluations. This is an area that evaluators need to understand clearly: the case law of the jurisdiction in which they practice. This will inform factors that will be weighed by the court to make an ultimate determination. Austin's (2008a, 2012) review of the relevant literature led to the finding that children are at substantial risk for poorer outcomes when families relocate. This research applied to intact as well as separated or divorced families. In custody cases involving parent relocation, Austin (2008a; 2008b, 2012) recommends a comparative analysis of the relative advantages and disadvantages to the child associated with living primarily with each parent in different communities and experiencing life in a long-distance parenting arrangement. Austin's empirically grounded model enumerates risk and protective factors that should be weighed in a relocation case. They include the age of the child, the geographic distance and travel time between the two homes, the psychological stability of the relocating parent and parenting effectiveness of each parent, the availability of specialized educational or therapeutic services for disabled children, the history of involvement by the nonresidential parent, and the history, if any, of high conflict or domestic violence between the parents. The evaluator must also assess the nature and extent of each parent's support for the child's relationship with the non-residential parent (an issue referred to as "parental gatekeeping") to understand whether the parent who wishes to relocate with the child also seeks to restrict the child's access to the other parent. The motivation for the relocation is also an important factor that needs to be assessed. Lastly, while there are some studies specifically regarding the effects of relocation on a child following a separation or divorce (Braver, Ellman, & Fabricius, 2003), further empirical research regarding child outcome data is still needed.

Intimate Partner Violence   Based on surveys of custody evaluators, Bow and Boxer (2003) found that 37% of CCEs included an allegation of intimate partner violence (IPV). Thus, this is a relatively common issue that must be assessed. Kelly and Johnson (2008) identify three major types of intimate partner violence (coercive controlling violence, violent resistance, situational couple violence) and one subtype of situational couple violence (separation-instigated violence). Several research studies have established a myriad of negative effects on children exposed to intimate partner violence, including emotional, behavioral, cognitive, and relationship effects, as well as increased risk of direct child abuse (Hardesty, Haselschwerdt, & Johnson, 2012).

To promote the safety and healthy adjustment of children, custody evaluators should be familiar with cutting-edge violence risk assessment models. Jaffe, Johnston, Crooks, and Bala (2008) suggest a differentiated approach for developing parenting plans when domestic violence is alleged. This includes assessing risk by screening for the potency, pattern, and primary perpetrator indicators of the violence as a foundation for generating hypotheses about parental functioning and the potential for future violence. Depending on the analysis of these factors, these authors also propose guidelines and criteria for developing parenting plans that might range from highly restricted access arrangements (no contact or supervised access) to relatively unrestricted ones, such a parallel parenting or even co-parenting. Austin and Drozd (2012) offer a revision of the above model, which is research based and expands on the types and identification of IPV (i.e., coercive controlling violence, intrusive violence, authoritarian violence, conflict-instigated violence, situation-specific violence, separation-associated violence, substance abuse-associated violence, and major-mental-disorder-associated violence). These authors then suggest analyzing each case utilizing ten behavioral dimensions of violence. They further propose that alternative parenting time schedules be developed in light of the type, severity, active-potency, and risk-threat assessment of the violence.

Child Alienation   Family courts frequently encounter families in which a child is either refusing or resisting contact with one of their divorcing or separated parents for reasons that seem out of proportion to any parental failings or the actual parent-child relationship. There is a rapidly growing literature in this area (Saini, Johnston, Fidler, & Bala, 2012), as claims of "parental alienation" arise with considerable frequency in high-conflict families. While initially referred to as "parental alienation syndrome" (Gardner 1992), alienation dynamics in a divorced family are more recently referred to as "children who resist post-separation parental contact" (Fidler, Bala, and Saini, 2012). An "alienated child," as defined by Kelly and Johnston (2001), is a child who expresses, freely and persistently, unreasonable negative feelings (such as anger, hatred, fear) toward a parent that are disproportionate to the child's actual experience with that parent.

Recent literature on alienation and divorce suggests that children's relatively sudden refusals to spend time with a parent are seldom just the result of one parent intentionally and systematically attempting to undermine the child's relationship with the other parent. Rather, there is often a more complex inter-play of factors operative within the family. (Friedlander & Walters, 2010). Drozd and Olesen (2004) outline a classification system for the identification of pathological and nonpathological parent-child relationships, ranging from children who are realistically estranged from a parent as a result of a history of abuse or mistreatment by that parent to those children who have developed an unjustified alienation in rejecting that parent.

Contrary to some past impressions, parental alienation is not a diagnostic syndrome but rather is considered to be a cluster of commonly recognized symptoms and/or behaviors. Because of the complexity of these cases, the evaluator's task is to conduct a comprehensive assessment of the various factors that may impede or facilitate parent-child contact problems. Awareness of the research on various treatment interventions for cases with alienation dynamics is crucial (Fidler & Bala, 2010).

Child Sexual Abuse Allegations   Allegations of child sexual abuse in custody disputes are among the most difficult to assess. Several preliminary studies have found that approximately 1% to 2% of contested custody cases involve an allegation of child sexual abuse, but Kuehnle and Kirkpatrick (2005) have opined that this appears to be a gross underestimate of the actual occurrence of sexual abuse allegations embedded in contested custody matters. There is no solid empirical evidence regarding the occurrence of false allegations of sexual abuse. Some authorities estimate the rate of false allegations involving "calculated lying" by a child to be in the range from 6% to 8%. However, if the criteria for false allegations are broadened to include inaccurate memories and false statements associated with suggestive questioning and socially desirable responding, others have estimated rates of 23% to 35% of false reports of sexual abuse (Poole & Lamb, 1998).

Child custody evaluations involving such allegations are typically ordered after child protective services has conducted their investigation and the findings have been determined to be either "unsubstantiated" or "inconclusive." Child custody evaluations of this nature should be completed by a FMHP who has substantial experience and training in forensic interviewing of children (Lamb, Sternberg, & Esplin; 1998; Kuehnle & Kirkpatrick, 2005). Competent evaluators should be familiar with research on normative sexual behaviors in children (Friedrich, 2002), as well as the extensive literature regarding children's memory and children's testimony (Ceci & Bruck, 1995; Ceci & Friedman, 2000; Goodman, Batterman-Faunce, Schaaf, & Kenny, 2002).

Evaluators must assess the circumstances under which the concern about sexual abuse arose and the methods by which the child's statements were elicited or triggered. Kuehnle and Connell (2009) have noted that evaluators can assist the court by conducting a careful analysis of the data that argue for and against a conclusion that a child has been sexually abused. Additionally, evaluators can describe the intersection between the child's developmental level and the factors that might have contributed to an atmosphere of suspicion. Relevant research bearing on an examination of the data should be noted, and evaluators should always discuss the potential limitations of their conclusions.

Best Practices

Ethical Guidelines and Model Standards of Practice for Child Custody Evaluations

In addition to gaining familiarity with state or local court rules, statues, and relevant case law, FMHPs who conduct child custody evaluations should be thoroughly familiar with the relevant professional guidelines and standards of practice. In the last ten years, the two most important sets of practice guidelines for child custody evaluations have undergone significant revision (American Psychological Association [APA], 2010; Association of Family and Conciliation Courts, 2007). Additionally, both the "Specialty Guidelines for Forensic Psychology" (APA, 2013) and the "Ethical Principles of Psychologists and Code of Conduct" (APA, 2002) provide FMHPs with additional guidance on ethical practice issues that impact how a CCE should be conducted. The focus in this chapter will be on the APA and AFCC (Association of Family and Conciliation Courts) guidelines, as they are most centrally related to CCE practice.

The Guidelines for Child Custody Evaluations in Family Law Proceedings (APA, 2010), a set of fourteen aspirational principles, specify that the purpose of the custody evaluation is to assist the trier of fact in determining the psychological best interests of the child and that "the evaluation focuses upon parenting attributes, the child's psychological needs, and the resulting fit" (p. 864). FMHPs must also strive to gain and maintain specialized competence in the field. Some states have codified this guideline by requiring potential evaluators to provide evidence of this specialty training. For example, California specifies that child custody evaluators must be licensed mental health professionals who have completed forty hours of initial general training related to CCEs, as well as sixteen hours of training related to domestic violence, prior to conducting any CCE. Additionally, according to California Rules of Court, rule 5.225, evaluations are required to complete eight hours of continuing education annually regarding CCE related issues, as well as four hours of education, annually, related to updates in domestic violence law and research. For each evaluation, FMHPs provide an affidavit to the court prior to beginning a case, confirming that these requirements have been completed. APA guidelines stress that FMHPs function as impartial evaluators and engage in nondiscriminatory practices. They offer some procedural guidelines regarding establishing the scope of the evaluation, obtaining informed consent, and using multiple methods of data collection including observational data and psychological testing.

The Model Standards of Practice for Child Custody Evaluation (AFCC, 2007) are the most detailed and useful guidelines to assist the FMHP in performing custody and access evaluations. Not only do the AFCC standards offer a series of twelve detailed standards but they also provide the closest thing to a "best-practice" document for the field. As with the APA guidelines, the AFCC standards are aspirational in nature. The model standards describe education, training, and experience requirements and emphasize that evaluators should utilize reliable and valid empirically based assessment methods when analyzing a case and offering recommendations. Among other things, evaluators should have reasonable knowledge of applicable statutes, case law, and rules of the court. The guidelines specifically emphasize the need for evaluators to reduce any source of potential bias and maintain forensic neutrality in the interest of providing an objective and impartial report. The importance of such role delineation is also emphasized, with cautions for evaluators not to take on multiples role and not to offer advice or therapeutic services, which might compromise the neutrality and objectivity of the evaluation.

Guidelines Offered in the Child Custody Evaluation Literature

Several books offer both novice and experienced practitioners a comprehensive discussion of guiding principles for conducting child custody evaluations. Gould (2006) and Gould and Martindale (2007) describe in detail the application of a forensic and scientifically informed model of practice that emphasizes the importance of utilizing multiple methods of data gathering to improve the validity and reliability of the evaluator's ultimate opinions and that includes the following principles:

- Identification of psycholegal questions provided by the court to guide the investigative process
- Multiple interviews with relevant parties and their children
- Use of valid and reliable tests and measure
- Direct behavioral observations, including parent-child interactions
- Review of relevant historical and current records
- Interviews with collateral sources to corroborate or disconfirm hypotheses
- Inclusion of a reference to the empirical literature in the report to justify and ground recommendations as having some empirical validity; application of reliable and relevant research

Of particular importance, Gould and Martindale (2007) highlight the need for the child custody evaluator to maintain a forensic role rather than a therapeutic one. This means recognizing the investigative nature of the task and, in the evaluation report, acknowledging the limitations inherent in the procedures. Several other textbooks (Ackerman, 2006; Fuhrman & Zibbell, 2012; Hynan, 2014; Stahl, 2011) offer important and well-researched information that can guide the conduct of a child custody evaluation.

Both novice and experienced evaluators should also keep abreast of the latest research, practice procedures, and emerging issues in the field by regularly reviewing the prominent journals relevant to the practice of CCEs. Among others, the *Family Court Review* and *Journal of Child Custody* present some of the latest thinking and research on best practices. For example, Pickar and Kaufman (2013) present a pragmatic best-practice model for writing child custody evaluation reports, which integrates forensic and clinical perspectives. Other recent articles have offered empirically based best-practice models for evaluating parenting skills (Moran & Weinstock, 2011), parent-child observations (Saini & Polak 2014), and the forensic interviewing of children in child custody evaluations (Saywitz, Camparo, & Romanoff, 2010).

The perception that child custody is a high-risk area of practice has been borne out over time. Two surveys have revealed that half of the respondents reported receiving a licensing board complaint in their work as evaluators (Bow and Martindale, 2009; Bow, Gottlieb, Siegel, & Noble, 2010). These authors also found that the most frequent type of complaint filed against custody evaluators was "bias." Bow et al. (2010) underscore that court-appointed evaluators must be aware of the various types of personal and cognitive bias that can impact their work, such as confirmatory bias (Martindale, 2005) or countertransference bias (Pickar, 2007a). While "bias" is a common charge levied against evaluators by parents who feel that the report did not support their position, utilizing a systematic method for organizing and weighing data can reduce the possibility of such charges. For example, to contend with the risk of cognitive errors and personal biases by custody evaluators, a notable book by Drozd, Olesen, and Saini (2013) offers a pragmatic scientifically based model that can be applied to data analysis and report writing. The approach is geared towards reducing bias and improving the accuracy of decision making. These authors propose using "decision trees" involving checklists and flow charts to help guide the evaluator through a systematic analysis and synthesis of the data gathered during the process of a child custody evaluation. Through such an analysis, pertinent issues are organized into themes that best fit the data and will ultimately inform parenting plan recommendations made by the evaluator. Such an approach also targets reduction of cognitive errors and bias that can unwittingly plague the evaluator's objectivity.

Lastly, there has been a recent trend in the child custody arena geared towards developing and utilizing risk-assessment models for use with special circumstances frequently encountered in child custody evaluations. Systematic weighing of multiple risk and protective factors should inform parenting plan recommendations to the court. For example, risk assessment models based on empirical research have been developed in areas such as parent relocation (Austin, 2008a; Austin, 2008b), domestic violence, (Austin, 2001; Jaffe, Johnston, Crooks, & Bala, 2008; Austin & Drozd, 2012), and special needs children (Pickar & Kaufman, 2015).

Conducting the Child Custody Evaluation

Child custody evaluations are unique in that *multiple individuals* are assessed. In addition, *multiple interpersonal relationships* and the *family system are also subjects of examination*. Every family referred for a CCE has at least two parents and one child. It is incumbent on the custody evaluator to report on the parenting competencies of each parent and the functioning of each child. In addition, each parent-child relationship must be understood and discussed, as well as the co-parenting relationship with respect to how parental conflict impacts the child (Pickar & Kaufman, 2013).

In general, custody evaluators must use multiple modes of data collection, including parent and other caretaker interviews, interviews of the child, parent-child observations, review of relevant documents and interviews of collateral sources of information. There has been considerable literature about the utility of psychological testing in custody evaluations (Flens, 2005). However, psychological testing is not a mandated component of the evaluation. Typically, either the court or the referring attorneys will specify whether testing is desired, or evaluators will state their preference for utilizing psychological testing as an additional source of CCE data.

Referrals for custody evaluations should include specific questions about which the court requires input, in addition to the more global issue of what parenting plan would be in the best interests of the child. This might include, for example, why is a child expressing a strong preference for spending more time with one parent? Does a parent suffer from a serious psychiatric or substance abuse disorder that significantly impacts his or her parenting capacity? Has a parent negatively influenced a child's relationship with the other parent, such that the child is refusing to spend time with that parent? Specific questions raised either by the court or by the parents themselves should be addressed in the custody evaluation report.

More specifically, comprehensive child custody evaluations will include the following procedures:

- Interview parents individually regarding:
  o Their views of custody related issues, including concerns about the children, the other parent(s), and the allegations and assertions;
  o Their response to allegations and assertions raised by the other parent;
  o The history of the parents' relationship, both prior to and subsequent to separation and/or divorce;
  o Their views of the functioning of each child and their understanding of the desires of each child;
  o Their individual family and relationship history;
  o Their views of the parent-child relationship;
  o Their views of the co-parenting relationship;
  o Their views of evaluation-specific issues (ex. domestic violence, allegations of sexual abuse, view of proposed relocation of a parent);
  o Their views of a parenting plan that will address the child's needs and their willingness to support the child's relationship with the other parent.
- Interviewing children regarding:
  o The structure and nature of their lives, including school, activities outside of school, and peer relations;
  o Their day-to-day routines in each parent's home;
  o Their views of their relationship with each parent (including step-parents and other significant caretakers) and siblings (including step-siblings);
  o How rewards and discipline are handled in each home;
  o Their views of the existing custody and access plan, if they have any;
  o Their experience of living in two households and managing day-to-day logistics;
  o Their moods, worries and concerns.
- Interviewing step-parents and other significant caretakers regarding:
  o Many of the same issues as with parents, though there is less emphasis on personal history.

- Parent-child observations
  - Depending on the age, this will take place in the evaluator's office and may include unstructured play between parent and child, as well as a structured task for a parent and child to do together.
  - Though not required, many evaluators conduct in-home parent-child observations. These preplanned visits have the advantage of observing children in settings in which they are comfortable and in which they conduct activities typical of their daily lives.
  - Recent literature (Saini & Polak, 2014) suggests that multiple observations of children across settings increases the ecological validity of the data obtained.
- Psychological testing
  - When psychological testing is part of a comprehensive custody evaluation, the Minnesota Multiphasic Personality Inventory-2 (MMPI-2; Butcher, Dahlstrom, Graham, Tellegen & Kaemmer, 1989) is the most commonly used assessment instrument. Other tests often used by custody evaluators include the Rorschach Inkblot Method, the Millon Clinical Multiaxial Inventory-III (MCMI-III; Millon, Millon, Davis, & Grossman, 2006), and the Personality Assessment Inventory (PAI: Morey, 2007).
  - Both AFCC Guidelines and APA Guidelines for Child Custody Evaluations offer cautions about the use of psychological testing for parents in custody evaluations. These issues, as well as the appropriate forensically informed use of these instruments have been discussed extensively in the child custody literature (Flens, 2005; Otto, Edens & Barcus, 2000). While some tests have been developed specifically to test parenting abilities, none of them have the requisite validity and reliability to meet the admissibility criteria for use in court.
  - In the case discussed in this chapter, the evaluator utilized the MMPI-2 and the Rorschach. Both instruments have sound and long-standing empirical bases, are used regularly in forensic evaluations, and meet both Frye and Daubert standards for use in court. The MMPI-2 is primarily a measure of psychopathology and is particularly useful for identifying personality disorders and clinical syndromes that *may* interfere with day-to-day parenting. These could include, for example, significant anxiety or depression, deficits in capacity for empathy, problems with reality testing, and resistance to following rules and orders. The primary drawback of the MMPI-2 in custody cases is the high incidence of defensive profiles, wherein parents are unwilling to report even minor faults, much less more significant problems in living. This response set can often render their MMPI-2 protocols invalid.
  - The Rorschach Inkblot Method (RIM) has long been described as a "projective" test. Especially with the development of the Rorschach

Performance Assessment System (R-PAS; Meyer, et al., 2011), it is most accurately defined as a performance based personality measure that adds incremental validity to self-report offered in interviews of custody litigants (Erard, 2014). Many of the concerns about the normative sample and statistical validity of some structural variables developed with the Comprehensive System (CS) have been addressed by R-PAS. The empirical base of the instrument when scored and analyzed via R-PAS has been strengthened and has led to increased use of the procedure in custody evaluations (Ackerman & Pritzl, 2011). There is ample research supporting the notion that the RIM, particularly when scored with R-PAS, yields enormously helpful information regarding stable and enduring personality characteristics that underlie parenting capacities. It is especially useful for revealing how individuals manage stressful situations, how individuals behave in intimate partner relations, and how their patterns of thinking and feeling emerge over time (Viglione & Meyer, 2008; Mihura et al., 2013; Erard & Viglioni, 2014).

- Information from collateral sources:
  o Written documents submitted to the evaluator that typically include declarations, pleadings, reports, and other materials submitted to the evaluator by the attorneys and the parents;
  o Interviews with third parties who have had contact and interaction with the parents, the children, or the family as a whole. These often include mental health professionals, medical providers, teachers, visitation supervisors, tutors, child-care providers, friends, and other family members.

The Child Custody or Parenting Plan Report

The CCE report is a forensic work product, which addresses the legal questions posed by the court and consequently should adhere to guidelines for forensic psychological reports (deMirer, 2012). These include discussions of data that are weighed to analyze rival hypotheses and lead to the evaluator's conclusions and recommendations. Pickar & Kaufman (2013) note that, in reality, CCE reports will be read and utilized by parents and attorneys and, potentially, by various professionals who are assisting families in addition to bench officers. Therefore, reports should be written with these multiple "clients" in mind by avoiding jargon, denoting parenting strengths as well as weaknesses, and creating a sense of hope for families in turmoil. In addition, the well-crafted custody report makes good use of insightful clinical impressions and understanding. As noted by Pickar and Kaufman (2013), "If anything, report writing grounded not only in science, but in sophisticated and well-reasoned clinical judgment, plays an essential role in helping the court understand complex and seemingly contradictory reports from parents, complicated histories, and the needs of children who are often too young to articulate feelings and needs at sufficient level of emotional maturity" (p. 23).

Custody evaluation reports that are helpful to the court and to parents alike provide a clear presentation of the data collected, whether the data are from interviews, observations, documentary evidence, or psychological testing. Effective reports lay out the scope of the assessment and the psycholegal questions. Readers should be able to understand how the evaluator weighed evidence, including conflicting reports from parents, to arrive at conclusions. This includes discussing evidence and data that do not necessarily support the evaluator's conclusions. Given how emotionally charged custody work can be, evaluators should be particularly careful to avoid describing parents in a polarized fashion, as bias is the most common complaint lodged against evaluators by custody litigants. In particular, evaluators are well advised to work hard to incorporate what is termed "the voice of the child" in their reports. This includes not only the child's stated preferences but also a picture of how the child experiences family life.

Most often, CCEs culminate in a set of recommendations regarding both legal and physical custody. These terms mean, respectively, how decisions are made regarding the children and how the children divide their time between homes. This typically includes specific timeshare schedules during the school year, as well as a plan for holidays and vacations. It is not unusual for reports to offer additional recommendations that could aid the family. These might include, for example, mental health treatment for individuals and/or the family, methods for addressing interventions related to substance abuse and/or domestic violence, and supervision for visitation or any other intervention or structure needed.

It is important to note that there has been controversy as to whether custody evaluators should be offering specific recommendations at all to the court, versus providing analysis of data to the trier of fact, who in turn will make decisions on these key issues (Tippins & Wittmann, 2005). While there is no argument that judges are charged with making ultimate determinations, there is some evidence that judicial officers want evaluators to make recommendations, though the recommendations are considered a starting point for the court, with the judge then likely to hear additional evidence at hearings or in trial (Ackerman, Ackerman, Steffen, & Kelley-Poulos, 2004; Stahl, 2014).

The Impact of the Evaluation Process

Custody evaluators should be cognizant of the fact that it is invariably stressful for parents and children to participate in these comprehensive assessments. Parents arrive at the evaluation process when other means of resolving disputes have failed and when parents have effectively turned critical decisions about their children over to third parties. Additionally, the need to have input from the children directly means that the children are thrust into the midst of their parents' disagreements. Depending on their age, children are often aware that their input could affect the evaluator's views and recommendations. This is especially so since custody evaluators are required to provide all participants, including children, with informed consent and an understanding of the evaluation process. Additionally, one cannot ignore the fact that custody evaluations, especially comprehensive family assessments, can take as much as three or more months to complete, and these evaluations are financially costly. While custody evaluators must keep appropriate neutrality and distance during the assessment process, they should be careful to treat participants with respect and strive to ensure that parents and children alike feel that their views have been understood. Application of "forensic empathy" (Brodsky & Wilson, 2012) can be particularly salient in child custody evaluations.

Case Vignette

Reasons for Referral

Ms. Frankel was 36 years of age and worked as an administrator at a financial institution. Mr. Frankel, age 42, was employed as a program developer for a software company. They had one daughter, Julia, age 4-and-three-quarters, who at the time of the evaluation was enrolled in a local prekindergarten program. The parents live within the same county, approximately eight miles from each other. The family was referred for a comprehensive child custody evaluation by a Family Court Services mediator shortly after their separation and after the mother filed for divorce. The parents had separated once earlier for a period of three months, but reconciled and remained together for another three years prior to the final separation and filing. The ultimate separation took place after an incident at their home in which the parents had an angry argument and confrontation in front of their daughter, during which Mr. Frankel called the police and alleged that his wife had been violent towards him. Ms. Frankel was ordered to leave the home and Mr. Frankel filed for a restraining order against her. He was also awarded sole custody of Julia, although, after an emergency hearing, a plan was adopted that allowed Ms. Frankel to have visits with their daughter that were supervised by the mother's family. These visits, which did not include overnights, lasted approximately one month, at which time the parents went for county-mandated mediation. Mr. Frankel withdrew his restraining order, and the Family Court Services mediator recommended a temporary plan in which the parents had joint legal custody and shared physical custody, on a rotating "2–2–3" schedule each week. With this schedule,

---

The case vignette has been redacted and all identifying information removed. It is not meant to serve as a forensic report. Any likeness to a case is purely coincidental.

Julia was with one parent on Mondays and Tuesdays and with the other parent on Wednesdays and Thursdays, followed by a return to the first parent's home for the weekend (Friday, Saturday, and Sunday). These time periods then alternated on a continuous rotating basis. The parents agreed to this plan and agreed to seek a private custody evaluation.

By the time the custody evaluation commenced, the timeshare plan had been in place for four months. From Mr. Frankel's perspective, the timeshare and schedule were working well. Still, he had significant concerns about Ms. Frankel's emotional stability. He characterized her as generally being very controlling, both of him and their daughter, but also prone to abrupt mood swings and outbursts of anger. He emphasized that there had been no fewer than five prior incidents in which the police were called due to her behavior, and he was concerned about the ill effects of such incidents on their daughter. Mr. Frankel noted that since the court had been involved, Ms. Frankel had been on better behavior. Although his job required some international travel, Mr. Frankel insisted that it was not as extensive as has been depicted by the mother. He requested that a system be put in place that would enable him to receive "make-up time" for days he misses with their daughter. He also proposed a somewhat different custody schedule that would have Julia in each home for longer blocks of time. That way, he could better plan his business trips to take place when he did not have his daughter and therefore would need to ask for fewer changes in the schedule due to his work.

From Ms. Frankel's perspective, the temporary schedule was not working well for Julia. She described Mr. Frankel as disorganized, a poor planner, and overwhelmed by work demands. Consequently, Mr. Frankel had frequently asked her to trade custodial time or to provide backup for him when he could not care for their daughter. This included sometimes dropping Julia off at Ms. Frankel's house early in the morning so Mr. Frankel could participate in work calls to clients in Asia or Europe. Ms. Frankel further asserted that, because of their daughter's age, Julia would do better spending more time with her, though she also acknowledged that Julia loves her father and that "he is a lot of fun." Ms. Frankel was critical of Mr. Frankel for not keeping Julia on consistent agreed-upon routines like bedtime and naps. She also strenuously disagreed with Mr. Frankel's characterization of her as volatile and suggested that Mr. Frankel was both provocative and "passive aggressive." She believed that Mr. Frankel should have custody of their daughter every other weekend, with some midweek dinner visits, if he could consistently maintain them.

Evaluation Process

The parents' attorneys contacted the evaluator and a stipulation to conduct the custody evaluation was drafted, signed by the parties and their counsel, and filed with the court. Each parent met with the evaluator individually on three separate occasions for a total of six hours each. During the initial meeting, the evaluator reviewed with the parties the terms and conditions of the evaluation process in detail and also fielded their questions and concerns. Over the course of the meetings, the parents reviewed their goals for the assessment, their views of relevant issues that were specific to the custody assessment, their views of their child, their personal history, and the history of their relationship. In addition, each parent completed the Minnesota Multiphasic Personality Inventory-2 (MMPI-2) and was administered the Rorschach Inkblot Method. Each also completed a comprehensive questionnaire regarding their history and concerns, and further completed the Behavior Assessment System for Children, Second Edition (BASC-2), which assisted the evaluator in understanding each parent's view of their child's behavioral and emotional functioning.

Each parent was seen for a one-hour in-office observation with their daughter. The evaluator also conducted a two-hour parent-child observation in each of the parent's homes. This was in addition to two individual sessions with Julia. For balance, each parent brought Julia to a session and waited for her in the evaluator's waiting room. Both parents submitted letters of reference from friends and family members. With written consent of the parents, the evaluator also spoke with the child's pre-K teacher, a former baby sitter, a former couple's therapist, and the mother's current therapist. Court pleadings and declarations were also reviewed, as were police reports from all incidents noted.

Relevant Background

Both parents were born in an Eastern European country, though they emigrated at different times of their lives. They met via an online dating service and, within a few months, they began cohabitating. Both parents reported that the early part of their relationship was passionate and exciting, though they were also prone to episodic arguing and conflict. Arguments focused on the demanding nature of Mr. Frankel's work life and Ms. Frankel's frustration that they did not spend enough time together. There were several times that Mr. Frankel would leave the home for a few days or a week but then offer a very romantic gesture, after which Ms. Frankel would ask him to return. There was a lengthier period of separation after a particularly volatile incident, but the parents eventually reconciled. During one romantic weekend away, Julia was conceived. While the parents had talked at different times about having a child, this pregnancy was not planned. Not long thereafter, Mr. Frankel moved back into Ms. Frankel's home. They married when Ms. Frankel was four months pregnant.

Over the ensuing two years, there remained instability in their relationship. Calm periods were punctuated by romantic reconciliations. The parents also started to argue over parenting issues. On three occasions, Mr. Frankel called the local police and alleged that Ms. Frankel was negligent and hence endangering their daughter or that Ms. Frankel had been violent and rageful, including handling Julia in a rough way. During one incident, when Julia was 4 years of age, Mr. Frankel produced a restraining order that he procured previously unbeknownst to Ms. Frankel. He presented it to the police who ordered Ms. Frankel to leave the home without their daughter. Over the next two months, Ms. Frankel had visitation with Julia almost every day, though there were no overnights. Eventually, the couple mediated the timeshare agreement that was in place at the beginning of the custody evaluation.

In terms of the parents' earlier family history, each had endured serious difficulties during their childhood and adolescent years. Mr. Frankel and his family came to the United States when he was an elementary school child, and the family suffered some economic hardship after their relocation, as his parents were unable to find employment in the fields in which they were trained. Mr. Frankel felt that there was a significant cultural divide between his parents and him, as he had grown up largely in the American culture. He also described his father as dictatorial, controlling, and threatening to the point of being abusive. After one particularly bad physical confrontation during his senior year of high school, Mr. Frankel moved out of the family home and lived with another family, returning only shortly before his graduation. He went on to college and never returned to the family home. While Mr. Frankel was able to reconcile with his father some years later, there always remained tension and a deep cultural divide in the relationship.

Ms. Frankel immigrated to the United States when she was 19 years of age. After her parents divorced, Ms. Frankel had no further contact with her father other than one letter when she was an early teenager. Since that time, she has had no contact with any of her paternal relatives. Ms. Frankel reported that it was not uncommon in her culture for men to disappear and create different families after divorce. Thus, Ms. Frankel was raised by her own mother, whom she described as caring and respectful.

Collateral Contacts

Several professionals were contacted to obtain independent third-party information. Current and former teachers and childcare professionals confirmed that Julia was developing well in terms of cognitive abilities and social skills. They further noted that Julia was generally happy, well adjusted, and eager to see whichever parent picked her up from preschool or child care. Julia's teacher at the time Julia was separated from her mother reported that she was uncharacteristically sad and dysregulated for those weeks. In addition, Julia seemed confused about when she would see her mother. The parents' former couple's therapist reported that the treatment only lasted six sessions. Mr. Frankel had initiated the counseling and reported that Ms. Frankel was prone to angry outbursts and was demeaning and controlling of him. He alleged that she "got in my face" and complained that he didn't make enough money. Ms. Frankel said she was disappointed in Mr. Frankel and that he needed to be more responsible and reliable. She acknowledged getting frustrated and impatient, but denied being confrontational. The therapist said that the parents had difficulty getting beyond the mutual allegations and were unable to be empathic towards the other. Treatment ended about three weeks prior to the incident that led to the couple's separation.

Mental Status Examinations

In individual interviews, both parents were cooperative and well engaged, and both expressed a great commitment to the positive care of their child. Neither parent demonstrated evidence of a thought disorder in their clinical presentation or exhibited overt signs of depression or significant anxiety. Both parents were intelligent and articulate individuals and evidenced a range of emotions in ways that were appropriate to the situation. Mr. Frankel was rather charming and had a boyish quality about him. He could also be warm and humorous. Ms. Frankel was extremely well organized, articulate, very respectful, and composed. She did, however, become tearful when discussing the imposed separation from her daughter.

Across the multiple individual meetings with Julia, as well as the parent-child observations, it was clear that Julia was bright, engaging, and energetic and did not suffer any developmental delays. She was also very responsive to and affectionate with both parents. Both parents' home lives appeared to center around their daughter, who seemed to be familiar and comfortable with the routines in each home.

Psychological Measures: Child and Family Observations

There were noteworthy differences in the parent-child observations in the evaluator's office. Ms. Frankel arrived for the observation meeting with a number of toys and play materials. From the onset, she guided and structured the daughter's play thorough different activities, and the daughter was very compliant with her mother's directions. Ms. Frankel also rewarded Julia frequently for her good performance, which made the daughter become brighter and more animated. At the same time, she corrected her daughter for relatively minor "mistakes," even during an art project. Ms. Frankel also led Julia through some reading games and, at the end of the session, reported that she wanted the evaluator to get a good sense of Julia's capabilities.

The home visit with Julia and her mother was somewhat more relaxed, though Ms. Frankel also took charge of decision making regarding the activities that we could all play together. During a board game, the Julia tried to manipulate the materials so she would get an optimal score and win every time. Ms. Frankel assured Julia that she would win, but when she tried to set a limit with her, Julia became petulant and verbally balked, insisting on getting her way. Eventually, Ms. Frankel had to convince the daughter to switch games.

For Mr. Frankel's in-office visit, he did not bring any of Julia's play materials, which had been an option suggested by the evaluator. Rather, he relied on toys, games, and art materials already in the office. Julia gravitated towards some art materials and, for some time, she was engaged in building and creating, with Mr. Frankel offering suggestions, encouragement, and enthusiastic reinforcement. As Julia became more engrossed in the activity, Mr. Frankel started to recede and become less engaged, although he did offer some periodic assistance to his daughter.

During the visit and observation at Mr. Frankel's home, Julia was animated and playful. She and her father were also playing with a soccer ball and, at times, she kicked it quite hard and with agility. The daughter also took out some dolls and started to create scenes and narratives in which her father participated. He also directed her to some educational materials they had been using so Julia could show that she was learning her numbers. Still, Julia continued to gravitate to games on her iPad. Mr. Frankel suggested that perhaps she could show the evaluator some dance moves that she had been practicing or making up. Much time was spent with Julia demonstrating her skills, which she seemed happy to do, and garnering enthusiastic rewards from her father.

Julia was also seen in separate individual sessions in the office. She was brought to each meeting by a different parent and her presentation in each session was roughly equivalent. She had no difficulty separating from either parent. Julia was well engaged, as well as focused during the interviews. Typical for children her age, Julia spoke in relatively concrete or practical terms regarding her life in each home. She explained that her father had to travel, so sometimes she had to go to her mother's home early in the morning, which was hard as she had to wake up early. Julia expressed affection for each parent, and she particularly liked her pre-K class. Julia expressed relief that she no longer had to listen to her parents fighting, since when she did hear her parents fighting, she would get scared. In addition, Julia did not understand why she had to stay only at her father's home for the weeks after the parents' most dramatic argument (i.e., after Mr. Frankel obtained a restraining order against Ms. Frankel). In general, Julia reported no negative information about either parent, but rather, she expressed that she liked to spend time in each parent's home.

Psychological Measures: Results from Psychological Testing

Both parents completed the MMPI-2 and were administered the Rorschach Inkblot Method. It should be noted that there are no psychological tests that directly assess parenting abilities with acceptable validity and reliability. Both the MMPI-2 and the Rorschach have been used extensively in child custody evaluations, and both tests have met standards for admissibility in court. There is sound empirical support for using these instruments to generate hypotheses regarding personality characteristics and qualities that are important in effective parenting. These include, among many others, capacity for empathy, accuracy of reality testing, ability to express emotions in ways that are neither overly constricted nor labile, and presence of significant psychopathology. While both parents were born in a foreign country, they were bilingual. Mr. Frankel's native language was spoken in his childhood home, but he was educated in English since elementary school. While Ms. Frankel knew limited English when she came to the United States, she took classes and ultimately obtained a college degree from an American institution. She became fluent in English, and her reading capabilities far surpassed the eighth-grade level required for the MMPI-2.

Mr. Frankel's response pattern on the MMPI-2 was straightforward and did not indicate a conscious attempt to portray himself in an overly positive light. The profile was valid. His MMPI-2 revealed a moderate level of emotional distress. There was a significant elevation on scale 7 (Psychasthenia) with secondary significant elevations on scale 8 (Schizophrenia) and scale 6 (Paranoia). Analysis of the MMPI-2 code types and subscales indicated that Mr. Frankel was experiencing moderate dysphoria and some agitation. He tended to brood over life situations and worry about his social effectiveness and lack self-confidence. On the positive side, the MMPI-2 findings were consistent with an individual who is analytical, sensitive, and creative, though, overall, rather cautious about taking risks. In terms of interpersonal relations, Mr. Frankel's MMPI-2 profile revealed him to be passive and have difficulty forming close meaningful bonds. His responses also suggested that he often felt isolated and lonely, with a long history of hurt feelings and resentments. While the MMPI-2 results did not reveal Mr. Frankel to be a fundamentally angry or aggressive individual, there were indications that periods of passivity could sometimes give way to instances of unpredictable acting out.

Mr. Frankel was also administered the Rorschach Inkblot Method, scored using the Rorschach-Performance Assessment System (R-PAS; Meyer, et al. 2011), and the results were statistically valid. A review of his Rorschach profile indicated that Mr. Frankel's characteristic coping mechanism was to avoid awareness of any emotional aspects of relationships or situations that caused him distress or made coping too complex and difficult. His tendency was to restrict his feelings and inhibit expression of emotions as a form of defense. This is not especially adaptive, and when Mr. Frankel does experience strong emotions, he becomes prone to acting out in a passive-aggressive manner. The Rorschach structural data also suggested that his psychological and emotional resources were strained, particularly by situational factors, leading him to be impulsive at times and have difficulty restoring emotional equilibrium. At the time of the evaluation, Mr. Frankel was feeling helpless and at a loss for how to cope effectively with his life. A problem for Mr. Frankel was that he did not spend enough time gathering information and understanding people and situations in adequate depth. Thus, he tended to come to conclusions and strategies for solving problems with inadequate information and insufficient forethought. Essentially a risk avoidant individual, Mr. Frankel would typically seek relatively quick or easy solutions. He was particularly weak in the area of understanding the nuances of relationship dynamics so that, especially in close relationships that were laden with conflict, his judgment and assessment of others tended to falter.

Ms. Frankel approached the MMPI-2 with a degree of caution. The validity scale scores indicated that she was an individual who was reluctant to admit personal faults, and who characteristically adopted a moralistic stance when viewing others and interpersonal relations. Ms. Frankel's approach to the MMPI-2 was essentially self-protective. None of the clinical scale scores reached a criteria level that would suggest severe psychopathology, but again, her self-protection and defensiveness no doubt suppressed scale elevations. Her highest score was on scale 6 (Paranoia). Ms. Frankel's MMP-2 profile suggested a high level of investment in correct outward behavior, especially in social situations. She expressed positive beliefs in her capabilities, but at the same time, was hypersensitive when hearing criticism from others. The MMPI-2 results suggested that Ms. Frankel had relatively limited insight into her own behavior and a distinct tendency to project blame outside of herself. Resentments, particularly of family members, were fixed. Ms. Frankel tended to vacillate between excessive self-control and attempts to control others, with periods of impatience leading to impulsive behavior. Her profile suggested sound ego strength and a good ability to meet responsibilities on a day-to-day basis, but she was also prone to feeling mistreated by others and quick to resent people and feel morally righteous. She was socially confident and placed value on her personal independence. Ms. Frankel also tested as someone who could be very rational, logical and extremely loyal. She would work hard to remain above any criticism, but she also likely had difficulties letting go of past resentments.

On the Rorschach Inkblot Method, Ms. Frankel produced a valid profile, but one suggesting that she was warding off more dysphoric feelings and self-doubts than she would acknowledge. Ms. Frankel's profile suggested that she was prone to exerting control in close relationships as a defensive attempt to avoid being hurt or criticized. Her tendency was to overwork or be perfectionistic in order to avoid criticism. She was quite alert and hypervigilant to what was taking place in her environment in an attempt to shield herself from anticipated criticism. Additionally, the test showed that Ms. Frankel typically avoided deep emotional involvement and had trouble trusting others beyond the superficial. Still, she was shown to be capable of realistic and conventional relationships that are positive, so long as they are not too demanding. However, unmet dependency needs made it difficult for Ms. Frankel to engage with people intimately and to let down her guard. Her fear of losing emotional control caused her to expend a great deal of energy to keep painful emotions out of her awareness, for fear of not controlling her emotions in the presence of others. Ms. Frankel's general coping resources were adequate for dealing with the demands of her environment.

Clinical Summary and Opinions

Determinations of custody and access for this family are based on the "best interests of the child" standard. In turn, this evaluation shed light on several factors central to a BIC analysis. They include the following:

- Parent strengths and weaknesses
- Functioning of the child
- Parent-child relationships
- Allegations of domestic violence
- Co-parenting relationship
- Additional factors that impact timeshare determinations

Parenting Strengths and Weaknesses: Father   While these parents certainly shared a deep love and affection for their daughter and, while both could also recognize the importance of the other parent in their daughter's life, they had differences and disputes on several fronts. Their relationship had also been episodically volatile, with allegations of domestic violence. With regard to Mr. Frankel, he had clearly been a devoted and dedicated parent. He had been consistently motivated to be an active and influential part of his daughter's life. The evaluation found him to be a sensitive individual who can be emotional, very warm and caring, and who loves to be in his daughter's presence. His parenting style could be described as relaxed, flexible, and not overbearing. He was at his best in low-stress situations. Mr. Frankel was consistent about picking up his daughter from child care. Despite the serious allegations Mr. Frankel levied against Ms. Frankel, he acknowledged during the evaluation that she had been a highly capable and caring parent. To his credit, Mr. Frankel was able to respond to his daughter's expressed desire to spend more time with her mother when the daughter missed her.

Mr. Frankel's relaxed and very likeable external presentation masks a somewhat more complex psychological picture. Though clearly competent and highly intelligent, assessment findings revealed him to have an emotionally needy and dependent side to his personality. This was particularly evident from the psychological testing, which raised a concern as to whether Mr. Frankel focused too much attention on his daughter to fill an emotional hole or the pain caused by the separation and divorce. Psychological testing, combined with some historical data, also indicated that Mr. Frankel could be unpredictable in his emotional control when anger or anxiety arises and, at such times, he was prone to excessive agitation or dramatic emotional reactions. In terms of direct parenting, Mr. Frankel's general skills were assessed to be sound. However, Mr. Frankel was more authoritative and less indulgent with Julia. Because he wanted to be liked by his daughter so much, when Julia misbehaved or required limit setting, Mr. Frankel had been too passive and reluctant to go against Julia's immediate desires. Thus far, Julia has been a child who very much wanted to please and perform for her parents. However, over the course of her development, Julia would, no doubt, pose more challenges for both parents. This would require Mr. Frankel to expand his parenting skills and be firmer and less conflict avoidant. The evaluation raised additional concerns that Mr. Frankel had not developed an adequate support network independent of Ms. Frankel. While it was positive that he had been willing to allow Julia additional time with Ms. Frankel when Julia asked for it, his reliance on Ms. Frankel to help him manage his work schedule was problematic. This arrangement worked adequately during those periods when conflict between the parents was low. However, these were not co-parents who could maintain reasonable calm for very long. Furthermore, the evaluation validated Ms. Frankel's concern that Mr. Frankel's poor organizational skills impacted planning around Julia's needs.

Parenting Strengths and Weaknesses: Mother   Ms. Frankel presented as a high-energy and effective person in her day-to-day life. The evaluation revealed her to be extremely well organized and socially poised, though Ms. Frankel also presented as someone who is often on guard, exacting and overly vigilant. Ms. Frankel's love for Julia was palpable and observable. She took great pride in her daughter's accomplishments and her winning personality and was spontaneously affectionate in ways that seemed genuine and heartfelt. Ms. Frankel had especially good organizational and coping skills for managing the diverse challenges of both work and parenting.

The findings from the evaluation did not support Mr. Frankel's allegations that Ms. Frankel was negligent at home with their daughter. If anything, she was observed to be attentive to detail, if not excessively so at times. This impression was confirmed by independent reports from people such as child care providers. Despite the episodic parental conflict, the police reports, and the domestic violence allegations, this evaluation did not reveal Ms. Frankel to be an individual who was aggressive or had persistent problems with anger and/ or impulse regulation. The evidence suggested that Ms. Frankel was an exacting individual who demanded much from others and had been disappointed by Mr. Frankel. She had likely expressed her frustration in forceful ways, but it was important to note that there had not been a finding that she had perpetrated domestic violence against Mr. Frankel. Ms. Frankel also understood that Julia's relationship with her father was important and must be supported. Ms. Frankel cooperated with the temporary-custody schedule, though she did not believe it was optimal, and accommodated the father's requests for changes in custodial time around his work travel.

Despite her many strengths, the evaluation raised some concerns about Ms. Frankel's parenting skills. Data suggested that over time, she may have difficulty letting Julia make age-appropriate choices and determine her own interests, particularly if they differed from own desires. There could also be continued challenges for Ms. Frankel regarding co-parenting. While she accepted and acknowledged the importance of Mr. Frankel's role in Julia's life, she had questioned his competency in a number of areas. Ms. Frankel expressed a high degree of confidence in her view of what is best for Julia and did not appear to view Mr. Frankel as an equal parent. Accepting that Mr. Frankel may have different, but equally valuable, ways of approaching some aspects of parenting was a recommended goal for Ms. Frankel in co-parenting counseling. Still, clinical interviews and psychological testing revealed that she was an individual of sound mental health, with no serious social and/or emotional problems. She was a highly competent parent, and despite her ambivalence towards Mr. Frankel, it is likely that she would provide very competent and consistent parenting and facilitate continuing contact between Julia and Mr. Frankel.

Re: Julia   As for Julia, this assessment revealed her to be a delightful girl who can be outgoing, creative, and effervescent. Reports from both parents and the collateral interviews indicated that she was generally happy and cognitively and developmentally advanced, and she had no serious social or emotional problems. Over the times that she was seen by this evaluator, Julia was very sweet, active, and enthusiastic. She was very comfortable and secure with each parent, and when she did push boundaries or become mildly oppositional, it was in ways that were age appropriate. The parents expressed different views of how Julia responded after the domestic violence charges and the sudden separation from her mother. Reports from collateral sources who saw Julia at the time reported that, not unexpectedly, Julia did have emotional difficulties, not only from the exposure to the episodic angry arguments but also, most significantly, from the abrupt separation from her mother. The collateral source information also suggested that Julia recovered well from this difficult situation, and by all indications, she was ready to start kindergarten next year.

A main area of concern was that Julia felt compelled to please her parents so much. She had already been exposed to too much overt conflict between them, and there was also some concern that she could eventually be compelled to take on the role of peacemaker between her parents. By both parents' reports, Julia had enjoyed the time when the parents were together with her. It is very typical for children her age to be invested in their parents' reconciling or remaining together, so these parents will need to be careful not to give Julia an inaccurate impression of their relationship. It was determined that Julia would benefit from more stability in her schedule, with clear limit setting and rules and less volatility between the parents. Fundamentally, Julia had been very well cared for by both parents. Reports from the preschool also indicated that Julia was an empathic child who was also well liked by her peers. Thus, barring further instability or conflict between the parents, the trajectory for Julia was determined to be positive.

Evaluation-Specific Issues

Domestic Violence and Volatility   Regarding the issues of domestic violence, this evaluator reviewed the police reports, each parent's declarations, and the parents' direct accounts of the multiple incidents in which the police were called. There had not been a court finding of domestic violence in this case, and this evaluator's review of the evidence revealed that there had not been a persistent pattern of battering or serious abuse perpetrated by either party. There had, however, been too much volatility and arguing, some of which had taken place in front of Julia. It was very difficult, if not impossible, to determine which of the two parents had been the more volatile or who has instigated the arguments and conflicts more than has the other. Both parents were very strong-willed, and neither had especially good interpersonal conflict-resolution skills, particularly in close interpersonal relations. Mr. Frankel's allegation that Ms. Frankel was a violent individual did not appear to have much basis in fact. If Mr. Frankel was fearful of Ms. Frankel, it would have been highly unusual that, very soon after obtaining a restraining order against Ms. Frankel, he would spend time with her and Julia on family outings or at Julia's activities. It is possible that Mr. Frankel felt fearful when Ms. Frankel became angry, but the data did not reveal those instances to be extreme or persistent. Mr. Frankel's actions raised a question as to whether his calls to the police were the result of a sincere need for protection or, rather, were driven by a combination of his inability to manage the interpersonal conflict and his desire to create a record of the couple's domestic problems. Overall, there was no evidence that precluded the parents from having a joint-custody timeshare arrangement.

Respective Allegations about Parenting Skills   Both parents levied allegations and concerns about some aspect of the other party's direct parenting skills. Mr. Frankel suggested that Ms. Frankel not only indulged Julia but also treated her as a much younger child, including allowing her to drink from a bottle. He also alleged that Ms. Frankel was somewhat neglectful at home, letting Julia play with hot or dangerous appliances without supervision. This allegation was inconsistent with other information Mr. Frankel provided, as frequently he described Ms. Frankel as exacting and demanding, if not compulsive. While custody evaluations involve a limited sampling of parental behavior under direct observation, this evaluator viewed the mother as a vigilant parent who was also very oriented to detail in her environment. In her presence, Julia did not ask to be treated in ways that were inappropriate, nor did Ms. Frankel treat her like a much younger child to the extent that Mr. Frankel claims. It was true that Ms. Frankel had been indulgent with Julia and tried to avoid her experiencing even inevitable disappointments (ex. making sure she wins every game on the home visit), but there was little difference between the parents in this regard.

   Ms. Frankel's main concern about Mr. Frankel was that he had been unable to meet the demands of a half-time parent due to the challenging nature of his work life, which frequently involved travel, as well as his general disorganization. She offered some statistical evidence showing that he needed her to cover significant portions of his custodial time to accommodate his work. Mr. Frankel did not refute Ms. Frankel's statistics or deny that he had frequently relied on her for backup child care. Mr. Frankel described his travel schedule differently at different times during the evaluation. He also portrayed it as less demanding than Ms. Frankel did. While Ms. Frankel had been willing to assist Mr. Frankel with child care, this was not a long-term solution, especially as Mr. Frankel had needed help very early in the morning. Over time, this could be experienced as intrusive by Ms. Frankel. It did appear to be accurate that Mr. Frankel's job responsibilities made it difficult for him to maintain consistently the current temporary custodial timeshare plan. The situation was further complicated by the historically accurate fact that these parents can suddenly have significant conflict at any time and for any reason. Thus, the current plan for Ms. Frankel to serve as Mr. Frankel's backup for childcare was not sustainable.

Timeshare Considerations   For over a year, Julia's schedule had placed her in the custodial care of each parent equally, on a rotating "2–2–3" basis. Julia greatly benefitted from substantial time with each parent. At the time of the evaluation, Julia was almost 5 years of age and was scheduled to enter kindergarten in a few months. Children her age can certainly benefit from an equally shared parenting plan, so long as attachment relationships are sound and firmly established and parents enjoy a co-parenting relationship that is also stable and relatively low conflict. This also assumes that both parents are competent and reasonably skilled in terms of direct parenting abilities and neither parent suffers from significant interfering psychopathology. It also assumes that both parents are available to maintain the custodial schedule consistently.

It is noteworthy, however, that since the court's intervention and the antici-pation of a custody evaluation, the parents enjoyed a period of relatively low conflict and positive collaboration. This evaluator had noted that Julia was developing well and was fundamentally a happy girl, despite being exposed to the parents' arguing. There were some indications, however, that she had missed her mother, as she had asked with some regularity to spend more time with Ms. Frankel. To his credit, Mr. Frankel had accommodated his daugh-ter's requests, which did not appear to come about by Ms. Frankel's undue influence. The findings of this evaluation indicated that Ms. Frankel had been the more constant parenting figure. She had regularly assumed more custodial time with Julia due in large measure to the father's work demands. She pre-sented her accounting of how custody time had actually been split, with her having significantly more custodial time due to father's work schedule. This accounting was not disputed by Mr. Frankel.

Mr. Frankel had requested a custodial plan that gave each parent longer blocks of time, such as a week with each parent. He claimed that this would enable him to plan the majority of his travel during times when Julia would be with her mother. Such a plan was not a realistic option for a girl of this developmental stage, given that Mr. Frankel still wanted to maintain a 50% time-share arrangement. Thus the schedule he proposed, which included Julia having regular six-to-eight-day separations from her mother, would have caused Julia to experience too much distress. There was already evidence that, even with the current temporary schedule, she was missing her mother and was asking for additional time with her. Mr. Frankel had struggled to maintain an equal custody arrangement, given the demands of his job, so it is not real-istic to believe that he can sustain 50% custody of his daughter. The situation was compounded by his organizational skills, which sometimes were quite weak. Aspects of Mr. Frankel's handling of the demands of this custody evalu-ation only verified that he struggled with planning and organizing his time, as well as prioritizing his daughter over his work life. Another factor considered was that Mr. Frankel's schedule also required the parents to negotiate frequent adjustments in the schedule. While this was not a large problem for the cur-rent year, it had the potential for creating increased conflict in the future.

This evaluator considered the option of leaving the existing 2–2–3 custody schedule in place; however, for the reasons cited above, this did not seem to be a reasonable parenting plan at the time. As previously stated, Julia would ben-efit from somewhat more time with her mother, and there remained a concern that Mr. Frankel, though well intended, could not really maintain the custodial schedule with necessary consistency. Therefore, it was recommended that the custodial schedule shift to allow Julia to spend every other weekend with each parent and some limited mid-week time with her father. This would enable Mr. Frankel to more easily plan his travel around the basic custodial schedule, hopefully minimizing disruptions. It would also enable Julia to have somewhat more time with her mother at this particular juncture. It was also hoped that, with the assistance of skilled professional help, these parents could improve their co-parenting relationship, which might allow for more flexibility in the future. It was certainly reasonable to assume that Julia would benefit from a fully shared parenting plan when she entered first grade, as she would be 6-and-a-half by that time. This assumed that the father's work schedule will allow for this. At that time a 2–2–5–5 schedule (Monday and Tuesday with one parent, Wednesday and Thursday with the other parent, with the parents then alternating weekends with Julia) would be best suited to this family's situation.

Recommendations

1. The parents will have joint legal custody.
2. The parents will have joint physical custody as follows:
   A. Julia will spend a larger percentage of parenting time with her mother.
   B. Julia will be with each parent on alternating weekends from Friday pick-up at school until drop-off at school the following Monday.
   C. Julia will also be with her father on the Tuesday following the mother's custodial weekend from pick-up at school or 4:00 p.m. (whichever applies) until drop-off at school or 9:00 a.m. the following morning. In addition, the daughter will be with the father on Thursday following his custodial weekend, from pick-up at school or 4:00 PM (whichever applies) until drop-off at school the following Friday morning.
   D. At all other times, Julia will be in her mother's custody.
3. When Julia enters first grade, she will split her time equally between the parents' homes on a "2–2–5–5" basis. That is, she will be with one parent each week on Monday and Tuesday, the other parent on Wednesday and Thursday, and weekends will be alternated, from Friday pick-up at school until return to school on Monday morning.

A vacation and holiday schedule was recommended that equally splits holidays and vacations each year. There was also a recommendation for co-parent counseling for a minimum of six months.

Legal Standards Considered in the Child Custody Evaluation

The recommendations to the court just described were based upon the legal standard of "the best interests of the child" (BIC). Because this case was conducted in California, several family law statutes that define the BIC standard in greater detail needed to be considered. These included California Family Codes §§3011, 3111, 3020, 3040, and 3080. In addition to the general factors that are part of the BIC standard (listed at the beginning of the chapter), these family codes describe several other factors the court must consider regarding a parenting plan. These include, among others, which parent is likely to allow the child frequent and continuing contact with the other parent; whether either parent has a mental health or substance abuse disorder or history of abusive behavior towards the child, which could negatively impact the health, safety, and welfare of the child. The evaluation report noted that, although they had conflict, these parents appreciated the role of the other parent and were capable of supporting the child's relationship with the other parent. Neither parent was found to have a significant mental health or substance abuse disorder, which would necessitate restricting his or her contact with their child.

This case also involved consideration of California Family Code §3044, the domestic violence statute, which states that there is a rebuttable presumption that a perpetrator of domestic violence shall not have joint or sole physical or legal custody of one's child. Although there were allegations of domestic violence in the case, the evaluator noted that there was not a court finding of domestic violence. In addition, analysis of the data did not find evidence of domestic violence that would preclude a joint legal and physical custody recommendation.

Common Pitfalls and Considerations

Among the various roles played by FMHPs in the forensic arena, conducting child custody evaluations must be considered as one of the most complex, demanding, and formidable endeavors that one can undertake. The case described posed a variety of challenges for the evaluator. As is typical in custody cases, there were conflicting portrayals about incidents that occurred in the past that influenced the parents' relative positions in the litigation, as well as their feelings about each other. Evaluators' ability to determine the "truth" amid such conflicting reports is often limited, especially in the absence of compelling third party information. In addition, the evaluator had to be cognizant of the most common pitfalls in conducting custody evaluations. These include forming strong impressions too early in the case and then looking for evidence or data to corroborate those impressions rather than giving adequate weight to divergent information (confirmatory bias). The evaluator also had to notice, but not be swayed by themes, behavior, or interactions described by the parents that might resonate with the evaluator's own personal experience in ways that could compromise the evaluator's ability to maintain neutrality and a forensic stance (countertransference bias).

In this particular case, the evaluator had to rely on indirect reports and cumulative evidence to determine that the father was not physically at risk with the mother and that the child had not been traumatized by witnessing the conflict between the parents. One of the dilemmas in this case was how to sustain and support father's relationship with his daughter, given the constraints of his work schedule, the father's inability to maintain half-time custody, and the fact that the daughter was craving additional time with her mother. The evaluator therefore suggested a plan that the father could maintain consistently, without having to rely on the mother to assist him with child care. There was also an attempt to affirm the father's role with his daughter by recommending a developmentally appropriate but equally shared parenting plan in the not too distant future.

The evaluator also had to deal with conflicting reports about potential domestic violence in the co-parenting relationship. There had been police involvement with the family, and the father had had a restraining order against mother. This fact, coupled with reports from both parents, suggested that they had had a volatile and acrimonious relationship with each other. On the other hand, since the custody evaluation was ordered, the parents had been working more cooperatively with each other, with considerable flexibility and mutual respect. The evaluator came to believe that there needed to be firmer boundaries between the parents given concerns about father's dependency on mother and the likelihood that the current collegial relationship was fragile and prone to additional conflict once the court was no longer actively involved in their lives. The evaluator anticipated that mother could become more rigid under other circumstances and that father could become more needy and demanding as he sought to maintain contact both with his daughter and his ex-wife. The evaluator was, however, impressed with both parents' desire for professional input on what would be best for their daughter. He deemed those desires to be sincere.

In addition to the demands of conducting an evaluation of multiple family members while also assessing the complex relationships among those family members, writing a CCE report is also one of the most challenging tasks of analysis and synthesis encountered in forensic psychology practice. Child custody remains a highly contentious area of practice. While the vast majority of CCE reports do lead to a custody settlement without a trial, evaluators still face the distinct possibility of being deposed or subpoenaed and having their results and conclusions challenged in court. As Stahl noted (2014), to be an effective evaluator, one must develop a thick skin, because one or more parents are likely to be upset with the recommendations.

Even with the risks involved, FMHPs in child custody cases can glean many rewards and considerable gratification. The evaluator can be tremendously helpful to the court with respect to providing input about parenting skills and deficits, the child's developmental needs and preferences, as well as the potential psychological risks associated with various custody arrangements. One of the most compelling reasons for engaging in CCEs is the opportunity to have a positive impact on the lives of children in the midst of very difficult family circumstances. In the midst of very high family conflict, the custody evaluator can refocus parents' attention on the best interests of their children and assist families to move forward in a healthier direction. As Pickar (2007b) noted, "add to this the fact that the role of the child custody evaluator is somewhat akin to being a sleuth, and you have a task which is rich in complexity" (p. 113).

References

Ackerman, M. J. (2006). *Clinician's guide to child custody evaluations* (3rd ed.). Hoboken, NJ: Wiley.

Ackerman, M. J., & Pritzl, T. B. (2011). Child custody evaluation practices: A 20-year follow-up. *Family Court Review, 49*, 618–628. doi:10.1111/j.1744-1617.2011.01397.x

American Psychological Association. (2002). Ethical principles of psychologists and code of conduct. *American Psychologist, 57*, 1060–1073.

American Psychological Association. (2010). Guidelines for child custody evaluation in family law proceedings. *American Psychologist, 65*(9), 863–867. doi:10.1037/a0021250

American Psychological Association. (2013). Specialty guidelines for forensic psychology. *American Psychologist, 68*(1), 7–19. doi.org/10.1037/a0029889

Association of Family and Conciliation Courts. (2007). Model standards of practice for child custody evaluation. *Family Court Review, 45*(1), 70–90. doi:10.1111/ j.1744-1617 .2007.129_3.x

Austin, W. G. (2001). Partner violence and risk assessment in child custody evaluation. *Family Court Review, 39*(4), 483–496.

Austin, W. G. (2008a). Relocation, research, and forensic evaluation, Part I: Effects of residential mobility on children of divorce. *Family Court Review, 46*(1), 137–150.

Austin, W. G. (2008b). Relocation research, and forensic evaluation, Part II: Research in support of the relocation risk assessment model. *Family Court Review, 46*(2), 347–365.

Austin, W. G. (2012). Relocation, research, and child custody disputes. In K. Kuehnle & L. M. Drozd (Eds.), *Parenting plan evaluations: Applied research for the family court* (pp. 540–559). New York, NY: Oxford University Press.

Austin, W. G., & Drozd, L. M. (2012). Intimate partner violence and child custody evaluation, Part I: Theoretical framework, forensic model, and assessment issues. *Journal of Child Custody, 9*(4), 250–309.

Bow, J. N., & Boxer, P. (2003). Assessing allegations of domestic violence in child custody evaluations. *Journal of Interpersonal Violence, 18*, 1394–1410.

Bow, J. N., Gottlieb, M. C., Siegel, J. C., & Noble, G. S. (2010). Licensing board complaints in child custody practice. *Journal of Forensic Psychology Practice, 10*, 403–418. doi:10.1080/1528932.2010.489851

Bow, J. N., & Martindale, D. A. (2009). Developing and Managing a Child Custody Practice. *Journal of Forensic Psychology Practice, 9*(2), 127–137.

Braver, S. L., Ellman, I. M., & Fabricus, W. V. (2003). Relocation of children after divorce and children's best interests. New evidence and legal considerations. *Journal of Family Psychology, 17*, 206–219.

Brodsky, S. L., & Wilson, J. K. (2012). Empathy in forensic evaluation: A systematic reconsideration. *Behavioral Sciences & the Law, 31*(2) 192–202.

Butcher, J. N., Dahlstrom, W. G., Graham, J. R., Tellegen, A, & Kaemmer, B. (1989). *The Minnesota Multiphasic Personality Inventory-2 (MMPI-2): Manual for administration and scoring.* Minneapolis, MN: University of Minnesota Press.

Ceci, S. J., & Bruck, M. (1995). *Jeopardy in the courtroom: A scientific analysis of children's testimony.* Washington, DC: American Psychology Association.

Ceci, S. J., & Friedman, R. D. (2000). The suggestibility of children: Scientific research and legal implications. *Cornell Law Review, 34*–108.

DeMier, R. L. (2013). Forensic report writing. In R. K. Otto and I. B. Weiner (Eds.), *Handbook of psychology: Vol. 11. Forensic psychology* (2nd ed.; pp. 75–98). New York, NY: Wiley.

DiFonzo, J. H. (2014). From the rule of one to shared parenting: Custody presumptions in law and policy. *Family Court Review, 52*(2), 213–239.

Drozd, L., Olesen, N., & Saini, M. (2013). *Parenting plan and child custody evaluations: Using decision trees to increase evaluator competence and avoid preventable errors.* Sarasota, FL: Professional Resources Press.

Drozd, L. M., & Olesen, N. W. (2004). Is it abuse, alienation, and/or estrangment? A decision tree. *Journal of Child Custody, 65*–106.

Emery, R. E., Otto, R. K., & O'Donohue, W. (2005). Custody disputed. *Scientific American Mind, 65*–67.

Erard, R. E., & Viglione, D. J. (2014). The Rorschach Performance Assessment System (R-PAS) in child custody evaluations. *Journal of Child Custody, 11*(3), 159–180.

Fidler, B., & Bala, N. (2010). Children resisting post-separation contact with a parent: Concepts, controversies and conundrums. *Family Court Review, 48,* 10–47.

Fidler, B. J., Bala, N., & Saini, M. A. (2013). *Children who resist post-separation parental contact: A differential approach for legal and mental health professionals.* New York, NY: Oxford University Press.

Flens, J. R. (2005). The responsible use of psychological testing in child custody valuations. Selection of tests. *Journal of Child Custody: Research, Issues, and Practices, 2*(1/2), 5–31.

Friedlander, S., & Walters, M. G. (2010). When a child rejects a parent: Tailoring the intervention to fit the problem. *Family Court Review, 48,* 97–110.

Friedrich, W. N. (2002). *Psychological assessment of sexually abused children and their families.* Thousand Oaks, CA: Sage.

Fuhrmann, G. S., & Zibell, R. A. (2012). *Evaluation for child custody.* New York, NY: Oxford University Press.

Gardner, R. A. (1992). *The parental alienation syndrome: A guide for mental health and legal professionals.* Cresskill, NJ: Creative Therapeutics.

Goodman, G. S., Batterman-Faunce, J. M., Schaaf, J. M, & Kenny, R. (2002). Nearly 4 years after an event: Children's eyewitness memory and adult's perception of children's accuracy. *Child Abuse and Neglect, 26*(8), 849–884.

Gould, J. W. (2006). *Conducting scientifically crafted child custody evaluations.* Sarasota, FL: Professional Resources Press.

Gould, J. W., & Martindale, D. A. (2007). *The art and science of child custody evaluations.* New York, NY: Guilford.

Hardesty, J. L., Haselschwendt, M. L., & Johnson, M. P. (2012). Domestic violence and child custody. In K. Kuehnle & L. M. Drozd (Eds.), *Parenting plan evaluations: Applied research for the family court* (pp. 442–475). New York, NY: Oxford University Press.

Hynan, D. J. (2014). *Child custody evaluation: New theoretical applications and research.* Springfield, IL: Charles C. Thomas.

Jaffe, P. G., Johnston, J. R., Crooks, C. V., & Bala, N. (2008). Custody disputes involving allegations of domestic violence: Towards a differentiated approach to parenting plans. *Family Court Review, 46*(3), 500–522.

Kelly, J. B. (2012). Risk and protective factors associated with child and adolescent adjustment following separation and divorce: Social science applications. In K. Kuehnle & L. M. Drozd (Eds.), *Parenting plan evaluations: Applied research for the family court* (pp. 49–84). New York, NY: Oxford University Press.

Kelly, J. B., & Johnson, M. P. (2008). Differentiation among types of intimate partner violence: Research update and implications for interventions. *Family Court Review, 46*(3), 476–499.

Kelly, J. B., & Johnston, J. R. (2001). The alienated child: A reformulation of parental alienation syndrome. *Family Court Review, 39*(3), 249–266.

Kirkland, K, & Kirkland, K. L. (2001). Frequency of complaints and related disciplinary action: A survey of the Association of State and Provincial Psychology. *Professional Psychology: Research and Practice, 32*(2), 1711–1174.

Kuehnle, K., & Connell, M. (Eds.). (2009). *The evaluation of child sexual abuse allegations.* Hoboken, NJ: Wiley.

Kuehnle, K., & Drozd, L. (Eds.). (2012). *Parenting plan evaluations: Applied research for the family court.* New York, NY: Oxford University Press.

Kuehnle, K., & Kirkpatrick, H. D. (2005). Evaluating allegations of child sexual abuse within complex child custody cases. *Journal of Child Custody, 2*(3), 3–39.

Lamb, M. E. (2012). Critical analysis of research on parenting plans and children's well-being. In K. Kuehnle & L. M. Drozd (Eds.), *Parenting plan evaluations: Applied research for the family court* (pp. 214–243). New York, NY: Oxford University Press.

Lamb, M. E., Sternberg, K. J., & Esplin, P. W. (2000). Effects of age and delay on the amount of information provided by alleged sex abuse victims in investigative interviews. *Child Development, 71*(6), 1586–1596.

Martindale, D. (2005). Confirmatory bias and confirmatory distortion. *Journal of Child Custody, 2*(1/2), 31–48. doi:10.1300/J190v02n01_03

McIntosh, J. E., Pruett, M. K, & Kelly, J. B. (2014). Parental separation and overnight care of young children, Part II: Putting theory into practice. *Family Court Review, 52*(2), 256–262.

Meyer, G. J., Viglione, D. J., Mihura, J. L., Erard, R. E., & Erdberg, P. (2011). *Rorschach Performance Assessment System: Administration, coding, interpretation, and technical manual.* Toledo, OH: Rorschach Performance Assessment System.

Mihura, J. L., Meyer, G. J., Dumitrascu, N., & Bombel, G. (2013). The validity of individual Rorschach variables: Systematic reviews and meta-analyses of the Comprehensive System. *Psychological Bulletin, 139*(3), 548–605.

Millon, T., Millon, C., Davis, R., & Grossman, S. (2006). *MCMI-III manual* (3rd ed.). Minneapolis, MN: Pearson Education.

Moran, J. A., & Weinstock, D. K. (2011). Assessing parenting skills for the family court. *Journal of Child Custody, 8*(3), 166–188.

Morey, L. C. (2007). *The Personality Assessment Inventory professional manual.* Lutz, FL: Psychological Assessment Resources.

Otto, R. K., Edens, J. F., & Barcus, E. H. (2000). The use of psychological testing in child custody evaluations. *Family Court Review, 38,* 312–340. doi:10.1111/j.174-1617.2000.tb00578.x

Pickar, D. B. (2007a). Countertransference bias in the child custody evaluator. *Journal of Child Custody, 4*(3/4), 45–67. doi:10.1300/J190v04n03_04

Pickar, D. B. (2007b). On being a child custody evaluator. *Family Court Review, 45*(1), 103–115.

Pickar, D. B., & Kaufman, R. L. (2013). The child custody evaluation report: Toward an integrated model of practice. *Journal of Child Custody, 10*(1), 17–53.

Pickar, D. B., & Kaufman, R. L. (2015). Parenting plans for special needs children: Applying a risk assessment model. *Family Court Review, 53*(1), 113–133.

Poole, D. A., & Lamb, M. E. (1998). *Investigative interviews of children: A guide for helping professionals.* Washington, DC: American Psychological Association.

Pruett, M. K., & DiFonzo, J. H. (2014). Closing the gap: Research, policy, practice and shared parenting. *Family Court Review, 52*(2), 152–174.

Pruett, M. K., McIntosh, J. E., & Kelly, J. B. (2014). Parental separation and overnight care of young children Part I: Consensus through theoretical and empirical investigation. *Family Court Review, 52*(2), 240–255.

Saini, M., Johnston, J. R., Fidler, B. J., & Bala, N. (2012). Empirical studies of alienation. In K. Kuehnle & L. M. Drozd (Eds.), *Parenting plan evaluations: Applied research for the family court* (pp. 399–441). New York, NY: Oxford University Press.

Saini, M. S., & Polak, S. (2014). The ecological validity of parent-child observations: A review of empirical evidence related to custody evaluations. *Journal of Child Custody, 11*(3). 181–201.

Saywitz, K., Camparo, L. B., & Romanoff, A. (2010). Interviewing children in custody cases: Implications of research and policy for practice. *Behavioral Sciences and the Law, 28,* 542–562. doi:10.1002/bsl.945

Shuman, D. W., & Berk, A. S. (2012). Judicial impact: The best interests of the child and the Daubert and Frye evidentiary frameworks. In K. Kuehnle & L. M. Drozd (Eds.), *Parenting plan evaluations: Applied research for the family court* (pp. 563–573). New York, NY: Oxford University Press.

Stahl, P. M. (2011). *Conducting child custody evaluations: From basic to complex issues.* Thousand Oaks, CA: Sage.

Stahl, P. M. (2014). Conducting child custody and parenting evaluations. In I. B. Weiner & R. K. Otto (Eds.), *The handbook of forensic psychology* (pp. 137–169). Hoboken, NJ: Wiley.

Tippins, T. M., & Wittmann, J. P. (2005). Empirical and ethical problems with custody recommendations. *Family Court Review, 43,* 193–222.

Viglione, D. J., & Meyer, G. J. (2008). An overview of Rorschach psychometrics for forensic practice. In C. B. Gacono & F. B. Evans (Eds.), with N. Kaser-Boyd & L. A. Gacono, *The handbook of forensic Rorschach assessment* (pp. 21–53). Mahwah, NJ: Erlbaum.

12

Overview of the Juvenile Justice System and Best Practices

Jeannie S. Brooks and Kendell L. Coker

Juvenile offenders have historically been viewed as a special population within the criminal justice system, constituting a distinct group of young individuals who were generally considered to be more amenable to rehabilitative efforts in comparison with their adult counterparts. Many authors have suggested that juvenile justice reform has been promulgated by the idea that children, in and of themselves, are inherently innocent, and an assumption of public responsibility is inherent within the historical framework of how juvenile offenders are handled. The juvenile justice system has evolved, in large part, due to case law that emerged as a function of concerns regarding perceived excessive leniency and harsh punitive sanctions for juvenile offenders (Lubit & Billick, 2003). Relatedly, the *parens patriae* doctrine is based on the premise that juveniles require certain legal protections from their own immaturity (which supposedly drives child/adolescent behavior). This mandate for increased legal/procedural safeguards is deemed applicable, irrespective of a child/adolescent's status as being in the care and custody of his or her biological parent(s) or legal guardian(s). It may also be considered within the context of cases involving allegations of child abuse and/or neglect, foster care, medical decision making, and juvenile delinquency.

Fundamentally, the *parens patriae* doctrine attempts to focus on regulating juvenile behavior, as a child/adolescent is presumed to be unable to do so independently in an effective, adaptive, and prosocial manner (Abrams, 2014). Ongoing vacillation between a punitive and interventional/rehabilitative model to restorative justice for juvenile offenders has apparently waxed and waned over the years, perhaps as a function of greater latitude afforded to juvenile judges in handling such cases. According to Trepanier (1999) for instance, pertinent changes have emerged for handling juvenile criminal cases at differing stages in the legal process since the 1960s and the application of the *parens patriae* doctrine. The doctrine has apparently been intended to operate under the assumption that the courts are responsible for handling juvenile cases by balancing a reduction of personal risk with the facilitation of protective legal functions. It is postulated that, over time, legal policies largely focused on juvenile justice have gradually transitioned in the direction of the adult criminal court model. Juvenile courts have apparently sought to distinguish juvenile offenders from their adult counterparts, and several concepts appear to delineate such efforts (e.g., the presumption that juveniles may receive pre-adjudicatory detention that ensures separation from adults). As such, the relevancy of the *parens patriae* doctrine has apparently decreased at various stages in time, and across the country.

While the adult criminal justice system has vacillated between adopting a punitive versus a rehabilitative model over the years, the juvenile justice system has been subject to sweeping case law and reform to maintain the perspective that juvenile offenders, unlike adult offenders, should be afforded greater opportunities for interventions as opposed to sanctions. Segregation of juvenile from adult offenders was delineated in the Selected Rules from the United Nations Standard Minimum Rules for the Administration of Juvenile Justice ("the Beijing Rules") that was adopted in 1985 (U.N. General Assembly, 1985; Benekos & Merlo, 2014). These "rules" delineated fundamental procedural safeguards (e.g., the presumption of innocence, right to notification of charges, protection against self-incrimination, right to legal counsel, the right to have a parent/guardian present, the right to confront/cross-examine witnesses, and the right to appeal during all stages of juvenile legal proceedings). Furthermore, juveniles who were detained pending trial were to be maintained separately from adults, and restrictions on a juvenile offender's personal liberty was to only be imposed subsequent to careful consideration and was to be limited as much as possible (U.N. General Assembly, 1985). Irrespective of the ultimate intentions set forth in these standards, however, significant changes occurred with respect to how juvenile offenders were largely perceived by society and with respect to related modifications to existing legal policy. Benekos and Merlo (2014) point out that in the 1990s, increasing numbers of juvenile offenders were waived into the adult criminal court system for against-person offenses (e.g., homicide, aggravated assault); albeit, such transfers have reportedly decreased since the mid-1990s, perhaps due to statutory exemptions and lower crime rates. Examining these trends on a large scale, however, may not fully account for the myriad cases in which innocence was lost, families were disrupted, and opportunities for a prosocial lifestyle were hindered. Accordingly, the timing and nature of an individual juvenile's commitment of a criminal offense may impact the outcome of individual cases. More recent decreases in the overall volume of juvenile arrests appear related to greater focus on a rehabilitative model of juvenile justice.

Given the nuances and the broad ability of judges in the juvenile courts to influence diversion, disposition, and other aspects of juvenile legal cases, a best-practices approach to the structure and function of the juvenile justice system should be delineated. Inherently, the process by which those with legal decision-making authority and other professionals involved in juvenile case outcomes (e.g., psychologists and psychiatrists) that work to assess each individual juvenile offender should hold themselves accountable for remaining familiar with empirical studies relevant to juvenile justice service delivery and reform. In this way, steps can be taken to ensure the appropriateness of services and other interventions to serve the best interests of society and the juvenile in question.

Juvenile court proceedings differ from their adult counterparts in several ways. For example, differing terminology is used to refer to various stages in juvenile proceedings (e.g., the term "disposition" is applied rather than "sentencing"), and outcomes in juvenile cases may often involve service referrals with the intention of providing intervention and rehabilitation rather than a more finite, punitive outcome that would put an end to the case (Lubit & Billick, 2003). Invariably then, examination of the quality of interventional and/or rehabilitative efforts is of paramount importance, as such variables can significantly influence the direction of an individual juvenile offender's legal case, and the likelihood that he or she will remain free of a pervasive life of crime into adulthood. Thus, when one thinks of the criminal courts in a general sense, an adversarial process likely comes to mind. In the case of juvenile justice however, there appears to be an inherent need to strike an effective balance between traditional criminal legal proceedings (largely viewed in punitive terms), with a more dynamic and future-oriented approach to handling legal cases involving juvenile offenders. The role of psycholegal constructs in paving the way for an ideal model of restorative justice for juveniles then may be viewed as highly relevant and dynamic. To elaborate on this idea, there appears to be a shift in thought from consideration of mostly static variables (e.g., prior criminal history) to ascertain the most appropriate outcome/disposition in criminal cases; albeit, a more future-oriented and scientific approach to juvenile case disposition and intervention/rehabilitation may bring an element of abstract reasoning to determining appropriate outcomes for individual juveniles.

Evolution of Best Practices within the Juvenile Justice System

Given the continuously evolving nature of the juvenile justice system, it is imperative to remain aware of growing research to delineate a best-practices approach to intervening with juvenile offenders. As previously noted, the juvenile justice system as a whole appears to operate under the assumption that the model is intended to maintain a rehabilitative focus, and the juvenile justice system presumes that the courts are well informed when it comes to determining the most beneficial sanctions and services to apply in cases involving juvenile offenders. Although perhaps well intentioned, research efforts appear to delineate various intervention strategies and/or model guidelines to conducting forensic psychological evaluations and applying interventions with juvenile offenders. Such efforts appear to build on pertinent case law, albeit, with a more rehabilitative focus that appears inherently clinical in nature. As juvenile offenders have increasingly been afforded greater legal protections and opportunities for rehabilitation—with most responsibility being placed on larger systems—research efforts have focused on determining what factors constitute a best-practice model for service delivery within the juvenile justice system.

Some examples of landmark cases that influenced reform in the juvenile justice system include *Kent v. United States* (1966), the first U.S. Supreme Court case that highlighted the critical impetus of the waiver of a juvenile offender into the adult criminal justice system, in which the court held that a juvenile offender retained the right to representation by legal counsel at all stages of the legal process. Subsequently, the U.S. Supreme Court stated *In re Gault* (1967) that juvenile offenders have the right to be notified of charges, to receive legal counsel, to confront and cross-examine witnesses, and to receive protection under the Fifth Amendment. The case *In re Winship* (1970) established that juvenile delinquency adjudication must be beyond a reasonable doubt. However, subsequently landmark cases such as the 1971 case, *McKeiver v. Pennsylvania*, held that juvenile cases do not necessarily have a constitutional right to a trial by jury. In the case of *Schall v. Martin* (1984), the Court held that juveniles could be detained as a means of self-protection and societal safeguards. Examination of these cases appears to highlight the inherent notion that juveniles (by their chronological age alone) may not consistently be viewed as free and competent members of society and as a result are not always afforded the same rights and freedoms that adult offenders receive. This invariably creates an assumption that the courts may be expected to remain aware of what is in the best interests of a child or juvenile offender and balance that knowledge carefully with the needs of society as a whole.

A review of relevant research on best-practice approaches to clinical service delivery for delinquent youth focuses on individual factors and risk. There are numerous individual barriers and needs that may be identified in any given case in which scientifically validated delivery and assessment models concerning juvenile offenders may be considered relevant. For example, in cases involving juvenile offenders that experience comorbid substance abuse and/ or dependence, an exploration of relevant research would appear indicated to ensure service delivery that aligns with best practices. As Chassin (2008) points out, substance use in juveniles may increase susceptibility for delinquency, and in turn, specialized treatment models that are informed by valid science may be considered applicable. One such widely applied used approach to recidivism reduction consists of Juvenile Drug Court, which first evolved in the 1990s. This systemic approach to curtailing juvenile delinquency is not only based on empirical evidence of comorbid substance-related problems among juvenile offenders but also on the notion that appropriate clinical service delivery to reduce or eliminate substance abuse/dependence can thus reduce recidivism risk. With that being said, however, the research indicates that there is no single treatment model that has, to date, been identified as most useful in terms of outcome. Conversely, a best-practice approach to juvenile offenders that is prescriptive and individualized in nature and that incorporates services that are empirically validated and widely accepted within the standards of care for a specific discipline (e.g., psychiatry and/or psychology) is indicated. Chassin (2008) further emphasized that when clinical interventions are applied to juvenile offenders experiencing substance-related difficulties, a multi-layered and systemic approach to service provision is generally recommended and deemed accessible; albeit, limitations in terms of service availability remains an inherent area of concern.

The MacArthur Foundation is perhaps one of the largest organizations devoted to promoting best practices in juvenile justice reform. According to its website (www.macfound.org), the MacArthur Foundation prides itself on furthering educational efforts to assist decision makers in developing the most effective policies and practices for juvenile offenders. The idea behind this centers on increasing awareness of fundamental differences among children, adolescents, and adults, and highlights the probability that treating juvenile offenders the same as their adult counterparts will only result in negative outcomes to juveniles and society as a whole. The MacArthur Foundation supports scientific study to promote an evidence-based approach to juvenile justice. By furthering such investigative efforts and maximizing education for those with legal decision-making authority, the foundation posits that an evidence-based approach to juvenile justice can facilitate an effective balance among personal accountability, rehabilitation, public safety, and lowered costs. In 2003, the MacArthur Foundation implemented a novel initiative dubbed "Models for Change: Systems Reform in Juvenile Justice," to promote system-wide reform that could be generalized around the world. This project sought to identify methods of improving system performance and outcomes initially in four core states (i.e., Pennsylvania, Illinois, Washington, and Louisiana) and, as of April 2014, had expanded to sixteen states. This initiative focuses on specific factors such as racial/ethnic variables, evidence-based practices, and distinguishing factors between the juvenile and adult criminal justice systems.

Although well intentioned and apparently active, the MacArthur Foundation's efforts are dynamic and ongoing, as data continues to be gathered and used as an informative guide to system reform and service delivery from a best-practices perspective. As there are numerous variables that warrant consideration in terms of their applicability to juvenile justice, significant time and effort appears needed to account for individual differences in juvenile offenders and particularly special-needs populations of juvenile offenders that present with unique concerns that might not have been extensively studied. Furthermore, it is important to emphasize the role of accountability as it relates to not only personal accountability for the offender but also accountability of the courts in terms of ensuring that those with legal decision-making authority keep abreast of the most current and emerging research trends to be considered when rendering dispositions in juvenile cases. Accordingly, several questions remain, including, who should be held accountable for ensuring that best practices are used in juvenile justice intervention? Who should be held accountable for ensuring consistent application of best practice models from case conception to disposition? Furthermore, is it possible to account for all variables that might impact juvenile offenders on an individualized level at any given time? In many cases involving juvenile offenders, information regarding personal characteristics that may influence delinquency can only be extrapolated from self-report. Certain jurisdictions might not consider implementing a comprehensive evaluative process with each individual juvenile offender that stands before the court, as such efforts may prove to be too costly and/or time-intensive. In some jurisdictions, comprehensive assessments of individual juveniles may not be considered until a juvenile is facing removal from their home and society as a whole. These concerns highlight a need for more sweeping reform in terms of what is most pertinent and salient when it comes to evaluating individual differences and interventional strategies within the juvenile justice system.

Review of Juvenile Justice Best Practices Literature

There is growing research that examines pertinent variables as they relate to juvenile offenders that may be considered when approaching system reform to espouse a best practices perspective. For example, various forms of abuse and/or neglect that juveniles might encounter in their homes and communities could arguably influence criminality and recidivism. Additional relevant variables to consider include gender, age, familial socioeconomic status, intelligence, the presence of a learning disorder, Attention-Deficit/Hyperactivity Disorder (ADHD), traumatic brain injury (TBI), and various types of offenses. In one study conducted by Conrad et al. (2014), juvenile female offenders generally reported higher rates of sexual abuse victimization in comparison with nonoffending females. This study found that even after other risk factors were accounted for (e.g., prior legal history and conduct problems), a history of sexual victimization was the most salient predictor of recidivism in female juvenile offenders. This study highlights the need for development of gender-specific and responsive interventions to lower recidivism. Another study conducted by Hampton, Drabick, and Steinberg (2014) examined whether intelligence test scores constituted a moderating variable in the relationship between psychopathy and juvenile offending. Their analysis of 1,354 juvenile offenders included assessments of intellectual ability, psychopathy, and self-reporting of offending behaviors at three time intervals (i.e., at the time of initial interview, and 36 and 84 months later). Results of this study indicated that although greater levels of psychopathy were associated with increased rates of offending, the greatest levels of offending were observed in juveniles that possessed both higher levels of psychopathy and higher intelligence test scores.

To further address treatment considerations and dynamics relevant to juvenile offenders, it is imperative to analyze outcomes that are delivered in various settings. Placement within an out-of-home setting (i.e., foster care) may be relevant when determining treatment application from a best practices perspective. Multidimensional Treatment Foster Care (MTFC) is an effective family-based model of intervention that is designed to curtail delinquency. MTFC has its roots in social learning theory and is essentially a behavioral reinforcement model implemented within foster care settings, utilizing caregivers who have received training in effective parent management. Generally speaking, one of the fundamental objectives of MTFC is to afford youth a normalized experience of life in various settings (i.e., school), while creating lasting positive environmental modifications that would otherwise serve to reinforce problem behaviors (Chamberlain, 2005).

To examine effectiveness of MTFC in female offenders, Kerr et al. (2014) cited that female juvenile offenders might be at an increased level of risk for suicidality and depression. The authors sought to examine long-term outcomes utilizing MTFC on a sample of 166 females. Trajectories of suicidality and depressive symptomatology using MTFC in comparison with a control group that received traditional group intervention revealed that MTFC (in comparison with other group treatments) resulted in greater reductions in depression, only slightly greater decreases in suicidal ideation, and no effect on suicide attempts.

Although a good deal of research appears to focus primarily on the efficacy of MTFC in females, it is also important to consider such data with regard to male offenders that might also be in the foster care system at the time of treatment delivery. In a study conducted by Chamberlain and Reid (1998), treatment outcomes using MTFC were assessed in a population of male juvenile offenders who were identified as exhibiting chronic and severe degrees of delinquency. The study sample consisted of 79 males who received either MTFC or standard group care. Results indicated that the participants who received MTFC exhibited significantly less criminal referrals, and they were also more likely to resume living with relatives in comparison with participants who received the alternative form of treatment. The authors also stated that receipt of either treatment modality predicted criminality upon follow-up, well beyond that of other identified risk factors related to juvenile delinquency (e.g., age at first offense and volume of prior offenses).

Perhaps one of the most thoroughly studied interventional models for juvenile offenders is Multi-Systemic Therapy (MST). According to a study conducted by Robinson et al. (2014), MST and other evidence-based treatments that are intended to target juvenile delinquency have been well-researched; albeit, empirical studies on the potential influence of contextual variables on treatment outcomes is relatively scarce. Thus, factors such as socioeconomic status, community variables, and other factors that influence parental monitoring may interplay with treatment efficacy. The researchers in this study sought to specifically examine the influence of socioeconomic status and community factors in moderating parental monitoring. Results indicated that community factors did interact with parental monitoring (e.g., parental monitoring predicted decreased externalizing behavior only for juveniles residing in neighborhoods with fewer risk factors). Conversely, socioeconomic status was reportedly unrelated to changes in externalizing behaviors that responded to MST. Collectively, the authors asserted that the results highlight a need for greater understanding of the potential role of the juvenile offender's larger social environment to predict outcomes when MST is applied.

There is a plethora of literature highlighting the applicability and effectiveness of MST as an interventional approach with juvenile offenders. Although an extensive review of outcome studies concerning this treatment modality is beyond the scope of this chapter, it is worthy of exploration when delineating best practices in juvenile justice service delivery. For instance, a study conducted by Weiss et al. (2013) examined treatment outcomes when MST was utilized with a sample of 164 adolescents who were not court-referred to treatment. Although this particular study was not specific to those juveniles legally mandated to engage in MST, it is deemed relevant, as some of the factors explored underlie and may predate a juvenile's entrance into the juvenile justice system. In this study, independent examination of MST efficacy on juvenile conduct problems and larger-scale systemic variables was conducted. Participants in the study were assessed eighteen months after receiving treatment using self and collateral ratings as well as a review of criminal records. Analysis of treatment outcomes also occurred two-and-a-half years post baseline. Collectively, results showed that MST was related to a significant decrease in externalizing problem behaviors, and favorable outcomes concerning MST in relation to familial functioning on a more global scale were also indicated.

Tighe et al. (2012) also sought to explore the efficacy of MST directly from a familial perspective. In addition to disseminating findings that suggest MST is an effective treatment model that may be deemed appropriate for use with juvenile offenders, the authors posited that certain adaptions of the traditional application of MST (e.g., increased clinical focus on the influence of negative peer associations and ensuring individual families are afforded necessary supports to facilitate active and consistent engagement in services to increase the likelihood of positive outcomes) were also highlighted. Such a multilayered and systemic focus to service delivery appears to delineate the importance of multiple interactional mechanisms for lasting change. As juveniles do not function mutually exclusive from their respective environments, consideration of treatment outcomes while accounting for more global influencing factors (particularly as they relate to treatment outcomes) appears highly relevant to determining what truly constitutes best practices.

Given the significant impact that juvenile criminality likely has on family functioning as a whole, it is not surprising that research has also focused rather heavily on examining systemic approaches to service delivery with juveniles who engage in delinquent behaviors. Researchers have sought to examine the efficacy of group- and family-based models of interventions for quite some time. For instance, Wunderlich, Lozes, and Lewis (1974) highlighted historical factors associated with group therapy, specifically in relation to drug-related juvenile court cases. One such approach to treatment originated within Prince George's County Juvenile Court in 1968. Guidance, Understanding, and Information in Drug Evaluation (GUIDE) was intended to provide brief group treatment to a population of adolescents who abused substances, and GUIDE also serviced parents. Parent and youth group sessions were conducted independently, and the primary objective of the model was to improve communication between parents and youth, so as to foster more adaptive problem-solving and conflict-resolution strategies within family systems. Interestingly, negative emotions displayed by parents toward their children occurred, in part, as a result of the interplay between different variables (e.g., dishonesty exhibited by the youth themselves in relation to their substance abuse and due to interactions with representatives of the juvenile court system). Thus, the model of intervention developed focused on decreasing such negative emotions since quite often, criminality in juveniles may constitute a symptom that is reflective of greater underlying dysfunction within a family system.

Studies have demonstrated efficacy in terms of family treatment outcomes on adult criminal conduct. In theory, it is not surprising that similar treatment models may also prove beneficial in terms of reducing recidivism in juvenile offenders. One such intervention that has shown promise with juvenile offenders is functional family therapy (FFT). FFT is designed primarily for youth between 11 and 18 years of age who have behavioral or emotional problems and who have a history of involvement in juvenile justice or the child welfare system. In a study conducted by Datchi and Sexton (2013), for instance, the researchers discovered that, among participants who received evidence-based, family-focused intervention, such as FFT, improvement was noted in terms of individual and relational functioning, as well as in terms of decreased reports of familial discord, distress, and higher levels of cohesion and organization within family systems. This study was reflective of preliminary evidence for the relevance of a family-focused approach to service delivery with adult and youthful offenders.

FFT may be conceptualized as a systemic and behaviorally based approach to family treatment that addresses concerns or symptoms via an ecological perspective (Rohde et al., 2014). Importantly, Flicker et al. (2008) also indicated that FFT has been rigorously studied and empirically supported. It is oftentimes relied on as an intervention of choice for youth who exhibit acting-out behaviors across diverse ethnic and racial groups. Importantly, the authors posit that FFT allows for a good deal of flexibility to be applied clinically, as each intervention is to be customized to the unique characteristics that may be associated with an individual family. FFT also relies heavily on interpersonal needs, which may facilitate consumers to view the treatment model as being particularly supportive.

In terms of selecting the most appropriate treatment modality with any juvenile offender and/or their families, it is important to note that the element of choice does not appear limited in terms of efficacy. For example, in a study conducted by Baglivio et al. (2014), the effectiveness of MST and FFT were evaluated in a sample of juvenile offenders, with the outcome being assessed based on the number of probation and offense violations, both during the time treatment was delivered and twelve months posttreatment. Collectively, results identified few significant differences in the effectiveness of these two treatment approaches, with the exception that in comparison with females in MST, females who received FFT exhibited decreased recidivism and low risk youth referred to FFT had fewer rates of new arrests and violations of probation than did low risk youth referred to MST.

One growing, although limited, area of research to inform best practices in juvenile justice concerns juvenile sexual offenders. According to Hunter (2001), sexual offenses perpetrated by juveniles reached a peak in the early 1990s and declined since then (as of the date of this study). Furthermore, female juvenile sexual offenders were said to account for only about 2% of such crimes at the time. Differing factors among individual juvenile sexual offenders lead some to be viewed as more treatment-resistant than others. This invariably confounds efforts to identify the most appropriate intervention models for both male and female juvenile sexual offenders; albeit, child maltreatment (e.g., both sexual and physical abuse victimization) has been identified as a salient developmental variable to consider when intervening with juveniles who exhibit sexually offensive behaviors.

Hunter and Figueredo (2000) identified four distinct variables that differentiated male children who were previously sexually abused and who went on to commit sexual offenses as adolescents from males who were similarly victimized but who did not offend in adolescence. To elaborate, children who were sexually victimized and subsequently committed sexual offenses in adolescence tended to have been victimized at younger ages and more often than their nonoffending counterparts. These subsequent offenders also reported waiting longer periods of time before disclosing their histories of victimization and, upon reporting past abuse, perceived their families were less supportive than were families of those adolescents who did not commit sexual offenses in adolescence. Collectively, these findings appear to imply that adolescents with more intense and severe developmental trauma are more likely to experience residual debilitating effects. Furthermore, these findings highlight the importance of familial and social support to facilitate adaptive coping mechanisms and successful resolution of past trauma.

The roles that individual and system factors play in juvenile delinquency highlight the importance of conducting comprehensive and culturally sensitive evaluations of offending youth. Given the possibility that many juveniles might not report or overtly evidence certain risk factors or other variables that could potentially inform intervention strategies, the value of comprehensive assessment on the juvenile's initial contact with the legal system should not be minimized. Through the careful selection and appropriate utilization of various psychological test measures, clinical interviewing, and examination of collateral sources (e.g., case documentation and interviews with third party sources), such assessment efforts may prove significantly useful in identifying those factors most relevant to treatment efforts and in targeting cases that require more specialized treatment models to curtail juvenile offending behaviors before they transition into adulthood.

Numerous types of forensic psychological evaluations may be deemed applicable to juvenile offenders. It is imperative for those with legal decision-making and policy-enhancing authority to identify and utilize only those professionals who possess the requisite knowledge, training, and expertise with evaluating juvenile offenders. This can further reduce the likelihood of misdiagnosis and cursory assessments that might be ineffective and perhaps even more problematic in exacerbating distress and other variables that have influenced delinquent conduct. Furthermore, it is important to note that, irrespective of whether a forensic evaluator is well intentioned and adequately informed regarding assessment procedures to utilize with juvenile offenders, it may not always be possible to administer all available tests to ascertain the presence of certain risk factors or other psychological variables that might inform an appropriate course of intervention/treatment. Again, the issue of self-report comes into play, as in some cases, juvenile offenders and/or their family culture might not support disclosure of certain experiences or feelings that could provide useful clinical data. Whenever possible, then, a sound forensic evaluation should consider consistency among multiple data sources and utilization of psychological test measures that have been scientifically studied and deemed psychometrically sound.

One area in which juvenile forensic assessment is often utilized concerns competency to proceed to trial evaluations. Borum and Grisso (1995) emphasize that there is a good deal of variability in terms of the methodologies and testing that may be utilized in competency-to-proceed-to-trial evaluations, and guidelines pertaining to the practice of forensic psychology offer little details regarding the content and structure of various types of evaluations. Examining standards in the practice of forensic psychological assessment with juvenile offenders is pertinent to delineating a best-practices approach to service delivery.

Ryba, Cooper, and Zapf (2003) analyzed the standard of practice for evaluating juvenile offenders when a question of competency to proceed to trial arose. These authors surveyed psychologists to identify pertinent elements that may be included in such assessment reports. They noted that the majority of respondents indicated that the use of forensic and psychological assessment measures was relevant and pertinent. Those respondents who noted relying on psychological test data in rendering conclusions identified intelligence testing as the most highly used instruments, with personality testing and, finally, achievement testing, weighing in.

When evaluating juvenile offenders, external variables and situational factors should also be considered. Hecker and Steinberg (2002) posed the question as to whether predisposition psychological evaluations of juvenile offenders have a measurable effect on legal decision making. The authors of this study examined 172 predispositional psychological evaluation reports from a Philadelphia-area juvenile court jurisdiction and the relationship between report quality and the judges' willingness to accept recommendations proffered in those reports. Results of this study highlighted the importance of psychologists and judges becoming more aware of what the relevant domains of assessment are and what constitutes a quality report. Guidelines have been proposed in the absence of clearly defined standards for conducting psychological evaluations of juvenile offenders. Detailed and comprehensive assessment of a juvenile's functioning across time and settings that are relevant to juvenile case disposition have been identified as pertinent and relevant, along with psychometrically sound test measures used to evaluate a juvenile's specific skills and abilities (e.g., intellectual, achievement, and vocational skills). In addition, thorough evaluation of the juvenile's family system may be beneficial to identify etiological factors associated with conduct-disordered behaviors. Furthermore, an assessment of the juvenile's community environment may also be considered relevant to guide placement and treatment recommendations. Professionals conducting psychological evaluations of juvenile offenders should receive necessary educational and training opportunities to provide meaningfully relevant information. As there appears to be a lack of informative consensus regarding what constitutes report quality, a need for further research and delineation of appropriateness in relation to psychological evaluations and report quality is indicated.

To further guide forensic psychological evaluations in juvenile cases when considering potential placement recommendations, an assessment of risk appears indicated and should be informed via delineation of psychologically meaningful risk variables. According to Hanson (2009), it is imperative not only to identify relevant risk factors at a superficial level but also to work towards identifying the potential source(s) that led to the formation and maintenance of risk factors. Distinguishing between static risk factors (i.e., historical variables that are not malleable) and dynamic risk factors (i.e., those that may be amenable to certain interventions) is also relevant in this discussion. Further, ensuring accurate operational definitions of terminology often used in psychological reports (i.e., "anger management problems") should be clearly explained to prevent misunderstanding and possible overgeneralization of problematic displays of aggression across time and settings.

Bailey, Gunn, and Law (2014) recommend that any course of study in forensic psychiatry should include principles of adolescent psychiatry. Distinctions between clinical screening and assessment in forensic and nonforensic settings are worthy of mention, as an assessment of danger to others may be considered highly relevant to decision making in relation to policy reform and legislative modification. Such risk assessment, however, differs fundamentally from a needs-based assessment. A risk assessment fundamentally combines statistical information with clinical data in ways that integrate historical or static variables along with current personal or dynamic factors within a contextual framework. Although some of these identified variables may highlight potential areas of need, the two approaches to assessment are somewhat distinct, albeit, intertwined. Via early identification of a juvenile offender's mental health needs, diversion from detention may be more likely by way of community-based models of care and intervention. The authors posit that pre-adjudicatory dispositions should be informed by the best possible evaluative processes, as specific measures may prove useful to delineate various forms of psychopathology and ongoing risk to self and others.

In a study conducted by Fonagy (2003), the authors asserted that aggression and violence are apparently present at a young age, and substantially higher rates of physically aggressive behaviors have been observed in children and adolescents who meet diagnostic criteria for Attention-Deficit/Hyperactivity Disorder (ADHD) and Conduct Disorder. Thus, the presence of these two comorbid diagnoses in childhood/adolescence may be said to significantly increase a juvenile's risk for engaging in conduct-disordered acts that may in turn place them at a greater likelihood of coming into contact with the juvenile justice system. At the same time, the possibility of misdiagnosis may be considered, as children and adolescents that exhibit symptomatology consistent with diagnoses of both ADHD and Conduct Disorder might actually be best accounted for by other etiology (e.g., behavioral reenactments of past trauma). This highlights the import of conducting sound, comprehensive evaluations for children/adolescents and, particularly, juvenile offenders. Given the potential traumatic response that may be associated with an out-of-home placement and the possibility of increased exposure to peers who exhibit similar or more severe behavioral problems, accurate diagnostic clarification may be paramount to identifying both risk factors and individual needs.

Additional diagnostic considerations worthy of further examination in juvenile offenders might include Autism Spectrum Disorders (ASD), Posttraumatic Stress Disorder (PTSD), and substance abuse/dependence. As these conditions might not occur exclusively (i.e., in the absence of other co-morbid diagnoses), it will be imperative to maximize efforts at conducting comprehensive and scientifically informed evaluation procedures to facilitate diagnostic clarification in an accurate and meaningful way. Bailey, Gunn, and Law (2014) discuss specialized medico-legal assessments and the import of considering an individual's age, level of maturity, intellectual abilities, and emotional capacities when a juvenile has been charged with a criminal offense. Certain difficulties (i.e., a specific learning disability and/or residual deficits from traumatic brain injury) might impact a juvenile's ability to adequately assist with various processes that occur at differing stages of juvenile legal proceedings and may also affect competency to proceed to trial. Thus, various psychological assessment measures that have been subject to empirical investigation for use with juvenile offenders are a relevant topic of discussion.

In terms of assessing for static variables, Villar-Torres, Romero, and Gomez-Fraguela (2014) sought to examine the validity of the Psychopathic Checklist: Youth Version (PCL: YV) on a sample of Hispanic youth that were involved with the juvenile justice system. Specifically, the others sought to generalize results from previous studies that examined the utility of this measure in the Anglo-Saxon literature. These prior studies reportedly supported the PCL: YV as a useful tool for predicting recidivism and subsequent violence; albeit, such data on Hispanic and other minority youth were less prevalent. Importantly, the authors of this study concluded that their analysis supports the utility of the PCL: YV with Hispanic youth. The measure is said to provide a convenient method that is deemed appropriate for use with such populations, specifically, to assess psychopathic traits and risk for criminality.

Due to the possibility that youth involved with the juvenile justice system might present with a history of trauma and other complex mental health symptomatology, a comprehensive approach to forensic psychological assessment with juvenile offenders may be most appropriate to delineate patterns of test results and to obtain consistency across data sources. The Child Report of Post-Traumatic Symptoms (CROPS) is a brief measure with demonstrated reliability and validity in evaluating a range of symptoms believed to be associated with posttraumatic stress in children between 7 and 17 years of age in myriad settings (Greenwald & Rubin, 1999). Furthermore, the Behavior Assessment System for Children, Second Edition, Self-Report Profile—Adolescent (BASC-2 SRP-A) is a widely used self-report measure that assesses various domains of behavioral and emotional functioning. The BASC-2-SRP-A includes clinical scales that tap into maladjustment, as well as adaptive scales that assess inter- and intrapersonal functioning (Reynolds & Kamphous, 2004). Perkins, Calhound, and Glaser (2014) examined the BASC-2-SRP-A and CROPS profiles that were generated from a sample of adjudicated youth. Results indicated that symptoms of posttraumatic stress are often identified in juvenile offenders. Youth who reported clinically significant levels of posttraumatic symptomatology on the CROPS were also found to have been increasingly likely to endorse increased mental health symptoms on the BASC-2-SRP-A.

A juvenile offender assessment that seeks to identify consistencies and inconsistencies among multiple data points may be considered most useful and relevant to identify risk level and needs. Moreover, comprehensive assessment may be needed to ascertain whether a juvenile possesses the requisite capacity to comprehend and to remain involved with the legal proceedings; albeit, such evaluation of a juvenile's individual capacities might not be applied early in a juvenile legal case for various reasons (e.g., the concerns might not have been identified and/or raised by the involved parties). This again highlights the importance of using multiple data sources to obtain an accurate and comprehensive picture of the risks and needs for each juvenile offender.

It is also important to consider problematic response styles on testing and general defensiveness during the clinical interview in any forensic psychological evaluation. Establishing rapport with juvenile offenders may be a daunting task, even for the most seasoned clinician. Ensuring informed consent and an adequate understanding of matters pertaining to limited confidentiality and other key components of forensic psychological evaluations may also pose additional barriers to establishing rapport and maximizing accurate self-disclosure. These matters should also be considered when disclosing one's status as a mandated reporter of abuse or neglect (and in some cases, the need to report concerns of self-harm and/or harm to others). In such instances, a juvenile may be reluctant to discuss past or ongoing abuse, neglect, and/or suicidal or homicidal ideation out of fear of punishment. Thus, a carefully balanced approached to forensic psychological evaluations with juvenile offenders that is not rushed or cursory and that is corroborated by as many credible data sources as possible (e.g., collateral records and interviews with third party sources) may prove invaluable when it comes to delineating risk factors and accurate diagnostic formulations. Relatedly, diagnostic prevalence rates should be considered prior to rendering conclusions. In many cases, professionals may be quick to apply several commonly seen diagnostic categories to collective sums of juvenile offenders (e.g., Conduct Disorder), when the true etiology for various manifestations of delinquency and other forms of mental health symptomatology may be related to other variables (e.g., those related to trauma). To elaborate, if the *Diagnostic and Statistical Manual for Mental Disorders, Fifth Edition* or *DSM-5* (2013) identifies a diagnostic category as having a very low prevalence rate, albeit the diagnosis appears readily applied to large numbers of individuals, then the possibility exists that the assessment may not be adequately informed.

As previously mentioned, there are several treatment modalities and intervention settings that may be utilized with juvenile offenders. Although some treatment approaches have been deemed applicable and useful when intervening with juvenile offenders, a prescriptive approach to psychotherapy may be most beneficial to determine the best treatment for each individual's unique needs. For example, although MST appears to be one of the most thoroughly studied treatment modalities with this population, an examination of the juvenile offender's family system would appear indicated to determine the appropriateness of utilizing this model. If a juvenile's family is not open to receiving services and/or to allowing professionals into their home, this may increase resistance to the therapeutic process and limit the possibility of positive treatment outcomes. Furthermore, CBT (which tends to rely heavily on verbal interventions) might not be most appropriate for a juvenile with a verbal learning disability who may struggle with comprehension and/or grasping concepts that others might not encounter. Amenability to services delivered within residential or institutional settings may be impacted by a juvenile's perception that treatment is solely punitive and that providers are aligned with those who possess legal decision-making authority. This may not only limit the establishment of a strong and trusting therapeutic relationship but also may result in the juvenile resisting treatment delivered in such a setting at all costs. For juveniles who have encountered significant trauma/abuse, the idea of receiving therapeutic interventions in a punitive setting may serve to increase resistance.

Even when juveniles have been comprehensively assessed prior to their case disposition, the importance of ongoing periodic evaluation of functioning and treatment progress and/or barriers is needed to identify and implement effective modifications to service delivery. Only then can such efforts be delivered from a best-practices perspective and truly account for programmatic strengths and areas for further development. Ongoing research is needed to identify various needs and areas for improvement in this regard, so as to reduce the likelihood of wasted resources and recidivism. Also worthy of consideration is the possibility that a juvenile who experiences a negative treatment encounter during his or her involvement with the juvenile justice system (and who subsequently recidivates) may prove less amenable to treatment efforts in the future. In some cases, this may result in treatment being delivered at a higher level of care, during which the juvenile might be at risk of developing thought patterns that equate any treatment services with punishment.

The phrase "continuity of care" may be used to reference several aspects of an individual's involvement in a system of treatment. For juvenile offenders, continuity of care may be operationally defined as collaborative assessment and treatment efforts among mental health providers, legal professionals, the juvenile's family members, and other professionals and nonprofessionals who may influence the outcome of a case. Although generally viewed as a connection between care that an individual receives in an acute inpatient setting (i.e., a hospital) and collaborative efforts for discharge planning, continuity of care for juveniles also involves ongoing planning to prevent recidivism and to mitigate emotional distress and other risk factors. Thus, comprehensive initial and periodic assessment of a juvenile's needs and level of risk is necessary to reduce the likelihood of continued involvement with the juvenile justice system and other deficiencies in functioning. Selecting the most appropriate assessment and intervention methods can be instrumental in maximizing a juvenile offender's functioning and opportunities for success in adopting a prosocial lifestyle that extends beyond the life of their legal case.

Continuity of care for juvenile offenders requires familiarity with treatment outcome studies and case collaboration. For example, when a psychological evaluation is performed on a juvenile offender to assist the trier of fact with decisions regarding placement, it is important to ensure that those with legal decision-making authority receive a thorough understanding of individualized variables that warrant ongoing attention via further assessment. In cases involving juvenile offenders who have encountered significant trauma, for example, treatment recommendations geared specifically towards this population may not be sufficient to ensure that retraumatization and/or recidivism does not occur. In such cases, the importance of clearly defining methods of ongoing needs and risk assessment and treatment progress is paramount. A study conducted by Thompson et al. (2012) sought to examine the relationship between past traumatic experience and predictions and/or expectations concerning various outcomes (e.g., educational, academic, and occupational). Several variables were noted to come into play with regards to these constructs (instability, maltreatment, and exposure to violence). Accordingly, continuity of care and ongoing assessment of an individual juvenile's internal experience and an environment that might not be conducive to promoting long-term treatment gains should be considered and clearly documented for those involved in case disposition.

As previously noted, there exists a differentiation between static and dynamic variables as they relate to both risk and protective constructs. When identified, dynamic variables may be addressed and periodically assessed to evaluate treatment progress and barriers. Thompson and McGrath (2012) point out that a sufficient number of empirical studies have been conducted to delineate the clinical utility of measures used for risk assessment purposes. However, individual jurisdictions and/or treatment program might not find these useful in assessing treatment outcomes and ongoing needs. This highlights a need for ongoing educational efforts to maximize development of a widely accepted approach and appropriate standard for continuity of care based on a juvenile offender's functioning at the time of assessment.

Conclusion

This chapter was intended to highlight the evolution of the juvenile justice system in response to several perceived shortcomings and the need for greater accountability and consideration of individual and culturally specific variables when intervening with juvenile offenders. In order for rehabilitative efforts to be successful, evidence-based approaches to service delivery and interventional models should be utilized and considered comprehensively with multiple sources of credible data. Although just a few examples of relevant and effective treatment models and strategies for reducing recidivism were discussed in this chapter, the following chapters shall more clearly explain additional pertinent variables to consider with regard to treatment and evaluative efforts within the juvenile justice system. The need for ongoing assessment of juveniles and the justice system as a whole is recommended to ensure that a best-practices model is consistently implemented to reduce recidivism and to further improve the overall quality of service delivery.

At times, evaluators may have large caseloads and feel the time pressure of meeting court deadlines. However, it is critical that evaluators do not sacrifice comprehensiveness in an attempt to improve efficiency. This can not only negatively impact an evaluator's professional reputation when there is a pattern of failure to gather critical information but also harm the juvenile because their needs are not accurately identified. Furthermore, evaluators should appreciate the importance of culture and the role it plays in behavior. Evaluators should expand their cultural framework "lens" and realize that culture is more than just nationality; it is also race, gender, class, disability, and a myriad of other factors that help shape our identity and experience (Sue & Sue, 2013). These factors can also contribute to the possibility of juveniles being given strong diagnostic labels (Rubio, Krieger, Finney, & Coker, 2014). Evaluators should be aware of these issues as well as being mindful of their cultural biases and the cultural differences that exist between them and the juveniles they evaluate. Having biases is not the problem, but rather ignorance or failure to acknowledge biases can lead to false assumptions and negative judgments that can "seep" into an evaluation.

Also, understanding a juvenile's cultural context on an individual, community, and societal level can give an evaluator critical insight in the underlying factors that motivate and sustain certain behaviors. For instance, a study by Stewart and Simons (2009) found that adoption of certain types of cultural norms (i.e., Code of the Street) that develop as a result of racism and marginalization (Anderson, 1999) predicts violence in African American youth. Exposure to trauma and community violence can lead to a juvenile's problematic behaviors and even cause them to rationalize and justify their transgressive behaviors (McMahon, Felix, Halpert, & Petropoulos, 2009; Coker, Ikpe, Brooks, Page, & Sobell, 2014).

Although it may not be possible to account for each and every nuance of individual factors pertaining to juvenile offenders, a comprehensive and scientifically informed approach to service delivery within the juvenile justice system may be more widely accepted as the norm, rather than the exception when appropriate education becomes increasingly available to those with the ability to bring about even greater legislative changes and reform. Through increased accountability at the individual, familial, and larger system levels, it remains hopeful that significant and positive changes to our juvenile justice system can be realized.

References

Abrams, D. E. (2014). A primer on juvenile protective legislation. *Juvenile & Family Court Journal, 65*(3).

American Psychiatric Association. (2013). *Diagnostic and statistical manual for mental disorders* (5th ed.). Arlington, VA: American Psychiatric Association.

Anderson, E. (1999). *Code of the street: Decency, violence and the moral life of the inner city.* New York: W.W. Norton.

Baglivio, M. T., Jackowski, K., Greenwald, M. A., & Wolff, K. T. (2014). Comparison of multisystemic therapy and functional family therapy effectiveness: A multiyear statewide propensity score matching analysis of juvenile offenders. *Criminal Justice and Behavior, 41*(9), 1033–1056.

Bailey, S., Gunn, J., & Law, H. (2014). *Forensic Psychiatry: Clinical, Legal and Ethical Issues* (2nd ed.). CRC Press.

Benekos, P. J., & Merlo, A. V. (2014). *Juvenile Justice: International Perspectives, Models and Trends.* CRC Press.

Borum, R. & Grisso, T. (1995). Test use in criminal forensic evaluations. *Professional Psychology: Research and Practice, 26*(5), 465–473.

Chamberlain, P. (2005). Intervention outcomes for girls referred from juvenile justice: Effects on delinquency. *Journal of Consulting and Clinical Psychology, 73*(6), 1181–1185.

Coker, K. L., Ikpe, U., Brooks, J., Page, B., & Sobell, M. (2014). Social problem solving skills mediates the relationship between traumatic stress and moral disengagement among inner-city African American high school students. *Journal of Child and Adolescent Trauma, 7*(2), 87–95.

Conrad, S. M., Tolou-Shams, M., Rizzo, C. J., Placella, N., & Brown, L. K. (2014). Gender differences in recidivism rates for juvenile justice youth: The impact of sexual abuse. *Law and Human Behavior, 38*(4), 305–314.

Datchi, C. C., & Sexton, T. L. (2013). Can family therapy have an effect on adult criminal conduct? Initial evaluation of functional family therapy. *Couple and Family Psychology: Research and Practice, 2*(4), 278–293.

Flicker, S. M., Turner, C. W., Waldron, H. B., Brody, J. L., & Ozechowski, T. J. (2008). Ethnic background, therapeutic alliance, and treatment retention in functional family therapy with adolescents who abuse substances. *Journal of Family Psychology, 22*(1), 167–170.

Fonagy, P. (2003). The development of psychopathology from infancy to adulthood: The mysterious unfolding of disturbance in time. *Infant Mental Health Journal, 24*(3), 212–239.

Greenwald, R., & Rubin, A. (1999). Brief assessment of children's post-traumatic symptoms: Development and preliminary validation of parent and child scales. *Research on Social Work Practice, 9*, 61–75.

Hampton, A. S., Drabick, D. A. G., & Steinberg, L. (2014). Does IQ moderate the relation between psychopathy and juvenile offending? *Law and Human Behavior, 38*(1), 23–33.

Hanson, R. K. (2009). The psychological assessment of risk for crime and violence. *Canadian Psychology/Psychologie Canadienne, 50*(3), 172–182.

Hecker, T., & Steinberg, L. (2002). Psychological evaluation at juvenile court disposition. *Professional Psychology: Research and Practice, 33*(3), 300–306.

Hunter, J. A. (2001). *Practical aspects of rape investigation: A multidisciplinary approach.* CRC Press.

Hunter, J. A., & Figueredo, A. J. (2000). The influence of personality and history of sexual victimization in the prediction of juvenile perpetrated child molestation. *Behavior Modification, 24*(2): 241–263.

Kerr, D. C. R., DeGarmo, D. S., Leve, L. D., & Chamberlain, P. (2014). Juvenile justice girls' depressive symptoms and suicidal ideation 9 years after multidimensional treatment foster care. *Journal of Consulting and Clinical Psychology, 82*(4), 684–693.

Lipsey, M. W., Howell, J. C., Kelly, M. R., Chapman, G., & Carver, D. (2010). Improving the effectiveness of juvenile justice programs: A new perspective on evidence-based practice. Paper for the Center for Juvenile Justice Reform. Retrieved from http://cjjr.georgetown.edu/pdfs/ebp/ebppaper.pdf

Lubit, R. H., & Billick, S. B. (2003). *Principles and Practice of Forensic Psychiatry* (2nd ed.). CRC Press.

McMahon, S. D., Felix, E. D., Halpert, J. A., & Petropoulos, L. A. N. (2009). Community violence exposure and aggression among urban adolescents: testing a cognitive mediator model. *Journal of Community Psychology, 37*(7), 895–910.

Perkins, A., Calhoun, G. B., & Glaser, B. A. (2014). An examination of the CROPS and BASC-2-SRP-A among adjudicated youth. *Journal of Forensic Psychology Practice, 14*(3), 193–212.

Reynolds, C. R., & Kamphous, R. W. (2004). *Behavior assessment system for children* (2nd ed.). New York, NY: Pearson.

Robinson, B. A., Winiarski, D. A., Brennan, P. A., Foster, S. L., Cunningham, P. B., & Whitmore, E. A. (2014). Social context, parental monitoring, and multisystemic therapy outcomes. *Psychotherapy,* Advance Online Publication.

Rohde, P., Waldron, H. B., Turner, C. W., Brody, J., & Jorgensen, J. (2014). Sequenced versus coordinated treatment for adolescents with comorbid depressive and substance use disorders. *Journal of Consulting and Clinical Psychology, 82*(2), 342–348.

Rubio, J. S., Krieger, M. A., Finney, E. J., & Coker, K. L. (2014). A review of the relationship between sociocultural factors and juvenile psychopathy. *Aggression and Violent Behavior, 19*(1), 23–31.

Ryba, N. L., Cooper, V. G., & Zapf, P. A. (2003). Juvenile competence to stand trial evaluations: A survey of current practices and test usage among psychologists. *Professional Psychology: Research and Practice, 34*(5), 499–507.

Sexton, T., & Turner, C. W. (2011). The effectiveness of functional family therapy for youth with behavioral problems in a community practice setting. *Couple and Family Psychology: Research and Practice, 1*, 3–15.

Stewart, E. A., & Simons, R. L. (2009). Code of the street and African-American adolescent violence. Washington, DC: U.S. Department of Justice, National Institute of Justice. Retrieved from: https://www.ncjrs.gov/pdffiles1/nij/223509.pdf

Sue, D. W., & Sue, D. (2013). *Counseling the culturally diverse: Theory and practice* (6th ed.). Hoboken, NJ: Wiley.

Tighe, A., Pistrang, N., Casdagli, L., Baruch, G., & Butler, S. (2012). Multisystemic therapy for young offenders: Families' experiences of therapeutic processes and outcomes. *Journal of Family Psychology, 26*(2), 187–197.

U.N. General Assembly. (1985). *United Nations standard minimum rules for the administration of juvenile justice ("The Beijing Rules"):resolution/adopted by the General Assembly*, November 29, 1985, A/RES/40/33. Retreived from http://www.refworld.org /docid/3b00f2203c.html

Villar-Torres, P., Luengo, M. A., Romero, E., Sobral, J., & Gómez-Fraguela, X. A. (2014). Assessing psychopathy in young people: The validity of the psychopathic checklist: Youth version for a sample of Spanish offenders. *Psychology, Crime & Law, 20*(9), 865–883.

Weiss, B., Han, S., Harris, V., Catron, T., Ngo, V. K., & Caron, A. Guth, C. (2013). An independent randomized clinical trial of multisystemic therapy with non-court-referred adolescents with serious conduct problems. *Journal of Consulting and Clinical Psychology, 81*(6), 1027–1039.

Wunderlich, R. A., Lozes, J., & Lewis, J. (1974). Recidivism rates of group therapy participants and other adolescents processed by a juvenile court. *Psychotherapy: Theory, Research & Practice, 11*(3), 243–245.

13

Sentencing Evaluations in Juvenile Court

Michael P. Brown

Once juveniles are adjudicated delinquent, it is customary for judges to order the juvenile probation department to conduct a presentence investigation and, from that investigation, produce a presentence report. It is sometimes called a social investigation report, a social study, or a social background report. Regardless of its name, the primary purpose of the presentence report is to provide judges with the information needed to make informed sentencing decisions. Presentence reports may include, but are not limited to, information about family history, school performance, substance abuse history, mental health treatment, and delinquent behaviors. Usually, the information found in presentence reports provides the foundational information needed to make informed sentencing decisions. However, there are occasions when cases are unusually complex, offenders appear to be especially dangerous to themselves or others, or information is needed to more fully understand the mental health status of adjudicated delinquents. In such cases, forensic evaluations are ordered by juvenile courts—upon a motion from the prosecutor—or they are requested by defense attorneys. A sentencing evaluation in juvenile court is used to assess how mental health problems, social circumstances, and environmental influences are related to delinquent behaviors. While prosecutors are seeking information that will help them respond appropriately to the needs of juveniles and the risks they pose to the safety of communities, defense attorneys are seeking information that will allow them to be better advocates for their clients (Melton, Perila, Poythress, & Slobogin, 2007).

When preparing forensic evaluations for juvenile cases, forensic evaluators apply their expertise in a truly unique legal culture. The contemporary juvenile court is charged with sentencing juveniles in a way that strikes a balance between what is in the child's best interest and protecting the community from that child. Grounded in the *parens patriae* philosophy, the juvenile court—acting as a parent—is supposed to provide children with care, custody, and treatment. This is done, in part, by keeping in mind two core principles of juvenile justice. First, juvenile court judges should impose the least detrimental alternative available in order to promote healthy child development. Second, judges should rely on the least restrictive alternative necessary to meet children's needs and at the same time protect society. Seasoned professionals sometimes say that these principles are merely guidelines because the practice of juvenile justice is neither ideal nor principled. Indeed, it is most often a compromise between what "should" happen and what "will" happen because of available resources and what parents are willing or able to do for their children.

Ascertaining the appropriate disposition is a complex endeavor. However, forensic evaluators can provide insights into psychosocial aspects of behavior that judges, prosecutors, and defense attorneys find helpful in performing their jobs. Forensic evaluators who perform work in this arena are specialists who understand the legal system and know how and when to use forensic assessment instruments and techniques; they understand the intersection between legal doctrines and mental health evaluations; they know the mental health literature, and they understand the ins and outs of being an expert witness (Melton, Perila, Poythress, & Slobogin, 2007).

In this chapter, the author will examine sentencing evaluations for juvenile court cases. The first part of the chapter involves an examination of relevant case law, a review of the literature, and a review of best practices in sentencing evaluations. The second part of this chapter is a case vignette that allows readers to apply what they learned from the first part of the chapter.

Relevant Case Law

An examination of how case law affects forensic evaluations conducted for the purpose of informing juvenile court sentencing decisions requires a review of the Fifth and Sixth Amendments to the U.S. Constitution. It is important to mention that, while delinquency proceedings have been described as quasi-criminal in nature, the U.S. Supreme Court held in *In re Gault* (1967) that the Fourteenth Amendment and due process rights apply to juvenile delinquency proceedings as well. So, although the court cases described here are appeals that originated in criminal courts, the decisions rendered also apply to juvenile courts.

The Fifth Amendment guarantees protection against self-incrimination (U.S. Const. amend. V) stating that an individual may not "be compelled in any criminal case to be a witness against himself." This protection is for testimonial evidence that is presented in court, which is an important consideration when it comes to forensic evaluations.

Initially, it was in the case of *Thornton v. Corcoran* (1969) that the D.C. Circuit Court stated "the words of the accused are critically important in determining his mental condition." Several years later the U.S. Supreme Court, agreeing in principle with the *Thornton* decision, concluded in *Estelle v. Smith* (1981) that clinical evaluations—depending on the type of evaluation and how the information contained in the evaluation is used—are in fact a form of testimonial evidence.

Estelle v. Smith (1981) was a death penalty case appealed to the U.S. Supreme Court. A critical part of the *Estelle* decision was a reference to a quotation in the American Psychiatric Association's amicus brief that asserted "absent a defendant's willingness to cooperate as to the verbal content of his communications a psychiatric examination . . . would be meaningless." (*Estelle v. Smith*, 1981, n. 8). Hence, in *Estelle v. Smith* (1981), the U.S. Supreme Court held that in the context of psychiatric evaluations, defendants are protected by the Fifth Amendment right against self-incrimination at the penalty phase. Evaluators have a duty to inform the defendant that information he or she provides during the course of the evaluation could be used against him or her in a court of law and that the defendant has a right to remain silent. Statements given during court-ordered evaluations, while the defendant is in custody, can be used in the penalty phase if the offender has been apprised of his or her rights and has knowingly decided to waive them (*Estelle v. Smith*, 1981).

A similar ruling was made by the U.S. Supreme Court for noncapital cases. In *Mitchell v. United States* (1999), the U.S. Supreme Court held that defendants may assert their Fifth Amendment right to remain silent and not incriminate themselves in matters pertaining to sentencing. The justices said that the defendant has reason to be concerned when testimony is given prior to sentencing. The testimony could sway the judge, and lengthier incarceration sentences could be just one of the consequences (*Mitchell v. U.S.*, 1999). Therefore, the accused may refuse to speak about the crime, even after adjudication, during presentence interviews.

The issue surrounding the Sixth Amendment and forensic evaluations has to do with whether defendants have the right to legal counsel. Although the U.S. Supreme Court held that, while the defendant's counsel is entitled to be notified when a forensic evaluation is ordered by the state, the accused does not enjoy the right to have an attorney present during forensic evaluations. The primary concern with having an attorney present centers around the potentially adverse effects it may have on the evaluation (*Estelle v. Smith*, 1981). However, the fact remains that a forensic evaluation has the potential of adversely affecting sentence lengths and the loss of liberty. As a conceptual middle ground, courts sometimes allow for forensic evaluations to be video recorded and reviewed at a later date by the defense attorney. On other occasions, courts have allowed an expert working for the defense attorney to observe the forensic interview in person (Melton, Perila, Poythress, & Slobogin, 2007).

Review of the Literature

Researchers have found a variety of risk factors for delinquency. For example, delinquency has been found to be associated with behavioral and emotional disorders including depression, attention deficit hyperactivity disorder (ADHD), and oppositional defiant disorder; (Akse, Hale, Engles, Raaijmakers, & Meeus, 2007; Grisso, 2004; Wasserman, Ko, & McReynolds, 2004; Teplin, McClelland, Dulcan, & Mericle, 2002); substance use disorders (Shek, 2005; Loeber, Burke, Lahey, Winters, & Zera, 2000); sensation-seeking behaviors (Loeber, & Farrington, 2000); post-traumatic stress disorder (PTSD) resulting from child abuse (Dixon, Howie, & Starling, 2005); developmental delays in such things as language, moral reasoning, and social interactions (Brownlie, Beitchman, Escobar, Young, Atkinson, Johnson, Wilson, & Douglas, 2004; Chandler & Moran, 1990); truancy and poor school performance (Chang, Chen, & Brownson, 2003; Barkley, 2003); family risk factors such as criminal parents or inadequate monitoring; (Gebo, 2007; Resnick, Ireland & Borowsky, 2005; Loeber & Farrington, 2000); delinquent peers (Hinshaw & Lee, 2003; Brody, Ge, Conger, Gibbons, Murry, Gerrard, M., & Simons, 2001); and poor communities and high-crime neighborhoods (Chung & Steinberg, 2006; Henry, Tolan, & Gorman-Smith, 2001; Guerra, Huesmann, Tolan, Van Acker & Eron, 1995).

For many juveniles, the juvenile justice system is the first place in which their mental health problems are identified by professionals and where attempts are made to treat them (O'Donnell & Lurigio, 2008). The juvenile justice system is likewise often the first response to other delinquency risk factors, such as substance abuse, child abuse, inadequate supervision, and truancy. While it is unfortunate that treatment and other interventions are often not used until behaviors rise to a level that a legal response by the justice system is considered necessary, the reality is that youths who come into contact with the juvenile court often suffer from and/or are exposed to a variety of individual, environmental, and social risk factors of delinquency.

While forensic evaluations are ordered to inform the court about concerns related to care and custody, do they affect the types of sentences imposed on delinquent youths? That is, do forensic evaluations influence judicial decision making? A review of the literature suggests that there are two answers to this question.

On the one hand, there is research that has examined how legal factors *predict* the sentences judges impose. Research indicates that factors most predictive of sentences imposed by judges include legal variables such as offense history, the seriousness of the current offense, and past incarceration sentences (Cauffman, Piquero, Kimonis, Steinberg, Chassin, & Fagan, 2007). Risk factors associated with the family, adolescent peer groups, school performance, substance use, and other risk factors, for instance, have very little (and sometimes no) predictive power related to the type of sentence imposed (Campbell & Schmidt, 2000).

On the other hand, there is research that has examined how forensic evaluations *influence* the type of sentences imposed. While there are no studies that have used an experimental design to determine whether forensic evaluations influence juvenile court sentences (Cappon & Vander Laenen, 2013), there have been studies concluded to ascertain whether recommendations from forensic evaluations influence depositions. For instance, several studies have shown that when appropriate controls are utilized, associations between forensic evaluations and juvenile court depositions are revealed. For example, after controlling for legal variables, the mention of mental disorders in forensic evaluations are correlated with the type of sentence imposed by juvenile court judges (Cauffman, Piquero, Kimonis, Steinberg, Chassin, & Fagan, 2007). Hecker and Steinberg (2002) found that when forensic evaluations contained information about mental health history or had information related to drug or alcohol abuse histories, judges were more likely to accept the sentencing recommendations found in forensic evaluations (see also, Campbell & Schmidt, 2000).

Similarly, Kempf-Leonard and Sontheimer (1995), Gebo (2007), and Wordes, Bynum, and Corley (1994) found that when forensic reports included references to mental disorders, juvenile court sentences were more likely to involve institutional placements than those without such diagnoses. Cauffman, Piquero, Kimonis, Steinberg, Chassin, and Fagan (2007) found that juveniles who were charged with substance abuse offenses or whose forensic evaluations noted that they were struggling with substance addictions were more likely to be institutionalized.

Best Practices

Before preparing sentencing evaluations, forensic evaluators should be familiar with a variety of issues. For instance, they should know and understand statutes related to sentencing evaluations. Those statutes delineate standards and regulations that govern sentencing evaluations within the practicing jurisdiction. Also, before evaluations are performed, forensic evaluators should know the research associated with the psychological tests they believe are most appropriate for the case at hand. Depending on the nature of the case, forensic evaluations may therefore include psychological tests that measure intellect, academic abilities, and vocational skills (Kavanaugh, Clark, Masson, & Kahn, 2006; Hecker & Steinberg, 2002). Cognitive and personality tests may also be given in order to gain insight into responsiveness to treatment. When interpreting the results of the tests that are used, evaluators should be careful to not infer beyond that which the scientific literature has validated (Kavanaugh, Clark, Masson, & Kahn, 2006; Heinbrun, 1992). Psychological test results can be helpful in sentencing decisions because they provide judges with information directly related to the mental health status of juveniles (Melton, Perila, Poythress, & Slobogin, 2007).

Furthermore, forensic evaluators should make every effort to avoid conflicting interests, especially when those interests may affect impartiality, competency, or professional effectiveness (American Psychological Association, 2013). They must know the scope of their competencies. Those competencies should be based on professional experiences, training, and relevant education. Forensic evaluators should know the justice system and the rights afforded those who are accused of breaking the law (The American Psychological Association, 2013).

The American Psychological Association (2013) asserts that agreements with clients should specify the services to be delivered, the compensation, and the scope and timeframe in which the services are to be delivered. Forensic evaluators should make every effort to honor the agreements they enter into, and services should be competently and promptly delivered. Clients should be regularly informed about the status of the agreed-on services until the agreement is satisfied.

While gathering information and preparing sentencing evaluations, attempts should be made to ascertain mental health needs. Gathering information about social institutions (e.g., the family, peer group, and school) can shed light on levels of support and prosocial or antisocial influences. Can delinquency in the case be traced back to social institutions? And, what community-based resources are available that might meet the child's needs (Hecker & Steinberg, 2002)? Answers to those questions should be included in forensic reports so as to inform judges why sentences and conditions were recommended.

While forensic evaluations for juvenile court dispositions have not been empirically validated, there is general agreement among psychological professionals about the methodology used and what should be included within them (Hecker & Steinberg, 2002). Forensic evaluators should thoroughly review the child's file, concentrating their efforts on compiling detailed information about how each child and the circumstances surrounding the child's offenses differs from common stereotypical beliefs that legal professionals may possess. In addition, evaluators should conduct multiple clinical interviews, collateral contacts, and administer psychological testing if relevant to the referral question(s). Combining all data sources will undoubtedly humanize the juvenile and shed light on the importance of individualized sentences (Melton, Perila, Poythress, & Slobogin, 2007). Additionally, according to the American Psychological Association (2013), forensic evaluators must have integrity and be impartial and fair as they provide expert opinions to judges and other legal decision makers. Opinions presented in writing or verbally expressed by way of testimony should be grounded in scientific principles (American Psychological Association, 2013).

Case Vignette

Reason for Referral

Marcus Aaron, a 15-year-old male was found guilty of theft at the Pearson County Juvenile Court. This sentencing evaluation came in response to Judge Dunn's request for clinical information. The court considered the following sentencing options: a probation sentence with conditions related to community-based services, Multisystemic Therapy (MST) while remaining in the community, or residential placement. The court was interested in knowing Marcus's mental health needs, the risk and protective factors for recommending a particular sentencing option, and why one sentencing option may be more appropriate for Marcus than the others.

Efforts were made to interview Marcus's mother, Ms. Aaron, on four separate occasions, but each time she neither kept the scheduled appointments nor attempted to reschedule them. The court asked this evaluator to complete the evaluation without interviewing Marcus's mother. Additionally, a social investigation report was not received prior to conducting this evaluation.

A 30-minute phone interview was conducted with Ms. Mack, school counselor, and a 15-minute interview was performed with Probation Officer Sheen. Before obtaining information from Ms. Mack and Probation Officer Sheen, the interviewees were informed about the nonconfidential nature of this evaluation, and they agreed to participate.

Three clinical interviews were conducted with Marcus. In total, the interviews lasted one hour and 40 minutes. Marcus was administered the Wide Range Achievement Test, Fourth Edition (WRAT-4) Reading Subsection, Wechsler Intelligence Scale for Children, Fourth Edition (WISC-IV),[1] and the Personality Assessment Inventory-Adolescent (PAI-A). Marcus was informed about the purpose of the evaluation, and the information obtained from the interviews would not be confidential, that it would be included in a forensic evaluation and used when giving oral testimony. He was told that the evaluation would be prepared even if he did not participate. Marcus was also instructed of his rights and informed that he could stop answering questions at any time and answer some questions and not others. Marcus indicated that he understood that the evaluation might be used by the judge to determine his sentence. Marcus agreed to fully participate in the evaluation.

The case vignette has been redacted and all identifying information removed. It is not meant to serve as a forensic report. Any likeness to a case is purely coincidental.

Sources of Information

The records reviewed for this evaluation were obtained from the Pearson County General Hospital, Belleville, the Department of Children and Family Services, and Marcus's high school. According to available records, Marcus was hospitalized on two occasions (all hospitalizations occurred at 14 years of age) for mental health reasons. His first hospitalization followed being taken into custody by the police for "violent behaviors toward his mother." Marcus noted that he was angry because his mother promised him money if he cleaned the bathroom and then she refused to pay him after he finished. Marcus admitted to hospital staff that he was "using alcohol and marijuana" prior to the incident involving his mother. While at the hospital, Marcus participated in individual and group therapy. Ms. Aaron refused to participate in family therapy. Hospital staff worked with Marcus to develop prosocial ways to express his emotions. Upon discharge, Marcus was prescribed psychotropic medication and ordered to participate in substance abuse treatment.

Marcus was hospitalized for the second time after he reportedly hit his mother, drank alcohol, used marijuana, and was noncompliant with taking prescription medications. Marcus was belligerent upon being taken into custody by the police; he was also "uncooperative" during admission into the hospital. Marcus denied ever hitting his mother. A urine toxicology test showed positive results for cannabinoids and his blood alcohol level was elevated. While there, Marcus was diagnosed with several psychological and psychiatric disorders and prescribed psychotropic medication.

Marcus was later admitted to Belleville, a residential facility, and returned home after one month due to insurance payment difficulties reported by Ms. Aaron. He admitted to feeling "so sad" on some days that he "did not want to get out of bed." Marcus admitted that his violent behavior was "tied to smoking marijuana and drinking alcohol." While at Belleville, Marcus reported that he began using cannabis and alcohol at 12 years of age. Marcus stated, "I like to stay high most of the day. It's what I do with my friends." He reported a history of selling cocaine, but never used the drug. According to therapy records, Marcus had difficulty "processing emotions" and was often "frustrated." Additionally Marcus continued to be "protective about being touched," which was speculated as a result of reported physical abuse from his biological father. Once again, Marcus was diagnosed with several psychological and psychiatric disorders and prescribed psychotropic medication. The residential facility recommended that he participate in individual, group, and family therapy.

The Department of Children and Family Services (DCFS) investigated two reports of child abuse involving Marcus and his biological father. The first investigation involved Marcus's father fracturing his jaw (occurred at 11 years of age). During the second investigation, a DCFS investigator noted a "bump" on Marcus's forehead and a bruise on his neck. Marcus's biological father admitted that, in frustration, he grabbed Marcus around the neck and slammed his head against the wall (occurred at 12 years of age). Marcus's father reportedly abandoned the family, and was never heard from again (occurred at 13 years of age). DCFS records also indicated investigations of maternal child neglect for not providing adequate supervision (13 years of age).

Based on school records, Marcus had a history of academic problems, dating back to the third grade. As a result, Marcus was retained in the third grade for an additional year. Over the past year, Marcus had frequent absences and was suspended from school on several occasions for fighting. Marcus had problems at school because he had difficulty listening to authority figures and following the rules. Marcus was easily frustrated by schoolwork and frequently distracted by his peers. Specifically, school records indicated that Marcus had "difficulty with reading comprehension and clarifying his thoughts and ideas." Marcus was recommended for special education several years ago; however, there was no indication of a special-education evaluation or that an Individualized Education Plan was completed.

Relevant Background Information

Marcus indicated that he was raised by his biological mother and godmother. His godmother passed away approximately two years ago and he was reportedly a witness to her death. He tearfully stated, "She was in a chair and I saw her take her last breath." Marcus has two siblings, an older brother (18 years of age) and a younger sister (10 months of age). Marcus reported having little contact with his older brother, who was incarcerated at the county jail, but expressed great love and affection for his sister.

Marcus reported that during the week, he lived with his mother. He managed a family-owned apartment complex and lived with a "family friend" on the weekend. Marcus indicated that this "family friend" was not in a gang, but used crack cocaine daily. About five years ago, when Marcus was 10 years of age, his mother was diagnosed with leukemia. Marcus reported that his mother attempted suicide soon after the diagnosis and was later hospitalized as a result. Marcus remembered that, when he was 11 years of age, his biological father punched him and broke his jaw. Marcus also recalled another incident (approximately one year after he was punched by his biological father) when his biological father slammed his head into the wall. Both cases were referred to the Department of Child and Family Services. He refused to elaborate on the incidents. Marcus denied any abuse and/or neglect from his mother despite records that indicated investigations of maternal child neglect for not providing adequate supervision. He indicated, however, that when his mother wanted to punish him she forbade him from holding his sister. He stated that when he was not allowed to hold his sister, it "messed me up . . . she was my world." Marcus said that his relationship with his mother "fell apart" when his godmother died. He reported that when his mother was feeling stress and loss, she took her emotions out on him by saying that she "hated" him and he was "stupid, ugly, and useless." Marcus admitted that when his mother yelled or called him names that he yelled back. He believed that negative exchanges with his mother had "increased in recent months." While records indicated that Ms. Aaron reported Marcus hit her, he vehemently denied doing so. Marcus contended that his "mother lied to the police in order to have him arrested and placed in a hospital." During the collateral interview, Ms. Mack (school counselor) asserted that Marcus's "internal pain" was related to family issues and contributed to his problem behaviors.

When conflict existed between him and his mother, Marcus admitted that he often left home and spent time with friends who were gang-involved. Marcus reported that he was gang-involved soon after his godmother passed away, but left the gang shortly after his sister was born. Marcus asserted that he continued to be friends with gang members, but they allowed him to leave the gang due to his "situation [birth of sister]." This was consistent with collateral interview information obtained from Ms. Mack and Probation Officer Sheen.

Marcus admitted to a history of selling marijuana and cocaine while gang-involved, but reported that he was no longer selling drugs. He admitted to using marijuana and alcohol since 12 years of age. Marcus said that, at first, he used marijuana only occasionally, but over a short period of time he "got used to it and, in order to feel high, smoked about two blunts a day." Marcus reported drinking a pint of vodka about once a week. Marcus's violent conduct was reportedly related to his use of marijuana and alcohol. Since being detained at the Pearson County Temporary Juvenile Detention Center, Marcus contended that he had not smoked marijuana or drank alcohol.

Marcus admitted that he had a "hard time" controlling his anger. Marcus reported that, for the most part, he exhibited anger because his mother, kids at school, or strangers on the street "picked fights with him or called him names." Marcus stated that he developed ways of coping with people who provoked him, such as "walking away, exercising, drawing pictures, or writing poems." Marcus stated that all of his fights were because he "had to deal with people who wanted to cause him problems." He could not recall a time when he initiated or provoked a fight. Specifically, Marcus reported that all of the fights involved him defending himself or responding to provocations. Marcus admitted to fighting at school and engaging in three physical fights within the academic year, with each resulting in suspensions. During the collateral interview, Ms. Mack reported that Marcus engaged in verbally aggressive behavior at school and it was difficult for him to disengage without external prompting. Marcus stated that he "hated school" and his failures were due to being "bored" and because "teachers were out to get me." He admitted to having difficulty learning in school, but denied being enrolled in special education classes. This was consistent with collateral interview information from Ms. Mack and Probation Officer Sheen.

Marcus reported that, at 14 years of age, he was hospitalized on two occasions for psychiatric treatment. Marcus indicated that admissions to the psychiatric hospital followed arguments with his mother. He asserted that "she called the police, lied to them that I had hit her, and the police took me to the hospital." Although he denied hitting his mother, Marcus admitted to having a "hard time" controlling his anger. He reported that they prescribed psychotropic medications for "depression," the names of which were not known to him, but that he did not take them consistently once at home because "those meds don't mix well with alcohol and my mom stopped reminding me to take them." Marcus reported symptoms of depression (e.g., reduction in appetite, increased isolation, irritability, sadness, feeling hopeless) since his godmother's death, which increased in frequency and severity over the past couple years. He expressed feeling "alone" and asserted that "there is no one who can be trusted." He reported no suicidal or homicidal ideation. When asked about sentencing options, Marcus expressed a considerable desire to participate in community-based services or MST. He thought MST programming would be most beneficial to him and his family because services would be provided in the home. Marcus contended that if his "family problems were fixed" he would no longer have problems with the law. Probation Officer Sheen also recommended community-based services or MST, but raised concerns about Ms. Aaron's commitment to treatment services.

Mental Status Examination

Marcus was a fifteen-year-old male who appeared his stated age and was well-groomed. Marcus participated in this evaluation and answered all questions asked of him, with the exception of questions related to incidents of physical abuse perpetrated by his biological father. He exhibited no difficulty in understanding the questions asked of him and his memory appeared intact. He presented with depressed mood and tearful affect. Marcus reported experiencing depressive symptoms (e.g., reduction in appetite, increased isolation, irritability, sadness, feeling hopeless) since his godmother's death, which have increased in frequency and severity over the past couple years. While discussing his godmother and the nature of their relationship, Marcus became tearful while recalling her death and stated, "She was in a chair and I saw her take her last breath." Marcus presented with organized and logical thinking. There were no noted speech disturbances. He presented with no preoccupation or ruminations and no thought disturbances were observed. He reported no suicidal or homicidal ideation. His judgment was considered poor, particularly with regard to prosocial behavior. Marcus possessed limited insight into his problem behaviors and emotions.

Psychological Measures

WRAT-IV The Wide Range Achievement Test, Fourth Edition (WRAT-4) is designed to assess academic achievement. Marcus was administered the WRAT-4 Reading Subsection and his score suggested that he read at approximately the 6.4 grade level.

WISC-IV Marcus was administered the Wechsler Intelligence Scale for Children, Fourth Edition (WISC-IV). The WISC-IV measures aspects of an individual's verbal and non-verbal abilities. An Intelligence Quotient (IQ) between 90 and 109 is considered average functioning. Data was collected on a cross section of subjects from across the United States of various ages and socioeconomic levels. The group on which data was collected also included subjects from various racial groups based upon their representation in the general population according to census data. Marcus achieved a verbal comprehension score of 75, perceptual reasoning score of 75, working memory score of 62, and processing speed score of 75. He achieved a Full Scale IQ of 67. This placed him in the extremely low range of cognitive functioning in the 1st percentile for his age group.

PAI-A The Personality Assessment Inventory-Adolescent (PAI-A) is a well-standardized measure of adolescent personality. It possesses validity, clinical, interpersonal, and treatment scales. Marcus's validity scores fell within acceptable limits. The PAI-A clinical profile revealed significant elevations across several scales, indicating a broad range of clinical difficulties that were associated with marked distress and significant impairment in functioning. Specifically, the configuration of scores on the clinical scales suggested that Marcus was experiencing problems with emotional stability, problem behaviors, and depressive related symptomatology. With regard to emotional functioning, Marcus's scores suggested that he manifested fairly rapid and extreme mood swings resulting in episodes of poorly controlled anger. As a result, he was likely impulsive, prone to behaviors that were self-destructive/self-injurious, experienced involvement in intense and volatile relationships, and tended to be preoccupied with consistent fears of being abandoned or rejected. Marcus likely experienced difficulties with significant depression, as his scores suggested he experienced thoughts of worthlessness, hopelessness, and personal failure; feelings of sadness; loss of interest in normal activities, sense of pleasure in things that were previously enjoyed, and appetite; sleep disturbances; and decreased level of energy and drive. Marcus's interpersonal style seemed to be best characterized as withdrawn or introverted. The scores indicated that Marcus was prone to be self-critical, pessimistic, and dwell on past failures with considerable uncertainty and indecision about his plans for the future. In addition, Marcus's scores suggested that alcohol use had a negative impact on his life and behaviors. Marcus's scores also suggested that he perceived others as treating him inequitably and making a concerted effort to undermine his interests.

Sentence Recommendations

Based on records, Marcus has not been afforded the opportunity to engage in consistent mental health or community-based services to address his specific needs. In the interest of recommending the least restrictive alternative disposition and promoting healthy child development, it was recommended that Marcus be released into the community with several probation conditions, including individual therapy, social skills training, and substance abuse treatment. It was also recommended that Marcus's psychiatric needs be reassessed. Although community-based services were considered the least restrictive option, it should be noted that Ms. Aaron's lack of parental supervision and weak parental attachment were considered to be barriers to Marcus's potential success in treatment, as he would need encouragement and consistent transportation to services. Thus, it was recommended that, if Ms. Aaron would not engage consistently in community-based family therapy services and support her son's mental health treatment by ensuring transportation to community-based services, the court should consider MST as a secondary option. Given her refusal to engage in family therapy in the past, if Ms. Aaron did not demonstrate consistent commitment to this intensive treatment, residential treatment was considered as the next best option.

Individual Therapy   Based on Marcus's behavioral problems and depressive symptoms as evidenced by records, clinical interview information, and PAI-A outcomes/scores, it was recommended that he receive Cognitive Behavioral Therapy (CBT). CBT has proven to be effective in reducing depressive symptoms and behavioral problems. As such, it was recommended that individual therapy address the following treatment goals:

- Provide psychoeducation and improved insight into stressors;
- Provide stress management and improved coping skills;
- Provide improved decision-making strategies;
- Assist Marcus in identifying and connecting emotions, thoughts and behaviors;
- Provide appropriate coping skills to manage emotions;

- Address loss and grief of godmother and abandonment from father;
- Discuss emotions with regard to mother-child relationship and improve coping strategies when experiencing anger and frustration;
- Provide psychoeducation specific to substance abuse, monitor for substance use, and explore how marijuana and alcohol use may be related to negative states;
- Promote prosocial activities;
- Monitor for exacerbation of mental health symptoms;
- Collaborate with other mental health and substance abuse providers to provide continuity of care.

Family Therapy   Based on information obtained from clinical interviews and records, Marcus's relationship with his mother was extremely strained and there was some concern about her ability to adequately care for and protect Marcus. Thus, it was strongly recommended that Ms. Aaron and Marcus participate in family therapy. Without family therapy, it was determined that Marcus was at increased risk of recidivism. The following goals were recommended:

- Build a positive parent-child relationship and improve communication between Marcus and his mother;
- Discuss importance of consistent parental supervision and assist Ms. Aaron in better meeting Marcus's emotional needs;
- Provide and practice effective and consistent parenting management skills to better handle Marcus's problem behaviors.

Since Marcus was being detained, awaiting a dispositional hearing, it was recommended that family therapy begin immediately upon his return to his mother's home. This recommendation was intended to address concerns about appropriate levels of parental supervision. Marcus was living on his own during the weekend, and when at home during the week his mother provided very little parental supervision. Success in community-based treatment often requires parental support and encouragement.

As noted above, if Ms. Aaron was court ordered to attend family therapy but chose not to comply, it was recommended that residential treatment be considered.

Special Education Services   Given the administration of the WISC-IV and scores obtained in addition to the long-standing problem behaviors and learning difficulties in school, it was recommended that an Individualized Education Plan be completed that incorporated a full battery of academic and cognitive testing. This was essential in determining the most appropriate school placement for Marcus and the potential impact of his problem behaviors on academic learning.

Social Skills Training   It was recommended that Marcus attend highly structured after-school activities that would expose him to prosocial role models and assist him in learning appropriate prosocial behaviors across a variety of contexts. This structure may also reduce opportunities for Marcus to engage in delinquent behaviors.

Substance Abuse Treatment   If individual therapy could not adequately incorporate or address substance abuse concerns, it was recommended that Marcus receive specialized treatment for marijuana and alcohol use. Based on records and clinical interview information, substance use impacts his negative emotions (e.g., anger) and increases the risk for future violence or angry outbursts. While Marcus reported that he stopped using marijuana and alcohol while in detention, it seemed unlikely that he would not use substances if he were in less structured environments. It was recommended that his substance abuse treatment provider remain in contact with all of Marcus's treatment providers to ensure continuity of care.

Medication Management   Although Cognitive Behavioral Therapy was to play an integral role in the reduction of Marcus's mental health symptoms, it was also recommended that he be referred for a medication evaluation. Based on the PAI-A and clinical interview information, Marcus was experiencing symptoms of depression that were impacting his daily functioning. Marcus had not taken medication consistently and it was recommended that the prescribing physician or psychiatrist be aware of the historical barriers to medication compliance. It was recommended that the psychiatrist work closely with all mental health treatment providers to ensure continuity of care.

Common Pitfalls and Considerations

Forensic evaluators are asked to prepare sentencing evaluations to help juvenile courts respond appropriately to juvenile offenders. This is no easy task. It requires considerable knowledge, experience, and sophistication to do well. Below are three interrelated challenges that are commonly associated with preparing juvenile court sentencing evaluations.

First, sentencing evaluations attempt to answer complex and wide-ranging questions. For instance, to what extent does the juvenile pose a threat to the community? What mental health problems exist? How severe are they? Are there social circumstances and environmental influences at play in the case? What are they and how serious are they? Accurate answers to those and other questions are difficult to obtain and understand. However, that is what is being asked of forensic evaluators when they conduct sentencing evaluations.

Second, forensic evaluators are expected to recommend sentences they believe reflect what is appropriate given the circumstances of cases. Additionally, sentencing recommendations are fundamentally influenced by two overarching principles. These principles are as follows:

a) In order to promote healthy childhood development, juvenile court judges should impose the least detrimental alternative sentences.
b) Juvenile court sentences are not to be overly restrictive. That is, judges should strive to impose the least restrictive alternative necessary to meet children's needs and at the same time protect society.

Third, sentencing recommendations have both short- and long-term considerations. The juvenile justice system is interested in the welfare of children, behavioral change, and the safety of the community. To those ends, sentencing recommendations require that the eyes of forensic evaluators remain simultaneously on the present and the future. Hence, what do juveniles need now in order to keep the community safe? Is residential placement necessary? If not, can restrictions be placed on the juvenile in the community that will keep the community reasonably safe? How might immediate psychological and social concerns be addressed to reduce the risk of recidivism? What can be done to bring about conformity to the law and participation in conventional law-abiding activities? Are there measures that can be taken in the family to help create a more loving and supportive environment? Answers to those questions depend on how well forensic evaluators understand the juvenile justice system and the short- and long-term needs of juvenile offenders. Those needs are reflected in the circumstances surrounding the offense(s) of conviction, the information derived through interviews, collateral sources, official records, and information obtained from psychological tests.

Note

1. At the time of the evaluation, the WISC-V (current version of the Wechsler Intelligence Scale for Children) was not on the market or available to evaluator. The latest version at the time was the Wechsler Intelligence Scale for Children, Fourth Edition, and was the reason for its use at the time of the evaluation.

References

Akse, J., Hale, W. W., Engles, R., Raaijmakers, Q., & Meeus, W. H. L. (2007). Co-occurrence of depression and delinquency in personality types. *European Journal of Personality, 21*(2), 235–256.

American Psychological Association. (2013). Specialty Guidelines of Forensic Psychologists. *American Psychologist, 68,* 1, 7–19. Retrieved from (http://www.apa.org/practice/guidelines/forensic-psychology.aspx

Barkley, R. A. (2003). Attention-deficit/hyperactivity disorder. In E. J. Mash & R. A. Barkley (Eds.), *Child psychopathology* (2nd ed.; 75–143). New York, NY: Guilford Press.

Brody, G. H., Ge, X., Conger, R., Gibbons, F. X., Murry, V. M., Gerrard, M., & Simons, R. L. (2001). The influence of neighborhood disadvantage, collective socialization, and parenting on African American children's affiliation with deviant peers. *Child Development, 72,* 1231–1246.

Brownlie, E. B., Beitchman, J. H., Escobar, M., Young, A., Atkinson, L., Johnson, C., Wilson, B., & Douglas, L. (2004). Early language impairment and young adult delinquent and aggressive behavior. *Journal of Abnormal Child Psychology, 32*(4), 453–467.

Campbell, M. A., & Schmidt, F. (2000). Comparison of mental health and legal factors in the disposition outcome of young offenders. *Criminal Justice and Behavior, 27,* 688–715.

Cappon, L., & Vander Laenen, F. (2013). Mental health in juvenile judges' decision-making: Review of literature. *International Journal of Law and Psychiatry, 36,* 65–72.

Cauffman, E., Piquero, A. R., Kimonis, E., Steinberg, L., Chassin, L., & Fagan, J. (2007). Legal, individual, and environmental predictors of court disposition in a sample of serious adolescent offenders. *Law and Human Behavior, 31,* 519–535.

Chandler, M., & Moran, T. (1990). Psychopathy and moral development: A comparative study of delinquent and nondelinquent youth. *Development and Psychopathology, 2,* 227–246.

Chang, J. J., Chen, J. J., & Brownson, R. C. (2003). The role of repeat victimization in adolescent delinquent behaviors and recidivism. *Journal of Adolescent Health, 32,* 272–280.

Chung, H. L., & Steinberg, L. (2006). Relations between neighborhood factors, parenting behaviors, peer deviance, and delinquency among serious juvenile offenders. *Developmental Psychology, 42*(2), 319–331.

Dixon, A., Howie, P., & Starling, J. (2005). Trauma exposure, posttraumatic stress and comorbidity in female juvenile offenders. *Journal of the American Academy of Child and Adolescent Psychiatry, 44,* 798–806.

Estelle v. Smith 451 U.S. 454 (1981). Retrieved from https://supreme.justia.com/cases/federal/us/451/454/case.html

Gebo, E. (2007). A family affair: The juvenile court and family violence cases. *Journal of Family Violence, 22,* 501–509.

Grisso, T. (2004). Double jeopardy: Adolescent offenders with mental disorders. Chicago, IL: University of Chicago Press.

Guerra, N. G., Huesmann, L. R., Tolan, P. H., Van Acker, R., & Eron, L. D. (1995). Stressful events and individual beliefs as correlates of economic disadvantage and aggression among urban children. *Journal of Consulting and Clinical Psychology, 63,* 518–528.

Hecker, T., & Steinberg, L. (2002). Psychological evaluation at juvenile court disposition. *Professional Psychology: Research and Practice, 33,* 3, 300–306.

Heinbrun, K. (1992). The Role of psychological testing in forensic assessment. *Law and Human Behavior, 16,* 257–272.

Henry, D. B., Tolan, P. H., & Gorman-Smith, D. (2001). Longitudinal family and peer group effects on violence and nonviolent delinquency. *Journal of Clinical Child Psychology, 30,* 172–186.

Hinshaw, S. P., & Lee, S. S. (2003). Conduct and oppositional defiant disorders. In E. J. Mash & R. A. Barkley (Eds.), *Child psychopathology* (2nd ed.; 144–198). New York, NY: Guilford Press.

Kavanaugh, A., Clark, J., Masson, T., & Kahn, B. (2006). Obtaining and utilizing comprehensive forensic evaluations: The applicability of one clinic's model. *Nevada Law Journal, 6,* 890–912.

Kempf-Leonard, K., & Sontheimer, H. (1995). The role of race in juvenile justice processing in Pennsylvania. In K. Kempf-Leonard, C. Pope, & W.H. Feyerherm (Eds.), *Minorities in juvenile justice* (pp. 98–127). Thousand Oaks, CA: Sage.

Loeber, R., Burke, J. D., Lahey, B. B., Winters, A., & Zera, M. (2000). Oppositional defiant and conduct disorder: A review of the past 10 years, part I. *Journal of the American Academy of Child and Adolescent Psychiatry, 39,* 1468–1484.

Loeber, R., & Farrington, D. P. (2000). Young children who commit crime: Epidemiology, developmental origins, risk factors, early interventions, and policy implications. *Development and Psychopathology, 12,* 737–762.

Melton, G. B., Perila, J., Poythress, N. G., & Slobogin, C. (2007). *Psychological evaluations for the courts: A handbook for mental health professionals and lawyers* (3rd ed.). New York, NY: Guilford Press.

Mitchell v. United States 526 U.S. 314 (1999). Retrieved from https://supreme.justia.com/cases/federal/us/526/314/

O'Donnell, P. C., and Lurigio, A. J. (2008). Orders in a juvenile court psychosocial predictors of clinicians' recommendations and judges' placement orders in a juvenile court. *Criminal Justice and Behavior, 35,* 1429–1448.

People v. Rosenthal, 617 P.2d 551 (Colo. 1980). Retrieved from http://law.justia.com/cases/colorado/supreme-court/1980/80sa221-0.html

Resnick M. D., Ireland, M., & Borowsky, I. (2004). Youth violence perpetration: What protects? What predicts? Findings from the National Longitudinal Study of Adolescent Health. *Journal of Adolescent Health, 35,* 5, 1–10.

Shek, D. L. (2005). Paternal and maternal influences on the psychological well-being, substance abuse, and delinquency of Chinese adolescents experiencing economic disadvantage. *Journal of Clinical Psychology, 61,* 3, 219–234.

Teplin, L. A., Abram, K. M., McClelland, G. M., Dulcan, M. K., & Mericle, A. A. (2002). Psychiatric disorders in youth in juvenile detention. *Archives of General Psychiatry, 59,* 1133–1143.

Thornton v. Corcoran, 407 F.2d 695, 700 (D.C. Cir. 1969). Retrieved from https://casetext.com/case/thornton-v-corcoran

U.S. Const. amend. I–XXVII. Retrieved from Find Law/Thomas Reuters website: http://constitution.findlaw.com/amendments.html

Wasserman, G. A., Ko, S. J., & McReynolds, L. S. (2004). Assessing the Mental Health Status of Youth in Juvenile Justice Settings. Juvenile Justice Bulletin, U.S. Department of Justice Office of Justice Programs, Office of Juvenile Justice and Delinquency Prevention.

Wordes, M., Bynum, T. S., & Corley, C. J. (1994). Locking up youth: The impact of race on detention decisions. *Journal of Research on Crime and Delinquency, 31,* 149–165.

14

Juvenile Competence
to Stand Trial

Nancy Ryba Panza

Juvenile competence to stand trial (JCST) is a newer area of practice in relation to many of the other types of forensic assessment that are commonly conducted for the courts. Essentially, a JCST evaluation is used to assess the functioning of a child or adolescent who has become involved in the legal system. Questions about competence may arise when there is concern about the presence of deficits in functioning or limitations in development that cause a young offender to not be able to function in the role of defendant. Despite the recency in development of this area of forensic clinical practice, there is a great deal of information available to aid those who wish to conduct this type of evaluation. Important aspects of the law and of clinical practice are reviewed in order to highlight the most essential considerations to which one must attend when conducting such evaluations.

Relevant Statutes and Case Law

The issue of competence to stand trial for juvenile offenders was rarely encountered prior to the mid-1990s, as it was mostly irrelevant. Since the first juvenile court was created in 1899, the primary focus was to aid in the rehabilitation of wayward youth (Steinberg & Schwartz, 2000). The idea behind the juvenile court movement was to hold youth accountable for legal wrongdoing by providing supervision and guidance in a way that promoted the child's well-being. Punishment of wrongdoing was not the focus, instead the court acted in what has been termed a parens patriae approach in which judges used their discretion to provide remediation in a manner that supported the "best interests of the child" (Kruh & Grisso, 2009; Steinberg & Schwartz, 2000).

Two major changes shifted the focus of the juvenile court away from rehabilitation and toward punishment. The first major change occurred in the 1960s when the U.S. Supreme Court decided the cases of *Kent v. United States* (1966) and *In re Gault* (1967). Both decisions stemmed from a realization that the juvenile court's well-intentioned lack of due process requirements was being abused, and youth were, at times, unfairly detained and punished without the benefit of the procedural protections that are in place for adults in criminal court. As a result, the *Kent* and *Gault* decisions put in place many of the due process requirements provided for adults (Grisso, 2013; Steinberg & Swartz, 2000). While this drastically changed the adjudication process for juveniles, it tended to be the case that sentencing in juvenile court was still used as a time to focus on rehabilitation and helping youth to become more functional and law-abiding citizens (Kruh & Grisso, 2009). It wasn't until the mid-1990s that the second major change occurred. During the late 1980s and early 1990s, arrests for juvenile violent crime increased, and state legislatures responded both by increasing the range of penalties available within the juvenile court and by making the procedures for transferring a youth to face trial in adult court much easier (Steinberg & Swartz, 2000). Taken together, these changes created a juvenile court that was very different from its informal, rehabilitation-focused origins, and it was these changes that prompted the need for consideration of competency to stand trial in the juvenile court system.

The issue of competence to stand trial has been relevant in the American criminal court system since its creation. With its basis in English common law, the idea that defendants must have a basic understanding and awareness of the proceedings they face was considered essential to fair and just legal procedures (Melton, Petrila, Poythress, Slobogin, Lyons & Otto, 2007). To try an individual who is unaware of what is happening, who cannot assist in the defense, or who cannot comprehend the possible loss of liberty that may result was believed to be a violation of the fundamental rights provided to those facing legal charges. Every state requires that a criminal court defendant be competent prior to the commencement of legal proceedings, and the U.S. Supreme Court set the standard for competence in the 1960 case of *Dusky v. United States*. The *Dusky* decision held that the test for competence to stand trial was "whether he [the defendant] has sufficient present ability to consult with his attorney with a reasonable degree of rational understanding and a rational, as well as factual, understanding of the proceedings against him (p. 402). Thus, to face trial, one must have some degree of understanding of the legal proceedings and must be able to work with an attorney to help prepare the legal case. In many circumstances, the defendant must also be able to work with the attorney to make important legal decisions, such as whether to testify on one's own behalf or whether to accept a plea agreement. In these cases, it is important that the defendant be able to make such decisions rationally (Grisso, 2013). If it is the case that a defendant is lacking in any of these capacities, he or she will be found incompetent, and efforts to remediate or restore competence will be enacted.

While the *Dusky* standard for competence to stand trial applies nationwide in adult court, it was not inherently clear whether this standard was relevant for juvenile court cases. Since competence in juvenile court was infrequently questioned prior to the mid-1990s, there was rarely a need to consider the issue. However, as the juvenile court became more structured and punitive in nature, more attorneys began to voice concerns over whether their youthful clients were able to understand the legal proceedings and work with them to prepare a proper defense (Kruh & Grisso, 2009). By the late 1990s, these referrals were becoming commonplace.

The *Dusky* decision provided a nationwide standard for competence for adults but was silent on whether the standard applied to juvenile offenders. Therefore, each state was left to determine whether, and how, to apply this legal standard of competence in juvenile court. Beyond this, many states note in statutes that, for adults, deficits in competence must be the direct result of a mental illness or an intellectual disability. However, as JCST evaluations became more commonplace, it was clear that the reasons underlying incompetence for young offenders were often quite different than were those in adults (Grisso, 2013; Kruh & Grisso, 2009).

According to recent data, all but six states in the United States have now developed court rules, statutes, or case law that speaks directly to the issue of juvenile competence to stand trial, and of these, only one state has ruled that competence is not relevant in juvenile court (Szymanski, 2013). Of the vast majority of jurisdictions in the United States that consider competence as relevant to juvenile court proceedings, most have adopted the *Dusky* standard as the basis for determining competence; however, there are differences in how *Dusky* is applied. Many believe the standard for competence should be applied in juvenile court just as it is in adult court; however, there are also arguments for applying *Dusky* in an alternate manner more fitting for the juvenile court. As Kruh and Grisso (2009) discuss, there are generally three alternative approaches offered: a lower bar, an adjusted bar, or a flexible bar. Essentially, applying *Dusky* under a lower bar holds juveniles to the same abilities required for adults, but at a lower level. Under an adjusted bar, only the basic understanding and communication abilities are considered necessary, and the more complex appreciation and decision-making abilities are not considered necessary; under a flexible bar, the level of competence needed is considered on the basis of the demands of the legal case and the seriousness of the possible penalties faced. There are benefits and drawbacks to each approach, and a consensus has yet to be reached on whether one of these approaches may be best or whether juveniles do indeed need to be held to the same level of competence required for adults (Kruh & Grisso, 2009).

Review of the Literature on Incompetence in Young Offenders

Beyond level of impairment, the types of impairment that are considered acceptable causes of deficits in competence also vary across jurisdictions. Most states specify that deficits in competence must be the result of a mental illness or deficits in cognitive functioning, as it is most often the case that incompetence in adults stems from impairments related to symptoms of a psychotic disorder or the presence of very low intellectual functioning, such as in those diagnosed with an Intellectual Disability (Kruh & Grisso, 2009; Melton et al., 2007). While it is the case that juveniles with serious cognitive deficits or severe mental illness are more likely to be found incompetent, the sources of deficits in young offenders often go beyond these two factors. In fact, research has identified a number of correlates of incompetence for youth, and they tend to look quite different from those seen in adults. The factors most commonly identified as being relevant to juvenile competence include age, cognitive functioning, mental illness, and developmental immaturity; many states have begun to adopt statutes that address the factors that are specifically relevant to juvenile competence (Kruh & Grisso, 2009).

Age

In the studies that have explored the correlates of incompetence in juvenile offenders, the most common and consistent finding is that younger defendants are more likely to show impairments in competence than are those who are older (Grisso, 2013; Kruh & Grisso, 2009). While studies include a variety of age ranges and measure competence in varying ways, it is generally accepted that youth under the age of 14 pose a high risk of incompetence, those in mid-adolescence ages 14 to 15 are at a heightened risk for impairments, and those who are 16 or older are more likely to function at a level similar to adults and therefore pose a lower risk of deficits (Grisso, 2013; Grisso et al., 2003; Kruh & Grisso, 2009). While looking at age provides a good starting point for determining one's overall risk of incompetence, focusing on age alone is not likely to be helpful as research has demonstrated that other factors, such as cognitive functioning, academic achievement, mental illness, and immature development, are likely to play a role in the relation between age and incompetence (LaVelle Ficke, Hart, & Deardorff, 2006; Grisso et al., 2003; Viljoen & Roesch, 2005; Warren, Aaron, Ryan, Chauhan, & DuVal, 2003).

Cognitive Functioning

As is the case for adult offenders, juveniles who have significant deficits in cognitive functioning are likely to show deficits in competence abilities.

Specifically, juveniles diagnosed with Intellectual Disability are likely to show deficits in competence, and correlations between low intelligence and low scores on competence measures are a consistent finding in the literature (Colwell, Cruise, Guy, McCoy, Fernandez, & Ross, 2005; Grisso et al., 2003; Kivisto, Moore, Fite, & Seidner, 2011; Kruh, Sullivan, Ellis, Lexcen, & McClellan, 2006; LaVelle Ficke et al., 2006; Viljoen & Roesch, 2005). However, recent research has moved beyond looking at overall IQ and toward identifying particular aspects of cognition that are most important to competence. Thus far, studies have shown links between competence and lower scores of tests of verbal abilities and attention (Viljoen & Roesch, 2005). Beyond these findings, there is also mounting evidence that young age and deficits in cognitive functioning interact in a way that those who are younger and who also have lower intelligence are likely to be at particularly high risk for deficits in competence (Grisso et al., 2003; LaVelle Ficke et al., 2006; Viljoen & Roesch, 2005).

Mental Illness

Far less consistent results have been found when it comes to investigations of the relations between various mental disorders and deficits in competence. While most studies have shown that, like adults, juveniles diagnosed with psychotic disorders are likely to be found incompetent (Cowden & McKee, 1995; Kruh et al., 2006), the findings for other diagnoses have been far less consistent. For instance, there is evidence both for (Viljoen, Klaver & Roesch, 2005) and against (Kruh et al., 2006) the relation between a diagnosis of ADHD and incompetence. Inconsistent findings have also surfaced for mood, anxiety, and substance use disorders, and to further complicate the matter, variation is often found across different competency measures and across different aspects of competence (i.e., understanding versus decision-making abilities; Baerger, Griffin, Lyons & Simmons, 2003; Grisso et al., 2003; Kruh et al., 2006; Warren et al., 2003). Because of this lack of clarity, forensic evaluators must attend carefully to the presence of symptoms of mental illness and the possible influence on competence abilities.

Developmental Immaturity

Perhaps the most complex and least understood factor relevant to juvenile competence is that of developmental immaturity. While adults are presumed to have the capacity for competence unless some debilitating impairment is present (i.e., mental illness or cognitive deficit), the same is not necessarily true for juveniles. Because young offenders are still maturing, it may be the case that they have not yet achieved a level of functioning in terms of cognition or social and emotional skills that allows them to possess the abilities necessary for competence (Grisso, 2005b). In these cases, a juvenile may be deficient in competence abilities, not due to the presence of mental illness or some other specific impairment, but instead due to the incomplete development of the abilities needed to understand, appreciate, or reason in the context of the legal setting. In such cases, the juvenile would indeed appear incompetent but would be so in the absence of some specific impairment short of a simple lack of development.

The courts have struggled with this issue, and many jurisdictions have begun to make statutory changes to directly address the lack of clarity. Some have specifically noted that incompetence can be due to "age or developmental immaturity" (i.e., Georgia, Idaho, Maine, Maryland, Vermont), while others have specifically rejected this notion and hold that one cannot be found incompetent without an identifiable impairment that goes beyond a simple lack of development (i.e., Arizona, Connecticut, Delaware, Montana, Virginia; Szymanski, 2013). This leaves the role of developmental immaturity in competency evaluations rather unclear. To further complicate the matter, both the courts and forensic evaluators alike have struggled to find a consistent definition or conceptualization of immaturity as it relates to competence (Grisso, 2005b; Ryba, Cooper & Zapf, 2003a). Many aspects of development may be relevant to consider in terms of deficits in competence, but to simply state that a young offender is immature and, therefore, incompetent would be far too general an opinion to offer the courts (Kruh & Grisso, 2009). Therefore, it is important for evaluators to be clear on what aspect(s) of development are in question (i.e., cognitive, biological, psychosocial; Borum & Grisso, 2007). Further, evaluators should indicate that a young offender has incomplete or delayed development in some area, while being clear about the comparisons implied herein ("incomplete" is generally in comparison to adults; "delayed" is generally in comparison to same-aged peers; Kruh & Grisso, 2009). Finally, it is important to note the concept of maturity goes beyond one's chronological age and can vary greatly across different domains.

Other Factors

A host of other factors have been studied to determine the relevance of each to deficits in competence, and most have shown little influence. For instance, it appears prior experience with the legal system, race and minority status, socioeconomic status, gender, and the nature of the charges all have little to no relation with competency status (see Grisso & Kruh, 2009, for a more detailed summary of these findings).

Best Practices in JCST Evaluations

With the variation in legal definitions and the potential sources of deficits underlying incompetence being much broader for juveniles than adults, conducting evaluations of competence to stand trial with juvenile offenders is more complex. First, due to the absence of a nationwide standard for JCST, it is essential for an evaluator to be familiar with the statutes governing the jurisdiction in which one is practicing. Knowledge of local law is best gained via contact with psychological and legal practitioners in one's area of practice. Second, JCST evaluations require a unique set of skills, and an evaluator should be familiar with issues pertinent to conducting good competency evaluations in general as well as issues related specifically to child and adolescent development. Fortunately, there are a number of recent publications available to forensic evaluators to aid in gaining an understanding of best practices in JCST evaluations. In the highly practical *Best Practices in Forensic Mental Health Assessment* series, Kruh and Grisso (2009) have written a book entitled *Evaluations of Juveniles' Competence to Stand Trial*. This text provides an in-depth look at the issues discussed above while also providing detailed guidance on the methods and procedures involved in conducting these evaluations. Additionally, Grisso (2013) recently published a revised edition of his groundbreaking text *Forensic Evaluation of Juveniles* in which he devotes a chapter to JCST evaluations. Finally, as will be discussed in more detail below, Grisso (2005a, 2005b) has also published guides for legal professionals and forensic evaluators who deal with issues of juvenile competence, the latter of which contains a detailed interview guide that practitioners can use to structure competence interviews to ensure consideration of the information most important in competency determinations. All of these sources should be required readings for anyone conducting JCST evaluations.

Conceptualization of the Evaluation

The primary goal of conducting a JCST evaluation is to provide the courts with information about the present functioning of the offender in the context of how his or her functioning may or may not impede the ability to be an active participant in the defense. Grisso (2005b, 2013) summarizes his five-part conceptualization of the considerations necessary to make such a determination. The first main task of the evaluation is to describe the youth's functioning in terms of the abilities necessary for standing trial. This description of functional abilities is typically focused on the aspects of functioning delineated in the *Dusky* standard, but may differ across jurisdictions depending on how competence is defined. While alternate approaches exist, the most commonly accepted conceptualization of *Dusky* entails a consideration of one's ability to understand (i.e., have a basic knowledge of the legal process, proceedings, and key players involved), appreciate (have the ability to grasp the personal relevance of the legal situation), and reason (have the ability to apply one's understanding to the legal situation and to make rational decisions based on the information available; Grisso, 2013). Within these areas, one's ability to work effectively with his or her defense attorney is considered, as is the ability to participate in the courtroom proceedings (Grisso, 2013). Therefore, it is of utmost importance that an evaluator consider these aspects of functioning and present a clear description of the youth's abilities as they relate to each.

Beyond describing the functional abilities related to competence, the evaluator must also make a connection between any deficiencies in these abilities and the possible causes (Grisso, 2005b, 2013). Therefore, the evaluation must include an investigation into potential problems areas that can explain any deficits identified. For juveniles, problems may stem from the presence of any of the types of impairment described previously or from incomplete development in some important area. Once this link is established, the third important objective is to explain the interactions between the deficits in competence abilities and the demands of the legal proceedings the individual will face. This approach involves a highly individualized approach to considering competence. For each case, the demands of the legal case must be considered and any deficits in the abilities identified must be considered in light of these demands. It may be that two youth with similar levels of functioning and similar levels of deficits may be seen differently in terms of competence, if one faces a much more complex legal case that will involve important decision making or a higher level of participation at trial (Grisso, 2013). Once deficiencies have been described, underlying causes for the deficiencies have been specified, and a connection between the deficits and demands of the legal situation have been identified, the last two objectives for the evaluation are making a determination about competence and, if incompetence is likely, making recommendations for remediation of the deficits noted. Using this five-step approach to conceptualize the nature of the evaluation is an excellent way to keep the evaluation process on target and to ensure the information gathered and decisions made are done so with the legal standard and needs of the court as the primary focus (Kruh & Grisso, 2009).

Evaluation Procedures

While the objectives of the JCST evaluation are rather unique, the procedures involved in gathering clinical data are similar to those in any clinical forensic evaluation. Generally, the process begins with the receipt of the referral either from the court or from an attorney, ex parte. While there are some differences in the outcomes of the evaluation process that depend on the referral source (see Kruh & Grisso, 2009, for a description of these issues), the first step after receiving a referral is to contact the defense attorney to clarify the nature of the referral question, to understand any procedural issues that are relevant to the case, and to enlist help in obtaining any important records or reports (Grisso, 2005b, 2013). In *Evaluating Juveniles' Adjudicative Compe-tence: A Guide for Clinical Practice*, Grisso (2005b) includes the Attorney CST Questionnaire, a concise two-page form that asks questions that help clarify the nature of the referral question. This form can be quickly and easily com-pleted by the attorney and can be a very useful source of information relevant to the reasons for referral as well as the demands of the legal proceedings the defendant is expected to face.

It is often the case in adult competency evaluations that the records review will be quite limited and focused primarily on existing mental health records; however, because JCST deficits may stem from a wider range of impairments than is typical for adults, JCST evaluations often require a review of school, court, social services, medical, and mental health records (Grisso, 2005b; Kruh & Grisso, 2009). Therefore, it is important to obtain and review any potentially relevant sources of information prior to conducting any in-person interviews. Having this information beforehand will aid forensic evaluators in determining what parties will need to be interviewed and what, if any, testing may be to be conducted with the offender. While it may be the case in other types of evaluations that an interviewer may wish to "go in blind" and inter-view the client without having prior access to information about the client, this is not advised in JCST evaluations. In fact, it is quite necessary to understand as much as possible about the child or adolescent and the specific legal case at hand so that the interview questions can be tailored to potential deficits and questions directly relevant to the legal case can be asked.

Interviews with the youth and any primary caretakers will be important in order to clarify and elaborate on information obtained from the records review as well as to gather information specific to the identification of com-petence deficits. Many of the tasks in these interviews mirror those in any clinical evaluation, such as reviewing important historical information (i.e., medical, mental health, family, social, educational, legal, etc.) and inquiring about one's current mental status and clinical functioning. However, addi-tional interview tasks are very specific to the forensic question and include a review of the current legal issue, questioning about competence abilities, and explorations of how any deficits seen in this line of questioning can be explained by the present functioning (Grisso, 2005b; 2013; Kruh & Grisso, 2009). It may also be necessary to interview the youth on more than one occasion. This is typically the case when one's understanding is questionable and attempts to educate the youth are made. In these cases, it is best practice to follow up at some point in time later to determine whether the efforts to improve one's understanding are lasting or not (Grisso, 2005b). Oftentimes, it is helpful to use structured interviews or formal psychological testing to supplement the data obtained from the records and interviews; however, the usefulness of psychological testing will vary greatly from one evaluation to the next and should be considered a potential, but not required, aspect of JCST evaluations (Kruh & Grisso, 2009).

Psychological Testing

There are generally two reasons to use psychological testing in JCST evaluations: one is to clarify whether there are deficits in competence abilities, and the other is to determine the nature of the underlying cause of such deficits. In the case of identifying deficits in competence abilities, CST-specific instruments can be useful, and a number are available to forensic evaluators, although each has its benefits and drawbacks. Since the 1960s, over a dozen instruments have been developed for use in competency evaluations (Grisso, 2003; Kruh & Grisso, 2009). These instruments vary in terms of both structure and data produced. Thus, the selection of a particular instrument should consider the appropriateness of the tool for the particular client (Kruh & Grisso, 2009). Most importantly, none of these instruments were developed for use with juveniles and, while some studies have provided preliminary support for the use of some tests with young offenders (Viljoen, Slaney, & Grisso, 2009; Viljoen, Vincent & Roesch, 2006), no formal measures have juvenile-specific norms available (Grisso, 2013).

In fact, the only tool that has been developed specifically for use in JCST evaluations is the Juvenile Adjudicative Competence Interview (JACI; Grisso, 2005b). This semistructured interview guide includes items that mirror the abilities identified in *Dusky* as important to competence and provides standardized questions applicable to most juveniles. It allows for flexibility in what information is relevant to a particular case, includes opportunities for education on relevant issues with a means for following up on educational efforts at a later interview, and aids the examiner in using a developmental approach to considerations of competence (Grisso, 2005b, 2013; Kruh & Grisso, 2009). The JACI is not a scored instrument, nor does it allow for any normative comparisons. For an extensive review of the strengths and weaknesses of all of the CST instruments, see Grisso (2003) or Kruh and Grisso (2009).

General psychological testing can also be useful in JCST evaluations in that these instruments can help to clarify the nature of any aspects of functioning that may underlie deficits in competence abilities. Because the deficits that may affect juveniles' functioning can vary widely, the types of tests that may be informative also vary (Grisso, 2005b, 2013). Prior surveys and reviews of test use indicate practitioners rely on an array of tests in their JCST evaluations; the most commonly used include intelligence tests, achievement tests, personality tests, clinical inventories, neuropsychological tests, behavior checklists and response style instruments (Kruh & Grisso, 2009; Ryba, Cooper & Zapf, 2003b). While this list of tests is extensive, it is important to note that the goal of a JCST evaluation is not to include an extensive battery of psychological tests in order to rule out any and all possible psychological issues but instead to limit testing to those instruments needed to clarify the nature and extent of those deficits indicated via data gleaned from records and interviews.

Forming and Presenting an Opinion to the Courts

After all data for the evaluation are collected, the evaluator must formulate an opinion and communicate the evaluation results to the court in the form of a report and, possibly, in-person testimony. It is often most useful to structure the report according to the following sections: summary of the referral issue, method and process of the evaluation, summary of developmental and clinical history, summary of current clinical status and results of psychological testing, summary of competence abilities, and summary of interpretations and opinions for the courts. Alternative formats and methods for presenting data are described in the various texts available (Grisso, 2005b, 2013; Kruh &Grisso, 2009); however, the nature of the information included remains generally the same across all approaches. Essentially, the examiner should elucidate the nature of the referral, provide all information about the youth that is relevant to the referral, provide a contextual understanding of the nature of any deficits in competence as well as the underlying causes of such deficits and the connection between the deficits and the demands of the case, and provide an opinion regarding competence and/or remediation, as appropriate. In preparing a report for the court, examiners should be aware of issues related to offering ultimate opinions, as jurisdictions vary as to whether judges expect forensic evaluators to offer opinions on the legal question or limit their input to the clinical issue (Kruh & Grisso, 2009). Further, forensic evaluators should be aware of whether or not a flexible opinion approach is considered acceptable in their jurisdiction. In a flexible opinion, the examiner can take a contextual approach a step further and offer an "if this, then that" approach to the opinion (Zapf & Roesch, 2009). For instance, it may be that a juvenile appears to possess the abilities necessary for competence because the demands of the case are relatively low; however, should the demands of the case increase and require more of the defendant in a way that may go beyond his or her capacities, competence would then become unlikely. A flexible opinion gives the court the option to proceed as long as the demands of the case remain low. Again, jurisdictions vary in the acceptability of this approach to formulating and communicating opinions. Finally, on the more practical side, all reports should be written in clear, jargon-free language and should be free from pejorative information and opinions that are not firmly grounded in data obtained during the evaluation process (Kruh & Grisso, 2009).

Case Vignette

The following information is drawn from a JCST report. All names and identifying information have been changed, and some details have been altered to aid in the clarity of the information presented.

Reason for Referral

Joe was a 13-year-old male who is currently on a secure hold at the Residential Treatment Unit of County Hospital. He faced juvenile court charges of breaking and entering and larceny that stemmed from an incident in which Joe and another youth were arrested for being found on school grounds after hours and in possession of school property. Mr. White, a public defender, was assigned to Joe's case at arraignment. After their initial meeting Mr. White became concerned about Joe's competence to stand trial due to Joe's confusion over some of the legal issues discussed during that meeting. Juvenile Court Judge Black ordered the present evaluation, which was then conducted through the County Juvenile Court Services Program.

Method and Process of the Evaluation

The evaluation process included the following interviews: two interviews with Joe spaced apart by one week (interview 1 lasting 2 hours, interview 2 last 40 minutes) and brief in-person interviews with nursing and correctional staff at the hospital. Phone interviews were conducted with (a) Joe's attorney, Mr. White; (b) the ADA assigned to the case, Ms. Grey; (c) Joe's school guidance counselor, Ms, Scarlet; and (d) a social worker who is assigned to work with Joe's family, Ms. Green. In addition, the defense attorney, Mr. White, provided copies of relevant records, including the police report, court intake notes, psychological testing from County Middle School (conducted 6 months prior), and a summary report from the Department of Social Services (DSS). No contact was made with Joe's mother, Ms. Peach, as she was hospitalized and receiving mental health treatment.

Psychological Measures

Mr. White was given Grisso's Attorney CST Questionnaire to complete. The questionnaire revealed concerns over Joe's level of cognitive functioning. Specifically, Mr. White indicated that during his initial meeting with Joe, he attempted to explain some of the likely steps in the legal proceedings that Joe would face and, when he asked Joe to repeat back the information, Joe was unable to do

---

The case vignette has been redacted and all identifying information removed. It is not meant to serve as a forensic report. Any likeness to a case is purely coincidental.

so. Mr. White was unclear as to whether Joe was having trouble understanding the information, whether Joe was understanding but having trouble explaining things in his own words, or whether Joe was simply not actively engaged in the discussion. One of Mr. White's specific concerns was whether Joe would be able to understand the concept of a plea bargain, as he felt this was a likely possibility since this was the first time he had faced legal charges.

During the interviews with Joe, the Juvenile Adjudicative Competence Interview (JACI) was used to guide questions about Joe's understanding, appreciation, and reasoning regarding the legal process. The results of the JACI are incorporated into the description of Joe's competence abilities below.

Due to the recency of past intellectual and academic testing and the consistency of Joe's presentation with the results of those test results, no further cognitive measures were given during the present evaluation. In addition, current hospital records included screens for clinical issues, such as depression and psychosis; no further psychological testing was deemed necessary.

Summary of Relevant Background Information

The following information was drawn from the in-person and phone interviews conducted, as well as from the records reviewed.

According to Joe's report and the information received from the DSS worker, Ms. Green, Joe was primarily raised by his mother, Ms. Peach. He has had no contact with his biological father since shortly after his birth. The only father figure(s) Joe had in his life were the series of men with whom his mother had relationships, although Joe had not established a bond or parental-type relationship with any of these men. Joe's family life can be described as chaotic and unstable as his family had moved often, necessitating several changes in schools and often leading to frequent absences. Joe's mother had a long history of alcohol and drug use and mental illness, although the nature of her diagnoses remained unclear. According to the DSS report, Joe was recently removed from his mother's care due to charges of neglect that stemmed from her inability to provide consistent care and supervision for him. Ms. Peach was currently hospitalized and undergoing court-ordered treatment services.

Joe had been physically healthy and had no history of prior medical concerns. He had no history of mental health issues or treatment, although DSS records indicated that the family was referred for counseling three years ago. There was no evidence that any services were obtained, and Ms. Green reported the lack of follow-up care was due to inconsistency in the family's living arrangements, which made it difficult for DSS to locate the family. Interviews with hospital staff revealed that while Joe was thin and possibly a bit undernourished, he did not presently suffer from any physical ailments or disabilities and had been a quiet and cooperative patient since his arrival on the unit. Nursing staff reported that Joe was rather withdrawn and that he interacts minimally with other patients. Hospital records indicated screenings for depression and other mental health issues were conducted upon admission and revealed no significant areas of concern.

According to Joe's guidance counselor, Ms. Scarlet, as well as the school records provided by Mr. White, Joe was currently in 8th grade at County Middle School. Mr. Scarlet described Joe as "somewhat below average" academically and indicated that he did not have problems in school behaviorally, but instead kept to himself and rarely interacted with teachers or administrative staff. She noted that he appeared to spend time with a small circle of friends. He had not failed any grades previously, but his grades were consistently below average and his teachers indicated that frequent absences caused him to fall behind the level that is typical for his same-grade peers.

According to Ms. Scarlet and the school records reviewed, approximately six months ago, Joe received psychological testing within the school system to determine his current level of functioning academically and to rule out the possibility of learning disabilities or below average intellectual functioning. The results of this testing, revealed his overall intellectual functioning to be slightly below average (Full Scale IQ of 89, 95% confidence interval 83–96) with his verbal abilities substantially lower than his nonverbal abilities (Verbal IQ of 85, Performance IQ of 93).[1] Achievement testing indicated that his performance in reading and writing were somewhat below what would be expected for someone of his chronological age and grade level, and additional testing indicated Joe had particularly low scores in the area of expressive language abilities. While his test results revealed a weakness in language skills, particularly expressive language skills, the underlying source of the impairment appeared to be more likely explained by Joe's lack of engagement with the academic material than by a specific learning disorder. Prior to being hospitalized the school counselor was working with Joe to monitor his attendance and to attempt to increase his motivation to complete his work both in and out of school. Joe had also been receiving tutoring in language skills and was expected to receive follow-up testing during the next academic school year to continue to monitor his progress.

Socially, Joe was consistently described by others as fairly shy and withdrawn. Joe agreed with this assessment of his personality and noted that he preferred to only spend time with a few close friends and that he did not feel very comfortable around adults. The school counselor noted that it was her impression that Joe appeared to have a desire to make friends and that, at times, he tended to do whatever he thought his friends wanted him to do in order to be liked and accepted.

Joe reported having no prior arrests or legal charges and information from the ADA assigned to his case confirmed this report. Aside from his current admission, Joe had not received mental health services or been hospitalized for psychiatric reasons in the past. He admitted to experimenting with drugs (i.e., marijuana) and alcohol in the past, but he said that he did not use either on a regular basis, stating he had "no way to buy that stuff even if I wanted to."

Mental Status Examination

Joe was interviewed two times, one week apart, on the residential treatment unit of County Hospital. During both meetings, Joe was appropriately dressed and well groomed. He is of average height and weight and appears his stated age. He was cooperative during the interviews, but he spoke quietly and had poor eye contact, often looking down when answering questions and frequently responding, "I don't know." When given adequate time and encouragement, Joe was able to provide answers to many questions to which he initially replied, "I don't know," although he struggled to find words to express his thoughts and feelings. His vocabulary was limited for his age, and when faced with trying to explain something he found difficult, he tended to shut down and become withdrawn.

During the interviews, Joe displayed a fairly low level of energy and sat in his chair a bit slumped over. He displayed no signs of hyperactivity or overt distractibility, although he did get restless during the first interview and began rocking back and forth in his chair when discussing particularly sensitive topics, like his mother's recent hospitalization and being removed from her care by DSS. When asked to focus on a particular topic, Joe was able do so. When asked about his present concerns, he mostly focused on recent family events and concerns over what would happen with his legal case and his living situation should he be released from custody. Clinically, Joe displayed no symptoms of psychosis or thought disorders, and he was in touch with reality and appropriately oriented. He reported that he had felt sad often in the past and feels this way at present due to his legal situation, being held at the hospital, and being removed from his family home. He denied any suicidal ideation and had no thoughts of harming others.

Competency Abilities

The information in this section was drawn from the interviews with Joe, the results of the JACI, and from information received about Joe's legal case form his defense attorney, Mr. White, and from the ADA assigned to the case, Ms. Grey.

In terms of demonstrating an understanding and appreciation of the charges, possible penalties, and plea agreements, Joe was able to state the current charges against him, describe what those charges meant, and indicate that he could go "to juvie if they find me guilty." When asked about the seriousness of the charges, he indicated they were "kinda bad" but that "it's not like I killed someone or something." When asked to describe what happened at a trial, he struggled to find words to describe the process. At first, he replied "I don't know," but when asked more concrete questions, he was able to provide answers. For instance, when asked what he will do during the trial, he stated, "I sit in a chair by my lawyer and listen to him talk and argue with the other lawyer." When asked about what happens after the lawyers finish talking, he stated, "the judge tells you if you go to juvie or not." When asked about pleading guilty or not guilty, again he struggled to find the words to explain these concepts and frequently replied ,"I don't know," but when questioned more concretely or when offered yes/no or multiple choice type options, he was able to provide answers that indicated a simplistic, but accurate, understanding of these concepts. However, when asked about what a plea bargain was, even with simplistic and concrete questions, he was not able to demonstrate an understanding. This concept was explained to him during the first interview and then he was questioned about this topic again during the second meeting. At that time, he still replied, "I don't know" initially, but when asked direct questions or given multiple choices, he demonstrated a much better understanding of what a plea agreement entails. Joe was able to demonstrate an understanding of the range of possible penalties that may result if he is found guilty.

In terms of demonstrating an understanding and appreciation of the trial participants and their roles, Joe's performance was very similar to that described above related to the trial process. He consistently struggled to find the language to express his thoughts, but when questioned in a simplistic and concrete manner, he was able to show an adequate understanding of the roles of his defense attorney ("to help me get clear"), the district attorney ("to lock me up"), and the judge ("to keep the attorneys in line and tell me if I go home or not"). The judge's role in overseeing the trial, determining what evidence may be presented, and deciding the outcome of the case were explained to him during the first meeting and, when questioned about these facts during the second meeting, Joe was able to describe the judge's role, albeit in simplistic language.

In terms of his ability to assist counsel, Joe understood that his defense attorney was "on my side" and that it was good to talk with him about the case. When asked to recount the events surrounding the legal incident in question, Joe was able to give a superficial account of the case, but when questioned about details that were in the police report but not in Joe's account, he responded, "I don't know" and was unable to elaborate further. While Joe verbalized an understanding of his attorney's role in helping him to present case, Joe appeared reluctant to fully rely on or trust Mr. White.

In terms of his ability to make decisions about his legal case, Joe was able to grasp the nature of what it meant to plead guilty or not guilty and, after some education about what a plea agreement entailed, he was able to concretely express his understanding of that process as well. When given an example of someone taking a lesser penalty by agreeing to accept a guilty plea, Joe was able to explain why this might be a good option (i.e., "you get out of juvie and get to go home instead of having to maybe stay in there a long time"). In terms of Joe's decision making outside of the legal context, he appears very eager to please his friends but reluctant to engage with adults that he does not know well. This hesitance may prove challenging for his attorney until Joe develops some sense of familiarity and trust in him.

Clinical Summary and Opinion

Based on the data obtained, it was this evaluator's opinion that Joe appeared to possess the very minimum of capacities necessary to be considered competent to stand trial in juvenile court and that because Joe's competence was right on the border, he was someone for whom a functional assessment of competence abilities was appropriate. A functional assessment means that the specifics of his case and the demands for his involvement in the legal proceedings must be considered when determining his competency to proceed. More specifically, if the demands of Joe's case remained relatively low and the court was willing to work with Joe to ensure his understanding and engagement throughout the trial process, then Joe appeared competent to proceed; however, if the demands of his case become greater than expected, Joe's capacities would very likely be exceeded, and he would not be able to actively participate and/or assist the defense attorney in the case.

In terms of Joe's legal situation, he was facing relatively serious charges, but his defense attorney had indicated that, if the case goes to trial, Joe's in-person testimony would not be required and that instead, Joe would primarily be required to follow along with testimony and to provide information as his attorney prepares his defense. The attorney further expected that the court was willing to make concessions to aid Joe in his ability to follow along (i.e., allow the defense attorney additional time to explain complex terms, to check in to ensure Joe's understanding, etc.), and the ADA concurred with these expectations. If this was the case, Joe was likely to possess the abilities necessary to understand and assist in his defense. On the other hand, should the legal parties involved be unwilling or unable to make these concessions or should the complexity of Joe's participation at trial increase, it was likely the demands of the trial would exceed Joe's current capacities.

Overall, Joe demonstrated a simplistic, but accurate, understanding and appreciation of the trial process, the potential consequences of his trial, and the roles of the key legal players involved. While his understanding was limited at times, he was able to gain a greater understanding after an explanation was provided, and he was able to maintain that knowledge when questioned again a week later. Therefore, while Joe's understanding of legal issues was minimal, he demonstrated the capacity to learn and retain information about the legal process. Joe's difficulties demonstrating his knowledge of the legal issues likely stemmed from his below average expressive language skills (as documented in the school testing), as such difficulties often caused trouble in formulating verbal responses. For Joe, these limitations likely impeded his ability to explain and convey his understanding of court information, and it would likely take him longer and require more effort than is typical to find the language necessary to explain his thoughts. However, when given time and assistance, Joe was able to express his thoughts adequately.

Beyond these issues, Joe's abilities to assist his attorney and make decisions about his case were intact, but tentative as well. Joe was able to describe events surrounding his case and to work with his attorney; however, his limited trust and tendency to answer "I don't know" when uncomfortable or struggling for language put him at risk. Should his attorney be able to work closely with Joe to develop a good working relationship and provide time and opportunity for Joe to formulate answers beyond Joe's default "I don't know" response, then Joe's ability to assist his defense counsel and provide input in important decision making would likely to be adequate.

The fragility of Joe's understanding and appreciation of the trial process and the limitations in his ability to assist counsel appear to be directly related to the documented impairments in expressive language skills and to his hesitancy to trust unfamiliar adults. Both issues are clearly documented in the prior academic testing and throughout interviews with those most familiar with Joe. His language skills and hesitance to trust unfamiliar adults certainly make Joe's participation at trial tentative. However, information from interviews with others as well as from the present interviews indicated that, with patience, careful formulation of questions, and a slow pace of interactions, Joe does have the capacity to understand information presented to him and to develop his own responses to questions or inquiries presented to him. Further, given time and patience in working with Joe, it is likely his attorney can develop a working relationship with Joe that will be adequate for allowing Joe to work effectively to assist with his own defense.

While it is the opinion of this examiner that Joe possesses the minimal capacities necessary to stand trial in juvenile court, the potential effect of Joe's limitations regarding understanding the trial process was very important to consider. It is likely that Joe will be an active and able participant in the trial process if the judge and the attorneys (particularly Joe's defense attorney) are willing to slow the pace of information down to a level Joe can understand.

Further, Joe should be given enough information and time to formulate his responses and to make decisions. Should the nature of the trial become highly complex or require Joe to make complicated decisions or explanations, it is likely Joe will not be able to comply and will thereby be unable to actively participate in the trial process. Should the options for various pleas be presented in a manner that does not consider his limited vocabulary and should complex answers be expected in response, Joe is likely to have difficulties. Also, if the court determines that such alterations are not possible or that the necessity of making such alterations is too burdensome, Joe is most likely going to be unable to proceed to trial. In this case, remediation efforts might focus on strengthening his knowledge and understanding of court procedures as well as working with him to increase his ability to use verbal communication more effectively. However, the demands related to the provision of complex in-person testimony are likely to be unaffected by remediation efforts as Joe's expressive language difficulties are likely to be unaffected by educational efforts.

Common Pitfalls and Considerations

Conducting JCST evaluations is a complex endeavor, and while the above information is intended to give a thorough overview of the history and current state of practice in this area, reviewing a short chapter alone is obviously not nearly enough training to begin taking on cases of this nature. A review of the texts mentioned above combined with in-person training offered by one of the many forensic psychology professional organizations would be strongly advised, as would working with a professional experienced in the area to receive supervision on cases both in the beginning and whenever a particularly difficult case is undertaken. Further, whenever evaluations of children or adolescents are conducted, one must use extreme caution in formulating diagnoses and making conclusions due to the challenges that are inherent when communicating with young people about complex issues, as is always the case in JCST evaluations. The best protection against making poor judgements or harmful decisions in clinical work is good training and ongoing supervision.

With that said, there are difficulties inherent in all clinical forensic work and particularly with competency evaluations. For instance, it is always a struggle to know how much information is sufficient and how much is too much. The courts tend to prefer concise and direct reports, while forensic evaluators are often trained to include any and all possibly relevant information. Learning to balance these demands is important. In evaluations of JCST, a more thorough review of background information and records may be necessary than is typical for CST evaluations with adults. However, this does not mean that any and every detail from one's past is relevant and important to include. In addition, the desire to administer every possible test that may be relevant can be strong, but it is also unnecessary. While one should always conduct testing when it will reveal important information about the youth's present abilities as they relate to standing trial, it is not necessary to administer a full battery of tests merely to provide the court with as much information as possible. This is generally not favorable to judges and attorneys who wish to know the bottom line of whether the offender is competent or incompetent to proceed.

Finally, there are a few cautions to all who conduct forensic evaluations. As with other clinical forensic work, one must be cautious not to align with either the defense or prosecution and to always indicate accurately the level of certainty one has in the data that are included in a report. Any time an expert is hired by either the prosecution of the defense, the tendency to align is strong. The evaluator wants to please the person who has retained them as an expert, and our tendencies to be biased in our work is well documented in the literature (Murie, Boccaccini, Guarnera, Rufino, 2013). Therefore, all forensic evaluators are cautioned to be aware of this literature and to continually evaluate themselves and their work to minimize potential sources of bias. Along these lines, classic texts have advised evaluators to cross check information that is included in reports and, whenever possible, to only include information that can be corroborated by more than one source (Melton et al, 2007). Cross-checking one's work and ensuring accountability of the information included in all reports is a practice sure to improve the quality and accuracy of one's work and is strongly recommended.

Note

1. At the time of this evaluation, the WISC-III was used, which produced these scores rather than the four index scores one would see on the WISC-IV currently.

References

Baerger, D. R., Griffin, E. F., Lyons, J. S., & Simmons, R. (2003). Competency to stand trial in preadjudicated and petitioned juvenile defendants. *Journal of the American Academy of Psychiatry and the Law, 31*, 314–320.

Borum, R., & Grisso, T. (2007). Developmental considerations for forensic assessment in delinquency cases. In A. Goldstein (Ed.), *Forensic psychology: Emerging topics and expanding roles*. Hoboken, NJ: Wiley.

Colwell, L. H., Cruise, K. L., Guy, L. S., McCoy, W. K., Fernandez, K., & Ross, H. H. (2005). The influence of psychosocial maturity on male juvenile offenders' comprehension and understanding of the *Miranda* warning. *Journal of the American Academy of Psychiatry and the Law, 33*, 444–454.

Cowden, V. L., & McKee, G. R. (1995). Competency to stand trial in juvenile delinquency proceedings—Cognitive maturity and the attorney-client relationship. *Journal of Family Law, 33*, 629–660.

Dusky v. United States, 362 U.S. 402 (1960).

Grisso, T. (2003). *Evaluating competencies: Forensic assessments and instruments* (2nd ed.). New York, NY: Kluwer Academic/Plenum Press.

Grisso, T. (2005a). *Clinical evaluations for juveniles' competence to stand trial: A guide for legal professionals.* Sarasota, FL: Professional Resource Press.

Grisso, T. (2005b). *Evaluating juveniles' adjudicative competence: A guide for clinical practice.* Sarasota, FL: Professional Resource Press.

Grisso, T. (2013). *Forensic evaluation of juveniles* (2nd ed.). Sarasota, FL: Professional Resource Press.

Grisso, T., Steinberg, L., Woolard, J., Cauffman, E., Scott, E., Graham, S., Lexcen, F., Repucci, D., & Schwartz, R. (2003). Juveniles' competence to stand trial: A comparison of adolescents' and adults' capacities as trial defendants. *Law and Human Behavior, 27,* 333–363.

In re Gault, 387 U.S. 1 (1967).

Kent v. United States, 283 U.S. 541 (1966).

Kivisto, A. J., Moore, T. M., Fite, P. A., & Seidner, B. G. (2011). Future orientation andcompetence to stand trial: The fragility of competence. *Journal of the American Academy of Psychiatry and the Law, 39,* 316–326.

Kruh, I., & Grisso, T. (2009). *Evaluation of juveniles' competence to stand trial.* New York, NY: Oxford University Press.

Kruh, I. P., Sullivan, L., Ellis, M., Lexcen, F., & McClellan, J. (2006). Juvenile competence to stand trial: A historical and empirical analysis of a juvenile forensic evaluation service. The *International Journal of Forensic Mental Health, 5,* 109–123.

LaVelle Ficke, S., Hart, K. J., & Deardorff, P. A. (2006). The performance of incarcerated juveniles on the MacArthur Competence Assessment Tool-Criminal Adjudication. Journal of the *American Academy of Psychiatry and the Law, 34,* 360–373.

Melton, G., Petrila, J., Poythress, N., Slobogin, C., Lyons, J., & Otto, R. (2007). *Psychological evaluations for the courts* (3rd ed.). New York, NY: Guilford Press.

Murie, D. C., Boccaccini, M. T., Guarnera, L. A., & Rufino, K. A. (2013). Are forensic experts biased by the side that retained them? *Psychological Science, 24,* 1889–1897.

Ryba, N. L., Cooper, V. G., & Zapf, P. A. (2003a). Assessment of maturity in juvenile competency to stand trial evaluations: A survey of practitioners. *Journal of Forensic Psychology Practice, 3,* 23–45.

Ryba, N. L., Cooper, V. G., & Zapf, P. A. (2003b). Juvenile competence to stand trial evaluations: A survey of current practices and test usage among psychologists. *Professional Psychology: Research and Practice, 34,* 499–507.

Steinberg, L., & Schwartz, R. (2000). Developmental psychology goes to court. In T. Grisso & R. Schwartz (Eds.), *Youth on trial: A developmental perspective on juvenile justice* (pp. 9–31). Chicago, IL: University of Chicago Press.

Szymanski, L. A. (2013). *Juvenile competency procedures. Juvenile justice: Geography, policy, practice, statistics.* Pittsburg, PA: National Center for Juvenile Justice.

Viljoen, J. L., Klaver, J., & Roesch, R. (2005). Legal decisions of preadolescent and adolescent defendants: Predictors of confessions, pleas, communication with attorneys, and appeals. *Law and Human Behavior, 29,* 253–277.

Viljoen, J. L., & Roesch, R. (2005). Competence to waive interrogation rights and adjudicative competence in adolescent defendants: Cognitive development, attorney contact, and psychological symptoms. *Law and Human Behavior, 29,* 723–742.

Viljoen, J. L., Slaney, K. L., & Grisso, T. (2009). The use of the MacCAT-CA with adolescents: An item response theory investigation of age-related measurement bias. *Law and Human Behavior, 33,* 283–297.

Viljoen, J. L., Vincent, G. M., & Roesch, R. (2006). Assessing adolescent defendant's adjudicative competence: Interrater reliability and factor structure of the Fitness Interview Test-Revised. *Criminal Justice and Behavior, 33,* 467–487.

Warren, J. I., Aaron, J., Ryan, E., Chauhan, P., & DuVal, J. (2003). Correlates of adjudicative competence among psychiatrically impaired juvenile offenders. *Journal of the American Academy of Psychiatry and the Law, 31,* 299–309.

Zapf, P. A., & Roesch, R. (2009). *Evaluation of competence to stand trial.* New York, NY: Oxford University Press.

15

Juvenile Miranda Waiver: A Naïve Teenager, Neurodevelopmental Disorder, and the "Interested Adult"

Joseph J. Begany

[T]he greatest care must be taken to assure that [a minor's] admission was voluntary, in the sense that it was not coerced or suggested, but also that it was not the product of ignorance of rights or of adolescent fantasy, fright or despair.

—Justice Abraham Fortas, Associate Justice to the U.S. Supreme Court, 1965–1969, *In Re Gault*, 387 U.S. 1 (1967)

Relevant Case Law

In 1967, the U.S. Supreme Court decided that 15-year-old Gerald Gault had not been afforded procedural due process rights when:

- Without prior written notice to him or his parents informing them of the issue(s) to which they must attend, the Gila County Sheriff went to Gerald's home and took Gerald into custody while his parents were at work;
- During the subsequent custodial interrogation, Gerald made incriminating statements as to his alleged involvement in the incident[1] for which he had been detained. Gerald made the statements in the juvenile court judge's chambers in the presence of the judge, his parents, and a probation officer;
- The alleged victim was not present and Gerald was not afforded the protection of defense counsel;
- There was no recording or transcript of the hearing, and at the time, Arizona state law prohibited appellate review in juvenile court cases.

The 14th amendment of the U.S. Constitution states that "No state shall . . . deprive any person of life, liberty, or property, without due process of law; nor deny to any person within its jurisdiction the equal protection of the laws." In 1966, the U.S. Supreme Court ruled in the landmark case of *Miranda v. Arizona* that whenever the police take a person into their custody, they must inform him or her of their right against making self-incriminating statements.

The test for determining whether a suspect has effectively waived his rights under *Miranda* has been stated as follows: "First, the relinquishment of the right must have been voluntary in the sense that it was the product of a free and deliberate choice rather than intimidation, coercion, or deception. Second, the waiver must have been made with a full awareness of both the nature of the right being abandoned and the consequences of the decision to abandon it." *Moran v. Burbine,* 475 U.S. 412, 421 (1986).

The question of how the issue of competence to waive Miranda rights applies to a juvenile delinquency proceeding in Massachusetts is not fully clear from the statutes, and this issue has never been the subject of appellate review.

The Interested Adult

In 1974, the Pennsylvania Supreme Court decided that juvenile defendants were unable to comprehend adequately their Miranda rights without the benefit of consultation from an "interested adult." This decision would establish one of the foundational criteria of the per se approach to determining the validity of a juvenile's waiver of their Miranda rights. The court held that juveniles undergoing custodial interrogation must have the opportunity to consult with an interested adult who himself or herself has been informed of the juvenile's rights, as well as of the consequences of waiving those rights. According to Grisso (1980), courts that adhere to the "interested adult" standard must decide whether the adult who was present during the juvenile's interrogation was "genuinely concerned with the juvenile's welfare. They must also determine whether the adult was informed of the juvenile's rights, whether the adult understood those rights, whether the child and the adult had an adequate opportunity to confer in private and whether the conference was meaningful" (p. 1142).

Review of the Literature

The question of whether a child or adolescent who has been taken into police custody and who subsequently chose to participate in a police interrogation did so knowingly and voluntarily can be thought of as a psycholegal problem defined by the nexus between the impact of a child's mental health functioning, broadly speaking, and the legal requirements for producing a valid juvenile Miranda waiver. In considering the mental health functioning relevant to the waiver, the evaluating clinician must be attentive to variables of mental functioning such as what the child's developmental stage is, whether the child suffers from a psychiatric illness, and whether the child suffers from a neuro-developmental (e.g., Communication Disorder) or acquired condition (e.g., Traumatic Brain Injury) that might reduce the child's ability to produce a valid Miranda waiver.

The Question of Developmental Immaturity

There is a growing body of literature aimed at explicating the hypothesized relationship between child and adolescent development and the competence to waive Miranda protections. For instance, in his two 1980 studies of juveniles' appreciation of Miranda rights, Grisso (1980) identified two groups of accused juveniles under 17 years of age who were unable to demonstrate understanding of their Miranda rights with even minimal adequacy: one group of juveniles younger than 15 (i.e., 11–15) and a second group of 15- and 16-year-olds with Full Scale IQ scores equal to or less than 80 demonstrated deficits in understanding their Miranda rights to the extent that "their waivers cannot be considered meaningful" (p. 1161).

There appears to be a significant disparity between the percentages of juvenile defendants who waive their Miranda rights, compared with adult defendants (Rogers et al., 2008). In fact, Rogers et al. (2005) found that 75% of the 11 to 15-year-old juvenile participants in their study waived their Miranda rights while nearly 90% of all juveniles under 17 years of age waive their Miranda rights during interrogation (Feld, 2006; Grisso et al., 1978). This contrasts with only about 20% (Rogers et al., 2005) to 60% (Redlich et al., 2004) of accused individuals aged 17 years and older waiving their rights to silence and legal representation during interrogation.

Comprehensibility of Miranda Language

Researchers focused on the comprehensibility of juvenile Miranda warnings have been finding a remarkable lack of uniformity across U.S. jurisdictions. For instance, Rogers et al. (2008) analyzed 122 juvenile Miranda warnings from across the United States according to the number of words that comprised the warnings, reading level required to comprehend the vocabulary and syntax, and content. They found that juvenile Miranda warnings seem to be even more variable than general Miranda warnings. According to Rogers, the juvenile warnings

> ranged from 52 to 526 words; inclusion of Miranda waivers and other material substantially increased these numbers (64–1,020 words). Flesch-Kincaid

reading estimates varied dramatically from Grade 2.2 to post-college. Differences in content included such critical issues as (a) right to parent/guardian input, (b) specification of free legal services for indigent defendants, and (c) statements of right to counsel in conditional terms.

Mental Health Issues, Neurodevelopmental Disorders, and Miranda Comprehension

Researchers estimate that about 30% to 70% of children and teenagers before juvenile courts on delinquency matters suffer from some kind of mental disorder. The most common conditions seen in populations of juvenile court-involved youth include ADHD, Learning Disorders, Communication Disorders, Depression, Anxiety and Disruptive Behavior Disorders. Increasingly, children and teens suffering from Autism Spectrum Disorders are also coming before juvenile courts for a range of offenses including sexual and physically violent offenses (Sondenaa et al., 2014; Salseda, 2011).

Neurodevelopmental disorders are disorders that stem from prenatal and/or postnatal disruption in the development of the brain or central nervous system. There is a strong heritability factor associated with neurodevelopmental disorders, but they can also be acquired via some kind of neurological insult such as prenatal alcohol and/or drug exposure or lead exposure/poisoning in early childhood. The disruption(s) can result in a wide variety of functional impairments including deficits in intellectual abilities, attention, learning, memory, executive functions, motor functions, social cognition and self-regulation, which, in turn, can lead to a wide variety of problems meeting the demands of everyday life, such as social, academic, and family-based demands. Common neurodevelopmental disorders include the different forms of Attention Deficit Hyperactivity Disorder (ADHD), Communication Disorders, Autism Spectrum Disorders (ASD), and Intellectual Disabilities (ID).

While there is a great deal of overlap in functional impairments across neurodevelopmental conditions, many of these conditions are characterized by the prominence of certain specific functional impairments among a range of often less prominent (but nonetheless problematic) neurodevelopmental deficits. For instance, impaired attention is common to most neurodevelopmental conditions, but particularly so with ADHD. Social skills deficits can be features of a variety of neurodevelopmental disorders, but social communication and social interaction deficits along with repetitive behaviors and restricted interests (Troyb et al., 2010, in Fein, 2011; Hill and Frith, 2003) are the hallmark characteristic of Autism Spectrum Disorders. Communication Disorders include expressive and receptive language deficits. Individuals suffering with expressive language impairments struggle to use written and spoken language to convey their thoughts and feelings and to engage in fluent discourse. Individuals struggling with receptive language problems have deficits in their ability to understand spoken language. Expressive and receptive language deficits often co-occur, and these deficits can result in substantial social, academic, and vocational deficits.

Intellectual and neuropsychological deficits can bear substantially on juveniles' understanding of their Miranda rights (Grisso, 1980; Nestor et al., 1999; Viljoen & Roesch, 2005) and on their ability to consider the long-term consequences of waiving those rights during interrogation. The following vignette illustrates some of the ways in which the impairing action of a communication disorder, of ADHD, and of the pressures of an adult [i.e., Edgar's mother) whose status as a genuinely "interested adult," from a statutory standpoint, is arguable, converge to produce a Miranda waiver of highly questionable validity.

Best Practices

The evaluation of a juvenile Miranda waiver is called for when a juvenile taken into police custody has chosen to waive his or her right to counsel and has then made inculpatory statements to the police during the custodial interrogation. Defense attorneys who are attentive to the standards of a valid juvenile Miranda waiver (e.g., an "interested adult" must be present during the waiver and interrogation, there must be an appreciation for the potential legal consequences of the waiver and subsequent statements) will seek an evaluation of the validity of their juvenile client's decision to waive the right to counsel and to then provide the police with evidence, often in the form of inculpatory statements, as to their involvement in an unlawful act. As previously noted in this chapter, the test for determining whether a Miranda waiver was valid was stated as follows in *Moran v. Burbine*, 475 U.S. 412, 421 (1986):

> First, the relinquishment of the right must have been voluntary in the sense that it was the product of a free and deliberate choice rather than intimidation, coercion, or deception. Second, the waiver must have been made with a full awareness of both the nature of the right being abandoned and the consequences of the decision to abandon it. (*Moran v. Burbine*, 475 U.S. 412, 421, 1986)

The evaluation of the validity of a juvenile's Miranda waiver should focus building a database on which to rest a forensic opinion as to whether the juvenile's waiver was voluntary and knowing: that is, that the child chose freely to waiver his or her rights, and that he or she did so with adequate appreciation of the rights themselves, as well as of the potential legal (e.g., a guilty finding in the court) and social (e.g., loss of liberty, exclusion from mainstream school setting) consequences of the inculpatory statements that he or she made during a custodial interrogation. Such an evaluation can be used specifically to assist the trier of fact in determining whether the juvenile's waiver was valid and whether the juvenile's statements made subsequent to the waiver, should be allowed as evidence.

Best practices dictate that the evaluator in a juvenile Miranda waiver case develop a well-rounded database with data gathered from multiple sources in order to adequately address the psycholegal question as to whether psychological factors interfered with a child's ability to knowingly and voluntarily waive their Miranda rights. Accessing multiple sources of information is standard practice in forensic assessment, and it is particularly important in the forensic evaluation of children (G. Koocher in Sparta & Koocher, 2006). When evaluating a child as to the validity of their Miranda waiver, sources should include at least one interview of the child focused on explicating their mental status, current substance abuse, school performance, social milieu, and experience with the legal system. Sources should also include interviews with educational and mental health providers, as well as caregivers, and a review of relevant educational and mental health records. Assessing a child's understanding and appreciation of their Miranda rights and of waiving those rights could be included in the first interview or reserved for a second meeting. Grisso's Miranda Rights Comprehension Instruments (Grisso et al., 2012) is the most widely used assessment tool in juvenile Miranda waiver evaluations.

Finally, it is of critical importance that the evaluating clinician be familiar with the statutory requirements of a valid juvenile Miranda waiver. For instance, some jurisdictions rely on the totality of the circumstances approach to determining whether a child's Miranda waiver was valid, while other jurisdictions (including the jurisdiction from which the case vignette below originated) rely on the per se approach to determining the validity of a juvenile Miranda waiver. There is nothing less useful to a juvenile defendant, a juvenile defense attorney, and by extension, a juvenile court judge, than an evaluation that does not address the psycholegal question at hand according to the statutory requirements of that jurisdiction.

In addition to ensuring a level of familiarity with jurisdictional requirements of a valid juvenile Miranda waiver that will hold up under the competent cross examination, evaluating clinicians also need to consider several other factors before undertaking a given evaluation. Such factors include, but are certainly not limited to, a child's suggestibility during interrogation, the language in which he or she is most fluent, as well as the language of primary fluency of the interested adult present during the interrogation, the mental status of the interested adult at the time of interrogation, and the child's level of effort during the evaluation.

Case Vignette

Reason for Referral

Edgar was the 14-year-old Hispanic son of Ms. Vic, a single mother. Edgar's father had been incarcerated, since Edgar was a very little boy, in an out-of-state prison for attempted murder and drug-related offenses. At the time of the evaluation, Edgar lived with his mother, his older sister (16), older brother (15), and younger sister (8) in a neat, clean double-decker two-family house in a coastal urban setting. Edgar was a special education middle school student who recently began attending an alternative public school placement, after being transferred from a regular education middle school within the district, owing to the delinquency charges against him (see below). Before moving to the new school district, Edgar had been receiving special education support services for a long-standing and well-documented health disability (i.e., ADHD) and a Communication Disorder (i.e., Mixed Expressive-Receptive Language Disorder). However, the current school district changed his IEP eligibility because of a district psychologist's evaluation, which stated that Edgar struggled with an "underlying emotional disorder" per the findings of a poorly conducted psychological evaluation. At the time of the evaluation, he was prescribed and reportedly compliant with a long-acting stimulant medication that his primary care physician prescribed.

This was Edgar's first experience with the juvenile delinquency system. Edgar was before the juvenile court facing one count of indecent assault and battery on a child under 14 years of age. The charged stemmed from an incident that occurred in the winter of 2013 just after Edgar moved from out of state to his current coastal urban location. It was being alleged that during a recess period on the playground of the middle school, and at the prodding of two other male schoolmates, Edgar ran over to a 13-year year-old female peer who was talking with several friends. As he ran by her, he reached out his hand, grazed her vaginal area over her pants, and then ran off. Edgar's mother became aware of the incident from the school officials who immediately intervened, informing the police and suspending Edgar. School administrators informed Ms. Vic of the incident that afternoon. The victim's parents also filed a police complaint that afternoon. According to Edgar's defense attorney, Ms. Vic "marched Edgar down the police station the following morning and prevailed upon him to make statements about his alleged involvement in the incident." Ms. Vic stated to this evaluator that, as a recovering heroin addict steeped in the 12-step recovery program, she lived by "the rules of God" and insisted that "It's my job to make sure that my son does the right thing and tells the truth and owns up to what he did."

The case vignette has been redacted and all identifying information removed. It is not meant to serve as a forensic report. Any likeness to a case is purely coincidental.

Because of the alleged sexual assault on his female schoolmate, Edgar was facing not only the possibility of Department of Youth Services committed time as well as probation thereafter, he was also facing the specter of court court-ordered registration with the state's Sex Offender Registry Board (SORB), as a sex offender for up to 20 years if found guilty of the sexual assault charge. He would face restrictions on his proximity to other children his age and younger and on his living circumstances as well as those of his mother and siblings.

Edgar's juvenile defense attorney requested that a forensic evaluator assess Edgar in connection with the charges he was facing before the Juvenile Court. Specifically, she asked this evaluator to conduct an assessment of Edgar's abilities directly related to his competence to waive his Miranda rights owing to concerns that Edgar may not have knowingly and voluntarily waived those rights prior to the police interrogation. The defense attorney indicated that Edgar's mother "dragged him down to the police station to confess." She noted Edgar suffered from cognitive impairments for which he had been receiving special education services since early elementary school. Defense counsel expressed concern that Edgar's cognitive deficits, his young age, and his mother's undue pressure may have converged to interfere with his ability to competently waive his Miranda rights.

As with adult clients, it is necessary to gain consent for the juvenile client to participate in an evaluation. Therefore, it was necessary for the evaluator to explain the parameters of the evaluation to Edgar. However, this also requires the presence of the interested adult, as the mediator of the information and facilitator of the child's understanding of the conditions of the evaluation. To that end, at the outset of both of our meetings, the evaluator explained to Edgar and his mother that whatever was discussed or produced during testing could be shared with Edgar's defense attorney, and if she requested it, the evaluator could prepare a report and/or testify in court. It was further explained to them that Edgar was not required to answer the evaluator's questions and that he could refuse the interview and/or testing. The evaluator explained that if there were some questions he wished not to answer, he could decline to answer them and could end the meeting at any time.

In response to the evaluator's request that he explain his understanding of what had just been explained, Edgar stated, "I don't actually remember what you said." The explanation was repeated and Edgar was again asked whether the content of meetings would be kept private, and he said, "No." He was then asked if he was required to participate in the evaluation and he said, "Not really, but I will." When Edgar was asked if he could selectively respond to questions and stop his participation at any time and he replied, "I think so." He looked to his mother and she affirmed his answer with a nod of her head. She then nodded at me, indicating that he understood the parameters. Based on Edgar's responses to my questions, and on his mother's acknowledgement of his understanding, it was my opinion that Edgar's ability to agree to participate in the evaluation and his understanding of the limits of confidentiality were at least minimally adequate.

Summary of Relevant Records

In addition to ongoing consultation with the defense attorney and conducting approximately three hours of interviews and testing with Edgar over the course of two meetings separated by about six weeks, the evaluator interviewed Edgar's mother and the school social worker. The evaluator also reviewed relevant records from the police department and juvenile court, as well as educational records from the current and past school districts that included the IEP, psychological testing, and incident reports, and primary care medical records. It is common in forensic evaluations that some records will not be available in a timely manner. The evaluator did not receive child protective services records from either state. These records would have provided important relevant information about the relationship between Edgar and Ms. Vic, who was the interested adult present during the interrogation in which Edgar reluctantly participated and who prevailed on him to participate in the interrogation. Data gathered from relevant records was integrated into the presentation of the background information detailed in the following section.

Relevant Background Information

Ms. Vic indicated that Edgar's father suffered from ADHD and substance abuse problems and would become aggressive and violent. She indicated that he had never been a part of Edgar's life, and was currently incarcerated in the federal prison system on drug and attempted murder convictions.

Ms. Vic indicated that depression was common on her side of the family but stated that, to her knowledge, none of her family members had ever been psychiatrically hospitalized. Ms. Vic had a history of addiction that began when Edgar was a child. Ms. Vic indicated that her addictions included different opioids but maintained that she did not use drugs or alcohol during pregnancy with Edgar. Ms. Vic indicated that she and her children moved out of state when Edgar was about 4 years of age and that she was able to maintain sobriety for a few months after their relocation, but she then relapsed into drug abuse. The out-of-state child protective services (CPS) removed Edgar from her care for about one month while she sought substance abuse treatment. The family also had in-state CPS involvement before moving out of state, in part because when Edgar was about 2 years of age, he set a fire in the family's apartment. Edgar and his family moved back to the local area in December 2013.

Edgar was born via C-section after an uncomplicated and healthy pregnancy. He sustained a hypoxic injury at birth as well as hyperglycemia. During his early development, Edgar exhibited substantial developmental motor and language delays, neither walking nor talking until 3 years of age. There is no report of Edgar receiving early intervention services, but he did attend Head Start at 3 years of age. In addition, at 3 years of age, he began showing significant aggression (e.g., throwing things at preschool, hitting adults) at home and at school. The public school district evaluated Edgar at that time and found him eligible for special education services based on "conduct problems, learning disabilities and language difficulties."

Edgar's learning and behavior problems persisted through the third grade. The out-of-state school district transferred Edgar from a supported regular educational setting to an alternative therapeutic educational placement where "his distress and instability continued, and where staff restrained [him] regularly." Prior school-based psychological test findings indicated that Edgar had a history of intellectual weaknesses primarily in the language-based domain of cognitive functions. A spring 2010 evaluation of Edgar's intellectual and speech and language abilities yielded impaired performances on two of three tests of language-based cognitive functions. His overall Verbal IQ (i.e., Verbal Comprehension Index score) was impaired at the 6th percentile. Edgar's visuoperceptual abilities (so-called "nonverbal" abilities represented in the WISC-IV Perceptual Reasoning Index) were measured at average compared with his peers at the 27th percentile. Speech and language testing from October 2010 yielded impaired scores on expressive and receptive language tests.

Edgar gradually began making progress in school. In the sixth grade, Edgar attended an alternative middle school during the time he and his family lived out of state, because his social and academic problems persisted. School records described Edgar in a variety of ways. For instance, his IEP stated the following:

> Edgar is a polite, funny and sensitive 12-year-old 6th grader at the out-of-state school. He has a playful and impish personality. Edgar is able to contribute to class discussion, and seems to enjoy science when he is focused. . . . He has been able to establish friendships with students both inside and outside of his age group.

His IEP also described him in the following terms:

> Edgar struggles with overall academics and maintaining focus in class. He has difficulty expressing his ideas and emotions. . . . He appears to struggle with auditory processing of information. . . . Edgar is slow to process information; he lags behind; his speech is monotone and slow. . . . Edgar needs time to process; requires clarification . . . [and] he needs guidance with certain things.

According to his school records, when Edgar became overwhelmed in the face of the demand to process more information than he can readily handle, he "shut down . . . became argumentative, and at times, aggressive." According to records, he struggled with misinterpreting situations, has difficulty expressing dissatisfaction appropriately (often shutting down), and struggled with overall academics and maintaining focus in class.

After Edgar and his family returned to the local school district in December 2013, Edgar began attending the regular education middle school. January 2014 psychological testing that a school district psychologist conducted suggested that Edgar did not suffer from ADHD, and that his difficulties may be better explained by an "underlying emotional disorder and precociousness regarding his sexual development." However, that report relied only on WISC-IV and invalid and unreliable testing procedures (i.e., Rorschach, Thematic Apperception Test, and various so-called projective drawings) to generate unreliable data from which to draw opinions about the nature of Edgar's difficulties. The school district psychologist did not attempt to access collateral data. The WISC-IV test findings yielded the following index scores: Verbal Comprehension = 71, 3rd percentile; Perceptual Reasoning = 96, 28th percentile; Working Memory = 74, 4th percentile; Processing Speed = 78, 7th percentile; Full Scale IQ = 73, 4th percentile. The school psychologist concluded that Edgar did not appear to meet criteria for ADHD because he did not produce an "ADHD profile" in his test performance. It is important to point out that ADHD is a heterogeneous neurological condition, and by definition, no such profile exists.

Edgar had no history of psychiatric hospitalization or major mental illness. The alternative school clinical director indicated that Edgar seemed to have a problem with bullying and being bullied." Ms. Buckley characterized Edgar's negative peer interactions as a part of mutual acclimation between him and his peers. She indicated that he "has had no major [behavioral] events" since beginning at the alternative school.

Edgar had a history of outpatient individual counseling in which he was engaged inconsistently owing in large part to his mother's ambivalence about him "telling his business to a stranger." At the time of incident in question, he had not been in counseling for about eight months, but his mother claimed that she had put him on the waiting list a local community mental health clinic.

Mental Status Examination

The forensic evaluator met Edgar at his home for both meetings. He initially presented as apprehensive and guarded until it was explained to him that he was not in trouble and that his lawyer asked this evaluator to meet with him. Edgar then relaxed and became more engaged and cooperative. Edgar was generally quiet during the meeting. However, he was particularly interested in talking about his involvement with a local arts group that specializes in working with children and teens. Edgar participated in the evaluation without refusal.

Edgar described his current mood as "fine." He indicated that he usually feels "good." Edgar did not endorse symptoms of anxiety, depression, mood instability, mania, hallucinations, delusions, obsessions, compulsions, or traumatic stress. He did not endorse having the burden of suicidal thoughts and feelings, and he did not endorse preoccupations with harm to others. The content of Edgar's speech appeared normal. His receptive language abilities appeared weak based on his apparent reticence to initiate discussion, his need to have instructions repeated, and he had what seemed to be a tendency to misunderstand test instructions. Regarding his expressive language abilities, Edgar demonstrated word-finding problems during conversation, which may be reflective of problems with expressive language, semantic memory or both. Edgar also had difficulty maintaining goal-directed speech in that he frequently inserted off-topic comments, such as a long digression focused on a new action movie.

Edgar told the evaluator that he has struggled with attention in school since he was a little boy. He indicated that he had particular difficulty controlling his attention during times when the topics of discussion or instruction are not of interest to him. He indicated that he was usually distracted by his own thoughts, generally related to extracurricular activities. Edgar's thinking was concrete and organized. His social judgment appeared deficient, based on his explanation of the interactions with his peers that led to his current delinquency charges.

Psychological Measures

The use of psychological test measures in evaluating a juvenile's understanding of Miranda is critical in addressing the question of whether the juvenile's waiver of his or her right to counsel was knowing and voluntary. In this case, it seemed to hold additional importance given what appeared to have been some degree of coercion on his mother's part through behavior that she explained as having been morally driven. As a first time alleged offender, Edgar had no experience with the juvenile justice system, so that measurement of his understanding of and full appreciation for the waiver of his Miranda rights via the Miranda Rights Comprehension Inventory (Grisso et al., 2012) was indicated in order to establish Edgar's baseline level of Miranda understanding going forward, as well as establishing his likely level of understanding and appreciation of a Miranda waiver at the time of the interrogation. Kalbeitzer, Zelle, and Riggs-Romaine (2011) noted that the new version of the Miranda assessment instrument includes a juvenile sample in the normative data. They found the MRCI to have good reliability and validity. In Edgar's case, it was particularly important to measure objectively whether Edgar possessed adequate independent ability to knowingly and voluntarily waive his Miranda rights and then to make inculpatory statements or whether he relied completely on his mother to provide him the protection of an interested adult who was ostensibly able to fully, or at least adequately, appreciate the implications of her son's Miranda waiver and subsequent making of inculpatory statements but who may have been acting out of her own moralistic motivations, naïve about the potential serious and long-term implications of her son's statements.[2]

The Gudjonsson Suggestibility Scale (Gudjonsson, 1995) is a test of a defendant's susceptibility to suggestive interrogation techniques. While it was not specifically designed for use with juvenile defendants, juveniles as young as 15 were used in the initial reliability and validity studies. Given that Edgar was subjected to interrogation in the presence of three authority figures (i.e., two police officers and his mother, whose ability to provide the protections of the interested adult according to legal standards may have been prohibitively compromised), it was important to be able to gauge objectively the extent to which he might acquiesce to the pressures of authority figures during interrogation, as many teenagers tend to do. In Edgar's case, it was particularly important to assess his degree of suggestibility to his mother's pressure, which included the threat of physical punishment for refusing to confess to the crime (see Interview with Edgar below).

The Wechsler Individual Achievement Test, Third Edition, Reading Comprehension subtest is a measure of a child's reading comprehension skills. In providing an arrested person with their Miranda rights, the police are required to verbally convey the Miranda warning, and they typically provide the arrested person with a sheet on which the Miranda rights are printed, to supplement the verbal warning. The reading levels of those warnings vary greatly across jurisdictions, so it is important to know whether the arrested child was able to read and comprehend the written version of the warning the police provided. When measuring a child's reading level, percentile scores should be used to compare the child's reading comprehension level with a national sample of their age peers, as it is the most psychometrically robust comparison as opposed to comparing with grade level peers. Edgar scored in the 4th percentile on that reading comprehension test.

The Test of Memory Malingering (TOMM; Tombaugh, 1996) is test of malingered memory symptoms. It is used to gauge performance validity in the context of psychological evaluations. While the published norms apply to those 17 years and older, Kirkwood et al. (2011) and others have validated the use of the TOMM in children as young as six years of age. The Dot Counting Test (DCT; Boone, Lu, et al., 2002) is also an assessment of test-taking effort.

While it is normed for individuals 17 years of age and older, it too has been validated for use in children as young as 13 years of age.

Test Results Bearing on Juvenile Miranda Waiver

Suggestibility during Questioning   The *Gudjonsson Suggestibility Scale* is a test of a defendant's susceptibility to suggestive interrogation techniques. The first section of the test involves reading the defendant a narrative passage and then asking him to immediately recall as much information from the passage as possible. After a 40-minute delay, Edgar was able to recall 3 of 39 target details from the passage, placing his score below the 1st percentile (i.e., the lowest score out of 100) compared with the general population, or in the 9th percentile (i.e., below average) compared with a clinical forensic sample of patients.

Following the second recall condition, the defendant was asked a series of 20 questions about the passage, only four of which he answered from the passage correctly. The remaining questions tested interrogative suggestibility and are presented in a manner in which the participant is forced to choose between two incorrect choices. The questions are structured to suggest that a particular response is desired over the other response choice. The number of answers a person provides for the suggestive questions is then scored. Edgar's score of 16 on this section of the test (named Yield 1) is placed in the 99.6th percentile (compared to forensic sample; mean score = 7, standard deviation [SD] = 3.5).

The second edition of the test (named Yield 2) is designed to test a defendant's suggestibility due to negative feedback from the test administrator and, by extension, an interrogator. After several moments during which the test administrator is instructed to appear as if he were scoring the first set of responses, the administrator is instructed to firmly state to the participant that he performed poorly on the test, that he gave a number of incorrect responses, and that the questions would have to be asked again. The participant is encouraged to try harder, the 20 questions are repeated, and the number of questions to which the participant changes his initial responses is noted and scored. Edgar changed a total of 9 of 20 of his responses. Edgar's score was within the average range (mean score of 7, SD = 3.5) when compared to forensically involved patients and the general population (mean score of 4, SD = 3).

The Yield 1 and Yield 2 scores are added together to provide a rating of overall suggestibility. The average score for the general population is 7 (SD = 5). Edgar's score (16 + 9) of 25 is approximately 3.25 standard deviations above the average score of 7, placing his score above the 99th percentile. According to the manual, the average score for a forensically involved population is "about 10 with a standard deviation of 5.5" (Gudjonsson, G, H., 1997, p. 53). Edgar's score of 25 is approximately 2.8 SDs above the forensic population, placing him in the 99.7th percentile. His overall scores strongly suggest that, out of 100 forensically involved people, he would likely be extremely vulnerable to interrogative suggestibility during interrogation.

The second edition of Grisso's (2012) *Miranda Rights Comprehension Instruments (MRCI)* was used to assess Edgar's knowledge of and appreciation for his Miranda rights.

Regarding Comprehension of Miranda Rights   The forensic evaluator administered the test titled *Miranda Rights Comprehension Instruments* (MRCI; Grisso, 2012) to assess Edgar's understanding of Miranda warnings. The test is divided into four sections. The first section, titled Comprehension of Miranda Rights, assesses a person's understanding of Miranda rights by asking him to state in his own words the meaning of the sentences comprising the Miranda warning. The results are scored from 0 to 10. Edgar achieved a score of 3. According to the normative data, Edgar's score was comparable to the mean score of other 12 and 13 years-of-age juvenile defendants with Full Scale IQ scores of 71–80 (M = 1.5, SD = 2.12). About 10% of the entire sample of juvenile defendants earned a score lower than Edgar's, indicating that his score was well below the average range compared to that of most juvenile offenders. Of note was Edgar's explanation of his understanding of the following statement, "You do not have to make a statement and have the right to remain silent." Edgar indicated that, to him, that statement meant, "Angry—I don't know—like you have to be quiet or something."

The second section is titled Comprehension of Miranda Rights, Recognition. During this task, a person is given the target sentences from the Miranda warning and then read alternative sentences that are either synonymous with the target sentence or different in meaning. The person is then asked to indicate whether the sentence read to him is the same as or different from the target Miranda sentence. Scores range from 0 to 15. Edgar earned a score of 6, which was approximately 2.5 SD below the mean score for 12 and 13-year-old juvenile defendants with Full Scale IQ scores between 71 and 80. In comparing Edgar's score to the overall sample of juvenile defendants (n = 181), 0% of the juvenile sample had scores lower than Edgar's.

Regarding Comprehension of Miranda Vocabulary   The third section of the test is titled Comprehension of Miranda Vocabulary. The purpose of this task is to assess a person's understanding of key words used throughout the Miranda warning. The person is read a target word, it is used in a sentence, and then it is repeated. The person is then asked to define the word. Scores can range from 0 to 32. Edgar earned a score of 12, which was approximately 1.5 SDs below the mean for 12- and 13-year-old juvenile defendants with Full Scale IQ scores ranging from 71–80 (M = 19.67, SD = 5.15). In comparing

Edgar's score with the standardization sample, 4.6% of the standardization sample scored lower than Edgar on this task, indicating that he scored well below the average range.

Regarding Functions of Rights in Interrogation   The fourth section of the test is titled Functions of Rights in Interrogation. It is divided into three subsections and is designed to assess a person's understanding of the nature of interrogation, the right to be represented by an attorney, and the right to silence. Edgar's total score of 11 (out of a possible 30 points) was slightly more than 3 SDs below the mean score for 12- and 13-year-old juvenile defendants with Full Scale IQ scores between 71 and 80. Almost all (99.4%) of the entire juvenile sample ($n = 169$) earned total scores higher than Edgar's.

In the first subsection of this task that assessed an understanding of the nature of interrogation, Edgar scored 4 out of possible 10 points, which was approximately 5 SDs below the mean score of other 12 and 13-year-old juvenile defendants (mean = 9.36, SD = 1.05). Less than 1% of the entire juvenile sample ($n = 169$) scored below Edgar's score. Edgar's score on the second section pertaining to his understanding of the right to counsel of 5 out of a possible 10 points was 1 SD below the mean score for 12- and 13-year-old juvenile defendants (mean = 7.73, SD = 1.83). About 98% of the entire juvenile sample scored above Edgar's score on this subsection of the test. Edgar's score of 2 on the section pertaining to his understanding of the right to silence (also out of a possible 10 points) was 1 SD below the mean score of other 12- and 13-year-old juvenile defendants (mean = 4.67, SD = 2.09); 6.6% of the entire juvenile sample scored below Edgar's score on this subsection of the MRCI.

Test Performance Credibility   The question of whether a defendant might be purposely performing poorly on tests of competence and related abilities (in this case, competence to waive Miranda and interrogative suggestibility) should always be considered when poor performance on those tests could increase the likelihood of avoiding prosecution (i.e., secondary gain in failing the tests). Edgar's score of 50 out of a possible 50 on the first trial of the TOMM is a passing score. His score of 21 on the Dot Counting Test was well above the cutoff for learning disabled individuals (≤ 14). Taken together, these performance credibility test scores strongly suggested that his other test performances were credible.

In summary, test results show that Edgar is extremely susceptible to interrogative pressure, which in turn causes him to show a strong tendency toward suggestibility during interrogation; his knowledge and appreciation of his Miranda rights is deeply deficient; and his performance on these tests is credible.

Additional Information Specifically Pertaining to Validity of Miranda Waiver

Interview with Edgar   In discussing his case with the forensic evaluator, Edgar was able to convey the facts of the incident in a coherent manner, but he required support (i.e., cuing during the discussion) to elaborate beyond the basic facts of the circumstances. Edgar recalled that the school principal suspended him and then sent him home. He remembered that when his mother arrived home from work, she was angry with him and disappointed in his behavior. Edgar indicated that she gave him the choice of accompanying her to the police station to "own up to what he did" or face physical punishment. He said, "I'm more scared for (sic) her than the cops. She (sic) beat my ass! She (sic) done it before! She be hittin' my [16-year-old] brother, too."[3] When asked whether he would have spoken to the police if they had come to his house and arrested him, Edgar replied, "I don't know. I didn't give a F&@% about talking to them."

When asked whether he knew at the time that his statements to the police could lead to the judge ordering him to register as a sex offender with the Sex Offender Registry Board, which would likely mean that he would not be able to attend regular school or continue to live in his current neighborhood. Edgar replied, "I do now." When asked again, Edgar confirmed that he was unaware of the possibility that his statements could lead to a guilty finding in court and subsequent SORB registration and all of its proscriptions.

Interview with Ms. Vic   In addition to having provided detailed information pertaining to Edgar's history, his mother, Ms. Vic, discussed the incident in question and her decision to press her son into participating in the police interrogation. Ms. Vic immediately began discussing her history of drug addiction, which included having engaged in various addiction driven crimes such as armed and unarmed robbery, exchanging sex for drugs, leaving her small children alone during drug binges, and allowing "men in and out of my place when my children were there." She explained that when she finally began to recover from addiction, she felt compelled "to get right with God" and atone for her crimes (e.g., she completed terms of probation that included community service of some kind). Ms. Vic adamantly insisted that she would not fail her children again and that she would fulfill what she saw as her parental duty to ensure that her son "own up" to his allegedly assaultive behavior, with the full force of her convictions. When asked about whether physical punishment would be a part of her efforts to prevail on her son to talk with the police, she looked over her shoulder from the kitchen stove (the interview took place in their apartment) and said "You (sic) damn right! And his ass know (sic) it, too!"

This evaluator asked Ms. Vic if she informed the police of Edgar's lifelong special education status, including the specific impairments of language processing for which school districts had been providing services. She stated, "Yo, I'm not trying to make excuses for him and what he did. If he did it, then he (sic) gonna tell them the truth and own up to it like a man. I understand that maybe he was just trying to fit being the new kid at school and all, but he gotta learn he can't jump off a bridge just because them boys dared him to."

Ms. Vic discussed the possibility that Edgar's statements to the police might result in the court requiring him to register with the state's Sex Offender Registry Board for up to 20 years should the court find him guilty of the charges. Ms. Vic was adamant that "my son ain't no sex offender! He did something stupid because as a dare and he learned his lesson! Ain't no judge gonna say he's a sex offender from that. I don't care what Edgar's lawyer say (sic)." I informed her that in fact, the judge could very well mandate Edgar's SORB registration if he determines that Edgar is at risk for reoffense. She simply replied, "God ain't gonna let that happen."

Review of Digital Audio Recording   Edgar's interrogation lasted 16 minutes and 54 seconds. Two detectives conducted the questioning. Edgar's mother was present during the questioning. At the outset of the interrogation, one of the officers asked Edgar whether he was allowed adequate time before the interrogation to discuss his participation with his mother. Edgar said, "Yea. I guess so." The officer then asked Edgar whether he was willing to talk about what happened, and Edgar's mother interjected, "He's gonna talk to you." The police officers accepted her statement of Edgar's willingness to participate. One of the officers then said to Edgar, "We just want to find out what happened on the playground with you and the girl. Nobody's getting arrested here." The other officer then asked Edgar, "So tell us what happened there on the playground with you and the girl." Edgar's mother then asserted, "Tell them the truth, Edgar. Tell them everything." Edgar then provided the police officers with his recollection of the incident, which included inculpatory statements.

Disposition

The suppression hearing lasted approximately 45 minutes, most of which consisted of the evaluator's testimony; the presiding juvenile court judge in this case rejected Edgar's motion to suppress his statements. The judge's written opinion stated that his denial of the motion was primarily based on Edgar's statement that he "didn't give a F&@%" about having made inculpatory statements to the police. The judge misconstrued Edgar's statement as an indication that Edgar understood adequately the implications of confessing to the police, that his mother had provided Edgar with adequate support and consultation during the interrogation, and the police had taken "the greatest care" in ensuring that Edgar's waiver was knowing and voluntary. The judge rendered his decision despite the weight of the evidence to the contrary. Edgar's defense attorney did not appeal the decision. Edgar eventually pled to a lesser charge and was given 18 months probation, which he violated by getting into a fight with the alleged victim's older male cousin, who physically assaulted Edgar on his way home from school the following school year, reportedly in retaliation for Edgar's behavior toward her the year before. Edgar was held in detention for 90 days after the court found him dangerous according to statutory criteria. He was released to the custody of the state's child protective services and placed in a group home for troubled teens where he remains as of this writing.

Common Pitfalls and Considerations

Among the many possible barriers that juvenile forensic evaluators might encounter over the course of an evaluation, there are those that will always remain beyond our ability to control. For instance, while a skilled evaluator might be able to communicate with a child and family in such a way that might maximize the chances for good rapport and participation, ultimately, we have very little influence over the motivation and willingness of a given child and their family/caregivers to participate in an evaluation. Also, try as we might, collateral providers are sometimes reticent to provide information to an evaluating clinician for fear of being called to court to testify to their statements. There will nearly always be someone who you consider to be of critical importance to your evaluation, who does not return your calls and e-mails. Further, it is not uncommon that a forensic clinician's written request for mental health or educational records goes unheeded, leaving the clinician with a gap in their otherwise pristine database. However, there are two common pitfalls that could be considered as fatal flaws to a juvenile Miranda waiver database that are easily avoided.

An error considered of the fatal variety to any juvenile forensic evaluation is the failure to test for effort in the child being evaluated. Many children and most teenagers are capable of understanding the benefit to them of the increased likelihood of avoiding prosecution if the court finds they were not competent to waive their Miranda rights and then suppresses their statements to the police. Kirkwood et al. (2012) showed that children as young as eight years of age are capable of intentionally putting forth poor effort during an evaluation. The Test of Memory Malingering, a commonly used test of performance validity, has been shown to be appropriate to administer to children as young as six years of age. Other measures of performance validity known to be appropriate for children include Green's Word Memory Test, the forced choice measure of the California Verbal Learning Test, Second Edition, and the Discriminability measure of the California Verbal Learning Test, Children's Edition. It is of critical importance that one be able to testify to the validity of the database. Whether the data presented represents a reasonable facsimile of the truth is a major concern to the trier of fact.

Failure to collect third party data in the form of interviews and records substantially limits the interferences that one can defensibly draw from interview and test data. It is necessary to interpret the child's interview and test data in the context of what is known about their academic skills, cognitive abilities, and prior experience with the juvenile court system in order to meaningfully apply that data to the psycholegal question of whether their Miranda waiver was knowing and voluntary.

Inexperienced evaluators sometimes provide what is referred to as "the ultimate opinion" in their reports, stating whether the child was or was not competent to waive their Miranda rights at the time of interrogation. The role of the forensic evaluator who is addressing the question of whether a child's Miranda waiver was knowing and voluntary is to provide the finder of fact with data as to how the child's mental functioning effected their waiver. Whether the child was competent to waive their Miranda rights and whether the waiver was valid is a legal decision to be rendered only by the trier of fact. However, if during testimony the judge were to ask a direct question of the testifying evaluator for their opinion as to the child's competence to waive their Miranda rights, then this evaluator would recommend providing the ultimate opinion with the following qualifying statement: "Whether the child was competent to waive his or her Miranda rights at the time of interrogation is a legal determination reserved for the finder of fact, but since your honor has instructed me to provide my opinion in that regard, then I will do so. It is my opinion that child X [was or was not] competent to waive their Miranda rights at the time of the police interrogation."

Notes

1. On the morning of June 8, 1964, the Gila County Sheriff took custody of Gerald Gault after a neighbor accused him of calling her on the phone and making lewd sexual comments. At the time, he was already on probation for being in the company of another boy who had stolen a wallet from a woman's purse.

2. In Edgar's case, he was facing the prospect that, if found guilty, he could be required by the court to register with the state as a sex offender for at least 15 years postconviction. Such a classification would limit his life in a range of ways including limiting his access to housing, limiting his access to school placement, and forcing an increase in his socialization with court-involved peers.

3. Edgar's disclosure raised obvious protective concerns pertaining to physical abuse in the home. After our meeting, I fulfilled my legally mandated reporting obligations per Massachusetts state law.

References

Bishop, D. M., & Farber, H. B. (2007). Joining the legal significance of adolescent developmental capacities with the legal rights provided by *In Re Gault*. *Rutgers Law Review, 60*(1), 125–173.

Boone, K., Lu, P., et al. (2002). *The Dot Counting Test*. WPS.

Farber, H. B. (2004). The role of the parent/guardian in juvenile custodial interrogations: Friend or foe? *American Criminal Law Review, 41*, 1277–1312.

Feld, B. (2006). Juveniles' competence to exercise Miranda rights: An empirical study of policy and practice. *Minnesota Law Review, 26–100*.

Feld, B. (2013). Real interrogation: What actually happens when cops question kids. *Law & Society Review, 47*, 1–35.

Grisso, T., & Pomicter, C. (1978). Interrogation of juveniles: An empirical study of procedures, safeguards and waiver rights. *Law and Human Behavior, 1*(4), 321–342.

Grisso, T. (1980). Juveniles' capacities to waive Miranda rights: An empirical analysis. *California Law Review, 68*(6), 1134–1166.

Grisso, T., Goldstein, N., & Zelle, H. (2012). *Miranda rights comprehension instruments: Manual for juvenile and adult evaluations*. Professional Resource Services.

Gudjonsson, Gisli H. (1997). *Gudjonsson Suggestibility Scales* (pp. 1–56). Psychology Press.

King, K. J. (2006). Waiving childhood goodbye: How juvenile courts fail to protect children from unknowing, unintelligent, and involuntary waivers of Miranda rights. *Wisconsin Law Review, 431–477*.

Redlich, A. D., Silverman, M., Chen, J., & Steiner, H. (2004). The police interrogation of children and adolescents. In D. G. Lassiter (Ed.), *Interrogations, confessions, and entrapment: Perspectives in law & psychology* (Vol. 20, pp. 107–125).

Rogers, R., Shuman, D. W., & Blackwood, H. L. (2008). The comprehensibility and content of juvenile Miranda warnings. *Psychology, Public Policy and Law, 14*(1), 63–87.

Salseda, L. M., Dixon, D. R., Fass, T., Miora, D., & Leark, R. A. (2011). An evaluation of Miranda rights and interrogation in autism spectrum disorders. *Research in Autism Spectrum Disorders, 5*(1), 79–85.

Sondenaa, E., Helverschou, S. B., Steindal, K., Rasmussen, K., Nilson, B., & Nottestad, J. A. (2014). Violence and sexual offending behavior in people with autism spectrum disorder who have undergone a psychiatric forensic examination. *Psychological Reports: Disability & Trauma, 115*(1), 32–43.

Viljoen, J. L., & Roesch, R. (2005). Competence to waive interrogation rights and adjudicative competence in adolescent defendants: Cognitive development, attorney contact, and psychological symptoms. *Law and Human Behavior, 29*(6), 723–742.

16

Transfer Evaluations in Juvenile Justice

Alison R. Flaum and Antoinette Kavanaugh

Relevant Case Law

Every state in the country has a juvenile justice system that is separate from the criminal justice system in which adults are tried. Every state also has a jurisdictional cutoff—usually age 18—that determines, by and large, which cases are directed to which system. But, in recent decades, this dividing line has been blurred by laws allowing certain young people below the age cutoff to be prosecuted as adults. These "transfer laws" vary greatly from state to state in terms of which young people are eligible for transfer and how the transfer decision is made. Some states designate every young person charged with a crime as transfer-eligible, providing criteria and standards for assessing each case. Other states deem certain charges "automatic transfer" offenses, meaning that any child facing those charges is sent directly to criminal court without a hearing of any kind. But virtually every state has some category of cases for which transfer is discretionary and for which courts—sometimes in the juvenile system, sometimes in the criminal system—are tasked with determining whether to try a particular young person as an adult.[1]

Forensic evaluators are essential to this process. Courts holding such hearings are ordered to consider various "transfer factors" that are best understood with the assistance of an expert clinician. In fact, clinicians not only are ideally suited for collecting and evaluating data on certain specific transfer factors—such as a youth's mental health history or her amenability to rehabilitation—but may also be called on to educate the court more generally about relevant topics, such as adolescent development. As discussed below, specific transfer factors vary by jurisdiction, as do the standards and presumptions involved. In some transfer cases, the court will render a decision based on "the best interests of the community"; in other cases, the ultimate legal question is whether the child at issue "is amenable to rehabilitation." Thus, clinicians will want to become familiar with not only the transfer factors at play in their jurisdiction but also the exact legal question or questions to be decided by the court. Indeed, the "Specialty Guidelines for Forensic Psychology" (hereafter referred to as "Specialty Guidelines") clearly state that a forensic psychologist should be competent in and knowledgeable regarding specific relevant legal issues and standards (APA, 2013). In addition, other aspects of transfer law may be helpful for a forensic evaluator to know—such as what types of evidence are admissible at the hearing or whether the transfer decision is to be made pre- or posttrial. These mechanics, and more, are discussed below.

Regardless of how the transfer question is framed or litigated in a given jurisdiction, transfer decisions have great impact on all the parties involved.[2] With limited exceptions, young people transferred to criminal court are subjected to the same penalties as every other criminal defendant.[3] Young people who are transferred also lose access to the confidentiality and supportive services provided by the juvenile justice system and may well be held in adult jail and prison facilities.[4] In addition, criminal prosecution of young people has implications for community safety—both the United States Department of Justice and the Centers for Disease Control have concluded that youth who are prosecuted in the criminal system are more likely to commit additional crimes upon release.[5]

Raising the stakes even further, these debates take place against the backdrop of cases and research that increasingly reexamine the overarching wisdom of equating juveniles and adults. Indeed, in recent years, the United States Supreme Court, as well as various lower courts across the country, have declared youth to be "categorically less culpable"[6] and cautioned against effacing the essential distinctions between those who commit crimes as children and those commit crimes later in life. Interestingly, these legal findings are grounded in large part on the work of psychology professionals who have established both the unique neuropsychological features of adolescence and their impact on a young person's judgment, actions, and rehabilitative potential.[7]

Still, every year, thousands of young people are subject to transfer proceedings.[8] Though the specific features of these hearings vary from state to state, as a general matter, a forensic psychologist should expect that

- The transfer decision will be made by a judge, usually in juvenile court.
- Although transfer statutes vary by state, most statutes will set out
  o The factors to be considered by the court;
  o The standard of proof (i.e., how certain the court needs to be before rendering its decision);
  o The burden of proof (i.e. whether juvenile court or criminal court is the default in a given case, and which party has the burden of overcoming that presumption);

○ Any other legal presumptions (e.g., whether certain crimes or certain transfer factors must be weighted more heavily than others are or must incline the court for or against transfer);

○ The ultimate legal question (i.e., whether the court is directed to resolve the transfer question based on what is best for the community, what is best for public safety, whether the child can be rehabilitated, etc.).

- A forensic evaluator may be retained by either the defense or the prosecution—or appointed by the court.[9]
- There may be limits on the forensic evaluator's access to the child in question and/or on whether the child may be questioned about the alleged crime, especially if the transfer hearing happens pretrial.
- The forensic evaluator's observations and findings may not be privileged or confidential and may be subject to the rules of discovery.

While transfer factors also vary by jurisdiction, common factors on which a clinician may be asked to opine include:

- The child's medical history;
- The child's history of out of home placements and mental health services;
- The child's educational history, including (but not limited to) special education needs and services;
- Evidence of abuse or neglect;
- The child's role in the alleged offense;
- Whether the child acted in an aggressive or premeditated manner in the alleged offense;
- The child's suggestibility and the role of peer pressure, or pressure by adults, in the alleged offense;
- Whether the child was able to foresee what occurred during the alleged offense, especially if the child is charged via "accountability" (i.e. where the child is being held legally responsible for another person's actions);
- Whether the child is amenable to rehabilitation;
- The advantages of treatment in the juvenile justice system relative to the criminal justice system.

Although it is the judge who will issue the ultimate transfer ruling, the forensic evaluator in a transfer case arguably plays an even more important role, providing both essential case-specific facts and, crucially, context for understanding how those facts relate to larger psychological phenomena, such as adolescent development or adolescent resilience. Essentially, a transfer court is tasked with determining whether the child in question can be rehabilitated—a weighty and challenging prospect under any circumstances but especially when the triggering allegation is a serious one. As both field reporter and neutral expert interpreter, no other evidence or witness carries more weight than a clinician with regard to this crucial question. In fact, a recent study regarding "reverse waivers" (hearings to determine if a child who has been transferred to criminal court ought to be returned to juvenile court) found that the forensic evaluator's opinion was the most influential factor in the judge's decision about whether a case would remain in the adult jurisdiction or be transferred back to the juvenile court (Means, Heller, & Janofsky, 2012).

At the same time, a clinician must take care not to undercut his or her influence by neglecting to translate findings into lay terms—a recent national survey of juvenile court judges found that forensic evaluators' reports were less helpful when they contained jargon and were not written at a level that could be understood by nonmental health practitioners (Brannen et al. 2006).

Review of the Literature

Materials Regarding Transfer Policy, Transfer Data, and Related Juvenile Justice Issues

A great deal of literature exists regarding the wisdom and implications of trying young people as adults; transfer reform is a subject of fierce and ongoing policy debate. Studies and discussions along these lines can be found via the websites of juvenile justice and sentencing policy organizations.[10] Additional materials—and rich data—may be found via various government entities, including the Centers for Disease Control and the Department of Justice's Office of Juvenile Justice and Delinquency Programs.

Resources are also available regarding related issues and fields, including recidivism studies,[11] studies regarding the impact of incarceration on youth (and on families and communities),[12] examinations of the relationship between transfer and deterrence (Redding, 2008; Jordan & Myers, 2011; Ward, 2003; McGowan, Hahn, Liberman & Crosby, 2007), evaluations of juvenile risk for violence (e.g., Hoge & Andrews, 2010), and assessments of malingering and deception in adolescents (e.g., McCann, 1998) and studies regarding youthful resilience (e.g., Steinberg, 2014).

In cases where the forensic evaluator may be called on to opine about the relative treatment options—and likely outcomes—in a jurisdiction's youth and adult prisons, the Office of Juvenile Justice and Delinquency Prevention, which is part of the United States Department of Justice, offers a great resource in its Model Programs Guide (MPG), which is available at http://www.ojjdp .gov/mpg/. The MPG contains information about, and evaluations of, many evidence-based intervention, prevention, and reentry programs.

Additional Psychological Issues Germane to Transfer Evaluations

The issue of how to conduct transfer evaluations began to appear in forensic psychology publications in the 1980s (e.g., Barnum, 1987). Since then, more attention has been paid to the various issues related to conducting these assessments (Salekin, 2002; Penney & Moretti, 2005; Grisso, 2010 and Grisso, 2013).

Heilbrun and DeMatteo (2012) have articulated the need for establishing standards of practice in juvenile forensic mental health assessments. As such, they propose that the assessment of juveniles is a specialty area within the domain of forensic assessment, which requires knowledge of both relevant legal concepts as well as concepts relevant to normal and abnormal developmental immaturity. The following is a brief summary of the topics related to conducting forensic transfer evaluations and aspects associated with presenting one's findings, be they in written form or via testimony.

Psychosocial Maturity   A clinician conducting forensic evaluations must be familiar with the growing body of research regarding issues related to normative developmental processes of psychosocial maturity as well as the various courses of youth violence. The clinician needs to be familiar with developmental differences related to impulsivity, resistance to peer influence, and risk-taking (Steinberg & Monahan, 2007; Steinberg et al., 2008; Steinberg, Cauffman, Woolard, Graham & Banich, 2009), as well as the body of empirical literature related to the manner in which the adolescent and adult brain differ (Weinberger, Elvevåg & Giedd, 2005; Lenroot & Giedd, 2006). Finally, the clinician conducting transfer evaluations should be familiar with literature that explains the developmental and normative course of youth violence. Moffitt (2003) reviews this literature. A recent OJJDP publication empirically examined the relationship between these trajectories and psychosocial immaturity. In short, most adolescents engaging in antisocial activities stop engaging in these behaviors by the time they are in their 20s (Steinberg et al., 2015). Those who frequently engage in antisocial behaviors during adolescence tend to be less psychosocially mature; however, as they mature, their engagement in antisocial behaviors tends to decrease or stop (Steinberg et al., 2015).

Risk Assessment   Many states have transfer statutes that implicitly or explicitly indicate the judge is to consider the risk the youth poses to society, and this is within the domain of a clinical forensic evaluator. However, when the defendant is a juvenile, the risk assessment requires a different set of factors, tools, and instruments than what one would use when conducting a risk assessment of an adult. Consequently, it is imperative that the clinician conducting transfer evaluations be well versed in this area and be familiar with writings that discuss the utility of different instruments in juvenile proceedings, such as those by Hoge and Andrews (2010) and Urquhart and Viljoen (2014), in addition to studies such as those written by Spice, Viljoen, Gretton, and Roesch (2010) that empirically examine the utility of different instruments in juvenile proceedings.

Additionally, the clinician should understand the potential sentencing options and how each may impact the assessment of risk. For example, if the youth is not going to be returned to the community in the near future, then the risk that youth poses may be different than if he or she were in the community, and the risk assessment should take this into account. Therefore, the evaluator may want to be familiar with literature regarding institutional infractions of youth in different justice settings (e.g., Kuanliang, Sorensen, & Cunningham, 2008).

Psychopathology and Issues Related to Diagnoses and Treatment   The clinician should be familiar with the mental health needs of youth in the juvenile justice system as well as potential controversies surrounding this issue. The literature regarding mental health needs among youth in the juvenile justice system is rich (e.g., MacKinnon-Lewis, Kaufman, & Frabutt, 2002; Cauffman & Grisso, 2005; Osterlind, Koller & Morris, 2007). In the areas of controversies, the clinician should be familiar with diagnostic nosology controversies as they pertain to youths. For example, Moffitt et al. (2008) present a review of research and controversies related to the *DSM-5* and conduct disorder.

Many jurisdictions ask the fact-finder to consider whether the youth needs treatment and, if so, which system is better suited to meet these clinical needs. Consequently, it is imperative the clinician be familiar with which treatments are effective for which disorders and in which settings or conditions. The latter issue requires the clinician to contact treatment providers in the potential setting. However, the former issue requires the clinician to be familiar with empirical literature regarding the efficacy of treatment and to review publications such as Hoge (2009), Lipsey (2009), Lipsey et al. (2010), and Underwood, Warren, Talbott, Jackson, & Dailey (2014).

Materials Regarding Best Practices

Books have been written about conducting forensic evaluations of juveniles (e.g., Grisso, 2013; Grigorenko, 2012, Salekin, 2015), as well as books on the screening and assessment of youth in the juvenile justice system (e.g., Grisso, Vincent & Seagrave, 2005) and chapters on conducting transfer evaluations (e.g., Chen & Salekin, 2012; Grisso, 2013; Salekin, Price, Adams, Ang, & Rosenbaum, 2013). The clinician conducting forensic transfer evaluations should be familiar with these texts and those germane to conducting forensic assessments in general (e.g., Heilbrun et al., 2014, and Heilbrun & Grisso, 2008). Additionally, the clinician needs to be familiar with potential ethical pitfalls (e.g., Allan & Grisso, 2014), as well as potential biases related to forensic evaluations (Neal & Grisso, 2014).

In short, evaluators conducting forensic evaluations will want to make sure this is an area in which they are competent to practice and understand the legal issue at hand. With the assistance of the referring party, the clinician identifies which statutory factors are clinically relevant and whether the clinician will discuss the alleged offense with the juvenile. The latter issue requires both the youth and the attorney to weigh the possibility of putting the offense in a developmental context with giving up rights related to self-incrimination.

The clinician should collect data by reviewing records and conducting a series of interviews with the minor exploring multiple domains of the youth's life, including academics, life in the community, home life, peers, substance use, mental health treatment, prior juvenile justice involvement, willingness to engage in treatment, and issues related to prosocial development. Additionally, the evaluator will want to interview the youth's parents or guardians and collect data on these domains as well. As part of the evaluation, the clinician may choose to administer general psychological instruments such as those that assess cognitive functioning, mental health status and personality, as well as a forensic assessment instrument such as the Structured Assessment of Violence Risk in Youth (SAVRY; Borum et al. 2006) or the Risk-Sophistication-Treatment Inventory (RSTI; Salekin, 2004).

Also, with the consent of the referral source, the clinician will want to conduct collateral interviews with a variety of sources ranging from those who knew the youth prior to his or her arrest and can provide information related to the youth's psychosocial development to those who can explain what types of services would be available to the youth in the juvenile or criminal justice systems.

Consistent with the "Specialty Guidelines," it is recommended the clinician present data in a manner that separates the data from the clinical opinion. The clinician is advised to present the relevant data points from each source, followed by a clinical summary in which an opinion is offered regarding each of the relevant statutory factors. In offering a clinical opinion, the clinician should use the data collected to clearly support the rationale for the opinion.

Some, but not all, written clinical reports will result in the clinician being asked to provide testimony in court. In such a case, it is imperative the clinician meet with the retaining party or, in the case of a court-ordered evaluation, the party for whom the clinician will testify, to go over the clinician's testimony as well as potential questions the opposing party may ask of the clinician. The clinician can refer to texts by Greenfield and Gottschalk (2008), Karson and Nadkarni (2013), and Otto, DeMier, and Boccaccini (2014) to assist them in presenting the data to the court via a written report or testimony.

Case Vignette

Reason for Referral[13]

Jason, a 15-year-old African American male, was referred by his attorney because he was facing a discretionary transfer hearing. At the time of the referral, Jason was in the detention center charged with first-degree reckless homicide, hit and run resulting in death(s), and operating a vehicle without the owner's consent. He had been in the detention center seven months awaiting hearing. During the initial contact with the attorney, the forensic evaluator requested records related to the current offense, Jason's previous mental health and substance abuse treatment history, academic records, and prior juvenile justice records, as well as social services records. During the initial conversation, the evaluator and attorney also identified which of the statutory criteria were to be considered. Lastly, as part of the initial conversation, the evaluator received permission from the attorney to discuss the alleged incident with the attorney's client. It is important that this issue be clarified initially as the information obtained from the defendant could be self-incriminating, and obtaining such information may not be consistent with the plan the attorney had for the case.

Evaluation Techniques

Jason was interviewed in private at the Great County Temporary Detention Center on April 13 and 16, 2014, for a three-and–a-half hours and two hours and fifteen minutes, respectively. As part of the evaluation, the Personality Assessment Inventory-Adolescent (PAI-A) was administered and the Risk-Sophistication-Treatment Inventory (RSTI) was utilized.

Jason's mother, Ms. Jones, and his grandmother, Ms. Victor, were interviewed separately at the evaluator's office on April 25, 2014. The interview with his maternal grandmother lasted two-and-a-half hours while the interview with his mother lasted approximately one hour. Three collateral telephone interviews were conducted. On May 1, 2014, Jason's detention caseworker, Mr. Mathews, was interviewed for approximately twenty minutes. Dr. Johnson, program director at the State Department of Corrections, Juvenile Division, and Dr. Smith, program director at the State Department of Corrections, were interviewed separately on May 3, 2014, and each interview lasted approximately thirty minutes. Prior to conducting each interview or assessment, the interviewee was informed of the purpose and limits of confidentiality of the interview.

Records reviewed and relied on in forming the clinical opinion were Officer Smith's arrest report dated January 15, 2014; Officer Price's supplemental report dated January 15, 2014; and Jason's report cards from Achievement Academy.

The case vignette has been redacted and all identifying information removed. It is not meant to serve as a forensic report. Any likeness to a case is purely coincidental.

Summary of Relevant Records

Per police reports, Jason and his friends stole two cars and were playing "car tag" when the car Jason was driving fatally hit a victim who was riding a bicycle. The cars fled the scene and, less than a mile later, an officer stopped the car Jason was driving because he was speeding. Jason acknowledged hitting the bicyclist and insisted it was an accident. Those in the car were arrested at the scene.

School records revealed Jason was not a special education student and that he attended a school ranked in the top 10% in the city. Jason's report cards for the three years prior to the offense indicated he attended school regularly, was rarely late, and typically earned As and Bs.

Relevant Background Information

Jason, his mother and his grandmother were the source of information for this section of the report. Jason lived exclusively with his maternal grandmother for the first ten years of his life because of his mother's drug addiction. His mother had abstained from any drugs or alcohol for the previous six years and, as a result, Jason had divided his living arrangements between his mother's and his maternal grandmother's residences during the past five years. In order to obtain a complete developmental, academic, and psychosocial history, Jason's mother and grandmother were interviewed separately. Highlights of their interviews are as follows:

A freshman in high school, Jason had performed reasonably well in school. He was not a special education student, and he had never failed or skipped a grade. While living with his grandmother or mother, he occasionally violated curfew but always called his guardian to let her know where he was, typically at a friend's house playing video games. He attended church regularly with his grandmother and occasionally had odd jobs mowing grass or shoveling snow.

Jason denied any significant medical or trauma history and had not received any mental health or substance abuse treatment. Although he denied drinking alcohol, he acknowledged that for the past year he had started smoking marijuana on a weekly basis.

Jason denied any gang involvement but acknowledged that some of his peers had arrest records or were on probation. Although his only prior arrest was for a shoplifting charge at 12 years of age—a charge that was later dropped—he admitted to stealing cars with two of his friends and their girlfriends for the previous three months. He described doing this on the weekends, late at night, or early in the morning. He explained that he got permission to spend the night at one of these friend's houses, and they snuck out from that location to steal cars and joy ride.

Jason's Account of the Offense

Jason was interviewed extensively about the alleged offense so the evaluator could place the offense in a psychosocial developmental context. Jason explained he and his friends frequently stole cars to go for joy rides. Never before had they hurt anyone nor had they damaged a car other than stripping the steering wheel to drive the car. Jason explained he always wanted to learn to drive but neither his mother nor grandmother could afford the cost of the driver's education class. He explained that his friends taught him to drive and, over time, taught him how to steal a car. He said he only stole cars when he was with his friends.

Regarding the night at hand, Jason explained that he sped up after his friends and the car behind him tapped the bumper of the car he was driving. Once they did that, he turned around to tell them to stop. As he did, he was not watching the road and hit the cyclist. He said he did not realize he killed the cyclist and thought the cyclist was just hurt. When asked why he didn't stop at that point, Jason explained that he was scared and that his friends were yelling at him to keep driving. Consistent with the police report, Jason explained once the police stopped him and asked why he was speeding he began crying and told the police he thought he hit a person on a bike. In describing the offense, unsolicited, Jason described how badly he felt for the victim and his family. Jason repeatedly voiced regret for his actions and insisted that when he and his friends took the car for a joy ride, he never thought anyone would get hurt.

Collateral Contacts

Relevant Data from Mr. Mathews, Jason's Detention Center Caseworker

Jason's caseworker, Mr. Mathews, indicated he had been Jason's caseworker during his entire stay in the detention center. Mr. Mathews stated Jason's mother and grandmother had not missed a visit and had participated in every family programming opportunity. He explained Jason had been on the highest behavioral level since his second month in the facility. Mr. Mathews described Jason as a "helpful" young man whose "behavior had been remarkable." He described an incident when, unprompted, Jason told staff he had learned about another resident who had threatened to sexually assault a third and younger resident. Mr. Mathews indicated when he spoke with Jason about this incident, Jason said he brought it to the staff's attention because he feared for the younger resident's safety. Finally, Mr. Mathews said Jason volunteered to join the Resident Advisory Board. Only fourteen of the two hundred residents participate on the board, which makes decisions regarding programming and commissary requests for residents.

Relevant Data from Dr. Johnson, Program Director at the State Department of Corrections, Juvenile Division   Dr. Johnson said that, if sentenced as a juvenile, Jason could be held until his 21st birthday, and he would be eligible for a variety of services including individual and group cognitive-behavioral treatment, instruction until he completed a GED or diploma, and opportunities for family engagement.

Dr. Johnson also explained that the front line and clinical staff were all trained on various aspects of adolescent development and the units utilize a behavioral management (or point system) that reflect adolescents' developmental needs, their behavior, and their progress toward their therapeutic and academic goals.

Relevant Data from Dr. Smith, Program Director at the State Department of Corrections   Dr. Smith said the Department of Corrections has designated units for those under 18 years of age, so that adolescents do not have contact with older inmates. Staff who work on the youth units, however, have no specialized training in adolescent development. All incarcerated youth are expected to attend school, but they do not receive any other programming until sixty days before their release date.

Psychological Measures

The statute indicated that the judge should consider Jason's treatment needs and risk to the community. Consequently, reliable and valid instruments with embedded validity scales were used to gather data related to these factors. Since Jason did not have a clinical history and the Millon Adolescent Clinical Inventory was normed on a clinical sample, this test was determined to be not appropriate for this case. As Jason was not a special education student and his academic records indicated an above-grade reading level, the evaluator considered administering the Personality Assessment Inventory-Adolescent (PAI-A) and/or the Minnesota Multiphasic Personality Inventory Adolescent (MMPI-A), ultimately choosing the PAI-A.

To determine the his risk for violence, utilization of the Structured Assessment of Violence Risk in Youth (SAVRY) and/or the Risk Sophistication Treatment Inventory (RSTI) was considered. The evaluator chose to administer the RSTI because it provides additional information such as the maturity of the youth and the youth's willingness to engage in treatment, which the court would consider when rendering its opinion.

Personality Assessment Inventory-Adolescent (PAI-A)   The PAI-A is a 264-item, self-report instrument designed to aid in the clinical assessment of youths 12–18 years of age. Jason produced a valid PAI-A profile indicating that he responded in a consistent and forthright manner. None of the clinical scales reached a clinically significant level, and the scales in his profile for depression, paranoia, antisocial features, drug problems, and alcohol problems, as well as the aggression scale, were in the normal range for adolescents. His profile was not clinically significant but was consistent with youth who have an inflated self-esteem.

Risk-Sophistication-Treatment Inventory (RSTI)   The RSTI is a rating scale designed to aid the clinician in assessment of risk for dangerousness, sophistication/maturity, and treatment amenability for youths 9–18 years of age. The RSTI is unique in that it compares a youth with other youths who are in the juvenile justice system. Compared with other juvenile offenders, Jason scored within the low range on the Risk for Dangerousness Scale. A good prognostic indicator was compared with other juvenile offenders; his psychopathic features were in the low offender range, indicating he has fewer psychopathic features than the average juvenile offender. Youth who score in the low range on the Psychopathic Features subscale display a normal range of remorse and guilt and are not more manipulative or deceptive than one would expect.

Jason appeared more mature than most youth in the juvenile justice system. He scored in the 98th percentile on the Sophistication-Maturity Scale of the RSTI. Youth in the juvenile justice system who score high on this scale have a greater emotional awareness and possess the skills needed to make good judgment most of the time. The behavior he had displayed in the detention center was consistent with what one would expect given his score on this scale.

Finally, regarding the Treatment and Amenability scale, his score was in the high range, which suggested he was more willing to engage in treatment than most juvenile offenders.

Clinical Summary and Opinion

Space limitations prevent the author from presenting a detailed version of what would have been offered to the court. In this case there were several legal factors that were clinically relevant. What follows is the sample of statutorily defined factors, which were both clinically and legally relevant to the court in determining whether Jason was to be transferred to the adult jurisdiction. As these factors were derived from the statute and are typically presented individually in the statute, it is good form for the clinician to reference and respond to each factor individually in their report.

Section 670.032(1)(c): Any Previous Abuse or Neglect History of the Minor   Jason did not have a history of abuse or neglect. In fact, as caseworker Mathews reported, his mother and grandmother had been a great support to

Jason while he has been detained. His lack of abuse history coupled with the level of family support weighed in favor of keeping this case in the juvenile justice system as family support is a key component in successfully addressing juvenile delinquency.

Section 670.032(1)(d): The Seriousness of the Crime   The death of a human is always a serious event. Jason expressed remorse for his actions. Consistent with this, although he did not stop at the scene, when he was apprehended for speeding moments later, he acknowledged the act and expressed regret for it.

Jason contended that, when he was in the car with his friends, he did not appreciate the likelihood that someone could get hurt. It is important to understand this contention from a developmental perspective. Research has shown when adolescents are with their peers, they tend to make riskier decisions than they make on their own or compared with their adult counterparts.

For example, using a standard video game paradigm, Chein (2011) and his colleagues studied three groups of subjects—adolescents 14–18 years of age, young adults 19–22 years of age, and adults 24–29 years of age—and demonstrated that adolescents took more risks when they thought their peers were watching than did adults, which resulted in more disastrous outcomes.

While they performed the tasks, subjects were connected to a machine that measured which parts of the brain were being engaged. Chein et al. (2011) demonstrated that the reward system was more active in adolescents compared with adults when their peers were watching. Additionally, adults engaged or used the prefrontal cortex more, regardless of whether they were in the presence of their peers or not.

Although the crime itself was serious, the manner in which it occurred was consistent with normative developmental differences between adults and adolescents. As such, it was yet another factor that indicated the case should remain in the jurisdiction of the juvenile courts.

Section 670.032(1)(g): Is Transferring Jurisdiction Necessary to Deter This Minor or Other Juveniles from Committing the Crime for Which the Minor Is Charged?   It is unlikely that transferring jurisdiction would deter Jason or other juveniles. Little empirical evidence exists supporting the concept that transferring a youth to adult court is a deterrent to youth who are transferred. Based on a systematic review of literature, McGowan et al. (2007) concluded, "On the basis of strong evidence that juveniles transferred to the adult justice system have greater rates of subsequent violence than juveniles retained in the juvenile justice system, the Task Force on Community Preventive Services concludes that strengthened transfer policies are harmful for those juveniles who experience transfer. Transferring juveniles to the adult justice system is counterproductive as a strategy for deterring subsequent violence" (p. S15). Furthermore, research consistently demonstrates that those youths who are transferred to, and prosecuted in, adult court recidivate more quickly and at higher rates than do their counterparts who were prosecuted in the juvenile justice system (Fagan, 1995; Bishop, Frazier, Lanza-Kaduce & Winner, 1996; Myers, 2003; Bishop & Frazier, 2000). Similarly, the Office of the Juvenile Justice Delinquency Prevention found "the bulk of the empirical evidence suggests that transfer laws have little or no general deterrent effect" (Redding, 2008, p. 2).

Likewise, little evidence exists indicating that transferring a youth is deterrence to other youths. For example, Redding and Fuller (2004) used a unique perspective to examine general deterrence. They asked questions of youth who were charged with felonies including murder. The vast majority of those who had already been transferred to adult court reported that, prior to their arrest, they did not know they could be charged as an adult for the offense (Redding & Fuller 2004). This demonstrates that the transfer laws were not a deterrent to those youths who went on to commit a transferable offense. Another way to demonstrate this is to examine the change in the rate of juvenile crime following changes in the law that make it more likely that youth will be transferred. As cited in Myers (2003), changes in the law in New York and Idaho "had little measurable effect on juvenile crime, and in the case of Idaho, it may have actually backfired by contributing to an increase in juvenile offending. Thus, these laws did not produce the general deterrent effect expected by policy makers." (p. 80).

The opinion that it is unlikely transferring Jason would be a deterrent to him or other juveniles can be understood when viewed from a developmental lens. As discussed previously, research has demonstrated, compared with their adult counterparts, juveniles are less likely to accurately anticipate the consequences of their actions and perceive rewards rather than risks. These two lines of research shed light on why the concept of deterrence would apply for adults but, when viewed in the context of the normal developmental process, are less likely to apply to juveniles.

Consistent with best practice standards, the clinician did not provide an ultimate opinion. Instead, data were provided for each clinically relevant factor. In doing so, the clinician indicated whether each factor weighted for or against transferring the case or whether the data were mixed for the specific factor.

Common Pitfalls and Considerations

Transfer evaluations, as is the case with most forensic evaluations, present some potential ethical issues. First and foremost, consistent with sections 2.01 and 2.03 of the "Ethical Principles of Psychologists and Code of Conduct" (EPPCC) it is important that transfer evaluations be an area of competence for the clinicians conducting them. Clinicians can obtain and maintain their competence in a variety of ways, including staying abreast of the most current literature, attending conferences such as those offered by the Division 41 of the American Psychological Association, or attending continuing education workshops offered by the American Academy of Forensic Psychology. When conducting any forensic evaluation, the clinician's attention to record-keeping must go beyond those articulated in the EPPCC to include relevant aspects of the "Specialty Guidelines," the law, and the rules of discovery.

Clinicians conducting this or any type of forensic evaluation should understand how different types of bias could impact their work and strive to reduce this influence (see Kassin, Dror, & Kukucka, 2013, and Gutheil & Simon, 2004, for discussions on bias in assessment and testimony). Clinicians are encouraged to ask themselves a series of questions such as "Is the money affecting my judgment (especially, for example, in taking on a case outside my expertise)?" or "Am I unduly fixed on winning, pleasing the retaining attorney and making a name for myself on this case?" as a means of reducing the influence of bias (Gutheil & Simon, 2004, p. 268). Alternatively, actively considering rival hypotheses could be a means of minimizing the effects of confirmation bias.

Unlike most forensic evaluations, transfer evaluations typically require the clinician to consider the following question as it applies to the juvenile and adult justice systems: "Can the system provide the services to meet *this particular* youth's needs?" In most jurisdictions, the juvenile justice and adult systems offer different programmatic and therapeutic services, and what is offered may change in response to changes in budget and in personnel. Consequently, collateral interviews with administrators or direct service providers in each system are very important. The clinician is warned that it may take longer than expected to identify and get in touch with these types of collateral sources. Additionally, the evaluator should not be surprised if a potential collateral source wants to consult with his or her supervisor before speaking with the evaluator. Regardless, as is the case with any forensic evaluation, it is important all successful and unsuccessful efforts made to obtain data are noted in the report.

Notes

1. For a brief but thorough history of the nation's transfer laws and trends, *see* U.S. Department of Justice, Office of Justice Programs, Office of Juvenile Justice and Delinquency Prevention, *Trying Juveniles as Adults: An Analysis of State Transfer Laws and Reporting* (September 2011) at 8–10. For more in-depth data regarding discretionary transfer, *see* U.S. Department of Justice, Office of Justice Programs, Office of Juvenile Justice and Delinquency Prevention, *Delinquency Cases Waived to Criminal Court, 2011* (December 2014).

2. *See, generally, Kent v. United States,* 383 U.S. 541 (1966; "the waiver of jurisdiction is a critically important action determining vitally important statutory rights of the juvenile").

3. A small minority of states allow criminal court judges to exempt young defendants from certain criminal penalties, under limited circumstances. *See An Analysis of State Transfer Laws and Reporting, supra,* at 7.

4. Though state laws vary widely as to whether youth can be housed in adult facilities, recent surveys by the U.S. Department of Justice have established that approximately 10,000 young people are held in adult jails and prisons on any given night. *See* U.S. Department of Justice, Bureau of Justice Statistics, *Jail Inmates at Midyear 2009* (June 2010); U.S. Department of Justice, Bureau of Justice Statistics, *Prison Inmates at Midyear 2009* (June 2010).

5. *See* Centers for Disease Control, *Effects on Violence of Laws and Policies Facilitating the Transfer of Youth from the Juvenile to Adult Justice System* (November 2007; finding that placing youth in the adult criminal court system increases the likelihood that they will commit future crimes by 34%); U.S. Department of Justice, Office of Justice Programs, Office of Juvenile Justice and Delinquency Prevention, *Juvenile Transfer Laws: An Effective Deterrent to Delinquency?* (June 2010; finding that public safety increases when young people are tried in the juvenile court system). *See also* Patrick Griffin, Sean Addie, Benjamin Adams, and Kathy Firestine, *Trying Juveniles as Adults: An Analysis of State Transfer Laws and Reporting,* Juv. Offenders and Victims: Nat'l Rep. Series, at 24, 26 (September 2011; sending children to adult prison has a "counter-deterrent effect" of increased recidivism).

6. *Roper v. Simmons,* 543 U.S. 551, 569 (2005; children have a "lack of maturity and an underdeveloped sense of responsibility . . . [that] lead[s] to recklessness, impulsivity, and heedless risk-taking. . . . [Children also] are more vulnerable . . . to negative influences and outside pressures [and have limited] contro[l] over their own environment"); *Graham v. Florida,* 560 U.S. 48, 50, 68 (2009; children have diminished culpability and greater prospects for reform and are accordingly "less deserving of the most severe punishments"); *Miller v. Alabama,* 132 S. Ct. 2455, 2464, (children "lack the ability to extricate themselves from horrific, crime-producing settings. . . . [A] child's character is not as well formed as an adult's; his traits are less fixed and his actions less likely to be evidence of irretrievabl[e] deprav[ity]"; internal citations omitted).

7. *Roper, supra,* at 569–70; *Miller, supra,* at 2464.

8. Only a handful of states publicly report their transfer data; it is impossible to know exactly how many youth are transferred each year. *See An Analysis of State Transfer Laws and Reporting* (September 2011) at 1. We can be confident, however, that the number is significant—a 2007 report including data from only 21 states documented nearly 14,000 transfers that year. *Id.*

9. Of course, regardless of who the retaining party is, the forensic psychologist should strive to be unbiased and impartial (APA, 2013 Specialty Guideline 1.02).

10. *See, e.g.,* the Campaign for Youth Justice Resource List, available at http://www .campaignforyouthjustice.org/about-resources.html

11. *See, e.g.,* University of Pittsburgh, Center for Research on Health Care, *Pathways to Desistance: A Longitudinal Student of Serious Adolescent Offenders.* (2011)

12. *See, e.g.,* Justice Policy Institute, *The Dangers of Detention: The Impact of Incarcerating Youth in Detention and Other Secure Facilities.* (2006)

13. Space limitations prevent the author from presenting a detailed version of what would have been offered to the court. Jason's mental status was fairly unremarkable except that he endorsed signs and symptoms of depression, but these appeared to be related his current legal circumstances.

References

Allan, A., & Grisso, T. (2014). Ethical principles and the communication of forensic mental health assessments. *Ethics & Behavior, 24*(6), 467–477.

American Psychological Association. (2010). Ethical principles of psychologists and code of conduct. Retrieved from http://www.apa.org/ethics/code/index.aspx

American Psychological Association. (2013). Specialty guidelines for forensic psychology. *American Psychologist, 68*(1), 7–19. Retrieved from http://www.apa.org/practice/guidelines/forensic-psychology.pdf

Barnum, R. (1987). Clinical evaluation of juvenile delinquents facing transfer to adult court. *Journal of the American Academy of Child and Adolescent Psychiatry, 26*(6), 922–925. doi:10.1097/00004583-198726060-00018

Bishop, D. M., & Frazier, D. (2000). Consequences of transfer. In J. Fagan & F. Zimring (Eds.), *The changing borders of juvenile justice: Transfer of adolescents to the criminal court* (pp. 13–43). Chicago, IL: University of Chicago Press.

Bishop, D. M., Frazier, C. E., Lanza-Kaduce, L., & Winner, L. (1996). The transfer of juveniles to criminal court: Does it make a difference? *Crime & Delinquency, 41*, 171–191. doi:10.1177/0011128796042002001

Borum, R., Bartel, P., Forth, A., & Psychological Assessment Resources, Inc. (2006). *SAVRY: Structured assessment of violence risk in youth: professional manual*. Lutz, FL: PAR.

Brannen, D. N., Salekin, R. T., Zapf, P. A., Salekin, K. L., Kubak, F. A., & DeCoster, J. (2006). Transfer to adult court: A national study of how juvenile court judges weigh pertinent Kent criteria. *Psychology Public Policy and Law*. doi:10.1037/1076-8971.12.3.332

Cauffman, E., & Grisso, T. (2005). Mental health issues among minority offenders in the juvenile justice system. In *Our children, their children: Confronting racial and ethnic differences in American juvenile justice* (pp. 390–412). Chicago, IL: University of Chicago Press.

Chein, J., Albert, D., O'Brien, L., Uckert, K., & Steinberg, L. (2011). Peers increase adolescent risk taking by enhancing activity in the brain's reward circuitry. *Developmental Science*, pp. F1–F10.

Chen, D. R., & Salekin, R. T. (2012). Transfer to adult court: Enhancing clinical forensic evaluations and informing policy. *Handbook of Juvenile Forensic Psychology and Psychiatry*, 105–125.

Fagan, J. (1995). Separating the men from the boys: The comparative advantage of juvenile versus criminal court sanctions on recidivism among adolescent felony offenders. In J. C. Howell, B. Krisberg, J. D. Hawkings, & J. J. Wilson (Eds.), *A sourcebook: Serious violent and chronic juvenile offenders* (pp. 238–260). Thousand Oaks, CA: SAGE.

Greenfield, D. P., & Gottschalk, J. A. (2008). *Writing forensic reports: A guide for mental health professionals* (1st ed.). New York, NY: Springer Publishing Company.

Grigorenko, E. L. (2012). *Handbook of juvenile forensic psychology and psychiatry*. New York, NY: Springer.

Grisso, T. (2010). Clinicians' transfer evaluations: How well can they assist judicial discretion? *Louisiana Law Review, 71*(1).

Grisso, T. (2013). *Forensic evaluation of juveniles* (2nd ed.). Professional Resource Press.

Grisso, T., Vincent, G., & Seagrave, D. (2005). *Mental health screening and assessment in juvenile justice* (1st ed.). New York, NY: Guilford Press.

Gutheil, T. G., & Simon, R. I. (2004). Avoiding bias in expert testimony. *Contemporary Psychiatry*, 260–270.

Heilbrun, K., & DeMatteo, D. (2012). Toward establishing standards of practice in juvenile forensic mental health assessment. *Handbook of Juvenile Forensic Psychology and Psychiatry*, 145–155. doi:10.1007/978-1-4614-0905-2_10

Heilbrun, K., DeMatteo, D., & Holliday, S. B. (2014). *Forensic mental health assessment: A casebook* (2nd ed.). Oxford University Press.

Heilbrun, K., Grisso, T., & Goldstein, A. (2008). *Foundations of forensic mental health assessment*. New York, NY: Oxford University Press.

Hoge, R. (2009). Advances in the assessment and treatment of juvenile offenders. *Kriminologija & Socijalna Integracija*, *17*(2), 49–69.

Hoge, R. D., & Andrews, D. A. (2010). *Evaluation for risk of violence in juveniles*. Oxford, UK: Oxford University Press.

Jordan, K. L., & Myers, D. L. (2011). Juvenile transfer and deterrence: Reexamining the effectiveness of a "get-tough" policy. *Crime & Delinquency*. doi:10.1177/0011128708319111

Karson, M., & Nadkarni, L. (2013). *Principles of forensic report writing*. Washington, DC: American Psychological Association.

Kassin, S. M., Dror, I. E., & Kukucka, J. (2013). The forensic confirmation bias: Problems, perspectives, and proposed solutions. *Journal of Applied Research in Memory and Cognition*, *2*, 42–52. Retrieved from http://dx.doi.org/10.1016/j.jarmac.2013.01.001

Kuanliang, A., Sorensen, J., & Cunningham, M. (2008). Juvenile inmates in an adult prison system: Rates of disciplinary misconduct and violence. *Criminal Justice and Behavior*, *35*(9), 1186–1201. doi:10.1177/0093854808322744

Lenroot, R., & Giedd, J. (2006). Brain development in children and adolescents: Insights from anatomical magnetic resonance imaging. *Neuroscience & Biobehavioral Reviews*, *30*(6), pp. 718–729.

Lipsey, M. W. (2009). The primary factors that characterize effective interventions with juvenile offenders: A meta-analytic overview. *Victims & Offenders*. doi:10.1080/15564880802612573

Lipsey, M. W., Howell, J. C., Kelly, M. R., Chapman, G., & Carver, D. (2010). *Improving the effectiveness of juvenile justice programs: A new perspective on evidence-based practice*. Retrieved from Center for Juvenile Justice Reform, Georgetown University website: http://cjjr.georgetown.edu/pdfs/ebp/ebppaper.pdf

MacKinnon-Lewis, C., Kaufman, M., & Frabutt, J. (2002). Juvenile justice and mental health: Youth and families in the middle. *Aggression and Violent Behavior*, *7*(4), 353–363. doi:10.1016/S1359-1789(01)00062.3

McCann, J. T. (1998). *Malingering and deception in adolescents: Assessing credibility in clinical and forensic settings*. Washington, DC: American Psychological Association.

McGowan, A., Hahn, R., Liberman, A., & Crosby, A. (2007). Effects on violence of laws and policies facilitating the transfer of juveniles from the juvenile justice system to the adult justice system: A systematic review. *American Journal of Preventive Medicine*, *32*, S7–S28.

Means, R. F., Heller, L. D., & Janofsky, J. S. (2012). Transferring juvenile defendants from adult to juvenile court: How Maryland forensic evaluators and judges reach their decisions. *Journal American Academy of Psychiatry & Law*, *40*.

Miller v. Alabama, Supreme Court of the United States, Certiorari to the Court of Criminal Appeals of Alabama, No. 10-9646, Argued March 20, 2012–Decided June 25, 2012.

Moffitt, T. (2003). Life-course-persistent and adolescence-limited antisocial behavior: A 10-year research review and a research agenda. In *Causes of Conduct Disorder and Juvenile Delinquency* (pp. 49–75). New York, NY: Guilford Press.

Moffitt, T., Arseneault, L., Jaffee, S., Kim-Cohen, J., Koenen, K., Odgers, C., & Viding, E. (2008). Research review: DSM-V conduct disorder: Research needs for an evidence base. *Journal of Child Psychology and Psychiatry, 49*(1), 3–33. doi:10.1111/j.1469-7610.2007.01823.x

Myers, D. L. (2003). Adult crime, adult time: Punishing violent youth in the adult criminal justice system. *Youth Violence and Juvenile Justice, 1*, 173–197. doi:10.1177/154120 4002250878

Neal, T., & Grisso, T. (2014). The cognitive underpinnings of bias in forensic mental health evaluations. *Psychology, Public Policy and Law, 20*(2), 200–211. doi:10.1037/a0035824

Osterlind, S. J., Koller, J. R., & Morris, E. F. (2007). Incidence and practical issues of mental health for school-aged youth in juvenile justice detention. *Journal of Correctional Health Care, 13*(4), 268–277. doi:10.1177/1078345807306802

Otto, R. K., DeMier, R. L., & Boccaccini, M. L. (2014). *Forensic reports and testimony: A guide to effective communication for psychologists and psychiatrists.* Wiley.

Penney, S. R., & Moretti, M. M. (2005). The transfer of juveniles to adult court in Canada and the United States: Confused agendas and compromised assessment procedures. *International Journal of Forensic Mental Health, 4*(1), 19–37. doi:10.1080/14999013.2005 .10471210

Redding, R. E. (2008). *Juvenile transfer laws: An effective deterrent to delinquency?* Retrieved from US Department of Justice/Office of Juvenile Justice and Delinquency Prevention website: https://www.ncjrs.gov/pdffiles1/ojjdp/220595.pdf

Redding, R. E., & Fuller, E. J. (2004). What do juvenile offenders know about being tried as adults? Implications for deterrence. *Juvenile and Family Court Journal*, 35–44.

Salekin, R. T. (2002). Clinical evaluation of youth considered for transfer to adult criminal court: Refining practice and directions for science. *Journal of Forensic Psychology, 2*, 55–72.

Salekin, R. T. (2015). Forensic Evaluation and Treatment of Juveniles: Innovation and Best Practice, American Psychological Association.

Salekin, R. T., Price, K., Adams, E., Ang, X., & Rosenbuam, J. (2013). Evaluation for disposition and transfer of juvenile offenders. In Roesch, R., & Zapf, P. A. (2013). *Forensic assessments in criminal and civil law: A handbook for lawyers* (pp. 249–263). New York, NY: Oxford University Press.

Salekin, R. T., & Psychological Assessment Resources. (2004). *RSTI, risk-sophistication-treatment inventory; risk for dangerousness sophistication-maturity treatment amenability: Professional manual.* Lutz, FL: PAR, Psychological Assessment Resources.

Spice, A., Viljoen, J. L., Gretton, H. M., & Roesch, R. (2010). Psychological assessment for adult sentencing of juvenile offenders: An evaluation of the RSTI and the SAVRY. *International Journal of Forensic Mental Health, 9*, 124–137. doi:10.1080/14999013.20 10.501846

Steinberg, L. (2014). *Age of opportunity: Lessons from the new science of adolescence.* New York, NY: Houghton Mifflin Harcourt.

Steinberg, L., Albert, D., Cauffman, E., Banich, M., Graham, S., & Woolard, J. (2008). Age differences in sensation seeking and impulsivity as indexed by behavior and self-report: Evidence for a dual system model. *Developmental Psychology, 44*(6), 1764–1778.

Steinberg, L., Cauffman, E., & Monahan, K. C. (2015). Psychosocial maturity and desistance from crime in a sample of serious juvenile offenders. *Highlights from Pathways to Desistance.* U.S. Department of Justice, Office of Justice Programs, Office of Juvenile Justice and Delinquency Prevention.

Steinberg, L., Cauffman, E., Woolard, J., Graham, S., & Banich, M. (October 2009). Are adolescents less mature than adults? Minors' access to abortion, the juvenile death penalty, and the alleged APA "flip-flop." *American Psychologist,* 583–594.

Steinberg, L., & Monahan, K. (2007). Age differences in resistance to peer pressure. *Developmental Psychology, 43*(6), 1531–1543.

Underwood, L. A., Warren, K. M., Talbott, L., Jackson, L., & Dailey, F. (2014). Mental health treatment in juvenile justice secure care facilities: Practice and policy recommendations. *Journal of Forensic Psychology Practice, 14*(1), 55–85. doi:10.1080/15228932.2014.865398

Urquhart, T., & Viljoen, J. (2014). The use of the SAVRY and YLS/CMI in adolescent court proceedings: A case law review. *The International Journal of Forensic Mental Health, 13*(1), 47–61. doi:10.1080/14999013.2014885470

Ward, J. M. (2003). Deterrence's difficulty magnified: The importance of adolescent development in assessing the deterrence value of transferring juveniles to adult court. *UC Davis Journal of Juvenile Law & Policy, 7,* 253–284.

Weinberger, D. R., Elvevåg, B., & Giedd, J. (2005). *The adolescent brain: A work in progress* (pp. 1–36). Washington, DC: The National Campaign to Prevent Teen Pregnancy. Retrieved from http://web.calstatela.edu/faculty/dherz/Teenagebrain.workinprogress.pdf

17

Introduction to School-Based Risk Assessments

Jeff D. Stein and Jill G. Durand

Relevant Case Law

School-based risk assessments diverge from other topics in this forensic psychology compendium because there is no legal standard or statutory guideline on which to form a clinical opinion. Rather, the issue of school violence has, until the late 1990s, typically been addressed after a tragic event, often attributed to some form of bullying. In the last fifteen years, legislatures in forty-five states have directed their respective school districts to adopt policies to address bullying (U.S. Department of Education, 2011). The fruits of those efforts are yet to be seen, however, as indicated by the National Center for Education Statistics (Robers et al., 2014). For example, as of 2012, students were more likely to be victimized at school than away from school, and there were 5.2 victimizations for every 100 students across the United States. The previous year, 2011, 28% of students across the country reported being bullied at school, and 7% of students were threatened or injured with a weapon, such as a gun, knife, or club, on school property. Some have indicated that schools are relying on profiling, as opposed to research-based risk assessments, as a means of identifying those students at risk of committing acts of violence (Reddy et al., 2001; Sewell & Mendelsohn, 2000).

A school-based risk assessment may include, but does not require, involvement by outside agencies or individuals such as law enforcement or the legal system. This type of psychological evaluation requires the consent of the juvenile's legal parent or guardian for the evaluation to occur, and typically the results are provided to the educational setting or school district. As a result, there are many risk management factors for the evaluator to consider, such as ensuring that all parties are aware of the limits of confidentiality, the duty to warn, who is paying for the evaluation, and who is entitled to receive the results or a copy of a written report. A school-based risk assessment is considered to fall within the jurisdiction of "forensic psychology," primarily because handling the ethical and management issues needed to address concerns about school violence requires a systematic approach to data collection familiar to clinicians in forensic mental health. Psychologists conducting school-based risk assessments must have a firm understanding of the ethical issues that underlie such evaluations, as outlined by the American Psychological Association (2010, 2012).[1]

This first section of this chapter is dedicated to the scientific "ancestry" of school-based risk assessments, including General Issues in Risk Assessments, Developmental Pathways of Aggression, and School Risk Assessments. The second section will consist of a case vignette.

General Issues in Risk Assessment

A commonly utilized approach to conducting a violence risk assessment in general is referred to as "structured professional judgment," which involves determining whether an individual possesses characteristics of known, aggregate factors associated with risk of violence and establishing an opinion about the strength of the individual's risk compared to those base rates. There are several published instruments, such as the Violence Risk Appraisal Guide (VRAG; Harris et al., 1993) and the Historical Clinical Risk Management-20 (HCR-20; Webster et al., 1997), which provide a numerical risk score based on an algorithmic calculation of an individual's presenting factors. A current perspective on these risk assessment instruments is that no single instrument is demonstrably more effective in predicting risk than another and that any instrument applied to an individual should be selected on the basis of the purpose of that evaluation (Monahan & Skeem, 2014).

Much of the literature that addresses violence among adolescents is still in its infancy, and has focused largely on juvenile offenders—adolescents who have been adjudicated for a criminal act. As a result, the lens through which these risk assessments have been viewed came from adult assessment, including the application of measures originally designed for adults and later modified for younger individuals. Examples of juvenile forensic instruments used include the SAVRY (Structured Assessment for Violence Risk in Youth; Borum, Bartel & Forth, 2003), the PCL: YV (Psychopathy Checklist: Youth Version; Forth et al., 2003), and the MAYSI-2 (Massachusetts Youth Screening Instrument—Version 2; Grisso & Barnum, 2006). However, assessing for psychopathy in juveniles is controversial. In one survey of forensic evaluators by Viljoen et al. (2010), for example, a majority (79%) reported using structured psychopathy measures on adolescents while also cautioning that juveniles should not be labeled as psychopaths. Overall, there is insufficient evidence of a direct link between psychopathic traits starting in childhood or adolescence and persisting into adulthood, and measures of psychopathy are unlikely to yield a reliable estimate of violence on their own, particularly in the long-term (Edens et al., 2001). An alternative and potentially valuable source of psychological data can also be obtained from the use of well-researched, structured instruments that assess personality traits or behavioral patterns, such as the Millon Adolescent Clinical Inventory (MACI; Millon 1993) and the Behavior Assessment System for Children, Second Edition (BASC-2; Reynolds & Kamphaus 2004).

Any risk assessment is a "snapshot" in time of an individual's functioning and potential for violence because, although some risk factors are static and unchangeable (i.e., gender and history of violence), others may change with time or intervention (i.e., employment and substance abuse). As noted by Appelbaum (2011), "the unknowable contingencies of life" (p. 819) can immediately alter any prediction offered in an individual assessment. This is particularly true for juveniles because, compared with adults, personality features and cognitive capacities vary and evolve quickly during this stage of development. Borum (2006) suggests incorporating research-driven data on known risk factors that are correlated to violence with individual dynamic (changeable) factors, such as the home environment and peer influence.

When considering the current state of the field regarding evaluations of risk for harm, much of the focus is on adults who may act in a violent manner. In fact, the definition of "risk assessment" has often been characterized as estimating the probability that an act of physical violence will be perpetrated on others (see, e.g., Kraemer et al., 1997; Skeem & Monahan, 2011). Yet the role that risk assessments play in legal arenas and health care has continued to grow over the last few decades, underscoring the need to carefully gather important data and communicate that information to those who are responsible for making decisions. Such communications can potentially be misleading and have far-reaching consequences, including the implementation of limits on an individual's well-being, liberty, and livelihood (Heilbrun et al., 2000). In addition, rather than simply providing a statistical estimate of probability that an act of violence will occur, a school-based risk assessment should identify the presence of both risk and protective factors. Through that process, one may discover concerns that an identifiable individual is being targeted for a harmful act, prompting a pressing *Tarasoff*-type circumstance (Borum & Reddy, 2001).

Developmental Pathways of Aggression

Before assessing risk, it is important for evaluators to understand the different types of violence as well as developmental factors that can lead to aggressive and violent behaviors among children and adolescents.

First, research has often separated youthful aggressive behavior into two subtypes: reactive and proactive aggression. Reactive aggression is a retaliatory response to a perceived threat and is the most common form of violence among youth. Youth who engage in this type of aggression are often sensitive to hostile or aggressive cues or misperceive benign social cues. The aggressive act is often impulsive, and the youth may have a psychiatric condition. The behavior may be defensive or a reaction to a highly stressful situation. In comparison, proactive aggression is often controlled and goal-directed. It is instrumental, or used to achieve a particular outcome. Youth who engage in proactive aggression often believe that aggression is a legitimate tool to achieve a goal (Borum, 2006).

In general, regardless of whether such conduct is reactive or proactive, or even very serious, the commission of a violent act during adolescence does not indicate that a youth is at risk of being a long-term or serious offender as an adult. While many engage in delinquent and aggressive acts as teenagers, the majority do not continue with such behavior as adults. Most delinquent and aggressive behavior is limited to adolescence. Moffitt (1993, 1997) has identified two primary types of delinquent patterns: adolescent-limited and life-course persistent. Most fall into the first category. There are developmental factors and influences, which tend to increase the likelihood that a child will continue to demonstrate aggressive behaviors into adulthood. This factor is important to consider when assessing the risk of future violence.

Assessing risk of future violence requires careful consideration to developmental and contextual factors that may influence behavior. However, research to date has focused mainly on male children and adolescents. Given the low base rate of female children and adolescents who engage in violent behavior, the risk factors identified below may not directly apply to this population. Furthermore, while research has consistently demonstrated that there are historical, clinical, personality, and environmental factors that increase the risk of violent behavior, there is no definitive combination to allow for prediction of future violence. Research has shown that various conditions can lead to the same outcome (equifinality), while the presence of such risk factors may not lead to aggression or violence at all (multifinality; Cichetti et al., 1996).

For those juveniles who continue to display aggressive and delinquent behaviors into adulthood, research has shown that the critical historical factors that increase the likelihood of future violence include a history of antisocial behaviors prior to age 13 and past engagement in proactive violence. Male gender also raises risk. Clinical and individual factors that increase risk include low intelligence, mental disorders, hyperactivity, early expression of antisocial personality traits, poor attitudes toward school, poor academic progress, and early substance use. There are numerous environmental factors that also raise the likelihood of violence, including low socioeconomic status, antisocial parents, parental discipline styles (harsh, lax or inconsistent), exposure to violence on television, separation from parents, poor parent-child relationships, abuse and neglect, and antisocial peer groups. For adolescents, additional risk factors include weak social connections, antisocial peer groups, and gang membership (U.S. Surgeon General's Report, 2011). For those children who engage in aggressive behaviors but do not continue to offend into adulthood, research has identified the following features: childhood histories that are relatively free from difficulty (e.g., fewer behavior problems, less likely to have a co-occurring disorder), antisocial behaviors that do not emerge until after age 13, a lower incidence of predatory violence, and an ability to develop and maintain appropriate attachments to others (Moffitt, 1993, 1997).

With regard to individual and personality factors, children who demonstrate antisocial tendencies, particularly conduct problems and psychopathic traits, are more likely to show aggressive behaviors in childhood and adolescence and likely to continue to demonstrate antisocial behavior into adulthood (Frick and Loney, 1999). Research has shown that after controlling for other risk factors such as prior offenses, drug use, and delinquent peers, the presence of callous-unempathic personality traits predicts later antisocial behavior (Salekin, 2008) and is more predictive of severe, stable, and aggressive behaviors (Edens et al., 2007; Leistico et al., 2008). Youth who present with callous-unemotional traits have been shown to demonstrate aggression that is both reactive and proactive, while antisocial youth without such traits show less overall aggression and less proactive aggression in particular (Frick & Viding, 2009). However, the same temperamental risk factors may have different outcomes, depending on the nature of exposure to varying parenting styles and environmental factors.

Given that most children and adolescents who engage in violent acts do not continue to do so into adulthood, it is important to also consider the unique developmental issues of this group. Adolescents are more vulnerable to external influences, particularly peer pressure, and interactions with an antisocial peer group can have a significant impact on decision making. In general, adolescent social development is marked by an increase in the importance of peers, and adolescents are far more likely to commit crimes in groups than are adults (Zimring, 1998). While some may be directly influenced by peer pressure, in general there is a greater desire for peer approval and a fear of rejection, which may lead adolescents to act in ways they might not otherwise, including aggressive acts. Furthermore, risk-taking may be "activated" by the presence of peers or emotional arousal, and "the net result is that adolescents are more likely than either children or adults to change their decisions and alter their behavior in response to peer pressure" (Scott & Steinberg, 2008, p. 20).

Finally, adolescence is a period of great malleability and personality formation. Both psychosocial and neurological development continue into early adulthood, and behaviors that are present in adolescence may not continue into adulthood. Adolescents differ from adults in three salient ways: their developing capacity for mature judgment and decision making, vulnerability to external negative influences, and identity growth. Furthermore, the research in neuroscience has provided evidence and supported the developmental research findings, demonstrating that adolescent brains are not fully developed in the regions responsible for executive functions (i.e., impulse control, planning, assessing risk) and that the limbic system (emotional, impulsive responses) is more readily activated during this period of development compared with adulthood. Adolescents are less likely to consider future consequences for their actions, and their decisions tend to be short-sighted. They are more likely to choose smaller, immediate rewards over larger, longer-term rewards, and they prefer immediate gratification as opposed to long-term consequences (Cauffman & Steinberg, 2000.)

Best Practices in School-Based Risk Assessments

For the purposes of conducting an evaluation of an individual for potentially harmful behavior in a school, Halikias (2004) described two groups of students who may be referred for a risk assessment—those juveniles who have a history of impulsive violence and anger problems (dangerousness), and those who select targets and carefully plan an act of violence (threat). The basis for a school seeking a risk assessment regarding a student is often because a specific incident—such as a physical altercation, an incendiary Internet communication, or a threatening statement made in the presence of others—served as a trigger for worry about dangerousness or a threat. These signals, which Meloy and O'Toole (2011) conceptualize as "leakage," may indicate the need for a forensic professional to determine the likelihood, severity, and imminence of an act of violence.

When conducting a school risk assessment, critical data points should mirror research-driven factors known to be associated with violence, similar to those that are captured by the SAVRY (Borum, 2006). Those include the following:

1. Static factors such as history of family violence, childhood abuse or maltreatment, disrupted attachment relationships, and family criminality;
2. Individual risk factors such as antisocial attitudes/perceptions, impulsivity and substance abuse, anger problems, and lack of empathy;
3. Social risk factors such as delinquent peers, poor parental monitoring, and community dysfunction.

The critical factors outlined above should be obtained from multiple sources. Interviews with the student and family members, as well as collateral information from objective professional sources such as a mental health provider and physician, provide the data from which the evaluator can form hypotheses and confirm or disconfirm clinical appraisals about the level of risk posed by the juvenile. Among several other questions that require clarification, the evaluator will want to know about the juvenile's behavioral patterns, signs of mental illness, self-perceptions and need for attention, ability to cope with frustration, rejection and failure, social inclusiveness and isolation, use of information technology and social media, range of extracurricular interests and motivation, and level/nature of parental and family involvement. These points of information are used to determine the juvenile's motivation, preparation, and contributing factors to engaging in an act of violence and, equally important, to delineate the mediating factors and possible interventions that will reduce this risk. For example, social supports, positive attachment relationships, good working relationships with authority, and resiliency are known protective factors against risk of violence. Participation in support services such as mental health treatment and organized activities might also mitigate this risk.

Case Vignette

Reason for Referral

Billy was a 16-year-old junior at a suburban high school. He was referred for a risk assessment by school administrators who were concerned about a statement Billy made in class that he was going to "bring in an AK and shoot everyone up." At the time of the threat, police were called to the scene and took Billy to a hospital for an inpatient evaluation, two days after which he was psychiatrically cleared. However, upon a police follow-up visit to his home to interview Billy and his parents, a collection of knives and other weapons were confiscated, and police charged him with two criminal offenses related to the threatening statements he made at school. In addition to a question about whether Billy was a risk to himself or others, school personnel intended to use the results as a supplement to determine the appropriateness of his academic placement.

As part of the evaluation process, Billy participated in a clinical interview lasting for one hour, and he completed a self-report, psychological assessment instrument, the Millon Adolescent Clinical Inventory (MACI). The examiner also conducted separate interviews of each of his parents, lasting a total of two hours and thirty minutes, and a collateral phone conversation with his current therapist. The following records were reviewed: 1) Billy's psychoeducational

---

The case vignette has been redacted and all identifying information removed. It is not meant to serve as a forensic report. Any likeness to a case is purely coincidental.

testing report, completed when he was in the 10th grade, and 2) discharge records from the psychiatric hospitalization following the index threat incident at school. At the initial meeting with all parties and collateral sources, the purpose of the risk assessment and the limits of confidentiality were explained. All participants provided a satisfactory understanding of the explanation and consented to participate.

Relevant Background Information

The following information was obtained during the course of the evaluation: Billy is the oldest of three children. Billy's father, Mr. Smith, was a nationwide real estate developer, and his mother, Ms. Smith, is a homemaker. There were no indications of parental psychiatric illness, substance abuse, or domestic violence. In describing Billy's early development, both parents reported he performed at an average level academically, but he was subjected to teasing and ridicule by his peers when he was in third grade. He also made a vague threat to "kill" a peer following one conflict that year. Billy was also physically bullied by a school peer who lived nearby. In an effort to gain popularity at school, when he was in the fifth grade, Billy brought a toy gun to school and, on another occasion, empty machine gun shell casings from his father's World War II memorabilia collection. By the eighth grade, Billy was exhibiting poor social skills, characterized by impulsivity and immaturity in his verbal communications. Billy's mother initiated a change in schools for Billy in the fifth grade and ninth grade because of parental dissatisfaction with how school administrators responded to his adjustment issues. His grades showed a slow decline through middle school and entering high school. His parents also reported that Billy had difficulty modulating his statements and that he did not comprehend rules of social conduct, particularly when larger groups of his peers were engaging in normal mild, disruptive behavior in class. They said that Billy had difficulty making and keeping friends, because he was impulsive, loud, and competitive. At the same time, they reported that he had managed to maintain a part-time job for two years at an outfitter's surplus warehouse, selling gear for fishing, camping, and hunting.

Both parents described "walking on eggshells" around Billy at home, due to his overreactions when he is disciplined. They reported one incident in the last year when, after Mr. Smith physically removed an air gun from his possession, Billy retreated to his room and smashed a large television to pieces. Mr. Smith acknowledged that he is impatient with his son, and Ms. Smith stated that Billy appears less stressed and irritable when Mr. Smith is away on business for longer periods of time. Billy's parents reported that their son did not use drugs or alcohol, and he had not exhibited signs of psychoses or severe mental illness, but they acknowledged long-standing irritability, oppositional conduct at home, and excessive anger in response to limit setting, such as when video game playing is restricted. Following the school incident during which Billy made a general homicidal threat, his parents expressed concern that their son's life had been upended in that he had been suspended from school, he was not working at his part-time job, and his plans to be a police officer or join the army were now in question.

When asked about reports of Billy having a collection of weapons, his parents explained that he enjoyed whittling with knives and engaging in target practice using air guns with plastic BBs. Mr. Smith noted that he took away some of Billy's knives several months ago because the weapons looked "treacherous" and because Billy would leave the knives lying around, unsecured, yet refused to discuss the issue. He said that Billy had purchased a samurai blade online, without the parents' awareness, which was discovered following the police investigation of weapons in the household. Ms. Smith acknowledged there was some miscommunication about when Billy could have his weapon collection back following Mr. Smith's departure on a one-month sales trip. Mr. Smith acknowledged that he (Mr. Smith) also had a collection of knives and firearms, which were kept under lock and key. Both parents acknowledged that Mr. Smith worried that Billy would attack him with a knife out of impulsive frustration over their tense relationship. Ms. Smith said that Billy slams his door and yells loudly but exhibited physical harm toward anyone at home. Neither of Billy's younger siblings were exhibiting developmental deficits or social/behavioral problems.

Interview with Billy

Billy was cooperative and spontaneous in response to interview questions. He acknowledged having a hard time socially, which he attributed to being the "new kid" who is typically shunned by others who are more familiar with each other. He acknowledged that he formed relationships with peers who were more likely to get in trouble but that he did not spend time with them outside of school hours. He acknowledged there were "a lot of bad influences there," such as a peer group involved with drug and alcohol use. Billy admitted that he had used marijuana on a periodic basis, usually by himself. He also expressed daily enjoyment of popular simulated video games, particularly war gaming.

When asked to explain events leading up to his current suspension from school, Billy said that he was being "loud and goofy," which created conflicts, and when one of the kids in his engineering class was engaging in a routine of disruptive behavior, Billy thought he would give the peer "a taste of his own medicine" by hiding his hat. He said that the peer became angry, and other students in the class also began yelling, so Billy threatened to "be the next school shooter." He said that "everyone freaked out," and he regretted it. When asked why he felt regret, Billy said, "I guess it scared people."

When asked for basic information about himself, Billy said he gets along well with his mother but not with his father, which he attributed to his father's criticisms of him. Billy mentioned a particular neighborhood peer who had been harassing him for several years. When asked how he would react if this peer were accidentally killed, Billy reported that he would be sad. He added that he is often disciplined when he retaliates against others who bully him, and although he feels the world is "not fair," he wants to obtain justice by "proving someone else wrong."

Billy acknowledged he loves collecting knives in particular because of their utility and the way they feel in his hand. He said that his mother does not have a problem with his weapons collection, but from his mother's perspective, his father "didn't feel safe with [Billy] having them." He acknowledged having a temper, which is evoked by "mostly being told 'no' or being threatened," such as his mother or father telling him he is not permitted to do something or having some of his belongings taken away. Billy denied hearing voices or having strange sensations; he denied feeling as though someone is out to get him; and he denied any thoughts or plans of killing himself, either past or present.

Collateral Contacts

In a collateral phone contact, Dr. Jones, a psychologist, reported that for the past two years he had been providing weekly counseling to Billy, who was periodically accompanied by his mother but not his father. Dr. Jones said that Billy presents with attention and impulse-control problems, consistent with his long-standing diagnosis of ADHD, but also a cluster of other symptoms, such as oppositional behavior, irritability, and poor interpersonal skills. He was aware Billy had amassed a collection of knives, but there were no signs that Billy ever fantasized about violence or that he might be prone to a planned attack on anyone. He agreed that Billy and others might be at risk if Billy were to carry a knife as a means of self-protection from bullying and react impulsively. Dr. Jones also suggested that Billy's educational setting was not sufficient to address his ongoing mental health/emotional difficulties and that he may need a therapeutically informed educational program in order to graduate high school. Dr. Jones acknowledged that he had not shared such an opinion with Billy or his parents, and he was unsure how that would be received, but it was his clinical belief that sharing such an opinion outweighed any risk that doing so would pose for the therapeutic relationship.

Psychological Measures

As noted above, Billy was administered the MACI, which was chosen as a structured, objective measure of his developing personality traits and any relevant mental health symptoms. Results of this psychological measure produced a valid profile that highlighted Billy's social anxiety and guardedness. He responded similarly to adolescents who possess a strong desire for acceptance, which is countered by anticipation of humiliation and rejection. Such adolescents are uncomfortable in social situations and retreat from the normal reciprocity involved in interpersonal relationships. Also salient in the testing results was Billy's apparent indifference to the behaviors and feelings of others. He responded similarly to those who are irresponsible and careless, fail to anticipate consequences for actions, and are easily bored. Diagnostically, the test highlighted Schizoid, Avoidant, and Antisocial traits, accompanied by a Depressive Disorder.

School records indicated psychoeducational testing prior to his sophomore year of high school. The results revealed intelligence skills in the average range, along with significant deficits in receptive and expressive language and difficulties with behavioral and emotional regulation. Hospital discharge records from his inpatient admission immediately following the school threat included Mood Disorder Not Otherwise Specified (MD-NOS), Posttraumatic Stress Disorder (PTSD) with history of bullying, Attention Deficit Hyperactivity Disorder (ADHD) by history, and episodic substance abuse (alcohol and cannabis abuse).

Clinical Summary and Opinion

Billy Smith was a 16-year-old junior in high school who lived with his parents. His early development was positive for deficits in fine motor control and organizational skills. He was subjected to bullying by peers for several years in school and became the object of scrutiny by school officials on several occasions (i.e., threatening a peer, bringing symbolic weapons to school, and disrupting class). Dissatisfied with the school's response to their son's difficulties, Billy's parents changed his schools a few times. His academic skills continued to decline, and he started using marijuana since early puberty. A comprehensive psychoeducational evaluation completed when he was 15 years of age revealed notable signs of executive function difficulties, such as poor impulse control, organizational skills, and language comprehension deficits.

Concurrent with Billy's cognitive function deficits revealed by his previous psychoeducational testing, there have also been long-standing signs of problematic interpersonal skills and social alienation. Without adaptive peer relationships, Billy's principal sources of social skill building had apparently come through playing violent video games and working part-time at a commercial retailer of outdoor sporting goods. In the evaluator's opinion, this dynamic created a bridge between an imaginary world of conflict resolution through violence and easy access to a wide variety of potential weaponry (toward which he had developed a fascination).

Regarding his threat made in a school classroom, the evaluator was of the opinion that Billy did not present with identifiable patterns of physical harm toward others. His threat of harm was not directed at any one individual but rather was made impulsively and without a true appreciation until well afterward, when he recognized the fear that such a comment might cause in others. There was no evidence that Billy has had a particular plan to harm someone. The incident appeared to reflect what was referred to earlier in this chapter as "reactive aggression," given that Billy was impulsive, had a long history of using poor judgment with his verbal commentary, and struggled to maintain healthy peer relationships. He had only one identified incident of physical aggression, in which he destroyed property at home following a conflict with his father, but overall his functioning did not translate to a high risk of actual physical violence in the absence of a plan, history, or other identified factors associated with violence (i.e., psychotic thought process, lack of insight or empathy, or a substance abuse disorder). Finally, there were protective factors in place, such as having involved parents with no history of problematic adjustment (i.e., substance abuse, domestic violence, incarceration) and Billy's participation in therapy with a psychologist who was very familiar with the factors involved in Billy's current difficulties. That said, there was, without question, a risk that Billy could lash out in anger at an individual whom he perceived to be tormenting him, even if he provoked a negative interchange by virtue of his social deficits or impulsivity.

The evaluation also revealed that Billy possessed a number of historical, clinical, and environmental risk factors that are associated with risk for violence. For this reason, there were understandable concerns that he was at risk for acting out against his father if he was feeling angry or thwarted. Therefore, Billy's access to weapons or involvement in violence-themed activities should be limited. It was recommended that Billy's goal for therapy should be to gain better insight about his impulsive propensities and the need to effect some protective measures for when he gets angry, particularly at home.

Furthermore, there was substantial data indicating the presence of a mood disorder, and in this evaluation circumstance the most appropriate *DSM-5* diagnosis would be Unspecified Depressive Disorder. He showed a developmental history and current functioning suggestive of a vulnerability for continued psychiatric dysfunction requiring ongoing mental health treatment including psychopharmacological consultation. Regarding Billy's educational needs, academic programming should include a substantial therapeutic support for his mental health condition, to supplement the goals of his special education plan. Given the pervasive social difficulties Billy has as a result of his mental health issues and executive (cognitive) deficits, both at home and school, consideration should also be given to Billy living outside the home in a residential program. Among the benefits to living in a treatment program, Billy's safety and that of others would be better managed, he would be provided more support and structure than he receives at home, and he would receive daily and consistent therapeutic support.

Common Pitfalls and Considerations

School risk assessments serve as a unique and complex service that forensically trained clinicians can offer educational institutions. These evaluations are based on a multitude of factors, including the individual and family functioning, demands of educational systems, community safety, and the pressure on a clinician to manage all of these issues while producing a thorough, forensic-based opinion of risk of harm. Like any forensic psychological evaluation, clinicians must be cognizant of the peripheral factors that could be at play and influence a clinical opinion. It is incumbent on the forensic assessor to inquire about and appreciate the history of support, conflict, distrust, and cooperation existing within the school community, between the school and the parents, between the parents and the student, and so on. For example, there may be significant financial motivations for either a school system to insist that a high-risk student can be managed internally or for a family to demand a costly, out-of-district therapeutic education for their child, resulting in an embellishment or exaggeration of various factors incorporated into the evaluation. There are often pulls, either internally or from the referral source, to make a certain prediction about whether violence is going to occur, and it behooves any clinician conducting school-based risk assessments to be familiar with what is professionally responsible and defensible. In short, the risk assessment must include the broader psychological and political climate within which the student and his behavior are embedded. Due to the high-stakes nature of making recommendations that could have a prominent, even lifelong impact on a young person's future, the authors would advise evaluators to ensure sufficient training has been obtained in conducting forensic mental health assessments and also to have access to colleagues from whom consultations can be obtained regarding complex cases.

Note

1. The "Specialty Guidelines for Forensic Psychology" of the APA (2012, p. 7) "apply in all matters in which psychologists provide expertise to judicial, administrative, and educational systems" such as offering expert opinion to administrators and in educational activities.

References

American Psychological Association. (2010). *Ethical principles of psychologists and code of conduct*. Retrieved from http://www.apa.org/ethics/code/index.aspx

American Psychological Association. (2012). Specialty guidelines for forensic psychology. *American Psychologist, 68*(1), 7–19.

Appelbaum, P. (2011). Reference guide on mental health evidence. In Federal Judicial Center, *Reference Manual on Scientific Evidence* (pp. 813–896). Washington, DC: National Academies Press.

Borum, R. (2006). Assessing risk for violence among juvenile offenders. In S. N. Sparta & G. P. Koocher (Eds.), *Forensic mental health assessment of children and adolescents* (pp. 190–202). New York, NY: Oxford Universities Press.

Borum, R., Bartel, P., & Forth, A. (2003). *Manual for the Structured Assessment of Violence Risk in Youth, version 1.1*. Tampa, FL: University of South Florida.

Borum, R., & Reddy, M. (2001). Assessing violence risk in *Tarasoff*-type situations: A fact-based model of inquiry. *Behavioral Sciences and the Law, 19*, 375–385.

Cauffman, E., & L. Steinberg. (2000). (Im)maturity of judgment in adolescence. *Behavioral Science and Law, 18*, 741–754.

Cichetti, D., & F. Rogosh. (1996). Equifinality and multifinality in developmental psychology. *Development and Psychopathology, 8*, 597–600.

Edens, J. F., & Cahill, M. A. (2007). Psychopathy in adolescence and criminal recidivism in young adulthood: Longitudinal results from a multiethnic sample of youthful offenders. *Assessment, 14*, 57–64.

Edens, J. F., Skeem, J. L., Cruise, K. R., & Cauffman, E. (2001). Assessment of "juvenile psychopathy" and its association with violence: A critical review. *Behavioral Sciences and the Law, 19*, 53–80.

Forth, A. E., Kosson, D., & Hare, R. D. (2003). *The Hare PCL: Youth Version*. Toronto, Ontario, Canada: Multi-Health Systems.

Frick, P., & Loney, B. (1999). Outcomes of oppositional defiant disorder and conduct disorder. In H. C. Quay & A. E. Hogan (Eds.), *Handbook of disruptive behavior disorders* (pp. 507–524). New York, NY: Kluwer Academic/Plenum.

Frick, P. J., & Viding, E. (2009). Antisocial behavior from a developmental psychopathology perspective. *Development and Psychopathology, 21*, 1111–1131.

Grisso, T., & Barnum, R. (2006). *Massachusetts Youth Screening Instrument—Version 2: User's manual and technical report*. Sarasota, FL: Professional Resource Exchange.

Halikias, W. (2004). School-based risk assessments: A conceptual framework and model for professional practice. *Professional Psychology: Research and Practice, 35*(6), 598–607.

Harris, G. T., Rice, M. E., & Quinsey, V. L. (1993). Violent recidivism of mentally disordered offenders: The development of a statistical prediction instrument. *Criminal Justice and Behavior, 20*, 315–335.

Heilbrun, K., O'Neill, M. L., Strohman, L. K., Bowman, Q., & Philipson, J. (2000). Expert approaches to communicating violence risk. *Law and Human Behavior, 24*(1), 137–148.

Kraemer, H., Kazdin, A., Offord, D., Kessier, R., Jensen, P., & Kupfer, D. (1997). Coming to terms with the terms of risk. *Archives of General Psychiatry, 54*, 337–343.

Leistico, A. M., Salekin, R. T., DeCosta, J., & Rogers, R. (2008). A large scale meta-analysis relating the Hare measures of psychopathy to antisocial conduct. *Law and Human Behavior, 32*, 28–45.

Millon, T. (1993). Millon Adolescent Clinical Inventory (MACI). Minneapolis, MN: National Computer Systems.

Moffit, T. (1993). Adolescent limited and life course persistent antisocial behavior: A developmental taxonomy. *Psychological Review, 100*, 674–701.

Moffitt, T. (1997). Adolescence-limited and life-course persistent offending: A complementary pair of developmental theories, In T. Thornberry (Ed.), *Developmental theories of crime and delinquency* (pp. 11–54). New Brunswick, NJ: Transaction.

Monahan, J., & Skeem, J. L. (2014). The evolution of violence risk assessment. *CNS Spectrums, 19*, 419–424.

Reddy, M., Borum, R., Berglund, J., Vossekuil, B., Fein, R., & Modzeleski, W. (2001). Evaluating risk for targeted violence in schools: Comparing risk assessment, threat assessment, and other approaches. *Psychology in the Schools, 38*(2), 157–172.

Reynolds, C. R., & Kamphaus, R. W. (2004). Behavioral Assessment System for Children, 2nd Edition (BASC-2). Minneapolis, MN: Pearson Assessment.

Robers, S., Kemp, J., Rathbun, A., & Morgan, R. E. (2014). *Indicators of School Crime and Safety: 2013* (NCES 2014-042/NCJ 243299). National Center for Education Statistics, U.S. Department of Education, and Bureau of Justice Statistics, Office of Justice Programs, U.S. Department of Justice, Washington, DC.

Salekin, R. T. (2008). Psychopathy and recidivism from mid-adolescence to young adulthood: Cumulating legal problems and limiting life opportunities. *Journal of Abnormal Psychology, 117*(2), 386–395.

Scott, E. S., & Steinberg, L. (2008). Adolescent development and the regulation of youth crime. *The Future of Children, 18*(2), 15–33.

Sewel, K. W., & Mendelsohn, M. (2000). Profiling potentially violent youth: Statistical and conceptual problems. *Children's Services: Social Policy, Research, and Practice, 3*, 147–169.

Skeem, J. L., & Monahan, J. (2011). Current directions in violence risk management. *Current Directions in Psychological Science, 20*(1), 38–42.

Steinberg, L., & E. Scott. (2003). Less guilty by reason of adolescence: Developmental immaturity, diminished responsibility, and the juvenile death penalty. *American Psychologist, 58*(12), 1009–1018.

U.S. Department of Education. (2011). Analysis of state bullying laws and policies. Washington, DC: Author.

U.S. Department of Health and Human Services. (2001). Youth violence: A report of the Surgeon General. Rockville, MD: Author.

Viljoen, J. L., McLachlan, K., & Vincent, G. M. (2010). Assessing violence risk and psychopathy in juvenile and adult offenders: A survey of clinical practices. *Assessment, 17*, 377–395.

Webster, C. D., Douglas, K. S., Eaves, D., & Hart, S. D. (1997). *HCR-20: Assessing risk for violence, version 2*. Burnaby, British Columbia, Canada: Simon Fraser University, Mental Health, Law, & Policy Institute.

Zimring, F. (1998). *American Youth Violence*. New York, NY: Oxford.

Appendix

Forensic Psychology Organizations

American Board of Forensic Psychology—http://www.abfp.com/

American Board of Professional Psychology—http://www.abpp.org/i4a /pages/index.cfm?pageid=3356

American Psychological Association—http://www.apa.org/

American Psychological Association Ethical Principles of Psychologists and Code of Conduct—http://www.apa.org/ethics/code/index.aspx#

American Psychology-Law Society—www.ap-ls.org

Articles, Research, and Resources in Psychology—http://www.kspope.com /index.php

Association of Family and Conciliation Courts—afccnet.org

National Criminal Justice Reference Service—https://www.ncjrs.gov /whatsncjrs.html

Online Resources

APA-Law Society Division 41 reference—http://www.apadivisions.org /division-41/education/programs/internship.aspx

Forensic Psychology Online—http://www.forensicpsychologyonline.com/

Huffington Post—http://www.huffingtonpost.com/news/forensic -psychology//

Masters in Psychology Guide.com—http://mastersinpsychologyguide.com /specializations/forensic-psychology

National Criminal Justice Reference Service—https://www.ncjrs.gov /whatsncjrs.html

Payscale—http://www.payscale.com/research/US/Job=Forensic_Psychologist /Salary

Psychology Degree Guide.org—http://psychologydegreeguide.org/job -resources/

Psychology Information Online—http://www.psychologyinfo.com/

Reddy's Forensic Page—http://www.forensicpage.com/new31.htm

About the Editor and Contributors

Editor

TIFFANY R. MASSON, PsyD, is a licensed clinical psychologist with extensive training and experience in forensic psychology. In addition to maintaining a private forensic practice, Dr. Masson has held a variety of faculty and administrative positions with increasing responsibility at The Chicago School of Professional Psychology, where she is currently an associate professor and vice president of E-Learning and Global Innovation.

During the decade she has spent at The Chicago School, Masson served as director of the Forensic Center, the practice arm of the Forensic Psychology Department, where she introduced Parent-Child Interaction Therapy (PCIT) and trained graduate students to implement this evidenced-based treatment with families involved in court-mandated parent skills training. She also codeveloped a country-specific 12-day trauma training program (Global HOPE Training Initiative), which has been successfully implemented in Rwanda and Zambia. The initiative trains teachers to effectively recognize, assess, and intervene with traumatized children, using culturally based practices. She has worked with local government and educational systems to assess the efficacy, overall impact, and sustainability of the program as a first step in building a strong paraprofessional counseling infrastructure in those countries.

She has an expertise in forensic assessments (e.g., juvenile, criminal, child protection, and civil matters), complex trauma, and evidenced-based treatment, and she speaks internationally about these issues. She has provided expert testimony and coauthored articles on issues of juvenile justice, child protection, and conducting competent Termination of Parental Rights Evaluations.

Contributors

VIRGINIA BARBER-RIOJA, PhD, earned her doctorate in clinical forensic psychology from John Jay College of Criminal Justice (City University of New

York). Although originally from Spain, she is currently based in New York City and works as the clinical director of EAC Network's Brooklyn and Staten Island court mental health diversion programs and jail and prison reentry programs. From 2009 to 2011 Dr. Barber-Rioja was the clinical director of the Queens TASC (Treatment Alternatives to Safer Communities) Mental Health Diversion Program, which works in collaboration with the Queens Mental Health Court. She subsequently worked as an attending psychologist in the Forensic Inpatient Unit at Bellevue Hospital Center, providing services to psychiatrically acute inmates. She currently serves as a clinical instructor in the Department of Psychiatry of New York University School of Medicine, and as an adjunct professor in the Psychology Master's Program of New York University. Dr. Barber-Rioja has published several chapters and articles in peer-reviewed journals on the topics of diversion and risk assessment in the context of alternatives to incarceration programs. She has presented numerous workshops and papers on criminal justice diversion and violence risk assessment in the context of diversion. Her research interests include criminal justice diversion, risk assessment, therapeutic jurisprudence, forensic assessment in general and in the context of immigration proceedings specifically, and cross-cultural psychological assessment.

JOSEPH J. BEGANY, PhD, is a forensic neuropsychologist in private practice at Psychological Consulting Services, Salem, Massachusetts, providing a wide range of forensic evaluations for children, teens, and adults. Begany has particular expertise providing forensic evaluations to psychiatrically complicated children and teens who suffer from intellectual disabilities, neurodevelopmental disorders such as autism and ADHD, seizure disorders, and neurological impairments acquired from traumatic brain injuries. Evaluations include competence to stand trial, criminal responsibility, competence to waive Miranda rights, aid to disposition and sentencing, malingering/feigned cognitive impairment, risk assessments for juvenile sex offenders, and evaluations of parents and children involved with the Massachusetts Department of Children and Families. Begany also provides consultation to school districts and private schools through neuropsychological evaluations of students, risk assessments of troubled students, and special education program evaluations. As a juvenile court clinician certified by the Massachusetts Department of Mental Health and UMass Medical School, Begany worked for five years providing evaluations to children and families involved with the Suffolk and Essex County Juvenile Courts. He recently completed the Massachusetts Department of Mental Health adult forensic certification program, after three years of conducting court-ordered forensic evaluations of adult defendants in Massachusetts district and superior courts.

DAWN M. BLACKER, PhD, graduated from the California School of Professional Psychology-Alameda in 1998. She currently serves as associate director at the UC Davis Children's Hospital CAARE Center. She is also the co-training director of an American Psychological Association accredited predoctoral internship. She provides training in Parent Child Interaction Therapy and Trauma Informed System of Care and conducts Trauma Focused-Cognitive Behavioral Therapy and Dialectical Behavior Therapy. Areas of focus include treatment of child physical and sexual abuse, developmental assessment of maltreated children, complex trauma, implementation of Empirically Based Treatment's, Commercial Sexual Exploitation of Children, and early intervention.

JEANNIE S. BROOKS, PsyD, is a Florida and New York State licensed psychologist in private practice, specializing in clinical forensic evaluations. Brooks has published quite extensively in the areas of domestic violence law, juvenile corrections, cognitive-behavioral therapy, and patient satisfaction. After graduating from Nova Southeastern University (where she completed a specialty track in forensic psychology), Dr. Brooks was one of the first forensic interns at the University of Medicine and Dentistry of New Jersey (UMDNJ), and she subsequently completed her postdoctoral fellowship within NYU/Bellevue Hospital Center's Inpatient Forensic Psychiatry Service. Her clinical and research endeavors are quite diverse, encompassing forensic evaluations within the context of dependency court, family and criminal law, and neuropsychological evaluations. Dr. Brooks maintains a thriving practice and proffers expert witness testimony within various court systems throughout Florida. She also consults with attorneys regularly regarding best practices, ethical considerations in forensic evaluations, and child protection matters, and she provides trainings to various professionals, including attorneys and other mental health providers.

MICHAEL P. BROWN, PhD, earned his degree in sociology, with concentrations in criminal justice and social psychology, from Western Michigan University in 1992. Brown holds the rank of professor of criminal justice and criminology at Ball State University, Muncie, Indiana. He teaches courses in juvenile delinquency, community corrections, and comparative criminology. Brown has published numerous journal articles, book chapters, invited manuscripts, and research reports. He consults with probation and prisoner reentry programs.

BLAKE D. CARMICHAEL, PhD graduated from the California School of Professional Psychology-Alameda in 2001. He is currently the Evaluation Program Manager at the UC Davis Children's Hospital CAARE Center. He conducts psychological and child welfare evaluations, including parent-child relationship assessments, differential diagnosis, treatment/reunification planning, juvenile competency, and juvenile/adult recidivism risk assessment.

Within the CAARE Center's American Psychological Association accredited internship program, Carmichael provides training in conducting child welfare and psychological evaluations, as well as conducting Trauma Focused Cognitive Behavioral Therapy (TF-CBT). For the past 10 years, Carmichael has provided consultation to social service and forensic programs throughout Northern California regarding child sexual abuse disclosure, emergent mental health concerns, treatment needs, and adoption/placement planning. His areas of focus include assessing the impact of violence and maltreatment on families, conducting quality child welfare evaluation services, providing evidence based practices for maltreated children, and decreasing placement disruption for children in foster care.

KENDELL L. COKER, PhD, JD, is a full-time assistant professor at University of New Haven (UNH) for the College of Arts & Sciences with a dual appointment in the Department of Criminal Justice. Dr. Coker is a faculty researcher at the Tow Youth Justice Institute at the University of New Haven. His research in juvenile justice is supported by a grant from the Tow Foundation. Kendell received his PhD in clinical psychology, with a specialization in forensic psychology from Nova Southeastern University. He completed his clinical postdoctoral training through Northwestern University at the Cook County Juvenile Court Clinic where he conducted sentencing evaluations on youth involved with the Department of Probation. Kendell then received his JD from Loyola University Chicago School of Law where he graduated with cum laude honors, was an entering Health Law Scholarship recipient, and also served as the editor-in-chief for the law school's health law and policy review, *Annals of Health Law*. He served as a council member on the Juvenile Defense Resource Institute at Northwestern University School of Law, which was a project designed to strategize ways to reduce recidivism and improve legal representation of juveniles involved in the criminal justice system. Kendell also completed a National Institute of Drug Abuse (NIDA) T-32 postdoctoral fellowship at Yale University in the Department of Psychiatry's Forensic Drug Diversion Program (FORDD). This chapter is dedicated to Dr. Coker's close friend, Herbie Gonzalez.

ANGEL DANIELS, PhD, received a bachelor of science degree in psychology in 2001 from Santa Clara University, a master of arts degree in forensic psychology from Marymount University in 2006, and a doctorate in clinical psychology in 2012 from Palo Alto University, in California. Her clinical work has focused on the various dynamics involved in sexual abuse, violence, and exploitation. She specializes in both trauma-informed therapy for survivors of sexual violence and the evaluation and treatment of the perpetrators of sexual violence. Daniels is currently an assistant professor in the Department of Forensic and Legal Psychology at Marymount University in Arlington, Virginia, and she provides sex offender treatment and evaluation in a private outpatient clinic. In addition, Daniels is the founder and executive director of the not-for-profit Sexual Abuse, Violence, & Exploitation Research Group, which conducts research on the various elements of sexual behavior and victimization and provides a range of services to survivors of sexual exploitation and the organizations that serve them.

JILL G. DURAND, PsyD, is a licensed psychologist in Massachusetts. Durand earned her doctorate from William James College and went on to work as a juvenile court clinician for seven years. Durand is currently a psychologist with Psychological Consulting Services, LLC. Her practice focuses on clinical and forensic evaluation of children, adolescents, and adults. Durand's professional interests include assessing court-related competencies, assessing risk of violence and fire-setting behavior, and assessing the impact of trauma on childhood development.

SAMUEL WITTA DWORKIN, MA, is a mitigation specialist and private investigator with over nine years' experience in capital defense. He was previously employed at the Northern Virginia Capital Defender Office for over five years. In early 2012, Sam started his own practice, Dworkin Investigations, LLC, and he has been appointed to capital cases in Virginia and throughout the country. He has an undergraduate degree in psychology from the Pennsylvania State University and a graduate degree in forensic psychology from Marymount University. Dworkin has worked on capital cases at both trial and postconviction stages and at both state and federal levels. He is devoted to indigent and criminal defense cases, sentencing, and merits investigations. Since the fall of 2013, he has also been an adjunct professor, coteaching the course The Death Penalty and Mitigation to graduate level students at Marymount University's Department of Forensic and Legal Psychology.

STEVE K. D. EICHEL, PhD, ABPP, is a licensed and board-certified psychologist in independent practice in Newark, Delaware. He has a highly varied professional history that includes extensive experience working with and running programs for traumatized and high-risk, adjudicated youth. He is considered a national expert on undue influence and destructive cults, and he currently serves as president of the International Cultic Studies Association (ICSA). His forensic experience in both civil and criminal courts has ranged from malpractice and custody evaluations to sex offending and capital cases. In 2003, he served as one of the expert witnesses in the death-penalty defense of "Beltway Sniper" Lee Boyd Malvo, who was accused of murdering over a dozen people while under the physical and psychological control of John Muhammad.

ALISON R. FLAUM, JD, is the legal director of the Children & Family Justice Center, a clinical program housed at Northwestern University Law School, where she is also an associate clinical professor of law. Flaum has practiced criminal and juvenile defense for 20 years and specializes in children being prosecuted as adults. She holds an AB from Brown University, a law degree from Yale University, and an LLM in advocacy from the Georgetown University Law Center.

ANNA FLOREK, PsyD, recently completed her post-doctoral fellowship and is now a staff psychologist at the DuPage County Jail in Wheaton, Illinois. Florek's clinical interests have been predominantly focused in the area of criminal forensic evaluations and correctional psychology. As a student-practitioner, she performed court-ordered psychological evaluations for Kane County, Illinois and conducted diagnostic evaluations in the Indiana and Colorado correctional systems, respectively. Florek received the Excellence Award during her internship at the Colorado Department of Corrections for her assistance in a governor-requested task to improve the assessment, treatment, and placement process of mentally ill offenders in administrative segregation. Florek completed her bachelor of arts degree in psychology at the University of Kansas in 2006. She relocated to Chicago, where she completed her master's degree in 2009 in forensic psychology, and later her doctorate in clinical forensic psychology in 2014, both at The Chicago School of Professional Psychology. She currently teaches assessment and correctional psychology courses as an adjunct faculty member at The Chicago School of Professional Psychology. Aside from civil commitment, her other professional interests include jury consultation, criminal responsibility, competence to stand trial, the application of culture in the context of criminal defense, and mental health in corrections. She is a member of the American Psychological Association and the American Psychology-Law Society.

EMILY D. GOTTFRIED, PhD, earned her doctoral degree in clinical psychology from Florida State University. She completed an internship at Patton State Hospital and a postdoctoral fellowship in forensic psychology at Georgia Regents University in a partnership with East Central Regional Hospital in Augusta, Georgia. After completing her fellowship, she accepted a position as a contractor and clinical instructor in the Community and Public Safety Psychiatry Division of the Department of Psychiatry and Behavioral Sciences at the Medical University of South Carolina. Gottfried's research interests include the accurate assessment of malingering during criminal forensic evaluations, personality predictors of poor treatment outcomes, suicide risk assessment, and female offenders.

MICHELLE HOY-WATKINS, PsyD, is an associate faculty member in the Department of Forensic Psychology at The Chicago School. Prior to joining

The Chicago School, Hoy-Watkins worked in a variety of clinical, correctional, and forensic settings. She graduated from the California School of Professional Psychology, Alameda, in 1997. She completed her internship at the Federal Bureau of Prisons' Metropolitan Detention Center—Los Angeles. In 1998, Hoy-Watkins completed a forensic postdoctoral fellowship at the United States Medical Center for Federal Prisoners in Springfield, Missouri. Upon completion of her fellowship, Hoy-Watkins worked at the Forensic Treatment Program in Elgin Mental Health Center—Forensic Treatment Program where she performed risk assessment evaluations for individuals acquitted through not guilty by reason of insanity and fitness to stand trial evaluations. Hoy-Watkins later became the director of the Mental Health Juvenile Justice Initiative in Cook County. She also worked as a contractual forensic psychologist for the Metropolitan Correctional Center—Chicago, where she conducted court-ordered criminal forensic evaluations. Hoy-Watkins has also provided consultative services, performing preemployment screenings and fitness for duty evaluations for local law enforcement agencies, fitness evaluations, mental health disability reviews, and school-based violence prevention programming with youth. She joined The Chicago School in 2002 as an adjunct faculty member and has been a full-time faculty member with the Forensic Department since January 2003. She became the associate chair of the Clinical Forensic PsyD Program in 2008 and served as the chair of the Department of Forensic Psychology from August 2010–2015.

ELIZABETH L. JEGLIC, PhD, is a professor of psychology at the John Jay College of Criminal Justice in New York City. Jeglic's research focuses broadly on the assessment and treatment of sex offenders.

LISA KALICH, PsyD, ABPP, is employed as a forensic psychologist at the California Department of Corrections and Rehabilitation, Board of Parole Hearings, Forensic Assessment Division, where she is responsible for conducting violence risk assessments for life term inmates eligible for parole. In her career, Kalich has been employed in a variety of forensic settings and has conducted evaluations in areas including sexual offender risk assessment, termination of parental rights, and disability determination. She obtained her doctorate of clinical psychology from the California School of Professional Psychology and completed her internship and postdoctoral fellowship at the University of California Davis, Medical Center, CAARE Center. Kalich is also board certified in forensic psychology by the American Board of Professional Psychology.

ROBERT L. KAUFMAN, PhD, ABPP, is a clinical and forensic psychologist in independent practice in the San Francisco Bay Area. He is board certified in forensic psychology and has worked on a wide range of both civil and criminal cases. For over 20 years, a large focus of his practice has been family law, where he has served as a court-appointed custody evaluator, mediator, co-parenting counselor, and consultant to attorneys. He has taught and trained other mental health professionals, attorneys, and bench officers, and he has published a number of articles relevant to child custody matters. Kaufman is currently on the board of the California Chapter of the Association of Family and Conciliation Courts and is past-board president of the Family and Children's Law Center in San Rafael, CA. For more than 15 years, he has been a senior trial consultant with Bonora-Rountree, LLC, a trial and litigation consulting firm in San Francisco.

ANTOINETTE KAVANAUGH, PhD, is board certified in forensic psychology by the American Board of Professional Psychology. She is the former clinical director of the Juvenile Justice Division—Cook County Juvenile Court Clinic and served as a clinical professor at Northwestern University's School of Law for 10 years. Currently, Dr. Kavanaugh is a Lecturer at the Feinberg School of Medicine, Northwestern University, Chicago, IL. In private practice since 1999, Kavanaugh evaluates youth and adults on a variety of forensic issues including competence to understand Miranda rights, competence to stand trial, transfer to adult court, wrongful convictions, ability to form intent, disputed confessions, pleas of not guilty by reason of insanity, and mitigation, and she has been retained in multiple *Miller v. Alabama* cases. Additionally, she testifies regularly in state and federal courts. As an author, Kavanaugh writes in the area of forensic training, forensic evaluations, and providing useful clinical information to the court. She also conducts presentations and consults with a variety of national organizations, including the Office of Juvenile Justice and Delinquency Prevention, on issues related to juvenile justice and adolescent development.

ERIC G. MART, PhD, ABPP, is a board-certified forensic psychologist in private practice in Portsmouth, New Hampshire. He is licensed in Vermont, New Hampshire, Virginia, and Massachusetts. Mart received his PhD in school psychology from Ferkauf Graduate School of Yeshiva University in 1983, and he subsequently retrained in clinical and forensic psychology. His practice includes child custody and parenting assessments, evaluations of civil and criminal competencies, personal injury assessment, and school consultation. Mart is the author of *Issue Focused Forensic Child Custody Assessment*, *Munchausen's Syndrome by Proxy Reconsidered*, and *Getting Started in Forensic Psychology Practice*. He has appeared on *20/20*, *NBC News*, BBC4, and National Public Radio, and he has been featured in articles in the *New York Times*, *Psychology Today*, and the *New Yorker*.

NANCY RYBA PANZA, PhD, completed her doctorate in clinical psychology, with a concentration in psychology and saw, at the University of Alabama in 2004. She spent four years working as an assistant professor in the Psychology Department at John Jay College of Criminal Justice in New York City before accepting her current position at California State University, Fullerton. Dr. Panza's clinical work and research focuses on criminal forensic assessment and police psychology. Dr. Panza has worked within county, state, and federal facilities providing clinical and forensic services for juvenile and adult offenders. She is currently licensed to practice psychology in New York and California.

DANIEL B. PICKAR, PhD, ABPP, is a board-certified child psychologist. He completed his undergraduate studies at Brown University and received his PhD from the California School of Professional Psychology—Berkeley. In his private practice, he conducts child custody evaluations, mediation, consultation to family law attorneys, and psychoeducational evaluations of children. He previously served as chief of Child and Family Psychiatry at Kaiser Permanente Medical Center in Santa Rosa, California, for 12 years. He has published articles in the areas of child custody evaluation and mediation and serves on the editorial board of the *Journal of Child Custody*.

AMANDA ROSINSKI, MS, is from Brooklyn, NY. She is a doctoral student in the Clinical Psychology PhD program at the CUNY Graduate Center, hosted at John Jay College of Criminal Justice. As a doctoral student, Amanda researches cross-cultural issues in clinical forensic assessment, under the mentorship of Rebecca Weiss. She earned her master's degree in forensic psychology from John Jay College of Criminal Justice, also under the supervision of Weiss. Amanda received her bachelor's degree in criminal justice from Utica College of Syracuse University in Utica, NY.

MERRILL ROTTER, MD, is a forensic psychiatrist working at Albert Einstein College of Medicine where he is associate clinical professor of psychiatry and director of the Division of Law and Psychiatry for the Department of Psychiatry. Dr. Rotter received his BA/MD from the Boston University Six-Year Combined Liberal Arts Medical Education Program. Trained in clinical psychiatry at Columbia and in forensic psychiatry at Yale, Dr. Rotter leads a program of teaching, research, and clinical service for Einstein as well as the New York State Office of Mental Health (NYSOMH). In his OMH role, Dr. Rotter is senior forensic consultant to the commissioner of NYSOMH and the director of the Division of Forensic Services at Bronx Psychiatric Services. In addition, Dr. Rotter is the medical director of the EAC Network, whose Criminal Justice Division provides mental health diversion services in Brooklyn, Queens, the Bronx, and Staten Island (including serving the mental health courts therein), and reentry services for inmates leaving Rikers Island and NYS prison. Dr. Rotter is creator and project director of SPECTRM, a research, training, and treatment program aimed at helping to meet the needs individuals with mental illness who have a history of incarceration. Dr. Rotter's research interests include risk assessment, violence risk management, mental health diversion, and assessing and addressing the medical, behavioral health, social service, and engagement challenges of individuals with seriously mental illness and criminal justice contact. In 2009 Dr. Rotter received the award for Best Teacher in a Forensic Psychiatry Fellowship from the American Academy of Psychiatry and the Law.

ALLISON M. SCHENK, PhD, earned her doctoral degree in clinical psychology from West Virginia, University with an emphasis in forensic psychology. She completed an internship at the United States Medical Center for Federal Prisoners and a postdoctoral fellowship in forensic psychology at Georgia Regents University in a partnership with East Central Regional Hospital in Augusta, Georgia. After completing her fellowship, she accepted a position as a clinical psychologist at the United States Medical Center for Federal Prisoners in Springfield, Missouri. Schenk's research interests include cyberbullying, risk predictors for prison violence, female offenders, and best practices for forensic evaluations.

FAITH SCHOMBS, MA, is currently a forensic case manager at EAC Brooklyn TASC Mental Health Diversion. She received her master of arts in general psychology with a concentration in forensic psychology from New York University in May 2015.

MEGAN E. SHAAL, PsyD, HSPP, is a licensed psychologist with an endorsement of health service provider in psychology in Indiana. She is the staff psychologist for the Isaac Ray Treatment Center at Logansport State Hospital in Logansport, Indiana, where she conducts evaluations for competency to stand trial. During 2012–2013, her doctoral dissertation, "Cross-Validation of the RRASOR, the SSPI, and the Static-99 with Indiana Sex Offenders," was awarded an American Academy of Forensic Psychology Dissertation Award. Shaal completed her American Psychological Association-accredited predoctoral internship at the Colorado Mental Health Institute at Pueblo (CMHIP), Colorado's primary forensic hospital. She also completed a postdoctoral fellowship in forensic psychology at The Chicago School Forensic Center, the practice arm of the Department of Forensic Psychology at The Chicago School of Professional Psychology. Her predoctoral clinical training took place at Indiana State Prison in Michigan City, Indiana; Hartgrove Hospital in Chicago, Illinois; and the Metropolitan Correctional Center—Chicago (Federal Bureau of Prisons). Prior to graduate school, she worked in professional practice for several years in a range of settings, including inpatient and outpatient psychiatric settings, community/residential settings, and corrections.

CASEY SHARPE, PsyD, obtained her master's degree in forensic psychology in 2005 and doctoral degree in clinical psychology in 2009. She currently holds the position of assistant professor in the Forensic Psychology department at The Chicago School of Professional Psychology. In addition to her role as faculty, Dr. Sharpe also serves as a supervising psychologist at The Chicago School Forensic Center, where she conducts fitness to stand trial evaluations and violence risk assessments for individuals court ordered to treatment after being found unfit to stand trial. She also provides expert testimony and provides supervision to students in clinical training at The Chicago School's Forensic Center. Prior to joining the faculty at The Chicago School, Dr. Sharpe was a postdoctoral fellow in forensic psychology at the University of Massachusetts Medical School, Law & Psychiatry program. She conducted forensic evaluations (competency to stand trial, criminal responsibility, aid in sentencing, civil commitment/risk assessments) at state hospitals in Massachusetts. She provided expert testimony in cases involving civil commitment for individuals with mental illness and risk for violence, as well as dangerousness related to drug/alcohol abuse. Sharpe also conducted individual therapy with clients who were civilly committed after a finding of not guilty by reason of insanity (NGRI). Additionally, she performed competence to stand trial and criminal responsibility screening evaluations, as well as assessments related to civil commitment and treatment for drug and alcohol abuse at various court clinics throughout the state of Massachusetts. In addition to her faculty and clinical responsibilities at The Chicago School, Dr. Sharpe also conducts psychological evaluations on a contractual basis for various entities in Illinois, including psychological pre-employment screening evaluations and fitness for duty evaluations for the Chicago police department, and works as a psychological consultant for the Social Security Administration.

JEFF D. STEIN, PhD, is a clinical and forensic psychologist in Massachusetts, where he performs a wide range of psychological assessments for attorneys, judges, schools, government agencies, and corporations. He has a particular interest in matters involving child and adolescent psychological development, family relationships, and identifying risk and protective factors associated with adaptive functioning. For 10 years, he has been working in a private group practice, Psychological Consulting Services, in Salem, MA.

ANTHONY J. URQUIZA, PhD, is a clinical psychologist, professor in pediatrics at UC Davis Children's Hospital, and director of both the CAARE Center and the UC Davis PCIT Training Center. He earned undergraduate and graduate degrees at the University of Washington and completed an internship at Primary Children's Medical Center in Salt Lake City, Utah. The CAARE Center provides medical evaluations, psychological assessments, and a range of mental health treatment services primarily for abused and neglected children. He is a nationally recognized expert in the areas of trauma, child maltreatment, mental health treatment for victims of interpersonal violence, and the implementation of mental health interventions.

MICHAEL J. VITACCO, PhD, earned his doctoral degree from the University of North Texas. He completed an internship at the University of North Carolina School of Medicine and a postdoctoral fellowship at the University of Massachusetts School of Medicine. He is currently an associate professor at Georgia Regents University, where he serves as the director of Forensic Psychology Training. Vitacco's research interests include psychopathy, violence risk assessment, malingering, and conditional release with insanity acquittees.

REBECCA WEISS, PhD, is an assistant professor of forensic assessment at John Jay College and a licensed clinical psychologist in the state of New York. Before joining the faculty at John Jay, she completed her clinical training at Yale University School of Medicine. She received her PhD and MA in clinical psychology from Fordham University. She received her BA in psychology and international studies from Northwestern University. Her research interests include the effect of group membership (e.g., culture, intellectual disabilities) on validity in psychological assessment and the impact of trauma on the treatment and development of aggression and substance use disorders.

ANNA M. L. WESTIN, PhD, currently works as a licensed psychologist at the Children's Hospital and Medical Center in Omaha, NE, specializing in child trauma. Westin completed her PhD in clinical child and community psychology at the University of Maryland, Baltimore County, in 2014. She completed her American Psychological Association accredited internship and postdoctoral fellowship at the UC Davis CAARE Center specializing in child maltreatment. She has experience in child welfare evaluations and empirically supported treatments for trauma. Westin is also chair of the Early Career Psychologist (ECP) committee of APA Division 37's Section on Child Maltreatment.

GEORGIA M. WINTERS is a clinical psychology PhD student at John Jay College of Criminal Justice and the Graduate Center, City University of New York. Georgia is a member of the Sex Offender Research Lab at John Jay College.

Index

Note: Page numbers followed by *n* indicate note numbers.